Macroeconomics

SECOND EDITION

PRENTICE HALL SERIES IN ECONOMICS

Adams/Brock, *The Structure of American Industry, 9/e*

Blanchard, *Macroeconomics, 2/e*

Blau/Ferber/Winkler, *The Economics of Women, Men, and Work, 3/e*

Boardman/Greenberg/Vining/Wiemer, *Cost Benefit Analysis: Concepts and Practice*

Bogart, *The Economics of Cities and Suburbs*

Case/Fair, *Principles of Economics, 5/e*

Case/Fair, *Principles of Macroeconomics, 5/e*

Case/Fair, *Principles of Microeconomics, 5/e*

Caves, *American Industry: Structure, Conduct, Performance, 7/e*

Collinge/Ayers, *Economics by Design: Principles and Issues, 2/e*

DiPasquale/Wheaton, *Urban Economics and Real Estate Markets*

Feiner, *Race and Gender in the American Economy: Views Across the Spectrum*

Folland/Goodman/Stano, *Economics of Health and Health Care, 2/e*

Froyen, *Macroeconomics: Theories and Policies, 6/e*

Greene, *Econometric Analysis, 4/e*

Heilbroner/Milberg, *The Making of an Economic Society, 10/e*

Heyne, *The Economic Way of Thinking, 9/e*

Hirschleifer/Hirschleifer, *Price Theory and Applications, 6/e*

Keat/Young, *Managerial Economics, 3/e*

Milgrom/Roberts, *Economics, Organization, and Management*

O'Sullivan/Sheffrin, *Economics: Principles and Tools*

O'Sullivan/Sheffrin, *Macroeconomics: Principles and Tools*

O'Sullivan/Sheffrin, *Microeconomics: Principles and Tools*

Petersen/Lewis, *Managerial Economics, 4/e*

Pindyck/Rubinfeld, *Microeconomics, 4/e*

Reynolds/Masters/Moser, *Labor Economics and Labor Relations, 11/e*

Roberts, *The Choice: A Fable of Free Trade and Protectionism*

Sachs/Larrain, *Macroeconomics in the Global Economy*

Schiller, *The Economics of Poverty and Discrimination, 7/e*

Weidenbaum, *Business and Government in the Global Marketplace, 6/e*

MACROECONOMICS

SECOND EDITION

Olivier Blanchard | *Massachusetts Institute of Technology*

Prentice Hall, Upper Saddle River, New Jersey 07458

Acquisitions Editor: Rod Banister
Developmental Editor: Michael Elia
Associate Editor: Gladys Soto
Editorial Assistant: Marie McHale
Editor-in-Chief: PJ Boardman
Vice President/Editorial Director: James C. Boyd
Marketing Manager: Lori Braumberger
New Media Project Manager: William Minick
Production Editor: Richard DeLorenzo
Permissions Coordinator: Monica Stipanov
Associate Managing Editor: Cynthia Regan
Senior Manufacturing Supervisor: Paul Smolenski
Manufacturing Manager: Vincent Scelta
Design Manager: Patricia Smythe
Interior Design: Amanda Kavanagh
Photo Research Supervisor: Melinda Lee Reo
Image Permission Supervisor: Kay Dellosa
Photo Researcher: Teri Stratford
Cover Design: Kevin Kall
Cover Illustration/Photo: Marjory Dressler
Composition: Progressive Information Technologies

Photo Credits

Page 302, SuperStock
Page 538, CORBIS/Beltmann
Page 539, *Top to bottom*: CORBIS/Owen Franken; Michael Marsland/Yale University; AP/Wide World Photos; Lawrence L. Klein/University of Pennsylvania, Philadelphia
Page 540, *Top to bottom*: CORBIS/Roger Ressmeyer; Professor Edmund Phelps/Columbia University
Page 541, *Top to bottom*: Charles Bennett/AP/Wide World Photos; Thomas J. Sargent/Hoover Institution, Stanford, CA; Robert J. Barro/Harvard University
Page 543, *Top to bottom*: Robert E. Hall/Stanford University; Rudiger Dornbusch/MIT Dept. of Economics; Stanley Fischer/International Monetary Fund; John B. Taylor/Stanford University
Page 544, Edward C. Prescott/Federal Reserve Bank of Minneapolis
Page 545, *Top to bottom*: George A. Akerlof/The Brookings Institution; Paul Romer/University of California-Berkeley

Library of Congress Cataloging-in-Publication Data
Blanchard, Olivier (Olivier J.)
    Macroeconomics / Olivier Blanchard.—2nd ed.
      p.   cm.
    A multimedia teaching/learning package for instructors/students supplements the text.
    Includes bibliographical references and index.
    ISBN 0-13-013306-X
    1. Macroeconomics.   I. Title.
HB172.5.B573   1999
339—dc21   99-049531
                                      CIP

Prentice-Hall International (UK) Limited, London
Prentice-Hall of Australia Pty. Limited, Sydney
Prentice-Hall Canada, Inc., Toronto
Prentice-Hall Hispanoamericana, S.A., Mexico
Prentice-Hall of India Private Limited, New Delhi
Prentice-Hall of Japan, Inc., Tokyo
Prentice-Hall (Singapore) Pte. Ltd.
Editora Prentice-Hall do Brasil, Ltda., Rio de Janeiro

Printed in the United States of America

10 9 8 7 6 5 4 3 2 1

To the Student:

If your textbook did not come bundled with the *"Active Graphs CD-ROM to Accompany MACRO-ECONOMICS, 2/e,"* you may order it for purchase separately through your bookstore using this ISBN: 0-13-017271-5. The CD-ROM contains 48 Active Graphs which correspond to important figures in the text. With each graph, you can change certain variables and see the effects on the equilibrium.

A NOELLE

Olivier Blanchard is the Class of 1941 Professor of Economics at MIT. He is also Chairman of the Department of Economics at MIT. He did his undergraduate work in France, and received a Ph.D. in economics from MIT in 1977. He taught at Harvard from 1977 to 1982, and has taught at MIT since 1983. He has frequently received the award for best teacher in the department of economics, most recently in 1999.

He has done research on many macroeconomic issues, from the effects of fiscal policy, to the role of expectations, to price rigidities, to speculative bubbles, to unemployment in Western Europe, and more recently transition in Eastern Europe. He has done work for many governments and many international organizations, including the *World Bank,* the *IMF,* the *OECD,* the *EU commission* and the *EBRD.* He has published over 150 articles and edited or written over 15 books, including *Lectures on Macroeconomics* with Stanley Fischer.

He is a research associate of the National Bureau of Economic Research, a fellow of the Econometric Society, a member of the American Academy of Arts and Sciences, and a past Vice President of the American Economic Association.

He lives in Cambridge, with his wife, Noelle. He has three daughters, Marie, Serena, and Giulia.

BRIEF CONTENTS

CONTENTS

C O N T E N T S

BOXES

PREFACE

I had two main goals in writing this second edition:

- To make close contact with current macroeconomic events.

  What makes macroeconomics exciting is the light it sheds on what is happening around the world, from the introduction of a new currency in Western Europe, to the elimination of budget deficits in the United States, to the transformation of Eastern Europe, to the crisis in Asia. These events—and many more—are described in the book, not in footnotes, but in detailed boxes, each box showing how macroeconomics can be used to get an understanding of what happened. My hope is that these boxes not only convey the fun of macroeconomics, but also reinforce the lessons from the models, making them more concrete, and easier to grasp.

- To provide an integrated view of macroeconomics.

  The book is built around one underlying model, a model that concentrates on the implications of equilibrium conditions in three sets of markets: the goods market, financial markets, and the labor market. Depending on the issue at hand, the parts of the model relevant to the issue are developed in more detail while the others are simplified or left in the background. But the underlying model is always the same. My hope is that, as a result, readers of this book will see macroeconomics as a coherent whole, not as a collection of models drawn from a hat.

The response to the first edition, in the United States and around the world, has shown that I share these goals with many instructors and students of macroeconomics. At the same time, feedback from teachers and students has also led me to make two important changes relative to the first edition.

- I have changed the organization of the book.

  The book is now organized around two main parts, a **core** and a set of three major **extensions**. The core gives an integrated view of the short run, the medium run, and the long run. The three extensions examine the role of expectations, the implications of openness, and pathologies, from high unemployment to hyperinflation. This has two advantages:

  It allows the reader to **quickly get an integrated view of macroeconomics**, from short-run fluctuations to growth.

  It gives **more flexibility** to instructors in using the book. Once the core has been covered, any one of the three extensions can be taught without the need to cover the other two.

- I have tried to recreate the dialogue that takes place in the classroom, but is typically absent from textbooks.

  I have done this by introducing margin notes running in parallel to the text. These notes serve many purposes: to emphasize an important point, to help with a derivation, to relate an argument to an earlier one, to summarize a series of steps, to suggest further readings, to give a related fact, or to tell a related anecdote. My belief is that these notes make reading the book and learning from it much easier.

Organization

The book has two central components, a core and the set of three major extensions. An introduction precedes the core. The set of extensions is followed by a review of the role of policy. The book ends with an epilogue (the structure of the book is highlighted by the flowchart on the front end paper of the text).

- Chapters 1 and 2 introduce the basic facts and issues of macroeconomics. Chapter 1 offers a tour of the world, from the United States, to Europe, to Asia. Some instructors may prefer to cover it later, perhaps after Chapter 2, which introduces basic concepts, articulates the notions of short run, medium run, and long run, and gives a quick tour of the book.

  While Chapter 2 gives the basics of national income accounting, I have moved a detailed treatment of national income accounts to Appendix 1 at the end of the book. This both decreases the burden on the beginning reader, and allows for a more thorough treatment in the appendix.

- Chapters 3 to 13 constitute the **core**.

  Chapters 3 to 5 focus on the **short run**. They characterize equilibrium in the goods market and in the financial markets, and they derive the basic model used to study short-run movements in output, the *IS–LM* model.

  (I have removed the chapter in the first edition which focused on dynamics and on the use of econometrics in macroeconomics. It came too early in the book and proved too hard for students to master. It has been partially replaced by Appendix 3 on econometrics at the end of the book. Some instructors may want to use it to show how macroeconomists actually estimate relations between variables, how they try to distinguish between correlation and causality. This can be done at any point during the course.)

Chapters 6 to 9 focus on the **medium run**. Chapter 6 focuses on equilibrium in the labor market and introduces the natural rate of unemployment. Chapters 7 to 9 develop a model based on aggregate demand and aggregate supply, and show how that model can be used to understand movements in activity and in inflation, both in the short and in the medium run. Chapter 9, which looks at the dynamic relation between inflation and activity, is a bit harder, and is optional.

Chapters 10 to 13 focus on the **long run**. Chapter 10 describes the facts, showing the evolution of output over countries and over long periods of time. Chapters 11 and 12 develop a model of growth, focusing on the determinants of capital accumulation and technological progress and the role of each in growth. Chapter 13, which is optional, focuses on the effects of technological progress not only in the long run, but also in the short and the medium run. This topic is typically not covered in textbooks but is an important one. Also the chapter shows how one can integrate the short run, the medium run, and the long run—an example of the payoff to an integrated approach to macroeconomics.

- Chapters 14 to 24 cover the three major extensions.

Chapters 14 to 17 focus on the role of **expectations** in the short run and in the medium run. Expectations play a major role in most economic decisions, and, by implication, in the determination of output. Chapter 14, which introduces basic tools, is simplified relative to the first edition. Also, many readers rightly suggested it was both easier and more natural to start with the role of expectations in financial markets. Thus, the order of the chapters on financial and goods markets, Chapters 15 and 16, has been inverted relative to the first edition.

Chapters 18 to 21 focus on the implications of **openness** of modern economies. Much has happened in the world since the first edition: Many countries have adopted new exchange rate regimes, and a number of countries have gone through serious exchange rate crises. These developments, and

what we have learned from them, are reflected in Chapter 21, which is largely new.

Chapters 22 to 24 focus on **pathologies**, times when something in the economy appears to go very wrong. Chapter 22 looks at periods of high unemployment. Chapter 23 looks at episodes of hyperinflation. Chapter 24 looks at two of the main events of the 1990s, transition in Eastern Europe and the Asian crisis.

- Chapters 25 to 27 return to **macroeconomic policy**.

While most of the first 24 chapters discuss macroeconomic policy in one form or another, the purpose of chapters 25 to 27 is to tie the threads together. Chapter 25 looks at the role and the limits of macroeconomic policy in general. Chapters 26 and 27 review monetary and fiscal policy. Some teachers may want to use parts of these chapters earlier. For example, it is easy to move forward the discussion of the government budget constraint in Chapter 27.

- Chapter 28 serves as an **epilogue**. It puts macroeconomics in historical perspective, showing the evolution of macroeconomics in the last 50 years and discussing current directions of research.

Alternative Course Outlines

I have made the chapters shorter than is standard in textbooks and, in my experience, most chapters can be covered in an hour and a half. A few (Chapters 5 and 7 for example) may require two lectures to sink in. Within the book's broad organization, there is plenty of opportunity for alternative course organizations:

- Short courses (15 lectures or less)

A short course can be organized around the two introductory chapters and the core. Leaving aside Chapters 9 and 13, both optional, gives a total of 11 lectures. Informal presentations of one or two of the extensions, based for example on Chapters 14 and 15 for expectations, and on Chapter 18 for the open economy, can then follow, for a total of 14 lectures.

A short course may leave out instead the study of growth (the long run). In this case, the course can be organized around the introductory chapters, and Chapters 3 to 8 in the core; this gives a total of 8 lectures, leaving enough time to cover, for example, Chapters 14 to 16 on expectations, and Chapters 18 to 20 on the open economy, for a total of 14 lectures.

- Longer courses (20 to 25 lectures)

A full semester course gives more than enough time to cover the core, plus at least two extensions, and the review of policy.

The extensions assume knowledge of the core, but are otherwise mostly self contained (one exception: The analysis of the Asian crisis in Chapter 24 requires knowledge of the first two extensions). Given the choice, the order in which they are best taught is probably the order in which they are presented in the book. Starting with the study of the role of expectations is useful for example in understanding the interest parity condition, and the nature of exchange rate crises.

One of the choices facing teachers is likely to be whether to teach growth (the long run) or not. If growth is taught, there may not be enough time to cover all three extensions and have a thorough discussion of policy. In this case, it may be best to leave out the study of pathologies. If growth is not taught, there should be time to cover most of the other topics in the book.

Features

I have made sure never to present a theoretical result without relating it to the real world. For this purpose, in addition to discussions of facts in the text itself, I have introduced three types of boxes:

- **Focus** boxes, which expand on a point made in the text.
- **In Depth** boxes, which look at a particular macroeconomic episode in detail.
- **Global Macro** boxes, which look at macroeconomic episodes from around the world.

As described earlier, a major innovation in this edition is the presence of margin notes running parallel to the text. Their function is to create a dialogue with the reader, to smooth the more difficult passages, and to allow for a deeper understanding of the concepts and the results derived along the way.

For students who want to explore macroeconomics further, I have introduced the following three features:

- **Digging deeper** notes, which expand on an argument in the text, often by indicating how an implicit assumption in the text could be relaxed, and what the implications might be.
- **Short appendixes** to some chapters, which show how a proposition in the text can be derived more rigorously or expanded.
- A **Further readings** section at the end of each chapter, indicating where to find more information, including a number of key internet addresses.

Each chapter ends with three ways of making sure that the material in the chapter has been thoroughly understood:

- A **summary** of the chapter's main points.
- A list of **key terms**.
- A series of **end-of-chapter exercises**, some of them requiring access to the internet, some of them requiring the use of a spreadsheet program. More challenging exercises, web based or otherwise, are indicated by an asterisk (*).

The Teaching and Learning Package

The book comes with a number of supplements to help both students and instructors.

For instructors:

- **Instructor's Manual**. Written by Mark Moore, of University of California-Irvine, the Instructor's Manual discusses pedagogical choices, alternative ways of presenting the material, and ways of reinforcing students' understanding. For each chapter of the book, the manual has 7 sections: objectives, in the form of a motivating question; why the answer matters; key tools concepts and assumptions; summary; pedagogy; extensions; and observations and additional exercises. The Instructor's Manual also includes the answers to all end-of-chapter questions and exercises.

- **Test Item File**. Written by David Findlay of Colby College, the test bank is completely revised with an additional 25 new multiple-choice questions per chapter, for a total of over 1200 questions.

- **Prentice Hall Test Manager**, **Version 4.1**. This computerized version of the Test Item File allows instructors to add, delete, edit, and save custom exams, as well as create data files to store and compare student scores.

- **Transparency Masters**. A complete set of transparency masters for all of the figures and tables in the text can be downloaded by adopters from www.prenhall.com/blanchard. Contact your Prentice Hall representative for a password.

- **PowerPoint Lecture Slides**. Created by Jeffrey Caldwell and Steve Smith, these electronic slides provide outlines, summaries, equations, and graphs for each chapter, and can be downloaded from www.prenhall.com/blanchard.

For students:

- **Study Guide**. David Findlay, of Colby College, has done an outstanding job of writing a student-friendly study guide. Each chapter begins with a presentation of objectives and a review. It is organized in the form of a tutorial, covering the important points of the chapter, with learning suggestions along the way. The tutorial is followed by quick self-test questions, review problems, and multiple-choice questions. Solutions are provided for all Study Guide problems.

- **Active Graphs CD-ROM**. Stephen Perez, of Washington State University, and Gregory M. Werner, have created a series of 48 active graphs corresponding to the most important figures in the book. Each graph allows the student to change the value of a variable and look at the effects on the equilibrium. Experience indicates that using graphs in this way considerably strengthens the students' intuition and understanding of the mechanisms at work.

For both instructors and students, **Prentice Hall's Learning on the Internet Partnership and Companion Website** (www.prenhall.com/blanchard) offers Internet exercises, activities, and resources related specifically to the second edition of Macroeconomics. All internet resources are updated every two weeks.

For students, PHLIP includes:

- **Research Area**. A collection of tips and resources helps students to harness the research potential of the Internet through tutorials, links to virtual libraries, and a wealth of search engines.

- **Current Events Articles** and **Exercises**. Relevant articles fully supported by group activities, critical thinking exercises, discussion questions, reference resources, key topics, and the like, which help keep students up-to-date with today's events.

- **Companion Website Interactive Study Guide**. Written by Rashid Al-Hmoud of Texas Tech University, this on-line self-assessment offers multiple-choice, true/false, and essay questions for every chapter. Graded by the Prentice Hall server, these quizzes provide students with immediate feedback, including additional help and section references linked to the text. Results for these activities, as well as the on-line quizzes and exams, can be sent to as many as four e-mail addresses.

- A **Student Study Hall**, which helps develop study skills through:

- **Ask the Tutor**. Virtual office hours that allow students to post questions from any supported discipline and receive monitored responses from the dedicated PHLIP faculty team.

- **Talk in the Hall**. A format for students to ask each other questions on-line.

- **Writing Skills**. On-line writing assistance that provides links to on-line directories, thesauruses, writing tutors, style and grammar guides, and additional tools.

- **Study Skills**. A resource center with links to academic and professional sites dedicated to helping students achieve their college goals through good study habits.

- **Study Tips**. An area providing helpful tips designed to help students develop better study skills.

- **Career Resources**. A section to help students investigate potential employment situations on the web, get career information, view sample resumes, and even apply for jobs on-line.

For faculty, PHLIP includes:

- **Downloadable supplements**. Ancillaries include Instructor's Manual, PowerPoint presentation, and transparency masters.

- **On-line faculty support**. Includes additional cases, current events articles, links, and full support for exercises posted on the Student Page.

- **Syllabus Manager**. Easy-to-use, this program allows faculty to create on-line custom syllabi hosted on Prentice Hall server. Syllabus Manager provides instructors with an easy, step-by-step process to create and revise syllabi, with direct links into Companion Web site and other on-line content. Changes you make to your syllabus are immediately available to your students at their next log in. For more information, please visit the on-line demo located at www.prenhall.com/demo.

- A **Faculty Lounge** where you can find:

  - **Teaching Archive**. Teaching resources from professors throughout the world, that enables instructors to share tips, techniques, academic papers, and sample syllabi.

  - **Talk to the Team**. A moderated and password-protected faculty chat room that allows instructors to communicate with other professors on-line. Instructors can share new teaching ideas, make suggestions, and ask questions, which gives them the opportunity to take advantage of the experiences and knowledge of other professors.

- **Computer Help**. An on-line computer-assistance section that offers tips and links to tutorials, helping instructors master spreadsheets, word processing, and presentation software.

Acknowledgments and Thanks

This book owes much to many.

I thank Adam Ashcraft, Peter Berger, Efe Cakarel, Jeromin Zettelmeyer, Gaurav Tewari, Stacy Tevlin, David Hwang, Harry Gakidis, Tobias Adrian, Emek Basker, Peter Benczur, Astrid Dick, Martin Eiras, John Simon, and Corissa Thompson for their assistance. I thank the generations of students in 14.02 at MIT who have freely shared their reactions to the book over the years.

I have benefited from comments from many colleagues and friends. Among them are John Abell, Roland Benabou, Samuel Bentolila and Juan Jimeno (who have adapted the book in a Spanish edition), François Blanchard, Roger Brinner, Ricardo Caballero, Luigi Chincarini, Larry Christiano, Andres Conesa, Peter Diamond, Martin Eichenbaum, David Findlay, Francesco Giavazzi (who has adapted the book in an Italian edition), Paul Krugman, Peter Montiel, Bill Nordhaus, Angelo Melino (who has adapted the book in a Canadian edition), Jose Carlos Miranda (who has adapted the book for a Brazilian edition), Tom Michl, Athanasios Orphanides, Jim Poterba, Watanabe Shinichi (who has adapted the book for a Japanese edition), Changyong Rhee, Julio Rotemberg, Robert Solow, Andre Watteyne, and Michael Woodford. I have also benefited from often stimulating suggestions from my daughters, Serena, Giulia, and Marie; I did not however follow all of them.

I have benefited from comments from many reviewers and class testers. Among them:

- Carol Adams, Cabrillo College
- Terence Alexander, Iowa State University
- Robert Archibald, College of William & Mary
- Charles Bean, London School of Economics and Political Science
- David C. Black, University of Toledo
- Scott Bloom, North Dakota State University
- Pim Borren, University of Canterbury, New Zealand
- Brad DeLong, University of California-Berkeley
- Wouter Denhaan, University of California-San Diego
- F. Trenery Dolbear, Brandeis University
- John Edgren, Eastern Michigan University
- J. Peter Federer, Clark University
- Rendigs Fels, Vanderbilt University
- David Findlay, Colby College
- Marc Fox, Brooklyn College
- Randy Grant, Linfield College
- Reza Hamzaee, Missouri Western State College
- Thomas Havrilesky, Duke University
- John Holland, Monmouth College
- John A. James, University of Virginia
- Fred Joutz, George Washington University
- Miles Kimball, University of Michigan
- Paul King, Denison University
- Ng Beoy Kui, Nanyang Technical University, Singapore
- Leonard Lardaro, University of Rhode Island
- Hsien-Feng Lee, National Taiwan University
- Carol Scotese Lehr, Virginia Commonwealth University
- Frank Lichtenberg, Columbia University
- Mark Lieberman, New York University
- Mathias Lutz, University of Sussex
- Bernard Malamud, University of Nevada, Las Vegas
- Rose Milbourne, University of New South Wales
- Jack Osman, San Francisco State University
- Allen Parkman, University of New Mexico
- Gavin Peebles, National University of Singapore
- Jack Richards, Portland State University
- Kehar Sangha, Old Dominion University
- Peter Sephton, University of New Brunswick
- Ruth Shen, San Francisco State University
- Kwanho Shin, University of Kansas
- David Sollars, Auburn University
- Abdul Turay, Radford University
- Frederick Tyler, Fordham University
- Susheng Wang, Hong Kong University
- Mark Wohar, University of Nebraska, Omaha
- Michael Woodford, Princeton University
- Ip Wing Yu, University of Hong Kong
- Chi-Wa Yuen, Hong Kong University of Science and Technology.

They have all helped me beyond the call of duty, and each has made a difference to the book.

I have many people to thank at Prentice Hall, from Stephen Dietrich for convincing me to write this book in the first place, to Rod Banister, the senior editor for Economics, to Gladys Soto, the associate editor, to William Becher, the editorial assistant, to Rick DeLorenzo, the production editor, to Kevin Kall, senior designer, and Lori Braumberger, senior marketing manager. I want to single out both Steve Rigolosi, the outstanding editor for the first edition, and Michael Elia, the equally outstanding development editor for the second edition. Steve forced me to clarify. Michael has forced me to simplify. Together, they have made all the difference to the process and to the book. I thank both of them deeply.

At MIT, I continue to thank John Arditi for his absolute reliability.

At home, I continue to thank Noelle for preserving my sanity.

Olivier Blanchard
Cambridge, MIT
October 1999

MACROECONOMICS

SECOND EDITION

INTRODUCTION

The first two chapters introduce you to the issues and the approach of macroeconomics.

CHAPTER 1

Chapter 1 takes you on a macroeconomic tour of the world, from the long U.S. expansion of the 1990s, to the introduction of a common currency in Western Europe, to the recession in Japan and the crisis in Asia.

CHAPTER 2

Chapter 2 then takes you on a tour of the book. It defines the three central variables of macroeconomics, output, unemployment, and inflation. It then introduces the three concepts around which the book is organized, the short run, the medium run, and the long run.

CHAPTER 1 | A Tour of the World

W hat is macroeconomics? The best way to answer this question is not to give you a formal definition, but rather to take you on an economic tour of the world, to describe both the main economic evolutions and the issues that keep macroeconomists and macroeconomic policy makers up at night.

At the time of this writing, macroeconomists and policymakers are not sleeping very well. In the United States, they worry that the long output expansion of the 1990s may be coming to an end. In Europe, they worry about unemployment, which has been high now for more than two decades. But the main worries concern Asia. After many decades of fast growth, Japan is in the middle of a severe recession. And a major economic crisis has also hit many of the other fast-growing Asian countries, from Thailand to South Korea.

This chapter looks more closely at what is happening in these three parts of the world. Read it as you would read an article in a newspaper. Do not worry about the exact meaning of the words, or about understanding all the arguments in detail. Regard it as background, intended to introduce you to the issues of macroeconomics; the words will be defined and the arguments articulated in later chapters. Indeed, once you have read the book, come back to this chapter; see where you stand on the issues, and judge how much progress you have made in your study of macroeconomics.

When they look at an economy, macroeconomists focus first on three measures.

- *Output*, the level of production of the economy as a whole, and its rate of growth.
- The *unemployment rate*, the proportion of workers in the economy who are not employed and are looking for a job.
- The *inflation rate*, the rate at which the average price of the goods in the economy is increasing over time.

By all three measures, the United States is doing well. Look at Table 1–1. The first column gives the average value of output growth, unemployment, and inflation since 1960; the next three columns give the numbers for 1997 to 1999 (the numbers for 1999 are forecasts, as of June 1999).

The United States entered the 1990s with a *recession*—a decrease in output. At the end of 1991, that recession gave way to an *expansion*—an increase in output—and output growth has remained positive every year since. Output growth for 1998 was 3.9%, a number higher than the average rate of growth since 1960.

The unemployment rate has steadily declined since the end of the recession. The unemployment rate for 1998 stood at 4.6%, more than one percentage point below the average unemployment rate since 1960. And inflation is low. In 1998, the average rate of increase of prices was only 1.0%, a full 3.0% below the average inflation rate since 1960.

Will this expansion last forever? If history is any guide, alas, no. Sooner or later, there will be a recession, followed by another expansion, and so on. Macroeconomists refer to these alternating periods of expansion and recession as *business cycles* or *fluctuations*. Can we predict when the next recession will come? Again, using history as a guide, the answer is no: Timing is very difficult to predict. But there are signs of danger, some from low unemployment rates, some from high stock market prices.

FIGURE 1-1

The United States

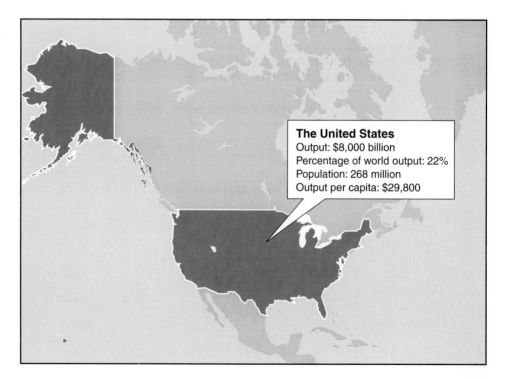

The United States
Output: $8,000 billion
Percentage of world output: 22%
Population: 268 million
Output per capita: $29,800

(in percent)	1960–1998	1997	1998	1999 (forecast)
Output growth rate	3.1	3.9	3.9	3.6
Unemployment rate	6.0	4.9	4.6	4.2
Inflation rate	4.0	1.9	1.0	1.1

Growth rate: annual rate of growth of gross domestic product (GDP). *Unemployment rate*: average over the year. *Inflation rate*: annual rate of change of the GDP deflator.

Sources: 1960 to 1998: Bureau of Economic Analysis; 1997 to 1999: *OECD Economic Outlook*, June 1999.

Is Unemployment Too Low?

Some macroeconomists worry that the unemployment rate may actually be too low. It is not that they like high unemployment; rather, they worry that low unemployment may lead to an increase in inflation. They argue that when the unemployment rate is as low as it is now, inflation typically starts rising: Firms that want to keep their workers or hire new ones have to pay higher wages, higher wages lead to higher prices, higher prices lead to further increases in wages, and so on. If the same thing happens again and inflation increases, they argue, *the Fed* (the central bank in charge of monetary policy in the United States, more formally known as the Federal Reserve Board) will have to tighten monetary policy, and this may lead to a recession. The last time the unemployment rate was as low as it is today was in 1969, at the end of a decade-long expansion; inflation increased, and there was a recession in 1970.

It may be because of statements like this that economics is often called "the dismal science."

Others argue that, this time, a low unemployment rate is not cause for worry and will not lead to higher inflation. They first point out that inflation has not yet increased. They argue that changes in the labor market now allow the U.S. economy to operate at a lower rate of unemployment than in past decades. One of the changes they identify is the decline of the power of unions: Despite low unemployment, workers may not be in a strong enough bargaining position to demand wage increases. Thus, they conclude, low unemployment is no cause for concern.

Is the Stock Market Too High?

The other worry is, again somewhat paradoxically, the strong performance of the stock market. The expansion of the 1990s has come with a very large increase in stock prices. If you watch the news, you are familiar with the *Dow Jones index*, an average of the stock prices of 30 large U.S. companies. The Dow Jones index was at 2,700 at the beginning of 1990. In the spring of 1999, it was above 10,000.

Some economists believe that this increase in stock prices simply reflects the strong performance of the U.S. economy. Financial investors, they argue, see and anticipate high profits for U.S. firms, now and in the future; so they are willing to pay high prices for stocks. Thus, these economists conclude, there is no reason to worry: High stock prices reflect high profits in the future, high *fundamentals*, nothing more.

Other economists believe that stock prices are too high, that financial investors are too optimistic about the future. One such observer is Alan Greenspan, the chairman of the Fed who, in December 1996, suggested that the increase in the stock market might reflect "irrational exuberance." (After his remarks, the market fell. But since then, the market has risen another 40%.) Why is too high a stock market a matter for concern? If the increase in the stock market results from excessive optimism, it is likely to be followed by a sharp decline, or even by a crash. And, as we shall see when we look below at the story of Japan in the 1990s, a stock market decline may trigger a serious recession.

Turning to longer-term concerns, there are at least two important issues facing the U.S. economy. One is the decrease in the average growth rate of the U.S. economy since the mid-1970s. The other is increasing wage inequality.

Why Has Growth Slowed Down?

Although growth rates vary from year to year, the evidence suggests that the underlying rate of growth in the United States has decreased since the mid-1970s. You can see this in Figure 1–2, which plots the annual rate of growth of output since 1950. The average growth rate for the period 1950 to 1973 was 4.0%. Since 1974, it has been only 2.6%. Thus, average growth has been 1.4% lower since the mid-1970s.

A decrease in the average rate of growth of 1.4% per year—the difference between the average rate for 1950 to 1973 and the average rate for 1974 to 1997—may not seem very important, but it is. One way of thinking about it is this: If the average growth rate of output after 1973 had remained equal to the average rate from 1950 to 1973, U.S. output would be 39% higher today; output per capita would be $41,400 instead of its actual value (given in Figure 1–1) of $29,800.

Why has growth slowed down? The growth rates of most other rich countries have also decreased, so one should not look for explanations specific to the United States. Some economists argue that rich countries have lost their edge, that the research process is less productive than it used to be. Others claim that countries are not investing enough in new capital. Still others say that the slowdown is largely a figment of the way data is constructed, that official measures of output underestimate the increase in the sophistication of new products and thus underestimate the growth rate of output. At this point all explanations are tentative, but the question clearly is a very important one.

If the growth rate had been 1.4% higher for the 24 years from 1974 to 1998, the level of output would be $(1.014)^{24} - 1 = 39\%$ higher than it is today. (For a review of exponents, see Appendix 2 at the end of the book.)

▷ "Output per capita" means "output per person" (Latin: *capita*, head).

FIGURE 1-2

U.S. Output Growth Since 1950

The average rate of growth has decreased since the mid-1970s.

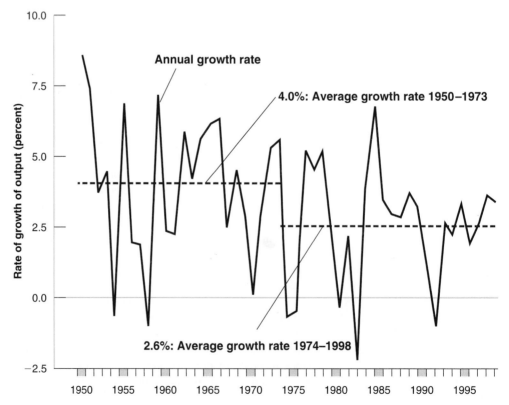

Why Has Wage Inequality Increased?

Wage inequality has increased in the United States since the late 1970s. Workers with fewer skills and less education have seen their wages decline relative to the average wage. Combined with low growth, this increase in wage inequality has led to an absolute wage decline for some workers. Since 1979, the average wage of workers who have not finished high school has *decreased* by roughly 1% per year (adjusted for inflation). During the same period, the average wage of workers with a graduate degree has increased by roughly 1% per year.

Where does this increase in wage inequality come from? Most economists see two main causes. The first is international trade. Unskilled workers are increasingly competing with the workers from countries with very low wages, and this competition is pulling down their wages. The second is the nature of technological progress. New technologies require increasingly skilled workers to operate them. Thus, the relative demand for skilled workers is steadily increasing, the relative demand for unskilled workers is steadily decreasing, and these two evolutions are reflected in the relative wages of skilled and unskilled workers.

Economists disagree about the relative importance of these two causes. Some believe that international trade is the main culprit; most believe that the nature of technological progress is to blame. Work on the causes of increasing wage inequality is one of the most active areas of research in economics today.

> There is evidence this increase in inequality may have slowed down or perhaps stopped since the mid-1990s. This would be an important change, but it is too early to be sure.

1-2 | The European Union

In 1957, six European nations—Belgium, France, Germany, Italy, Luxembourg, and the Netherlands—decided to form a common European market—an economic zone where people, goods, and factors of production could move freely. Since then, nine more—Austria, Denmark, Finland, Greece, Ireland, Portugal, Spain, Sweden, and the United Kingdom—have joined. This union is now known as the **European Union,** or **EU.** (Until a few years ago, the official name was the *European Community* or EC. You are likely to encounter both names.)

Not only has the number of members increased, but the ties among members have tightened. Together, they form a formidable power. As Figure 1–3 shows, their combined output is roughly equal to the output of the United States. And many of them have a standard of living, measured by the level of output per capita, close to or higher than the United States.

Recently however, the economic performance of the European Union has been disappointing. Look at Table 1–2. Growth has been low and unemployment has remained very high. In 1998, the average unemployment rate was 10.5%, and the forecast was for only a small decline in 1999. The unemployment numbers for some countries are astounding: In 1998, the unemployment rate in Spain stood at 19%.

The good news concerns inflation. Just as in the United States, inflation is low in the European Union, running at an annual rate of 1.8% in 1998, much lower than its average of 5.7% since 1960.

The European Union is confronting two major economic challenges at this point: the reduction of high unemployment; and the transition to a common currency, the *Euro.*

How to Reduce High Unemployment?

High unemployment is not a European tradition. Figure 1–4, which plots the evolution of unemployment rates in the European Union and the United States, shows how low the European unemployment rate was in the 1960s. At that time, the talk in the United States was about the European "unemployment miracle"; U.S. macroeconomists went to Europe in the hope of discovering the secrets of that miracle. But by the late 1970s, the miracle had vanished. And since the early 1980s, the unemployment rate in Europe has been much higher than in the United States.

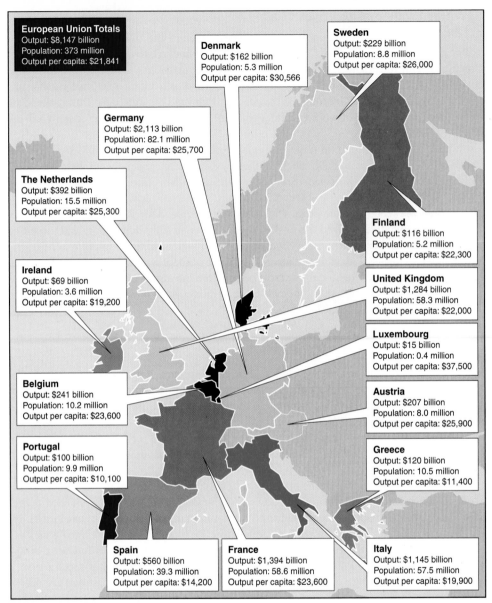

European Union Totals
Output: $8,147 billion
Population: 373 million
Output per capita: $21,841

Denmark
Output: $162 billion
Population: 5.3 million
Output per capita: $30,566

Sweden
Output: $229 billion
Population: 8.8 million
Output per capita: $26,000

Germany
Output: $2,113 billion
Population: 82.1 million
Output per capita: $25,700

The Netherlands
Output: $392 billion
Population: 15.5 million
Output per capita: $25,300

Finland
Output: $116 billion
Population: 5.2 million
Output per capita: $22,300

Ireland
Output: $69 billion
Population: 3.6 million
Output per capita: $19,200

United Kingdom
Output: $1,284 billion
Population: 58.3 million
Output per capita: $22,000

Luxembourg
Output: $15 billion
Population: 0.4 million
Output per capita: $37,500

Belgium
Output: $241 billion
Population: 10.2 million
Output per capita: $23,600

Austria
Output: $207 billion
Population: 8.0 million
Output per capita: $25,900

Portugal
Output: $100 billion
Population: 9.9 million
Output per capita: $10,100

Greece
Output: $120 billion
Population: 10.5 million
Output per capita: $11,400

Spain
Output: $560 billion
Population: 39.3 million
Output per capita: $14,200

France
Output: $1,394 billion
Population: 58.6 million
Output per capita: $23,600

Italy
Output: $1,145 billion
Population: 57.5 million
Output per capita: $19,900

FIGURE 1–3

The European Union

Source: International Financial Statistics, International Monetary Fund. Output is GDP in domestic currency in 1997, converted to dollars at the average exchange rate for 1997.

There are many views as to why European unemployment is high and what should be done to decrease it.

At one extreme are those who point to what they call "labor market rigidities." Europe, they argue, suffers from too high a level of unemployment benefits, too high a minimum wage, too high a level of worker protection. The solution, they conclude, is to remove these "rigidities," to make European labor markets more like the U.S. labor market.

At the other extreme are those who say that these so-called rigidities are, for the most part, not excessive, and that high unemployment comes primarily from misguided macroeconomic policies. They argue that a change in these policies—for example, a more expansionary monetary policy leading to lower interest rates—could lead to an increase in demand, and to a decrease in unemployment rates to levels similar to those of the United States.

TABLE 1-2	Growth, Unemployment, and Inflation in the European Union, 1960–1999			
(in percent)	1960–1998	1997	1998	1999 (forecast)
Output growth rate	3.1	2.7	2.8	1.9
Unemployment rate	6.4	11.2	10.5	10.1
Inflation rate	5.7	1.8	1.8	1.7

Growth rate: annual rate of growth of gross domestic product (GDP). *Unemployment rate*: average over the year. *Inflation rate*: annual rate of change of the GDP deflator.
Source: OECD Economic Outlook, June 1999.

Most macroeconomists stand somewhere between these two extremes. They believe that both changes in the labor market as well as some demand expansion are needed. The debate is far from settled, yet its outcome is crucial to Europe's future.

What Will the Euro Do for Europe?

In 1999, the European Union started the process of replacing national currencies with one common currency, called the Euro. Only 11 of the 15 EU countries are participating in the process. Greece did not satisfy the economic criteria for participation. Denmark, Sweden, and the United Kingdom have decided to wait and perhaps join in the future. The plan is the following: On January 1, 1999, each of the 11 countries fixed the parity of its currency to the Euro. For example, a Euro is now worth 6.56 French francs, 166 Spanish pesetas, and so on. On January 1, 2002, Euro notes and coins will start circulating together with national currencies. And from July 1, 2002, the Euro will be the only currency in circulation. By then, the 11 countries will have become a *common currency area*, just as the 50 states of the United States are today.

What to call the group of 11 countries that have adopted the Euro is not settled. "Euro-zone" sounds technocratic. "Euroland" reminds some of "Disneyland," but seems to be winning acceptance.

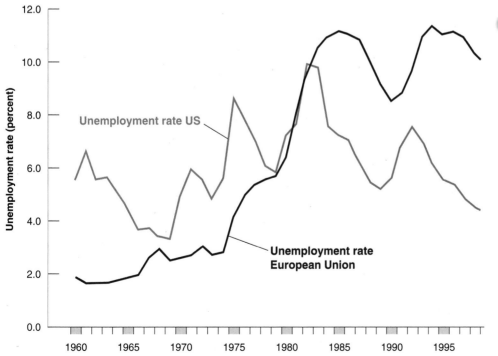

FIGURE 1-4

Unemployment rates: Europe versus the United States, 1960–1998

The European unemployment rate has gone from being much lower to being much higher than that of the United States.

Supporters of the Euro point to the enormous symbolic importance of the Euro. In light of the many past wars between European countries, what better proof that the page has definitely been turned than the adoption of a common money? They also point to the economic advantages of a common currency: no more exchange rate movements for firms to worry about, no more need to change currency when traveling between Euro countries. Together with the removal of other obstacles to trade between European countries which has taken place since 1957, the Euro will contribute, they argue, to the creation of a large, if not the largest, economic power in the world.

Others worry that the symbolism of the Euro may exact heavy economic costs. They point out that a common currency means a common monetary policy, and thus identical interest rates across the Euro countries. What if, they argue, one country plunges into a recession, while another sharply expands? The first country may need lower interest rates to increase demand and output; the second country may need higher interest rates to slow down its expansion. If interest rates have to be the same in both countries, what will happen? Isn't there the risk that the first country may remain in recession for a long time, or that the second country may not be able to slow down too strong an expansion?

This has been the debate in Europe for most of the 1990s. The question used to be, should Europe introduce the Euro? Now it has. The full move to the Euro in 2002 will be one of the main economic events of the start of the twenty-first century.

1-3 | Japan and East Asia

Forty years ago, Japan might not have been included in our economic tour. Its output per capita was very low compared to the United States or Europe. But things are very different today. As Table 1–3 shows, Japan's average annual rate of growth since 1960 has been close to 6%, nearly 3% above the average U.S. growth rate. And, as you can see from Figure 1–5, Japan's output is now more than half that of the United States; output per capita is higher than output per capita in the United States.

Although Japan's economic performance since 1960 is impressive, its economic performance in the 1990s has been dismal. Average growth since 1992 has been under 1.0%. Growth in 1998 was actually negative, and the forecast for 1999 is for roughly no growth. The unemployment rate—which traditionally has been very low in Japan—has increased to record highs. The unemployment rate for 1998 was 4.1%, a number that Europe can only dream of, but a post–World War II high for the Japanese economy.

Why Has Japan Done So Poorly in the 1990s?

Why has growth been so low in Japan in the 1990s? Most analysts point to the movement in stock prices from the mid-1980s to the early 1990s as one of the main culprits. Figure 1–6

TABLE 1–3 Growth, Unemployment, and Inflation in Japan, 1960–1999				
(in percent)	1960–1997	1997	1998	1999 (forecast)
Output growth rate	5.8	0.8	−2.8	−0.9
Unemployment rate	1.9	3.4	4.1	4.9
Inflation rate	4.8	0.6	0.4	−0.7

Growth rate: annual rate of growth of gross domestic product (GDP). *Unemployment rate*: average over the year. *Inflation rate*: annual rate of change of the GDP deflator.

Source: OECD Economic Outlook, June 1999.

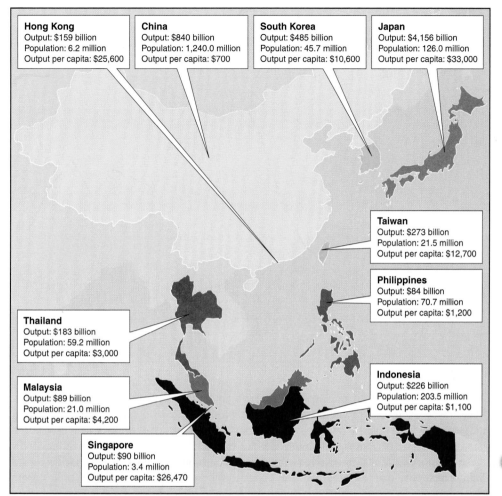

Hong Kong
Output: $159 billion
Population: 6.2 million
Output per capita: $25,600

China
Output: $840 billion
Population: 1,240.0 million
Output per capita: $700

South Korea
Output: $485 billion
Population: 45.7 million
Output per capita: $10,600

Japan
Output: $4,156 billion
Population: 126.0 million
Output per capita: $33,000

Taiwan
Output: $273 billion
Population: 21.5 million
Output per capita: $12,700

Philippines
Output: $84 billion
Population: 70.7 million
Output per capita: $1,200

Thailand
Output: $183 billion
Population: 59.2 million
Output per capita: $3,000

Malaysia
Output: $89 billion
Population: 21.0 million
Output per capita: $4,200

Singapore
Output: $90 billion
Population: 3.4 million
Output per capita: $26,470

Indonesia
Output: $226 billion
Population: 203.5 million
Output per capita: $1,100

FIGURE 1-5

East Asia

Source: IFS, The numbers for Japan are for 1997, the numbers for the other countries are for 1996.

shows the behavior of the *Nikkei index*, an index of stock prices in the Japanese stock market, since 1980. From 1985 to 1989, the Nikkei increased from about 13,000 to 35,000; in other words, the average price of a share in the Japanese stock market nearly tripled in less than four years. This sharp increase was followed in the early 1990s by an equally sharp decrease. In less than two years, from 1990 to 1992, the Nikkei fell from 35,000 to 16,000.

Many economists interpret this rise and fall of the Nikkei as a *speculative bubble*, an excessive increase in stock prices in the 1980s, followed by a sharp decline and a return to reality in the early 1990s. They point to similar movements in the prices of other assets, such as land or housing; real estate prices increased in line with the Nikkei, and since 1990 have declined even more than stock prices. They argue that the result of the stock market boom was a boom in demand and in output in the late 1980s, and that the result of the stock market fall was a sharp drop in demand and output in the 1990s.

The question now is how Japan can return to higher growth. In an effort to increase demand, the Japanese central bank has decreased interest rates to very low levels: Interest rates in Japan have remained under 1% since 1996. The government is also using fiscal policy to increase demand. It has cut taxes in order to stimulate spending by consumers and firms, and more tax cuts are planned for 1999. So far, however, these measures have not had much effect on output.

It is precisely this set of events that leads many economists to worry about the large rise—and the potential fall—of the U.S. stock market.

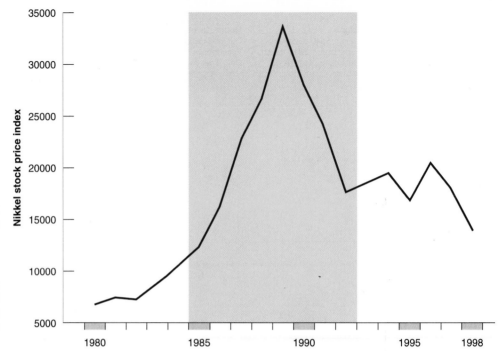

FIGURE 1-6

The Japanese Stock Market Index, 1980–1998

The large increase in the index in the second half of the 1980s was followed by a very sharp decline in the early 1990s.

This has led some to conclude that the problem is more serious, that the economy will not grow fast again before a number of structural problems are recognized and solved. During the stock and real estate boom of the 1980s, many banks made loans to stock market investors and to real estate developers. With the declines in stock and real estate prices in the 1990s, these banks have found themselves saddled with bad loans, loans that will not be repaid. Some banks have had to close; others are likely to follow. Without a healthy banking system, many economists argue, it will be difficult for Japan to return to steady growth.

What Was the Cause of the Asian Crisis of 1997?

Although it is the richest Asian country, Japan is not the only Asian country to have grown very fast over the last 30 years.

Four countries, often called the *four tigers*—Hong Kong, Singapore, Korea, and Taiwan—have followed close behind. As you can see from Table 1–4, since 1970 all four countries have had average growth rates of about 8%. Hong Kong and Singapore now have levels of output per capita close to those of the United States (Figure 1–4).

Behind the four tigers are many other Asian countries that are poor—with output per capita often less than one-tenth that of the United States—but growing fast. As Table 1–4 shows, Indonesia, Malaysia, the Philippines, and Thailand have all achieved high growth rates since 1970. Because of its size, China is in a category by itself. It is still poor, with output per capita around 700 dollars. But with a population of 1.2 billion and a growth rate of output of 9% a year since 1970, it is rapidly becoming one of the main economic powers in the world.

This impressive performance has been dubbed the *Asian miracle.* Economists have studied this miracle, trying to identify the factors behind such high growth in the hope of applying the lessons elsewhere. Since 1997, however, many of these countries have been in a serious economic crisis, known as—guess what?—the *Asian crisis.*

The crisis started in Thailand, when some foreign investors decided to remove their funds from Thailand. In the process of selling assets, and then selling bahts (the Thai currency) for dollars, they triggered sharp drops both in the stock market and in the value of the baht

Hong Kong is actually not a country. Until 1997, it was a British colony; in 1997, it became part of China.

| TABLE | 1–4 | Output Growth in East Asian Countries, 1970–1999 |

(in percent)	1970–1997	1997	1998	1999 (forecast)
Hong Kong	7.5	5.2	−5.1	−1.3
Singapore	8.2	7.5	1.5	0.5
Korea	8.4	5.5	−5.5	2.0
Taiwan	8.3	6.8	4.9	3.9
Indonesia	6.8	4.7	−13.7	−4.0
Malaysia	7.4	7.8	−6.8	0.9
Philippines	3.6	5.1	−0.5	2.0
Thailand	7.5	−0.4	1.0	3.0
China	9.1	8.8	7.8	6.6

Growth rate: annual rate of growth of gross domestic product (GDP).
Source: *World Economic Outlook*, May 1999.

against the dollar. By early 1998, several other Asian countries were suffering from the same ills. Figure 1–7 shows the evolution of the stock market index and of the value of the domestic currency in terms of dollars for Thailand, Malaysia, Indonesia, and Korea from January 1997 to December 1998. In each case, the value of the index is set equal to one in January 1997. All four countries experienced deep recessions—large decreases in output—in 1998, and the forecasts, shown in Table 1–4, are for low or negative growth for 1999.

Economists are still trying to assess exactly what happened. Did foreign investors see several serious economic problems ahead, and decide to move out as a result? Or was there,

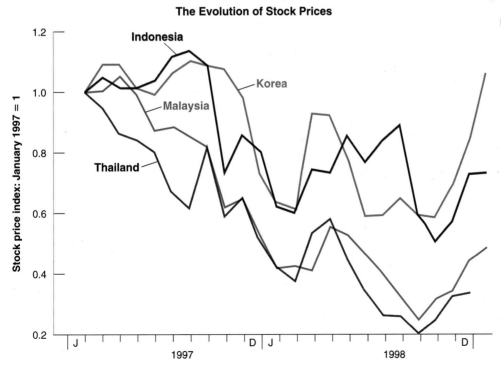

The Evolution of Stock Prices

FIGURE 1–7

The Fall in East Asian Stock Prices and Currencies, January 1997 to December 1998

In 1997 and early 1998, many East Asian economies saw both a sharp drop in stock prices and in the value of their currency against the dollar.

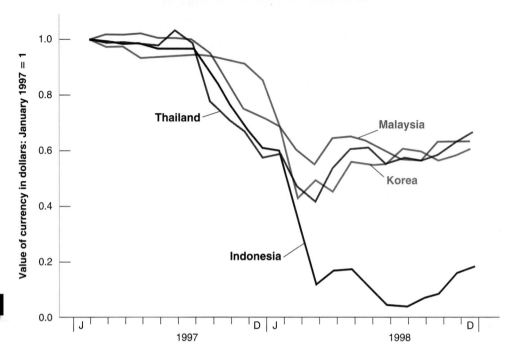

The Evolution of the Values of Currencies

FIGURE 1-7

(*continued*)

as the Prime Minister of Malaysia has argued, a series of unjustified speculative attacks against their currency, leading to an economic crisis only as a result of the speculative attack itself?

The answer is probably yes to both questions. Despite the fast growth, these economies were suffering from a number of structural problems, from corruption to poor regulation of financial institutions. Also, as in Japan in the late 1980s, stock and real estate prices were very high in 1997. Foreign investors had reasons to worry that things may not be as good in the future. But there is also no question that the sharp falls in stock prices and in the value of their currency have made the economic situation much worse. For example, many firms and banks had borrowed abroad in dollars. With the sharp increase in the dollar relative to their domestic currency, they found themselves with very high debts in terms of domestic currency. Some of them have gone bankrupt; others will soon.

The Asian crisis is still unfolding. But what happened in Asia in the late 1990s, how to avoid a repeat of a similar crisis elsewhere, and how to get Asian countries back on track are among the main questions facing macroeconomists today.

1-4 | Looking Ahead

This concludes our world tour. There are many other countries we might have looked at, from the nations of Eastern Europe (which shifted in the early 1990s from central planning to a market system) to Latin America (which has gone from very high to low inflation in the 1990s) to Africa (which may be starting to grow after decades of economic stagnation). But there is a limit to how much you can absorb in this first chapter. Think of the questions to which you have been exposed already:

● What determines expansions and recessions? Why has the United States had such a long expansion in the 1990s? What has been the role of monetary and fiscal policy? How will the Euro affect monetary policy in Europe?

● What are the interactions between the stock market, the foreign exchange market, and economic activity? Is the U.S. stock market too high? Can the poor performance of

Japan in the 1990s be attributed to the sharp decline in the Japanese stock market in the early 1990s?

- Why is inflation so much lower in the 1990s than in earlier decades? What is so bad about inflation? Should countries aim for zero inflation, as is now the case in Japan?
- Could the current U.S. unemployment rate be too low? Why is unemployment so high in Europe? Why has the Japanese unemployment rate been so low for so many years?
- Why do growth rates differ so much across countries, even over long periods of time? Why has Japan grown so much faster than the United States and Europe over the last 40 years? What are the factors behind the Asian miracle? Why has growth slowed down since the mid-1970s in most rich countries?

The purpose of this book is to give you a way of thinking about these questions. As I develop the tools you need, I shall show you how to use them, by returning to all these questions and showing what answers they suggest.

FOCUS

Gathering Macro Data

Where do the data we have examined in this chapter come from? For example, where does one find the number for inflation in Germany over the last two decades? Forty years ago, the answer would have been to learn German, find a library with German publications, find the page where inflation numbers were given, write them down, and plot them by hand on a nice clean sheet of paper. Today, improvements in the collection of data and the development of computers and electronic databases make the task much easier.

International organizations now collect data for many countries. For the richest countries, the most useful source is the **Organization for Economic Cooperation and Development (OECD)** based in Paris. Most of the world's rich economies belong to the OECD. The complete list includes Austria, Australia, Belgium, Canada, the Czech Republic, Denmark, Finland, France, Germany, Greece, Hungary, Iceland, Italy, Japan, Luxembourg, Mexico, the Netherlands, New Zealand, Norway, Poland, Portugal, Korea, Spain, Sweden, Switzerland, Turkey, the United Kingdom, and the United States. Together, these countries account for about 70% of world output. The *OECD Economic Outlook*, which is published twice yearly, gives basic data on inflation, unemployment, and other major variables for member countries, as well as an assessment of their recent macroeconomic performance. The data, going back to 1960, are available on diskettes; they are on most macroeconomists' hard disks.

For those countries that are not members of the OECD, information is available from other international organizations. The main world economic organization, a sort of world economic club, is the **International Monetary Fund (IMF)**. The IMF publishes the monthly *International Financial Statistics (IFS)*, which contains basic macroeconomic information for all IMF members. It also publishes the annual *World Economic Outlook*, an assessment of macroeconomic developments in various parts of the world. Although their language is sometimes stilted, both the *World Economic Report* and the *OECD Economic Outlook* are precious sources of information.

Because these publications sometimes do not contain sufficient details, you may need to turn to specific country publications. Major countries now produce remarkably clear statistical publications, often with an English translation available. In the United States, an extremely good buy is the *Economic Report of the President*, prepared by the Council of Economic Advisors and published annually. This report has two parts. The first is an assessment of current U.S. events and policy. The second is a set of data for nearly all relevant macroeconomic variables, usually for the entire post–World War II period.

A longer list of data sources, both for the United States and for the rest of the world, as well as how to access some of them through the Internet, is given in the appendix to this chapter.

KEY TERMS

- European Union (EU), 7
- Organization for Economic Cooperation and Development (OECD), 15

- International Monetary Fund (IMF), 15

An asterisk denotes a harder question. [Web] indicates that the question requires access to the Internet.

1. TRUE/FALSE/UNCERTAIN

Using the tables and graphs in this chapter, label each of the following statements *true*, *false*, or *uncertain*. Explain briefly.

a. Recently, inflation has been below its historical average in the United States, the European Union, and Japan.

b. In the 1960s and early 1970s, the United States had a higher rate of unemployment than Europe, but today it has a much lower rate of unemployment.

c. As the U.S. rate of unemployment has been very low since the early 1980s, wage inequality in the United States has decreased.

d. The collapse of the Japanese stock market in the early 1990s was followed by a sharp drop in Japanese output.

e. The European "unemployment miracle" refers to the extremely low rate of unemployment that Europe has been enjoying since the 1980s.

f. The 1997 collapse of the stock markets and many local currencies of East Asian countries is expected to have no effect on the growth rate of output in those countries.

2. ECONOMIC GROWTH IN THE RICHEST COUNTRIES

Using the actual rates of growth and the forecasts reported in Tables 1–1, 1–2, and 1–3, compute the average output growth rate forecast for the period 1997 to 1999 for each of the following regions: the United States, the European Union, and Japan.

a. For each of the three regions, compare the average rate of output growth for 1997 to 1999 computed earlier with the average rate over 1960 to 1998. In particular, how do the recent experiences of each of these regions compare to their respective long-run averages?

b. Are the preceding data consistent with a claim that there has been a slowdown in growth in rich countries since the mid-1970s? In particular, does the recent experience in the United States indicate that the slowdown in average growth since 1974 has been reversed?

3. [WEB] FLUCTUATIONS IN OUTPUT GROWTH

Although the growth rate of output is positive on average, there are periods during which the growth rate of output is negative. Periods of declining output that last at least two quarters are called recessions.

a. To examine recessions a little closer, obtain quarterly data on U.S. output growth for the period 1959 to 1996 from the Web site <http://www.bea.doc.gov/bea/sumnip-d.html>. Look at the data series for the percentage change in quarterly real gross domestic product (GDP). How many quarters do most recessions last? In terms of length and magnitude, which two recessions have been the most severe in this period?

b. In the text it is noted that the last time the unemployment rate was as low as in 1999 was in 1969, at the end of a decade-long expansion. By looking at data from 1968 to 1971, verify the claim that shortly thereafter, inflation increased and a recession began. Use the data series for the percentage change in the quarterly "Implicit Price Deflator for GDP" from the same Web page as in (a) as a measure of inflation. If history repeats itself, what are the prospects for the U.S. economy for the beginning of the next millennium?

4. WAGE INEQUALITY AND TECHNOLOGICAL CHANGE

Consider the share of total U.S. output in 1987 and 1996 produced by each of the following industries:

Industry	1987 (%)	1996 (%)
Mining, agriculture, and construction	8.4	7.1
Retail trade	9.3	8.7
Banking services	17.7	18.9
Business services	3.0	4.0

Source: U.S. Department of Commerce, Bureau of Economic Analysis, <http://www.bea.doc.gov/>

a. In which of these industries do you think that new technology has increased the relative demand for skilled workers?

b. Given your answer in (a) and the change in the composition of U.S. output presented in the table, why do you think that the wage gap between skilled and unskilled workers has increased?

5. CORRECT THE POLITICIANS

Politicians often tell only one side of the story. Consider each of the statements and comment on the other side of the story.

a. There is no such thing as a rate of unemployment that is too low. Unemployment is bad. The lower it is, the better.

b. There is no slowdown in growth, just a slowdown in the ability of economists to measure output correctly.

c. There is a simple solution to the problem of high European unemployment: Reduce labor market rigidities.

d. The crisis in Asia was well deserved because it was caused by corruption and poor regulation of the financial system.

e. What can be wrong about joining forces and adopting a common currency? The Euro is obviously good for Europe.

6. WHEN WILL CHINA CATCH UP?

Suppose that from now on, the output of the People's Republic of China will grow at an annual rate of 9% per year, whereas the output of the United States will grow at an annual rate of 3% per year.

a. Using the latest data available from this chapter on the level of output in each country, how long will it be before China's output becomes larger than that of the United States.

b. Suppose also that the population of both China and the United States will remain constant from now on. How long will it be before China's output per worker becomes larger than that of the United States.

FURTHER READING

This book has a Web page (http://www.prenhall.com/book-bind/pubbooks/blanchard/), which is updated regularly. For each chapter, the page offers discussions of current events, and includes relevant articles and Internet links. You can also use the page to make comments on the book, and start discussions with other readers.

The best way to follow current economic events and issues is to read *The Economist*, a weekly magazine published in England. The articles in *The Economist* are well informed, well written, witty, and strongly opinionated.

APPENDIX

WHERE TO FIND THE NUMBERS

The purpose of this appendix is to help you find the numbers you are looking for, be it inflation in Malaysia last quarter, or consumption in the United States in 1959, or youth unemployment in Ireland in the 1980s.

For a Quick Look at Current Numbers

- The best source for the most recent numbers on production, unemployment, inflation, exchange rates, interest rates, and stock prices for a large number of countries is the last four pages of *The Economist*, published each week (Internet address: http://www.economist.com). This Web site, as most of the Web sites listed below, contains both information available free of charge and information available only to subscribers.
- There exist several Web pages that collect and analyze recent data. One of the best is: http://www.yardeni.com, the home page of Dr. Edward Yardeni, Chief Economist of a large bank, Deutsche Morgan Grenfell.

For More Detail about the U.S. Economy

- For a detailed presentation of the most recent numbers, look at the *Survey of Current Business*, published monthly by the U.S. Department of Commerce, Bureau of Economic Analysis (Internet address: http://www. bea.doc.gov). A user's guide to the statistics published by the Bureau of Economic Analysis is given in the *Survey of Current Business*, January 1995, 36–52. It tells you what data are available, in what form, and at what price.
- Once a year, the *Economic Report of the President*, written by the Council of Economic Advisers and published by the U.S. Government Printing Office in Washington, gives a description of current evolutions, as well as numbers for most major macroeconomic variables, often going back to the 1950s. (The statistical tables in the report can be found at http://www.access.gpo.gov/eop/)
- The authoritative source for statistics going back as far as data have been collected is *Historical Statistics of the*

United States, Colonial Times to 1970, Parts 1 and 2, published by the U.S. Department of Commerce, Bureau of the Census (Internet address: http://www.census.gov/stat_abstract/).

- The standard reference for national income accounts is *National Income and Product Accounts of the United States.* Volume 1, 1929–1958, and Volume 2, 1959–1988, published by the U.S. Department of Commerce, Bureau of Economic Analysis (Internet address: http://www.bea.doc.gov).

- For data on just about everything, including economic data, a precious source is the *Statistical Abstract of the United States*, published annually by the U.S. Department of Commerce, Bureau of the Census (Internet address: http://www.census.gov/statab/www/).

Numbers for Other Countries

The OECD, located in Paris, publishes three extremely useful publications. The OECD includes most of the rich countries in the world. (The list is given earlier in this chapter.) (Internet address: http://www.oecd.org)

- The first is the *OECD Economic Outlook*, published twice a year. In addition to describing current macroeconomic issues, it includes data for many macroeconomic variables. The data typically go back to the 1970s, and are reported consistently, both across time and across countries.

- The second is the *OECD Employment Outlook*, published annually. It focuses more specifically on labor-market issues and numbers.

- Occasionally, the OECD puts together current and past data, and publishes the *OECD Historical Statistics*. At this point in time, the most recent is *Historical Statistics, 1960–1993*, published in 1995.

The main strength of the publications of the International Monetary Fund (IMF, located in Washington, D.C.) is that they cover most of the countries of the world (Internet address: http://www.imf.org).

The IMF issues four particularly useful publications:

- The first is the *International Financial Statistics* (IFS), published monthly. It has data for member countries, usually going back a few years, mostly on financial variables, but also on some aggregate variables (such as GDP, employment, and inflation).

- The second is the *International Financial Statistics Yearbook*, published annually. It has the same coverage of countries and variables as the IFS, but gives annual data for up to 30 years.

- The third is the *Government Finance Statistics Yearbook*, published annually, which gives data on the budget of each country, typically going back 10 years. (Because of delays in the construction of the numbers, data for the most recent years are often unavailable.)

- The fourth, the *World Economic Outlook*, published twice a year, describes major evolutions in the world and in specific member countries.

For long-term historical statistics for several countries, a precious new data source is *Monitoring the World Economy, 1820–1992,* Development Centre Studies, OECD, Paris, 1995. This study gives data going back to 1820 for 56 countries.

Finally, if you still have not found what you were looking for, here are two useful sites: The Macroeconomics Resources site of the Harvard Business School (http://www.hbs.edu/units/bgie/internet/), which assesses the quality of—and provides links with—a large number of other potentially useful Web sites.

A site maintained by Bill Goffe at the University of Mississippi (http://rfe.wustl.edu), which lists not only data sources but sources for economic information in general, from working papers, to jokes, to jobs in economics, and so on.

We invite you to visit the Blanchard page on the Prentice Hall Web site at:

http://www.prenhall.com/blanchard

for this chapter's World Wide Web exercises

CHAPTER 2 | A Tour of the Book

The words *output*, *unemployment*, and *inflation* appear daily in newspapers and on the evening news. So when I used them in Chapter 1, you were familiar with them, at least to the extent that you knew roughly what they meant. Now I need to define them precisely and this is what I do in the first two sections of this chapter. In section 2-1, I focus on aggregate output and show how we can look at aggregate output both from the production side and from the income side. In section 2-2, I look at the unemployment rate and at the inflation rate. Having defined the major macro-economic variables, I then take you, in section 2-3, on a tour of the book. In that tour, I introduce the three central concepts around which the book is organized:

- The *short run*—what happens to the economy from year to year.
- The *medium run*—what happens to the economy over a decade or so.
- The *long run*—what happens to the economy over a half century or more.

Building on these three concepts, I then give you a road map to the rest of the book.

Economists studying economic activity in the nineteenth century or during the Great Depression had no measure of aggregate activity (*aggregate* is the word macroeconomists use for *total*) on which to rely. They had to put together bits and pieces of information, such as the production of pig iron or sales at department stores, to infer what was happening to the economy as a whole.

It was not until the end of World War II that **national income and product accounts** (or national income accounts, for short) were put together in major countries. Measures of aggregate output have been published on a regular basis in the United States since October 1947. (You will find measures of aggregate output for earlier times, but these have been constructed retrospectively.)

Like any accounting system, the national income accounts define concepts, and then construct measures corresponding to these concepts. One needs only to look at statistics from countries that have not yet developed such accounts to realize how crucial such precision and consistency are. Without them, numbers that should add up do not; trying to understand what is going on often feels like trying to balance someone else's checkbook. I shall not burden you with the details of national income accounting here. But, because you will occasionally need to know the definition of a variable and how variables relate to each other, Appendix 1 at the end of the book gives you the basic accounting framework used in the United States (and, with minor variations, in most other countries). You will find it useful whenever you want to look at economic data on your own.

> Putting the national income accounts together was a gigantic intellectual achievement. The Nobel prize was awarded in 1971 to Simon Kuznets, from Harvard University, and in 1984, to Richard Stone, from Oxford University, for their contributions to the development of the national income and product accounts.

GDP, Value Added, and Income

The measure of **aggregate output** in the national income accounts is **gross domestic product**, or **GDP**, for short. There are three ways of thinking about an economy's GDP. Let's examine each one:

> You may encounter another term, **gross national product**, or **GNP**. There is a subtle difference between "domestic" and "national," and thus between GDP and GNP. We shall examine it in Chapter 18 (and also in Appendix 1). For the moment, you can ignore the difference between the two.

1. GDP Is the Value of the Final Goods and Services Produced in the Economy During a Given Period. The important word is *final*. To see why, consider the following example. Suppose that the economy is composed of just two firms.

- Firm 1 produces steel, employing workers and using machines. It sells the steel for $100 to Firm 2, which produces cars. Firm 1 pays its workers $80 and keeps what remains, $20, as profit.
- Firm 2 buys the steel and uses it, together with workers and machines, to produce cars. Revenues from car sales are $210. Of the $210, $100 goes to pay for steel and $70 goes to workers in the firm, leaving $40 in profit.

We can summarize this information in a table:

Steel company		
Revenues from sales		$100
Expenses (wages)		$80
Profit		$20
Car company		
Revenues from sales		$210
Expenses		$170
Wages	$70	
Steel purchases	$100	
Profit		$40

What is GDP in this economy? Is it the sum of the values of all production in the economy—the sum of $100 from the production of steel and $210 from the production of cars, $310? Or is it the value of the production of final goods, here cars, $210?

Some thought suggests that the right answer must be $210. Why? Because steel is an **intermediate good**, a good used in the production of the final good, cars, and thus should not be counted in GDP—the value of *final* output. We can look at this example in another way. Suppose the two firms merged, so that the sale of steel took place inside the new firm and was no longer recorded. All we would see would be one firm selling cars for $210, paying workers $80 + $70 = $150, and making $20 + $40 = $60 in profits. The $210 measure would remain unchanged—as it should.

This example suggests constructing GDP by recording and adding up the production of final goods—and this is indeed roughly the way actual GDP numbers are put together. But the example also suggests another way of thinking about and constructing GDP:

An intermediate good is a good used in the production of another good. Some goods can be both final goods and intermediate goods. When sold directly to consumers, potatoes are final goods. When used to produce chips, they are intermediate goods.

2. GDP Is the Sum of Value Added in the Economy During a Given Period. The term **value added** means exactly what it suggests. The value added by a firm in the production process is defined as the value of its production minus the value of the intermediate goods it uses in production.

In our two-firm example, the steel company does not use intermediate goods. Its value added is simply equal to the value of its production, $100. The car company, however, uses steel as an intermediate good. Thus, value added by the car company is equal to the value of the cars it produces minus the value of the steel it uses in production, $210 − $100 = $110. Total value added in the economy, or GDP, equals $100 + $110 = $210. Note that aggregate value added would remain the same if the steel and car firms merged and became one firm.

This definition gives us a second way of thinking about GDP. Put together, the two definitions imply that the value of final goods and services—the first definition of GDP—can also be thought of as the sum of the value added by all firms along the chain of production of those final goods—the second definition of GDP.

3. GDP Is the Sum of Incomes in the Economy During a Given Period. We have looked so far at GDP from the *production side*. A third way of looking at GDP is from the *income side*. Think about the revenues left to a firm after it has paid for intermediate goods.

- Some of the revenues are collected by the government in the form of taxes on sales—such taxes are called *indirect taxes.*
- Some of the revenues go to pay workers—this component is called *labor income.*
- The rest goes to the firm—that component is called *capital income.*

In short, looking at it from the income side, value added is the sum of indirect taxes, labor income, and capital income.

Let us return to our example. There are no indirect taxes. Of the $100 of value added by the steel manufacturer, $80 goes to workers (labor income) and the remaining $20 goes to firms as profit (capital income). Of the $110 of value added by the car manufacturer, $70 goes to labor income and $40 to capital income. For the economy as a whole, value added is $210, of which $150 ($80 + $70) goes to labor income and $60 ($20 + $40) goes to capital income.

In this example, labor income accounts for 71% of GDP, capital income for 29%, indirect taxes for 0%. Table 2–1 shows the breakdown of value added among the different types of income in the United States in 1960 and 1998. The table shows that, except for indirect taxes (which are equal to zero in our example), the proportions we have been using in our example are roughly those of the U.S. economy. Labor income accounts for 65% of U.S. GDP. Capital income accounts for 27%. Indirect taxes account for the remaining 8%. The proportions have not changed much since 1960.

(in percent)	1960	1998
Labor income	66%	65%
Capital income	26%	27%
Indirect taxes	8%	8%

Sources: *Economic Report of the President, 1999*, Tables B27 and B28.

To summarize: You can think about aggregate output—about *GDP*—in three different but equivalent ways.

- From the output side: GDP is equal to the value of the final goods and services produced in the economy during a given period.
- Also from the output side: GDP is the sum of value added in the economy during a given period.
- From the income side: GDP is the sum of incomes in the economy during a given period.

Nominal and Real GDP

U.S. GDP was $8,508 billion in 1998, compared to $526 billion in 1960. Was U.S. output 16 times higher in 1998 than in 1960? No. This leads us to the distinction between nominal GDP and real GDP.

> Warning! People often use "nominal" to denote small amounts. Economists use nominal for variables expressed in current prices. And economists surely do not refer to small amounts. The numbers you will see in this book are typically expressed in billions or even trillions of dollars.

Nominal GDP is the sum of the quantities of final goods produced times their current price. This definition makes it clear that nominal GDP increases over time for two reasons. First, the production of most goods increases over time. Second, the prices of most goods also increase over time. We produce more and more cars and their prices increase each year as well. If our intention is to measure production and its change over time, we need to eliminate the effect of increasing prices. That's why **real GDP** is constructed as the sum of the quantities of final goods times *constant* (rather than current) prices.

Let's look more closely at the construction of real GDP. If the economy produced only one final good, say, a particular car model, constructing real GDP would be easy. We could merely count the number of cars produced each year, and call that number real GDP. Or, if we wanted to have a measure in dollars rather than cars, we could use the price of cars in a given year, and then use it to multiply quantities in all years.

Suppose, for example, that the quantity produced and the price of cars in three successive years was as shown here:

Year	Quantity of Cars	Price of Cars	Nominal GDP
1991	10	$10,000	$100,000
1992	12	$12,000	$144,000
1993	13	$13,000	$169,000

Nominal GDP, which is equal to quantity of cars times their price, goes up from $100,000 in 1991 to $144,000 in 1992, a 44% increase, and from $144,000 in 1992 to $169,000 in 1993, a 16% increase.

How should we define real GDP, and by how much does it go up? We can define it as the number of cars: 10 in 1991, 12 in 1992, 13 in 1993. This implies a 20% increase in real GDP from 1991 to 1992, and an 8% increase from 1992 to 1993. Or we can define it by multiplying the number of cars in each year by a *common* price, say, the price of a car in 1992. This approach gives us in effect *real GDP in 1992 dollars*.

Using this approach, real GDP in 1991 (in 1992 dollars) is equal to $10 \times \$12,000 = \$120,000$. Real GDP in 1992 (in 1992 dollars) is equal to $12 \times \$12,000 = \$144,000$, the same as nominal GDP in 1992. Real GDP in 1993 (in 1992 dollars) is equal to $13 \times \$12,000 = \$156,000$. Note that, because we multiply the number of cars in each year by the *same* price, the increase in real GDP, when measured in 1992 dollars, is the same as when measured in cars: Real GDP in 1992 dollars increases by 20% from 1992 to 1993, and by 8% from 1993 to 1994. If we had decided to measure real GDP in 1993 prices, the level of real GDP would be different (because the prices are not the same in 1993 as in 1992), but its increase from year to year would be the same as above.

◄ Just to be sure: Compute real GDP in 1993 prices, and compute the rate of growth from 1991 to 1992, and from 1992 to 1993.

The main problem in constructing real GDP in practice is that there is more than one final good. Real GDP must be defined as a weighted average of the output of all final goods, which brings the question of what the weights should be. Relative prices of the goods would appear to be the natural weights. If a good costs twice as much per unit as another one, then it should clearly count twice as much in the construction of real output. But this raises another question. What if, as is often the case, relative prices change over time? Should we choose the relative prices in a given year as weights, or should we change the weights over time? More discussion of these issues, and of the way real GDP is constructed in the United States, is best left to an appendix to this chapter. What you should know is that the measure of real GDP in the U.S. national income accounts is called **real GDP in chained (1992) dollars** ("1992" because, as in our example, 1992 is the year when, by construction, real GDP is equal to nominal GDP). It is a measure of the output of the U.S. economy, and its evolution shows how U.S. output has increased over time.

Figure 2–1 plots the evolution of both nominal and real GDP since 1960. By construction, the two are equal in 1992. The figure shows that real GDP in 1998 was 3.3 times its level of 1960—a considerable increase, but clearly much less than the 16-fold increase in nominal GDP over the same years. The difference between the two results from the increase in prices over the period.

◄ Suppose that real GDP was measured in 1998 dollars rather than 1992 dollars. Where would the two graphs intersect?

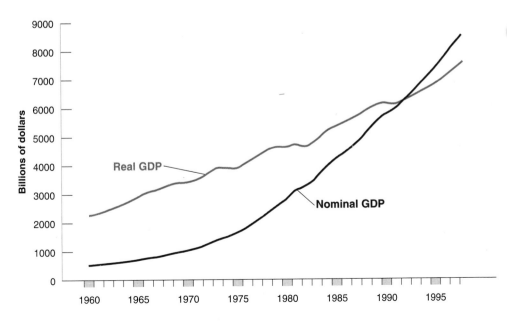

FIGURE 2–1

Nominal and Real U.S. GDP, 1960–1998

From 1960 to 1998, nominal GDP increased by a factor of 16. Real GDP increased by a factor of 3.3.

The terms *nominal GDP* and *real GDP* each have many synonyms, and you are likely to encounter them in your readings:

- *Nominal GDP* is also called **dollar GDP** or **GDP in current dollars**
- *Real GDP* is also called **GDP in terms of goods**, **GDP in constant dollars**, **GDP adjusted for inflation**, or **GDP in 1992 dollars**—if the year in which real GDP is set equal to nominal GDP is 1992, as is the case in the United States at this point.

This concludes your introduction to the main macroeconomic variable, GDP. In the chapters that follow, unless indicated otherwise, GDP will refer to real GDP and Y_t will denote *real* GDP in year t. Nominal GDP, and variables measured in current dollars, will be denoted by a dollar sign in front—for example, $\$Y_t$ for nominal GDP in year t.

Similarly, **GDP growth** in year t will refer to the rate of change of real GDP in year t. GDP growth equals $(Y_t - Y_{t-1})/Y_{t-1}$. Periods of positive GDP growth are called **expansions**. Periods of negative GDP growth are called **recessions**. To avoid calling just one quarter of negative growth a recession, macroeconomists usually use the word only if the economy goes through at least two consecutive quarters of negative growth. The U.S. recession of 1990 to 1991, for example, was characterized by three consecutive quarters of negative growth, the last two quarters of 1990 and the first quarter of 1991.

> Rate of output growth:
> $(Y_t - Y_{t-1})/Y_{t-1}$
>
> rate of growth > 0:
> expansion
>
> rate of growth < 0:
> recession

FOCUS

Real GDP, Technological Progress, and the Price of Computers

A tough problem in computing real GDP is dealing with changes in quality in existing goods. One of the most difficult cases is computers. Should we assume that a personal computer in 1999 is the same good as a computer produced in 1987? This would clearly be absurd: The same price or less clearly buys much more computing power in 1999 than it bought in 1987. The difficult question is, how much more? Does a 1999 computer provide 10 times, 100 times, or 1,000 times the computing power of a 1987 computer? How should we take into account improvements in internal speed, in the size of the RAM or of the hard disk, the fact that computers can access the Internet, and so on?

The approach used by economists to adjust for these improvements is to look at how the market values computers with different characteristics in a given year. An example will help. Suppose that the evidence from prices of different models on the market show that people are willing to pay 10% more for a computer with a speed of 400 rather than 300 megahertz. Suppose all new computers this year have a speed of 400 megahertz, compared to a

speed of 300 megahertz for new computers last year. And suppose the dollar price of new computers this year is the same as the dollar price of new computers last year. Then, economists in charge of computing the adjusted price of computers will assume that new computers are, in fact, 10% cheaper than last year.

This approach, which treats goods as providing a collection of characteristics (here speed, memory, and so on) each with an implicit price, is called **hedonic pricing** (*hedone* means "pleasure" in Greek). It is used by the Department of Commerce, which constructs estimates of real GDP, to estimate changes in the price of complex and fast-changing goods, such as automobiles and computers. Using this approach, the Department of Commerce estimates that the quality of new computers has increased on average by 15% a year since 1987. Put another way, it estimates that, although the dollar price of computers has declined by about 10% a year since 1987, their quality-adjusted price has fallen at an average rate of 15% + 10% = 25% per year.

2-2 | The Other Major Macroeconomic Variables

GDP is the main macroeconomic variable. Two others, unemployment and inflation, tell us about other important aspects of how an economy is performing.

The Unemployment Rate

The **unemployment rate** is defined as the ratio of the number of unemployed to the labor force:

$$u = \frac{U}{L}$$

unemployment rate = unemployed/labor force

The **labor force** is defined as the sum of those employed and those unemployed:

$$L \quad = \quad N \quad + \quad U$$
$$\text{labor force} = \text{employed} + \text{unemployed}$$

What determines whether a worker is counted as unemployed? Until the 1940s in the United States, and more recently in other countries, the number of people registered at unemployment offices was the only available source of data on unemployment, and only those workers who were registered in unemployment offices were counted as unemployed. This system led to a poor measure of unemployment. How many of the truly unemployed actually registered varied both across countries and across time. Those who had no incentive to register—for example, those who had exhausted their unemployment benefits—were unlikely to take the time to come to the unemployment office, so they were not counted. Countries with less generous benefit systems were likely to have fewer unemployed registering, and therefore smaller measured unemployment rates.

Today, most countries rely on large surveys of households to compute the unemployment rate. In the United States, this survey is called the **Current Population Survey** (**CPS**). It relies on interviews of 60,000 households every month. The survey classifies a person as employed if he or she has a job at the time of the interview; it classifies a person as unemployed if he or she does not have a job and has been looking for work in the last four weeks. Most other countries use a similar definition of unemployment. In the United States, estimates based on the CPS survey show that, during 1998, on average 131.4 million people were employed, and 6.2 million people were unemployed, so the unemployment rate was 6.2/(131.4 + 6.2) = 4.5%.

Note that only those *looking for work* are counted as unemployed; those not working and not looking for work are counted as **not in the labor force**. When unemployment is high, some of those without jobs give up looking for work and therefore are no longer counted as unemployed. These people are known as **discouraged workers**. Take an extreme case: If all workers without a job gave up looking, the unemployment rate would equal zero. This would make the unemployment rate a very poor indicator of what is happening in the labor market. More typically, high unemployment is associated with more workers dropping out of the labor force. Equivalently, a higher unemployment rate is typically associated with a lower **participation rate**, defined as the ratio of the labor force to the total population of working age. Since the start of economic reform in Eastern Europe in the early 1990s, unemployment has increased, often dramatically. But equally dramatic has been the drop in participation rates. In Poland in 1990 for example, 70% of the decrease in employment was accounted for by early retirements—by people dropping out of the labor force rather than becoming unemployed.

Macroeconomists care about unemployment for two main reasons: The unemployment rate tells them something about whether an economy is operating above or below its normal level. And unemployment has important social consequences. Let's look at each in turn.

Unemployment and Activity. In most countries, there is a clear relation between the change in unemployment and GDP growth. This relation is known as **Okun's law**, after the economist Arthur Okun, who first identified and interpreted it in the 1960s. The relation between these two variables in the United States since 1960 is plotted in Figure 2–2, which shows the change in the unemployment rate on the vertical axis and the rate of GDP growth on the horizontal axis. Each point in the figure shows the growth rate and the change in the unemployment rate for a given year. (Figures such as Figure 2–2, which plot one variable against another over time, are called **scatter diagrams**.)

The figure shows that high output growth is typically associated with a decrease in the unemployment rate, and low output growth is associated with an increase in the unemployment rate. This makes sense: High output growth leads to high employment growth, as firms hire more workers to produce more. High employment growth leads to a decrease in unemployment.

Okun's law:

High output growth ⟹ unemployment rate ↓

Low output growth ⟹ unemployment rate ↑

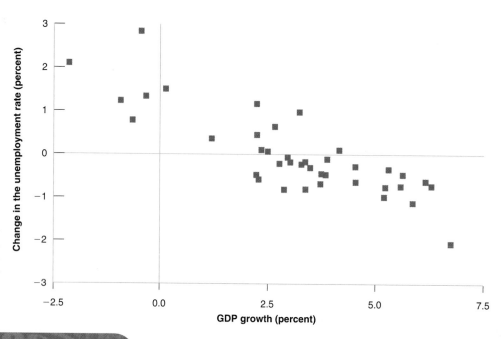

FIGURE 2-2

**Change in the U.S.
Unemployment Rate versus
U.S. GDP Growth
1960–1998**

High output growth is typically associated with a decrease in the unemployment rate. Conversely, low output growth is typically associated with an increase in the unemployment rate.

Does Spain Really Have a 19% Unemployment Rate?

In 1998, the official unemployment rate in Spain was a very high 19%. Yet there were no riots and Spain looked nothing like the United States did during the Great Depression. There were few homeless, and most cities looked prosperous. Can we really believe that nearly one-fifth of the Spanish labor force was looking for work?

To answer this, we must examine how the Spanish unemployment figure is put together. Much as in the United States, it comes from a large survey of 60,000 households. People are classified as unemployed if they indicate that they are not working but are seeking work.

Can we be sure that people tell the truth? No. Although there is no obvious incentive to lie—answers to the survey are confidential and are not used to determine whether people are eligible for unemployment benefits—those who are working in the underground economy may prefer to play it safe and report that they are unemployed instead.

The **underground economy** is that part of economic activity that is not measured in official statistics, either because the activity is illegal or, more importantly here, because firms and workers would rather not report it and thus not pay taxes. The size of the underground economy is an old issue in Spain. And because of that we actually know more about it than in many other countries. In 1985, the Spanish government tried to find out more by organizing a detailed survey of 60,000 individuals. To try to elicit the truth from those interviewed, the questionnaire asked interviewees for an extremely precise account of the use of their time, making it difficult to lie easily. The answers were interesting. The underground economy in Spain—defined as the number of people working without declaring income to the social security administration—accounted for between

10% to 15% of employment. But it was composed mostly of people who already had a job and were holding a second or a third job. The best estimate from the survey was that only about 15% of the unemployed were, in fact, working. This implied that the unemployment rate, which was officially 21% at the time, was, in fact, closer to 18%, still a very high number. The Spanish underground economy is significant, but it does not explain the high unemployment rate.

Do the unemployed survive because unemployment benefits are unusually generous in Spain? No. Except for very generous unemployment systems in two regions, Andalusia and Extremadura (which have even higher unemployment than the rest of the country), unemployment benefits are very much in line with those in other OECD countries. Benefits are typically 70% of the wage for the first six months, 60% thereafter. They are paid for a period of 4 to 24 months, depending on how long people have worked before becoming unemployed. The 30% of the unemployed who have been unemployed for more than two years do not receive unemployment benefits.

So how do the unemployed survive? A key to the answer lies in the Spanish family structure. The unemployment rate is highest among the young: It exceeds 40% for those between 16 and 19, and is around 40% for those between 20 and 24. The young typically stay at home until their late twenties, and have increasingly done so as unemployment has increased. Looking at households rather than at individuals, the proportion of households where nobody was employed in 1994 was less than 10%; the proportion of households that received neither wage income nor unemployment benefits was around 3%. In short, it is the family structure that has allowed many of the unemployed to survive.

GLOBAL MACRO

The relation has a simple implication. If the current unemployment rate is too high (what constitutes *too high* or *too low* will be the topic of many chapters later; we can leave this discussion until then), it will take a period of higher growth to reduce it. If, instead, the unemployment rate is about right, then output should grow at the rate that is consistent with an unchanged unemployment rate. The unemployment rate therefore provides macroeconomists with a signal of where the economy stands and what growth rate might be desirable. Return to our discussion of the current unemployment rate in the United States in chapter 1: Those economists who believe the current U.S. unemployment rate is currently *too low* would like to have lower output growth for some time, to allow unemployment to return to a higher level. This is why they advocate macroeconomic policies aimed at slowing down U.S. growth for a time.

From Figure 2–2, what is the rate of growth of output associated with roughly no change in the unemployment rate?

Social Implications of Unemployment. Macroeconomists also care about unemployment because of its direct effects on the welfare of the unemployed. Although unemployment benefits are greater today than they were during the Great Depression, unemployment is still associated with financial and psychological suffering. How much depends on the nature of the unemployment. One image of the unemployed is that of a stagnant pool, of people remaining unemployed for long periods of time. As we shall see later in the book, this image does not reflect what happens in the United States. In the United States each month, many people become unemployed, and many of the unemployed (on average, 30% of them) find jobs. But, even in the United States, some groups (often the young, the ethnic minorities, and the unskilled) suffer disproportionately from unemployment, remaining chronically unemployed and being most vulnerable to becoming unemployed when the unemployment rate increases.

The Inflation Rate

Inflation is a sustained rise in the general level of prices, a sustained rise in the **price level**. The **inflation rate** is the rate at which the price level increases.

The practical issue is how to define this price level. Macroeconomists typically look at two measures of the price level, at two *price indexes*: the GDP deflator and the consumer price index.

The GDP Deflator. Suppose nominal GDP, $\$Y_t$, increases, but real GDP, Y_t, remains unchanged. Then, the increase in nominal GDP must result from the increase in prices. This motivates the definition of the GDP deflator. The **GDP deflator** in year t, P_t, is defined as the ratio of nominal GDP to real GDP in year t:

$$P_t = \frac{\text{nominal GDP}_t}{\text{Real GDP}_t} = \frac{\$Y_t}{Y_t}$$

Note that, in the year in which, by construction, real GDP is equal to nominal GDP (1992 at this point in the United States), this definition implies that the price level is equal to 1. This is worth emphasizing: The GDP deflator is what is called an **index number**. Its level is chosen arbitrarily—here it is equal to 1 in 1992—and has no economic interpretation. But its rate of change has a clear economic interpretation: It gives the rate at which the general level of prices goes up over time—the rate of inflation.

Index numbers are often set to 100 rather than 1 in the base year. 100 is short for 100%, which in decimal terms, is equal to 1. If you look at the *Economic Report* (Table B3) you will see that the GDP deflator is equal to 100 for 1992 (the base year), to 102.6 in 1993, and so on.

One advantage to defining the price level as the GDP deflator is that it implies that a simple relation holds between nominal GDP, real GDP, and the price level. To see this, reorganize the previous equation to get

$$\$Y_t = P_t Y_t$$

Nominal GDP is equal to the GDP deflator times real GDP.

Rate of inflation:
$$(P_t - P_{t-1})/P_{t-1}$$

The Consumer Price Index. The GDP deflator gives the average price of the goods included in GDP—the final goods *produced* in the economy. But consumers care about the average price of the goods they *consume*. The two prices need not be the same: The set of goods produced in the economy is not the same as the set of goods bought by consumers. This is true for two reasons. Some of the goods in GDP are sold not to consumers but to firms (machine tools, for example), to the government, or to foreigners. And some of the goods bought by consumers are not produced at home, but rather imported from abroad.

To measure the average price of consumption, or equivalently, the **cost of living**, macroeconomists look at another index, the **consumer price index, (CPI)**. The CPI has been in existence since 1917, and is published monthly (in contrast, GDP numbers and the GDP deflator are published quarterly).

The CPI gives the cost in dollars of a specific list of goods and services over time. The list, which is based on a detailed study of consumer spending, attempts to represent the consumption basket of a typical urban consumer. It is revised approximately every 10 years. Each month, Bureau of Labor Statistics (BLS) employees visit stores to find out what has happened to the price of the goods on the list; prices are collected in 85 cities, from about 22,000 retail stores, car dealerships, gas stations, hospitals, and so on. These prices are then used to construct the consumer price index.

The CPI should not be confused with the PPI, or *producer price index*, which is an index of prices of domestically produced goods in manufacturing, mining, agriculture, fishing, forestry, and electric utility industries.

Like the GDP deflator, the CPI is an index. It is set equal to 1 in the period chosen as the base period and thus does not have a natural level. The current base period is 1982 to 1984, so that the average for the period 1982 to 1984 is equal to 1. In 1998, the CPI stood at 1.63; thus, it cost 63% more in dollars to purchase the same consumption basket than in 1982 to 1984.

Like the GDP deflator, the CPI is also typically set to 100 rather than to 1 in the base period (so, for example, equal to 163 rather than to 1.63 for 1998).

You may wonder how the rate of inflation differs depending on whether the GDP deflator or the CPI is used to measure it. The answer is given in Figure 2–3, which plots the two inflation rates since 1960 for the United States.

The plots on the graph yield two conclusions:

- The CPI and the GDP deflator move together most of the time. In most years, the two inflation rates differ by less than 1%.
- But there are clear exceptions. In both 1974 and 1979 to 1980, the increase in the CPI was significantly larger than the increase in the GDP deflator. The reason is not hard to find. Recall that the GDP deflator is the price of goods produced in the United States, whereas the CPI is the price of goods consumed in the United States. That means when the price of imported goods increases relative to the price of goods produced in the United States, the CPI increases faster than the GDP deflator. This is precisely what happened in both 1974 and 1979 to 1980. In each case, the price of oil doubled. And

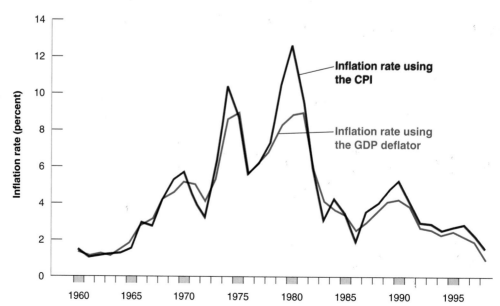

FIGURE 2-3

U.S. Inflation Rate, Using the CPI and the GDP Deflator, 1960–1998

The inflation rates, computed using either the CPI or the GDP deflator, are largely similar.

although the United States is a producer of oil, it produces much less than it consumes: It was and still is a major oil importer. Thus, in each case, there was a large increase in the CPI compared to the GDP deflator.

In what follows, I shall make no distinction between the two indexes unless the discussion requires us to focus on their difference. Thus, I shall simply talk about the *price level* and denote it by P_t, without indicating whether I have the CPI or the GDP deflator in mind.

Inflation and Unemployment. Is there a relation between inflation and either output or unemployment? Or does inflation have a life of its own? The answer: There is a relation, but it is far from mechanical—it varies across time and country.

The relation between unemployment and inflation in the United States since 1970 is shown in Figure 2–4. The change in the inflation rate (using the CPI)—that is, the inflation rate this year minus the inflation rate last year—is plotted on the vertical axis. The unemployment rate is plotted on the horizontal axis. The figure gives the combinations of unemployment rates and changes in inflation rates for each year since 1970.

Figure 2–4 shows a negative relation between the unemployment rate and the change in inflation. When the unemployment rate is low, inflation tends to increase. When the unemployment rate is high, inflation tends to decrease. This negative relation is called the Phillips relation, and the curve that fits the set of points best is called the **Phillips curve**, named for the economist who first documented the relation between unemployment and inflation. Where this relation comes from, why it changes through time and place, and what it implies, will be the focus of many later chapters.

Why Do Economists Care About Inflation? If higher inflation meant just a faster proportional increase in all prices and wages—a case called *pure inflation*—inflation would be only a minor inconvenience. Relative prices would not be affected by inflation. Take, for example, the workers' *real wage*—the wage measured in terms of goods rather than in dollars. In an economy with 10% inflation, prices would increase by 10% a year but so would wages—and real wages would remain the same. Inflation would not be entirely irrelevant; people would have to keep track of the increase in prices and wages in making decisions. But this would be a small burden, hardly justifying making control of the inflation rate one of the major goals of macroeconomic policy.

The Phillips curve:
Low unemployment ⇒
inflation ↑
High unemployment ⇒
inflation ↓

We shall see in Chapter 8 that the nature of the Phillips curve has changed since Phillips first documented it in 1958. But the name is still used.

This ignores the changes in real wages that would occur even if there were no inflation. A more accurate statement is that, under pure inflation, inflation would not affect the evolution of real wages.

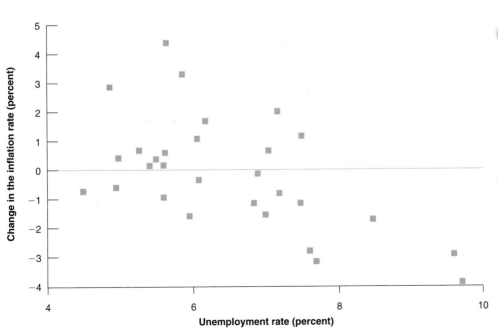

FIGURE 2–4

Change in the U.S. Inflation Rate versus the U.S. Unemployment Rate, 1970–1998

When the unemployment rate is low, inflation tends to increase. When the unemployment rate is high, inflation tends to decrease.

So, why do economists care about inflation? Precisely because there is no such thing as pure inflation. During periods of inflation, not all prices and wages rise proportionately. Because they do not, inflation affects income distribution. For example, retirees in many countries receive payments that do not keep up with the price level, so they lose in relation to other groups when inflation is high. This is not the case in the United States, where Social Security benefits automatically rise with the CPI, protecting retirees from inflation. But during the very high inflation that has taken place in Russia since the early 1990s, retirement pensions have not kept up with inflation, and many retirees have been pushed to near starvation.

Inflation also leads to distortions. Some prices, which are fixed by law or by regulation, lag behind the others, leading to changes in relative prices. Taxation interacts with inflation to create more distortions. If tax brackets are not adjusted for inflation, for example, people move into higher and higher tax brackets as their nominal income increases, even if their real income remains the same. Variations in relative prices also lead to more uncertainty, making it harder for firms to make decisions about the future, such as investment decisions.

To summarize: Economists see high inflation as affecting income distribution, and creating both distortions and uncertainty. How important these problems are, and whether they justify trying to achieve and maintain, say, zero inflation, are much debated questions. We shall take them up later in this book.

> This is known as *bracket creep*. In the United States, the tax brackets are adjusted automatically for inflation: If inflation is 5%, all tax brackets also go up by 5%—in other words, there is no bracket creep.

2-3 | A Road Map

Having defined the main variables, let's now turn to the central question of macroeconomics. What determines the level of aggregate output?

- Reading newspapers suggests one answer: Movements in output come from movements in the demand for goods. You probably have read news stories that begin, "Production and sales of automobiles were higher last month, apparently due to a surge in consumer confidence, which drove consumers to showrooms in record numbers." Such explanations point to the role of demand in determining aggregate output, as well as to factors ranging from consumer confidence to tax rates to interest rates.

- But, surely, no amount of consumers rushing to showrooms will increase India's output to the level of output in the United States. This suggests a second answer. What must matter is the supply side: how advanced the technology of the country is, how much capital it is using, the size and the skills of its labor force. These factors, not consumer confidence, must be the fundamental determinants of the level of output.

- One may want to push this argument one step further: Neither technology, nor capital, nor skills are given. The technological sophistication of a country depends on its ability to innovate and introduce new technologies. The size of its capital stock depends on how much people save. The skills of workers depend on the quality of the education system. Other factors may also be important. If firms are to operate efficiently, they need a clear system of laws under which to operate, and an honest government to enforce them. This suggests a third answer: The true determinants of output are factors such as the education system, the saving rate, and the quality of government. It is there that we must look if we want to understand what determines output.

Which of the three answers is the right one? The answer is all three. But each of them applies over a different time period.

- In the **short run**, say a few years or so, the first answer is the right one. Year-to-year movements in output are primarily driven by movements in demand. Changes in demand, which can arise from changes in consumer confidence or from any other source, can lead to a decrease in output (a recession), or an increase in output (an expansion).

- In the **medium run**, say, a decade or two, the second answer is the right one. Over the medium run, the economy tends to return to the level of output determined by supply factors: the capital stock, technology, and the size of the labor force. And over a decade or two, these factors do not move so much that it is a mistake to take them as given.

- In the **long run**, say, a half century or more, the third answer is the right one. To understand why Japan has grown so much faster than the United States over the last 50 years, we must explain why both capital and the level of technology have increased faster in Japan than in the United States. We must indeed look at factors such as the education system, the saving rate, and the role of the government.

This way of thinking about the determinants of output underlies macroeconomics, and it underlies the organization of this book.

A Tour of the Book

The book is organized in three main parts; first, the core; then, three extensions; and, finally, a look at the role of macroeconomic policy. This organization is shown in Figure 2–5. Let me now describe it in more detail.

The Core. The core is composed of three parts—the short run, the medium run, and the long run.

- Chapters 3 to 5 look at the determination of output in the short run.

  The focus is on the determination of the demand for goods. To focus on the role of demand, we assume that firms are willing to supply any quantity at a given price; in other words, we ignore supply constraints. Chapter 3 looks at the goods market. Chapter 4 focuses on financial markets. Chapter 5 puts goods and financial markets together. The resulting framework is known as the *IS-LM* model. Developed in the late 1930s, the *IS-LM*

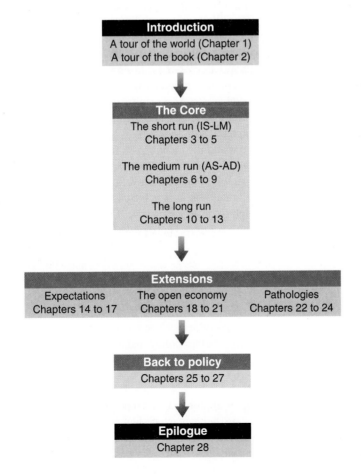

FIGURE 2-5

The Organization of the Book

model still provides a simple way of thinking about the determination of output in the short run, and it remains a basic building block of macroeconomics. It also allows for a first pass at studying the role of fiscal policy and monetary policy in affecting output.

- Chapters 6 to 9 reintroduce the supply side, and look at the determination of output in the medium run.

    Chapter 6 focuses on the labor market. Chapter 7 puts together goods, financial, and labor markets, and shows how one can think about the determination of output both in the short run and in the medium run. The model developed in that chapter is called the aggregate supply–aggregate demand (*AS–AD*) model of output. Chapters 8 and 9 show how the model can be used to think about several issues, such as the relation between output and inflation, and the role of monetary and fiscal policy both in the short run and in the medium run.

- Chapters 10 to 13 focus on the long run.

    Chapter 10 introduces the facts, and looks at the growth of output both across countries and across long periods of time. Chapters 11 and 12 then discuss the role and the determinants of both capital accumulation and technological progress in growth. Chapter 13 looks at the interaction between technological progress, wages, and unemployment.

Extensions. The core chapters give you a way of thinking about the determination of output (and unemployment, and inflation) over the short, medium, and long run. But they leave out several elements. These are explored in three extensions.

- The core chapters ignore the role of *expectations*. But expectations play an essential role in macroeconomics. Nearly all the economic decisions people and firms make — whether to buy bonds or whether to buy stocks, whether or not to buy a machine — depend on their expectations of future profits, of future interest rates, and so on. Fiscal and monetary policy affect activity not only through their direct effects, but also through their effect on expectations. Chapters 14 to 17 focus on the role of expectations, and their implications for fiscal and monetary policy.
- The core chapters treat the economy as *closed*, ignoring its interactions with the other economies of the world. But economies are increasingly *open*, trading with other countries both in goods and in financial assets. As a result, countries are more and more interdependent. The nature of this interdependence and the implications for fiscal and monetary policy are the topics of chapters 18 to 21.
- The core chapters on the short run and the medium run focus on fluctuations in output — on expansions, and on recessions. Sometimes, however, the word "fluctuations" does not accurately capture what is happening in the economy. Something goes very wrong. Inflation reaches extremely high rates. Or, as was the case during the Great Depression, unemployment remains very high for a very long time. Or, as is the case in Asia today, a crisis leads to a sharp, large drop in output. These *pathologies* are the topics of Chapters 22 through 24.

Back to Policy. Monetary and fiscal policies are discussed in every chapter of the book. But, once the core and the extensions have been covered, it is worth going back and assessing the role of policy.

- Chapter 25 focuses on general issues of policy, such as whether macroeconomists know enough to use policy at all, and on whether policy makers can be trusted to do what is right.
- Chapters 26 and 27 then assess the role of monetary and fiscal policy.

Epilogue. The final chapter, Chapter 28, looks at the recent history of macroeconomics and how macroeconomists have come to believe what they believe today. From the outside, macroeconomics often looks like a field divided between schools — Keynesians, monetarists, new classicals, supply-siders, and so on — hurling arguments at each other. The actual process of research is more orderly and more productive than this image suggests. I identify what I see as the main differences between macroeconomists, and the set of propositions that define the core of macroeconomics today.

SUMMARY

- We can think of GDP, the measure of aggregate activity, in three equivalent ways: (1) GDP is the value of the final goods and services produced in the economy during a given period; (2) GDP is the sum of value added in the economy during a given period; and (3) GDP is the sum of incomes in the economy during a given period.

- Nominal GDP is equal to the sum of the quantities of final goods produced times their current price. This implies that changes in nominal GDP reflect both changes in quantities and changes in prices. Real GDP is a measure of output. Changes in real GDP reflect changes in quantities only.

- The labor force is defined as the sum of those employed and those unemployed. The unemployment rate is defined as the ratio of the number of unemployed to the labor force. Somebody is classified as unemployed if he or she does not have a job and has been looking for work in the last four weeks.

- The empirical relation between GDP growth and the change in the unemployment rate is called Okun's law. The relation shows that high output growth is associated with a decrease in the unemployment rate and, conversely, that low growth is associated with an increase in the unemployment rate.

- Inflation is a rise in the general level of prices, in the price level. The inflation rate is the rate at which the price level increases. Macroeconomists look at two measures of the price level. The first is the GDP deflator, which gives the average price of goods produced in the economy. The second is the consumer price index (CPI), which gives the average price of goods consumed in the economy.

- The empirical relation between the inflation rate and the unemployment rate is called the Phillips curve. This relation has changed over time, and also varies across countries. In the United States today, it takes the following form: When the unemployment rate is low, inflation tends to increase. When the unemployment rate is high, inflation tends to decrease.

- Inflation leads to changes in income distribution, and increases distortions and uncertainty.

- Macroeconomists distinguish between the short run (a few years), the medium run (a decade or two), and the long run (a half century or more.) They think of output as being determined by demand in the short run, by the level of technology, the capital stock, and the labor force in the medium run, and by factors such as education, research, saving, and the quality of government in the long run.

KEY TERMS

- national income and product accounts, 20
- aggregate output, 20
- gross domestic product, or GDP, 20
- gross national product, or GNP, 20
- intermediate good, 21
- value added, 21
- nominal GDP, 22
- real GDP, 22
- real GDP in chained (1992) dollars, 23
- dollar GDP, GDP in current dollars, 24
- GDP in terms of goods, GDP in constant dollars, GDP adjusted for inflation, GDP in 1992 dollars, 24
- GDP growth, expansions, recessions, 24
- hedonic pricing, 24
- unemployment rate, 24
- labor force, 24

- *Current Population Survey* (CPS), 25
- not in the labor force, 25
- discouraged workers, 25
- participation rate, 25
- Okun's law, 25
- scatter diagrams, 25
- underground economy, 26
- price level, 27
- inflation rate, 27
- GDP deflator, 27
- index number, 27
- cost of living, 28
- consumer price index (CPI), 28
- Phillips curve, 29
- short run, medium run, and long run, 30–31

An asterisk denotes a harder question. [Web] indicates that the question requires access to the Internet.

1. TRUE/FALSE/UNCERTAIN

a. The share of labor income in GDP is much smaller than the share of capital income.

b. U.S. GDP in 1998 was 16 times higher than U.S. GDP in 1960.

c. If a high unemployment rate discourages workers from looking for work, then the unemployment rate can be a poor indicator of labor market conditions. To assess the situation, one must also look at the participation rate.

d. A reduction in the rate of unemployment requires high output growth.

e. If the Japanese CPI is currently at 108 and the U.S. CPI is at 104, then the Japanese rate of inflation is higher than the U.S. rate of inflation.

f. The rate of inflation computed using the CPI is a better index of inflation than the rate of inflation computed using the GDP deflator.

2. GDP AND ITS COMPONENTS

Suppose you are measuring annual U.S. GDP by adding up the final value of all goods and services produced in the economy. Determine the effect of each of the following transactions on GDP.

a. You buy $100 worth of fish from a fisherman, which you cook and eat at home.

b. A seafood restaurant buys $100 worth of fish from a fisherman.

c. Delta Airlines buys a new jet from Boeing for $200 million.

d. The Greek national airline buys a new jet from Boeing for $200 million.

e. Delta Airlines sells one of its jets to John Travolta for $100 million.

*3. MEASURED VERSUS TRUE GDP

Suppose that instead of cooking dinner for an hour, you decide to work an extra hour, earning an additional $12. You then buy some Chinese food for $10.

a. By how much does measured GDP increase?

b. Does true GDP increase by more or less? Explain.

4. MEASURING GDP

During a given year, the following activities occur:

i. A silver mining company pays its workers $200,000 to mine 75 pounds of silver. The silver is then sold to a jewelry manufacturer for $300,000.

ii. The jewelry manufacturer pays its workers $250,000 to make silver necklaces, which it sells directly to consumers for $1,000,000.

a. Using the "production of final goods" approach, what is GDP in this economy?

b. What is the value added at each stage of production? Using the "value added" approach, what is GDP?

c. What are the total wages and profits earned? Using the income approach, what is GDP?

5. NOMINAL AND REAL GDP

An economy produces three goods: cars, computers, and oranges. Production units and prices per unit for years 1998 and 1999 are as follows:

	1998		1999	
	Quantity	**Price**	**Quantity**	**Price**
Cars	10	$2,000	12	$3,000
Computers	4	$1,000	6	$500
Oranges	1,000	$1	1,000	$1

a. What is nominal GDP in 1998 and in 1999?

b. Using 1998 as the base year (i.e., using 1998 prices), what is real GDP in 1998 and 1999? By what percentage does real GDP increase from 1998 to 1999?

c. Using 1999 as the base year (i.e., using 1999 prices), what is real GDP in 1998 and 1999? By what percentage does real GDP increase from 1998 to 1999?

d. The growth rate we obtain for real GDP depends on which year is used as a base year. Is this statement true or false?

6. THE GDP DEFLATOR

Use the data from problem 5 to answer the following:

a. Using 1998 as the base year, what is the GDP deflator for 1998 and 1999? What is the rate of inflation over this period?

b. Using 1999 as the base year, what is the GDP deflator for 1998 and 1999? What is the rate of inflation over this period?

c. Does the choice of base year affect the rate of inflation computed using the GDP deflator?

7. CHAIN-TYPE INDEXES

As can be seen from problems 5 and 6, the use of base year prices to compute the rate of change of real GDP and the rate of inflation has some very unattractive properties. Every time a new base year is selected (*e.g.*, to reflect the growing share of services in GDP), all past growth rates of real GDP and all past rates of inflation based on the GDP deflator have to be revised. To avoid these problems, the U.S. Bureau of Economic Analysis started using chain-type indexes in 1995. In this problem, we shall see, using the economy described in problem 5, how chain-type indexes are constructed. Further discussion of this method can be found in the appendix to Chapter 2.

a. Construct real GDP for years 1998 and 1999 for the economy described in problem 5 by using the average price of each good over the two years.

b. By what percentage does real GDP increase from 1998 to 1999?

c. What is the GDP deflator in 1998 and 1999? What is the rate of inflation using the chain-type deflator?

d. Do you find this method of construction of real GDP growth and of the inflation rate attractive? Why or why not?

8. HEDONIC PRICING

As the first focus box of Chapter 2 explains, it is hard to measure the true increase in prices of goods whose characteristics change over time. Hedonic pricing offers a method of computing the quality-adjusted increase in prices.

a. Consider the case of a routine medical checkup. Name some reasons why you may want to use hedonic pricing to measure the increase in the price of this service.

Now consider the case of a medical checkup for a pregnant woman. Suppose that the year a new ultrasound method is introduced, the price of this checkup increases by 20%, and all doctors adopt the ultrasound simultaneously.

b. What information do you need in order to determine the quality-adjusted increase in pregnancy checkups?

c. Is that information available? Explain. What can you say about the quality-adjusted price increase of pregnancy checkups?

*9. [WEB] OKUN'S LAW

To answer this question, you will need monthly data on U.S. unemployment rates and annual data on U.S. real GDP growth rates. The former can be retrieved from the web page of the Bureau of Labor Statistics— <http://stats.bls.gov/> (look for "Labor Force Statistics from the CPS," "most requested series"). The latter can be retrieved from the Web page of the Bureau of Economic Analysis (look under "GDP and Related Data")— <http://www.bea.doc.gov/>. However, you should feel free to use any data source you wish (see the appendix to Chapter 1).

a. Examine Figure 2–2. What is the growth rate of GDP so that the unemployment rate stays constant?

b. What was the growth rate of real GDP in 1992? Was it close to the growth rate you reported in part (a)? What was the rate of civilian unemployment in January 1992 and in January 1993? Do your findings support Okun's law? Explain.

Looking at Figure 2–2, imagine a straight line joining the data point closest to zero change in the unemployment rate and the data point corresponding to the largest negative change in the unemployment rate.

c. In terms of the vertical axis, what is the approximate distance between these two points? What is the approximate distance between these two points in terms of the horizontal axis?

Suppose now that U.S. policy makers want to reduce the unemployment rate by one percentage point.

d. According to your answer to (c), by how much must the growth rate of GDP increase in order to reduce the unemployment rate by one percentage point in one year?

FURTHER READINGS

● If you want to know more about the definition and the construction of the many economic indicators that are regularly reported on the news—from the help-wanted index to the retail sales index—two easy-to-read references are

Norman Frumkin, *Tracking America's Economy*, 3rd ed. (New York: M.E. Sharpe, 1998).

The Staff of *The Economist, The Economist Guide to Economic Indicators: Making Sense of Economics.* (New York: Wiley and Sons, 1998).

- In 1995, the U.S. Senate set up a commission to study the construction of the CPI, and to make recommendations about potential changes. That commission concluded that the rate of inflation computed using the CPI was, on average, about 1% too high. If this conclusion is correct, this implies in particular that real wages (nominal wages divided by the CPI) have grown at 1% more a year than is currently reported. For more on the conclusions of the commission, and some of the ex-

changes that followed, read Michael Boskin et al., "Consumer Prices, the Consumer Price Index, and the Cost of Living," *Journal of Economic Perspectives*, Winter 1998, 3–26.

- For why it is hard to measure the price level and output correctly, read Paul Krugman, "Viagra and the Wealth of Nations" (web page http://web.mit.edu/krugman/www/).

APPENDIX

THE CONSTRUCTION OF REAL GDP, AND CHAIN-TYPE INDEXES

The example I used in the chapter had only one final good—cars—so constructing real GDP was easy. But how should one construct real GDP when there is more than one final good? This is the question taken up in this appendix.

All that is needed to make the relevant points is an economy where there are two goods. So, suppose that an economy produces cars and potatoes.

- In year 0, it produces 100,000 pounds of potatoes, at $1 a pound, and 10 cars at $10,000 a car.
- One year later, in year 1, it produces 100,000 pounds of potatoes at $1.20 a pound, and 11 cars at $10,000 a car.
- Nominal GDP in year 0 is therefore equal to $200,000, nominal GDP in year 1 equal to $230,000. This information is summarized in the following table.

Nominal GDP in Year 0 and in Year 1.

	Quantity	Year 0 $ Price	$ value
Potatoes	100,000	1.00	100,000
Cars	10	10,000.00	100,000
Nominal GDP			200,000
	Quantity	Year 1 $ Price	$ value
Potatoes	100,000	1.20	120,000
Cars	11	10,000.00	110,000
Nominal GDP			230,000

The increase in nominal GDP from year 0 to year 1 is equal to $30,000/$200,000 = 15 percent. But what is the increase in real GDP?

The basic idea in constructing real GDP is to evaluate quantities in both years using the same set of prices. Suppose we choose for example the prices of year 0; year 0 is then called the **base year**. The computation is then as follows:

- Real GDP in year 0 is the sum of quantities in year 0 times prices in year 0: $(100,000 \times \$1) + (10 \times \$10,000) = \$200,000$.
- Real GDP in year 1 is the sum of quantities in year 1 times prices in year 0: $(100,000 \times \$1) + (11 \times \$10,000) = \$210,000$.
- The rate of change of real GDP from year 0 to year 1 is thus $(\$210,000 - \$200,000)/\$200,000 = 5\%$.

However, this answer raises an important issue: Instead of using year 0 as the base year, we could have used year 1, or any other year for that matter. If, for example, we had used year 1 as the base year, then

- Real GDP in year 0 would be equal to $(100,000 \times \$1.2 + 10 \times \$10,000) = \$220,000$.
- Real GDP in year 1 would be equal to $(100,000 \times \$1.2 + 11 \times \$10,000) = \$230,000$.
- The rate of change of real GDP from year 0 to year 1 would be equal to $\$10,000/\$220,000 = 4.5\%$.

The answer using year 1 as the base year would therefore be different from the answer using year 0 as the base year. So, if the choice of the base year affects the constructed rate of change of output, what base year should one choose?

Until 1995 in the United States—and still today in most countries—the practice was to choose a base year and change it infrequently, say, every five years or so. For example, in the United States, the base year used from December 1991 to December 1995 was 1987. That is, measures of real GDP published, for example, in 1994 both for 1994 and for all earlier years were constructed using 1987 prices. In December 1995, national income accounts shifted to 1992 as a base year; measures of real GDP for all earlier years were recalculated using 1992 prices.

This practice was logically unappealing. Every time the base year was changed, and a new set of prices was used, all past real GDP numbers—and all past rates of change of real GDP—were recomputed: History was, in effect, rewritten every five years! Starting in December 1995, the U.S. Bureau of Economic Analysis (the government office that produces the GDP numbers) shifted to a new method, which does not suffer from this problem. The method requires three steps.

1. The rate of change of real GDP from each year to the next is computed using as the common set of prices the average of the prices for the two years. For example, the rate of change of real GDP from 1998 to 1999 is computed by constructing real GDP for 1998 and real GDP for 1999 using as the common set of prices the average of the prices for 1998 and 1999, and then computing the rate of change from 1998 to 1999.

2. An index for the level of real GDP is then constructed by linking—or chaining—the constructed rates of change for each year. The index is set equal to 1 in some arbitrary year. Right now, the year is 1992. Given that the constructed rate of growth for 1993 by the Bureau of Economic Analysis is 2.3%, the index for 1993 equals (1 + 2.3%) = 1.023. The index for 1994 is obtained by multiplying the index for 1994 by the rate of growth from 1993 to 1994, and so on. (You will find the value of this index—multiplied by 100—in the second column of Table B3 in the 1999 *Economic Report.* Check that it is 100 in 1992 and 102.3 in 1993, and so on.)

3. Finally, this index is multiplied by nominal GDP in 1992 to give real GDP in chained (1992) dollars. As the index is 1 in 1992, this implies that real GDP in 1992 equals nominal GDP in 1992. *Chained* refers to the chaining of rates of change described above. (*1992*) refers to the year where, by construction, real GDP is equal to nominal GDP (You will find the value of real GDP in chained [1992] dollars in the first column of Table B2 of the 1999 *Economic Report.*)

This index is more complicated to construct than the indexes used before 1995. But it is clearly better. The prices used to evaluate real GDP in two adjacent years are the right prices, namely, the average prices for those two years. And, because the rate of growth from one year to the next is constructed using the average prices in those two years rather than the set of prices in an arbitrary base year, history will not be rewritten every five years or so, as it used to be when, under the previous method for constructing real GDP, the base year was changed, and all past growth rates were recomputed.

KEY TERM

- base year, 36

We invite you to visit the Blanchard page on the Prentice Hall Web site at:

http://www.prenhall.com/blanchard

for this chapter's World Wide Web exercises

THE CORE

The Short Run

In the short run, demand determines output. Many factors affect demand, from consumer confidence to fiscal and monetary policy.

CHAPTER 3

Chapter 3 looks at equilibrium in the goods market and the determination of output. It focuses on the interaction between demand, production, and income. It shows how fiscal policy can be used to affect output.

CHAPTER 4

Chapter 4 looks at equilibrium in financial markets and the determination of the interest rate. It shows how monetary policy can be used to affect the interest rate.

CHAPTER 5

Chapter 5 looks at the goods market and financial markets together. It shows what determines output and the interest rate in the short run. It looks at the role of fiscal and monetary policy. The model developed in Chapter 5 is called the *IS-LM* model and is one of the workhorses of macroeconomics.

CHAPTER 3 | The Goods Market

When economists think about year-to-year movements in economic activity, they focus on the interaction between *production*, *income*, and *demand*. Changes in the demand for goods lead to changes in production. Changes in production lead to changes in income. And changes in income lead to changes in the demand for goods. This interaction is summarized in Figure 3–1. The cartoon on page 43 makes the point even better.

This chapter looks at this interaction and its implications.

FIGURE 3–1

Production, Income, and the Demand for Goods

3-1 | The Composition of GDP

"Output" and "production" are synonymous. There is no rule for using one or the other; use the one that sounds better.

Purchases of machines by firms depend on different factors than do purchases of food by consumers, or purchases of new combat airplanes by the federal government. If we are to think about what determines the demand for goods, it makes sense to decompose aggregate production (GDP) from the point of view of the different goods being produced, and the different buyers for these goods. The decomposition of GDP typically used by macroeconomists is given in Table 3–1 (A more detailed version, with more formal definitions, is given in Appendix 1 at the end of the book.)

- The first component of GDP is **consumption**, (C). These are the goods and services purchased by consumers, ranging from food to airline tickets, to vacations, to new cars, and so on. Consumption is by far the largest component of GDP, accounting for 68% of GDP in 1998.
- **Investment** (I) is sometimes called **fixed investment** to distinguish it from inventory investment. Investment is the sum of **nonresidential investment**, the purchase by firms of new plants or new machines (from turbines to computers), and **residential investment**, the purchase by people of new houses or apartments.

Warning! To the person in the street or the financial press, "investment" refers to the purchase of any asset, such as gold or shares of General Motors. Economists use investment to refer to the purchase of *new capital goods*, such as machines, buildings, or houses. When referring to the purchase of financial assets, economists say "financial investment."

  The two types of investment (residential and nonresidential) and the decisions behind them have more in common than might first appear. Firms buy machines or plants to be able to produce more output in the future. People buy houses or apartments to get *housing services* in the future. This is the justification for lumping both under "investment." Together, the two components of investment accounted for 15% of GDP in 1998.
- **Government spending**, (G), represents the purchases of goods and services by the federal, state, and local governments. The goods range from airplanes to office equipment. The services include services provided by government employees. In effect, the national income accounts treat the government as buying the services provided by government employees — and then providing these services to the public, free of charge.

  Note that G does not include **government transfers**, such as Medicare or Social Security, nor interest payments on the government debt. Although these are clearly government expenditures, they are not purchases of goods and services. That is why the number for government spending on goods and services in Table 3–1, 18% of GDP, is smaller than the number for total government spending including transfers and interest payments. That number, in 1998, was 31% of GDP.
- The sum of lines 1, 2, and 3 gives the purchases of goods and services by U.S. consumers, U.S. firms, and the U.S. government. To get to the purchases of U.S. goods and services, we must take two more steps.

TABLE 3–1 The Composition of U.S. GDP, 1998

		Billions of Dollars		Percent of GDP	
	GDP (Y)	8509		100	
1	Consumption (C)	5806		68	
2	Investment (I)	1308		15	
	Nonresidential		939		11
	Residential		369		4
3	Government spending (G)	1488		18	
4	Net exports	−154		−2	
	Exports (X)		958		11
	Imports (Q)		−1112		−13
5	Inventory investment (I_S)	61		1	

Source: *Survey of Current Business*, February 1999, Table 1–1.

First, we must subtract **imports** (Q), the purchases of foreign goods and services by U.S. consumers, U.S. firms, and the U.S. government. Second, we must add **exports** (X), the purchases of U.S. goods and services by foreigners.

The difference between exports and imports, ($X - Q$), is called **net exports**, or the **trade balance**. If exports exceed imports, a country is said to run a **trade surplus**. If exports are less than imports, the country is said to run a **trade deficit**. In 1998, exports accounted for 11% of GDP. Imports were equal to 13% of GDP, so the United States was running a trade deficit of 2% of GDP.

- The sum of lines 1 through 4 gives the purchases (equivalently, the sales) of U.S. goods and services in 1998. To get to U.S. production in 1998, we need one last step. Some of the goods produced in a given year are not sold in that year, but sold in later years. And some of the goods sold in a given year may have been produced in an earlier year. The difference between goods produced and goods sold in a given year—equivalently, between production and sales—is called **inventory investment** and is denoted I_S (Subscript S for **stocks** of goods, another term for inventories). If production exceeds sales, firms accumulate inventories. Inventory investment is positive. If production is less than sales, firms decrease inventories. Inventory investment is negative. Inventory investment is typically small—positive in some years, negative in others. In 1998, inventory investment was positive, and equal to 1% of GDP.

Exports−imports ≡ net exports ≡ trade balance

Exports > imports ⇔ trade surplus

Exports < imports ⇔ trade deficit

Production − sales = inventory investment

With this decomposition of GDP, we can now turn to our first model of output determination. The first step is to think about what determines the demand for goods.

3-2 | The Demand for Goods

Denote the total demand for goods by Z. Using the decomposition of GDP we just saw in Section 3-1, we can write Z as

$$Z \equiv C + I + G + X - Q$$

Note that this equation is an **identity** (which is why it is written using the symbol " $\equiv$ " rather than an equal sign). It defines Z as the the sum of consumption, plus investment, plus government spending, plus exports, minus imports.

A model nearly always starts with the word "assume" (or "suppose"). This is an indication that reality is about to be simplified in order to focus on the issue at hand.

Assume now that all firms produce the same good, which can be used by consumers for consumption, by firms for investment, or by the government. With this simplification, we need to look at only one market—the market for "the" good (thus the title of the chapter, "The Goods Market," rather than "The Goods Markets")—and think about what determines supply and demand in that market.

Assume further that firms are willing to supply any amount of the good at a given price, P. In other words, assume that the supply of goods is completely elastic at price P. This assumption will allow us to focus on the role of demand in the determination of output. As we shall see later in the book, this assumption is valid only in the short run. When we move to the study of the medium run (starting in Chapter 6), we shall need to give up this assumption.

Assume finally that the economy is *closed*, that it does not trade with the rest of the world: Both exports and imports are equal to zero. The assumption is clearly counterfactual: Modern economies trade with the rest of the world. Later on (starting in Chapter 18), we shall abandon this assumption and look at what happens when the economy is open. But, for the moment, this assumption will simplify things: We shall not have to think about what determines exports and imports.

Under this last assumption, $X = Q = 0$, and the demand for goods Z is the sum of consumption, investment, and government spending:

$$Z \equiv C + I + G$$

Let's discuss each of these three components in turn.

Consumption (C)

The main determinant of consumption is surely income, or more precisely **disposable income**, the income that remains once consumers have received transfers from the government and paid their taxes. When their disposable income goes up, people buy more goods; when it goes down, they buy fewer goods. Other variables affect consumption, but for the moment we shall ignore them.

Let C denote consumption, and Y_D denote disposable income. We can write

$$C = C(Y_D)$$
$$(+)$$

This is just a formal way of stating that consumption is a function of disposable income. The function $C(Y_D)$ is called the **consumption function**. The positive sign below Y_D reflects the fact that when disposable income increases, so does consumption. Economists call such an equation a **behavioral equation**, to indicate that the equation reflects some aspect of behavior—in this case, the behavior of consumers.

I shall use functions in this book as a simple but formal way of representing relations between variables. What you need to know about functions—which is very little—is described in Appendix 2 at the end of the book. This appendix develops the mathematics you need to go through this book. Do not worry: I shall always describe a function in words when I introduce it for the first time.

It is often useful to be more specific about the form of the function. Here is such a case. It is reasonable to assume that the relation between consumption and disposable income is given by

$$C = c_0 + c_1 Y_D \tag{3.1}$$

In words: It is reasonable to assume that the function is a **linear relation.** The relation between consumption and disposable income is then characterized by two **parameters**, c_0 and c_1.

The parameter c_1 is called the **propensity to consume**. (It is also called the *marginal propensity to consume*. I shall drop "marginal" for simplicity.) It gives the effect of an additional dollar of disposable income on consumption. If c_1 is equal to 0.6, then an additional dollar of income increases consumption by $\$1 \times 0.6 = 60$ cents. A natural restriction on c_1 is that it be positive: An increase in disposable income is likely to lead to an increase in consumption. Another natural restriction is that c_1 be less than 1: People are likely to consume only part of any increase in income, and to save the rest.

The parameter c_0 has a simple interpretation. It is what people would consume if their disposable income in the current year were equal to zero: If Y_D equals zero in equation (3.1), $C = c_0$. A natural restriction is that, if current income is equal to zero, consumption is still positive: People must eat! This implies that c_0 is positive. How can people have positive consumption if their income is equal to zero? The answer is by dissaving—by selling some of their assets, or by borrowing.

The relation between consumption and disposable income implied by equation (3.1) is drawn in Figure 3–2. Because it is a linear relation, it is represented by a straight line. Its intercept with the vertical axis is c_0; its slope is c_1. Because c_1 is less than 1, the slope of the line is less than 1: The line is flatter than a 45-degree line. (A refresher on graphs, slopes, and intercepts is also given in Appendix 2.)

Next we need to define disposable income. Disposable income is given by

$$Y_D \equiv Y - T$$

where Y is income and T is taxes paid minus government transfers received by consumers. This equation is an identity; thus the use of the symbol " $\equiv$ ". For short, I shall refer to T simply as taxes—but remember that it is equal to taxes minus transfers.

In the United States, the two major taxes paid by individuals are income taxes and Social Security contributions. The main sources of government transfers are Social Security benefits, Medicare (health care for retirees), and Medicaid (health care for the poor).

Replacing Y_D in equation (3.1) gives

$$C = c_0 + c_1(Y - T) \tag{3.2}$$

Consumption is a function of income and taxes. Higher income increases consumption, although less than one for one. Higher taxes decrease consumption, also less than one for one.

Investment (I)

Models have two types of variables. Some variables depend on other variables in the model, and are therefore explained within the model. Such variables are called **endogenous**. This is the case for consumption here. Other variables are not explained within the model but are instead taken as given. Such variables are called **exogenous**. This is how we shall treat investment here. We shall take investment as given, and write

$$I = \bar{I} \tag{3.3}$$

Two types of variables:
Endogenous variables— explained by the model
Exogenous variables— taken as given

Putting a bar on investment is a simple typographical way to remind us that we take investment as given.

The reason for taking investment as given is to keep our model simple. But the assumption is not innocuous. It implies that, when we look at the effects of changes in production later, we shall do so under the assumption that investment does not respond to such changes

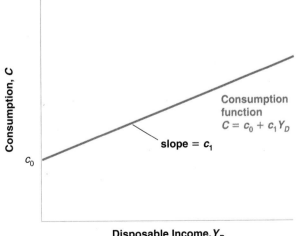

FIGURE 3–2

Consumption and Disposable Income

Consumption increases with disposable income, but less than one for one.

Consumption, C

Consumption function
$C = c_0 + c_1 Y_D$

slope = c_1

c_0

Disposable Income, Y_D

THE GOODS MARKET

in production. It is not hard to see that this implication may be quite bad as a description of reality: Firms that experience an increase in production may decide that they need more machines, and increase their investment. I leave this mechanism out of the model here, but I shall introduce a more realistic treatment of investment in Chapter 5.

Government Spending (G)

The third component of demand in our model is government spending, G. Together with taxes T, G describes **fiscal policy**—the choice of taxes and spending by the government. Just as we just did for investment, we shall take G and T as exogenous. But the rationale for this assumption is different from that for investment. It is based on two considerations.

Recall that "taxes" stands for taxes minus government transfers.

First, governments do not behave with the same regularity as consumers or firms, so there is no reliable rule we could write for G or T corresponding to the rule we wrote for consumption. This consideration is not fully convincing, however. Even if governments do not follow simple behavioral rules as consumers do, a good part of their behavior is predictable. We shall look at these issues later, in particular in Chapters 25 to 27, but we leave them aside until then.

Because we shall (nearly always) take G and T as exogenous, I shall not use a bar to denote their value. This will keep the notation lighter.

Second, and more importantly, one of the tasks of macroeconomists is to advise governments on spending and tax decisions. That means we do not want to look at a model in which we have already assumed something about their behavior. We want to be able to say, "If you were to choose these values for G and T, this is what would happen." The approach in this book will typically treat G and T as variables chosen by the government, and not try to explain them within the model.

If firms hold inventories, then the supply of goods need not equal production all the time: Firms can supply more than they produce by decreasing their inventories. Conversely, firms can increase inventories by producing more than they supply. It is easier to start thinking about the equilibrium by ignoring this possibility. (Think of an economy that produces only haircuts. There cannot be inventories of haircuts—haircuts produced, but not sold? Equilibrium requires production of haircuts be equal to demand for haircuts.)

3-3 | The Determination of Equilibrium Output

Let's collect the pieces we have introduced so far. Assuming that exports and imports are both zero, the demand for goods is the sum of consumption, investment, and government spending:

$$Z \equiv C + I + G$$

If we replace C and I from equations (3.2) and (3.3), we get

$$Z = c_0 + c_1(Y - T) + \bar{I} + G \qquad (3.4)$$

The demand for goods (Z) depends on income (Y), taxes (T), investment ($\bar{I}$), and government spending (G).

Let's now turn to **equilibrium** in the goods market. Assume that firms do not hold inventories, so that the supply of goods is equal to production Y. Then, **equilibrium in the goods market** requires that the supply of goods (Y) equals the demand for goods (Z):

$$Y = Z \qquad (3.5)$$

Three types of equations:
  identities
  behavioral equations
  equilibrium conditions

This equation is called an **equilibrium condition**. Models include three types of equations: identities, behavioral equations, and equilibrium conditions. We now have seen examples of each: The equation defining disposable income is an identity, the consumption function is a behavioral equation, and the condition that supply equals demand is an equilibrium condition.

Replacing demand (Z) using equation (3.4) gives

$$Y = c_0 + c_1(Y - T) + \bar{I} + G \qquad (3.6)$$

Equation (3.6) represents algebraically what we described informally at the beginning of this chapter. Production, Y, (the left side of the equation) must be equal to demand (the right side). And demand in turn depends on income, Y. Note that we are using the same symbol Y for production and income. This is no accident! As we saw in Chapter 2, production and income are identically equal: They are the two ways of looking at GDP—one from the production side, the other from the income side.

See Figure 3–1: Demand determines production (the equilibrium condition). Production is equal to income. And income determines demand (equation [3.4]).

Having constructed a model, we can solve it to look at what determines the level of output, how output changes in response to, say, a change in government spending. Solving a model means not only solving it algebraically but also understanding why the results are what they are. In this book, solving a model will also mean characterizing the results using graphs—sometimes skipping the algebra altogether—and describing the results and the mechanisms in words. Macroeconomists always use these three tools:

1. Algebra to make sure that the logic is right
2. Graphs to build the intuition
3. Words to explain the results

Make it a habit to do the same.

Using Algebra

Rewrite the equilibrium equation (3.6):

$$Y = c_0 + c_1 Y - c_1 T + \bar{I} + G$$

Move $c_1 Y$ to the left side and reorganize the right and the left sides:

$$(1 - c_1)Y = c_0 + \bar{I} + G - c_1 T$$

Divide both sides by $(1 - c_1)$:

$$Y = \frac{1}{1 - c_1} [c_0 + \bar{I} + G - c_1 T] \qquad (3.7)$$

Equation (3.7) characterizes equilibrium output, the level of output such that supply equals demand. Let's look at both terms on the right, beginning with the second one.

The second term, $[c_0 + \bar{I} + G - c_1 T]$, is that part of the demand for goods that does not depend on output. This term is called **autonomous spending**. Can we be sure that autonomous spending is positive? We cannot, but it is very likely to be. The first two terms in brackets, c_0 and $\bar{I}$, are positive. What about the last two, $G - c_1 T$? Suppose the government is running a **balanced budget**—taxes equal government spending. If $T = G$, and the propensity to consume (c_1) is less than one (as we have assumed), then $(G - c_1 T)$ is positive and so is autonomous spending. Only if the government ran a very large budget surplus—if taxes were much larger than government spending—could autonomous spending be negative. We can safely ignore that case here.

Turn to the first term, $1/(1 - c_1)$. Because the propensity to consume (c_1) is between zero and one, $1/(1 - c_1)$ is a number greater than one. This number, which multiplies autonomous spending, is called the **multiplier**. The closer c_1 is to one, the larger the multiplier.

What does the multiplier imply? Suppose that, for a given level of income, consumers decide to consume more. More precisely, assume that c_0 in equation (3.2) increases by \$1 billion. Equation (3.7) tells us that output will increase by more than \$1 billion. For example, if c_1 equals 0.6, the multiplier equals $1/(1 - 0.6) = 2.5$, so that output increases by $2.5 \times \$1$ billion $= \$2.5$ billion. We have looked here at an increase in consumption, but clearly any increase in autonomous spending—from an increase in investment to an increase in government spending to a reduction in taxes—will have the same qualitative effect: It will increase output by more than its direct effect on autonomous spending.

Where does the multiplier effect come from? Looking back at equation (3.6) gives the beginning of a clue. An increase in c_0 increases demand. The increase in demand then leads to an increase in production and income. But the increase in income further increases consumption, which further increases demand, and so on. The best way to strengthen this intuition is to use a graphical approach.

> Autonomous means independent—in this case, independent of output.

> If $T = G$
> $G - c_1 T = G - c_1 G$
> $\qquad = G(1 - c_1)$
> $\qquad > 0$ if $c_1 < 1$

Using a Graph

Equilibrium requires that the production of goods (Y) equals the demand for goods (Z). Figure 3–3 plots both production and demand as functions of income; the equilibrium is the point at which production and demand are equal.

First, look at the plot of production as a function of income. Production is measured on the vertical axis, and income is measured on the horizontal axis. Plotting production as a function of income is straightforward, as production and income are always equal. Thus, the relation between the two is simply the 45-degree line, the line with a slope equal to 1, in Figure 3–3.

FIGURE **3-3**

Equilibrium in the Goods Market

Equilibrium output is determined by the condition that production be equal to demand.

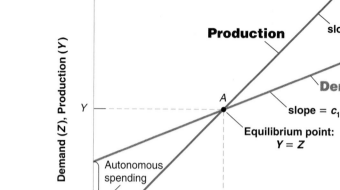

Second, look at the plot of demand as a function of income. The relation between demand and income is given by equation (3.4). Let's rewrite it here for convenience, regrouping the terms for autonomous spending together in the term in parentheses:

$$Z = (c_0 + \bar{I} + G - c_1 T) + c_1 Y$$

Demand depends on autonomous spending, and on income—through its effect on consumption. The relation between demand and income is drawn as ZZ in the figure. The intercept with the vertical axis—the value of demand when income is equal to zero— equals autonomous spending. The slope of the line is the propensity to consume, c_1: When income increases by 1, demand increases by c_1. Under the restriction that c_1 is positive but less than 1, the line is upward sloping but with slope less than 1.

Equilibrium holds when production equals demand. Thus, equilibrium output, Y, is given by the intersection, at point A, of the 45-degree line and the demand relation, ZZ. To the left of A, demand exceeds production; to the right, production exceeds demand. Only at A are the two equal.

Now return to the example we looked at earlier. Suppose that c_0 increases by $1 billion. At the initial level of income (the level of income associated with point A), consumers increase their consumption by $1 billion. What happens then is shown in Figure 3–4, which builds on Figure 3–3.

For any value of income, demand is higher by $1 billion. Before the increase in c_0, the relation between demand and income was given by the line ZZ. After the increase in c_0 by $1 billion, the relation between demand and income is given by the line ZZ', which is parallel to ZZ but higher by $1 billion. In other words, the demand relation shifts up by $1 billion. The new equilibrium is at the intersection of the 45-degree line and the new demand relation, at point A'. Equilibrium output increases from Y to Y'. It is clear that the increase in output, $(Y' - Y)$, which we can measure either on the horizontal or the vertical axis, is larger than the initial increase in consumption of $1 billion. This is the multiplier effect.

With the help of the graph, it becomes easier to tell how and why the economy moves from A to A'. The initial increase in consumption leads to an increase in demand of $1 billion. At the initial level of income, Y, the level of demand is now given by point B: Demand is $1 billion higher. To satisfy this higher level of demand, firms increase production by $1 billion. The economy moves to point C, with both demand and production higher by $1 billion. But this is not the end of the story. The higher level of production leads to an increase

The distance between Y and Y' on the horizontal axis is larger than the distance between A and B—which is equal to $1 billion.

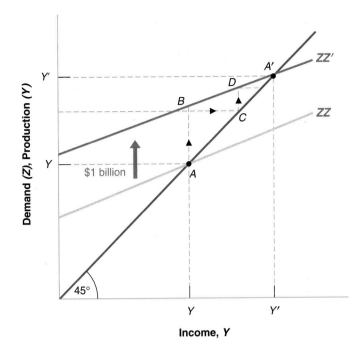

FIGURE 3-4

The Effects of an Increase in Autonomous Spending on Output

An increase in autonomous spending has a more than one-for-one effect on equilibrium output.

in income of $1 billion, and to a further increase in demand, so that demand is now given by point D. Point D leads to a higher level of production, and so on, until the economy is at A', where production and demand are again equal, and which is therefore the new equilibrium.

We can pursue this line of thought a bit more, and this will give us another way of thinking about the multiplier. The first-round increase in production—the distance AB in Figure 3–4—equals $1 billion. The second-round increase in production—the distance CD—in turn equals $1 billion (the increase in income in the first round) times the propensity to consume out of income, c_1—hence, $\$c_1$ billion. Following the same logic, the third-round increase in production equals $\$c_1$ billion (the increase in income in the second round), times c_1, the marginal propensity to consume out of income; it is thus equal to $\$c_1 * c_1 = \$c_1^2$ billion. Following this logic, the total increase in production after, say, n rounds equals $1 billion times the sum:

$$1 + c_1 + c_1^2 + \cdots + c_1^n$$

Such a sum is called a **geometric series**. Geometric series will come up often in this book. A refresher on their properties is given in Appendix 2. The main property of such series is that, when c_1 is less than one (as it is here) and as n gets larger and larger, the sum keeps increasing but approaches a limit. That limit is $1/(1 - c_1)$, making the eventual increase in output $\$1/(1 - c_1)$ billion.

The expression $1/(1 - c_1)$ should be familiar: It is the multiplier, derived another way. This gives us an equivalent, but more intuitive way of thinking about the multiplier. We can think of the original increase in spending as triggering successive increases in production, with each increase in production implying an increase in income, which leads to an increase in demand, which leads to a further increase in production, which leads . . . and so on. The multiplier is the sum of all these successive increases in production.

Using Words

How can we summarize our findings in words?

Production depends on demand, which depends on income, which is itself equal to production. An increase in demand, such as an increase in government or in consumer spending, leads to an increase in production and a corresponding increase in income. This increase in income leads to a further increase in demand, which leads to a further increase in production, and so on. The end result is an increase in output that is larger than the initial shift in demand, by a factor equal to the multiplier.

A trick question: Think about the multiplier as the result of these successive rounds. What would happen in each successive round if c_1, the propensity to consume, was larger than one?

The size of the multiplier is directly related to the value of the propensity to consume: the higher the propensity to consume, the higher the multiplier. What is the value of the propensity to consume in the United States today? To answer this question, and more generally to estimate behavioral equations and their parameters, economists use **econometrics**, the set of statistical methods used in economics. To give you a sense of what econometrics is and how it is used, Appendix 3 at the end of the book gives you a quick introduction, using as an application the estimation of the propensity to consume. The conclusion from the appendix is that, in the United States today, the propensity to consume is around 0.6. An additional dollar of income leads on average to an increase in consumption of 60 cents. This implies a multiplier equal to $1/(1 - c_1) = 1/(1 - 0.6) = 2.5$.[1]

How Long Does It Take for Output to Adjust?

Let's return to our example one last time. Suppose that c_0 increases by $1 billion. We know that output will increase by an amount equal to the multiplier $1/(1 - c_1)$ times $1 billion. But how long will it take for output to reach this new higher level?

Under the assumptions I have made so far, the answer is: Right away! In writing the equilibrium condition (3.5), I have assumed that production is always equal to demand—in other words, production responds to demand instantaneously. In writing the consumption function (3.1), I have assumed that consumption responds to disposable income instantaneously. Under these two assumptions, the economy goes instantaneously from point A to point A': The increase in demand leads to an increase in production right away, the increase in income associated with the increase in production leads to an increase in demand right away, and so on. We can think of the adjustment in terms of successive rounds as we did earlier, but all these rounds happen at once.

This instantaneous adjustment does not seem very plausible. And indeed it is not. A firm that faces an increase in demand may decide to wait before adjusting its production, drawing down its inventories to satisfy demand. A consumer who gets a raise at work may not adjust her consumption right away. And these delays imply that the adjustment of output will take time.

Describing formally this adjustment of output over time—what economists call the **dynamics** of adjustment—would take us too far. But it is easy to do it in words.

Suppose that firms make decisions about their production level at the beginning of each quarter; once the decision is made, production cannot be adjusted for the rest of the quarter. If purchases are higher than production, firms draw down inventories to satisfy purchases. If purchases are lower than production, firms accumulate inventories.

Now, let's return to our example, and suppose consumers decide to spend more, that they increase c_0. During the quarter in which this happens, demand increases, but—because of our assumption that production was set at the beginning of the quarter—production does not yet change. Therefore, income does not change either. In the following quarter, firms having observed an increase in demand in the previous quarter are likely to set a higher level of production. This increase in production leads to a corresponding increase in income and a further increase in demand. If purchases still exceed production, firms further increase production in the following quarter, and so on. In short, in response to an increase in consumer spending, output does not jump to the new equilibrium, but rather increases over time from Y to Y'. How long this adjustment takes depends on how and how often

---

[1]**DIGGING DEEPER.** In reality, the multiplier is smaller than 2.5, for two reasons.

We have assumed that taxes, T, were given. But in reality, when income increases, taxes increase. This means disposable income increases less than one for one with income, and this implies that consumption increases less than we have assumed here. (This is explored in more detail in problem 6 at the end of the chapter.)

We have assumed that imports and exports were equal to zero. But in reality, when income increases, some of the increase in demand falls not on domestic goods but on foreign goods. In other words, the demand for domestic goods increases by less than we have assumed here. We shall explore this in more detail in Chapter 19.

firms revise their production schedule. The more often firms adjust their production schedule, and the larger the response of production to past increases in purchases, the faster the adjustment.

I shall often do in the book what I just did in the last two paragraphs. Having looked at changes in equilibrium output, I shall then describe informally how the economy moves from one equilibrium to the other. This will not only make the description of what happens in the economy feel more realistic, but it will often reinforce our intuition about why the equilibrium changed in the first place.

We have focused in this section on *increases* in demand. But the mechanism is symmetric: Decreases in demand lead to decreases in output. The 1990–1991 recession in the United States was largely the result of a sudden drop in consumer confidence, leading a sharp decrease in consumption demand, which led, in turn, to a sharp decline in output. The origins of the 1990–1991 recession are examined in the In Depth box "Consumer Confidence and the 1990–1991 Recession."

In Depth: Consumer Confidence and the 1990–1991 Recession

In the third quarter of 1990, after the invasion of Kuwait by Iraq but before the beginning of the Persian Gulf war, U.S. GDP growth turned negative and remained negative for the following two quarters. As we saw in Chapter 2, economists use the term "recession" to denote at least two consecutive quarterly decreases in GDP, so this episode is known as the 1990–1991 recession.

The second column of the accompanying table gives real GDP—in billions of 1992 dollars—from the second quarter of 1990 to the second quarter of 1991. The third column gives the change in GDP from one quarter to the next. Note that GDP is measured at *an annual rate,* so the numbers are equal to four times their true value for the quarter. Reporting monthly or quarterly variables at an annual rate may at first appear confusing. But reporting

all variables (whether daily, monthly, or quarterly) at an annual rate—and thus at a common rate—makes comparison among them easier. In 1990:3, 1990:4 and 1991:1, the change in GDP is negative. This is the 1990–1991 recession.

The 1990–1991 recession was not predicted by macroeconomists. To a large extent, it was the result of the effects of shifts in spending that had not been anticipated. This is clear from columns (4) and (5) of the table. Column (4) gives the forecasts made during the preceding quarter for each subsequent quarter. For example, the forecast of GDP made in the second quarter for the third quarter of 1990 was $6,199 billion. Column (5) gives the **forecast error**, the difference between the actual value of GDP and the

(continued)

TABLE 1				GDP, consumption, and forecast errors, 1990:2 to 1991:2		
(1) Quarter	(2) Real GDP	(3) Change in GDP	(4) Forecast of GDP	(5) Forecast error for GDP	(6) Forecast error for c_0	(7) Consumer Confidence
1990:2	6,171	19	6,189	−17	−23	105
1990:3	6,142	−29	6,199	−57	−1	90
1990:4	6,078	−63	6,167	−88	−37	61
1991:1	6,047	−31	6,074	−27	−30	65
1991:2	6,074	27	6,027	47	8	77

Notes for headings:
Column (2)—Real GDP: Billions of 1992 dollars, at an annual rate.
Column (3)—Change in GDP: Change from last quarter, at annual rate.
Column (4)—Forecast of GDP for the current quarter, as of the previous quarter.
Column (5)—Forecast error for GDP: GDP minus forecast of GDP.
Column (6)—Forecast error for c_0, from article cited at the end of the box.
Column (7)—Consumer confidence index.

forecast value. A positive forecast error indicates that actual GDP turned out to be higher than expected; a negative forecast error indicates that actual GDP turned out lower than expected. To pursue our example: Because the actual value of GDP in the third quarter of 1990 was $6,142 billion, the forecast error for that quarter was $6,142 - 6,199$, or $-$57 billion.

As you can see, the forecast errors are negative during all three quarters of the recession. They are actually larger than the actual declines in GDP in each of the first two quarters of the recession. Put another way, at the beginning of each of these two quarters, the forecasts were of positive growth, whereas growth actually turned out negative. For example, the forecast made in the second quarter for the third quarter was for an increase in GDP of $6,199 - 6,171 = $28 billion. The actual movement in GDP was a decrease of $29 billion.

Where did these forecast errors come from? In terms of equation (3.7), which of the determinants of spending was the main culprit? Was it c_0, or I, or G, or T? Research looking at the evolution of each of the components of spending suggests that the main cause, for the last two quarters of the recession, was an adverse shift in consumption, an unexpected decrease in c_0. Forecast errors of c_0 are given in the sixth column of the table. There are two large negative errors for the last two quarters of the recession.

A large decrease in c_0 is a drop in consumption given disposable income. Why did consumption drop so much, given disposable income, in late 1990 and early 1991?

The direct cause is shown in the last column of the table, which gives the value of the **consumer confidence index**. This index is computed from a monthly survey of about 5,000 households; the survey asks consumers how confident they are about both current and future economic conditions, from job opportunities to their expected family income six months ahead. As you can see, there was an unusually large decrease in the index in the fourth quarter of 1990. Consumers lost confidence, leading them to cut consumption given disposable income, and triggering the recession.

This brings us to the last question: Why did consumers lose confidence in late 1990? Why did they become more pessimistic about the future? Even today, economists are not sure. It is more than likely that this change in mood was related to the increasing probability of a war in the Middle East—a war that started in early 1991, after the beginning of the recession. People worried that the United States might get involved in a prolonged and costly war. They also worried that a war in the Middle East could lead to a large increase in oil prices and to a recession: The two previous large increases in oil prices in the 1970s had both been associated with recessions. Whatever the reason, the decrease in consumer confidence was a major factor behind the 1990–1991 recession.

Source: Olivier Blanchard, "Consumption and the Recession of 1990–1991," *American Economic Review*, May 1993. Updated using revised NIPA series for consumption and GDP.

3-4 | Investment Equals Saving: An Alternative Way of Thinking About Goods-Market Equilibrium

Thus far we have thought about equilibrium in terms of equality between the supply and the demand for goods. An alternative—but equivalent—way of thinking about equilibrium focuses on *investment* and *saving* instead. This is how John Maynard Keynes first articulated this model in 1936, in *The General Theory of Employment, Interest and Money*.

By definition, **private saving (S)**, saving by consumers, is equal to their disposable income minus their consumption

$$S \equiv Y_D - C$$

Using the definition of disposable income, we can rewrite private saving as income minus taxes minus consumption:

$$S \equiv Y - T - C$$

Now return to the equation for equilibrium in the goods market. Production must be equal to demand, which in turn is the sum of consumption, investment, and government spending:

$$Y = C + I + G$$

Subtract taxes (T) from both sides and move consumption to the left side

$$Y - T - C = I + G - T$$

The left side of this equation is simply private saving (S), so that

$$S = I + G - T$$

Or equivalently,

$$I = S + (T - G) \qquad (3.8)$$

If taxes exceed government spending, the government is running a budget surplus—public saving is positive. If taxes are less than government spending, the government is running a budget deficit—public saving is negative.

The term on the left is investment. The first term on the right is *private saving*. The second term is **public saving**—taxes minus government spending.

Equation (3.8) thus gives us another way of looking at equilibrium in the goods market. Equilibrium in the goods market requires that investment equals **saving**—the sum of private and public saving. This way of looking at equilibrium explains why the equilibrium condition for the goods market is called the **IS relation**, for "**I**nvestment equals **S**aving." What firms want to invest must be equal to what people and the government want to save.

To strengthen your intuition for equation (3.8), think of an economy where there is only one person, who has to decide how much to consume, invest, and save—a "Robinson Crusoe" economy. For Robinson Crusoe, the saving and the investment decisions are one and the same: What he invests (say, by keeping rabbits for reproduction, rather than eating them), he automatically saves. In a modern economy, however, investment decisions are made by firms, whereas saving decisions are made by consumers and the government. In equilibrium, equation (3.8) tells us, all those decisions have to be consistent: Investment must be equal to saving.

The two equivalent ways of stating the condition for equilibrium in the goods market:

Supply of goods
      = demand for goods

   Investment = Saving

We can study the characteristics of the equilibrium using equation (3.8) and the behavioral equations for saving and investment. Note first that *consumption and saving decisions are one and the same*: Given their disposable income, once consumers have chosen con-

The Paradox of Saving

As we grow up, we are told of the virtues of thrift. Those who spend all their income are condemned to end up poor. Those who save are promised a happy life. Similarly, governments tell us, an economy that saves is an economy that will grow strong and prosper! Equation (3.7), however, tells a different and quite surprising story.

Suppose that, at a given level of disposable income, consumers decide to save more. In terms of equation (3.2), the equation describing consumption, they decrease c_0, therefore decreasing consumption and increasing saving at a given level of disposable income. What happens to output and to saving?

Equation (3.7) makes it clear that equilibrium output decreases when c_0 decreases. As people save more at their initial level of income, they decrease their consumption. But this decreased consumption decreases demand, which decreases production.

Can we tell what happens to saving? Return to the equation for private saving (by assumption, there is no change in public saving, so saving and private saving move together):

$$S = -c_0 + (1 - c_1)(Y - T)$$

On the one hand, $-c_0$ is higher: Consumers are saving more at any level of income; this tends to increase saving.

But, on the other hand, Y is lower: This decreases saving. The net effect would seem to be ambiguous. In fact, we can tell which way it goes. Remember that we can think of the equilibrium condition as the condition that saving equals investment, equation (3.8). By assumption, investment does not change. So, the equilibrium condition tells us that in equilibrium, saving does not change either. Although people want to save more at a given level of income, income decreases by an amount such that saving is unchanged. This means that attempts by people to save more lead both to a decline in output and to unchanged saving. This surprising pair of results is known as the **paradox of saving**.

So should you forget the old wisdom? Should the government tell people to be less thrifty? No. The results of this simple model are of much relevance in the *short run*. The desire of consumers to save more led to the 1990–1991 recession (see the In Depth box earlier in this chapter). But—as we shall see later in this book when we look at the *medium* and the *long run*—other mechanisms come into play over time and an increase in the saving rate is likely to lead to higher saving and higher income. An important warning remains, however: Policies that encourage saving may be good in the medium and the long run, but may lead to a recession in the short run.

sumption, their saving is determined, and vice versa. The way we specified consumption behavior implies that private saving is given by

$$S = Y - T - C$$
$$= Y - T - c_0 - c_1(Y - T)$$

Rearranging, we get

$$S = -c_0 + (1 - c_1)(Y - T)$$

In the same way that we called c_1 the propensity to consume, we can call $(1 - c_1)$ the **propensity to save**. The propensity to save tells us how much people save out of an additional unit of income. The assumption we made earlier that the propensity to consume (c_1) is between zero and one implies that the propensity to save $(1 - c_1)$ is also between zero and one. Private saving increases with disposable income, but by less than one dollar for each additional dollar of disposable income.

In equilibrium, investment must be equal to saving, the sum of private and public saving. Replacing private saving in equation (3.8) by its expression from above

$$I = -c_0 + (1 - c_1)(Y - T) + (T - G)$$

Solving for output,

$$Y = \frac{1}{1 - c_1}[c_0 + \bar{I} + G - c_1 T]$$

This is exactly the same expression as equation (3.7) earlier. This should come as no surprise. We are looking at the same model, just in a different way. This alternative way will prove useful in various applications later in the book. Such an application is given in the Focus box, "The Paradox of Saving."

3-5 | Is the Government Omnipotent? A Warning

Equation (3.7) implies that the government, by choosing the level of spending (G) or the level of taxes (T), can choose the level of output it wants. If it wants output to increase by, say, $1 billion, all it needs to do is to increase G by $(1 - c_1)$ billion; this increase in government spending, in theory, will lead to an output increase of $(1 - c_1)$ billion times the multiplier $1/(1 - c_1)$, thus $1 billion.

Can governments really choose the level of output they want? The existence of recessions makes clear the answer is no. There are many aspects of reality that we have not yet incorporated in our model. We shall do so in due time. But it is useful to list them in brief here:

You may want to have a ▶ glimpse at the longer list given in the Focus box "Fiscal Policy: What Have We Learned and Where?" in Chapter 27.

- Changing government spending or taxes may be far from easy. Getting the U.S. Congress to pass bills always takes time, and can often turn into a president's nightmare (Chapters 25 and 27).
- The effects of spending and taxes on demand are much less mechanical than equation (3.7) makes them appear. They may happen slowly, consumers and firms may be scared of the budget deficit and change their behavior, and so on (Chapters 5 and 17).
- Maintaining a desired level of output may come with unpleasant side effects. Trying to achieve too high a level of output may, for example, lead to accelerating inflation and may become unsustainable in the medium run (Chapters 7 and 8).
- Cutting taxes or increasing government spending may lead to large budget deficits, and an accumulation of public debt. Such debt will have adverse implications in the long run (Chapters 11 and 27).

As we refine our analysis, the role of the government in general, and the successful use of fiscal policy in particular, will become increasingly difficult. Governments will never again have it so good as in this chapter.

What you should remember about the components of GDP:

- GDP is the sum of consumption, plus investment, plus government spending, plus exports, minus imports, plus inventory investment.

- Consumption (C) is the purchase of goods and services by consumers. Consumption is the largest component of demand.

- Investment (I) is the sum of nonresidential investment—the purchase of new plants and new machines by firms—and of residential investment—the purchase of new houses or apartments by people.

- Government spending (G) is the purchase of goods and services by federal, state, and local governments.

- Exports (X) are purchases of U.S. goods by foreigners. Imports (Q) are purchases of foreign goods by U.S. consumers, U.S. firms, and the U.S. government.

- Inventory investment (I_S) is the difference between production and purchases. It can be positive or negative.

What you should remember about our first model of output determination:

- In the short run, demand determines production. Production is equal to income. And income determines demand.

- The consumption function shows how consumption depends on disposable income. The propensity to consume describes how much consumption increases for a given increase in disposable income.

- Equilibrium output is the point at which supply (production) equals demand. In equilibrium, output equals autonomous spending times the multiplier. Autonomous spending is that part of demand that does not depend on income. The multiplier is equal to $1/(1 - c_1)$, where c_1 is the propensity to consume.

- Increases in consumer confidence, in investment demand, or in government spending, or decreases in taxes all increase equilibrium output in the short run.

- An alternative way of stating the goods-market equilibrium condition is that investment must be equal to saving, the sum of private and public saving. For this reason, the equilibrium condition is called the IS relation (I for investment, S for saving).

- consumption (C), 42
- investment (I), 42
- fixed investment, 42
- residential investment, 42
- nonresidential investment, 42
- government spending (G), 42
- government transfers, 42
- imports (Q), 43
- exports (X), 43
- net exports ($X - Q$), 43
- trade balance, 43
- trade surplus, 43
- trade deficit, 43
- inventory investment (I_S), 43
- stocks, 43
- identity, 43
- disposable income (Y_D), 44
- consumption function, 44
- behavioral equation, 44
- linear relation, 44
- parameter, 44

- propensity to consume (c_1), 44
- endogenous variables, 45
- exogenous variables, 45
- fiscal policy, 46
- equilibrium, 46
- equilibrium in the goods market, 46
- equilibrium condition, 46
- autonomous spending, 47
- balanced budget, 47
- multiplier, 47
- geometric series, 49
- econometrics, 50
- dynamics, 50
- forecast error, 51
- consumer confidence index, 52
- private saving (S), 52
- public saving ($T - G$), 53
- saving, 53
- IS relation, 53
- paradox of saving, 53
- propensity to save, 54

An asterisk denotes a harder question. [Web] indicates that the question requires access to the Internet.

1. TRUE/FALSE/UNCERTAIN

a. The largest component of GDP is consumption.

b. Government spending, including transfers, was equal to 18% of GDP in 1998.

c. The propensity to consume has to be positive, but beyond that it can take on any positive value.

d. Fiscal policy describes the choice of government spending and taxes, and is treated as exogenous in our goods market model.

e. The equilibrium condition for the goods market states that consumption equals output.

f. An increase of one unit in government spending leads to an increase of one unit in equilibrium output.

2. A SIMPLE ECONOMY

Suppose that the economy is characterized by the following behavioral equations:

$$C = 160 + 0.6Y_D$$
$$\bar{I} = 150$$
$$G = 150$$
$$T = 100$$

Solve for

a. equilibrium GDP (Y)

b. disposable income (Y_D)

c. consumption spending (C)

3. THE CONCEPT OF EQUILIBRIUM

For the economy in question 2,

a. Assume output is equal to 900. Compute total demand. Is it equal to production? Explain.

b. Assume output is equal to 1,000. Compute total demand. Is it equal to production? Explain.

c. Assume output is equal to 1,000. Compute private saving. Is it equal to investment? Explain.

4. THE U.S. ECONOMY

a. For the economy in question 2, compute each component of demand as a percentage of GDP. Are your results roughly consistent with the 1998 composition of U.S. GDP?

b. Consider the decline in real GDP during the 1990–1991 recession as presented in the box "Consumer Confidence and the 1990–1991 Recession." From the beginning of the period in question to the worst point in the recession, what was the decline in GDP in percentage terms?

*c. By how much should c_0 in question 2 decrease in order to achieve the same percentage change in equilibrium GDP as the one you reported in part (b)?

*d. In terms of units (i.e. *not* in percentage terms), is the decrease in c_0 required in part (c) greater or less than the decrease in output that it causes? Why?

5. THE BALANCED BUDGET MULTIPLIER

For both political and macroeconomic reasons, governments are often reluctant to run budget deficits. Here we examine whether policy changes in G and T that maintain a balanced budget are macroeconomically neutral. Put another way, we examine whether it is possible to affect output through changes in G and T so that the government budget remains balanced. Start with equation (3.7).

a. By how much does Y increase when G increases by one unit?

b. By how much does Y decrease when T increases by one unit?

c. Why are your answers to (a) and (b) different?

Suppose that the economy starts with a balanced budget: $T = G$. If the increase in G is equal to the increase in T, then the budget remains in balance. Let us now compute the balanced budget multiplier.

d. Suppose that both G and T increase by exactly one unit. Using your answers to parts (a) and (b), what is the change in equilibrium GDP? Are balanced budget changes in G and T macroeconomically neutral?

*e. How does the propensity to consume affect your answer? Why?

*6. AUTOMATIC STABILIZERS

So far in this chapter we have been assuming that the fiscal policy variable T is independent of the level of income. In the real world, however, this is not the case. Taxes typically depend on the level of income, and so tend to be higher when income is higher. In this problem we examine how this automatic response of taxes can help reduce the impact of changes in autonomous spending on output.

Consider the following model of the economy:

$$C = c_0 + c_1 Y_D$$
$$T = t_0 + t_1 Y$$
$$Y_D = Y - T$$

G and $\bar{I}$ are both constant

a. Is t_1 greater or less than one? Explain.

b. Solve for equilibrium output.

c. What is the multiplier? Does the economy respond more to changes in autonomous spending when t_1 is zero or when t_1 is positive? Explain.

d. Why is fiscal policy in this case called an "automatic stabilizer"?

*7. BALANCED BUDGET VERSUS AUTOMATIC STABILIZERS

It is often argued that a balanced budget amendment would actually be destabilizing. To understand this argument, consider the economy of question 6.

a. Solve for equilibrium output.

b. Solve for taxes in equilibrium.

Suppose that the government starts with a balanced budget and that there is a drop in c_0.

c. What happens to Y? What happens to taxes?

d. Suppose that the government cuts spending in order to keep the budget balanced. What will be the effect on Y? Does the cut in spending required to balance the budget counteract or reinforce the effect of the drop in c_0 on output? (Don't do the algebra. Give the answer in words.)

 We invite you to visit the Blanchard page on the Prentice Hall Web site at:

http://www.prenhall.com/blanchard

for this chapter's World Wide Web exercises

CHAPTER | Financial Markets

Barely a day goes by without the media speculating whether the Federal Reserve Bank, the U.S. central bank (the Fed for short), is going to increase or decrease interest rates and what this is likely to do to the economy. The model of economic activity we developed in chapter 3 did not include interest rates. This was a strong simplification, and it is time to relax it. This requires that we take two steps. First, we must look at what determines interest rates, and the role of the Fed in this determination. This is the topic of this chapter. Second, we must look at how interest rates affect economic activity. This is the topic of the next chapter.

To understand what determines interest rates, we must look at **financial markets.** The task appears daunting: In modern economies, there are thousands of financial assets, and thousands of interest rates—interest rates on short-term bonds, on long-term bonds, on government bonds, on corporate bonds, and so on. To make progress, we must simplify. Just as we did assume, in looking at the goods market in chapter 3, that there was only one type of good, we assume in this chapter that there is just one type of bond, and therefore just one interest rate. We can then think about the determinants of *the* interest rate. As we shall see, the interest rate is determined by the condition that the demand for money is equal to the supply of money. And, because the central bank can change the supply of money, monetary policy has a direct effect on the interest rate.

The chapter has three sections. Section 4-1 looks at the demand for money. Section 4-2 looks at the determination of the interest rate under the assumption that the supply of money is directly under the control of the central bank. Section 4-3 (which is optional) introduces banks as suppliers of money, and revisits the determination of the interest rate, and the role of the central bank.

Before we start, a warning: Discussions of financial markets and financial issues are fraught with semantic traps. Words such as "money" or "wealth" have very specific meanings in economics, and these are often not the same meanings as in everyday conversations. The purpose of the Focus box "Semantic Traps: Money, Income, and Wealth" is to help you avoid some of these traps. Read it carefully, and come back to it once in a while.

Semantic Traps: Money, Income, and Wealth

In everyday life we use the word "money" to denote many things. We use it as a synonym for income: "making money." We use it as a synonym for wealth: "she has a lot of money." In economics, you must be more careful. Here is a basic guide to some terms and their precise meanings.

Income is what you earn from working plus what you receive in interest and dividends. It is a **flow**—that is, it is expressed per unit of time: weekly income, monthly income, or yearly income. J. Paul Getty was once asked what his income was. Getty answered, "$1,000." He meant but did not say: per minute.

Saving is that part of after-tax income that is not spent. It is also a flow. If you save 10% of income and your income is $3,000 per month, then you save $300 per month. Savings (plural) is sometimes used as a synonym for wealth—the value of what you have accumulated over time. To avoid potential confusion, I shall not use it in the book.

Your **financial wealth**, or simply **wealth**, is the value of all your financial assets minus all your financial liabilities. In contrast to income or saving, which are flow variables, financial wealth is a **stock** variable. It is the value of wealth at a given moment of time. At a given moment of time, you cannot change the total amount of your financial wealth. You can do this only over time, as you save or dissave, or

as the value of your assets change. But you can change the composition of your wealth; you can for example decide to pay back part of your mortgage by writing a check on your checking account. This leads to a decrease in your liabilities (a smaller mortgage) and a corresponding decrease in your assets (a smaller checking account balance); but it does not change your wealth.

Financial assets that can be used directly to buy goods are called money. Money includes currency and checkable deposits, deposits against which you can write checks. Money is also a stock. Someone can have a large wealth but small money holdings, for example, $1,000,000 worth of stocks, but only $500 in his checking account. Or someone can have a large income but small money holdings, for example, be paid $10,000 a month, but have a very small positive balance in her checking account.

Investment is a term economists reserve for the purchase of new capital goods, from machines to manufacturing plants to office buildings. When you want to talk about the purchase of shares or other financial assets, you should refer to **financial investment**.

Learn how to be economically correct: Do not say "Mary is making a lot of money"; say "Mary receives a high income." Do not say "Joe has a lot of money"; say "Joe is very wealthy."

4-1 | The Demand for Money

Assume that you have the choice between only two financial assets:

- Money, which can be used for transactions, but pays zero interest. In reality, there are two types of money: **currency**, the coins and bills issued by the central bank, and **checkable deposits**, the bank deposits on which you can write checks. The distinction between the two will be important later when we look at the supply of money. But for the moment, it does not matter.

Checkable deposits often pay a small interest rate. We ignore this here.

- Bonds, which cannot be used for transactions, but pay a positive interest rate, i. In reality there are many other assets than money, and in particular many types of bonds, each associated with a specific interest rate. As discussed earlier, we shall also ignore this aspect of reality for the moment.

Suppose that, as a result of having steadily saved part of your income in the past, your financial wealth today is $50,000. You may intend to keep saving in the future and to increase your wealth further, but its value today is given. The choice you have to make today is how to allocate this $50,000 between money and bonds.

Make sure you see the difference between the decision about how much to save (a decision that determines how wealth changes over time), and the decision about how to allocate a given stock of wealth between money and bonds.

Think of buying or selling bonds as implying some cost, for example, a phone call to a broker and the payment of a transaction fee. How much of your $50,000 should you hold in money, and how much in bonds?

Holding all your wealth in the form of money is clearly very convenient. You will never have to call a broker or pay transaction fees. But it also means you won't receive interest income. Holding all your wealth in the form of bonds implies receiving income as interest on all your wealth. But having to call your broker whenever you need money to take the subway or pay for a cup of coffee is a rather inconvenient way of living. Therefore, it is clear that you should hold both money and bonds. In what proportions? This depends mainly on two variables:

- Your *level of transactions*. You want to have enough money on average to avoid having to sell bonds to get money too often. Say that you typically spend $5,000 a month. You may want to have on average, say, two months worth of spending on hand, or $10,000 in money, and the rest, $50,000 − $10,000 = $40,000 in bonds. If, instead, you typically spend $6,000 a month, you may want to have $12,000 in money and thus only $38,000 in bonds.
- The *interest rate on bonds*. The only reason to hold any of your wealth in bonds is that they pay interest. If bonds paid no interest, you would hold all of your wealth in money: Bonds and money would pay the same interest rate (namely zero), and money, which can be used for transactions, would therefore be more convenient.

  The higher the interest rate, the more you will be willing to incur the hassle and the costs associated with buying and selling bonds. If the interest rate is very high, you may decide to squeeze your money holdings to an average of only two weeks' worth of spending, or $2,500 (assuming your monthly spending is $5,000). This means you will be able to keep, on average, $47,500 in bonds, getting more interest as a result.

Let's make this last point more concrete. Most of you probably do not hold bonds directly; few of you have a broker. But many of you hold bonds indirectly, through a money market account. **Money market funds** receive funds from people and firms, and use these funds to buy bonds, typically government bonds. Money market funds pay an interest rate close to the interest rate on the bonds that they hold—the difference coming from the administrative costs of running the funds and from their profit margin.

In the early 1980s, with the interest rate on money market funds reaching 14% per year, people who had previously kept all their financial wealth in their checking accounts (which paid no interest) realized how much interest they could earn by holding part of those funds in a money market account instead. Money market funds became the rage. Since then, however, the interest rate has decreased. In 1998, the interest rate paid by money market funds was down to under 5.0%. This is better than zero—the rate paid on many checking accounts—but much less attractive than the rate in 1981. As a result, most people put less in their money market fund and more in their checking account than they did in 1981.

Let's formalize this discussion. Denote the amount of money people want to hold—their *demand for money*—by M^d (the superscript d stands for *demand*). I just argued that an individual's money demand depends on two variables, his level of transactions, and the interest rate. The demand for money for the economy as a whole is just the sum of all individual demands for money. Thus, money demand for the economy as a whole depends on the overall level of transactions in the economy and on the interest rate. The overall level of transactions in the economy is hard to measure. But it is reasonable to assume that it is roughly proportional to nominal income: If nominal income increases by 10%, it is reasonable to think that the amount of transactions in the economy also increases by roughly 10%. So we write the ◀ relation between the demand for money, nominal income, and the interest rate as

$$M^d = \$Y\,L(i) \qquad (4.1)$$
$$(-)$$

where $\$Y$ denotes nominal income. This equation says that the demand for money is equal to nominal income times a function of the interest rate, denoted $L(i)$. The minus sign under i in $L(i)$ captures the fact that the interest rate has a negative effect on money demand: An increase in the interest rate *decreases* the demand for money.

This equation summarizes what we have learned so far:

- The demand for money increases in proportion to nominal income. If income doubles, increasing from $\$Y$ to $\$2Y$, then the demand for money increases from $\$Y\,L(i)$ to $\$2Y\,L(i)$; it also doubles.

Revisit chapter 2's example of an economy composed of a steel and a car company. Calculate the total volume of transactions in that economy, and its relation to GDP. If the steel and the car companies double in size, what happens to transactions and to GDP?

What matters here is nominal income—income in dollars, not real income. If real income does not change but prices double, leading to a doubling of nominal income, people will need to hold twice as much money to buy the same consumption basket.

- The demand for money depends negatively on the interest rate. This is captured by the function $L(i)$ and the negative sign underneath: An increase in the interest rate decreases the demand for money.

The relation between the demand for money, nominal income, and the interest rate implied by equation (4.1) is represented graphically in Figure 4–1. The interest rate, i, is measured on the vertical axis. Money, M, is measured on the horizontal axis.

The relation between the demand for money and the interest rate, for a given level of nominal income, is represented by the M^d curve. The curve is downward sloping: The lower the interest rate (the lower i), the higher the amount of money people want to hold (the higher M).

At any interest rate, an increase in nominal income increases the demand for money. In other words, an increase in nominal income shifts the demand for money to the right, from M^d to $M^{d'}$. For example, at interest rate i, an increase in nominal income from $\$Y$ to $\$Y'$ increases the demand for money from M to M'.

Money Demand and the Interest Rate: The Evidence

How well does equation (4.1) fit the facts? In particular, how much does the demand for money respond to changes in the interest rate?

To get at the answer, first divide both sides of equation (4.1) by $\$Y$:

$$\frac{M^d}{\$Y} = L(i) \tag{4.2}$$

The term on the left side of the equation is the ratio of money demand to nominal income—in other words, how much money people want to hold in relation to their income. Thus, if equation (4.1)—and by implication equation (4.2)—is a good description of reality, we should observe an inverse relation between the ratio of money to nominal income and the interest rate. This provides the motivation for Figure 4–2, which plots the ratio of money to nominal income and the interest rate against time, for the period 1960 to 1998.

The ratio of money to nominal income is constructed as follows. Money, M, is the sum of currency (the coins and bills issued by the Fed), traveler's checks, and checkable deposits

$L(i)$ is a decreasing function of the interest rate i. Equation (4.2) predicts that when the interest rate is high, the ratio of money to nominal income should be low. When the interest rate is low, the ratio of money to nominal income should be high.

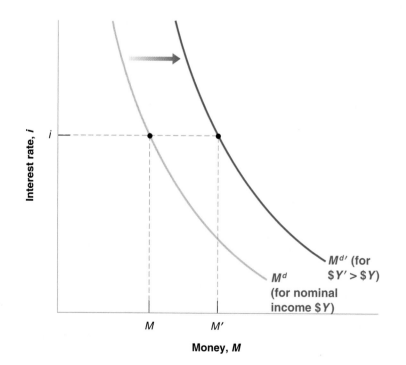

FIGURE 4–1

The Demand for Money

For a given level of nominal income, a lower interest rate increases the demand for money. For a given interest rate, an increase in nominal income increases the demand for money.

Interest rate, i

$M^{d'}$ (for $\$Y' > \$Y$)

M^d (for nominal income $\$Y$)

M M'

Money, M

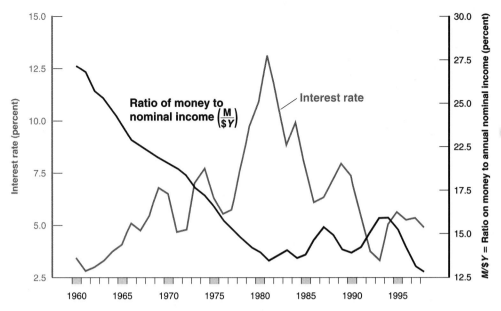

FIGURE 4-2

The Ratio of Money to
Nominal Income and the
Interest Rate, 1960–1998

The ratio of money to nominal income has decreased
over time. Leaving aside this
trend, the interest rate and
the ratio of money to nominal income typically move in
opposite directions.

(deposits against which checks can be written.) This measure of money, is called **M**1.
Nominal income is measured by nominal GDP, $Y. The interest rate, i, is the average interest
rate paid by government bonds during each year.

> More precisely, the inter-
> est rate is the average over
> the year of the one-year
> Treasury bill rate. A pre-
> cise definition of Treasury
> bills is given in section
> 4-2.

Figure 4–2 has two characteristics:

(1) The first is the large decline in the ratio of money to nominal income since 1960. The interest rate was roughly the same in 1998 as it was in the early 1960s. Yet the ratio of money
to nominal income was about half what it was in 1998 (13% compared to 27% in 1960).

Economists sometimes refer to the inverse of the ratio of money to nominal income—
that is, to the ratio of nominal income to money—as the **velocity** of money. The word "velocity" comes from the intuitive idea that when the ratio of nominal income to money is
higher, the number of transactions for a given quantity of money is higher, and it must be the
case that money is changing hands faster; in other words, the *velocity* of money is higher.
Therefore, another, equivalent, way of stating the first characteristic of Figure 4–2 is that the
velocity of money has increased from about 3.7 (1/0.27) in 1960 to about 7.6(1/0.13) in
1998.

$$\frac{1}{(M/\$Y)} = \frac{\$Y}{M}$$
$$= velocity$$

Why has velocity roughly doubled over the last 40 years? The reason is not hard to
guess. Many innovations in financial markets have made it possible to hold lower money
balances for a given amount of transactions. Perhaps the most important development is the
increased use of credit cards. At first glance, credit cards would appear to be money: When
we go to a store, aren't we asked whether we want to pay with cash, check, or credit card?
But, despite what they may seem, credit cards are not money. You actually do not pay when
you use your credit card at the store; you pay when you receive your bill and send your
monthly payment. What credit cards allow you to do is to concentrate many of your payments in one day, and thus to decrease the average amount of money you need to have during the rest of the month. You would expect the introduction of credit cards to reduce money
demand in relation to nominal income over time. Figure 4–2 shows that this indeed has been
the case.

> Some (but not all) credit
> cards also allow you to de-
> fer payment, and thus to
> borrow, often at a high in-
> terest rate. This is a sepa-
> rate service, and not one
> that is relevant here.

(2) The second is the negative relation between year-to-year movements in the ratio of money
to nominal income and the interest rate. The trend decline in the ratio of money to nominal income in Figure 4–2 makes it difficult, however, to see this relation clearly. A better way to
look at year-to-year movements is with a scatter diagram. Figure 4-3 plots the *change in the
ratio of money to nominal income* versus the *change in the interest rate* from year to year.

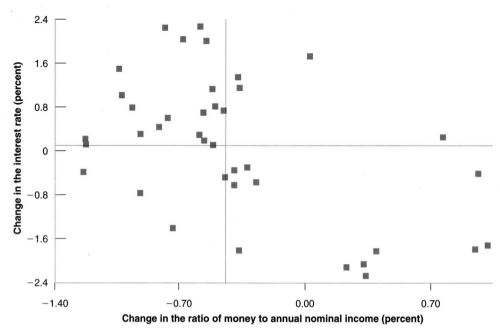

FIGURE 4-3

Changes in the Ratio of Money to Income and Changes in the Interest Rate, 1960–1998

Increases in the interest rate are typically associated with a decrease in the ratio of money to nominal income, decreases in the interest rate with an increase in that ratio.

Note that most of the points lie either in the upper-left quadrant (increases in the interest rate, decreases in the ratio) or the lower-right quadrant (decreases in the interest rate, increases in the ratio).

Changes in the interest rate are measured on the vertical axis. Changes in the ratio of money to nominal income are measured on the horizontal axis. Each point (shown as a square) in the figure corresponds to a given year. The vertical and horizontal lines give the mean values of the change in the ratio and in the interest rate for the period of 1960 to 1998. The figure shows a negative relation between year-to-year changes in the interest rate and changes in the ratio. The relation is not tight, but if we were to draw a line that best fits the cloud of points, it would clearly be downward sloping, as predicted by our money demand equation.

4-2 | The Determination of the Interest Rate: I

We have looked at the demand for money. We now need to look at the supply of money. In reality, there are two suppliers of money: banks supply checkable deposits and the central bank supplies currency. In this section, we shall assume that all money is currency, supplied by the central bank. In the next, we shall reintroduce checkable deposits, and look at the role of banks. Introducing banks makes the discussion more realistic. But it also makes the mechanics of money supply more complicated, and it is better to build the intuition in two steps.

Money Demand, Money Supply, and the Equilibrium Interest Rate

Throughout this section, "money" stands for "central bank money," or "currency."

The name of the relation (*LM*) is more than 50 years old. *L* stands for liquidity: Economists use liquidity as a measure of how easily and how cheaply an asset can be exchanged for money. Money is fully liquid, other assets less so; we can think of the demand for money as a demand for liquidity. *M* stands for money. The demand for liquidity must equal the supply of money.

Suppose that the central bank decides to supply an amount of money equal to M. (Let's leave aside for the moment the issue of how the central bank chooses and changes the amount of money in the economy. We shall return to it in a few paragraphs.)

Equilibrium in financial markets requires that money supply be equal to money demand, that $M^s = M^d$. Using equation (4.1) for money demand, the equilibrium condition is

$$\text{Money supply} = \text{Money demand}$$
$$M = \$Y\,L(i) \tag{4.3}$$

This equation tells us that the interest rate must be such that people are willing to hold an amount of money equal to the existing money supply. This equilibrium relation is called the **LM relation.**

This equilibrium condition is represented graphically in Figure 4–4. Just as in Figure 4–1, money is measured on the horizontal axis, and the interest rate is measured on the vertical axis. The demand for money, M^d, drawn for a given level of nominal income, is

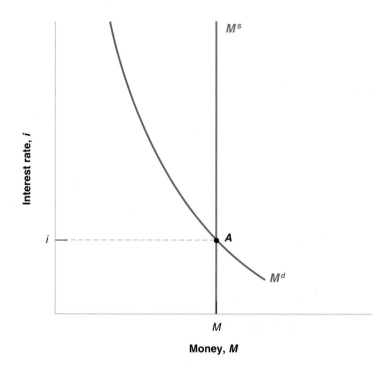

FIGURE 4-4

The Determination of the Interest Rate

The interest rate must be such that the supply of money is equal to the demand for money.

ACTIVE GRAPH

downward sloping: A higher interest rate implies a lower demand for money. The supply of money is drawn as the vertical line denoted M^s: The money supply equals M, and is independent of the interest rate. Equilibrium is at point A, with interest rate i.

With this characterization of the equilibrium, we can then look at the effects of changes in nominal income or in the money stock on the equilibrium interest rate.

Figure 4–5 shows the effects of an increase in nominal income on the interest rate. The figure replicates Figure 4–4, and the initial equilibrium is at point A. An increase in nominal in-

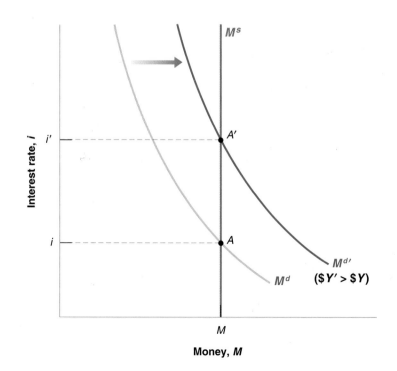

FIGURE 4-5

The Effects of an Increase in Nominal Income on the Interest Rate

An increase in nominal income leads to an increase in the interest rate.

ACTIVE GRAPH

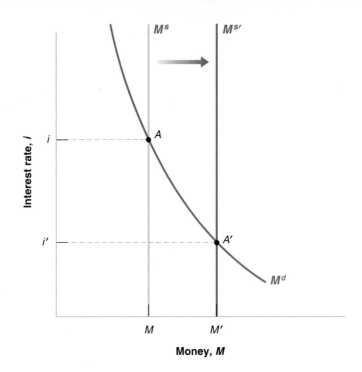

FIGURE 4–6

The Effects of an Increase in the Money Supply on the Interest Rate

An increase in the supply of money leads to a decrease in the interest rate.

come increases the level of transactions, which increases the demand for money at any interest rate. The demand curve shifts to the right, from M^d to $M^{d'}$. The equilibrium moves along the fixed money supply, from A to A', and the equilibrium interest rate increases from i to i': *An increase in nominal income leads to an increase in the interest rate.* The reason: At the initial interest rate, the demand for money exceeds the unchanged supply. An increase in the interest rate is needed to decrease the amount of money people want to hold and reestablish equilibrium.

Figure 4–6 shows the effects of an increase in the money supply on the interest rate. The initial equilibrium is at point A, with interest rate i. An increase in the money supply, from M to M', leads to a shift of the supply curve to the right, from M^s to $M^{s'}$. The equilibrium moves from A to A', and the interest rate decreases from i to i'. Thus, *an increase in the supply of money leads to a decrease in the interest rate.* The decrease in the interest rate increases the demand for money so it equals the larger money supply.

Monetary Policy and Open Market Operations

We can get a better intuition for the results in Figures 4–5 and 4–6 by looking more closely at how the central bank actually changes the money supply, and what happens when it does so.

Assume that the central bank changes the amount of money in the economy by buying or selling bonds in the bond market. If it wants to increase the amount of money in the economy, it buys bonds and pays for them by printing money. If it wants to decrease the amount of money in the economy, it sells bonds, and removes from circulation the money it receives in exchange for the bonds. Such operations are called **open market operations**, so called because they take place in the "open market" for bonds. They are the standard method central banks use to change the money stock in modern economies.

The balance sheet of a bank (or firm or individual) is a list of its assets and liabilities. The assets are the sum of what the bank owns and what is owed to the bank, the liabilities are what the bank owes to others.

The balance sheet of the central bank is given in Figure 4–7. The assets of the central bank are the bonds that it holds in its portfolio. Its liabilities are the stock of money in the economy. Open market operations lead to equal changes in assets and liabilities. If the central bank buys, say, $1 million worth of bonds, the amount of bonds it holds is higher by $1 million, and so is the amount of money in the economy. If it sells $1 million worth of bonds, both the amount of bonds held by the central bank and the amount of money in the economy are lower by $1 million.

Assets	Liabilities
Bonds	Money (currency)

FIGURE 4-7

The Balance Sheet of the Central Bank

The assets of the central bank are the bonds it holds. The liabilities are the stock of money in the economy. An open market operation in which the central bank buys bonds and issues money increases both assets and liabilities by the same amount.

The other step we need to take is to look at the relation between bond prices and interest rates. We have focused so far on the interest rate on bonds. In fact, what is determined in bond markets is not interest rates, but bond *prices*; the interest rate on a bond can then be inferred from the price of the bond. Understanding the relation between the interest rate and the price of a bond will prove useful both here and later in the book.

Suppose the bonds in our economy are one-year bonds — bonds that promise a payment of a given number of dollars, say, $100, a year hence. In the United States, such bonds, when issued by the government and promising payment in a year or less, are called **Treasury bills** or **T-bills.** You can think of the bonds in our economy as one-year T-bills. Let the price of a bond today be P_B, where B stands for "bond." If you buy the bond today and hold it for a year, the rate of return on holding the bond for a year is equal to $(\$100 - \$P_B)/\$P_B$. Therefore, the interest rate on the bond is

◄ What you get for the bond a year from now ($100) minus what you pay for the bond today (P_B), divided by the price of the bond today, (P_B).

$$i = \frac{\$100 - \$P_B}{\$P_B}$$

If P_B is $95, the interest rate equals $5/$95 = 0.053, or 5.3%. If P_B is $90, the interest rate is 11.1%. *The higher the price of the bond, the lower the interest rate.*

Equivalently, if we are given the interest rate, we can infer the price of the bond. Reorganizing the formula above, the price today of a one-year bond paying $100 a year from today is given by

$$\$P_B = \frac{\$100}{1 + i}$$

The price of the bond is equal to the final payment divided by 1 plus the interest rate. If the interest rate is positive, the price of the bond is less than the final payment. The higher the interest rate, the lower the price today. When newspapers write that "bonds markets went up today," they mean that *the prices of bonds went up*, and therefore that *interest rates went down.*

We are now ready to return to the effects of an open market operation. Consider an **expansionary open market operation** — an operation in which the central bank increases the supply of money. In such a transaction, the central bank buys bonds in the bond market and pays for them by creating money. As the central bank buys bonds, the demand for bonds goes up, increasing the price of bonds. Equivalently, the interest rate on bonds goes down. When the central bank wants instead to decrease the supply of money — a **contractionary open market operation** — it sells bonds. This leads to a decrease in their price, an increase in the interest rate.

To summarize:

- The interest rate is determined by the equality of the supply of money and the demand for money.
- By changing the supply of money, the central bank can affect the interest rate.
- The central bank changes the supply of money through open market operations, which are purchases or sales of bonds for money.
- Open market operations in which the central bank increases the money supply by buying bonds lead to an increase in the price of bonds — equivalently, a decrease in the interest rate.
- Open market operations in which the central bank decreases the money supply by selling bonds lead to a decrease in the price of bonds — equivalently, an increase in the interest rate.

Our economy with its two assets, money and bonds, is a much simplified version of actual economies with their many financial assets and many financial markets. But, as we shall see later in the book, the basic lessons we have just seen apply very generally. The only change we shall have to make is to replace "interest rate" in our conclusions by "short-term interest rate." We shall see that the short-term interest rate is determined by the condition that money supply equals money demand; that the central bank can, through open market operations, change the amount of money and the short-term interest rate; and that open market operations are indeed the basic tool used by most modern central banks, including the Fed, to affect interest rates.

The complication: The short-term interest rate—the rate directly affected by monetary policy—is not the only interest rate in the economy. The determination of other interest rates and asset prices (such as stock prices) is the topic of chapter 15.

There is one dimension, however, in which our model must be extended. We have assumed that all money was currency, supplied by the central bank. In the real world, money includes not only currency but also checkable deposits. Checkable deposits are supplied not by the central bank, but by (private) banks. How the presence of banks, and of checkable deposits, changes our conclusions, is the topic of the next section. The section is optional. For those of you who decide to skip it, let me state its basic conclusion. In an economy in which money includes both currency and checkable deposits, the central bank no longer controls the total amount of money directly. It does, however, control it indirectly. In particular, it can still use open market operations—purchases and sales of bonds—to increase or decrease the supply of money and affect the interest rate.

*4-3 | The Determination of Interest Rates: II

To understand what determines the interest rate in an economy with both currency and checkable deposits, we must first look at what banks do.

What Banks Do

Modern economies are characterized by the existence of many types of **financial intermediaries**, institutions that receive funds from people and firms, and use these funds to buy bonds or stocks, or make loans to other people and firms. Their liabilities are the funds that they owe to the people and firms from whom they have received funds. Their assets are the stocks and bonds they own, and the loans they have made.

Banks are one type of financial intermediaries. What makes banks special—and the reason we focus on banks here rather than financial intermediaries in general—is that their liabilities are money: People can pay for transactions by writing checks up to the amount of their account balance. Let's look at what they do more closely.

Banks receive funds from depositors. They keep some of these funds as reserves, and use the rest to make loans and purchase bonds. Their balance sheet is shown in Figure 4-8(a). Their liabilities consist of checkable deposits, the funds deposited by people and firms. Their assets consist of reserves, loans, and bonds.

Banks receive funds from people and firms who either deposit funds or have funds sent to their checking account (their paycheck, for example.) At any point in time, people and firms can write checks or withdraw up to the full amount of their account balance. Thus, the liabilities of the banks are equal to the total value of *checkable deposits.*[2]

[2]**DIGGING DEEPER**. This description simplifies reality in two ways. First, banks also offer other types of deposits, such as savings and time deposits. These cannot be used directly in transactions, so they are not money. I shall ignore this part of the banks' activity, which is not central for our purposes. Also, banks are the main but not the only financial intermediary to offer checkable deposits; some savings institutions and credit unions also offer such deposits. I also ignore this complication here and use "banks" to denote all suppliers of checkable deposits.

* This section is optional.

(a) **Banks**

Assets	**Liabilities**
Reserves Loans Bonds	Checkable deposits

(b) **Central Bank**

Assets	**Liabilities**
Bonds	Central Bank Money = Reserves + Currency

FIGURE 4–8

The Balance Sheet of Banks (a) and the Balance Sheet of the Central Bank Revisited (b)

Banks keep as **reserves** some of the funds they have received. These reserves are reserves of central bank money; they are held partly in cash, partly on an account the banks have at the central bank, on which they can draw when they need to.

Why do banks hold reserves? For three reasons:

- On any given day, some depositors withdraw cash from their checking account, whereas others deposit cash into their account. There is no reason for the inflows and outflows of cash to be equal, so the bank must keep some cash on hand.
- In the same way, on any given day, people with accounts at a bank, bank A, write checks to people with accounts at other banks, and people with accounts at other banks write checks to people with accounts at bank A. What bank A, as a result of these transactions, owes to other banks may be greater or smaller than what other banks owe to bank A. For this reason also, a bank needs to keep reserves.
- The first two reasons imply that banks would want to keep some reserves even if they were not required to. But, in addition, banks are subject to legal reserve requirements, which require them to hold reserves in some proportion to checkable deposits. In the United States, reserve requirements are set by the Fed, and vary by size of deposits as well as over time. They can be set by the Fed anywhere between 7% and 22% of deposits. The actual **reserve ratio**, the ratio of bank reserves to checkable deposits, is about 10% in the United States today.

Leaving aside reserves, banks use the remainder of their funds to make loans to firms and consumers or to buy bonds. Loans represent roughly 70% of banks' nonreserve assets. Bonds account for the rest, thus 30%. The distinction between bonds and loans is unimportant for our purpose—understanding the determination of the money supply. So, in what follows, I shall assume for simplicity that banks do not make loans and thus hold only reserves and bonds as assets. But the distinction between loans and bonds is important for other purposes, from the likelihood of bank runs to the role of federal deposit insurance. These topics are explored in the Focus box "Bank Runs."

Figure 4-8(b) gives the balance sheet of the central bank in an economy with banks. It is very similar to the balance sheet in Figure 4–7. The asset side is the same as before: The assets of the central bank are the bonds that it holds. The liabilities of the central bank are the money it has issued, **central bank money**. The new feature is that not all of central bank money is held as currency by the public. Some is held as reserves by banks.

The Supply and Demand for Central Bank Money

The easiest way to think about the determination of the interest rate in this economy is by thinking in terms of the supply and the demand for central bank money. The demand for central bank money is equal to the demand for currency by people plus the demand for reserves by banks. The supply of central bank money is under the direct control of the central bank.

Bank Runs

Making a loan to a firm and buying a government bond are more similar than they may seem. In one case, one lends to a firm. In the other, one lends to the government. This is why, for simplicity, I have ignored in the text the fact that banks both make bank loans and hold government bonds, and I have assumed that they held only bonds.

But, in one respect, making a loan is very different from buying a bond. Bonds, especially government bonds, are very liquid; in case of need, they can be sold easily in the bond market. Loans are often not liquid at all. Calling them back may be impossible: The firm, which has used the loan to buy inventories or a new machine, no longer has the cash. Selling the loan itself to a third party may be very difficult, because potential buyers know little about how reliable the firm is as a borrower.

This fact has one important implication. Take a healthy bank, a bank with a good portfolio of loans. Suppose rumors start that the bank is not doing well and some loans will not be paid back. Believing that the bank may fail, people with deposits at the bank will want to close their accounts and get cash. If enough people do so, the bank will run out of reserves. Given that the loans cannot be called back, the bank will not be able to satisfy the demand for cash, and it will have to close.

Therefore, the belief that a bank may close may lead it to close, even if all its loans are good. The financial history of the United States up to the 1930s is full of such **bank runs**. One bank fails for the right reason (that is, it has made bad loans), leading depositors at other banks to get

scared and run on their own banks, thus forcing them to close, whether or not their loans are good. You may have seen *It's a Wonderful Life*, an old movie with James Stewart that runs on TV every year around Christmas. Because of the failure of another bank in town, depositors at the savings and loan of which James Stewart is the manager get scared and come to get their money back. It takes all of James Stewart's persuasion to avoid closure. The movie has a happy ending. In real life, most bank runs didn't.

What can be done to avoid such runs? The way the United States has dealt with this problem is by creating, in 1934, a system of **federal deposit insurance**. The U.S. government insures each account up to a ceiling of $100,000. There is no reason for depositors to run and get their money out, and healthy banks do not fail.

However, federal deposit insurance leads to problems of its own. Depositors, who do not have to worry about their deposits, no longer look at the activities of the banks in which they have their deposits, and banks may misbehave. Banks may make risky loans, they would not have made absent the insurance.

An alternative solution is **narrow banking**. Narrow banking would restrict banks to holding liquid, safe, government bonds such as T-bills. It would eliminate bank runs, as well as the need for federal insurance. Loans to firms could be made by other financial intermediaries. Narrow banking has often been proposed, but, so far, never implemented.

Be careful in this section to distinguish among:

The demand for money (demand for currency and checkable deposits)

The demand for bank money (demand for checkable deposits)

The demand for central bank money (demand for currency by people, and demand for reserves by banks)

The equilibrium interest rate is such that the demand and the supply for central bank money are equal.

Figure 4–9 shows the structure of demand and supply in more detail. Start from the left side. The demand for money is a demand for both checkable deposits and currency. Banks have to hold reserves against checkable deposits: The demand for checkable deposits leads to a demand for reserves by banks. The demand for central bank money is equal to the demand for reserves by banks plus the demand for currency by people. The supply of central bank money is determined by the central bank. The interest rate must be such that the demand and the supply are equal.

Let's go through each of the steps in Figure 4–9 and ask: What determines the demand for checkable deposits and the demand for currency? What determines the demand for reserves by banks? How does the interest rate reconcile the demand and the supply of central bank money?

FIGURE 4–9

Determinants of the Demand and the Supply of Central Bank Money

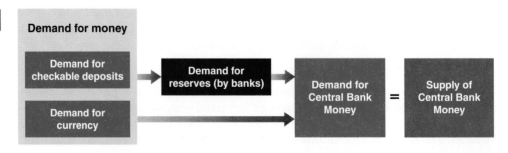

The Demand for Money. When people can hold both currency and checkable deposits, the demand for money involves two decisions. First, people must decide how much money to hold. Second, they must decide how much of this money to hold in currency and how much to hold in checkable deposits.

It is reasonable to assume that the overall demand for money is given by the same factors as before. People will hold more money, the higher the level of transactions, and the lower the interest rate on bonds. So we assume that overall money demand is given by the same equation as before (equation [4.1])

$$M^d = \$Y\,L(i) \tag{4.4}$$
$$(-)$$

That brings us to the second decision. How do people decide how much to hold in currency, and how much in checkable deposits? Currency is more convenient for small transactions. Checks are more convenient for large transactions. Holding money in your checking account is safer than holding it in cash. I shall simply assume here that people hold a fixed proportion of their money in currency—call this proportion c—and, by implication, a fixed proportion $(1-c)$ in checkable deposits. In the United States, people hold 40% of their money in the form of currency; so think of c as equal to 0.4.

Call the demand for currency CU^d (CU for currency, and d for demand). Call the demand for checkable deposits D^d (D for deposits, and d for demand). The two demands are thus given by

$$CU^d = cM^d \tag{4.5}$$
$$D^d = (1-c)M^d \tag{4.6}$$

Equation (4.5) gives the first component of the demand for central bank money, the demand for currency by the public. Equation (4.6) gives the demand for checkable deposits. This demand for checkable deposits leads to a demand by banks for reserves, the second component of the demand for central bank money. To see how, let us turn to the behavior of banks.

The Demand for Reserves. The larger the amount of checkable deposits, the larger the amount of reserves the banks must hold, both for precaution and for legal reasons. Let θ (the Greek lowercase letter theta) be the reserve ratio, the amount of reserves banks hold per dollar of checkable deposits. Let R denote the dollar amount of reserves of banks. Let D denote the dollar amount of checkable deposits. Then, by the definition of θ, the following relation holds between R and D:

$$R = \theta D \tag{4.7}$$

We saw earlier that, in the United States today, the reserve ratio is roughly equal to 10%. Thus, θ is roughly equal to 0.1.

If people want to hold D^d in deposits, then, from equation (4.7) banks must hold θD^d in reserves. Combining equations (4.6) and (4.7), the second component of the demand for central bank money—the demand for reserves by banks—is given by

$$R^d = \theta(1-c)M^d \tag{4.8}$$

The Determination of the Interest Rate. We are now ready to characterize the equilibrium. Let H be the supply of central bank money; H is directly controlled by the central bank, which can change the amount of H through open market operations. The demand for central bank money is equal to the sum of the demand for currency and the demand for reserves. The equilibrium condition is that the supply of central bank money be equal to the demand for central bank money

$$H = CU^d + R^d \tag{4.9}$$

Replace CU^d and R^d by their expressions from equations (4.5) and (4.8) to get

$$H = cM^d + \theta(1-c)M^d = [c + \theta(1-c)]M^d$$

A Fed study suggests that more than half of U.S. currency is held abroad! It is a reasonable guess that part of these foreign holdings of U.S. currency is associated with illegal transactions, and that U.S. currency is the currency of choice for illegal transactions around the world.

More on open market operations coming next.

Finally, replace the overall demand for money, M^d, by its expression from equation (4.4) to get

$$H = [c + \theta(1 - c)]\$Y L(i) \qquad (4.10)$$

The supply of central bank money (the left side) is equal to the demand for central bank money (the right side), which is equal to the term in brackets times the overall demand for money.

Look at the term in brackets more closely. Assume that people only hold currency: $c = 1$. Then, the term in brackets is equal to 1, and the equation is exactly the same as equation (4.3) in section 4-2 (with the letter H replacing the letter M on the left side, but both H and M standing for the supply of central bank money). In this case, people hold only currency, and banks play no role in the supply of money.

Assume instead that people do not hold currency at all, but hold only checkable deposits. In this case $c = 0$, and the term in brackets is equal to θ. Suppose for example that $\theta = 0.1$, so that the term in brackets equals 0.1. Then, the demand for central bank money is one-tenth of the overall demand for money. This is easy to understand: People hold only checkable deposits. For every dollar they want to hold, banks need to have 10 cents in reserves. The demand for reserves is one-tenth of the overall demand for money.

Leaving aside these two extreme cases, note that, as long as people hold some checkable deposits (so that $c < 1$), the term in brackets is less than 1: The demand for central bank money is less than the overall demand for money. This comes from the fact that the demand for reserves by banks is only a fraction of the demand for checkable deposits.

The equilibrium condition in equation (4.10) is represented graphically in Figure 4–10. The figure looks the same as Figure 4–4, but with central bank money rather than money on the horizontal axis. The interest rate is measured on the vertical axis. The demand for central bank money, $CU^d + R^d$, is drawn for a given level of nominal income. A higher interest rate implies a lower demand for central bank money for two reasons. The demand for currency goes down; the demand for checkable deposits also goes down, leading to a decrease in the demand for reserves by banks. The supply of money is fixed, and is represented by a vertical line at H. Equilibrium is at point A, with interest rate i.

FIGURE 4–10

The Determination of the Interest Rate When Money Includes Both Currency and Checkable Deposits

The equilibrium interest rate is such that the supply of central bank money is equal to the demand for central bank money.

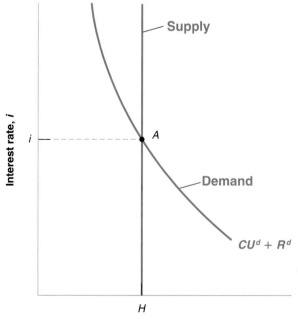

The effects of either changes in nominal income or changes in the supply of central bank money are qualitatively the same as in the previous section. In particular, an increase in the supply of central bank money leads to a shift in the vertical supply line to the right. This leads to a lower interest rate. As before, an increase in central bank money leads to a decrease in the interest rate; symmetrically, a decrease in central bank money leads to an increase in the interest rate. The rest of this section is spent exploring this result further.

Two Alternative Ways of Looking at the Equilibrium

We have looked at the equilibrium through the condition that the supply and the demand of central bank money be equal. There are two alternative ways of looking at the equilibrium. One is through the condition that the supply and demand of reserves be equal. The other is through the condition that the supply and the demand of money are equal. Going through each will strengthen your intuition.

The Supply and Demand for Reserves. Take the equilibrium condition (4.9) and move the demand for currency to the left side, to get

$$H - CU^d = R^d$$

The left side gives the *supply of reserves* as the amount of central bank money minus what people hold as currency. The right side gives the *demand for reserves*. The equilibrium condition now reads: The supply of reserves must be equal to the demand for reserves.

This way of looking at the equilibrium is attractive because, in the United States, there is indeed a market for reserves, in which the interest rate that reconciles the demand and the supply of reserves is determined. The market is called the **federal funds market**. Banks that have excess reserves at the end of the day lend them to banks that have insufficient reserves. In equilibrium, the total demand for reserves by all banks, R^d, must be equal to the supply of reserves, $H - CU^d$—the equilibrium condition above. The interest rate determined in the market is called the **federal funds rate**. Because the Fed can, in effect, choose the federal funds rate it wants by appropriately changing the supply of central bank money, H, many economists look at the federal funds rate as an indicator of U.S. monetary policy, reflecting what the Fed wants the interest rate to be.

The Supply and Demand for Money. Yet another, but still equivalent, way of looking at the equilibrium is as the condition that the overall demand for money is equal to the overall supply of money. To see this, take equation (4.10) and divide both sides by $[c + \theta(1 - c)]$ to get

$$\frac{1}{[c + \theta(1 - c)]} H = \$Y L(i) \qquad (4.11)$$

$$\text{Supply of money} = \text{Demand for money}$$

The right side of the equation gives the overall demand for money (currency plus checkable deposits). The left side gives the overall supply of money (currency plus checkable deposits). The equilibrium condition is that demand and supply be equal.

Note that the overall supply of money is equal to a constant term times central bank money. Note that because $c + \theta(1 - c)$ is less than one, its inverse—the constant term on the left of the equation above—is greater than one. This term is often called the **money multiplier**. Equation (4.11) then tells us that the overall supply of money is a multiple of the supply of central bank money, with the multiple given by the money multiplier. Suppose $c = 0.4$ and $\theta = 0.1$. Then $[c + \theta(1 - c)] = [0.4 + 0.1(0.6)] = 0.46$, and the multiplier equals $1/0.46$, or about 2.2. A multiplier of 2.2 implies that the overall money supply is equal to 2.2 times the supply of central bank money. To reflect the fact that the overall money supply in the end depends on central bank money, central bank money is often called **high powered money** (this is where the letter H we used to denote central bank money comes from), or the **monetary base**.

"High-powered" because increases in H lead to more than one-for-one increases in the supply of money—the left side of equation (4.11): Increases in H are high-powered.

The multiplier in equation (4.11) implies that a given change in central bank money has a larger effect on the money supply—and in turn a larger effect on interest rates—in an economy with banks than in an economy without banks. In an economy without banks—the economy we studied in section 4-2—the effect of a change in central bank money on the money supply is simply one-for-one, as central bank money and money are the same thing. Here the effect is given by the multiplier: The effect on the money supply is a multiple of the original change in central bank money. To give you more intuition for this result, the last subsection looks at the effects of an open market operation in an economy in which people hold checkable deposits.

Open Market Operations Revisited

Consider the special case where people hold only checkable deposits, so $c = 0$. In this case, the multiplier is $1/\theta$: An increase of one dollar of high-powered money leads to an increase of $1/\theta$ dollars in the money supply. Assume further that $\theta = 0.1$, so that the multiplier equals $1/0.1 = 10$. The purpose of what follows is to get more intuition for where this multiplier comes from, and, more generally, for how the initial increase in central bank money leads to a tenfold increase in the overall money supply.

Suppose the Fed buys $100 worth of bonds in an open market operation. It pays the seller—call him seller 1—$100, creating $100 in central bank money. At this point, the increase in central bank money is $100. When we looked earlier at the effects of an open market operation in an economy in which there were no banks, this was the end of the story. Here it is just the beginning:

There is a parallel be-
tween our interpretation of
the money multiplier as
the result of successive
purchases of bonds and
the interpretation of the
goods market multiplier
(chapter 3) as the result of
successive rounds of
spending. Multipliers can
often be derived as the
sum of a geometric series,
and be interpreted as the
result of successive
rounds of decisions. This
interpretation often gives a
better intuition for the
process at work.

- Seller 1 (who, we have assumed, does not want to hold any currency) deposits the $100 in a checking account at his bank—call it bank A. This leads to an increase in checkable deposits of $100.
- Bank A keeps $100 \times 0.1 = $10 in reserves, and buys bonds with the rest, $100 \times 0.9 = $90. It pays $90 to the seller of those bonds—call her seller 2.
- Seller 2 deposits $90 in a checking account in her bank—call it bank B. This leads to an increase in checkable deposits of $90.
- Bank B keeps $90 \times 0.1 = $9 in reserves, and buys bonds with the rest, $90 \times 0.9 = $81. It pays $81 to the seller of those bonds, call him seller 3.
- Seller 3 deposits $81 in a checking account in his bank, call it bank C. And so on.

By now, the chain of events should be clear. What is the eventual increase in the money supply? The increase in checkable deposits is $100 when seller 1 deposits the proceeds of his sale of bonds in bank A, plus $90 when seller 2 deposits the proceeds of her sale of bonds in bank B, plus $81 when seller 3 does the same, and so on. Let's write the sum as

$$\$100 \ (1 + 0.9 + 0.9^2 + \cdots)$$

See Appendix 2 at the end
of the book for a refresher
on geometric series.

The series in parentheses is a geometric series, so its sum is equal to $1/(1 - 0.9) = 10$. The money supply increases by $1,000, 10 times the initial increase in central bank money.

This derivation gives us another way of thinking about the money multiplier: We can think of the ultimate increase in the money supply as the result of *successive rounds of purchases of bonds*—the first by the Fed in its open market operation, the following ones by banks. Each successive round leads to an increase in the money supply; eventually the increase in the money supply is equal to 10 times the initial increase in the central bank money.

Work out the case where
$c > 0$. In each round, take
into account that not all
money is deposited in a
checking account.

To summarize: When we take into account the fact that money is composed of both currency and checkable deposits, the best way to think about the determination of the interest rate is as the condition that the demand for central bank money equals the supply of central bank money. Changes in the supply of the central bank money, carried out by the central bank through open market operations, affect the equilibrium interest rate. Increases in central bank money decrease the interest rate; decreases in central bank money increase the interest rate.

- The demand for money depends positively on the level of transactions in the economy, and negatively on the interest rate.

- Given the supply of money, an increase in income leads to an increase in the demand for money and an increase in the interest rate. An increase in the money supply leads to a decrease in the interest rate.

- The central bank affects the interest rate through open market operations. Open market operations in which the central bank increases the money supply by buying bonds lead to an increase in the price of bonds— equivalently, a decrease in the interest rate.

  Open market operations in which the central bank decreases the money supply by selling bonds lead to a decrease in the price of bonds—equivalently an increase in the interest rate.

- When people hold currency and checkable deposits, the central bank does not directly control the money supply. But it controls the supply of central bank money. The interest rate must be such that the supply of central bank money is equal to the demand for central bank money, which is itself the sum of the demand for currency by people, and of reserves by banks.

- In an economy where people hold both currency and checkable deposits, the effect on the money supply of a given change in central bank money is given by the money multiplier. The larger the money multiplier, the larger the effect of a given change in central bank money on the money supply, and in turn on the interest rate.

- Federal Reserve Bank (Fed), 59
- financial markets, 59
- income, 60
- flow, 60
- saving, 60
- savings, 60
- financial wealth, 60
- wealth, 60
- stock, 60
- investment, 60
- financial investment, 60
- money, 60
- currency, 60
- checkable deposits, 60
- bonds, 60
- money market funds, 61
- $M1$, 63
- velocity, 63

- LM relation, 64
- open market operation, 66
- Treasury bills, T-bills, 67
- Expansionary open market operations, 67
- Contractionary open market operations, 67
- financial intermediaries, 68
- reserves, 69
- reserve ratio, 69
- central bank money, 69
- bank runs, 70
- federal deposit insurance, 70
- narrow banking, 70
- federal funds market, 73
- federal funds rate, 73
- money multiplier, 73
- high-powered money, 73
- monetary base, 73

1. TRUE/FALSE/UNCERTAIN

a. Income and financial wealth are both examples of stock variables.

b. The demand for money does not depend on the interest rate because only bonds earn interest.

c. Given their financial wealth, if people are satisfied with the amount of money they hold, then they must also be satisfied with the amount of bonds they hold.

d. Financial innovations are the reason why velocity has increased dramatically in the past 35 years.

e. In the past 35 years, the ratio of money to nominal income has moved in the same direction as the interest rate.

f. The central bank can increase the supply of money by selling bonds in the market for bonds.

g. By construction, bond prices and interest rates always move in opposite directions.

2. MONEY DEMAND

Suppose that a person's wealth is $50,000 and that her yearly income is $60,000. Also suppose that her money demand function is given by

$$M^d = \$Y(.35 - i)$$

a. What is her demand for money and her demand for bonds when the interest rate is 5%? 10%?

b. Describe the effect of the interest rate on money demand and bond demand. Is it consistent with the theory in chapter 4? Why?

c. Suppose that the interest rate is 10%. In percentage terms, what happens to her demand for money if her yearly income is reduced by 50%?

d. Suppose that the interest rate is 5%. In percentage terms, what happens to her demand for money if her yearly income is reduced by 50%?

e. Summarize the effect of income on money demand. How does it depend on the interest rate?

3. BONDS AND THE INTEREST RATE

A bond promises to pay $100 in one year.

a. What is the interest rate on the bond if its price today is $75? $85? $95?

b. What is the relation between the price of the bond and the interest rate?

c. If the interest rate is 8%, what is the price of the bond today?

4. FINANCIAL MARKETS EQUILIBRIUM

Suppose that money demand is given by

$$M^d = \$Y(.25 - i)$$

where $Y is $100. Also, suppose that the supply of money is $20. Assume equilibrium in financial markets.

a. What is the interest rate?

b. If the Federal Reserve Bank wants to increase i by 10% (from, say, 2% to 12%), at what level should it, set the supply of money?

5. BOND DEMAND

Suppose that a person's wealth is $50,000 and that her yearly income is $60,000. Also, suppose that her money demand function is given by

$$M^d = \$Y(.35 - i)$$

a. Derive the demand for bonds. What is the effect of an increase in the interest rate of 10% (from, say, 2% to 12%) on the demand for bonds?

b. What are the effects of an increase in wealth on money demand and on bond demand? Explain in words.

c. What are the effects of an increase in income on money and on bond demand? Explain in words.

d. "When people earn more money, they obviously want to hold more bonds." What is wrong with this sentence?

6. THE MONEY MULTIPLIER

Suppose the following assumptions hold:

1. The public holds no currency.

2. The ratio of reserves to deposits is 0.1.

3. The demand for money is given by:

$$M^d = \$Y(.8 - 4i)$$

Initially, the monetary base is $100 billion and nominal income is $5 trillion.

a. What is the demand for high-powered money?

b. Find the equilibrium interest rate by setting the demand for high-powered money equal to the supply of high-powered money.

c. What is the overall supply of money? Is it equal to the overall demand for money at the interest rate you found in (b)?

d. What is the impact on the interest rate if high-powered money is increased to $300 billion?

e. If the overall money supply increases to $3,000 billion what will be the impact on i? (*Hint:* Use what you learned in [d])

7. ATMS AND CREDIT CARDS

In this problem we examine the effect of the introduction of ATMs and credit cards on money demand. For simplicity, let's examine a person's demand for money over a period of four days.

Suppose ATMs and credit cards do not exist, and a person goes to the bank once at the beginning of each four-day period and withdraws from his savings account all the money he needs for the next four days. He spends $4 per day.

a. How much does he withdraw each time he goes to the bank?

Compute the person's money holdings for days 1 through 4 (in the morning, before he spends any of the money he withdraws).

b. What is the amount of money he holds on average?

After advent of ATMs he now withdraws money once every two days.

c. How much does he withdraw each time he goes to the bank?

d. What is the amount of money he holds on average?

Finally, with the advent of credit cards, the person pays for all his purchases using his card. He withdraws no money from his savings account until the fourth day, when he withdraws the whole amount necessary to pay for his credit card purchases over the previous four days.

e. Compute the person's money holdings for days 1 through 4.

f. What is the amount of money he holds on average?

g. Based on your answers to (b), (d), and (f), what has been the effect of ATMs and credit cards on money demand?

8. THE VELOCITY OF MONEY

Let money demand be given by:

$$M^d = \$Y\, L(i)$$

a. Derive an expression for velocity as a function of i. How does it depend on i?

b. Look at Figure 4–2. What has happened to the velocity of money from the mid-1960s to the mid-1990s?

c. According to Figure 4–2, in the mid-1960s and in the mid-1990s the interest rate was approximately the same (around 5%). In light of this fact, how do you explain your answer to (b)? (*Hint*: Look at question 7.)

FURTHER READINGS

For a more detailed description of financial markets and institutions, you might want to look at a textbook on money and banking. An excellent one is by R. Glenn Hubbard, *Money, the Financial System and the Economy* (Reading, MA: Addison-Wesley, 1997).

The Fed maintains a useful Web site (http://www.bog.frb.fed.us) that contains data on financial markets as well as information on what the Fed does, on recent testimonies by the Fed chairman, and so on.

We invite you to visit the Blanchard page on the Prentice Hall Web site at:

http://www.prenhall.com/blanchard

for this chapter's World Wide Web exercises

CHAPTER 5

Goods and Financial Markets: The IS-LM Model

We looked at the goods market in chapter 3 and at financial markets in chapter 4. We now look at goods and financial markets together. By the end of this chapter you will have a framework to think about how output and the interest rate are determined in the short run.

In developing this framework we follow a path first traced by two economists, John Hicks and Alvin Hansen, in the late 1930s and the early 1940s. When Keynes's *General Theory* was published in 1936, there was much agreement that the book was both fundamental and nearly impenetrable. (Look at it, and you will agree.) There were many debates about what Keynes really meant. In 1937, John Hicks summarized what he saw as one of Keynes's main contributions: the joint description of goods and financial markets. His analysis was later extended by Alvin Hansen. Hicks and Hansen called their formalization the *IS-LM* model.

Macroeconomics has made substantial progress since the early 1940s. This is why the *IS-LM* model is treated in chapter 5 rather than in chapter 28 of this book. (Think of it: If you had taken this course 40 years ago, you would be nearly done.) But to most economists, the *IS-LM* model still represents an essential building block—one that, despite its simplicity, captures much of what happens in the economy in the short run. This is why the *IS-LM* model is still taught and used today.

5-1 | The Goods Market and the *IS* Relation

Let's first summarize what we learned in chapter 3:

The exact relation, from ▶ chapter 3:

$$Y = Z \Leftrightarrow$$
$$I = S + (T - G)$$

- We characterized equilibrium in the goods market as the condition that production, Y, be equal to the demand for goods, Z. We called this condition the *IS* relation, because it can be reinterpreted as the condition that investment be equal to saving.
- We defined demand as the sum of consumption, investment, and government spending. We assumed that consumption was a function of disposable income (income minus taxes), and took investment spending, government spending, and taxes as given. The equilibrium condition was given by

$$Y = C(Y - T) + \bar{I} + G$$

- Using this equilibrium condition, we then looked at the factors that changed equilibrium output. We looked in particular at the effects of changes in government spending and of shifts in consumption demand.

The main simplification of this first model was that the interest rate did not affect the demand for goods. Our first task in this chapter is to remove this simplification, to introduce the interest rate in our model of goods–market equilibrium. For the time being, we shall focus only on the effect of the interest rate on investment and take up a discussion of its effects on the other components of demand later.

We shall do this in chapter ▶ 16, where we shall look at the effects of interest rates on both consumption and investment.

Investment, Sales, and the Interest Rate

In our first model of output determination, investment was left unexplained—we assumed investment was constant, even when output changed. Investment—spending on new machines and plants by firms—is in fact far from constant, and it depends primarily on two factors:

- The level of sales. A firm facing an increase in sales needs to increase production. To do so, it may need to buy additional machines, or to build an additional plant. A firm facing low sales will feel no such need and will spend little if anything on investment.
- The interest rate. Consider a firm deciding whether to buy a new machine. To buy the new machine, the firm must borrow, either by taking a loan from a bank or by issuing bonds. The higher the interest rate, the less likely the firm is to borrow and buy the machine. At a high enough interest rate, the additional profits from the new machine will not cover interest payments, and the new machine will not be worth buying.

To capture these two effects, we write the investment relation as follows

$$I = I(Y, i) \tag{5.1}$$
$$(+,-)$$

Equation (5.1) states that investment depends on production, Y, and the interest rate, i. Although our discussion suggests that sales may be a more appropriate variable, we shall assume that sales and production are equal—in other words, we shall assume that inventory investment always equals zero—and use production instead. The positive sign under Y indicates that an increase in production leads to an increase in investment. The negative sign under the interest rate i indicates that an increase in the interest rate leads to a decrease in investment.

$$Y\uparrow \Rightarrow I\uparrow$$
$$i\uparrow \Rightarrow I\downarrow$$

The IS Curve

Taking into account the investment relation (5.1), the equilibrium condition in the goods market becomes

$$Y = C(Y - T) + I(Y,i) + G \tag{5.2}$$

The supply of goods (the left side) must be equal to the demand for goods (the right side). Equation (5.2) is our expanded *IS* relation. We can now look at what happens to output when the interest rate changes.

Start with Figure 5–1. Demand (the right side of equation [5.2]) is measured on the vertical axis. Output (equivalently, production or income) is measured on the horizontal axis. The curve ZZ plots demand as a function of output for a given value of the interest rate, i. As output, and thus income, increases, so does consumption; we studied this relation in chapter 3. As output increases, investment also increases; this is the relation between investment and production that we have introduced in this chapter. Through its effects on both consumption and investment, an increase in output leads to an increase in demand: ZZ is upward sloping.

Remember (1) production is a synonym for output, and (2) production and income are always equal.

Note that I have drawn ZZ so that it is flatter than the 45-degree line. Put another way, I have assumed that an increase in output leads to a less than one-for-one increase in demand. In chapter 3, where investment was constant, this restriction naturally followed from the restriction that consumers spend only part of their additional income on consumption. But now that we allow investment to respond to production, this restriction may no longer hold. When output increases, the sum of the increase in consumption and the increase in investment could exceed the initial increase in output. Although this is a theoretical possibility, the empirical evidence suggests that it is not the case in practice. That's why I shall assume the response of demand to output is less than one-for-one and draw ZZ flatter than the 45-degree line.

Since we have not assumed that the consumption and investment relations in equation (5.2) are linear, ZZ is in general a curve rather than a line. Thus, I draw it as a curve in Figure 5–1.

Equilibrium is reached at the point where demand equals production, at point A, the intersection of ZZ and the 45-degree line. The equilibrium level of output is given by Y.

We have drawn the demand relation, ZZ, for a given value of the interest rate. Suppose that the interest rate increases from its initial value i to a new higher value i'. At any level of output, investment decreases. The demand curve ZZ shifts down to ZZ': at a given level of output, demand is lower. The new equilibrium is at the intersection of the lower demand curve ZZ' and the 45-degree line, at point A'. The equilibrium level of output is now Y'.

Equilibrium in the goods market: $i\uparrow \Rightarrow Y\downarrow$

In words: An increase in the interest rate decreases investment. The decrease in investment leads to a decrease in output, which further decreases consumption and investment. In other words, the initial decrease in investment leads to a larger decrease in output through the multiplier effect.

Using Figure 5–1, we can find the equilibrium value of output associated with *any* value of the interest rate. The relation between equilibrium output and the interest rate is derived in Figure 5–2. Figure 5–2(a) reproduces Figure 5–1. The interest rate i implies a level of output equal to Y. The higher interest rate i' implies a lower level of output, Y'. Figure 5–2(b) plots equilibrium output Y on the horizontal axis against the interest rate on the vertical axis. Point A in Figure 5–2(b)

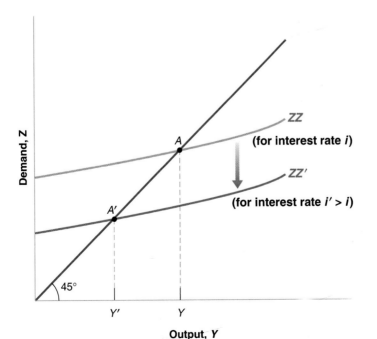

FIGURE 5–1

The Effects of an Increase in the Interest Rate on Output

An increase in the interest rate decreases the demand for goods at any level of output. Because we have not assumed that the consumption and investment relations in equation (5.2) are linear, ZZ is in general a curve rather than a line, as shown. But all the arguments that follow would apply if we assumed that the consumption and investment relations were linear, and that ZZ was a line instead.

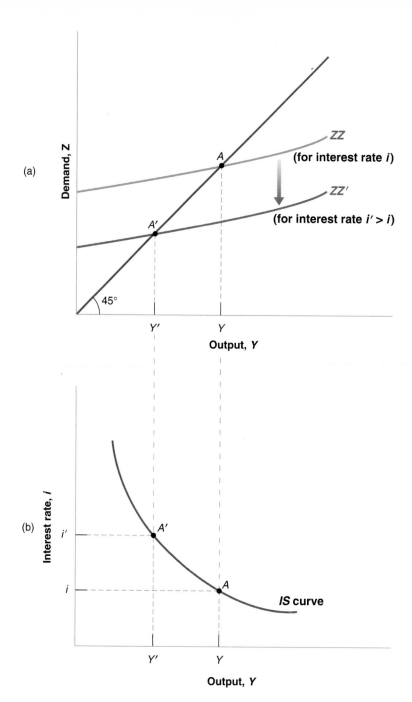

FIGURE 5-2

**The Derivation of the
IS Curve**

Equilibrium in the goods
market implies that output
is a decreasing function of
the interest rate. The *IS*
curve is downward sloping.

Equilibrium in the goods
market implies that output
is a decreasing function of
the interest rate. This relation is represented by the
downward sloping *IS* curve.

corresponds to point *A* in Figure 5–2(a), and point *A'* in Figure 5–2(b) corresponds to *A'* in
Figure 5–2(a). More generally, equilibrium in the goods market implies that the higher the interest
rate, the lower the equilibrium level of output. This relation between the interest rate and output is
represented by the downward-sloping curve in Figure 5–2(b). This curve is called the **IS curve**.[1]

---

[1]DIGGING DEEPER. Consider what happens to investment and saving as we move down the *IS* curve.
As we move down, the interest rate decreases and production increases; both factors increase investment. As we move down, income increases, so that saving increases. Thus, as income increases and
we move down the *IS* curve, both investment and saving increase; indeed, by the construction of the
IS curve, they increase by the same amount, so that investment remains equal to saving.

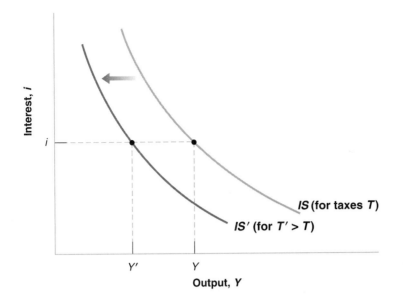

FIGURE 5-3

Shifts in the *IS* Curve

An increase in taxes shifts the *IS* curve to the left.

ACTIVE GRAPH

Shifts in the IS Curve

Note that we have derived the *IS* curve in Figure 5–2 for given values of taxes, *T*, and government spending, *G*. Changes in either *T* or *G* will shift the *IS* curve.

To see how, consider Figure 5–3. The *IS* curve gives the equilibrium level of output as a function of the interest rate. It is drawn for given values of taxes and spending. Now consider an increase in taxes, from *T* to *T'*. At a given interest rate, say, *i*, consumption decreases, leading to a decrease in the demand for goods and, through the multiplier, to a decrease in equilibrium output. The equilibrium level of output decreases, from, say, *Y* to *Y'*. Put another way, the *IS* curve shifts to the left: At any interest rate, the equilibrium level of output is lower than it was before the increase in taxes.

More generally, any factor that, for a given interest rate, decreases the equilibrium level of output, leads the *IS* curve to shift to the left. We have looked at an increase in taxes. But the same would hold for a decrease in government spending, or a decrease in consumer confidence (which decreases consumption given disposable income). In contrast, any factor that, for a given interest rate, increases the equilibrium level of output—a decrease in taxes, an increase in government spending, an increase in consumer confidence—leads the *IS* curve to shift to the right.

Let's summarize:

- Equilibrium in the goods market implies that output is a decreasing function of the interest rate.
- This relation is represented by the downward-sloping *IS* curve.
- Changes in factors that decrease or increase the demand for goods given the interest rate shift the *IS* curve to the left or to the right.

◄ For given *i*, $T\uparrow \Rightarrow Y\downarrow$
An increase in taxes shifts the *IS* curve to the left.

5-2 | Financial Markets and the *LM* Relation

Let's now turn to financial markets. We saw in chapter 4 that the interest rate is determined by the equality of the supply of and the demand for money.

$$M = \$Y\,L(i)$$

The variable *M* on the left side is the nominal money stock. I shall ignore here the details of the money-supply process, and simply think of the central bank as controlling *M* directly. The right side gives the demand for money, which is a function of nominal income, $\$Y$, and

◄ Left side: Money supply
$$M^s = M$$
Right side: Money demand
$$M^d = \$YL(i)$$

of the nominal interest rate, i; an increase in nominal income increases the demand for money; an increase in the interest rate decreases the demand for money. Equilibrium requires that money supply (the left side of the equation) be equal to money demand (the right side of the equation).

Real Money, Real Income, and the Interest Rate

The equation $M = \$Y\, L(i)$ gives a relation between money, nominal income, and the interest rate. It will be more convenient here to rewrite it as a relation between real money (that is, money in terms of goods), real income (that is, income in terms of goods), and the interest rate.

From chapter 2: $\$Y/P = Y$ ▸

Recall that nominal income divided by the price level equals real income, Y. Dividing both sides of the equation by the price level P (which we take as given here) gives

$$\frac{M}{P} = Y\, L(i) \tag{5.3}$$

Hence, we can restate our equilibrium condition as the condition that the *real money supply*—that is, the money stock in terms of goods, not dollars—be equal to the *real money demand*, which depends on real income Y and the interest rate i. The notion of a "real" demand for money may feel a bit abstract, so an example may help. Think not of your demand for money in general but just of your demand for coins. Suppose you like to have coins in your pocket to buy four cups of coffee during the day. If a cup costs 60 cents, you will want to keep about $2.40 in coins: This is your nominal demand for coins. Equivalently, you want to keep enough coins in your pocket to buy four cups of coffee. This is your demand for coins in terms of goods—here in terms of cups of coffee.

From now on, I shall refer to equation (5.3) as the *LM relation*. The advantage of writing things this way is that *real income*, Y, appears on the right side of the equation instead of *nominal income*, $\$Y$. And real income (equivalently real output) is the variable we focus on when looking at equilibrium in the goods market. To make the reading lighter, I shall refer to the right and left sides of equation (5.3) simply as "money supply" and "money demand" rather than the more accurate but heavier "real money supply" and "real money demand." Similarly, I shall refer to income rather than "real income."

The LM Curve

To see the relation between output and the interest rate implied by equation (5.3), let's start with Figure 5–4. Let the interest rate be measured on the vertical axis, and (real) money be measured on the horizontal axis. Money supply is given by the vertical line at M/P, and is denoted M^s. For a given level of income, Y, money demand is a decreasing function of the interest rate. It is drawn as the downward-sloping curve denoted M^d. Except for the fact that we measure real rather than nominal money on the horizontal axis, the figure is similar to Figure 4–4 in chapter 4. The equilibrium is at point A, where money supply is equal to money demand, and the interest rate is equal to i.

Now consider an increase in income from Y to Y', which leads people to increase their demand for money at any given interest rate. Money demand shifts to the right, to $M^{d'}$. The new equilibrium is at A', with a higher interest rate, i'. Why does an increase in income lead to an increase in the interest rate? When income increases, money demand increases. But the money supply is given. Thus, the interest rate must go up until the two opposite effects on the demand for money—the increase in income that leads people to want to hold more money, and the increase in the interest rate that leads people to want to hold less money—cancel each other. At that point, the demand for money is equal to the unchanged money supply, and financial markets are again in equilibrium.

Equilibrium in financial markets: For given M, $Y\uparrow \Rightarrow i\uparrow$ ▸

Using Figure 5–4, we can find out the value of the interest rate associated with *any* value of income for a given money stock. The relation is derived in Figure 5–5. Figure 5–5(a) reproduces Figure 5–4. When income is equal to Y, money demand is given by M^d and the

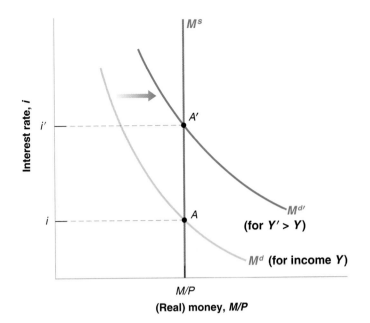

FIGURE 5-4

The Effects of an Increase in Income on the Interest Rate

An increase in income leads, at a given interest rate, to an increase in the demand for money. Given the money supply, this leads to an increase in the equilibrium interest rate.

equilibrium interest rate is equal to i. When income is equal to the higher value Y', money demand is given by $M^{d'}$ and the equilibrium interest rate is equal to i'. Figure 5–5(b) plots the equilibrium interest rate i on the vertical axis against income on the horizontal axis. Point A in Figure 5–5(b) corresponds to point A in Figure 5–5(a), and point A' in Figure 5–5(b) corresponds to point A' in Figure 5–5(a). More generally, equilibrium in financial markets implies that the higher the level of output, the higher the demand for money, and therefore the higher the equilibrium interest rate. This relation between output and the interest rate is represented by the upward sloping curve in Figure 5–5(b). This curve is called the **LM curve**. Economists sometimes characterize this relation by saying that "higher economic activity puts pressure on interest rates." Make sure you understand the steps behind this statement.

Equilibrium in financial markets implies that, for a given money stock, the interest rate is an increasing function of the level of income. This relation is represented by the upward sloping LM curve.

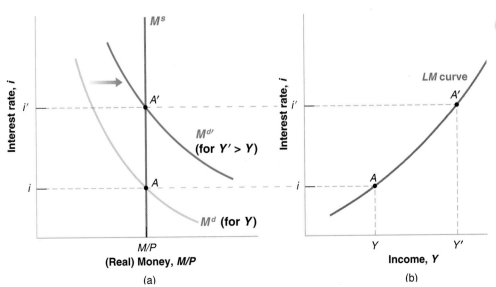

FIGURE 5-5

The Derivation of the _LM_ Curve

Equilibrium in financial markets implies that the interest rate is an increasing function of the level of income. The _LM_ curve is upward sloping.

FIGURE 5-6

Shifts in the LM Curve

An increase in money leads the LM curve to shift down.

The LM curve: interest rate i plotted against income Y, with LM (for M/P) shifting down to LM' (for $M'/P > M/P$); equilibrium interest rate falls from i to i'.

Shifts in the LM Curve

We have derived the LM curve in Figure 5–5 taking both the nominal money stock, M, and the price level, P—and, by implication, their ratio, the real money stock, M/P—as given. Changes in M/P, whether they come from changes in the nominal money stock, M, or from changes in the price level, P, will shift the LM curve.

To see how, consider Figure 5–6. The LM curve gives the interest rate as a function of the level of income. It is drawn for a given value of M/P. Now consider an increase in the nominal money supply, from M to M', so that, at an unchanged price level, the real money supply increases from M/P to M'/P. At a given level of income, Y, this increase in money leads to a decrease in the equilibrium interest rate from i to i'. Put another way, the LM curve shifts down; at any level of income, an increase in money leads to a decrease in the equilibrium interest rate. By the same reasoning, at any level of income, a decrease in money leads to an increase in the interest rate. A decrease in money leads the LM curve to shift up.

Let's summarize:

For given Y, $M/P\uparrow \Rightarrow i\downarrow$
An increase in money shifts the LM curve down.

- Equilibrium in financial markets implies that the interest rate is an increasing function of the level of income. This relation is represented by the upward-sloping LM curve.
- Increases in money shift the LM curve down; decreases in money shift the LM curve up.

Why do we talk about shifts of the IS curve to the left and to the right, but about shifts of the LM curve up or down?

We think of the goods market as determining Y given i; so we want to know what happens to Y when some exogenous variable changes. Y is measured on the horizontal axis, and moves right or left.

We think of financial markets as determining i given Y; so we want to know what happens to i when some exogenous variable changes. i is measured on the vertical axis, and moves up or down.

5-3 | The *IS-LM* Model: Exercises

We can now put the IS and LM relations together. At any point in time, the supply of goods must be equal to the demand for goods. And the supply of money must be equal to the demand for money. Both the IS and LM relations must hold

IS   relation $$Y = C(Y - T) + I(Y,i) + G$$

LM   relation $$\frac{M}{P} = Y L(i)$$

Figure 5–7 plots both the IS curve and the LM curve on one graph. Output—equivalently production or income—is measured on the horizontal axis. The interest rate is measured on the vertical axis.

Any point on the downward-sloping IS curve corresponds to equilibrium in the goods market. Any point on the upward-sloping LM curve corresponds to equilibrium in financial markets. Only at point A are both equilibrium conditions satisfied. That means point A, with associated level of output Y and interest rate i, is the overall equilibrium, the point at which there is equilibrium in both the goods market and the financial markets.

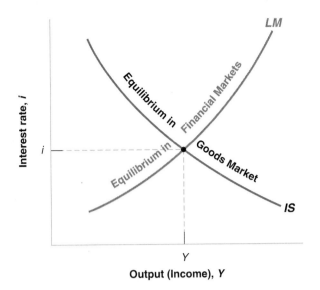

FIGURE 5-7

The *IS-LM* Model

Equilibrium in the goods market implies that output is a decreasing function of the interest rate. Equilibrium in financial markets implies that the interest rate is an increasing function of output. Only at point A are both goods and financial markets in equilibrium.

The *IS* and *LM* relations that underlie Figure 5–7 contain a lot of information about consumption, investment, money demand, and equilibrium conditions. But you may ask, so what if the equilibrium is at point *A*? How does this fact translate into anything directly useful about the world? Don't despair: Figure 5–7 does in fact hold the answer to many questions in macroeconomics. Used properly, it allows us to study what happens to output and the interest rate when the central bank decides to increase the money stock, or when the government decides to increase taxes, or when consumers become more pessimistic about the future, and so on.

Let's now see what the *IS-LM* model can do.

Fiscal Policy, Activity, and the Interest Rate

Suppose the government decides to reduce the budget deficit, and does so by increasing taxes while keeping government spending unchanged. Such a policy, aimed at reducing the budget deficit, is often called a **fiscal contraction** or a **fiscal consolidation**. (An *increase* in the deficit, either due to an increase in spending or to a decrease in taxes, is called a **fiscal expansion**.) What are the effects of such a fiscal contraction on output, on its components, and on the interest rate?

In answering this or any question about the effects of changes in policy, always follow these three steps:

Step 1. Ask how this change affects goods and financial markets equilibrium relations, how it shifts the *IS* or/and the *LM* curve.

Step 2. Characterize the effects of these shifts on the equilibrium.

Step 3. Describe the effects in words.

◁ Decrease in $G - T \Leftrightarrow$ fiscal contraction $\Leftrightarrow$ fiscal consolidation

Increase in $G - T \Leftrightarrow$ fiscal expansion

With time and experience, you will often be able to go directly to step 3; by then you will be ready to give an instant commentary on the economic events of the day. But until you achieve that level of expertise, go step by step.

Going through step 1, the first question is how the increase in taxes affects equilibrium in the goods market—that is, how it affects the *IS* curve.

Let's draw, in Figure 5–8(a), the *IS* curve corresponding to equilibrium in the goods market before the increase in taxes. Take an arbitrary point, *B*, on this *IS* curve. By construction of the *IS* curve, output Y_B and the corresponding interest rate i_B are such that the supply of goods is equal to the demand for goods.

Now, at the interest rate i_B, ask what happens to output if taxes increase from *T* to *T'*. We saw the answer in section 5-1. Because people have less disposable income, the increase in taxes decreases consumption, and through the multiplier, decreases output. At interest rate

Life Among the Econ: The *IS-LM* as a Totem

From the 1950s to the 1970s, the *IS-LM* model was the dominant model in macroeconomics. Nearly every question was recast in terms of whether the *IS* curve or the *LM* curve shifted, and how this shift led to a change in output.

The dominance of the *IS-LM* model led Axel Leijonhufvud, an economist at UCLA, to write a satire of macroeconomics. In "Life Among the Econ," he pretended to be an "econologist"—an anthropologist studying a tribe called the Econ. He described the tribe as divided into castes, the "Micros" and the "Macros," each with "elders" and "grads," each making "models," and each with their own totems. Here is how he describes macro and the *IS-LM*:

> Consider the totems of the Micro and the Macro. Both could be roughly described as formed by two carved sticks joined together in the middle somewhat in the form of a pair of scissors. [See Figure 1.]

> Certain ceremonies connected with these totems are of great interest to us. . . . The following account of the "prospecting" ceremony among the Macro brings out several riddles that currently perplex econologists working in the area:

> The elder grasps the LM *with his left hand and the* IS *with his right hand and, holding the totem out in front of himself, with elbows slightly bent, proceeds in a straight line—gazing neither left nor right, in the words of their ritual—out over the chosen terrain. . . . At long last, the totem vibrates, then oscillates more and more; finally, it points, quivering, straight down. The elder waits for the grads to gather around and then pronounces, with great solemnity: "Behold, the Truth and the Power of Macro."* . . .

> The Macro maintain that they strike gold this way. Some travellers and investigators support the contention, others dismiss it as mere folklore. The issues are much the same as those connected with attempts to appraise the divining-rod method of finding water. Numerous people argue that it works—but no scientific explanation of why it would has ever been advanced.

Source: Axel Leijonhufvud, "Life Among the Econ," *Western Economic Journal,* 1973, 327–337.

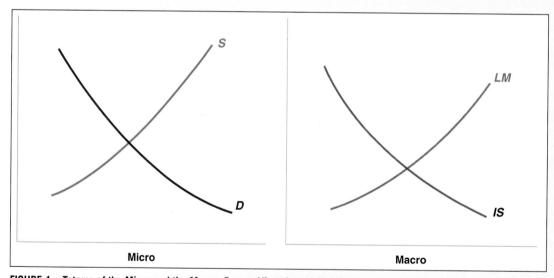

FIGURE 1   Totems of the Micro and the Macro. Demand/Supply and *IS-LM*

Taxes appear in the *IS* relation ⟺ taxes shift the *IS* curve.

i_B, output decreases from Y_B to Y_C. More generally, at *any* interest rate, higher taxes lead to lower output: The *IS* curve shifts to the left from *IS* to *IS'*.

Next, let's see if anything happens to the *LM* curve. Figure 5–8(b) draws the *LM* curve corresponding to financial-markets equilibrium before the increase in taxes. Take an arbitrary point, *F*, on this *LM* curve. By construction of the *LM* curve, the interest rate i_F and income Y_F are such that the supply of money is equal to the demand for money.

What happens to the *LM* curve when taxes are increased? The answer: nothing. At the given level of income Y_F, the interest rate at which the supply of money is equal to the de-

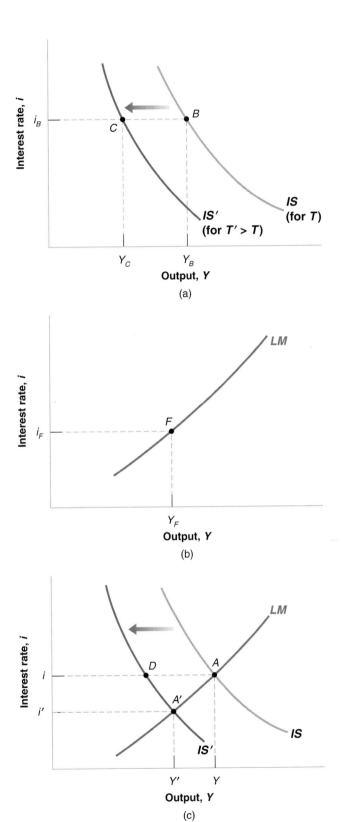

FIGURE 5-8

The Effects of an Increase in Taxes

An increase in taxes shifts the *IS* curve to the left, and leads to a decrease in equilibrium output and the equilibrium interest rate.

Taxes do not appear in the *LM* relation ⟺ taxes do not shift the *LM* curve.

A reminder. Exogenous variables are variables we take as given, unexplained within the model.

$T \uparrow \Rightarrow$ the *IS* curve shifts. The *LM* curve does not shift. The economy moves along the *LM* curve.

If the interest rate did not decline, the economy would go from point *A* to point *D* in Figure 5–8(c), and output would be directly below point *D*. Because of the decline in the interest rate—which stimulates investment—the decline in activity is only to point *A'*.

mand for money is the same as before, namely, i_F. In other words, because taxes do not appear in the *LM* relation, they do not affect the equilibrium condition. They do not affect the *LM* curve.

Note the general principle here: *A curve shifts in response to a change in an exogenous variable only if this variable appears directly in the equation represented by that curve.* Taxes enter equation (5.2), so the *IS* curve shifts. But taxes do not enter equation (5.3), so the *LM* curve does not shift.

Now let's consider the second step, the determination of the equilibrium. Let the initial equilibrium in Figure 5–8(c) be at point *A*, at the intersection between the initial *IS* curve and the *LM* curve. After the increase in taxes, the *IS* curve shifts to the left, and the new equilibrium is at the intersection of the new *IS* curve and the unchanged *LM* curve, at point *A'*. Output decreases from Y to Y'. The interest rate decreases from i to i'. Thus, as the *IS* curve *shifts*, the economy *moves along* the *LM* curve, from *A* to *A'*. The reason these words are italicized is that it is very important to distinguish *shifts in* curves (here the *IS* curve) and *movements along* a curve (here the *LM* curve). Many mistakes result from not distinguishing between the two.

The third and final step is to tell the story in words: The increase in taxes leads to lower disposable income, which causes people to consume less. This leads, through the multiplier effect, to a decrease in output and income. The decrease in income reduces the demand for money, leading to a decrease in the interest rate. The decline in the interest rate reduces but does not completely offset the effect of higher taxes on the demand for goods.

What happens to the components of demand? By assumption, government spending remains unchanged: We have assumed that the reduction in the budget deficit takes place through an increase in taxes. Consumption surely goes down, both because taxes go up and because income goes down: Disposable income goes down on both counts. But what happens to investment? On one hand, lower output means lower sales and lower investment. On the other hand, a lower interest rate leads to higher investment. Without knowing more about the exact form of the investment relation, equation (5.1), we cannot tell which effect dominates. If investment depends only on the interest rate, then investment surely increases; if investment depends only on sales, then investment surely decreases. In general, investment depends on both the interest rate and on sales, so we cannot tell. Contrary to what is often stated by politicians, a reduction in the budget deficit does not necessarily lead to an increase

---

FOCUS

Deficit Reduction: Good or Bad for Investment?

You may have heard the argument before: "Private saving goes toward either financing the budget deficit or financing investment. It does not take a genius to conclude that reducing the budget deficit leaves more saving available for investment, which increases investment."

This argument sounds simple and convincing. How do we reconcile it with what we just saw in the text, that deficit reduction may decrease rather than increase investment? Remember from chapter 3 that we can also think of the goods–market equilibrium condition as

$$I \quad = \quad S \quad + \quad (T - G)$$

Investment   Private saving + Public saving

In equilibrium, investment is equal to private saving plus public saving. If public saving is positive, the government is said to run a budget surplus; if public saving is negative, the government runs a budget deficit. So it is true

that given private saving, if the government reduces its deficit—either by increasing taxes or reducing government spending, so $T - G$ goes up—investment must go up. Given S, $T - G$ going up implies that I goes up.

The crucial part of this statement, however, is "given private saving." And a fiscal contraction affects private saving as well: A fiscal contraction leads to lower output, lower income; as consumption goes down by less than income, private saving also goes down. And it may go down by more than the reduction in the budget deficit, leading to a decrease rather than an increase in investment. In terms of the equation above: If S decreases by more than $T - G$ increases, then I will decrease, not increase. To sum up, a fiscal contraction may decrease investment. Or, looking at the reverse case, a fiscal expansion—a decrease in taxes or an increase in spending—may actually increase investment.

in investment. (The Focus box "Deficit Reduction: Good or Bad for Investment?" discusses this at more length.) We shall return to the relation between fiscal policy and investment many times in this book, and we shall qualify this first answer in many ways. But the result that *in the short run, deficit reduction may decrease investment*, will remain.

Monetary Policy, Activity, and the Interest Rate

An increase in the money supply is called a **monetary expansion**. A decrease in the money supply is called a **monetary contraction** or **monetary tightening**.

Increase in $M \Leftrightarrow$ monetary expansion.

Decrease in $M \Leftrightarrow$ monetary contraction $\Leftrightarrow$ monetary tightening.

Let's take the case of a monetary expansion. Suppose that the central bank increases nominal money, M, through an open market operation. Given our assumption that the price level is fixed, this increase in nominal money leads to a one-for-one increase in real money, M/P. Let us denote the initial real money supply by M/P, the new higher one by M'/P, and trace the effects of the money supply increase on output and the interest rate.

P fixed, M increases by 10% $\Rightarrow$ M/P increases by 10%.

The first step is again to see whether and how the IS and the LM curves shift. Let's look at the IS curve first. The money supply does not affect directly either the supply of or the demand for goods. In other words, M does not appear in the IS relation. Thus, a change in M does not shift the IS curve.

Money does not appear in the IS relation $\Leftrightarrow$ Money does not shift the IS curve.

Money enters the LM relation, however, so that the LM curve shifts when the money supply changes. As we saw in section 5–2, an increase in money shifts the LM down: At a given level of income, an increase in money leads to a decrease in the interest rate.

Money appears in the LM relation $\Leftrightarrow$ Money shifts the LM curve.

Putting things together, a monetary expansion shifts the LM curve and does not affect the IS curve. Thus, in Figure 5–9, the economy moves along the IS curve, and the equilibrium moves from point A to point A'. Output increases from Y to Y', and the interest rate decreases from i to i'. In words: The increase in money leads to a lower interest rate. The lower interest rate leads to an increase in investment and, through the multiplier, to an increase in demand and output.

$M \uparrow \Rightarrow$ The IS curve does not shift. The LM curve shifts down. The economy moves along the IS curve.

In contrast to the case of a fiscal contraction, we can tell exactly what happens to the different components of demand after a monetary expansion. With higher income and unchanged taxes, consumption goes up. With both higher sales and a lower interest rate, investment also unambiguously goes up. A monetary expansion is more investment friendly than a fiscal expansion.

To summarize:

- You should remember the method we have developed in this section to look at the effects of changes in policy on activity and the interest rate. We shall use it throughout the book.

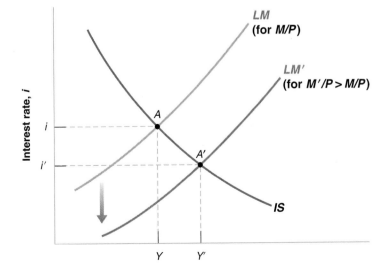

FIGURE 5-9

The Effects of a Monetary Expansion

A monetary expansion leads to higher output and a lower interest rate.

ACTIVE GRAPH

TABLE 5-1 The Effects of Fiscal and Monetary Policy

	Shift in *IS*	Shift in *LM*	Movement in Output	Movement in Interest Rate
Increase in taxes	left	none	down	down
Decrease in taxes	right	none	up	up
Increase in spending	right	none	up	up
Decrease in spending	left	none	down	down
Increase in money	none	down	up	down
Decrease in money	none	up	down	up

- We have used this method to look at the effects of fiscal and monetary policy on output and the interest rate. Table 5–1 summarizes what we have learned. But you can use the same method to look at other changes as well. For example, you may want to trace the effects of a decrease in consumer confidence through its effect on consumption demand, or of the introduction of new, more convenient credit cards through their effect on the demand for money.

The Clinton–Greenspan Policy Mix

When Bill Clinton was elected president at the end of 1992, he faced a tough macroeconomic problem. The federal budget deficit was 4.5% of the GDP—the second-largest percentage since World War II—and there was a wide consensus that something should be done about it. At the same time, the U.S. economy was just emerging from the 1990–1991 recession; although we now know that output growth was positive in 1992, many economists at the time worried that the recession had not yet ended. The problem facing Clinton was clear: As desirable as a deficit reduction might be, implementing it might lead to a decrease in demand, and perhaps put the United States back into recession. In terms of the *IS-LM* model, a shift of the *IS* to the left might lead to a decrease in output, to a recession.

Yet, five years later in 1998, the federal deficit was gone, replaced by a surplus of 0.8% of GDP, and the U.S. economy was in the seventh year of a sustained expansion. (Table 1 gives the basic numbers for the budget, output,

growth, and interest rates, from 1991 to 1998.) How did Clinton do it? He did it with the help of Alan Greenspan, and with quite a bit of luck.

Even before the election, Alan Greenspan had made clear he was worried about the size of the fiscal deficit. When Clinton was elected, Greenspan made clear he would be happy to help. Although not stating this explicitly, he indicated that if Clinton were to embark on a path of deficit reduction, the Fed would be willing to counteract the adverse effects of a fiscal contraction on economic activity with a more expansionary monetary policy. In terms of the *IS-LM* diagram in Figure 1, the Fed agreed (implicitly: nothing was signed, or written down) that, if deficit reduction took place (leading to a shift to the left of the *IS* curve, from *IS* to *IS'*), the Fed would shift the *LM* curve down (from *LM* to *LM'*). It agreed to offset the adverse effects of fiscal contraction on activity, leading the economy from *A* to *A'*, rather than to point *B*.

TABLE 1 Selected macro variables for the United States, 1991–1998

	1991	1992	1993	1994	1995	1996	1997	1998
Budget surplus (% of GDP) (minus sign: deficit)	−3.3	−4.5	−3.8	−2.7	−2.4	−1.4	−0.3	0.8
GDP growth (%)	−0.9	2.7	2.3	3.4	2.0	2.7	3.9	3.7
Interest rate (%)*	7.3	5.5	3.7	3.3	5.0	5.6	5.2	4.8

*Interest rate: Average interest rate over the year on one-year government bonds.
Source: Bureau of Economic Analysis.

On the basis of this implicit understanding, in February 1993 Clinton sent a deficit reduction plan to Congress. This plan was intended to gradually reduce the deficit to 2.5% by 1998. The reduction was divided in roughly equal parts between tax increases and spending decreases. The limited size of the deficit reduction was due to the worry that, even with help from the Fed, too fast a deficit reduction would lead to a recession. As this deficit reduction package was implemented, the Fed delivered on its implicit promise: Interest rates, which had already been reduced in 1991 and 1992, were further decreased in 1993 and 1994. The interest rate in 1994 was 3.3%, down from 7.3% in 1991. The result of this policy mix (fiscal contraction and monetary expansion) was a steady output expansion in the face of deficit reduction.

Was the expansion of output from 1992 to 1998 due only to a smart policy mix? No, it was also due to luck. Especially from 1995 on, various factors from unusually strong consumer and business confidence to a strong stock market, led to favorable shifts in the *IS* curve, and in turn to strong output growth. This had two implications:

- First, the Fed did not have to decrease interest rates further; shifts to the right in the *IS* curve were enough to sustain activity. Indeed, from 1994 on, the Fed had to slightly increase interest rates to prevent the economy from "overheating" (more on this in the next four chapters).

- Second, the mechanical effect of this strong expansion was to further reduce the deficit: When an economy grows, tax revenues (which depend directly on output)

tend to increase, whereas spending is largely unaffected. The deficit is automatically reduced. (A useful rule of thumb for the United States is that every additional increase in the growth rate of 1% per year leads to a decrease in the ratio of the deficit to the GDP of 0.5%.) Thus, the mechanical effect of sustained growth was a larger reduction of the deficit than had been anticipated, even by the Clinton administration.

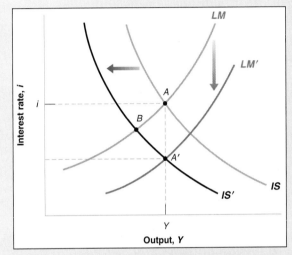

FIGURE 1   Deficit Reduction and Monetary Expansion.
The right combination of deficit reduction and monetary expansion can achieve a reduction in the deficit without adverse effects on output.

5-4 | Using a Policy Mix

We have looked so far at fiscal and monetary policy in isolation. Our purpose was to show how each worked. In practice, the two are often used together. The combination of monetary and fiscal policies is known as the **monetary–fiscal policy mix**, or simply the **policy mix**.

Sometimes monetary and fiscal policies are used for a common goal. For example, expansionary monetary policy is used to offset the adverse effect on the demand for goods of a fiscal contraction. This has been the case in the 1990s in the United States, where, used in combination, fiscal and monetary policy have delivered both sustained deficit reduction and output growth. How it was done, and how much of the credit should go to President Clinton, to Alan Greenspan (the chairman of the Fed), and to sheer luck, is described in the In Depth box "The Clinton–Greenspan Policy Mix."

Sometimes the monetary–fiscal mix emerges from tensions or even disagreements between the government (which is in charge of fiscal policy) and the central bank (which is in charge of monetary policy). A typical scenario is one in which the central bank, disagreeing with what it considers a dangerous fiscal expansion, embarks on a course of monetary contraction to offset some of the effects of the fiscal expansion on activity. An example of such a tension is what happened in Germany after unification in the early 1990s, described in the Global Macro box "German Unification and the German Monetary–Fiscal Tug-of-War".

Fiscal contraction ⇔ Reduction in budget deficit

See the box "Did Rules Help Reduce the U.S. Budget Deficit?" in Chapter 25.

See the boxes "German Unification, Interest Rates, and the EMS" in chapter 20, and "Anatomy of a Crisis: The September 1992 EMS crisis" in chapter 21.

German Unification and the German Monetary–Fiscal Tug-of-War

In 1990, East Germany and West Germany became one country again. Whereas the two parts had been at a roughly comparable level of economic development before World War II, this was no longer the case by 1990. West Germany was far richer and far more productive than East Germany. The economic consequences of unification were many. Our focus here will be limited to the implications for fiscal and monetary policy after unification.

Upon unification, it became clear that most firms in the Eastern Lander (as the ex–German Democratic Republic is now known) were not competitive. Many simply had to be closed in part or in total, and the others needed new and more modern equipment. It soon became obvious that transition would require large increases in government spending on new infrastructure, on cleaning up environmental damage, on unemployment benefits to workers losing their jobs, and on government subsidies to firms to keep them operating until they turned around.

Faced with this large increase in transfers and spending, the German government decided to rely partly on an increase in taxes and partly on a larger deficit. Table 1 gives basic numbers on some of the major macroeconomic variables from 1988 to 1991 (for West Germany only).

The numbers show that, even before unification, Germany was experiencing a strong expansion. GDP growth in 1988 and 1989 was close to 4%. Investment was booming. And, because tax revenues depend on economic activity, the strong growth in GDP was the source of high government revenues in 1989, leading to a fiscal surplus of 0.2% of GDP in 1989.

The effects of unification were to increase demand further. In 1990, the rate of growth of investment was even higher than in 1989. Because of the increase in spending and transfers resulting from unification, West Germany's fiscal position turned from a budget surplus in 1989 to a budget deficit of 1.8% of GDP in 1990. In terms of the *IS-LM* model, 1990 was thus characterized by a sharp increase in government spending, a large shift of the *IS* curve to the right, from *IS* to *IS'* in Figure 1.

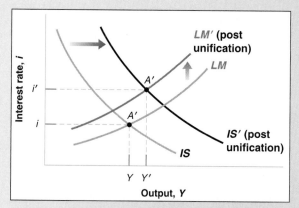

FIGURE 1 The Monetary–Fiscal Policy Mix in Post-Unification Germany

Seeing these developments, the German central bank (the Bundesbank) worried that growth was too strong, that the economy was operating at too high a level of activity, and that the result would be an increase in inflation (a mechanism we explore in the next four chapters). The central bank concluded that growth should be slowed. Even though the interest rate had already increased from 4.3% in 1988 to 7.1% in 1989, the Bundesbank decided on a policy of tight money; it let the interest rate rise even higher, to 9.2% in 1991. In terms of the *IS-LM* in Figure 1, the central bank decided to shift the *LM* curve up, in order to slow down economic activity.

In conclusion, one of the effects of German unification was fiscal expansion combined with tight monetary policy. The result was fast growth (from the fiscal expansion) and high interest rates (from tight money). These high interest rates had important implications not only for Germany, but for all of Europe. Indeed, they have been accused of being one of the main causes of the recession in the rest of Europe in the early 1990s. We discuss this argument in detail in chapter 20.

TABLE	1	Selected macro variables for West Germany, 1988–1991			
		1988	**1989**	**1990**	**1991**
GDP growth (%)		3.7	3.8	4.5	3.1
Investment* growth (%)		5.9	8.5	10.5	6.7
Budget surplus (% of GDP) (minus sign: deficit)		−2.1	0.2	−1.8	−2.9
Interest rate (short term)		4.3	7.1	8.5	9.2

*Investment refers to nonresidential investment.

Source: OECD Economic Outlook, June 1992.

GLOBAL MACRO

In chapter 3 we added dynamics to our description of the goods market and were able to describe the adjustment of output both more realistically and more intuitively. We do the same here.

Let's return first to the *IS* curve and examine the effects of a tax increase. As we have seen, a tax increase shifts the *IS* curve to the left. In Figure 5–10(a), the *IS* curve shifts from *IS* to *IS'*. At a given interest rate, say i_A, the equilibrium level of output decreases from Y_A to Y_B.

Will output really decline instantaneously from Y_A to Y_B? No. We saw some reasons why not in chapter 3: It may take a while for consumers to respond to the decrease in income. It takes a while for production to respond to the decrease in sales. Firms may initially accumulate inventories rather than cut production. We can now add to that list the fact that it may also take a while for firms to revise their investment plans in light of a decrease in sales. For all these reasons, the decline in output will occur only over time. In terms of Figure 5–10(a), output will decrease slowly from Y_A to Y_B.

More generally, it is reasonable to assume that when output is to the right of the equilibrium curve—which, in our case, after the tax increase, is *IS'*—output decreases slowly; when it is to the left of the equilibrium curve, output increases slowly. This basic conclusion is represented by the two large arrows on each side of *IS'* in Figure 5–10(a).

Now let's look at the *LM* curve and the effects of a monetary contraction. As we have seen, a monetary contraction shifts the *LM* curve up. In Figure 5–10(b), the *LM* curve shifts from *LM* to *LM'*: At a given level of income, say, Y_A, the interest rate increases from i_A to i_B. Will the interest rate increase instantaneously? In this case, the answer is yes. Interest rates adjust very quickly to changes in supply and demand. The market for government bonds (in which the Fed buys and sells bonds in the United States) is one of the most efficient markets in the world, and clears within seconds of changes in demand or supply. When the Fed does an open market operation, selling bonds in the bonds market, the interest rate adjusts almost instantaneously. Therefore, the right assumption is that the decrease in the money supply causes the interest rate to increase instantaneously from i_A to i_B in Figure 5–10(b). For the rest of the book, I shall assume that the adjustment of the interest rate to any change in the demand or the supply of money is so fast that *the economy is always on the LM curve.*

Equipped with these dynamics, let's reexamine the effects of a monetary contraction on activity and the interest rate. The adjustment is shown in Figure 5–11. Before the decrease in the money supply, the economy is at point *A*, with output *Y* and interest rate *i*. At the moment at which the central bank decreases the money supply, the *LM* curve shifts from *LM* to *LM'*. The economy jumps to point *A''*: Output does not change right away, and so the interest rate must do all the adjustment, increasing from *i* to *i''*. Over time, the higher interest rate leads to lower investment, a lower demand for goods, and lower output, so that output slowly decreases from its initial level. The economy moves along *LM'*, and eventually reaches point *A'*. At *A'*, the in-

Sources of dynamics in the goods market: (a) Production adjusts slowly to demand; (b) demand (consumption, and investment) adjusts slowly to income (production).

Slow adjustment of *Y* in goods markets

Fast adjustment of *i* in financial markets

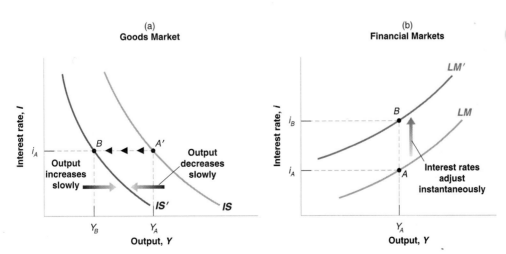

(a)
Goods Market

(b)
Financial Markets

FIGURE 5–10

Introducing Dynamics in the *IS-LM* Model

When output is above or below the level implied by the *IS* relation, it adjusts slowly to that level. In contrast, interest rates adjust quickly, so that the *LM* relation is always satisfied.

FIGURE 5-11

The Dynamic Effects of a Monetary Contraction

A monetary contraction leads to an increase in the interest rate. The increase in the interest rate leads, over time, to a decline in output.

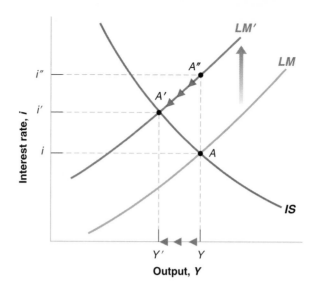

terest rate is equal to i' and output is equal to Y'. Note that the eventual increase in the interest rate is smaller than the initial increase in the interest rate: This is because, as output contracts, so does the demand for money, which puts some pressure on the interest rate to decrease.

▶ After a decrease in money: Interest rates initially increase and then decline, partially offsetting the initial increase. Output initially does not change, then declines over time.

In words: The monetary contraction leads initially to a sharp increase in the interest rate. Over time, this increase leads to a decrease in output. This time dimension is important, and there is a general lesson about policy to be drawn from it. Monetary policy can affect the interest rate quickly but cannot affect output right away. So the central bank must be careful not to be fighting the last battle. For example, there is no point in fighting a recession through a lower interest rate if the recession is already over when the lower interest rate starts affecting economic activity.

I shall let you look at the dynamic effects of a change in fiscal policy on your own. And, from now on, I shall often rely on these dynamics to tell more realistic stories of how changes in policy or behavior affect economic activity.

5-6 | Does the *IS-LM* Model Actually Capture What Happens in the Economy?

The *IS-LM* model gives us a way of thinking about the determination of output and the interest rate. But it is a theory based on many assumptions and many simplifications. How do we know that we have made the right simplifications? How much should we believe the answers given by the *IS-LM* model?

These are the questions facing any theory, whether in macroeconomics or anywhere else. A theory must pass two tests.

- First, the assumptions and the simplifications must be reasonable. What "reasonable" means is not entirely clear. Surely assuming—as we have done—that there is only one type of good in the economy is factually wrong. But it may still be a reasonable simplification of reality if allowing for more than one type of good led to a more complicated model, but roughly the same results for aggregate activity, the interest rate, and so on.
- Second, the major implications of the theory must be consistent with what we actually see in the world. This is easier to check. Using econometrics, we can trace the effects of changes in monetary policy and fiscal policy and see how close the effects correspond to the predictions of the *IS-LM* model. And it turns out that the *IS-LM* model does quite well.

Figure 5–12 makes this point nicely. It shows the results of a recent econometric study of the effects of changes in monetary policy on activity, using data from the United States from 1960 to 1990. The study focuses on the effects of changes in the *federal funds rate*, the

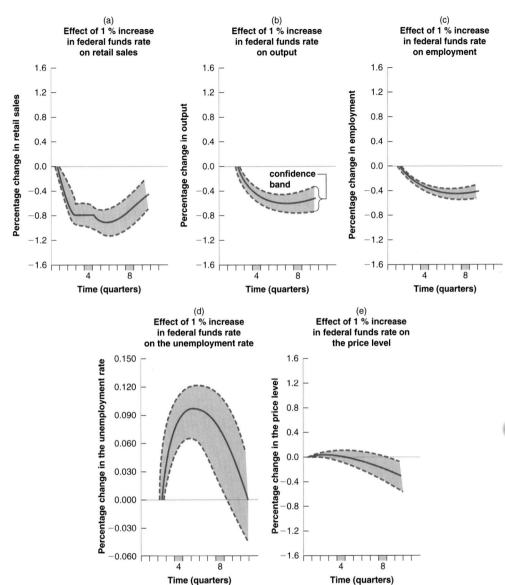

(a)
Effect of 1 % increase in federal funds rate on retail sales

(b)
Effect of 1 % increase in federal funds rate on output

(c)
Effect of 1 % increase in federal funds rate on employment

(d)
Effect of 1 % increase in federal funds rate on the unemployment rate

(e)
Effect of 1 % increase in federal funds rate on the price level

confidence band

Source: Lawrence Christiano, Martin Eichenbaum, and Charles Evans, "The Effects of Monetary Policy Shocks: Evidence from the Flow of Funds," Review of Economics and Statistics, February 1996, 78-1.

FIGURE 5–12

The Empirical Effects of an Increase in the Federal Funds Rate

In the short run, an increase in the federal funds rate leads to a decrease in output and to an increase in unemployment, but has little effect on the price level.

interest rate that is most directly affected by changes in monetary policy. It then traces the typical effects of such a change on activity.

Figure 5–12(a) shows the effects of an increase in the federal funds rate of 1% on retail sales over time. The percentage change in retail sales is plotted on the vertical axis; time, measured in quarters, on the horizontal axis. The figure plots three lines. The best estimate of the effect of the change in the interest rate on output is given by the solid-color line. But there is no such thing as learning the exact value of a coefficient or the exact effect of one variable on another. Rather, econometrics provides a best estimate—here, the solid-color line—and a measure of confidence we should have in the estimate. The true value of the effect lies within the two dotted lines with 60% probability. For this reason, the space between the two dashed lines is called a **confidence band**.

Focusing on the best estimate—the solid-color line—we see that the increase in the federal funds rate leads to a decline in retail sales. The largest decrease, −0.9%, is achieved after five quarters.

We discussed the federal funds market and the federal funds rate in chapter 4, section 4-3.

For an introduction to econometrics, see Appendix 3 at the end of the book.

$i\uparrow \Rightarrow Z\downarrow$

$$i\uparrow \Rightarrow Z\downarrow \Rightarrow Y\downarrow$$

Figure 5–12(b) shows how lower sales lead to lower output. In response to the decrease in sales, firms cut production, but initially by less than the decrease in sales. Put another way, firms accumulate inventories for some time. The adjustment of production is smoother and slower than the adjustment of sales. The largest decrease, -0.7% is reached after eight quarters.

Figure 5–12(c) shows how lower output leads to lower employment: As firms cut production, they also cut employment. As with output, the decline in employment is slow and steady, reaching -0.5% after eight quarters. The decline in employment is reflected in an increase in the unemployment rate, shown in Figure 5–12(d).

$$i\uparrow \Rightarrow Z\downarrow \Rightarrow Y\downarrow$$
$$\Rightarrow N\downarrow \Rightarrow U\uparrow$$

Figure 5–12(e) looks at the behavior of the price level. Remember that one of the *assumptions* of the *IS-LM* model is that the price level is given and so does not change in response to changes in demand. Figure 5–12(e) shows that this assumption is not a bad approximation in the short run. The price level is nearly unchanged for the first six quarters or so. Only after the first six quarters does the price level appear to decline. This gives a strong hint as to why the *IS-LM* model becomes less reliable as we look at the medium run: In the medium run, we can no longer assume that the price level is given, and movements in the price level become important.

Figure 5–12 is comforting. It shows that the implications of the *IS-LM* model are consistent with what we observe in the economy. This does not *prove* that the *IS-LM* model is right. It may be that what we observe in the economy is the result of a completely different mechanism, and that the fact that the *IS-LM* model fits well is a coincidence. But this seems unlikely. The *IS-LM* model looks like a solid basis on which to build to look at movements in activity in the short run. Later in the book, we extend the model to look at the role of expectations about the future (chapters 14 to 17) and the implications of openness in both goods and financial markets (chapters 18 to 21). Before we do this, we must first understand what determines output in the medium run. This is the topic of the next four chapters.

SUMMARY

- The *IS-LM* model characterizes the implications of equilibrium in both the goods and the financial markets.

- The *IS* relation and the *IS* curve show the combinations of the interest rate and the level of output that are consistent with equilibrium in the goods market. An increase in the interest rate leads to a decline in output.

- The *LM* relation and the *LM* curve show the combinations of the interest rate and the level of output consistent with equilibrium in financial markets. Given the real money supply, an increase in output leads to an increase in the interest rate.

- A fiscal expansion shifts the *IS* curve to the right, leading to an increase in output and an increase in the interest rate. A monetary expansion shifts the *LM* curve down, leading to an increase in output and a decrease in the interest rate.

- The combination of monetary and fiscal policies is known as the monetary–fiscal policy mix, or simply policy mix. Sometimes monetary and fiscal policy are used for a common goal. Sometimes, the monetary–fiscal mix occasionally emerges from tensions or even disagreements between the government (which is in charge of fiscal policy) and the central bank (which is in charge of monetary policy).

- The *IS-LM* model appears to describe well the behavior of the economy in the short run. In particular, the effects of monetary policy appear to be similar to those implied by the *IS-LM* model once dynamics are introduced in the model. An increase in the interest rate due to a monetary contraction leads to a steady decrease in output, with the maximum effect taking place after about eight quarters.

QUESTIONS & PROBLEMS

An asterisk denotes a harder question.

1. TRUE/FALSE/UNCERTAIN

a. The main determinants of investment are the level of sales and the interest rate.

b. If all the exogenous variables in the *IS* relation are constant, then a higher level of output can be achieved only at a lower interest rate.

c. The *IS* curve is downward sloping because goods–market equilibrium implies that an increase in taxes leads to a lower level of output.

d. If both government spending and taxes increase by the same amount, the *IS* curve does not shift.

e. The *LM* curve is upward sloping because a higher level of the money supply is needed to increase output.

f. An increase in government spending decreases investment.

g. An increase in output at a constant interest rate can only be achieved using a monetary–fiscal policy mix.

*2. INVESTMENT AND THE INTEREST RATE

The chapter argues that the reason investment depends negatively on the interest rate is the following: When the interest rate increases, the cost of borrowing funds also increases and this discourages investment. However, firms often finance their investment projects using their own funds. Because no borrowing actually occurs, will higher interest rates discourage investment in this case? Explain. *Hint*: Think of yourself as an owner of a firm who is considering financing new investment projects in your firm using the profits your firm just earned, or buying bonds. Will your decision to invest in new projects in your firm be affected by the interest rate?

3. THE MULTIPLIER REVISITED

Consider first the goods market model with constant investment that we saw in chapter 3:

$C = c_0 + c_1(Y - T)$, and *I*, *G*, and *T* are given.

a. Solve for equilibrium output. What is the value of the multiplier?

Now, let investment depend on both sales and the interest rate:

$$I = b_0 + b_1 Y - b_2 i$$

b. Solve for equilibrium output. At a given interest rate, is the effect of change in autonomous spending bigger than what it was in (a)? Why? (Assume $c_1 + b_1 < 1$).

Next, let's introduce the financial market equilibrium condition with real money demand equal to the real money supply.

$$M/P = d_1 Y - d_2 i$$

c. Solve for equilibrium output. (*Hint*: Eliminate the interest rate in the *IS* equation using the expression from the *LM* equation.) Derive the multiplier (the effect of a change of 1 in autonomous spending on output).

d. Is the multiplier you obtained smaller or larger than the multiplier you derived in your answer to [a]? Explain how your answer depends on the behavioral equations for consumption, investment, and money demand.

4. THE RESPONSE OF INVESTMENT TO FISCAL POLICY

a. Using the *IS-LM* graph, determine the effects on output and the interest rate of a decrease in government spending. Why is the effect on investment ambiguous?

With more information on the parameters of the IS and LM relation, we may be able to determine, for example, whether deficit reduction is good or bad for I in the short run. Consider the following equations for consumption, investment, and money demand:

$$C = c_0 + c_1(Y - T)$$
$$I = b_0 + b_1 Y - b_2 i$$
$$M/P = d_1 Y - d_2 i$$

b. Solve for equilibrium output. (*Hint*: You may want to work through question 3 if you're having trouble with this step.)

c. Solve for the equilibrium interest rate. (*Hint*: Use the LM relation.)

d. Solve for investment.

e. Under what condition on the parameters of the model (for example, c_0, c_1, and so on) will investment increase when G decreases?

f. Explain the condition you derived in (e).

5. MONETARY AND FISCAL POLICY: AN EXAMPLE

Consider the following $IS\text{-}LM$ model:

$$C = 200 + .25Y_D$$
$$I = 150 + .25Y - 1000i$$
$$G = 250$$
$$T = 200$$
$$(M/P)^d = 2Y - 8000i$$
$$M/P = 1,600$$

a. Derive the equation for the IS curve. (*Hint*: You want an equation with Y on the left hand side, all else on the right.)

b. Derive the equation for the LM curve. (*Hint*: It will be convenient for later use to write this equation with i on the left side, all else on the right.)

c. Solve for equilibrium real output. (*Hint*: Substitute the expression for the interest rate given by the LM equation into the IS equation and solve for output.)

d. Solve for the equilibrium interest rate. (*Hint*: Substitute the value you obtained for Y in (c) into either the IS or LM equations and solve for i. If your algebra is correct you should get the same answer from both equations.)

e. Solve for the equilibrium values of C and I and verify the value you obtained for Y by adding up C, I, and G.

f. Now suppose that the money supply increases to $M/P = 1840$. Solve for Y, i, C, and I, and explain in words the effects of expansionary monetary policy.

g. Set M/P equal to its initial value of 1,600. Now suppose that government spending increases to $G = 400$. Summarize the effects of expansionary fiscal policy on Y, i, and C.

*h. (Try this point only if you have already answered question 4.) Without solving for Y and i, can you tell whether contractionary fiscal policy will increase or decrease I? To verify your answer, set all exogenous variables back to their initial values and solve for investment when government spending decreases to $G = 100$.

*6. THE LIQUIDITY TRAP

a. Suppose the interest rate on bonds was negative. Would people want to hold bonds or to hold money? Explain.

b. Draw the demand for money as a function of the interest rate, for a given level of real income. How does your answer to (a) affect your answer? (*Hint*: Show that the demand for money becomes very flat as the interest rate gets very close to zero).

c. Derive the LM curve. What happens to the LM curve as the interest rate gets very close to zero? (*Hint*: It becomes very flat)

d. Take your LM curve. Suppose that the interest rate is very close to zero, and the central bank increases the supply of money. What happens to the interest rate at a given level of income?

e. Can an expansionary monetary policy increase output when the interest rate is already very close to zero?

This inability of the central bank to decrease the interest rate when it is already very close to zero is known as the "liquidity trap", and was first mentioned by Keynes in 1936 in his General Theory—which laid the foundations of the IS-LM model.

f. Keynes also mentioned that he was not aware of there ever having been a liquidity trap. Yet in 1998, Japan's interest rate was almost zero, and output had barely changed even in the face of expansionary monetary policy by the central bank of Japan. Do you think that Japan was experiencing a liquidity trap?

g. Also in 1998, the Japanese government pursued an expansionary fiscal policy in its effort to increase output. Do you agree with this course of action? Is fiscal policy more or less effective than monetary policy when there is a liquidity trap?

7. POLICY RECOMMENDATIONS

Suggest a policy or policy mix to achieve the following objectives:

a. Increase Y while keeping i constant.

b. Decrease the deficit while keeping Y constant. What happens to i? To investment?

FURTHER READINGS

Paul Krugman, an economist at MIT, regularly writes columns for several magazines, including *Fortune* and *Slate*. The columns are insightful and fun to read. You can find them on his home page (http://web.mit.edu/krugman/www/). One column "Vulgar Keynesians," discusses the role of monetary policy in the U.S. economy. Read it and try to see if you can restate his arguments in terms of the *IS-LM* model.

Another interesting home page is that of Brad DeLong, an economist at UC Berkeley (http://econ161.berkeley.edu/). For more information on deficit reduction and the Clinton–Greenspan policy mix, read his article, "The Budget Deficit."

We invite you to visit the Blanchard page on the Prentice Hall Web site at:

http://www.prenhall.com/blanchard

for this chapter's World Wide Web exercises

THE CORE

The Medium Run

The next four chapters focus on the medium run.

CHAPTER 6

Chapter 6 looks at equilibrium in the labor market. It derives the natural rate of unemployment as the unemployment rate to which the economy tends to return in the medium run. Associated with the natural rate of unemployment is a natural level of output.

CHAPTER 7

Chapter 7 looks at equilibrium in all three markets—goods, financial, labor—together. It shows how, in the short run, output can deviate from its natural level, and how it tends to return to this natural level in the medium run. The model developed in chapter 7 is called the *AS–AD* model, and is, like the *IS-LM* model, one of the workhorses of macroeconomics.

CHAPTER 8

Chapter 8 looks more closely at the relation between inflation and unemployment, a relation known as the Phillips curve. It shows that, in the United States today, low unemployment leads to an increase in inflation; high unemployment to a decrease in inflation.

CHAPTER 9

Chapter 9 looks at the determination of output, unemployment and inflation, and the effects of money growth. In the short run, decreases in money growth can trigger a recession. In the medium run however, they are neutral; they are reflected one for one in changes in the rate of inflation.

CHAPTER | The Labor Market

Think about what happens when firms respond to an increase in demand by stepping up production:

- Higher production requires an increase in employment.
- Higher employment leads to lower unemployment.
- Lower unemployment puts pressure on wages.
- Higher wages increase production costs, forcing firms in turn to increase prices.
- Higher prices lead workers to ask for higher wages, and so on.

In the previous three chapters, we ignored this sequence of events: We assumed that firms were able and willing to supply any level of output at a given price level. So long as our focus was on the *short run* this was an acceptable simplification. As our attention turns to what happens in the *medium run*, we must now relax this assumption, explore how prices and wages adjust over time, and how this, in turn, affects the response of output. This will be our task in this and the next three chapters.

At the center of the process described above is the *labor market*, the market in which wages are determined. This chapter starts with an overview of the labor market and takes a first pass at deriving equilibrium in the labor market. In particular, it derives the central notion of the *natural rate of unemployment*. The next three chapters then combine our earlier treatment of goods and financial markets with our newly acquired knowledge of the labor market. When we are done, you will know how to think about movements in output and the price level, both in the short run and in the medium run.

In 1998, about 62 million Americans were under 16 years old; 1.4 million were in the armed forces; 1.5 million were incarcerated.

The total U.S. population in 1998 was 270.2 million. Excluding those who were either under working age (under 16), in the armed forces, or in jail, the number of people potentially available for civilian employment, the **noninstitutional civilian population**, was 205.2 million (Table 6–1).

The **labor force**—the sum of those either working or looking for work—was, however, only 137.6 million. The other 67.6 million people were **out of the labor force**, neither working in the market place nor looking for work. The **participation rate**, defined as the ratio of the labor force to the noninstitutional civilian population, was therefore equal to 137.6/205.2, or 67%. The participation rate has steadily increased over time, reflecting mostly the increasing participation rate of women: In 1950, one woman out of three was in the labor force; now the number is close to two out of three.

Work in the home, such as cooking or raising children, is not classified as work in official statistics. The reason is the difficulty of measuring these activities; it is not meant as a value judgment concerning what is or is not work.

Of those in the labor force, 131.4 million were employed, and 6.2 million were unemployed. The **unemployment rate**, defined as the ratio of the unemployed to the labor force, was thus equal to 6.2/137.6 = 4.5%.

The Large Flows of Workers

Sclerosis, a medical term, means hardening of the arteries. In social sciences, it is used to describe institutions that do not adapt to changes in their environment, and, as a result, function less and less well over time.

To think further about unemployment, the following analogy will be helpful: Take an airport full of passengers. This may be because it is a busy airport; with many planes taking off and landing. Many passengers are quickly moving in and out of the airport. Or it may be because bad weather is delaying flights and passengers are stuck, waiting for the weather to improve. The number of passengers in the airport may be the same in both cases, but their plight is quite different. In the same way, a given unemployment rate may reflect two very different realities. It may reflect an active labor market, with many **separations** (workers leaving or losing their jobs), many **hires**, and lots of workers entering and exiting unemployment; or it may reflect a sclerotic labor market, with few separations, few hires, and a stagnant unemployment pool.

The series in Figure 6–1 are adjusted for a number of problems with the original data. These adjustments are available only for 1968 to 1986, which is why Figure 6–1 covers only that period.

Finding out what reality hides behind the aggregate unemployment rate requires data on the movements of workers. Such data are available in the United States from a monthly survey called the **Current Population Survey (CPS)**. Average monthly flows, computed from the CPS for the United States from 1968 to 1986, are reported in Figure 6–1. (For more on the ins and outs of the CPS, see the Focus box "The Current Population Survey.")

Figure 6–1 has three striking features:

1. *The size of the flows into and out of employment:* The average monthly flow into employment is 3.1 million: 1.6 million from unemployment plus 1.5 million from out of the labor force. The average monthly flow out of employment is 2.9 million: 1.3 to unemployment plus 1.6 to out of the labor force. Put another way, hires by firms and separations from firms are respectively equal to 3.3% (3.1/93.8) and 3.1% (2.9/93.8) of employment *each month.*

These numbers underestimate the true flows, because they do not include movements of workers directly from one job to another. These flows cannot be constructed from the information available in the CPS for that period, but we know from other sources that they are large as well, around 2.5% each month.

   Why are these flows so large? About half of separations (the flows from employment) are **quits**, workers leaving their jobs in search of a better alternative. The other half are **layoffs**, which come mostly from changes in employment levels across firms: The slowly changing aggregate employment numbers hide a reality of continual job destruction and job creation across firms. At any time, some firms are suffering decreases

TABLE 6–1	Population, Labor Force, Employment, and Unemployment in the United States (in millions), 1998
Total population	270.2
Civilian noninstitutional population	205.2
Civilian labor force	137.6
Employed	131.4
Unemployed	6.2

Source: Economic Report of the President, 1999, tables B34, B35.

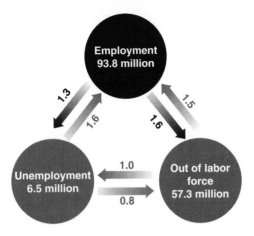

FIGURE 6-1

Average Monthly Flows Between Employment, Unemployment, and Nonparticipation in the United States, 1968–1986

(1) The flows of workers into and out of employment are large; (2) The flows into and out of unemployment are large in relation to the number of unemployed; (3) There are also large flows into and out of the labor force, much of it directly to and from employment.

in demand and decreasing their employment; others are enjoying increases in demand and increasing employment. A recent study shows that about 5% of existing jobs in U.S. manufacturing are ended every quarter (and a roughly equal number is created: total employment in manufacturing is roughly constant.) One function of the labor market in modern economies is to allow for this steady reallocation of labor across firms.

2. *The size of the flows into and out of unemployment in relation to the total number of unemployed.* The average monthly flow out of unemployment each month is 2.4 million: 1.6 million to employment plus 0.8 million to out of the labor force. Put another way, the proportion of unemployed leaving unemployment equals 2.4/6.5 or about one-third each month. Put yet another way, the average **duration of unemployment**—the average length of time people spend unemployed—is about three months.

This fact has an important implication. You should not think of unemployment in the United States as a stagnant pool of workers waiting indefinitely for jobs. For most of the unemployed, being unemployed is more a quick transition than a long wait between jobs: For the period 1968–1986, the proportion of unemployed getting a job was about 25% (1.6/6.5) each month. In this respect, the United States is unusual among OECD countries. As we shall see in chapter 21, evidence from Western Europe shows a much longer average duration of unemployment.

3. *The size of the flows into and out of the labor force.* You might have expected these flows to be small, composed on one side of those finishing school and entering the labor force for the first time, and on the other side of workers going into retirement. But these flows actually represent a small fraction of the total flows. Each month only about 350,000 new people enter the labor force, and about 200,000 retire. The actual flows into and out of the labor force are nearly 10 times larger. What this means is that many of those classified as "out of the labor force" are in fact willing to work, and move back and forth between participation and nonparticipation. Indeed, among those classified as out of the labor force, nearly 5 million report that although they are not looking, they want a job. What they mean exactly is unclear, but the evidence is that many do take jobs when offered.

This fact also has an important implication. The sharp focus on the unemployment rate by economists, policy makers, and news media is partly misdirected. Some of the people classified as "out of the labor force" are very much like the unemployed; they are in effect **discouraged workers**, and although they are not actively looking for a job, they will take it if they find it. This is why economists sometimes focus on the **nonemployment rate**, the ratio of population minus employment to population, rather than the unemployment rate. I shall follow tradition in this book and focus on the unemployment rate, but you should keep in mind that the unemployment rate may not be the best estimate of the number of people available for work.

◄ Think of it this way. Suppose the number of unemployed is constant. If each unemployed person remains unemployed for n months, then it must be that a proportion $1/n$ is leaving unemployment each month (and, as the number of unemployed is constant, an equal number enters unemployment.) More formally, the proportion of people leaving unemployment is the inverse of unemployment duration. Conversely, unemployment duration is the inverse of the proportion of people leaving unemployment.

◄ In the other direction, some unemployed may be unwilling to accept any job offered to them, and should probably not be counted as unemployed (that is, looking for a job.)

The Current Population Survey (CPS) is the main source of statistics on the labor force, employment, participation, and earnings in the United States.

When the CPS began in 1940, it was based on interviews of 8,000 households. The sample has grown considerably, and now more than 60,000 households are interviewed every month. The households are chosen so that the sample is representative of the U.S. population. Each household stays in the sample for four months, leaves the sample for the following eight months, then comes back for another four months before leaving the sample permanently.

The survey is now based on computer-assisted interviews. Interviews are either done in person, in which case interviewers use laptop computers, or by phone. Some questions are the same every month. Other questions are specific to a particular survey and are used to find out about particular aspects of the labor market.

Here are the main questions that are asked to determine whether somebody is employed or unemployed:

1. Last week, did you do any work for either pay or profit?
2. Last week (in addition to any business you may have), did you have a job, either full or part time? Include any job from which you were absent temporarily.
3. Last week, were you on layoff from a job?
4. Has your employer given you a date to return to work?
5. Have you been given any indication that you will be recalled to work within the next six months?
6. Have you been doing anything to find work during the last four weeks?

7. What are all the things that you have done to find work during the last four weeks?

People are classified as employed if they say "yes" to question 1 (and have worked at least 15 hours or received profit from the business), or 2.

People are classified as unemployed if they say yes to 3 and yes to either 4 or 5, or if they say yes to 6 and give a job-search method that could have brought them in contact with a potential employer in 7.

The Labor Department uses the data to compute and publish numbers on employment, unemployment, and participation by age, sex, education, and industry. Economists use these data, which are available in large computer files, in two ways. The first is to get snapshots of how things are at various points in time, to answer such questions as: What is the distribution of wages for Hispanic-American workers with only primary education, and how does it compare with the same distribution 10 or 20 years ago? The second, of which Figure 6–1 is an example, is by exploiting the fact that the survey follows people through time. By looking at those who are in the sample in two adjacent months, economists can find out for example how many of those who were unemployed last month are employed this month. This number gives them an estimate of the probability of finding a job for those who were unemployed last month.

For more on the CPS, read "How the Government Measures Unemployment" at (http://www.bls.gov/).

Differences across Workers

The aggregate picture we have just drawn is one of large flows between employment, unemployment, and nonparticipation. The picture is, however, different for different groups of workers. Table 6–2, again based on evidence from the CPS, shows some of the differences in separation rates by age and sex, during 1968 to 1986 (the same period as in Figure 6–1).

TABLE 6–2 Monthly Separation Rates for Different Groups, 1968–1986

Category		Monthly Separation Rate (%) (Quits and Layoffs)
Male:	Ages 16–19	15.9
	35–44	1.6
Female:	Ages 16–19	16.1
	35–44	5.0

Source: *Current Population Survey*. The separation rate is defined as the monthly flow out of employment divided by the initial level of employment. The number is the average separation rate for the period 1968–1986.

On average, 16% of workers ages 16 to 19 leave their jobs each month. But the rate is only 5.0% among female workers ages 35 to 44, and an even lower 1.6% among male workers ages 35 to 44. These different separation rates are reflected in different unemployment rates for the different groups. In 1998, when the aggregate unemployment rate was 4.5%, the rate of unemployment among young males ages 16 to 19 was a high 16.2%.

This means that the average duration of a job for workers 16 to 19 years old is only 1/0.16 = 6 months.

Why these differences? Many young people hold low-paying jobs—in the fast food industry, for example—and these jobs are often only marginally more attractive than unemployment. Also, young workers have little seniority and are often the first to be laid off when a firm reduces its work force. Thus, young workers frequently move between jobs, unemployment, and nonparticipation. Middle-aged males, in contrast, tend to keep the jobs they have. This is because the jobs are typically better, and because family responsibilities make it more difficult to give up a job for a chance of a better one.

The variations in labor-market experiences reflect in part life-cycle considerations, with the young going from one job to the next until they eventually find one they like and settle down. But they also reflect permanent differences among workers, including education level, skill, and race. Unskilled workers, whatever their age, typically have higher unemployment rates. So do African-Americans. In 1998, the unemployment rate among African-Americans was 8.9%, nearly twice the national average.

These differences across jobs and workers have sometimes led macroeconomists and labor economists to model the labor market as a **dual labor market** with (1) a **primary labor market** where jobs are good, wages are high, and turnover is low (workers do not change jobs very often), and (2) a **secondary labor market** where jobs are poor, wages are low, and turnover is high. This is not a distinction I shall pursue in this book, but it is one that can often be important and useful in thinking about the labor market.

6-2 | Movements in Unemployment

Let's now turn to movements in unemployment over time. Figure 6–2 shows the average value of the U.S. unemployment rate for each year since 1948. (The shaded areas represent years in which there was a recession—at least two consecutive quarters of output decline.)

Figure 6–2 yields two conclusions. First, there is evidence of a small upward trend in the unemployment rate. The average unemployment rate was 4.5% in the 1950s, 4.7% in the

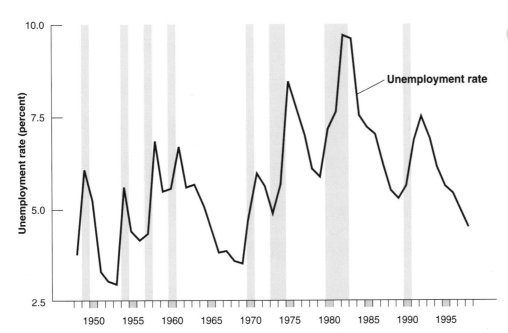

FIGURE 6–2

Movements in the U.S. Unemployment Rate, 1948–1998

Since 1948, the average yearly U.S. unemployment rate has fluctuated between 3% and 10%, with some evidence of a small upward trend.

1960s, 6.2% in the 1970s, 7.3% in the 1980s. In the 1990s however, average unemployment has been only 5.9%, and in 1998 it stood at 4.5%. This decrease has led some economists to conclude that the trend has been reversed, and that the U.S. economy is likely to operate at a lower average unemployment rate in the future than in the last twenty years. We shall return to this issue in Chapter 8.

See the In Depth box "Has the U.S. natural rate decreased in the 1990s?" in Chapter 8.

Second, the trend increase is dominated by large fluctuations in the unemployment rate. The fluctuations are closely associated with recessions and expansions. Note, for example, the last two peaks in unemployment. The most recent, in which unemployment peaked at 7.7%, was associated with the recession of 1990–1991 (the peak in unemployment actually came one year after the end of the recession, in 1992.) The one before, in which unemployment peaked at 9.7% (a postwar high) was during the recession of 1982.

The average unemployment rate for the year 1982 was less than 10%. But, in the month of November, the unemployment rate reached 10.8%.

How do fluctuations in the *aggregate unemployment rate* affect *individual workers*? This is an important question for two reasons. The answer determines both the effect of movements in unemployment on the welfare of workers—and the effect of unemployment on wages.

Think about how firms can decrease their employment in response to a decrease in demand. They can hire fewer new workers or they can lay off the workers they currently employ. Typically, firms prefer first to slow or stop the hiring of new workers, relying on quits and retirements to achieve a decrease in employment. But if the decrease in demand is large, this may not be enough, and firms may then have to lay off workers.

Now think about the implications for workers, employed or unemployed. If the adjustment takes place through a decrease in hires, the effect is to decrease the chance that an unemployed worker will find a job. Fewer hires means fewer job openings; higher unemployment means more job applicants. Fewer openings and more applicants combine to make it harder for the unemployed to finds jobs. If the adjustment takes place instead through higher layoffs, then the employed workers are at a higher risk of losing their jobs. In general, when firms use both margins of adjustment, the result is likely to be both a lower chance of finding a job if unemployed and a higher chance of losing one if employed. Figures 6–3 and 6–4 show these two effects at work in the United States over the period 1968 to 1986.

FIGURE 6–3

The Unemployment Rate and the Proportion of Unemployed Finding Jobs, 1968–1986

When unemployment is high, the proportion of unemployed finding jobs is low. Note that the scale on the right is an inverse scale.

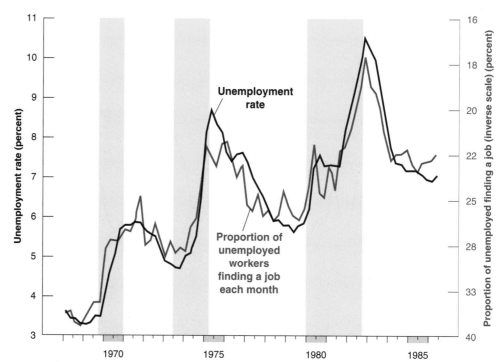

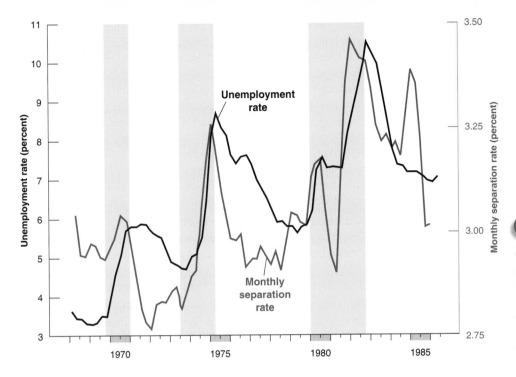

FIGURE 6-4

The Unemployment Rate and the Monthly Separation Rate from Employment, 1968–1986

When unemployment is high, a higher proportion of workers lose their jobs.

Figure 6–3 plots two variables against time: first, the unemployment rate; second, the proportion of unemployed workers finding a job each month. The proportion is constructed by dividing the flow from unemployment to employment during each month by the number of unemployed at the beginning of the month. To make the point clearer visually, the proportion is plotted on an inverted scale on the right: The proportion is lowest at the top, highest at the bottom. The close relation between movements in the proportion and the unemployment rate is striking: Periods of higher unemployment are associated with much lower proportions of unemployed workers finding jobs. At the peak of the 1980 to 1982 recession, the proportion of workers finding jobs was down to 17% per month, compared to an average value of 25% over the period 1968–1986.

Similarly, Figure 6–4 plots two variables against time: first, the unemployment rate; second, the monthly separation rate from employment. The separation rate is constructed by dividing the flow from employment (to unemployment and to "out of the labor force") during each month by the number of people employed at the beginning of the month. The relation between the separation rate and the unemployment rate is less tight than the relation plotted in Figure 6–3, but it is nevertheless quite clearly there. Higher unemployment implies a higher separation rate, a higher chance for employed workers to lose their jobs.

To summarize: When unemployment is high, workers are worse off in two ways. The probability that they lose their job is higher. And if they become unemployed, the probability that they will find another job is lower; equivalently, they can expect to be unemployed for a longer length of time.

> When unemployment is high, the proportion of unemployed workers finding jobs is low.

> Strictly speaking, we only learn from the figure that, when unemployment is higher, separations are higher. Separations are quits plus layoffs. We know from other sources that quits are lower when unemployment is high: It is more attractive to quit when there are plenty of jobs. So, if separations go up, and quits go down, this implies that layoffs go up more than separations.

6-3 | Wage Determination

Having looked at the nature of unemployment, let's turn to wage determination, and to the relation between wages and unemployment.

Wages are set in many ways. Sometimes they are set by **collective bargaining**, that is, bargaining between firms and unions. In the United States however, collective bargaining plays a limited role, especially outside manufacturing. Today, less than 25% of workers are covered by collective bargaining agreements. For the rest, wages are set either by employers, or by individual bargaining between the employer and the employee. The higher the skills needed to do the job, the more typical is individual bargaining. Wages offered for entry-level jobs at McDonald's are on a take-it-or-leave-it basis. New college graduates can typically negotiate a few aspects of their contract. CEOs and baseball stars can negotiate a lot more.

There are also large differences across countries. Collective bargaining plays an important role in Japan and in most European countries. Negotiations may take place at the level of the firm, at the level of industry, or at the national level. Contract agreements sometimes apply only to those firms that have signed the agreement; sometimes they are automatically extended to all firms and all workers in the sector or the economy.

Given these differences across workers and across countries, can we hope for anything like a general theory of wage determination? Yes. Although institutional differences play a role, there are common forces at work in all countries. Two sets of facts stand out:

1. Workers are typically paid a wage that exceeds their **reservation wage**, the wage that would make them indifferent to working or becoming unemployed. In other words, most workers are paid a high enough wage that they prefer to be employed rather than unemployed.

2. Wages typically depend on labor-market conditions: The lower the unemployment rate, the higher the wages.

To think about these facts, economists have focused on two broad lines of explanation. The first is that even in the absence of collective bargaining, workers have some bargaining power, which they can and do use to obtain wages above their reservation wage. The second is that firms themselves may, for a number of reasons, want to pay wages higher than the reservation wage. Let's look at each explanation.

Bargaining

How much **bargaining power** a worker has depends on two factors. The first is how easy it would be for the firm to replace him, were he to leave the firm. The second is how easy it would be for him to find another job, were he to leave the firm. The harder it is for the firm to replace him, or the easier it is for him to find another job, the stronger he will be in bargaining.

This has two implications. First, how much bargaining power a worker has depends on the nature of his job. Replacing a worker at McDonald's is not very costly; the required skills can be taught quickly, and typically a large number of willing applicants have already filled out job application forms. In this situation, the worker is unlikely to have much bargaining power. If he asks for a higher wage, the firm can lay him off and find a replacement at minimum cost. In contrast, a highly skilled worker who has proven unusually good at his job may be very difficult to replace. This gives him more bargaining power. If he asks for a higher wage, the firm may decide that it is best to give it to him.

Second, how much bargaining power workers have depends on labor market conditions. When the unemployment rate is low, it is more difficult for firms to find acceptable replacements, and it is easier for workers to find other jobs. Under such conditions, workers are in a stronger bargaining position, and may be able to obtain a higher wage. Conversely, when the unemployment rate is high, finding good replacements is easier for firms, whereas finding another job is harder for workers. Being in a weaker bargaining position, workers may have no choice but to accept a lower wage.

Efficiency Wages

Leaving aside workers' bargaining power, firms themselves may want to pay more than the reservation wage. Firms want their workers to be productive, and the wage can help them achieve that goal.

If, for example, it takes a while for workers to learn how to do a job correctly, firms will want their workers to stay. But if workers are paid just their reservation wage, they will be indifferent between staying or leaving. Many of them may quit, and turnover may be high. In such a situation, paying a wage above the reservation wage will make it financially attractive for workers to stay. It will decrease turnover, and increase productivity.

Behind this example lies a more general proposition: Most firms want their workers to feel good about their jobs. Feeling good promotes good work, which leads to higher productivity. Paying a high wage is one instrument the firm can use to achieve these goals. (See the Focus box "Henry Ford and Efficiency Wages.") Economists call the theories that link the *productivity* or the *efficiency* of workers to the wage they are paid **efficiency wage theories**.

Like theories based on bargaining, efficiency wage theories suggest that wages depend both on the nature of the job and on labor-market conditions.

- Firms—such as high-tech firms—that see employees' morale and commitment as essential to the quality of their work will pay more than firms in sectors where workers' activity is more routine.
- Labor-market conditions will affect the wage. Lower unemployment rate makes it more attractive for employed workers to quit: Lower unemployment makes it easier to find another job. A firm that wants to avoid an increase in quits will have to counteract the effects of lower unemployment by increasing the wage it pays its workers. In short, a lower unemployment will lead to higher wages.

> The evidence is that workers who operate more expensive machinery are typically paid more. Can efficiency wage theories explain this fact?

Henry Ford and Efficiency Wages

In 1914, Henry Ford—the builder of the most popular car in the world at the time, the model T—made a stunning announcement. His company would pay all qualified employees a minimum of $5 a day for an eight-hour day. This was a very large salary increase for most employees, previously earning on average $2.34 for nine-hour days. Although company profits were substantial, this increase in pay was far from negligible—it represented about half of the company's profits at the time.

What Ford's motivations were is not entirely clear. Ford himself gave too many reasons for us to know which ones he actually believed. The reason was not that the company had a hard time finding workers at the previous wage. But the company clearly had a hard time retaining workers. There was a very high turnover rate, as well as high dissatisfaction among workers.

Whatever the reasons behind Ford's decision, the results of the wage increase were astounding, as Table 1 shows.

The annual turnover rate (the ratio of separations to employment) plunged from a high of 370% in 1913 to a low of 16% in 1915. (An annual turnover rate of 370% means that on average 31% of the company's workers left each month, so that over the year the ratio of separations to employment was 31% × 12 ≈ 370%.) The layoff rate col-

lapsed from 62% to nearly 0%. Other measures point in the same direction. The average rate of absenteeism (not shown in the table), which ran at 10% in 1913, was down to 2.5% a year later. There is little question that higher wages were the main source of these changes.

Did productivity at the Ford plant increase enough to offset the cost of increased wages? The answer to this question is less clear. Productivity was much higher in 1914 than in 1913; estimates of productivity increases range from 30% to 50%. Despite higher wages, profits were also higher in 1914 than in 1913. But how much of this increase in profits was due to changes in workers' behavior and how much was due to the increasing success of model-T cars is harder to establish.

Although the effects support efficiency-wage theories, it may be that the increase in wages to $5 a day was excessive, at least from the point of view of profit maximization. But Henry Ford probably had other objectives as well, from keeping the unions out—which he did—to generating publicity for himself and the company—which he surely did as well.

Source: Dan Raff and Lawrence Summers, "Did Henry Ford Pay Efficiency Wages?" *NBER Working Paper*, 2101, December 1986.

TABLE 1	Annual turnover and layoff rates (%) at Ford, 1913–1915		
	1913	**1914**	**1915**
Turnover rate	370	54	16
Layoff rate	62	7	0.1

Wages and Unemployment

The following equation captures the main conclusions of our discussion of wage determination:

$$W = P^e F(u, z) \qquad (6.1)$$
$$(-, +)$$

where W, the nominal wage depends on three factors:

- The expected price level, P^e.
- The unemployment rate, u.
- A catchall variable, z, that stands for all other variables that affect the outcome of wage setting.

Let's look at each factor in turn.

The Expected Price Level. Leave aside first the difference between the expected and the actual price level, and ask, Why does the price level affect wages? Quite simply because workers and firms care about *real wages*, not nominal wages.

- Workers care not about how many dollars they receive, but about how many goods they can buy with their wages. In other words, they care about their wage in terms of goods, about W/P.
- In the same way, firms care not about the nominal wages they pay workers, but about the nominal wages they pay in terms of the price of the output they sell. So firms also care about W/P.

If both workers and firms knew that the price level was going to double, they would agree to doubling the nominal wage. This relation between the wage and the expected price level is captured in equation (6.1). A doubling in the expected price level leads to a doubling of the nominal wage chosen in wage setting.

$P^e \uparrow \Rightarrow W \uparrow$

Returning to the distinction we put aside at the start of the preceding paragraph: Why do wages depend on the *expected price level, P^e*, rather than the *actual price level, P*? Because wages are set in nominal (dollar) terms, and when they are set, what the relevant price level will be is not yet known. For example, in most U.S. union contracts nominal wages are typically set in advance for three years. Unions and firms have to decide what nominal wages will be over the following three years based on what they expect the price level to be over those three years. Even when wages are set by firms, or by bargaining between the firm and each worker, nominal wages are typically set for a year. If the price level goes up unexpectedly during the year, nominal wages are typically not readjusted. (How workers and firms form expectations of the price level will occupy us for much of the next three chapters; we leave this issue aside for the moment.)

The Unemployment Rate. Also affecting the aggregate wage in equation (6.1) is the unemployment rate. The minus sign under u indicates that an increase in the unemployment rate *decreases* wages.

This is one of the main implications of our earlier discussion of wage determination. If we think of wages as being determined by bargaining, higher unemployment weakens workers' bargaining power, forcing them to accept lower wages. If we think of wages as being determined by efficiency wage considerations, higher unemployment allows firms to pay lower wages and still keep workers willing to work.

$u \uparrow \Rightarrow W \downarrow$

The Other Factors. The third variable in equation (6.1), z, is a catchall variable that stands for all the factors that affect wages given the expected price level and the unemployment rate. By convention, z is defined in such a way that an increase in z leads to an increase in the wage—hence the plus sign under z. Our earlier discussion suggests a long list of such factors. For instance:

$z \uparrow \Rightarrow W \uparrow$

- Unemployment insurance offers workers protection from a complete loss of income if they become unemployed. There are good reasons why society should provide at least partial insurance to workers who lose a job and find it difficult to find another. But there is little question that, by making the prospects of unemployment less distressing, more generous unemployment benefits do increase wages. To take an extreme example, suppose unemployment insurance did not exist. Workers would then be willing to accept very low wages to avoid being unemployed. But unemployment insurance does exist, and it allows unemployed workers to hold out for higher wages. In this case, we can think of z as standing for the level of unemployment benefits: Higher unemployment benefits increase the wage.

- Suppose the economy undergoes a period of structural change, so more jobs are created and more jobs are destroyed, leading to larger flows into and out of unemployment. This implies that, at a given level of unemployment, there are more job openings, and thus a better chance of finding a job while unemployed. If it is easier to get a job while unemployed, then unemployment is less of a threat to workers. At a given level of unemployment, workers are in a stronger bargaining position and the wage increases. In this case, we can think of z as standing for an increase in the rate of structural change in the economy.

It is easy to think of other examples, from changes in minimum-wage legislation to changes in restrictions on firing and hiring, and so on. We shall explore the implications of some of these as we go along.

6-4 | Price Determination

Having looked at the determination of wages given expected prices, let's now look at the determination of prices given wages.

Prices depend on costs. Costs depend on the nature of the **production function**—the relation between the inputs used in production and the quantity of output produced. I shall assume that firms produce goods using labor as the only factor of production and according to the production function

$$Y = AN$$

where Y is output, N is employment, and A is labor productivity. This implies that **labor productivity**—the ratio of output per worker—is constant and equal to A.

It should be clear that this assumption is a drastic simplification of reality. Firms use other factors of production than labor. They use capital—machines and plants. They use raw materials—oil, for example. We know that there is technological progress, so that labor productivity (A) is not constant but instead steadily increases over time. We shall face these realities later. We shall introduce raw materials in chapter 7 when we discuss the oil crises of the 1970s. We shall focus on the role of capital and technological progress when we turn to the determination of output in the *long run* in chapters 10 to 13. For the moment, the simple relation between output and employment will make our life easier and still serve our purposes.

Given the assumption that labor productivity, A, is constant, we can make one further simplification. We can choose the units for output so that one worker produces one unit of output—so that $A = 1$. (This way we do not have to carry the letter A around, and this will simplify notation.) With that choice, the production function becomes

$$Y = N \tag{6.2}$$

The production function $Y = N$ implies that the cost of producing one more unit of output is the cost of employing one more worker, at wage W. Using the terminology introduced in your microeconomics course, the marginal cost of production is equal to W. If there were perfect competition in the goods market, the price of a unit of output would be equal to marginal cost: P would be equal to W. But many goods markets are not competitive, and firms charge a price higher than their marginal cost. A simple way of capturing this fact is to assume that firms set their price according to

$$P = (1 + \mu)W \tag{6.3}$$

◄ Using a term from microeconomics, this assumption implies *constant returns to labor* in *production*. If firms double the amount of labor they use, they can double the amount of output they produce.

If we had not put A equal to 1, then to produce one unit of goods, the firm would need 1/A units of labor, at cost W/A (the wage times the number of units of labor.) Thus, P would equal $(1 + \mu)W/A$.

where μ is the markup of price over cost. If goods markets were perfectly competitive, the price would simply equal the cost and μ would equal zero. To the extent that they are not competitive and that firms have market power, the price will be higher than the cost, and μ will be positive.

6-5 | The Natural Rate of Unemployment

Let's now look at the implications of wage and price determination for unemployment. Let's do so under the assumption that in wage determination, nominal wages depend on the actual price level, P, rather than on the expected price level, P^e (why we assume this will become clear soon.) Under this assumption, wage setting and price setting determine the equilibrium rate of unemployment. Let's see how.

An important assumption for the rest of the chapter: $P^e = P$.

The Wage-Setting Relation

Given the assumption that nominal wages depend on the actual price level (P) rather than on the expected price level (P^e), equation (6.1), which characterizes wage determination, becomes

$$W = P\, F(u,z)$$

Or, dividing both sides by the price level

"Wage setters" means unions and firms if wages are set by collective bargaining; it means individual workers and firms if wages are set in bilateral bargaining; it means firms if wages are set on a take-it-or-leave-it basis.

$$\frac{W}{P} = F(u, z) \qquad (6.4)$$
$$(-,+)$$

Wage determination implies a negative relation between the real wage, W/P, and the unemployment rate, u: *The higher the unemployment rate, the lower the real wage chosen by wage setters*. The intuition is straightforward: The higher the unemployment rate, the weaker workers are in bargaining, and so the lower the real wage.

This relation between the real wage and the rate of unemployment, let's call it the **wage-setting relation**, is drawn in Figure 6–5. The real wage is measured on the vertical axis. The unemployment rate is measured on the horizontal axis. The wage-setting relation is drawn as the downward-sloping curve WS (for wage setting): The higher the unemployment rate, the lower the real wage.

FIGURE 6–5

The Wage-Setting Relation, the Price-Setting Relation, and the Natural Rate of Unemployment

The real wage chosen in wage setting is a decreasing function of the unemployment rate. The real wage implied by price setting is constant, independent of the unemployment rate. The natural rate of unemployment is the unemployment rate such that the real wage chosen in wage setting is equal to the real wage implied by price setting.

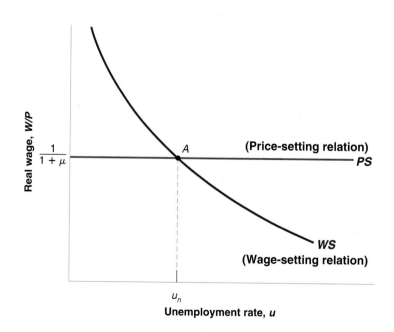

The Price-Setting Relation

Turn now to the implications of price determination. If we divide both sides of the price-determination equation (6.3), by the nominal wage, we get

$$\frac{P}{W} = 1 + \mu \tag{6.5}$$

The ratio of the price level to the wage implied by the price-setting behavior of firms equals 1 plus the markup. Now invert both sides of this equation to get the implied real wage

$$\frac{W}{P} = \frac{1}{1 + \mu} \tag{6.6}$$

Price-setting decisions determine the real wage paid by firms. An increase in the markup leads firms to increase prices given wages; equivalently, it leads to a decrease in the real wage.

The step from equation (6.5) to equation (6.6) is algebraically straightforward. But how price setting actually determines the real wage paid by firms may not be intuitively obvious. A numerical example will help. Suppose it takes one hour of work to produce one unit of output, firms pay a wage of $10 per hour, and the firms' markup is 20%, so they sell each unit of output for $10 \times 1.2 = 12. The real wage—how many units of the good workers can buy if they work for an hour—is $10/12 = 0.83$ units of the good. If firms increase their markup to 30%, the real wage falls to $10/13 = 0.76$ units. By choosing their markup, firms in effect determine the real wage. This is what is captured in equation (6.6).

The **price-setting relation** in equation (6.6) is drawn as the horizontal line *PS* (for price setting) in Figure 6–5. The real wage implied by price setting is constant, equal to $1/(1 + \mu)$, therefore independent of the unemployment rate.

Equilibrium Real Wages, Employment, and Unemployment

Equilibrium in the labor market requires that the real wage implied by wage setting be equal to the real wage implied by price setting. (This way of stating equilibrium may sound strange if you learned to think in terms of labor supply and labor demand in your microeconomics course. The relation between the wage-setting and price-setting relations on the one hand, and labor supply and labor demand on the other, is closer than it looks at first and is discussed in the Focus Box "Wage and Price Setting versus Labor Supply and Labor Demand." Wait however until you have read the whole section to read that box.) In Figure 6–5, equilibrium is therefore given by point *A*, with equilibrium unemployment rate u_n.

We can also characterize the equilibrium unemployment rate algebraically; eliminating *W/P* between equations (6.4) and (6.6) gives

$$F(u_n, z) = \frac{1}{1 + \mu} \tag{6.7}$$

The equilibrium unemployment rate, u_n, is such that the real wage chosen in wage setting—the left side of equation (6.7)—is equal to the real wage implied by price setting—the right side of equation (6.7).

The equilibrium unemployment rate (u_n) is called the **natural rate of unemployment** (which is why I have used the subscript *n* to denote it). The terminology has become standard, and I shall adopt it, but the word "natural" is a misnomer. It suggests a constant of nature, one that is unaffected by institutions and policy. As its derivation makes clear, the "natural" rate of unemployment is anything but natural. The positions of the wage-setting and price-setting curves, and thus the equilibrium unemployment rate, depend on both z and μ. Consider two examples:

- An increase in unemployment benefits. An increase in benefits can be represented by an increase in z: It increases the wage set by wage setters at a given unemployment rate. So it shifts the wage-setting relation up, from *WS* to *WS'* in Figure 6–6. The equilibrium moves from *A* to *A'*, and the natural unemployment rate increases from u_n to u_n'.

> More help with the intuition: If the firm in which I work increases its markup and so increases the price of its products, my real wage does not change very much if at all. I am still paid the same wage, and, even if one of the goods I buy is the good produced by the firm, it is at most a very small part of my consumption basket. But, if not only the firm I work for but all firms increase their markup and the price of their products, then the prices of all the goods I buy go up. My real wage goes down.

> "Natural," as defined by Webster's Dictionary, is "in a state provided by nature, without man-made changes."

FIGURE 6-6

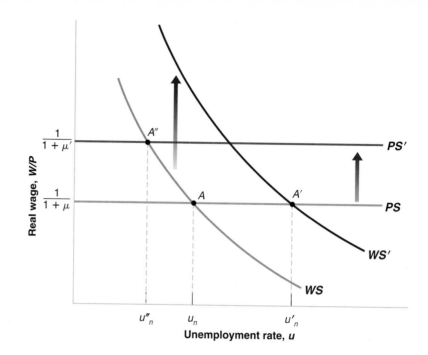

Unemployment Benefits, Markups, and the Natural Rate of Unemployment

An increase in unemployment benefits leads to an increase in the natural rate of unemployment. A decrease in the markup leads to a decrease in the natural rate of unemployment.

ACTIVE GRAPH

- A more stringent antitrust legislation. To the extent that such a legislation decreases the market power of firms, it leads to a decrease in the markup—a decrease in μ. The decrease in μ implies an increase in the real wage paid by firms, and so it shifts the price-setting relation up, from PS to PS' in Figure 6–6. The equilibrium moves from A to A', and the natural unemployment rate decreases from u_n to u''_n.

Factors such as the generosity of unemployment benefits or antitrust legislation can hardly be thought of as the result of nature. Rather, they reflect various structural characteristics of the economy. For that reason, a better name for the equilibrium rate of unemployment would be the **structural rate of unemployment**, but so far the name has not caught on.

This name has been suggested by Edmund Phelps, in his book, *Structural Slumps*, (Cambridge: Harvard University Press, 1994).

From Unemployment to Output

Associated with the natural rate of unemployment is a **natural level of employment**, the level of employment that prevails when unemployment is equal to its natural rate.

Let U denote unemployment, N employment, and L the labor force. Then

$$u \equiv \frac{U}{L} = \frac{L - N}{L} = 1 - \frac{N}{L}$$

The first step follows from the definition of the unemployment rate (u). The second follows from the fact that, from the definition of the labor force, the level of unemployment (U) is equal to the labor force (L) minus employment (N). The third step follows from simplifying the fraction: The unemployment rate equals 1 minus the ratio of employment to the labor force.

Rearranging to get employment as a function of the labor force and the unemployment rate

$$N = L(1 - u)$$

Employment equals the labor force, times 1 minus the unemployment rate. If the natural rate of unemployment is u_n, the natural level of employment N_n is given by $N_n = L(1 - u_n)$. For example, if the labor force is 100 million and the natural rate of unemployment is 5%, then the natural level of employment is 95 million.

If u_n is the natural rate of unemployment, $N_n = L(1 - u_n)$ is the natural level of employment.

Finally, associated with the natural level of employment is a **natural level of output**, the level of production when employment is equal to the natural level of employment. Given the

Wage- and Price-Setting Relations versus Labor Supply and Labor Demand

You may have seen in your microeconomics course a representation of labor market equilibrium in terms of labor supply and labor demand. How does the representation in terms of wage setting and price setting relate to the representation of the labor market in your microeconomics course?

In an important sense, the two representations are similar.

To see why, let's redraw Figure 6–5, but in terms of the real wage and the level of employment (rather than the unemployment rate). We do so in Figure 1. Employment, N, is measured on the horizontal axis. The level of employment must be somewhere between zero and L, the labor force. Employment cannot exceed the number of people available for work, the labor force. Note that for any employment level N, unemployment is given by $U = L - N$. Knowing that, we can measure unemployment by starting from L and moving to the left on the axis: Unemployment is given by the distance between L and N. As we move from left to right, employment increases, unemployment decreases and so does the unemployment rate. We now have the elements we need to characterize the equilibrium:

● An increase in employment implies a decrease in the unemployment rate, and so an increase in the real wage implied by wage setting. Thus, the wage-setting relation is now upward sloping: Higher employment implies a higher real wage.
● The price-setting relation is still a horizontal line at $W/P = 1/(1 + \mu)$.
● The equilibrium is given by point A, with "natural" employment level N_n (and an implied natural unemployment rate equal to u_n).

Note that in Figure 1 the wage-setting relation looks like a labor-supply relation. As the level of employment in-

creases, the real wage paid to workers increases as well. For that reason, the wage-setting relation is sometimes called the "labor supply" relation (in quotes).

What we have called the price-setting relation looks like a flat labor-demand relation. The reason it is flat rather than downward sloping has to do with our simplifying assumption of constant returns to labor in production. Had we assumed, more conventionally, that there were decreasing returns to labor in production, our price-setting curve would, like the standard labor-demand curve, be downward sloping: As employment increased, the marginal cost of production would increase, forcing firms to increase their price given the wage. In other words, the real wage implied by price setting would decrease as employment increased.

But, in spirit, the two approaches are different.

The standard labor-supply relation gives the wage at which a given number of workers are willing to work: The higher the wage, the larger the number of workers who are willing to work. In contrast, the wage corresponding to a given level of employment in the wage-setting relation is the result of a complex process of bargaining between workers and firms, or unilateral wage setting by firms. Factors such as the structure of collective bargaining or the use of wages to deter quits affect the wage-setting relation; they have no place in the standard labor-supply relation.

The standard labor-demand relation gives the level of employment chosen by firms at a given real wage. It is derived under the assumption that firms operate in competitive goods and labor markets and therefore take wages and prices—and by implication the real wage—as given. The price-setting relation takes into account the fact that in most markets firms actually set prices. Factors such as the degree of competition in the goods market affect the price-setting relation by affecting the markup; these factors have no place in the standard labor-demand relation.

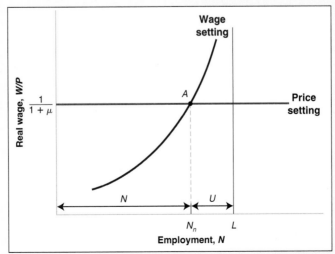

FIGURE 1   Wage and Price Setting and the Natural Level of Employment

If u_n is the natural rate of
unemployment, and if
$Y = N$, then $Y_n = N_n =$
$L(1 - u_n)$ is the natural
level of output.

production function we have been using in this chapter ($Y = N$), the relation takes the simple form $Y_n = N_n = L(1 - u_n)$.

For reference in the next chapter, note that, using equation (6.7) and the relations between the unemployment rate, employment and output we just derived, the natural level of output satisfies

$$F\left(1 - \frac{Y_n}{L}, z\right) = \frac{1}{1 + \mu} \tag{6.8}$$

The natural level of output (Y_n) is such that, at the associated rate of unemployment ($u_n = 1 - Y_n/L$), the real wage chosen in wage setting—the left side of equation (6.8)—is equal to the real wage implied by price setting—the right side of equation (6.8).

To summarize: Suppose that the expected price level is equal to the actual price level. Then, wage setting implies that the real wage is a decreasing function of the unemployment rate. The real wage implied by price setting is constant. Equilibrium in the labor market requires that the real wage chosen in wage setting be equal to the real wage implied by price setting. This condition determines the unemployment rate. This unemployment rate is known as the natural rate of unemployment. Associated with the natural rate of unemployment is a natural level of output.

6-6 | Where We Go From Here

We have just seen how equilibrium in the labor market determines the natural rate of unemployment, which then determines the natural level of output. So what have we been doing in the previous three chapters? If our primary goal was to understand the determination of output, why did we spend so much time looking at the goods and financial markets? What about our earlier conclusions that the level of output was determined by factors such as monetary policy, fiscal policy, consumer confidence, and so on—all factors that do not enter equation (6.7) and thus do not affect the natural level of output?

The key to the answers is simple, yet important.

- We have derived the natural rate of unemployment, and the associated levels of employment and output, under two assumptions. We have assumed equilibrium in the labor market. We have assumed that the price level was equal to the expected price level.

- There is no reason for the second assumption to be true in the *short run*. The price level may turn out to be different from what was expected by wage setters when nominal wages were set. Hence, in the short run, there is no reason for unemployment to be equal to the natural rate, or for output to be equal to its natural level. As we shall see in the next chapter, the factors that determine movements in output *in the short run* are the factors we focused on in the preceding three chapters: monetary policy, fiscal policy, and so on. Your time (or mine) was not wasted.

- But expectations of the price level are unlikely to be systematically wrong (say, always too high, or always too low) forever. That is why, in the medium run, unemployment tends to return to the natural rate, and output tends to return to the natural level. *In the medium run*, the factors that determine unemployment and output are the factors which appear in equations (6.7) and (6.8).

These, in short, are the answers to the questions asked in the first paragraph. Developing these answers in detail will be our task in the next three chapters.

- The labor force is composed of those who are working (employed) or looking for work (unemployed). The unemployment rate is equal to the ratio of the number of unemployed to the labor force. The participation rate is equal to the ratio of the labor force to the population of working age.

- The U.S. labor market is characterized by large flows between employment, unemployment, and out of the labor force. Each month, on average, more than one-third of the unemployed move out of unemployment, either to take a job or to drop out of the labor force.

- Many people who are not actively searching for jobs and are therefore not counted as unemployed are in fact willing to work if they find a job. This is one reason why the unemployment rate is an imperfect measure of the number of people not working but willing to work.

- There are important differences across groups of workers in terms of their average unemployment rate, and in terms of their average duration of unemployment. Unemployment rates are typically higher for the young, for the low-skilled, and for minorities.

- Unemployment is high in recessions, low in expansions. During periods of high unemployment, the probability of losing a job increases, and the probability of finding a job if unemployed decreases.

- Wages depend negatively on the unemployment rate. Wages depend positively on expected prices. The reason why wages depend on expected rather than actual prices is that wages are typically set in nominal terms for some period of time. During that time, even if prices turn out to be different from what was expected, wages are typically not readjusted.

- Prices set by firms depend on wages and on the markup of prices over wages. The higher the markup chosen by firms, the lower the real wage implied by price-setting decisions.

- Equilibrium in the labor market requires that the real wage chosen in wage setting be equal to the real wage implied by price setting. Under the additional assumption that the actual price level is equal to the expected price level, equilibrium in the labor market determines the unemployment rate. This unemployment rate is known as the *natural rate of unemployment*.

- In general, the actual price level may turn out to be different from what was expected by wage setters, and therefore the unemployment rate need not be equal to the natural rate. The coming chapters will show that, in the short run, unemployment and output are determined by the factors we focused on in the preceding three chapters, but that, in the medium run, unemployment tends to return to the natural rate, and output tends to return to its natural level.

KEY TERMS

- noninstitutional civilian population, 106
- labor force, 106
- out of the labor force, 106
- participation rate, 106
- unemployment rate, 106
- separations, 106
- hires, 106
- Current Population Survey (CPS), 106
- quits, 106
- layoffs, 106
- duration of unemployment, 107
- discouraged workers, 107
- nonemployment rate, 107
- dual labor market, 109

- primary labor market, 109
- secondary labor market, 109
- collective bargaining, 111
- reservation wage, 112
- bargaining power, 112
- efficiency wage theories, 113
- production function, 115
- labor productivity, 115
- wage-setting relation, 116
- price-setting relation, 117
- natural rate of unemployment, 117
- structural rate of unemployment, 118
- natural level of employment, 118
- natural level of output, 118

An asterisk denotes a harder question. [Web] indicates that the question requires access to the internet.

1. TRUE/FALSE/UNCERTAIN

a. Since 1950, the participation rate in the United States has remained roughly constant at 60 percent.

b. Each month, the flows in and out of employment are very small compared to the size of the labor force.

c. One-third of all unemployed workers exit the unemployment pool each year.

d. Although the job separation rates may differ across demographic groups, the unemployment rates are roughly similar.

e. The unemployment rate tends to be high in recessions, low in expansions.

f. Most workers are typically paid their reservation wage.

g. Workers who do not belong to unions have very little bargaining power.

h. It may be in the best interest of employers to pay wages higher than their workers' reservation wage.

i. The natural rate of unemployment is unaffected by policy changes.

2. LABOR-MARKET NUMBERS

Answer the following questions using the information about the United States provided in this chapter.

a. As a percentage of the employed workers, what is the size of the flows in and out of employment (that is, hires and separations) each month?

b. As a percentage of the unemployed workers, what is the size of the flows from unemployment into employment each month?

c. As a percentage of the unemployed, what is the size of the total flows out of unemployment each month? What is the average duration of unemployment?

d. As a percentage of the labor force, what is the size of the total flows in and out of the labor force each month?

e. What percentage of the flows in and out of the labor force do new workers entering the labor force and retirees leaving it make up?

3. THE LABOR MARKET AT A GLANCE [Web]

Go to the web site maintained by the U.S. Bureau of Labor Statistics at (http://stats.bls.gov). Look under the link "Economy at a glance."

a. What are the latest monthly data on the size of the U.S. civilian labor force, on the number of unemployed people, and on the unemployment rate?

b. How many people are employed?

c. Compute the change in the number of unemployed from the first available number to the most recent month in the table. Do the same for the number of employed workers. Is the decline in unemployment equal to the increase in employment? Explain in words.

*4. UNEMPLOYMENT SPELLS AND LONG-TERM UNEMPLOYMENT

According to the data presented in this chapter, one out of every three unemployed workers leaves unemployment each month.

a. What is the probability a worker will still be unemployed after one month? Three months? Six months?

b. What proportion of the unemployed has been unemployed for six months or more?

c. In Table B44 of the *Economic Report of the President*, look for the proportion of unemployed who have been unemployed 6 months or more (27 weeks or more). Does the number correspond to the answer obtained in (b)? Can you guess what the difference between the two may be due to? (*Hint*: Suppose that the probability of exiting unemployment goes down with how long you have been unemployed.)

5. RESERVATION WAGES

In the mid-1980s, a famous supermodel once said that she would not get out of bed for less than $10,000 (presumably per day).

a. What is your own reservation wage?

b. Did your first job pay more than your reservation wage at the time?

c. Relative to your reservation wage at the time you accept each job, which job pays more: your first one or the one you expect to have in ten years?

d. Explain your answers in terms of the efficiency wage theory.

6. BARGAINING POWER AND WAGE DETERMINATION

Even in the absence of collective bargaining, workers do have some bargaining power that allows them to receive a wage higher than their reservation wage. Each worker's bargaining power depends both on the nature of the job and on the economywide labor market conditions. Let's consider each factor in turn.

a. Compare the job of a delivery person and the job of a computer network administrator. In which of these jobs does a worker have more bargaining power? Why?

b. For any given job, how do labor-market conditions affect the workers' bargaining power? Which labor-market variable would you look at to assess labor-market conditions?

7. THE NATURAL RATE OF UNEMPLOYMENT

Suppose that the firms' markup over costs is 5%, and the wage-setting equation is $W = P(1 - u)$, where u is the unemployment rate.

a. What is the real wage as determined by the price-setting equation?

b. What is the natural rate of unemployment?

c. Suppose that the markup of prices over costs increases to 10%. What happens to the natural rate? Explain the logic behind your answer.

FURTHER READINGS

An in depth discussion of unemployment along the lines of this chapter is given by Richard Layard, Stephen Nickell, and Richard Jackman in *The Unemployment Crisis* (Oxford: Oxford University Press, 1994).

We invite you to visit the Blanchard page on the Prentice Hall Web site at:

http://www.prenhall.com/blanchard

for this chapter's World Wide Web exercises

CHAPTER 7

Putting All Markets Together. The AS–AD Model

We are now ready to think about the determination of output in both the short run and in the medium run. This requires taking into account equilibrium in *all* markets (goods, financial, and labor). We do so by deriving two relations:

- The aggregate supply relation captures the implications of equilibrium in the labor market; it builds on what we learned in chapter 6.
- The aggregate demand relation captures the implications of equilibrium in both the goods and financial markets; it builds on what we learned in chapter 5.

Using both relations, we can characterize the equilibrium level of output and prices over time. This is what we do in this and the next two chapters. This chapter develops a basic version of the model, called the *AS–AD* (for aggregate supply–aggregate demand) model. When confronted with macroeconomic questions, it is the model that I typically use to organize my thoughts. For some questions, however (in particular, for the study of inflation), it must be refined and extended. This is what we shall do in the next two chapters.

The **aggregate supply relation** captures the effects of output on the price level. It is derived from equilibrium in the labor market.

The Derivation of the Aggregate Supply Relation

Recall our characterization of wage and price determination in chapter 6:

$$W = P^e F(u,z)$$
$$P = (1 + \mu)W$$

- The nominal wage (W), set by wage setters, depends on the expected price level (P^e), on the unemployment rate (u), and on the catchall variable (z) that stands for all the other factors that affect wage determination, from unemployment benefits to the form of collective bargaining.
- The price level (P) set by price setters is equal to the nominal wage (W), times 1 plus the markup (μ).

Combining these two equations by replacing the wage in the second equation by its expression from the first gives

$$P = P^e(1 + \mu) F(u,z)$$

The price level is a function of the expected price level and the unemployment rate. It will be more convenient in this chapter to express the price level as a function of the level of output rather than as a function of the unemployment rate. To do this, recall from chapter 6 the relation between the unemployment rate, employment, and output

$$u \equiv \frac{U}{L} = 1 - \frac{N}{L} = 1 - \frac{Y}{L}$$

> A better name would be "the labor market equilibrium relation." But, because the relation looks graphically like a supply curve (that is, a positive relation between output and the price), it has become traditional to call it "the aggregate supply relation." I shall follow tradition.

The first step follows from the definition of the unemployment rate, the second from the definition of unemployment ($U \equiv L - N$). The last follows from our specification of the production function, which says that one unit of output requires one worker, so that $Y = N$.

Replacing u in the previous equation gives the aggregate supply relation between the price level, the expected price level, and output.

$$P = P^e(1 + \mu) F\left(1 - \frac{Y}{L}, z\right) \tag{7.1}$$

Note two things about equation (7.1):

> $P^e \uparrow \Rightarrow P \uparrow$

1. *A higher expected price level leads, one for one, to a higher actual price level.* For example, if the expected price level doubles, then the price level will also double. This effect works through wages: If wage setters expect higher prices, they set higher nominal wages. This in turn leads firms to set higher prices.

> $P^e \uparrow \Rightarrow W \uparrow$
> $W \uparrow \Rightarrow P \uparrow$

> $Y \uparrow \Rightarrow P \uparrow$

2. *An increase in output leads to an increase in the price level.* This is the result of four underlying steps:

> $Y \uparrow \Rightarrow N \uparrow$
> $N \uparrow \Rightarrow u \downarrow$

- An increase in output leads to an increase in employment.
- The increase in employment leads to a decrease in unemployment, therefore a decrease in the unemployment rate.

> $u \downarrow \Rightarrow W \uparrow$
> $W \uparrow \Rightarrow P \uparrow$

- The lower unemployment rate leads to an increase in nominal wages.
- The increase in nominal wages leads to an increase in costs, which leads firms to increase prices.

The aggregate supply relation between output and the price level is represented by the *aggregate supply curve AS* in Figure 7–1(a). This aggregate supply curve has two characteristics:

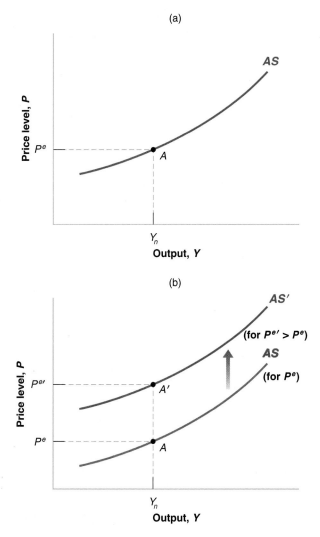

FIGURE 7–1

The Aggregate Supply Curve

(a) Given the expected price level, an increase in output leads to an increase in the price level. (b) An increase in the expected price level shifts the aggregate supply curve up.

- It is upward sloping: For a given value of the expected price level, P^e, an increase in output leads to an increase in the price level.
- It goes through point A, where $Y = Y_n$ and $P = P^e$. That is, if output is equal to its natural level Y_n, then the price level is equal to the expected price level: $P = P^e$. We know this from the definition of the natural level of output in chapter 6: We derived the natural rate of unemployment (and by implication the natural level of output) as the unemployment rate (and by implication the level of output) that prevails if the price level and the expected price level are equal.

Here is an informal way of saying the same thing: High activity puts pressure on prices.

  These characteristics have, in turn, two implications; both will be useful when we trace movements in equilibrium output later in this chapter:

- When output is above its natural level, the price level is higher than expected: $P > P^e$. Conversely: When output is below its natural level, the price level is lower than expected: $P < P^e$. This is shown in Figure 7–1(a). To the left of A, the price level is lower than was expected. To the right of A, the price level is higher than was expected.
- An increase in the expected price level shifts the aggregate supply curve up. Conversely, a decrease in the expected price level shifts the aggregate supply curve down.
    This second implication is shown in Figure 7–1(b). If the expected price level increases from P^e to $P^{e\prime}$, the aggregate supply curve shifts up: Instead of going through point A (where $Y = Y_n$ and $P = P^e$), it now goes through point A' (where $Y = Y_n$, $P = P^{e\prime}$).

To summarize: We have derived the *aggregate supply relation*, the first of the two relations we need to characterize the equilibrium. This relation is derived from equilibrium in the labor market. It says that the price level is an increasing function of the level of output, and of the expected price level. It is represented by an upward sloping curve. Changes in the expected price level shift the curve up or down.

7-2 | Aggregate Demand

The **aggregate demand relation** captures the effect of the price level on output. It is derived from equilibrium in the goods market and financial markets.

Borrowing from chapter 5, the two equations that characterize equilibrium in goods and financial markets are

(Goods market)   *IS*: $Y = C(Y - T) + I(Y,i) + G$

(Financial markets)   *LM*: $\dfrac{M}{P} = YL(i)$

Equilibrium in the goods market requires that the supply of goods equal the demand for goods—the sum of consumption, investment, and government spending. This is the *IS* relation.

Equilibrium in financial markets requires that the supply of money equal the demand for money; this is the *LM* relation. Note that what appears on the left side of the *LM* equation is the real money stock, *M/P*. We have focused so far on changes in the real money stock that came from changes in nominal money, *M*—monetary contractions or expansions implemented by the central bank. But changes in *M/P* also can come from changes in the price level. A 10% increase in the price level has the same effect on *M/P* as a 10% decrease in the stock of nominal money: Both lead to a 10% decrease in the real money stock.

Figure 7–2 derives the relation between the price level and output implied by equilibrium in the goods and the financial markets. Figure 7–2(a) draws the *IS* and *LM* curves. The *IS* curve is downward sloping: An increase in the interest rate leads to a decrease in demand and in output. The *LM* curve is upward sloping: An increase in output increases the demand for money, and the interest rate must increase so as to maintain equality of money demand and the (unchanged) money supply. The initial equilibrium is at point *A*.

While still looking at Figure 7–2(a), consider an increase in the price level from *P* to *P'*. Given the stock of nominal money, *M*, the increase in the price level decreases the real money stock, *M/P*, and the *LM* curve shifts up: At a given level of output, the lower real money stock leads to an increase in the interest rate. The equilibrium moves from *A* to *A'*; the interest rate increases from *i* to *i'*, and output decreases from *Y* to *Y'*. The increase in the price level leads to a decrease in output.

In words: As the price level increases, the demand for *nominal* money increases. Because the supply of nominal money is fixed, the interest rate must increase to induce people to decrease their demand for money, and reestablish equilibrium. The increase in the interest rate leads, in turn, to a decrease in the demand for goods and a decrease in output.

The implied negative relation between output and the price level is drawn as the downward-sloping curve *AD* in Figure 7–2(b). Points *A* and *A'* in Figure 7–2(b) correspond to points *A* and *A'* in Figure 7–2(a). An increase in the price level from *P* to *P'* leads to a decrease in output from *Y* to *Y'*. We shall call this curve the aggregate demand curve, and call the underlying negative relation between output and the price level the aggregate demand relation.

Any variable other than the price level that shifts either the *IS* curve or the *LM* curve in Figure 7–2(a) also shifts the aggregate demand curve in Figure 7–2(b). Take, for example, an increase in consumer confidence, which shifts the *IS* curve to the right and so leads to

A better name would be "the goods and financial markets equilibrium relation." But because this is a long name, and because the relation looks graphically like a demand curve (that is, a negative relation between output and the price), it has become traditional to call it the "aggregate demand relation." Be aware, however, that the aggregate supply and aggregate demand relations are very different from regular supply and demand curves.

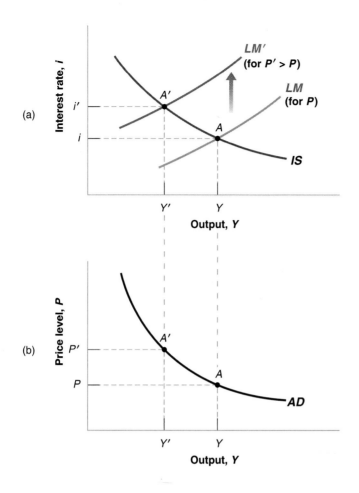

FIGURE 7–2

The Derivation of the Aggregate Demand Curve

An increase in the price level leads to a decrease in output. Any variable other than the price level that shifts either the *IS* curve or the *LM* curve in (a) also shifts the aggregate demand relation in (b).

ACTIVE GRAPH

higher output. At the same price level, output is higher: The aggregate demand curve shifts to the right. Or take a contractionary open-market operation, which shifts the *LM* curve up ◄ and decreases output. At the same price level, output is lower: The aggregate demand curve shifts to the left.

We represent the aggregate demand relation by

$$Y = Y\left(\frac{M}{P}, G, T\right) \qquad (7.2)$$
$$(+, +, -)$$

Recall that a contractionary open market operation is a decrease in nominal money, *M*, implemented through the sale of bonds by the central bank.

Output is an increasing function of the real money stock, an increasing function of government spending, and a decreasing function of taxes. Other factors, such as consumer confidence, could be introduced in this equation; I omit them for simplicity. Given monetary and fiscal policy—that is, given *M*, *G*, and *T*—an increase in the price level *P* leads to a decrease in the real money stock, *M/P*, which leads to a decrease in output. This is the relation captured by the *AD* curve in Figure 7–2(b).

To summarize: We have derived the *aggregate demand relation*, the second of the two relations we need to characterize the equilibrium. This relation is derived from equilibrium in the goods and financial markets. It says that the level of output is a decreasing function of the price level, and is represented by a downward sloping curve. Changes in monetary or fiscal policy—or more generally, in any factor that shifts the *IS* or the *LM* curves—shift the aggregate demand curve to the right or to the left.

We now put the *AS* and the *AD* relations together. From sections 7-1 and 7-2, the two relations are given by

$$AS \text{ relation} \qquad P = P^e(1 + \mu) F\left(1 - \frac{Y}{L}, z\right)$$

$$AD \text{ relation} \qquad Y = Y\left(\frac{M}{P}, G, T\right)$$

Figure 7–3 plots the two corresponding curves. The aggregate supply curve *AS*, drawn for a given value of P^e, is upward sloping. Recall from the derivation of the aggregate supply curve in section 7-1 that, when output is equal to its natural level, the price level is equal to the expected price level. This implies that the aggregate supply curve goes through point *B*—if output is equal to Y_n, the price level is equal to the expected price level P^e. The aggregate demand curve *AD* is downward sloping. Its position depends on the values of *M*, *G*, and *T*.

The equilibrium is given by the intersection of the two curves at point *A*. By construction, at point *A*, the goods, financial, and labor markets are *all* in equilibrium. The fact that the labor market is in equilibrium comes from the fact that point *A* is on the aggregate supply curve. The fact that goods and financial markets are in equilibrium comes from the fact that point *A* is also on the aggregate demand curve. The equilibrium level of output and price level are given by *Y* and *P*.

Note that there is no reason why, in general, equilibrium output *Y* should be equal to the natural level of output Y_n. Equilibrium output depends on both the position of the aggregate supply curve—thus on the value of P^e—and the position of the aggregate demand curve—thus on the values of *M*, *G*, and *T*. As I have drawn the two curves, the equilibrium is such that *Y* is larger than Y_n: The economy is operating above its natural level of output. But I could clearly have drawn the *AS* and the *AD* curves so that equilibrium output was smaller than its natural level. It all depends on the specific values of the expected price level, and the values of the variables affecting the position of aggregate demand.

> Equivalently, the unemployment rate is below the natural rate.

This gives us our first result: In the short run, there is no reason why output should equal its natural level. We can, however, go further and ask: What happens over time? More specifically, suppose that (as in Figure 7–3) output is above its natural level. Now suppose that the economy is left to itself; that is, policy and other exogenous variables remain constant. What will happen to output over time? Will it return to its natural level? If so, how? These are the questions we take up in the rest of this section.

FIGURE 7–3

Equilibrium Output and Price Level

The equilibrium is given by the intersection of the aggregate supply and the aggregate demand curves. At point *A*, the labor, goods, and financial markets are all in equilibrium.

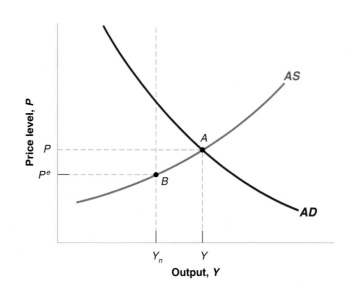

The Dynamics of Output and the Price Level

To study the movement of output over time, we must first specify how wage setters form expectations. In drawing Figure 7–3, we took the expected price level, P^e, as given. But P^e is likely to change over time: If the price level last year turned out to be different from what they expected, wage setters are likely to take this into account when forming expectations of what the price level will be this year. We shall assume in this chapter that wage setters always expect the price level this year to be equal to the price level last year. This assumption is too simple and we shall improve on it in the next two chapters. But starting with it will make it easier to understand the basic mechanisms at work.

As we now look at the evolution of output and other variables over time, the other thing we need to do is to introduce time indices. So, P_t will refer to the price level in year t, P_{t-1} to the price level in year $t - 1$, P_{t+1} to the price level in year $t + 1$, and so on.

Using this notation, the assumption that the expected price level equals the price level last year is written as

$$P_t^e = P_{t-1}$$

And the aggregate supply and demand relations must now be written as:

AS relation	$P_t = P_{t-1}(1 + \mu) F\left(1 - \dfrac{Y_t}{L}, z\right)$	(7.3)
AD relation	$Y_t = Y\left(\dfrac{M}{P_t}, G, T\right)$	(7.4)

Note that the parameters (μ, z) and the exogenous variables (L in the aggregate supply relation, M, G, and T in the aggregate demand relation) do not have a time subscript. This is because we shall assume they remain constant, so there is no need for a time subscript.

With the help of Figure 7–4, we can now look at the evolution of output over time.

1. Assume that in year t, the equilibrium is the same as the equilibrium characterized in Figure 7–3. So Figure 7–4(a), which gives the equilibrium for year t, replicates Figure 7–3; the only change is the presence of time indices. Under our assumption that the expected price level is equal to last year's price level, $P_t^e = P_{t-1}$, and the aggregate supply curve goes through point B, where output is equal to Y_n and the price level equals P_{t-1}.

Equilibrium is at point A, with output Y_t and price level P_t. Output Y_t is above its natural level Y_n. The price level P_t is higher than the expected price level P_t^e, hence higher than P_{t-1}.

2. Now turn to year $t + 1$. Equilibrium in year $t + 1$ is shown in Figure 7–4(b). The curves AS and AD repeat the AS and AD for year t from Figure 7–4(a).

To draw the aggregate supply curve for year $t + 1$, recall that *the aggregate supply curve always goes through the point where, if output is equal to its natural level, the price level is equal to the expected price level—which, under our assumptions, is itself equal to the price level the year before.* This implies, as we saw earlier, that the aggregate supply curve for year t goes through point B, where output equals Y_n and the price level is equal to P_{t-1}. Using the same logic, this implies that the aggregate supply curve for year $t + 1$ goes through point B', where output equals Y_n and the price level is equal to P_t. As P_t is higher than P_{t-1}, this implies that the aggregate supply shifts up from year t to year $t + 1$.

Make sure you understand the steps in the previous paragraph. But do not lose track of the basic intuition for why the aggregate supply curve shifts up. In year t, output is higher than its natural level, and so prices turn out to be higher than expected. This leads wage setters in year $t + 1$ to increase their price expectations, leading the aggregate supply curve to shift up.

Turn to the aggregate demand curve. Note that it does not shift: The aggregate demand curve gives the relation between output and the price level from goods and financial markets equilibrium, for given values of M, G, and T. And by assumption, M, G, and T remain constant.

FIGURE 7-4

The Dynamics of Adjustment to the Natural Level of Output

(a) Output is above its natural level. The price level is higher than expected. (b) As wage setters revise their price expectations up, the aggregate supply curve shifts up. Output declines. The price level increases. (c) The aggregate supply curve keeps shifting up, until, in the medium run, output is equal to its natural level.

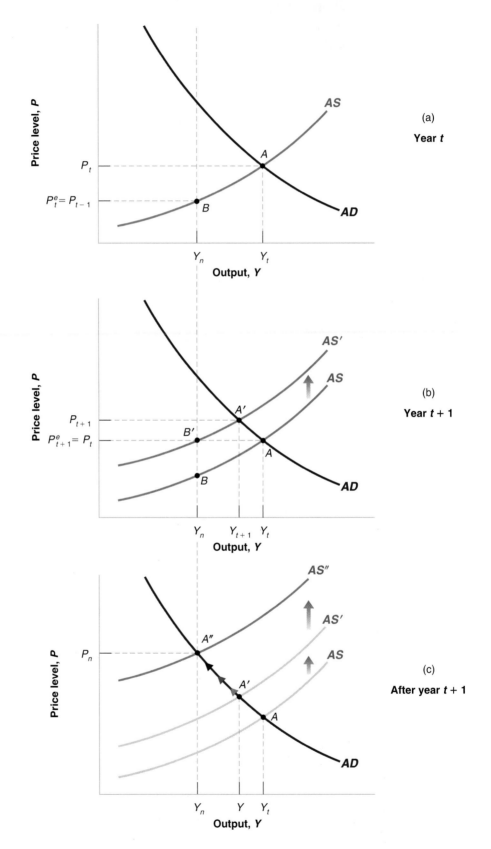

The shift in the aggregate supply curve implies that the economy moves from A in year t to A' in year $t + 1$. The price level P_{t+1} is higher than P_t. Output Y_{t+1} is lower than Y_t, thus closer to the natural level of output Y_n.

In words: Because output is above its natural level in year t, the price level in year t is higher than expected. This leads wage setters to increase their expectations of the price level in year $t + 1$, leading to a higher price level in year $t + 1$. Given nominal money, a higher price level leads to a lower real money stock in year $t + 1$. The lower real money stock leads to a higher interest rate. The higher interest rate leads to a lower demand for goods, and a lower level of output in year $t + 1$.

3. We have looked at what happens in year t and $t + 1$. What happens in the following years is now easy to describe and is shown in Figure 7–4(c). As long as output is higher than its natural level, the price level keeps increasing and the aggregate supply curve keeps shifting up. Output keeps decreasing. The economy moves up along the AD curve, until it eventually reaches point A''. At point A'', the aggregate supply curve is given by AS'' and output is equal to its natural level. There is no longer any pressure on prices to increase, and the economy settles at Y_n, with associated price level P_n.[1]

This is the basic mechanism through which the economy returns to its natural level. We shall use it in the next three sections to understand the dynamic effects of various shocks and changes in policy. But we already can draw two important lessons:

- In the *short run*, output can be above or below its natural level. Changes in any of the variables that enter either the aggregate supply or aggregate demand relation lead to changes in output and prices.
- In the *medium run*, however, output eventually returns to its natural level. The adjustment process works through prices. When output is above its natural level, prices increase. Higher prices decrease demand and output. When output is below its natural level, prices decrease, increasing demand and output.

We can now use the model to look at the dynamic effects of changes in policy or in the economic environment. We shall focus on three changes. The first two are old favorites by now: an open-market operation, which changes the stock of nominal money, and a decrease in the budget deficit. The third, which we could not examine until we had developed a theory of wage and price determination, is an increase in the price of oil. Each of these shocks is interesting in its own right. Monetary policy was responsible for the recession of 1980 to 1982. Budget deficit reduction made headlines throughout the 1990s. And increases in the price of oil were the main cause of the 1973 to 1975 recession.

7-4 | The Effects of a Monetary Expansion

What are the short- and medium-run effects of an expansionary monetary policy, say, an increase in the level of nominal money from M to M'?

The Dynamics of Adjustment

Assume that before the change in nominal money, output is at its natural level. In Figure 7–5, aggregate demand and aggregate supply cross at point A, and the level of output at A equals Y_n.

> Warning. There are many steps here: A higher expected price level leads to a higher price level. A higher price level leads to a lower real money stock. A lower real money stock leads to a higher interest rate. A higher interest rate leads to lower output. Make sure you understand each but don't worry: You will get more training in the next three sections.

> Short run $Y \neq Y_n$

> Medium run $Y \rightarrow Y_n$

> We leave the more difficult question of the effects of a change in the rate of growth of money—rather than a change in the level of money—to the next two chapters.

[1]**DIGGING DEEPER.** What if the aggregate supply curve shifts up so much from one period to the next that equilibrium output ends up below its natural level? That may happen. If so, with output below the natural level, the price level is lower than the expected price level, and the aggregate supply curve starts shifting down. In short, the return to the natural level may involve oscillations of output rather than a smooth adjustment of output to Y_n. These oscillations are not important for our purposes, and I shall not consider them further.

FIGURE 7-5

The Dynamic Effects of a Monetary Expansion

A monetary expansion leads to an increase in output in the short run, but has no effect on output in the medium run.

ACTIVE GRAPH

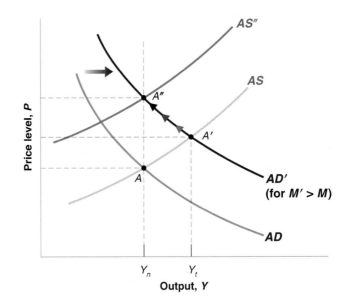

Output, Y

We think of shifts in the aggregate demand curve as shifts to the right and the left. It is because we think of the aggregate demand relation as giving output given the price level. We then ask: At a given price level, does output increase (a shift to the right) or decrease (a shift to the left)? We think of shifts in the aggregate supply curve as shifts up or down. It is because we think of the aggregate supply relation as giving the price level given output. We then ask: At a given output level, does the price level increase (a shift up) or decrease (a shift down)?

If M/P is unchanged, it must be that M and P increase in the same proportion.

Now consider an increase in nominal money. Recall the specification of aggregate demand from equation (7.4)

$$Y_t = Y\left(\frac{M}{P_t}, G, T\right)$$

For a given price level P_t, the increase in money leads to an increase in M/P_t, leading to an increase in output. The aggregate demand curve shifts to the right, from AD to AD'. The equilibrium moves from point A to A'. Output is higher, and so is the price level.

Over time, the adjustment of price expectations comes into play. Seeing higher prices, wage setters ask for higher nominal wages, which lead to higher prices. Prices keep rising. Equivalently, as long as output exceeds its natural level, the aggregate supply curve shifts up. The economy moves up along the aggregate demand curve AD'. The adjustment process stops when output has returned to its natural level. In the medium run, the aggregate supply curve is given by AS'', and the economy is at point A'': Output is back to its natural level, and the price level is higher.

We can pin down exactly the size of the eventual increase in the price level. If output is back to its natural level, the real money stock must also be back to its initial value. In other words, the proportional increase in prices must be equal to the proportional increase in the nominal money stock: If the initial increase in nominal money is equal to 10%, then the price level ends up 10% higher.

Looking Behind the Scene

It is useful to look behind the scene at what happens in terms of the underlying *IS-LM* model. This is done in Figure 7–6. Figure 7–6(a) reproduces Figure 7–5, showing the adjustment of output and the price level. Figure 7–6(b) shows the adjustment of output and the interest rate, by looking at the adjustment in terms of the *IS-LM* model.

Look at Figure 7–6(b). Before the change in money, the economy is at point A (which corresponds to point A in Figure 7–6(a)). Output is equal to its natural level, Y_n, and the interest rate is given by i. The short-run effect of the monetary expansion is to shift the *LM* curve down from *LM* to *LM'*, moving the equilibrium from A to A' (which corresponds to A' in Figure 7–6(a)). The interest rate is lower, output is higher. Note that there are two effects at work behind the shift in the *LM* curve:

● The increase in nominal money shifts the *LM* curve down to *LM''*. If the price level did not change—as was our assumption in chapter 5—the economy would move to point B.

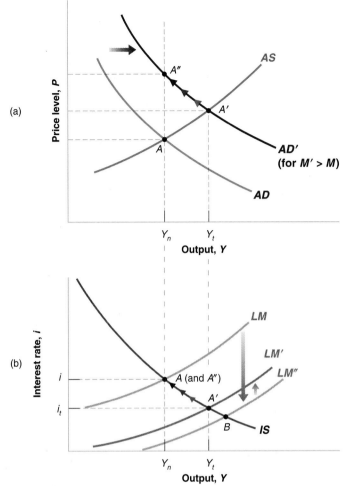

(a)

(b)

FIGURE 7-6

The Dynamic Effects of a Monetary Expansion on Output and the Interest Rate

The increase in nominal money initially shifts the *LM* curve down, decreasing the interest rate and increasing output. Over time, the price level increases, shifting the *LM* curve back up until output is back at its natural level.

- But even in the short run, the price level increases with output as the economy shifts along the aggregate supply curve. So, this increase in the price level shifts the *LM* curve upward from *LM″* to *LM′*, partially offsetting the effect of the increase in nominal money.

Over time (after the first year), the price level increases further, reducing the real money stock and shifting the *LM* back up. The economy thus moves along the *IS* curve: The interest rate increases and output declines. Eventually, the *LM* curve returns to where it was before the increase in nominal money. The economy ends up at point *A*, which corresponds to point *A″* in Figure 7–6(a). The increase in nominal money is then exactly offset by a proportional increase in the price level, which leaves the real money stock unchanged. With the real money stock unchanged, output is back to its initial value, Y_n, and the interest rate also returns to its initial value, *i*.

Why only partially? Suppose the increase in the price level fully canceled the increase in nominal money, leaving the real money stock unchanged. If the real money stock were unchanged, output would remain unchanged as well. But if output were unchanged, the price level would not increase, in contradiction with our premise.

The Neutrality of Money

Let's summarize what we have learned about the effects of monetary policy in this section:

- In the short run, a monetary expansion leads to an increase in output, a decrease in the interest rate, and an increase in the price level. How much of the initial effect falls on output and how much falls on prices depends on the slope of the aggregate supply curve. In chapter 5, we assumed that the aggregate supply curve was flat, so that the price level did not increase at all in response to an increase in output. This was a simplification, but empirical evidence shows that the initial effect of changes in output on prices is quite small. We saw this when we looked at estimated responses to changes in the federal funds rate in Figure 5–12: Despite the movement in output, the price level remained practically unchanged for nearly a year.

Actually, the way the proposition is typically stated is that money is neutral in the *long run*. This is because many economists use "long run" to refer to what I call in this book the "medium run." ▸

● Over time, prices increase, and the effects of the monetary expansion on output and the interest rate disappear. In the medium run, the increase in nominal money is reflected entirely in a proportional increase in the price level; it has no effect on output or the interest rate. (How long it takes for the effects of money on output to disappear is the topic of the In Depth box "How Long Lasting are the Real Effects of Money?") Economists refer to the absence of medium-run effects of money on output and the interest rate by saying that money is *neutral in the medium run*.

The **neutrality of money** does not imply that monetary policy cannot or should not be used: An expansionary monetary policy can, for example, help the economy move out of a recession and return faster to its natural level. But it is a warning that monetary policy cannot sustain higher output forever.

IN DEPTH

How Long Lasting are the Real Effects of Money?

How long lasting are the effects of an increase in money on output?

One way to answer is to turn to macroeconometric models. These models, which are used both to forecast activity and to look at the effects of alternative macroeconomic policies, are large-scale versions of the aggregate supply and aggregate demand model presented in the text. Figure 1 shows the effects in such a model—a model built by John Taylor of Stanford University—of a 3% permanent increase in nominal money. The increase in nominal money is assumed to take place over the four quarters of year 1: 0.1% in the first quarter, another 0.6% in the second, another 1.2% in the third, and another 1.1% in the fourth. After these four step increases, nominal money remains at its new higher level forever.

The effects of money on output reach a maximum after three quarters. By then, output is 1.8% higher than it would have been without the increase in nominal money. Over time however, prices increase and output returns to its natural level. In year 4, the price level is up by 2.5%,

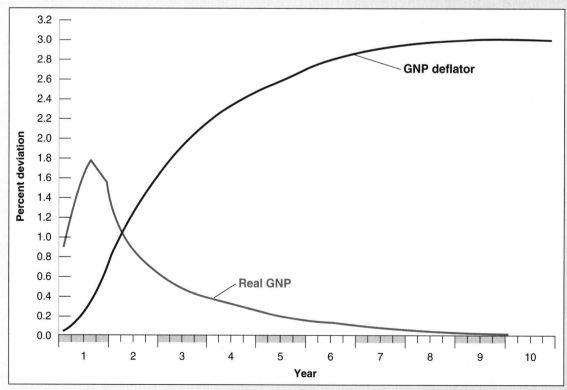

FIGURE 1   The Effects of an Expansion in Nominal Money in the Taylor Model

whereas output is up by only 0.3%. Therefore, the Taylor model suggests that it takes roughly four years for money to be neutral.

Some economists are skeptical of the results of simulations from such large models. Building such a model requires making decisions about which equations to include, which variables to include in each equation, and which ones to leave out. Some decisions are bound to be wrong. Because the models are so large, it is difficult to know how each of these decisions affects the outcome of a particular simulation. So, they argue, whenever possible, one should use simpler methods.

One such method is simply to trace out, using econometrics, the effects of a change in money on output. This method is not without its problems: A strong relation between money and output may not come from an effect of money on output, but rather from an effect of output on the conduct of monetary policy and thus on nominal money (the econometric problems raised by such two-way causation are discussed further in Appendix 3 at the end of the book). But the method can provide a useful first pass. The results of such a study by Frederic Mishkin, building on earlier work by Robert Barro, are summarized in Table 1.

Following Barro, Mishkin first separates movements in nominal money into those movements that could have been predicted based on the information available up to that time (a component he calls anticipated money) and those that could not (a component he calls unanticipated money). The motivation for this distinction should be clear from this chapter: If wage setters anticipate increases in money, they may expect the price level to be higher and ask for higher wages. Thus, to the extent that they are anticipated, changes in money may have a larger effect on prices and a smaller effect on output.

The results in Table 1 confirm that changes in money have stronger effects when they are unanticipated. Whether anticipated or unanticipated, the effects of changes in money on output peak after about two quarters. The effects are substantially larger than in the Taylor model (which looked at a 3% increase in nominal money; Table 1 looks at the effects of 1% increase). As in the Taylor model, the effects disappear after three to four years (12 to 16 quarters).

Although the results using the two approaches are not identical, they share a number of features. Money has a strong effect on output in the short run. But the effect is largely gone after four years. By then, the effect of higher nominal money is largely reflected in higher prices, not higher output.

Sources:

Figure 1 is reproduced from John Taylor, *Macroeconomic Policy in a World Economy* (New York: W.W. Norton, 1993), Figure 5–1A, p. 138.

Table 1 is taken from Frederic Mishkin, *A Rational Expectations Approach to Macroeconometrics* (Chicago: NBER and University of Chicago, 1983), Table 6.5, p. 122.

The study by Mishkin builds, in turn, on Robert Barro, "Unanticipated Money Growth in the United States," *American Economic Review*, March 1977, pp. 101–115.

TABLE 1	The effects of a 1% increase in nominal money, anticipated and unanticipated on output (percent)					
Quarters	0	2	4	6	12	16
Effects on output of:						
Anticipated money	1.3	1.9	1.8	1.3	0.7	− 0.6
Unanticipated money	2.0	2.3	2.2	2.0	0.5	− 0.4

7-5 | A Decrease in the Budget Deficit

The policy we just looked at—a monetary expansion—led to a shift in aggregate demand coming from a shift in the *LM* curve. Let's now look at the effects of a shift in the *IS* curve.

Suppose the government was running a budget deficit, and decides to eliminate it. It does so by decreasing government spending (*G*) while leaving taxes unchanged. How will this affect the economy in the short run and the medium run?

Assume that output is initially at its natural level, so that the economy is at point *A* in Figure 7–7: Output equals Y_n. The decrease in government spending shifts the aggregate demand curve to the left, from *AD* to *AD'*: At a given price level, the demand for output is lower. The economy therefore moves from *A* to *A'*, leading to lower output and lower prices. The initial effect of deficit reduction is thus to trigger a recession. We first derived this result in chapter 3, confirmed it in chapter 5, and it holds here as well.

FIGURE 7-7

The Dynamic Effects of a Decrease in the Budget Deficit

A decrease in the budget deficit leads initially to a decrease in output. Over time, output returns to its natural level.

That the price level decreases as the economy goes first from A to A' and then from A' to A'' over time feels strange: We rarely observe deflation. This result comes, however, from our assumption that there is no money growth, so that there is zero inflation in the medium run. In the real world, money growth is typically positive, and inflation is positive. Recessions generate a temporary decrease in inflation, not a decrease in the price level. We shall explore the implications of positive money growth in the next two chapters.

What happens over time? As long as output is below its natural level, the aggregate supply curve keeps shifting down. The economy moves down along the aggregate demand curve AD' until the aggregate supply curve is given by AS'' and the economy reaches point A''. By then, the initial recession is over, and output is back at Y_n.

So, just like an increase in nominal money, a reduction in the budget deficit does not affect output forever. Eventually, output returns to its natural level; unemployment returns to the natural rate. But there is an important difference between the effects of a change in money and the effects of a change in the deficit: At point A'', not everything is the same as before. Output is back to its natural level, but the price level and the interest rate are now lower than before the shift. The best way to see why is to look at the adjustment in terms of the underlying IS-LM model.

The Budget Deficit, Output, and the Interest Rate

Figure 7–8 shows the adjustment in terms of output and the interest rate. Figure 7–8(a) reproduces Figure 7–7. Figure 7–8(b) shows the adjustment in terms of the IS-LM model.

Look at Figure 7–8(b). The economy is initially at point A (which corresponds to A in Figure 7–8(a)). Output is equal to its natural level, Y_n, and the interest rate is equal to i. As the government reduces the budget deficit, the IS curve shifts to the left, to IS'. If the price level did not change, the economy would move from point A to point B. But, because prices decline in response to the decrease in output, the real money stock increases, leading to a partly offsetting shift of the LM curve downward, to LM'. The initial effect of deficit reduction is thus to move the economy from A to A'; point A' corresponds to point A' in Figure 7–8(a). Both output and the interest rate are lower than before the fiscal contraction. Note, for later use, that whether investment increases or decreases in the short run is ambiguous: Lower output decreases investment, but the lower interest rate increases it.

Over time, output below the natural level—equivalently, unemployment above the natural rate—leads to a further decrease in prices. As long as output is below its natural level, prices decrease, and the LM curve shifts down. The economy moves down from point A' along IS', and eventually reaches A'' (which corresponds to A'' in Figure 7–8(a)). At A'', the LM curve is given by LM''. Output is back at its natural level. But the interest rate is now equal to i'', lower than it was before deficit reduction. The composition of output is now different. To see how and why, let us rewrite the IS relation, taking into account that at A'', output is back at its natural level, so that $Y = Y_n$

$$Y_n = C(Y_n - T) + I(Y_n, i) + G$$

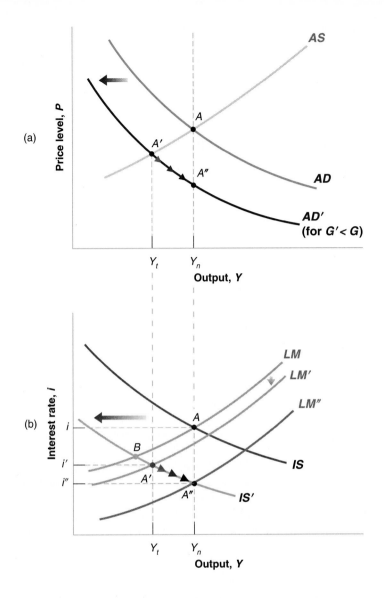

FIGURE 7-8

The Dynamic Effects of a Decrease in the Budget Deficit on Output and the Interest Rate

Deficit reduction leads in the short run to a decrease in output and in the interest rate. In the medium run, output returns to its natural level, whereas the interest rate declines further.

Because neither income nor taxes have changed, consumption is the same as before deficit reduction. By assumption, government spending, G, is lower than before; therefore investment, I, must be higher than before deficit reduction—higher by an amount exactly equal to the decrease in the budget deficit. Put another way, in the medium run, a reduction in the budget deficit unambiguously leads to a decrease in the interest rate and an increase in investment.

Budget Deficits, Output, and Investment

Let's summarize what we have learned about the effects of fiscal policy in this section:

1. In the short run, a budget deficit reduction, if implemented alone (that is, without an accompanying change in monetary policy) leads to a decrease in output, and may lead to a decrease in investment. However, note the qualification "without an accompanying change in monetary policy": In principle, these adverse short-run effects on output can be avoided by using the right monetary–fiscal policy mix. What is needed is for the central bank to decrease interest rates enough to offset the adverse effects of the decrease in government spending on demand. As we saw in chapter 5, this is what happened in the United States in the 1990s: The Fed made sure that even in the short run, deficit reduction did not lead to a recession and to a decrease in output.

2. In the medium run, output returns to its natural level, and the interest rate is lower. In the medium run, deficit reduction leads to an *increase* in investment. So far, we have not taken into account the effects of investment on capital accumulation, and the effects of capital on production (we shall do so from chapter 10 on when we look at the long run). But it is easy to see how our conclusions would be modified if we did. In the long run, a lower budget deficit leads to higher investment. Higher investment leads to a higher capital stock, which leads to higher output.

Everything we have just said about the effects of deficit reduction would apply equally to measures aimed at increasing private saving. An increase in the saving rate increases output and investment in the medium run and long run. But it may also create a recession and a decrease in investment in the short run.

Disagreements among economists about the effects of measures aimed at increasing either public saving or private saving often come from differences in time frames. Those concerned with short-run effects worry that such measures may create a recession and decrease saving and investment for some time. Those who look beyond the short run see the eventual increase in saving and investment, and emphasize the favorable medium- and long-run effects on output. We shall return to these issues again in Chapter 27.

> Effects of a deficit reduction:
>
> Short run: $Y\downarrow$ and $I\uparrow\downarrow$?
>
> Medium run:
> Y unchanged and $I\uparrow$
>
> Long run: $Y\uparrow$ and $I\uparrow$

7-6 | Changes in the Price of Oil

In the 1970s, the price of oil increased dramatically. This was the result of the formation of the Organization of Petroleum Exporting Countries (OPEC), a cartel of oil producers. Behaving as a monopolist, OPEC reduced the supply of oil and, in doing so, increased its price. Figure 7–9, which plots the ratio of the price of crude petroleum to the producer price index since 1960 (the price index is set to 100 in 1960), shows the effects of the formation of OPEC. The relative price of petroleum, which had remained roughly constant throughout the 1960s, almost tripled between 1970 and 1982. This was the result of two particularly sharp increases in the price, the first in 1973 to 1975 and the second in 1979 to 1981.

From 1982 on, however, the cartel became unable to enforce the production quotas it had set for its members. Some member countries started to produce more than their assigned quota, and the supply of oil steadily increased, leading to a large decline in the price. As Figure 7–9 shows, the breakdown of OPEC has led to a steady decline in the relative price

FIGURE 7-9

The Price of Crude Petroleum, 1960–1998

There were two sharp increases in the relative price of oil in the 1970s, followed by a decrease in the 1980s and the 1990s.

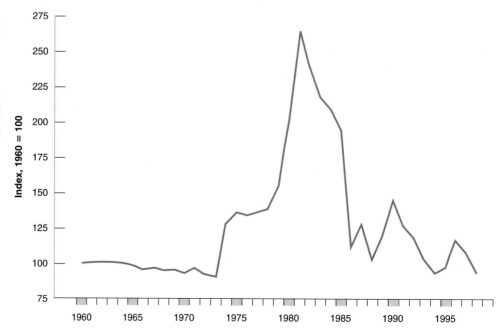

of crude petroleum. From a high of 264 in 1982, the price index stood in 1998 at 92, below its 1960 level.

In thinking about the macroeconomic effects of an increase in the price of oil, we face an obvious problem: The price of oil appears neither in our aggregate supply relation nor in our aggregate demand relation! The reason is that we have assumed thus far that output was produced using only labor. One way of proceeding would be to relax this assumption, recognize explicitly that output is produced using labor and other inputs (including energy), and derive the implications for the relation of prices to wages and the price of oil. I shall instead use a shortcut and capture the increase in the price of oil by an increase in μ, the markup of prices over wages. The justification is straightforward: Given wages, an increase in the price of oil increases the cost of production, forcing firms to increase prices.

We can then track the dynamic effects of an *increase in the markup* on output and prices. It is best here to work backward in time, to start by asking what happens in the medium run, and then working out the dynamics of adjustment.

Effects on the Natural Rate of Unemployment

Let's first ask what happens to the natural rate of unemployment as a result of the increase in the price of oil. Figure 7–10 reproduces the characterization of labor-market equilibrium from chapter 6. The wage-setting curve is downward sloping. The price-setting relation is represented by the horizontal line at $W/P = 1/(1 + \mu)$. The initial equilibrium is at point A, and the initial natural unemployment rate is u_n.

An increase in the markup leads to a downward shift of the price-setting line, from PS to PS': The higher the markup, the lower the real wage implied by price setting. The equilibrium moves from A to A'. The real wage is lower. The natural unemployment rate is higher: Getting workers to accept the lower real wage requires an increase in unemployment.

The increase in the natural rate of unemployment implies a decrease in the natural level of employment. If we assume that the relation between employment and output is unchanged—that is, that each unit of output still requires one worker, in addition to the energy input—then the decrease in the natural level of employment leads to an identical decrease in the natural level of output. In short, an increase in the price of oil leads to a decrease in the natural level of output.

The Dynamics of Adjustment

Let's now turn to dynamics. Suppose that before the increase in the price of oil, the economy is at point A in Figure 7–11, with output at its natural level, Y_n, and a constant price level (so that $P_t = P_{t-1}$). We have just established that the increase in the price of oil decreases

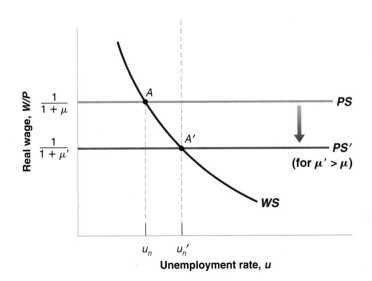

FIGURE 7–10

The Effects of an Increase in the Price of Oil on the Natural Rate of Unemployment

An increase in the price of oil leads to a lower real wage and a higher natural rate of unemployment.

ACTIVE GRAPH

FIGURE 7-11

The Dynamic Effects of an Increase in the Price of Oil

An increase in the price of oil leads, in the short run, to a decrease in output and an increase in the price level. Over time, output decreases further and the price level increases further.

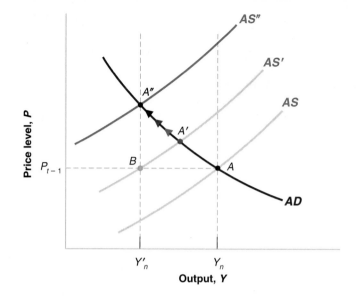

the natural level of output from Y_n to, say, Y'_n. We now want to know what happens in the short run and how the economy moves from Y_n to Y'_n.

Recall that the aggregate supply relation is given by

$$P_t = P_{t-1}(1 + \mu) F\left(1 - \frac{Y_t}{L}, z\right)$$

An increase in the markup leads to an increase in the price level (P_t) at a given level of output (Y_t). Thus, in the short run, the aggregate supply curve shifts up.

We can be more specific about the size of the shift, and this will be useful in what follows. We know from section 7-1 that the aggregate supply curve always goes through the point such that output equals its natural level and the price level equals the price level expected by wage setters. Before the increase in the price of oil, the aggregate supply curve goes through point A, where output equals Y_n and the price level is equal to P_{t-1} (as we are assuming that expectations of the price level are such that $P_t^e = P_{t-1}$). After the increase in the price of oil, the new aggregate supply curve goes through point B, where output equals the new lower natural level Y'_n and the price level equals the expected price level, P_{t-1}. Thus, the aggregate supply curve shifts from AS to AS'.

Does the aggregate demand curve shift as a result of the increase in the price of oil? There are many channels through which demand might be affected at a given price level. The higher price of oil may lead firms to change their investment plans, canceling some investment projects and/or shifting to less energy-intensive equipment. The increase in the price of oil also redistributes income from oil buyers to oil producers. Oil producers may have a higher propensity to save than oil buyers. Let's take the easy way here: Because some of the effects shift the aggregate demand curve to the right and others shift the aggregate demand curve to the left, let's assume simply that the effects cancel each other out and that aggregate demand does not shift.

In the short run, therefore, the economy moves from A to A'. The increase in the price of oil leads firms to increase prices; the increase in prices decreases demand and output. Note the different effects of adverse demand and supply shocks: Adverse demand shocks (for example, the reduction in the budget deficit we looked at in section 7-5) lead to lower output and lower prices. Adverse supply shocks (in this case, an increase in the price of oil) lead to lower output and *higher* prices.

What happens over time? Although output has decreased, the natural level of output has decreased even more: At point A', the economy is still above the new natural level of output Y'_n. This leads to a further increase in prices. The economy therefore moves over time from

This was the case in the 1970s. The OPEC countries realized that high oil revenues might not last forever. So most of them saved a large proportion of their income.

A' to *A"*. At point *A"* output is equal to its new natural level, and prices are higher than before the oil shock. Shifts in aggregate supply affect output not only in the short run but in the medium run as well.

How does our story compare to what actually happened after the first oil shock? Table 7–1 gives the basic macroeconomic facts.

From 1973 to 1975, the cumulative increase in petroleum prices (in dollars) was 77.3%. The results were very much what our model predicts: a combination of a recession and large

Why Has Japan Done So Poorly in the 1990s?

As we saw in chapter 1, Japan's growth rate, which had averaged close to 6.0% per year since 1960, has averaged only 1.0% since 1992. (Table 1 gives the values of the main macroeconomic variables for Japan since 1992.)

Why has growth been so low for nearly a decade? Most economists point to two causes:

- The first is the collapse of the Japanese stock market in the early 1990s. From 1990 to 1992, Japanese stock prices decreased by half (see chapter 1). The prices of land and real estate followed. By 1997, commercial land prices were at only 55% of their 1990 value.
- The second is the effect that the collapse in stock and land prices had on Japanese banks. Many of these banks had made loans to buyers of stocks or real estate. When stock and real estate prices collapsed, many of these borrowers could not repay their loans. In 1997, it was estimated that bad loans on the balance sheets of the largest 20 banks in Japan added up to 4% of Japan's GDP. With so many bad loans on their books, banks had to cut back drastically on any new lending to firms.

How these two factors combined to create low growth is more controversial and still the subject of research.

Most economists have focused on the effects of the decrease in stock and real estate prices, and the decrease in lending by banks on *aggregate demand*. A sharp fall has decreased the wealth of consumers and led them to cut spending. For many firms, a decrease in bank lending has meant being unable to finance investment. The result has been an adverse shift in aggregate demand, leading to low growth and low inflation—inflation was indeed negative (equivalently, prices declined) in 1995 and 1996. This diagnosis has led these economists to recommend both expansionary monetary policy and expansionary fiscal policy, and this is indeed what is happening. As you can see from Table 1, the Japanese central bank has cut the interest rate from 4.5% in 1992 to 0.7% in 1998. And the government has gone from running a budget surplus of 1.5% in 1992 to running a budget deficit of 6.1% in 1998.

Other economists believe that this is only part of the story. They point out that, despite very low interest rates and a large budget deficit, output has actually gone down in 1998. They think of the problems of the banking system as an adverse shift in aggregate supply. A banking system in bad shape is very much like an increase in the price of oil, or a decrease in productivity: It increases the cost of doing business, increases the cost of production, and decreases equilibrium output. These economists argue that Japan's problems cannot be solved only by increasing aggregate demand. The banking system must be repaired: Some banks must be closed; for the others, bad loans should be replaced in the balance sheet of banks by good assets, such as government bonds. Once this is done, the banking system can function again, and the Japanese economy can recover. The Japanese government has started to implement such a plan; it has committed to spend up to 6% of GDP to improve the health of the financial sector.

TABLE 1 — Japanese macroeconomic variables, 1992–1998

	1992	1993	1994	1995	1996	1997	1998
Output growth (%)	1.0	0.3	0.6	1.5	3.9	0.8	− 2.6
Inflation* (%)	1.7	0.6	0.2	− 0.6	− 0.5	0.6	0.7
Budget surplus (% of GDP)	1.5	− 1.6	− 2.3	− 3.6	− 4.3	− 3.3	− 6.1
Short-term interest rate	4.5	3.0	2.2	1.2	0.6	0.6	0.7

*Inflation: Rate of change of the GDP deflator.
Source: OECD Economic Outlook December 1998.

TABLE 7-1 The Effects of the Increase in the Price of Oil, 1973–1975

	1973	1974	1975
Rate of change of petroleum price (%)	10.4	51.8	15.1
Rate of change of GDP deflator (%)	5.6	9.0	9.4
Rate of GDP growth (%)	5.8	−0.6	−0.4
Unemployment rate (%)	4.9	5.6	8.5

Source: Economic Report of the President, 1997.

increases in prices. In 1974 and 1975, GDP growth was negative. In both 1974 and 1975, inflation (as measured by the rate of change of the GDP deflator) was higher than the year before. At the time, this combination of negative growth and high inflation—which was baptized **stagflation** to capture the combination of *stag*nation and in*flation*—came as a surprise to economists. It was the trigger for a large amount of research on the effects of supply shocks for the rest of the decade. By the time of the second oil shock in the late 1970s, macroeconomists were better equipped to understand it.

In the late 1990s, the price of oil has decreased further. One question is whether this decrease is one of the reasons the U.S. expansion has gone on far longer than was forecast.

Many questions still remain, however. One of the most intriguing is whether the effects of changes in oil prices are symmetric, that is, whether increases and decreases have symmetrical effects on output. The motivation for the question is the fact that the favorable effects on output of the large decrease in oil prices since 1982 appear to have been weaker than the negative effects of the increases in oil prices of the 1970s.

See the related box "Could the Great Depression Happen Again? Japan at the Crossroads" in chapter 22.

We have focused in this section on the effects of an increase in the price of oil. But, like shifts in aggregate demand, shifts in aggregate supply can come in many forms. Anything that affects labor productivity or leads to changes in the markup of prices over wages can potentially act as an aggregate supply shift. For example, one can think of the problems of Japan in the 1990s as being due in part to the problems of its banking sector, problems that have led to adverse shifts both in aggregate supply and in aggregate demand. This is explored at more length in the Global Macro box "Why Has Japan Done So Poorly in the 1990s?" on page 143.

7-7 | Conclusions

This has been an important chapter. Let me repeat and develop some of the conclusions.

The Short Run versus the Medium Run

One message of this chapter is that changes in policy or, more generally, changes in the economic environment (from changes in consumer confidence to changes in the price of oil) typically have different short-run and medium-run effects. We looked at the effects of a monetary expansion, of a deficit reduction, and of an increase in the price of oil. The main results are summarized in Table 7–2. A monetary expansion, for example, affects output in the short run but not in the medium run. In the short run, a decrease in the budget deficit decreases output and the interest rate, and may therefore decrease investment. But in the medium run, the interest rate decreases, output returns to the natural rate, and investment increases. An increase in the price of oil decreases output not only in the short run but also in the medium run. And so on.

This difference between the short- and medium-run effects of policies is one of the main reasons economists disagree in their policy recommendations. Some economists believe that the economy adjusts quickly to its medium-run equilibrium, and so they emphasize medium-run implications of policy. Others believe that the adjustment mechanism through which out-

	Short Run			Medium Run		
	Output Level	Interest Rate	Price Level	Output Level	Interest Rate	Price Level
Monetary expansion	increase	decrease	increase (small)	no change	no change	increase
Deficit reduction	decrease	decrease	decrease (small)	no change	decrease	decrease
Increase in oil price	decrease	increase	increase	decrease	increase	increase

put returns to its natural level is a slow one at best, so they put more emphasis on the short-run effects of policy. They are more willing to use active monetary policy or budget deficits to get out of a recession, even if money is neutral in the medium run, and budget deficits have adverse implications in the long run.

Shocks and Propagation Mechanisms

This chapter also gives you a general way of thinking about **output fluctuations** (sometimes called **business cycles**)—movements in output around its trend (a trend that we have ignored so far, but on which we shall focus in chapters 10 to 13):

The economy is constantly buffeted by **shocks** to aggregate supply, or to aggregate demand, or to both. These shocks may be shifts in consumption coming from changes in consumer confidence, shifts in investment, shifts in portfolio behavior, shifts in labor productivity, and so on. Or they may come from changes in policy—from the introduction of a new tax law, to a new program of infrastructure investment, to the decision by the central bank to fight inflation through tight money.

Each shock has dynamic effects on output and its components. These dynamic effects are called the **propagation mechanism** of the shock. Propagation mechanisms are different for different shocks. The effects on activity may be largest at the beginning and then they may decrease over time. Or the effects may build up for a while, and then decrease and eventually disappear. We saw, for example, that the effects of an increase in money on output peak after six to nine months and then slowly decline afterward, as prices eventually increase in proportion to the increase in money. Some shocks have effects even in the long run. This is the case for any shock that has a permanent effect on aggregate supply, such as a permanent change in the price of oil.

Fluctuations in output come from the constant appearance of new shocks, each with its own propagation mechanism. At times, some shocks are sufficiently bad, or come in sufficiently bad combinations, that they create a recession. The two recessions of the 1970s were due largely to increases in the price of oil; the recession of the early 1980s was due to a sharp change in monetary policy; the recession of the early 1990s was due primarily to a sudden decline in consumer confidence. What we call economic fluctuations are the result of these shocks and their dynamic effects on output.

Output, Unemployment, and Inflation

In developing the model of this chapter, we made the assumption that the nominal money stock was constant. That is, although we considered the effects of a one-time change in the level of nominal money (in section 7-4), we did not allow for sustained nominal money growth. One implication of that assumption was that the price level was constant in the medium run, that there was no inflation. We must now relax this assumption and allow for

We shall return to these issues many times in the book. See in particular chapter 22, which focuses on periods of sustained high unemployment, such as the Great Depression, and chapters 25 to 27, which look at macroeconomic policy in more detail.

How to define *shocks* is harder than it appears. Suppose a failed economic program in a foreign country leads to the fall of democracy in that country, which leads to an increase in the risk of nuclear war, which leads to a fall in domestic consumer confidence in our country, which leads to a drop in consumption. What is the "shock"? The failed program? The fall of democracy? The increased risk of nuclear war? Or the decrease in consumer confidence? In practice, we have to cut the chain of causation somewhere. Thus, we may refer to the drop in consumer confidence as "the shock," ignoring its underlying causes.

nominal money growth. Only by doing so can we explain why inflation is typically positive, and think about the relation between economic activity and inflation. Movements in unemployment, output, and inflation are the topics of the next two chapters.

SUMMARY

- The model of aggregate supply and aggregate demand describes the movements in output and prices when account is taken of equilibrium in the goods, financial, and labor markets.

- The aggregate supply relation captures the effects of output on the price level. It is derived from equilibrium in the labor market. It is a relation between the price level, the expected price level, and the level of output. An increase in output decreases unemployment, increasing wages and, in turn, increasing the price level. A higher expected price level leads, one for one, to a higher increase in the actual price level.

- The aggregate demand relation captures the effects of the price level on output. It is derived from equilibrium in the goods and financial markets. An increase in the price level decreases the real money stock, increasing interest rates and decreasing output.

- In the short run, movements in output come from shifts in either aggregate demand or aggregate supply. In the medium run, output returns to its natural level, which is determined by equilibrium in the labor market.

- An expansionary monetary policy leads in the short run to an increase in the real money stock, a decrease in the interest rate, and an increase in output. Over time, the price level increases, leading to a decrease in the real money stock until output has returned to its natural level. In the medium run, money is neutral: It does not affect output, and changes in money are reflected in proportional increases in the price level.

- A decrease in the budget deficit leads in the short run to a decrease in the demand for goods and thus a decrease in output. Over time, the price level decreases, leading to an increase in the real money stock and a decrease in the interest rate. In the medium run, output is back to its natural level, but the interest rate is lower and investment is higher.

- An increase in the price of oil leads, in both the short and the medium run, to a decrease in output. In the short run, it leads to an increase in prices, which decreases the real money stock and leads to a contraction of demand and output. In the medium run, it decreases the real wage paid by firms, increases the natural rate of unemployment, and in turn decreases the natural level of output.

- The difference between short- and medium-run effects of policies is one of the main reasons why economists disagree in their policy recommendations. Some economists believe that the economy adjusts quickly to its medium-run equilibrium, and thus emphasize medium-run implications of policy. Others believe that the adjustment mechanism through which output returns to its natural level is a slow one at best, and put more emphasis on short-run effects.

- Economic fluctuations are the result of a constant stream of shocks to aggregate supply or to aggregate demand, and of the dynamic effects of each of these shocks on output. Sometimes the shocks are sufficiently adverse, alone or in combination, that they lead to a recession.

KEY TERMS

- aggregate supply relation, 126
- aggregate demand relation, 128
- neutrality of money, 136
- anticipated money, 137
- unanticipated money, 137

- stagflation, 144
- output fluctuations, 145
- business cycles, 145
- shocks, 145
- propagation mechanism, 145

An asterisk denotes a harder question.

1. TRUE/FALSE/UNCERTAIN

a. The aggregate supply relation implies that an increase in output leads to an increase in the price level.

b. The natural level of output can be determined by looking only at the aggregate supply relation.

c. The aggregate demand relation implies that an increase in the price level leads to an increase in output.

d. In the absence of changes in fiscal and/or monetary policy, the economy will always remain at the natural level of output.

e. Expansionary monetary policy has no effect on the level of output in the medium run.

f. Fiscal policy cannot affect investment in the medium run, because output always returns to its natural level.

g. In the medium run, prices and output always return to the same value.

2. SPENDING SHOCKS AND THE MEDIUM RUN

Using the *AS–AD* model developed in this chapter, show the effects of each of the following shocks on the position of the *IS, LM, AD,* and *AS* curves in the medium run. Then show the effect on output, the interest rate, and the price level, also in the medium run. Assume that before the changes, the economy was at the natural level of output.

a. An increase in consumer confidence

b. An increase in taxes

3. SUPPLY SHOCKS AND THE MEDIUM RUN

Using the *AS–AD* model developed in this chapter, show the effects of each of the following shocks on the position of the *WS, PS, IS, LM, AD,* and *AS* curves in the medium run. Then state the effects on output, the interest rate, and the price level, also in the the medium run. Assume that before the changes, the economy was at the natural level of output.

a. An increase in unemployment benefits

b. A decrease in the price of oil

4. THE NEUTRALITY OF MONEY

a. In what sense is money neutral? Why is monetary policy useful even though money is neutral?

b. Fiscal policy, just like monetary policy, cannot change the natural level of output. Why then is monetary policy considered neutral but fiscal policy is not?

c. Discuss this statement: "Because neither fiscal nor monetary policy can affect the natural level of output, it follows that in the medium run the natural level of output is independent of all government policies."

*5. WHAT IF THE INTEREST RATE HAD NO EFFECT ON INVESTMENT?

Suppose that investment is not responsive to the interest rate.

a. Can you think of a situation where that may happen?

b. What does this imply for the *IS* curve?

c. What does this imply for the *LM* curve?

d. What does this imply for the *AD* curve?

Now suppose that the economy starts at the natural level of output and that due to a shock to the catchall variable *z*, the *AS* curve shifts up.

e. What is the short-run effect on prices and output?

f. What happens to output and prices over time? Explain in words.

6. INVESTMENT AND MONETARY POLICY

Consider the following model of the economy (we ignore the role of *G* and *T* on demand; also, to simplify the algebra, we assume that output depends on the difference between *M* and *P* rather than on their ratio):

$$AD: \quad Y = c(M - P)$$
$$AS: \quad P = P^e + d(Y - Y_n)$$

Where *c* and *d* are parameters

a. What is the natural level of output? If nominal money is equal to M_0, what is the initial price level? Call this initial price level P_0.

Suppose that in an effort to increase investment, the Fed decides to pursue an expansionary monetary policy, and doubles the nominal money stock: $M_1 = 2M_0$.

b. Solve for the equilibrium value of output in the short run.

c. What happens to investment behind the scene? Explain in words.

d. Solve for the equilibrium value of output in the medium run.

e. What happens to investment in the medium run? Explain in words.

CHAPTER | 8

The Phillips Curve

In 1958, A. W. Phillips drew a diagram plotting the rate of inflation against the rate of unemployment in the United Kingdom for each year from 1861 to 1957. He found clear evidence of a negative relation between inflation and unemployment: When unemployment was low, inflation was high, and when unemployment was high, inflation was low, often even negative.

Two years later, Paul Samuelson and Robert Solow replicated Phillips' exercise for the United States, using data from 1900 to 1960. Figure 8–1 shows their findings. (Figure 8–1 uses the rate of change of the CPI as the measure of the inflation rate. Samuelson and Solow used the rate of change of nominal wages, as did Phillips.) Apart from the period of very high unemployment during the 1930s (the years from 1931 to 1939 are denoted by black triangles and are clearly to the right of the other points in the figure), there appeared to be a negative relation between inflation and unemployment in the United States also.

This relation, which Samuelson and Solow baptized the **Phillips curve**, rapidly became central to macroeconomic thinking and policy. It appeared to imply that leaving aside such episodes as the Great Depression, countries could choose between different combinations of unemployment and inflation. They could achieve low unemployment if they were willing to tolerate higher inflation, or they could achieve price level stability—zero inflation—if they were willing to tolerate higher unemployment. Much of the discussion about macroeconomic policy became a discussion about which point to choose on the Phillips curve.

In the 1970s, however, the relation broke down. In both the United States and most OECD countries, there was both high inflation *and* high unemployment, clearly contradicting the original Phillips curve. A relation reappeared, but it was now a relation between the unemployment rate and the *change* in the inflation rate. Today in the United States, high unemployment leads not to low inflation, but instead to a decrease in inflation.

The purpose of this chapter is to explore the mutations of the Phillips curve and, more generally, to understand the relation between inflation and unemployment. We shall see that what Phillips discovered was the aggregate supply relation, and that the mutations of the Phillips curve came from changes in the way people and firms formed expectations.

FIGURE 8-1

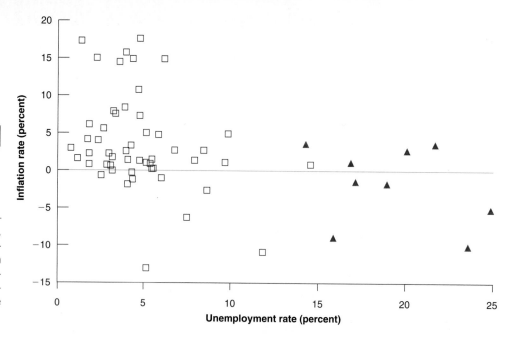

Inflation and Unemployment in the United States, 1900–1960

During the period 1900–1960 in the United States, low unemployment was typically associated with high inflation, and high unemployment was typically associated with low or negative inflation.

I shall from now on refer to the inflation rate as "inflation," and to the unemployment rate as "unemployment."

After deriving this relation ▷ in chapter 7, we replaced the unemployment rate by its expression in terms of output to obtain a relation between the price level, the expected price level, and output. It will be more convenient in this chapter to stay with the relation in terms of unemployment rather than output.

$P^e \uparrow \Rightarrow P \uparrow; u \uparrow \Rightarrow P \downarrow$ ▷

$\pi^e \uparrow \Rightarrow \pi \uparrow; u \uparrow \Rightarrow \pi \downarrow$ ▷

8-1 | Inflation, Expected Inflation, and Unemployment

Our first step will be to show that the aggregate supply relation we derived in chapter 7 can ▷ be rewritten as a relation between *inflation* and *unemployment*, given *expected inflation*.

To do this, go back to the relation between the *price level*, the *expected price level*, and ▷ the *unemployment rate* we derived in chapter 7:

$$P_t = P_t^e(1 + \mu)F(u_t, z)$$

Recall that the function F captures the effects on the wage of the unemployment rate, u_t, and of the other factors that affect wage setting, represented by the catchall variable z. It will be convenient here to assume a specific form for the function F:

$$F(u_t, z) = 1 - \alpha u_t + z$$

This captures the notion that the higher the unemployment rate, the lower the wage, and the higher z, the higher the wage. The parameter α (the Greek lowercase letter alpha) captures the strength of the effect of unemployment on wages: the larger α, the stronger the (negative) effect of unemployment on wages.

Replacing in the earlier equation gives

$$P_t = P_t^e(1 + \mu)(1 - \alpha u_t + z)$$

With a few manipulations, this relation can be rewritten as a relation between the *inflation rate*, the *expected inflation rate*, and the *unemployment rate*

$$\pi_t = \pi_t^e + (\mu + z) - \alpha u_t \tag{8.1}$$

where π_t denotes the inflation rate, defined as the rate of change of prices from last year to this year, and π_t^e denotes the corresponding expected inflation rate—the rate of change of prices from last year to this year, expected by wage setters as of last year.

In short, equation (8.1) tells us that *inflation depends positively on expected inflation and negatively on unemployment.*

- *Higher expected inflation leads to higher inflation.* We saw in chapter 7 how higher expected prices lead to higher nominal wages, which lead to higher prices. But note that, given last year's prices, higher prices this year imply higher inflation this year; similarly, higher expected prices imply higher expected inflation. So, higher expected inflation leads to higher actual inflation.
- *Given expected inflation, the higher the markup chosen by firms, μ, or the higher the factors that affect wage determination, z, the higher inflation.* We saw in chapter 7 how a higher markup leads to higher prices given expected prices. We can restate this proposition as follows: A higher markup leads to higher inflation given expected inflation. The same argument applies to increases in any of the factors that affect wage determination.
- *Given expected inflation, the higher unemployment, the lower inflation.* We saw in chapter 7 that given expected prices, a higher unemployment rate leads to lower prices. We can restate this proposition as follows: Given expected inflation, a higher unemployment rate leads to lower actual inflation.

With this reformulation of the aggregate supply relation, we can now return to the tribulations of the Phillips curve.

Going from the relation between the expected price level and the price level to a relation between inflation and expected inflation.

Start with:
$$P_t^e \uparrow \Rightarrow P_t \uparrow$$
Subtract P_{t-1} from both sides, and divide both sides by P_{t-1}:
$$(P_t^e - P_{t-1})/P_{t-1} \uparrow \Rightarrow$$
$$(P_t - P_{t-1})/P_{t-1}$$
Recall the definitions of expected inflation ($\pi_t^e = (P_t^e - P_{t-1})/P_{t-1}$) and actual inflation ($\pi_t = (P_t - P_{t-1})/P_{t-1}$), and replace:
$$\pi_t^e \uparrow \Rightarrow \pi_t \uparrow$$

8-2 | The Phillips Curve

Let's start with the relation between unemployment and inflation as it was first discovered by Phillips, Solow, and Samuelson, circa 1960.

The Early Incarnation

Think of an economy where inflation is positive in some years, negative in others, and on average equals zero. This is clearly not the way things are in the United States today: The last year during which inflation was negative—the last year during which there was **deflation**—was 1955, when inflation was −0.3%. But as we shall see later in this chapter, average inflation *was* close to zero during much of the period that Phillips, Samuelson, and Solow were examining.

Think of wage setters choosing nominal wages for the coming year and thus having to forecast what inflation will be over the year. With the average inflation rate equal to zero in the past, it is reasonable for them to expect that inflation will be equal to zero over the next year as well. Assuming that $\pi_t^e = 0$ in equation (8.1) gives the following relation between unemployment and inflation

$$\pi_t = (\mu + z) - \alpha u_t \qquad (8.2)$$

This is precisely the negative relation between unemployment and inflation that Phillips, Solow, and Samuelson found for the United Kingdom and for the United States. The story behind it is simple: Given expected prices, which workers simply take to be last year's prices, lower unemployment leads to higher nominal wages. Higher nominal wages lead to higher prices. Putting the steps together, lower unemployment leads to higher prices this year compared to last year's prices—that is, to higher inflation.

This mechanism has sometimes been called the **wage-price spiral**, and this phrase captures well the basic mechanism at work:

- Low unemployment leads to higher nominal wages.
- In response to higher wages, firms increase their prices.
- In response to higher prices, workers ask for higher nominal wages.
- Firms further increase prices, so workers ask for further increases in wages.
- And so on, with the result being steady wage and price inflation.

Mutations

The combination of an apparently reliable empirical relation, together with a plausible story to explain it, led to the adoption of the Phillips curve by macroeconomists and policy makers alike. U.S. macroeconomic policy in the 1960s was aimed at maintaining unemployment in the range that appeared consistent with moderate inflation. And, throughout the 1960s, the negative relation between unemployment and inflation provided a reliable guide to the joint movements in unemployment and inflation. Figure 8–2 plots the combinations of inflation and unemployment in the United States for each year from 1948 to 1969. Note how well the relation held during the long expansion of the 1960s. During the years 1961 to 1969, denoted by green diamonds in the figure, the unemployment rate declined steadily from 6.8% to 3.4%; the inflation rate steadily increased, from 1.0% to 5.5%.

From 1970 on, however, the relation broke down. Figure 8–3 gives the combination of inflation and unemployment in the United States for each year since 1970. The points are scattered in a roughly symmetric cloud: There is no relation between the unemployment rate and the inflation rate.

Why did the original Phillips curve vanish? There are two main reasons:

- As we saw in chapter 7, the United States was hit twice in the 1970s by a large increase in the price of oil. The effect of this increase in nonlabor costs was to force firms to increase their prices given wages, to increase μ. As shown in equation (8.1), an increase in μ leads to an increase in inflation, even at a given rate of unemployment, and this indeed happened twice in the 1970s. But the main reason for the breakdown of the Phillips curve relation was elsewhere:

- Wage setters changed the way they formed expectations. This change came from a change in the process of inflation itself. Look at Figure 8–4, which plots the U.S. inflation rate for each year since 1900. Starting around 1960 (indicated by the vertical bar in the figure), there was a clear change in the way the rate of inflation moved over time. First, rather than being sometimes positive, sometimes negative, as it had for the first part of the century, the rate of inflation became consistently positive. Second, inflation became more persistent. High inflation in one year became more likely to be followed by high inflation the next year.

The persistence of inflation led workers and firms to revise the way they formed their expectations. When inflation is consistently positive, expecting that prices this year will

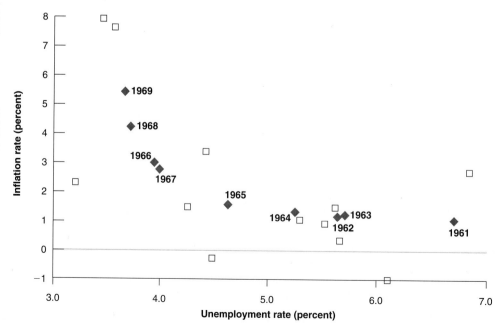

FIGURE 8–2

Inflation and Unemployment in the United States, 1948–1969

The steady decline in U.S. unemployment throughout the 1960s was associated with a steady increase in inflation.

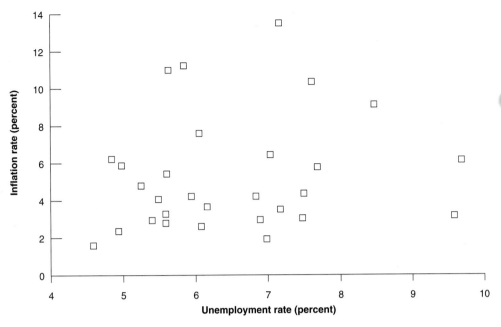

FIGURE 8-3

Inflation and Unemployment in the United States, 1970–1998

Beginning in 1970, the relation between the unemployment rate and the inflation rate disappeared in the United States.

be the same as last year becomes systematically incorrect; indeed, it becomes foolish. People do not like to make the same mistake repeatedly. So, as inflation became consistently positive and more persistent, expectations started to take into account the presence of inflation. This change in expectation formation changed the nature of the relation between unemployment and inflation.

To understand what happened, suppose expectations are formed according to

$$\pi_t^e = \theta\pi_{t-1} \tag{8.3}$$

The value of the parameter θ (the Greek lowercase letter theta) captures the effect of last year's inflation rate on this year's expected inflation rate. The higher the value of θ, the more

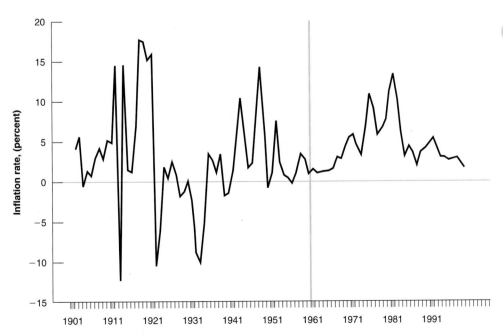

FIGURE 8-4

U.S. Inflation, 1900–1998

Since the 1960s, U.S. inflation has been consistently positive. Inflation has also become more persistent: High inflation this year is more likely to be followed by high inflation next year.

last year's inflation leads workers and firms to revise their expectations of what inflation will be this year and so the higher expected inflation.

We can then think of what happened from 1970 on as an increase in the value of θ over time. As long as inflation was low and not very persistent, it was reasonable for workers and firms to ignore past inflation and to assume that this year's price level would be roughly the same as last year's. For the period that Samuelson and Solow had looked at, θ was close to zero, expectations were roughly given by $\pi_t^e = 0$, and the relation between the inflation and unemployment rates was given by equation (8.2).

But, as inflation became more persistent, workers and firms started changing the way they formed expectations. They started assuming that if inflation had been high last year, inflation was likely to be high this year as well. The parameter θ, the effect of last year's inflation rate on this year's expected inflation rate, steadily increased. By the 1970s, the evidence is that people formed expectations by expecting this year's inflation rate to be the same as last year's—in other words, that θ was now equal to 1.

To see the implications of different values of θ for the relation between inflation and unemployment, replace equation (8.3) in equation (8.1). Doing so gives

$$\pi_t = \overbrace{\theta \pi_{t-1}}^{\pi_t^e} + (\mu + z) - \alpha u_t$$

- When θ equals zero, we get the original Phillips curve, a relation between the inflation rate and the unemployment rate.
- When θ is positive, the inflation rate depends not only on the unemployment rate but also on last year's inflation rate.
- When θ equals 1, the relation becomes (moving last year's inflation rate to the left side of the equation)

$$\pi_t - \pi_{t-1} = (\mu + z) - \alpha u_t \tag{8.4}$$

So, when $\theta = 1$, the unemployment rate affects not the inflation rate, but rather the *change* in the inflation rate: High unemployment leads to decreasing inflation; low unemployment leads to increasing inflation.

To distinguish equation (8.4) from the original Phillips curve (equation [8.2]), it is often called the **modified Phillips curve**, or the **expectations-augmented Phillips curve** (to indicate that the term π_{t-1} stands for expected inflation), or the **accelerationist Phillips curve** (to indicate that a low unemployment rate leads to an increase in the inflation rate and thus an *acceleration* of the price level). I shall simply call equation (8.4) the Phillips curve, and refer to the earlier incarnation, equation (8.2), as the *original* Phillips curve.

This discussion gives the key to what happened from 1970 on. As θ increased from 0 to 1, the simple relation between unemployment and inflation disappeared. This is what we saw in Figure 8–3. But equation (8.4) tells us what to look for: a relation between unemployment and the *change* in inflation. This relation is shown in Figure 8–5, which plots the change in the inflation rate versus the unemployment rate for each year since 1970. It shows a negative relation between unemployment and the change in inflation. The line that best fits the scatter of points for the period 1970–1998 is

$$\pi_t - \pi_{t-1} = 6.5\% - 1.0\, u_t \tag{8.5}$$

The corresponding line is drawn in Figure 8–5. For low unemployment, the change in inflation is positive. For high unemployment, the change in inflation is negative.

Back to the Natural Rate of Unemployment

The history of the Phillips curve is closely related to the discovery of the concept of the natural unemployment rate that we developed in chapter 6.

Original Phillips curve:

$$u_t \uparrow \Rightarrow \pi_t \downarrow$$

Modified Phillips curve:

$$u_t \uparrow \Rightarrow (\pi_t - \pi_{t-1}) \downarrow$$

This line is obtained using econometrics. (See Appendix 3 at the end of the book.) Note that the line does not fit the cloud of points very tightly. There are years when the change in inflation is much larger than implied by the line, years when the change in inflation is much less than implied by the line. We return to this point below.

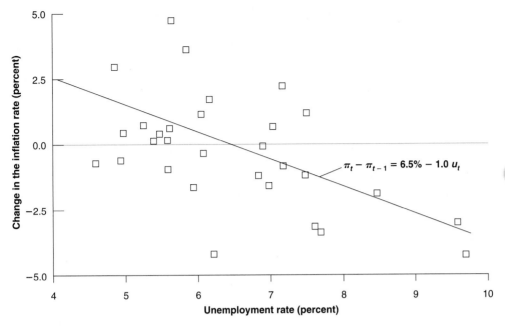

The equation labeled in the figure reads:

$$\pi_t - \pi_{t-1} = 6.5\% - 1.0\, u_t$$

FIGURE 8–5

Change in Inflation versus Unemployment in the United States, 1970–1998

Since 1970, there has been a negative relation between the unemployment rate and the change in the inflation rate in the United States.

The original Phillips curve implied that there was no such thing as a natural unemployment rate: If policy makers were willing to tolerate a higher inflation rate, they could maintain a lower unemployment rate forever.

In the late 1960s, and even while the original Phillips curve still gave a good description of the data, two economists, Milton Friedman and Edmund Phelps, questioned the existence of such a trade-off between unemployment and inflation. They questioned it on logical grounds. They argued that such a trade-off could exist only if wage setters systematically underpredicted inflation, and that they were unlikely to do so forever. They also argued that if the government attempted to sustain lower unemployment by accepting higher inflation, the trade-off would ultimately disappear; the unemployment rate could not be sustained below a certain level, a level they called the "natural rate of unemployment." Events proved them right, and the trade-off between the unemployment rate and the inflation rate indeed disappeared. (See the Focus box "Theory Ahead of the Facts: Milton Friedman and Edmund Phelps".) Today, most economists accept the notion of a *natural rate of unemployment*—subject to the many caveats we state in the next section.

Let's make explicit the connection between the Phillips curve and the natural rate of unemployment. By definition, the natural rate of unemployment is that unemployment rate such that the actual price level turns out equal to the expected price level. Equivalently, and more conveniently here, the natural rate of unemployment is the unemployment rate such that the actual inflation rate is equal to the expected inflation rate. Denote the natural unemployment rate by u_n. Then, imposing the condition that actual inflation and expected inflation be the same ($\pi_t = \pi_t^e$) in equation (8.1) gives

$$0 = (\mu + z) - \alpha u_n$$

Solving for the natural rate u_n:

$$u_n = \frac{\mu + z}{\alpha} \tag{8.6}$$

Thus, the higher the markup, μ, or the higher the factors that affect wage setting, z, the higher the natural rate.

In chapter 6, we derived the natural rate of unemployment as the rate of unemployment such that the expected and actual price level are the same. In chapter 7, when drawing the aggregate supply curve, we emphasized that, when output is equal to its natural level (hence unemployment is at the natural rate), the price level is equal to the expected price level.

If $P_t^e = P_t$, then

$$\pi_t^e \equiv (P_t^e - P_{t-1})/P_{t-1}$$
$$= (P_t - P_{t-1})/P_{t-1} = \pi_t$$

From equation (8.6), $\alpha u_n = \mu + z$. Replacing $(\mu + z)$ by αu_n in equation (8.1) and rearranging gives

$$\pi_t - \pi_t^e = -\alpha(u_t - u_n) \qquad (8.7)$$

If—as appears to be the case in the United States today—the expected rate of inflation (π_t^e) is well approximated by last year's inflation rate (π_{t-1}), the relation finally becomes

$$\pi_t - \pi_{t-1} = -\alpha(u_t - u_n) \qquad (8.8)$$

Calling the natural rate "the nonaccelerating inflation rate of unemployment" is actually wrong. It should be called "the non-increasing inflation rate of unemployment," or NIIRU. But NAIRU has now become so standard that it is too late to change it.

Equation (8.8) gives us another way of thinking about the Phillips curve, as a relation between the actual unemployment rate, the natural unemployment rate, and the change in the inflation rate: *The change in inflation depends on the difference between the actual and the natural unemployment rates. When the actual unemployment rate is higher than the natural unemployment rate, inflation decreases; when the actual unemployment rate is lower than the natural unemployment rate, inflation increases.*

Equation (8.8) also gives us another way of thinking about the natural rate of unemployment: It is the rate of unemployment required to keep inflation constant. This is why the natural rate is also called the **nonaccelerating inflation rate of unemployment**, or **NAIRU**.

What has been the natural rate of unemployment in the United States since 1970? In other words, what is the unemployment rate such that, on average, inflation has been constant? We can find the answer by returning to the estimated equation (8.5). Putting the change in inflation equal to zero in equation (8.5) implies a value for the natural unemployment rate of $6.5\%/1.0 = 6.5\%$. In other words, the evidence suggests that, since 1970 in the United States, the rate of unemployment required to keep inflation constant has been on average around 6.5%.

Theory Ahead of the Facts: Milton Friedman and Edmund Phelps

FOCUS

Economists are usually not very good at predicting major changes before they happen, and most of their insights are derived after the fact. Here is an exception.

In the late 1960s—precisely as the original Phillips curve relation was working like a charm—two economists, Milton Friedman and Edmund Phelps, argued that the appearance of a trade-off between inflation and unemployment was an illusion.

Here are a few quotes from Milton Friedman. Talking about the Phillips curve, he said,

Implicitly, Phillips wrote his article for a world in which everyone anticipated that nominal prices would be stable and in which this anticipation remained unshaken and immutable whatever happened to actual prices and wages. Suppose, by contrast, that everyone anticipates that prices will rise at a rate of more than 75% a year—as, for example, Brazilians did a few years ago. Then, wages must rise at that rate simply to keep real wages unchanged. An excess supply of labor will be reflected in a less rapid rise in nominal wages than in anticipated prices, not in an absolute decline in wages.

He went on to say,

To state [my] conclusion differently, there is always a temporary trade-off between inflation

and unemployment; there is no permanent trade-off. The temporary trade-off comes not from inflation per se, but from a rising rate of inflation.

He then tried to guess how much longer the apparent trade-off between inflation and unemployment would last in the United States:

But how long, you will say, is "temporary"? . . . I can at most venture a personal judgment, based on some examination of the historical evidence, that the initial effect of a higher and unanticipated rate of inflation lasts for something like two to five years; that this initial effect then begins to be reversed; and that a full adjustment to the new rate of inflation takes as long for employment as for interest rates, say, a couple of decades.

Friedman could not have been more right. A few years later, the original Phillips curve started to disappear, in exactly the way Friedman had predicted.

Source: Milton Friedman, "The Role of Monetary Policy," March 1968, *American Economic Review* 58-1, 1–17. (The article by Phelps, "Money-Wage Dynamics and Labor-Market Equilibrium," *Journal of Political Economy*, August 1968, part 2, 678–711, made the same points more formally.)

To summarize: The aggregate supply relation is well captured in the United States today by the Phillips curve, which is a relation between the change in the inflation rate and the deviation of unemployment from its natural rate (equation [8.8]). When unemployment exceeds the natural rate, inflation decreases. When unemployment is below the natural rate, inflation increases.

This relation has held quite well since 1970. But its earlier history points to the need for several warnings. All of them point to one main fact: The relation can change, and it often has.

The Inflation Process and the Phillips Curve

Recall how the U.S. Phillips curve changed as inflation became more persistent and the way wage setters formed inflation expectations changed as a result. The lesson is a general one: The relation between unemployment and inflation is likely to change with the inflation process. Evidence from countries with high inflation confirms this lesson. Not only does the way in which workers and firms form expectations change, but institutional arrangements change as well.

When the inflation rate becomes high, inflation also tends to become more variable. ◄ Workers and firms become more reluctant to enter into labor contracts that predetermine nominal wages for a long period of time: If inflation turns out to be higher than expected, real wages may plunge and workers may suffer a large cut in their standard of living. If inflation turns out to be lower than expected, real wages may explode and firms may go bankrupt.

For this reason, the form of wage agreements changes with the level of inflation. Nominal wages are set for shorter periods of time, down from a year to a month or even less. **Wage indexation**, a rule that increases wages automatically in line with inflation, becomes more prevalent.

These changes lead to a stronger response of inflation to unemployment. To see this, an example based on wage indexation will help. Think of an economy that has two types of labor contracts. A proportion λ (the Greek lowercase letter lambda) of labor contracts is indexed: Nominal wages in those contracts move one for one with variations in the actual price ◄ level. A proportion $1 - \lambda$ of labor contracts is not indexed: Nominal wages are set on the basis of expected inflation. Finally, assume expected inflation is equal to last year's inflation.

Under this assumption, equation (8.7) becomes

$$\pi_t = [\lambda \pi_t + (1 - \lambda)\pi_{t-1}] - \alpha(u_t - u_n)$$

The term in brackets on the right reflects the fact that a proportion λ of contracts responds to actual inflation (π_t), and a proportion $(1 - \lambda)$ responds to expected inflation, which we have assumed is equal to last year's inflation (π_{t-1}).

When $\lambda = 0$, all wages are set on the basis of expected inflation—which is equal to last year's inflation, π_{t-1}—and the equation reduces to equation (8.8). When λ is positive, however, a proportion λ of wages is set on the basis of actual rather than expected inflation.

Reorganizing the equation gives

$$\pi_t - \pi_{t-1} = -\frac{\alpha}{(1 - \lambda)}(u_t - u_n)$$

Indexation increases the effect of unemployment on inflation. The higher the proportion of indexed contracts—the higher λ—the larger the effect of the unemployment rate on the change in inflation—the higher the coefficient $\alpha/(1 - \lambda)$.

The intuition is as follows: Without indexation, lower unemployment increases wages, which in turn increases prices. But because wages do not respond to prices right away, there is no further effect within the year. With wage indexation, however, an increase in prices leads to a further increase in wages within the year, which in turn leads to a further increase in prices, and so on, so the effect of unemployment on inflation within the year is higher.

More concretely, when inflation runs on average at 5% a year, wage setters can be confident the rate will be, say, between 3% and 7%. When inflation runs on average at 30% a year, wage setters can be confident the rate will be, say, between 20% and 40%. If they set a nominal wage, their real wage may vary in the first case by 2% up or down relative to what they expected; in the second case, it may vary by as much as 10% relative to what they expected. There is much more uncertainty in the second case.

This assumption is actually too strong. Indexation clauses typically adjust wages not for current inflation (which is only known with a lag), but for inflation in the recent past, so there remains a short lag between inflation and wage adjustments. I ignore this lag here.

If and when λ gets close to 1 — when most labor contracts allow for wage indexation — small changes in unemployment can lead to very large changes in inflation. Put another way, there can be large changes in inflation with nearly no change in unemployment. This is indeed what happens in countries where inflation is very high: The relation between inflation and unemployment becomes more and more tenuous and eventually disappears altogether.

High inflation is the topic ▷ of chapter 23.

Differences in the Natural Rate Across Countries

Recall from equation (8.6) that the natural rate of unemployment depends on all the factors that affect wage setting, represented by the catchall variable z; on the markup set by firms μ; and on the response of inflation to unemployment, represented by α. To the extent that these

GLOBAL MACRO

The Japanese Unemployment Rate

The average unemployment rate in Japan since 1970 has been 2.3%, compared to 6.5% in the United States. The difference has little to do with different definitions. Using the standardized rates computed by the OECD, which adjust for differences in definitions, the rate in Japan has been 2.2%, compared to 6.4% for the United States.

If we take the average unemployment rate to be a rough estimate of the underlying natural rate, it would appear that the natural rate in Japan is equal to roughly one-third of the U.S. natural rate. Why the difference?

One of the main characteristics of the Japanese labor market is the widespread reliance on lifetime employment. The typical pattern of working life is one in which new workers quickly settle on a job and keep it until retirement. Table 1 shows the sharp contrast with the United States. By age 24, U.S. workers have had on average more than four jobs, Japanese workers only about two. By age 64, U.S. workers have had on average nearly 11 jobs; Japanese workers have had fewer than five.

To give workers incentives to stay in their jobs, Japanese firms offer wages that increase steeply with seniority, rely mostly on seniority-based promotions, and offer large lump-sum retirement payments. In exchange for job security, Japanese workers allow firms to reassign them to other divisions or even to affiliated companies. When car sales at Nissan went down in the 1980s, for example, Nissan sent some of its workers from idle production lines to the dealerships, to help promote sales.

One implication of these labor arrangements is that flows of workers through the labor market are much smaller in Japan than they are in the United States. In Japan there are no temporary layoffs and many fewer permanent layoffs. A much larger proportion of the needed relocation of workers takes place within firms rather than through the labor market.

Much lower flows into and out of employment are the main reason why the natural rate of unemployment is lower in Japan than in the United States. To see why, think of two countries that are identical in all respects except for the size of the labor-market flows. Country 1 has flows that are one-third those in country 2; put another way, the number of hires and separations in country 1 is one-third of those in country 2. If the two countries had the same number of unemployed workers, the probability of finding a job if unemployed (which is equal to the number of hires divided by the number of unemployed) would be one-third in country 1 of what it is in country 2. Wages, which depend in part on how easy it is to find a job if unemployed, would be much lower in country 1. For wages to be the same in both countries, the probability of getting a job if unemployed must be the same. Thus, unemployment in country 1 must be one-third what it is in country 2.

Reference

A good source on the Japanese economy in general, and the Japanese labor market in particular, is Takatoshi Ito, *The Japanese Economy* (Cambridge, MA: MIT Press, 1992).

TABLE 1	Cumulative number of jobs held by males of different ages, in Japan and the United States*				
Age Group	**16–19**	**20–24**	**25–29**	**⋯**	**55–64**
	Average No. of Jobs Held, by Person				
Japan	0.72	2.06	2.71	⋯	4.91
United States	2.00	4.40	6.15	⋯	10.95

*The numbers for Japan are for 1977, those for the United States for 1978.
Source: Takatoshi Ito. *The Japanese Economy* (Cambridge, MA: MIT Press, 1992).

factors differ across countries, there is no reason to expect different countries to have the same natural rate of unemployment. And indeed, natural rates differ across countries. Compare Japan and the United States. The natural rate is not directly observable, but under the assumption that the economy gravitates around it—sometimes above, sometimes below—a simple strategy is to look at the average unemployment rate over a long period of time. Since 1970, the unemployment rate in Japan has averaged 2.3%, compared to 6.5% in the United States. There is no question that the Japanese natural rate is much smaller than the U.S. natural rate.

The question of where the differences between the U.S. and the Japanese natural rates come from is taken up in the Global Macro box "The Japanese Unemployment Rate." The answer, in short, is that the internal organization of firms is very different in the two countries. Flows of separations and hires are much smaller in Japan than in the United States, resulting in a much lower natural rate of unemployment in Japan.

Variations in the Natural Rate Over Time

In estimating equation (8.6), we treated $\mu + z$ as a constant. But there is no reason to believe that μ and z are constant over time. The composition of the labor force, the structure of wage bargaining, the system of unemployment benefits, and so on, are likely to change over time, leading to changes in the natural rate of unemployment.

Changes in the natural unemployment rate over time are hard to measure. Again, the reason is that we do not observe the natural rate, only the actual rate. But broad evolutions can be established by comparing average unemployment rates across decades. We saw in chapter 6 that from the 1950s to the 1980s, the U.S. unemployment rate fluctuated around a slowly increasing trend: Average unemployment was 4.5% in the 1950s, 7.3% in the 1980s. In the 1990s, the trend appears to have been reversed. Average unemployment for 1990 to 1998 has been only 6.1%, and in 1998, inflation decreased despite the fact that the unemployment rate was down to 4.6%. This has led a number of economists to conclude that the natural rate of unemployment has decreased. Whether this is the case is discussed in the In Depth box "Has the U.S. Natural Rate of Unemployment Decreased in the 1990s?". The conclusion is that the natural rate has decreased; what is less clear is whether it will remain low in the future.

> In 1998, *actual* unemployment rates in the two countries were very close: 4.2% in Japan versus 4.6% in the United States. But this reflected that (1) Japan was in the middle of a recession, with an actual unemployment rate far above its natural rate, and that (2) the United States was in a strong expansion, with an actual unemployment rate at or perhaps below its natural rate.

The Limits of Our Understanding

The theory of the natural rate gives macroeconomists directions where to look for differences in natural rates across countries or for variations in the natural rate over time in a given country. But the truth is that macroeconomists' understanding of exactly which factors determine the natural rate of unemployment is still very limited. In particular, there is considerable uncertainty about the exact list of factors behind z, and about the dynamic effects of each factor on the natural unemployment rate.

Let's return, for example, to an increase in the price of oil. When we examined its effects in the previous chapter—capturing it by an increase in the markup, μ—we concluded that an oil price increase would lead to an increase in the natural rate of unemployment. (The same conclusion holds in equation (8.6): An increase in μ increases the natural rate.)

But there is in fact more uncertainty about the effects of an increase in the price of oil than our discussion let appear. Some of the bargaining models that underlie the wage-determination equation imply that workers may eventually accept a wage cut without a need for an increase in the unemployment rate. In terms of equation (8.6), these models suggest that when μ increases, z eventually decreases so that $\mu + z$, and thus the natural rate of unemployment $u_n = (\mu + z)/\alpha$, remains unchanged. Other models imply that although z may decrease in response to an increase in μ, the offset is only partial, so that an increase in the price of oil has a permanent effect on the natural rate.

> The two books on unemployment we mentioned in chapter 6 reach different conclusions on this point. Layard and colleagues argue that factors such as the price of oil, indirect taxes, the real exchange rate, and the real interest rate have no permanent effect on the natural rate. Phelps argues these factors can have permanent effects on the natural rate and explain a good part of the movements in unemployment in OECD countries over the last 20 years.

Has the U.S. Natural Rate of Unemployment Decreased in the 1990s?

The average U.S. unemployment rate for 1998 was 4.6%, its lowest value in three decades. Despite this low unemployment rate, the inflation rate was actually lower in 1998 (1.6%) than in 1997 (2.3%).

This has led some economists to proclaim the emergence of a "new labor market," where unemployment can be kept much lower without the risk of increasing inflation—an economy with a much lower natural rate of unemployment. What should we make of this claim?

The first step must be to look at whether the relation between the change in inflation and unemployment appears to have changed in the 1990s. Figure 1 replicates Figure 8–5, with the points corresponding to the years since 1990 indicated by diamonds. The line drawn in the figure gives the historical relation between the change in the inflation rate and the unemployment rate, based on observations from 1970 to 1998 (equation [8.5]). Note that the points corresponding to the years 1994 to 1998 all lie below this line. In words: Given the unemployment rate, the change in the inflation rate in each of these years has indeed been less than would have been predicted by the average relation between the change in inflation and the unemployment rate for the period 1970 to 1998.

Does this mean that the relation between the change in inflation and unemployment has shifted, that the line corresponding to the 1990s is lower than the line drawn in the figure? Figure 1 makes clear that the relation between the change in inflation and the unemployment rate has never been tight. There are many years since 1970 when the change in inflation was much larger or much smaller than predicted by the line: It would have been wrong to conclude, in each of those years, that the natural rate has drastically decreased or increased. The favorable outcomes from 1994 to 1998 could represent a series of lucky breaks, with the underlying relation between the change in inflation and unemployment remaining the same as before. But a series of lucky breaks five times in a row is not a very likely outcome, and the evidence points indeed to a downward shift in the relation, implying a decrease in the rate of unemployment consistent with zero change in inflation.

Where may this downward shift come from? To answer this, we must dig deeper. The next step is to look separately at wage and price inflation. Table 1 gives the basic numbers.

The table yields two conclusions. Low unemployment has led to an increase in wage inflation, from 2.8% in 1994 to 4.3% in 1998. But higher wage inflation has not translated into higher price inflation: Price inflation is lower in 1998 than it was in 1994.

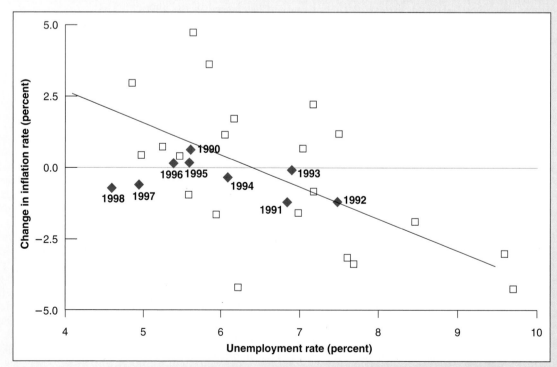

FIGURE 1 **The Change in the Inflation Rate versus the Unemployment Rate in the United States in the 1990s**

Why has price inflation been so flat despite the increase in wage inflation? Studies have identified three factors:

- Benefits paid to workers (health care, for example) by firms, which had increased rapidly early in the 1990s, have grown more slowly than wages since then. This has led to a smaller rate of increase in the total cost of labor to firms (wages plus benefits) than in wages.
- The dollar has appreciated, leading to cheaper prices for imports, which represent about 10% of the standard consumption basket (recall that the CPI is the average price of consumption).

- The prices of many raw materials, including the price of oil, have also decreased, leading to a decrease in nonlabor costs for firms.

In sum, the evidence at this point falls short of the claims that the U.S. labor market has become a "new labor market." Low unemployment still leads to pressure on wages. The good inflation performance of the late 1990s appears to be due more to an unusually slow increase in nonwage costs and import prices rather than to fundamental changes in the labor market. It is therefore reasonable to forecast that the natural rate will not remain as low as it appears to be in the late 1990s.

TABLE 1	Wage inflation, price inflation, and unemployment, 1994–1998				
	1994	**1995**	**1996**	**1997**	**1998**
Wage inflation (%)	2.8	2.8	3.4	3.9	4.3
Price inflation (%)	2.6	2.8	3.0	2.3	1.6
Unemployment rate (%)	6.1	5.6	5.4	4.9	4.6

*Wage inflation: rate of change of the wage and salaries component of the employment cost index for the private sector. Price inflation: rate of change of the CPI.

Source: *Economic Report of the President 1999*, Tables B48 and B60.

The fact that different models lead to different conclusions is not unusual; the way to decide which model is most appropriate is to see which fits the data best. In this case, the data do not speak very clearly and have so far been unable to give us precise answers. Whether changes in the price of oil have a permanent effect on the natural rate of unemployment, for example, is still very much an open question.

The limits of our understanding are particularly clear and painful in the case of Europe today. Recall our discussion of the evolution of European unemployment in chapter 1. The European unemployment rate, which until the early 1970s had been much lower than the unemployment rate of the United States, has steadily increased since. In 1998, the unemployment rate in the European Union was 10.6%, compared to 4.6% in the United States.

As a matter of logic, this high unemployment rate could reflect a large deviation of the actual unemployment rate from the natural rate, or a high natural rate. How can we tell? By looking at the change in inflation. If inflation is decreasing fast, this is an indication that the actual unemployment rate is far above the natural rate. If inflation is stable, this is an indication that the actual and the natural rate are roughly equal, and that the natural rate itself is high.

EU countries have had slowly declining inflation over the second half of the 1990s. So we can infer that the actual unemployment rate is above—but not far from—the natural rate. This point is made in Figure 8–6, which plots the change in the EU inflation rate against the unemployment rate for each year since 1971. The figure also gives the best-fitting line for the relation between the change in inflation and the unemployment rate using data since 1984 (the years since 1984 are denoted by black diamonds in the figure). The line sug-

Looking at the change in inflation to infer whether high unemployment reflects a high natural rate, or unemployment above the natural rate. From equation (8.8):

$$\pi_t - \pi_{t-1} = -\alpha(u_t - u_n)$$

So if $\pi_t - \pi_{t-1} < 0$, it must be that $u_t > u_n$
And if $\pi_t - \pi_{t-1} = 0$, it must be that $u_t = u_n$

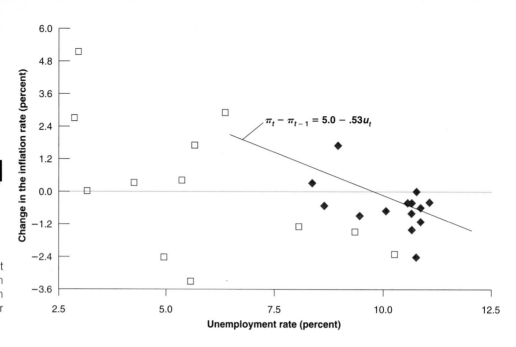

FIGURE 8-6

Change in Inflation versus Unemployment in the European Union, 1971–1998

The natural unemployment rate in the European Union is now around 9%, much higher than it was two or three decades ago.

The average unemployment rate for the countries now in the European Union was about 3% in the 1960s. If we take this average as an estimate of what the natural rate was then, the natural rate therefore has increased by about 6% since the 1960s.

gests that the natural rate—the unemployment rate at which inflation remains constant—is now around 9%, much higher than it was two or three decades ago.

Interestingly, much the same evolution took place in the United States during the 1930s. Recall Figure 8–1, which plotted the U.S. inflation rate against the U.S. unemployment rate since 1900. During the 1930s, which correspond to the period known as the Great Depression, high unemployment was associated with a much higher inflation rate than would have been predicted by the normal relation between unemployment and inflation (Given the very high unemployment rate, one would have expected that there would be deflation, indeed a large rate of deflation. In fact, deflation was limited, and from 1934 to 1937, inflation was actually positive). Put another way, the natural unemployment rate appears to have become much higher in the 1930s than in the preceding or the following decades.

Why is the natural rate of unemployment so high in Europe today? The question is sufficiently important that we shall spend a good part of chapter 22 trying to answer it. But be warned: Although this is one of the major economic questions of our time, there is little agreement on the answer.

SUMMARY

- The aggregate supply relation can be expressed as a relation between inflation, expected inflation, and unemployment. The higher expected inflation, the higher actual inflation. The higher unemployment, the lower inflation.

- When inflation is not very persistent, expected inflation does not depend very much on past inflation. Thus, the aggregate supply relation becomes a relation between inflation and unemployment. This is what Phillips in the United Kingdom, and Solow and

Samuelson in the United States, discovered when they looked in the early 1960s at the joint behavior of unemployment and inflation.

- As inflation became more persistent in the 1970s and 1980s, expected inflation became increasingly dependent on past inflation. In the United States today, the aggregate supply relation takes the form of a relation between unemployment and the change in inflation. High unemployment leads to decreasing inflation; low unemployment leads to increasing inflation.

- The natural unemployment rate is the unemployment rate at which inflation remains constant. When the actual unemployment rate exceeds the natural rate, inflation decreases; when the actual unemployment rate is less than the natural rate, inflation increases.

- Changes in the way the inflation rate varies over time affect the way wage setters form expectations and how much they use wage indexation. When wage indexation is widespread, small changes in unemployment can lead to very large changes in inflation. At high rates of inflation, the relation between inflation and unemployment disappears altogether.

- The natural rate of unemployment depends on many factors that differ across countries and can change over time. Thus, the natural rate varies across countries: It is much lower in Japan than in the United States. The natural rate also varies over time. In the United States, the natural rate appears to have increased by 1% to 2% from the 1960s to the 1980s, and to have decreased in the 1990s. In Europe, the natural rate has steadily increased since the 1960s.

KEY TERMS

- Phillips curve, 149
- deflation, 151
- wage-price spiral, 151
- modified Phillips curve, 154
- expectations-augmented Phillips curve, 154

- accelerationist Phillips curve, 154
- nonaccelerating inflation rate of unemployment (NAIRU), 156
- wage indexation, 157

QUESTIONS & PROBLEMS

[Web] indicates that the question requires access to the Internet.

1. TRUE/FALSE/UNCERTAIN

a. The original Phillips curve is the negative relation between unemployment and inflation first observed by Phillips for the U.K.

b. The original Phillips curve relation has proven to be very stable across both countries and time.

c. The aggregate supply relation is consistent with the Phillips curve as observed before the 1970s, but not since.

d. Policy makers can only temporarily exploit the inflation-unemployment trade-off.

e. Before the 1970s, there was no natural rate of unemployment, and policy makers could achieve as low a rate of unemployment as they wanted.

f. The expectations-augmented Phillips curve is consistent with workers and firms adapting their expectations following the macroeconomic experience of the 1960s.

2. THE PHILLIPS CURVE

Discuss the following statements:

a. The Phillips curve implies that when unemployment is high, inflation is low, and vice versa. Therefore, we may experience either high inflation or high unemployment, but we will never experience both together.

b. As long as we do not mind having high inflation, we can achieve as low a level of unemployment as we want. All we have to do is increase the demand for goods and services by using, for example, expansionary fiscal policy.

3. MAINTAINING LOW UNEMPLOYMENT

Suppose that the Phillips curve is given by:

$$\pi_t = \pi_t^e + 0.1 - 2u_t$$

where

$$\pi_t^e = \theta \pi_{t-1}$$

Also, suppose that θ is initially equal to zero.

a. What is the natural rate of unemployment?

THE PHILLIPS CURVE

Suppose that the rate of unemployment is initially equal to the natural rate. In year *t* the authorities decide to bring the unemployment rate down to 3% and hold it there forever.

b. Determine the rate of inflation in years *t*, *t* + 1, *t* + 2, *t* + 10, *t* + 15.

c. Do you believe the answer you gave in (b)? Why or why not? (*Hint:* think about how inflation expectations are formed.)

Now suppose that in year *t* + 5 θ increases from 0 to 1.

d. Why might θ increase like this? What is the effect on u_n?

Suppose that the government is still determined to keep *u* at 3% forever.

e. What will the inflation rate be in years *t* + 5, *t* + 10, and *t* + 15?

f. Do you believe the answer given in (e)? Why or why not?

4. INDEXATION OF WAGES

Suppose that the Phillips curve is given by:

$$\pi_t - \pi_t^e = 0.1 - 2u_t$$

where

$$\pi_t^e = \pi_{t-1}$$

Suppose that inflation in year *t* − 1 is zero. In year *t*, the authorities decide to keep the unemployment rate at 4% forever.

a. Compute the rate of inflation for years *t*, *t* + 1, *t* + 2, and *t* + 3.

Now suppose that half the workers have indexed labor contracts.

b. What is the new equation for the Phillips curve?

c. Repeat the exercise in (a).

d. What is the effect of indexation on the relation between π and *u*?

5. OIL SHOCKS, INFLATION, AND UNEMPLOYMENT

Suppose that the Phillips curve is given by:

$$\pi_t - \pi_t^e = 0.08 + 0.1\mu - 2u_t$$

where μ is the markup of prices over wages.

Suppose that μ is initially equal to 20%, but that as a result of a sharp increase in oil prices, μ increases to 40% in year *t* and after.

a. Why would an increase in oil prices result in an increase in μ?

b. What is the long run effect of the increase in μ on the natural rate of unemployment?

6. FAVORABLE OIL SHOCKS, UNEMPLOYMENT, AND INFLATION

In sharp contrast to the oil shocks of the 1970s, the price of oil has substantially declined in the 1990s.

a. Can this explain the good performance of both inflation and unemployment in the 1990s?

b. What has been the probable effect on the natural rate of unemployment?

7. ESTIMATING THE NATURAL RATE OF UNEMPLOYMENT [Web]

To answer this question, you will need data on the annual unemployment and inflation rates of the United States since 1970, which can be obtained from the web site of the Bureau of Labor Statistics at http://stats.bls.gov/

Look under "Data" and select the "Most requested series." Under "Employment and Unemployment," pick "Labor force statistics from the Current Population Survey" and make an extract of the "Unemployment Rate—Civilian Labor Force." This is a monthly series, so use the year's average for that year's unemployment rate.

Similarly, under the "Most requested series," look under "Prices and Living Conditions" and make an extract of the "Consumer Price Index—All Urban Consumers." Define the inflation rate in year *t* as the percentage change in the CPI between year *t* and year *t* − 1. Once you have computed the rate of inflation for each year, also compute the change in inflation from one year to the next.

a. Make a graph for all the years since 1970, with the change in inflation on the vertical axis and the rate of unemployment on the horizontal axis. Print out the graph. Is your graph similar to Figure 8–5?

b. Using a ruler, draw the line that appears to fit the set of points best. Approximately what is the slope of your line? What is the intercept? Write down the corresponding equation.

c. According to your analysis in (b), what has been the natural rate of unemployment since 1970?

8. CHANGES IN THE NATURAL RATE OF UNEMPLOYMENT [Web]

Repeat the exercise for question 7(a), drawing separate graphs for the period 1970 to 1990 and 1990 on. Do you find that the relation between inflation and unemployment is different in the two subperiods? If so, what does this imply for the natural rate of unemployment?

FROM THE AGGREGATE SUPPLY RELATION TO THE PHILLIPS CURVE

The purpose of this appendix is to derive equation (8.1), expressing the relation between inflation, expected inflation, and unemployment.

The starting point is the aggregate supply relation between the price level, the expected price level, and the unemployment rate derived in Chapter 7:

$$P_t = P_t^e(1 + \mu)(1 - \alpha u_t + z)$$

Divide both sides by last year's price level, P_{t-1}

$$\frac{P_t}{P_{t-1}} = \frac{P_t^e}{P_{t-1}}(1 + \mu)(1 - \alpha u_t + z) \qquad (8A.1)$$

Rewrite the fraction P_t/P_{t-1} on the left side as:

$$\frac{P_t}{P_{t-1}} = 1 + \frac{P_t - P_{t-1}}{P_{t-1}} = 1 + \pi_t$$

where the first equality follows from adding and subtracting 1, and the second from the definition of the inflation rate ($\pi_t \equiv (P_t - P_{t-1})/P_{t-1}$).

Do the same for the fraction P_t^e/P_{t-1} on the right side, using the definition of the expected inflation rate ($\pi_t^e \equiv (P_t^e - P_{t-1})/P_{t-1}$)

$$\frac{P_t^e}{P_{t-1}} = 1 + \frac{P_t^e - P_{t-1}}{P_{t-1}} = 1 + \pi_t^e$$

Replacing P_t/P_{t-1} and P_t^e/P_{t-1} in equation (8A.1) by the expressions we have just derived

$$(1 + \pi_t) = (1 + \pi_t^e)(1 + \mu)(1 - \alpha u_t + z)$$

This gives us a relation between inflation (π_t), expected inflation (π_t^e) and the unemployment rate (u_t). The remaining steps make the relation look more friendly:

Divide both sides by $(1 + \pi_t^e)(1 + \mu)$

$$\frac{(1 + \pi_t)}{(1 + \pi_t^e)(1 + \mu)} = 1 - \alpha u_t + z$$

As long as inflation, expected inflation, and the markup are not too large, a good approximation to this equation is given by (see Propositions 3 and 6 in Appendix 2 at the end of the book)

$$1 + \pi_t - \pi_t^e - \mu = 1 - \alpha u_t + z$$

Rearranging gives:

$$\pi_t = \pi_t^e + (\mu + z) - \alpha u_t$$

This is equation (8.1) in the text. The inflation rate depends on the expected inflation rate and the unemployment rate u_t. The relation depends on the markup μ, on the factors that affect wage setting, z, and on the effect of the unemployment rate on wages, α.

We invite you to visit the Blanchard page on the Prentice Hall Web site at:

http://www.prenhall.com/blanchard

for this chapter's World Wide Web exercises

CHAPTER 9

Inflation, Activity, and Money Growth

In October 1979, the Fed decided to reduce money growth and decrease inflation, which was then close to 14% a year. Five years later, but after a deep recession, inflation was down to less than 4% a year.

Why did the Fed decide to reduce inflation? How did it do it? Why was there a recession? More generally, what are the effects of money growth on inflation and on activity? Our treatment of expectations in chapter 7 was too simple to allow us to tackle these issues. But, with our discussion of expectations and the introduction of the Phillips curve relation in chapter 8, we now have what we need. In this chapter we answer these questions.

The first section looks at the links between output, unemployment and inflation. The next several sections put these links together, and discuss both the short-run and the medium-run effects of money growth on inflation and activity. The last section returns to the U.S. disinflation of the late 1970s.

9-1 | Output, Unemployment, and Inflation

In thinking about the interactions between output, unemployment, and inflation, you must keep in mind three relations:

1. **Okun's law**, which relates the change in unemployment to the deviation of output growth from normal.
2. **The Phillips curve**, which relates the change in inflation to the deviation of unemployment from the natural rate.
3. **The aggregate demand relation**, which relates output growth to the rate of growth of nominal money minus the rate of inflation.

This section looks at each relation on its own. The rest of the chapter looks at their joint implications.

Okun's Law: Output Growth and Changes in Unemployment

When we wrote the relation between output and unemployment in chapter 6, we did so under two convenient but restrictive assumptions. We assumed that output and employment moved together, so changes in output led to equal changes in employment. And we assumed the labor force was constant, so changes in employment were reflected one for one in opposite changes in unemployment.

We must now move beyond these assumptions. To see why, think about what they imply for the relation between the rate of output growth and the unemployment rate. As output and employment move together, a 1% increase in output leads to a 1% increase in employment. And because movements in employment are reflected in opposite movements in unemployment, a 1% increase in employment leads to a decrease of 1% in the unemployment rate.[1] Let g_{yt} denote the growth rate of output. Then, under these two assumptions, the following relation should hold

$$u_t - u_{t-1} = -g_{yt} \tag{9.1}$$

The change in the unemployment rate should be equal to the negative of the growth rate of output. If output growth is, say, 4%, then the unemployment rate should decline by 4%.

Contrast this with the actual relation between output growth and the change in the unemployment rate, the relation known as **Okun's law**. Figure 9–1 plots the change in the unemployment rate against the rate of output growth for each year since 1960. It also plots the regression line that best fits the scatter of points. The relation corresponding to the line is given by

$$u_t - u_{t-1} = -0.4(g_{yt} - 3\%) \tag{9.2}$$

Equation (9.2) differs in two ways from equation (9.1):

If g_{yt} = 3%, then

$u_t - u_{t-1}$
$= -0.4(3\% - 3\%)$
$= 0$

▶ • Annual output growth has to be at least 3% to prevent the unemployment rate from rising. This is because of two factors we have neglected so far—both the labor force and the productivity of labor are growing over time.

Suppose the labor force grows at 1.7% a year. To maintain a constant unemployment rate, employment must grow at the same rate as the labor force, at 1.7% a year.

---

[1]**DIGGING DEEPER**. This last step is only approximately correct. Remember the definition of the unemployment rate:

$$u \equiv U/L = 1 - N/L$$

If the labor force L is fixed,

$$\Delta u = \Delta U/L = -\Delta N/L = -(\Delta N/N)(N/L)$$

where the last equality follows from multiplying and dividing by N. If N/L is equal to, say, 0.95, then a 1% increase in employment leads to a decrease of 0.95% in the unemployment rate. The result in the text is based on approximating N/L by 1, so a 1% increase in employment leads to a decrease of 1% in the unemployment rate.

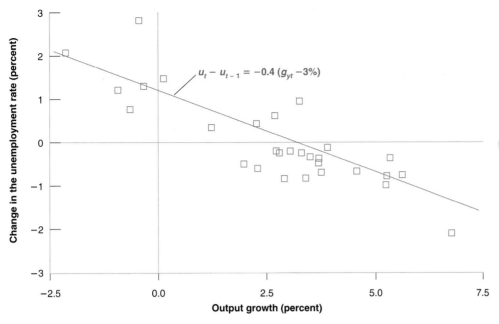

FIGURE 9-1

Changes in the Unemployment Rate versus Output Growth in the United States, 1960–1998

High output growth is associated with a reduction in the unemployment rate; low output growth is associated with an increase in the unemployment rate.

Suppose also that labor productivity—output per worker—is growing at 1.3% a year. If employment grows at 1.7%, and labor productivity grows at 1.3%, output will grow at 1.7% + 1.3% = 3%. In other words, to maintain a constant unemployment rate, output growth must be equal to 3%. In the United States, the sum of the rate of labor-force growth and of labor-productivity growth has been equal to 3% on average since 1960, and this is why the number 3% appears on the right side of equation (9.2). I shall call the rate of output growth needed to maintain a constant unemployment rate the **normal growth rate** in what follows.

● The coefficient on the deviation of output growth from the normal growth rate is −0.4 in equation (9.2), not −1.0 as in equation (9.1). Put another way, output growth of 1% in excess of the normal growth rate leads to only a 0.4% reduction in the unemployment rate rather than a 1% reduction. There are two reasons why:

1. Firms adjust employment less than one for one in response to deviations of output growth from the normal growth rate. More specifically, output growth that is 1% above normal for one year leads to only a 0.6% increase in the employment rate.

    One reason is that some workers are needed no matter what the level of output is. The accounting department of a firm, for example, needs roughly the same number of employees whether the firm is selling more or less than normal.

    Another reason is that training new employees is costly. That is why many firms prefer to keep current workers rather than lay them off when output is lower than normal, and ask them to work overtime rather than hire new employees when output is higher than normal. In bad times, firms in effect hoard labor; this behavior is called **labor hoarding**.

2. An increase in the employment rate does not lead to a one-for-one decrease in the unemployment rate. More specifically, a 0.6% increase in the employment rate leads to only a 0.4% decrease in the unemployment rate.

    The reason is that labor participation increases. When employment increases, not all the new jobs are filled by the unemployed. Some of the jobs go to people who were classified as *out of the labor force*, meaning they were not actively looking for a job. And, as labor-market prospects improve for the unemployed, some discouraged workers—who were previously classified as out of the labor force—decide to start actively looking for a job, and become classified as unemployed. For both reasons, the decrease in unemployment is smaller than the increase in employment.

Putting the two steps together:

1% increase in output above normal ⟹

0.6% increase in employment ⟹

0.4% decrease in the unemployment rate.

Okun's Law Across Countries

The coefficient β in Okun's law gives the effect on the unemployment rate of deviations of output growth from normal. A value of β of 0.4 tells us that output growth 1% above the normal growth rate for one year decreases the unemployment rate by 0.4%.

The coefficient β depends in part on how firms adjust employment in response to temporary deviations in output. This adjustment of employment depends in turn on such factors as the internal organization of firms and the legal and social constraints on hiring and firing. We would expect the coefficient to be different across countries, and it is. Table 1 gives the estimated coefficient β for four OECD countries.

The first column gives estimates of β based on data from 1960 to 1980. The United States has the highest coefficient, followed by Germany, the United Kingdom, and Japan.

The ranking in the first column fits well with what we know about the behavior of firms and the structure of firing/hiring regulations across countries. The coefficient β is smallest in Japan. As we saw in chapter 8, Japanese firms offer a high degree of job security to their workers, so variations in output have little effect on employment and thus on unemployment. The coefficient β is largest in the United States, where there are few social and legal constraints on firms' adjustment of employment. And legal restrictions on firing—from severance pay to the need for legal permission from the state to terminate employment—explain why the coefficients estimated for the two European countries are in between those of Japan and the United States.

The second column gives estimates based on data from 1981 to 1998. The coefficient is uniformly larger. This again fits with what we know about firms and regulations. Increased competition in goods markets since the early 1980s has led firms in most countries to reconsider and reduce their commitment to job security. And, at the urging of firms, legal restrictions on hiring and firing have been considerably weakened in many countries. Both factors have led to a larger response of employment to fluctuations in output, thus to a larger value of β.

TABLE 1	**Okun's law coefficients across countries and time**	
Country	1960–1980 β	1981–1998 β
United States	0.39	0.42
United Kingdom	0.15	0.51
Germany*	0.20	0.32
Japan	0.10	0.20

*For Germany, the second period is 1981–1989, rather than 1981–1998.
Source: Author's computations.

Using letters rather than numbers, let's write the relation between output growth and the change in the unemployment rate as

Okun's law:
$g_{yt} > \bar{g}_y \Rightarrow u_t < u_{t-1}$

$$u_t - u_{t-1} = -\beta(g_{yt} - \bar{g}_y) \tag{9.3}$$

where $\bar{g}_y$ is the normal growth rate of the economy (about 3% for the United States), and β (the Greek lowercase letter beta) tells us how growth in excess of normal growth translates into decreases in the unemployment rate. In the United States, β equals 0.4. (The evidence for other countries is given in the Global Macro box "Okun's Law Across Countries.")

The Phillips Curve: Unemployment and the Change in Inflation

We derived in chapter 8 the following relation between inflation, expected inflation, and unemployment (equation [8.7])

$$\pi_t = \pi_t^e - \alpha(u_t - u_n) \tag{9.4}$$

Inflation depends on expected inflation and on the deviation of unemployment from the natural rate.

We then argued that in the United States today, expected inflation appears to be well approximated by last year's inflation, so that we can replace π_t^e by π_{t-1}. With this assumption, the relation between inflation and unemployment takes the form

$$\pi_t - \pi_{t-1} = -\alpha(u_t - u_n) \tag{9.5}$$

Unemployment above the natural rate leads to a decrease in inflation; unemployment below the natural rate leads to an increase in inflation. The parameter α gives the effect of unemployment on the change in inflation. We saw in chapter 8 that since 1970 in the United States, the natural unemployment rate has been on average equal to 6.5%, and α roughly equal to 1.0. This value of α means that an unemployment rate of 1% above the natural rate for one year leads to a decrease in the inflation rate of about 1%. I shall refer to equation (9.5) as the Phillips curve.

Phillips curve:
$u_t < u_n \Rightarrow \pi_t > \pi_{t-1}$

We should call equation (9.5) the "Phillips relation," and reserve the expression "Phillips curve" for the curve that represents the relation. But the tradition is to use "Phillips curve" to denote equation (9.5). I shall follow tradition.

The Aggregate Demand Relation: Money Growth, Inflation, and Output Growth

In chapter 7, we wrote the aggregate demand relation as a relation between output and the real money stock, government spending, and taxes (equation [7.2]). To focus on the relation between the real money stock and output, I shall ignore changes in factors other than real money here, and write the aggregate demand relation simply as

$$Y_t = \gamma \frac{M_t}{P_t} \tag{9.6}$$

where γ (the Greek lowercase gamma) is a positive parameter. This equation states that the demand for goods, and thus output, is simply proportional to the real money stock. This simplification will make our life easier. You should keep in mind, however, that behind this relation hides the set of steps we saw in the *IS-LM* model:

- An increase in the real money stock leads to a decrease in the interest rate.
- The decrease in the interest rate leads to an increase in the demand for goods and, to an increase in output.

$M/P \uparrow \Rightarrow i \downarrow$
$i \downarrow \Rightarrow Y \uparrow$
Putting the two steps together: $M/P \uparrow \Rightarrow Y \uparrow$

For our purposes we need to move from the relation between levels (the output level, the level of nominal money, and the price level) in equation (9.6) to a relation between growth rates (of output, nominal money, and prices). Let g_{yt} be the growth rate of output. Let g_{mt} be the growth rate of nominal money, and let π_t be the growth rate of prices—the rate of inflation. Then, from equation (9.6), it follows that

$$g_{yt} = g_{mt} - \pi_t \tag{9.7}$$

If a variable is the ratio of two variables, its growth rate is the difference between the growth rates of these two variables (proposition 8 in Appendix 2 at the end of the book). So if $Y = \gamma M/P$, and γ is constant, $g_y = g_m - \pi$.

The growth rate of output is equal to the growth rate of nominal money minus the rate of inflation. Given money growth, high inflation leads to a decrease in the real money stock and a decrease in output; low inflation leads to an increase in the real money stock, and an increase in output.

Aggregate demand relation:
$g_{mt} > \pi_t \Rightarrow g_{yt} > 0$

9-2 | The Medium Run

Let's collect the three relations between inflation, unemployment, and output growth we derived in section 9-1. Okun's law relates the change in the unemployment rate to the deviation of output growth from normal (equation [9.3])

$$\underset{\text{unemployment rate}}{\underset{\text{Change in the}}{}} \quad \underset{\text{growth from normal}}{\underset{\text{Deviation of output}}{}}$$
$$u_t - u_{t-1} = -\beta(g_{yt} - \overline{g}_y)$$

The Phillips curve relates the change in inflation to the deviation of the unemployment rate from its natural rate (equation [9.5])

$$\begin{array}{cc} \text{Change in the} & \text{Deviation of unemployment} \\ \text{inflation rate} & \text{from the natural rate} \end{array}$$
$$\pi_t - \pi_{t-1} = -\alpha(u_t - u_n)$$

The aggregate demand relation relates output growth to the difference between nominal money growth and inflation (equation [9.7])

$$\begin{array}{cc} \text{Rate of growth} & \text{Rate of growth of nominal} \\ \text{of output} & \text{money minus rate of inflation} \end{array}$$
$$g_{yt} = g_{mt} - \pi_t$$

Our task is now to see what these three relations imply for the effects of money growth on output, unemployment and inflation. We can go some way already. Take for example a decrease in money growth:

$g_m \downarrow \Rightarrow g_m - \pi \downarrow \Rightarrow g_y \downarrow$

- From the aggregate demand relation, given inflation, lower money growth implies a decrease in output growth.

$g_y \downarrow \Rightarrow u \uparrow$
$u \uparrow \Rightarrow \pi \downarrow$

- From Okun's law, this decrease in growth leads to an increase in unemployment.
- From the Phillips curve, higher unemployment implies a decrease in inflation.

We can already see that the initial effects of lower money growth are to slow down output growth, increase unemployment, and decrease inflation. But what happens after this initial response is harder to tell: Does unemployment keep going up? What happens to inflation? The easiest way to answer these questions is to work backward in time, to start by looking at the medium run—that is, where the economy ends when all the dynamics have worked themselves out—and then to return to the dynamics. This section looks at the *medium run*. The following sections return to dynamics.

Assume that the central bank maintains a constant growth rate of nominal money, call it $\bar{g}_m$. What will be the values of output growth, unemployment, and inflation in the medium run?

- In the medium run, unemployment must be constant; unemployment cannot be increasing or decreasing forever. Putting $u_t = u_{t-1}$ in Okun's law implies that $g_{yt} = \bar{g}_y$. *In the medium run, output grows at its normal rate of growth, $\bar{g}_y$.*

Medium run: $g_y = \bar{g}_y$

- With money growth equal to $\bar{g}_m$ and output growth equal to $\bar{g}_y$, the aggregate demand relation implies that inflation is constant and satisfies

$$\bar{g}_y = \bar{g}_m - \pi$$

Moving π to the left, and $\bar{g}_y$ to the right, gives

$$\begin{array}{ccc} \text{Inflation rate} & \text{Rate of growth} & \text{Normal growth} \\ & \text{of nominal money} & \text{rate of output} \end{array}$$
$$\pi = \qquad \bar{g}_m \quad - \quad \bar{g}_y \qquad (9.8)$$

Medium run: $\pi = g_m - \bar{g}_y$

In the medium run, inflation is equal to nominal money growth minus normal output growth. It will be convenient to call nominal money growth minus normal output growth **adjusted nominal money growth**, so that this result can be stated as: *In the medium run, inflation equals adjusted nominal money growth.*

One way to think about this result is as follows: A growing level of output implies a growing level of transactions and thus a growing demand for real money. If output is growing at 3%, the real money stock must also grow at 3% per year. If the nominal money stock grows at a rate different from 3%, the difference must show up in inflation (or deflation). For example, if nominal money growth is 10%, then inflation must be equal to 7%.

- If inflation is constant, then $\pi_t = \pi_{t-1}$. Putting $\pi_t = \pi_{t-1}$ in the Phillips curve implies that $u_t = u_n$. *In the medium run, the unemployment rate must be equal to the natural rate.*

Medium run: $u = u_n$

These results are the natural extension of the results we derived in chapter 7. There, we saw that *changes in the level of money* were neutral in the medium run: They had no effect on either output or unemployment, but were reflected one for one in changes in the price

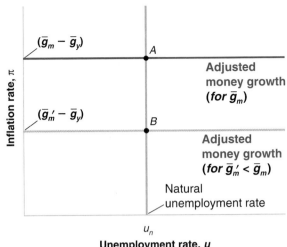

FIGURE 9-2

Inflation and Unemployment in the Medium Run

In the medium run, unemployment is equal to the natural rate, and inflation is equal to adjusted money growth.

level. We see here that a similar neutrality result applies to *changes in the rate of growth of money*. Changes in nominal money growth have no effect on output or unemployment in the medium run, but are reflected one for one in changes in the rate of inflation.

Another way to state this last result is that the only determinant of inflation in the medium run is adjusted money growth. Milton Friedman put it this way: *Inflation is always and everywhere a monetary phenomenon.* Unless they lead to higher nominal money growth, factors such as the monopoly power of firms, strong unions, strikes, fiscal deficits, the price of oil, and so on have no effect on inflation *in the medium run*.

We can summarize the results of this section with the help of Figure 9–2, which plots the unemployment rate on the horizontal axis, and the inflation rate on the vertical axis.

In the medium run, the unemployment rate is equal to the natural rate. The economy must thus be somewhere on the vertical line at $u = u_n$.

In the medium run, inflation must be equal to adjusted money growth—the rate of nominal money growth minus the normal rate of growth of output. This is represented by the horizontal line at $\pi = \bar{g}_m - \bar{g}_y$.

A decrease in nominal money growth from $\bar{g}_m$ to $\bar{g}'_m$ shifts the vertical line downward, moving the equilibrium from point A to point B. The inflation rate decreases by the same amount as the decrease in nominal money growth. There is no change in the unemployment rate, which is still equal to u_n.

Having looked at what happens in the medium run, we can now return to the dynamics of adjustment. This is the focus of the next three sections.

> In the medium run, changes in money growth have no effect on output or on unemployment. They are reflected one for one in changes in the rate of inflation.

> The "unless" qualification is important. When we study episodes of very high inflation in chapter 23, we shall see that fiscal deficits often lead to money creation, and to higher nominal money growth.

9-3 | Disinflation: A First Pass

Suppose the economy is in medium-run equilibrium: Unemployment is at its natural rate, and the rate of growth of output is equal to the normal growth rate. But the inflation rate is high, and there is a general consensus that it must be reduced.

We know from the previous section that achieving lower inflation requires lowering money growth. But we also know that a decrease in money growth will slow down output growth and increase unemployment, at least initially. Knowing this, how should the central bank achieve **disinflation**—that is, the decrease in inflation? Should it decrease money growth quickly or slowly? Let's see what our equations imply.

How Much Unemployment? And for How Long?

Start with the Phillips curve relation (equation [9.5])

$$\pi_t - \pi_{t-1} = -\alpha(u_t - u_n)$$

> What is so bad about high inflation if growth is proceeding at a normal rate, and unemployment is at its natural rate? To answer, we need to discuss the costs of inflation, and why policy makers take steps to decrease inflation. We shall do this in chapter 23.

When to use "percentage point" rather than "percent"? Suppose you are told that the unemployment rate, which was equal to 10%, has increased by 5 percent. Is it 5% of itself, in which case the unemployment rate is equal to $(1.05) \times 10\% = 10.5\%$? Or is it 5 percentage points, in which case it is equal to $10\% + 5\% = 15\%$? The use of "percentage point" rather than "percent" helps avoid the ambiguity. If you are told the unemployment rate has increased by 5 percentage points, this means that the unemployment rate is $10\% + 5\% = 15\%$.

This relation makes it clear that disinflation can be obtained only at the cost of higher unemployment. For the left side of the equation to be negative — that is, for inflation to decrease — the term $(u_t - u_n)$ must be positive: The unemployment rate must exceed the natural rate.

The equation actually has a stronger and quite startling implication: The total amount of unemployment required for a given decrease in inflation does not depend on the speed at which disinflation is achieved. In other words, disinflation can be achieved quickly, at the cost of very high unemployment for a few years; or it can be achieved more slowly, with a smaller increase in unemployment spread over more years. In both cases, the total amount of unemployment, summing over the years, will be the same.

Let's now see why this is. Define first a **point-year of excess unemployment** as a difference between the actual and the natural unemployment rate of one percentage point for one year. For example, if the natural rate is 6.5%, an actual unemployment rate of 9% four years in a row corresponds to $4 \times (9 - 6.5) = 10$ point-years of excess unemployment.

Now suppose a central bank wants to reduce inflation by x percentage points. To make things simpler, let's use specific numbers: Assume that the central bank wants to reduce inflation from 14% to 4%, so that x is equal to 10. Let's also assume that α equals 1.

Suppose it wants to achieve the reduction in inflation in just one year. Equation (9.5) tells us that what is required is one year of unemployment at 10% above the natural rate. In this case, the right side of the equation is equal to -10%, and the inflation rate decreases by 10% within a year.

Suppose it wants to achieve the reduction in inflation over a period of two years. Equation (9.5) tells us that two years of unemployment are required at 5% above the natural rate. During each of the two years, the right side of the equation is equal to -5%, so the inflation rate decreases by 5% each year, thus by 10% over two years.

By the same reasoning, reducing inflation over a period of five years requires five years of unemployment at 2% above the natural rate; reducing inflation over a period of 10 years requires 10 years of unemployment at 1% above the natural rate, and so on.

Note that in each case the number of point-years of excess unemployment required to decrease inflation is the same, namely 10: One year times 10% excess unemployment in the first scenario, 2 years times 5% in the second, 10 years times 1% in the last. The implication is straightforward: The central bank can choose the distribution of excess unemployment over time, but it cannot change the total number of point-years of excess unemployment.

We can state this conclusion another way. Define the **sacrifice ratio** as the number of point-years of excess unemployment needed to achieve a decrease in inflation of 1%. Then equation (9.5) implies that this ratio is independent of policy and simply equal to $(1/\alpha)$. If α roughly equals one, as the estimated Phillips curve suggests, then the sacrifice ratio is roughly equal to one.

If the sacrifice ratio is constant, does this imply that the speed of disinflation is irrelevant? No. Suppose that the central bank tried to achieve the decrease in inflation in one year. As we have just seen, this would require an unemployment rate of 10% above the natural rate for one year. With a natural unemployment rate of 6.5%, this would require increasing the actual unemployment rate to 16.5% for one year. From Okun's law, using a value of 0.4 for β and a normal output growth rate of 3%, output growth would have to satisfy

$$u_t - u_{t-1} = -\beta \ (g_{yt} - \bar{g}_y)$$
$$16.5\% - 6.5\% = -0.4(g_{yt} - 3\%)$$

This implies a value for $g_{yt} = -(10\%)/0.4 + 3\% = -22\%$. In words, output growth would have to equal -22% for a year! For comparison, the largest negative growth rate in the United States this century was -15% in 1931, during the Great Depression. It is fair to say that macroeconomists do not know with great confidence what would happen if monetary policy were aimed at inducing such a large negative growth rate. But most would surely be unwilling to try. The increase in the overall unemployment rate would lead, as we saw in chapter 6, to extremely high unemployment rates for some groups — specifically the young and the unskilled. Not only would the welfare costs for these groups be large, but such high unemployment might leave permanent scars. The sharp drop in output would most likely also lead to a large number of bankruptcies, with long-lasting effects on economic activity. In short, the disruptions from a fast disinflation might be very large.

This suggests very high unemployment may have long-lasting effects on the natural rate itself. This will be one of the questions we take up when looking at European unemployment in chapter 22.

Working Out the Required Path of Money Growth

Let's assume that based on the computations we just went through, the central bank decides to decrease the inflation rate from 14% to 4% in five years. Clearly it does not control either inflation or unemployment directly. What it controls is money growth. Using our equations, we can solve for the path of money growth that will achieve the disinflation.

As we saw in chapter 4, what the central bank actually controls is central bank money, not the money stock itself. We shall ignore this complication here.

Let's make the same numerical assumptions as before. Normal output growth is 3%. The natural rate of unemployment is 6.5%. The parameter α in the Phillips curve is equal to 1; β in Okun's law is equal to 0.4. Table 9–1 shows how to derive the path of money growth needed to achieve 10% disinflation over five years.

In year 0, before the disinflation, output growth is proceeding at its normal rate of 3%. Unemployment is at the natural rate, 6.5%; inflation is running at 14%; nominal money growth is equal to 17%. Real money growth equals 17% − 14% = 3%, the same as output growth.

The way to read the rest of this section is first to follow the logic of the step-by-step computations; do not worry about understanding the broader picture. When you have done this, step back and look at the way the economy adjusts over time. Make sure you can tell the story in words.

The decision is then made to reduce inflation from 14% to 4% over five years, starting in year 1.

The easiest way to solve for the path of money growth is to start from the desired path of inflation, find the required path of unemployment and the required path of output growth, and, finally, derive the required path of money growth.

- The first line of Table 9–1 gives the *target path of inflation*. Inflation starts at 14% before the change in monetary policy, decreases by 2 percentage points a year from year 1 to year 5, and then remains at its lower level of 4% thereafter.

  From the inflation path.

- The second line gives the required *path of unemployment* implied by the Phillips curve. If inflation is to decrease by 2 percentage points a year and $\alpha = 1$, the economy must accept five years of unemployment at 2 percentage points above the natural rate (5 × 2% = 10%, the required decrease in inflation). Thus, from year 1 to year 5, the unemployment rate must equal 6.5% + 2% = 8.5%.

  To the path of unemployment.

- The third line gives the required *path of output growth*. From Okun's law, we know that the initial increase in unemployment requires lower output growth. With β equal to 0.4, an initial increase in unemployment of 2% requires the rate of output growth to be lower than normal by 2%/0.4 = 5 percentage points. Given a normal growth rate of 3%, the economy must therefore have a growth rate of 3% − 5% = − 2% in year 1. There must be a recession in year 1.

  To the path of output growth.

TABLE 9–1 Engineering Disinflation

	Before	Disinflation					After		
Year	**0**	**1**	**2**	**3**	**4**	**5**	**6**	**7**	**8**
Inflation (%)	14	12	10	8	6	4	4	4	4
Unemployment rate (%)	6.5	8.5	8.5	8.5	8.5	8.5	6.5	6.5	6.5
Output growth (%)	3	−2	3	3	3	3	8	3	3
Nominal money growth (%)	17	10	13	11	9	7	12	7	7

From years 2 to 5, growth must proceed at a rate sufficient to maintain the unemployment rate constant at 8%. Thus, output must grow at its normal rate, 3%. In other words, from years 2 to 5, the economy grows at a normal rate, but has an unemployment rate that exceeds the natural rate by 2 percentage points.

Once disinflation is achieved, a burst of output growth in year 6 is needed to return unemployment to normal: To decrease the unemployment rate by 2 percentage points in a year, the rate of output growth must exceed normal growth by 2%/0.4, thus by 5%. The economy must therefore grow at 3% + 5% = 8% for one year.

To the path of nominal ▶ ● money growth. The fourth line gives the implied path of *nominal money growth*. From the aggregate demand relation, (equation [9.7]), we know that output growth equals nominal money growth minus inflation, or, equivalently, that nominal money growth equals output growth plus inflation. Adding the numbers for inflation in the first line and for output growth in the third gives us the required path for the rate of nominal money growth.

The path looks surprising at first: Money growth goes down sharply in year 1, then up again, then slowly down for three years, then up again in the year following disinflation, to finally reach its permanent lower level of 7%. But this is easy to explain:

To start disinflation, the central bank must induce an increase in unemployment. This requires a sharp contraction in money growth in year 1. The decrease in nominal money growth—from 17% to 10%—is much sharper than the decrease in inflation—from 14% to 12%. The result is thus a sharp decrease in real money growth, decreasing demand and output, which increases the unemployment rate.

For the next four years, monetary policy is aimed at maintaining unemployment at 8.5%, not at increasing unemployment further. Nominal money growth is aimed at allowing demand and therefore output to grow at the normal growth rate. Put another way, nominal money growth is set equal to inflation plus the normal growth rate of 3%. And as inflation decreases—because of high unemployment—so does nominal money growth.

At the end of the disinflation the central bank must allow unemployment to return to its natural rate (otherwise, inflation would continue to decrease.) This implies that it provides in year 6 a one-time increase in money growth before returning, from year 7 on, to the new lower rate of money growth.

Figure 9–3 shows the path of unemployment and inflation implied by this disinflation path. In year 0, the economy is at point *A*: The unemployment rate is 6.5% and the inflation

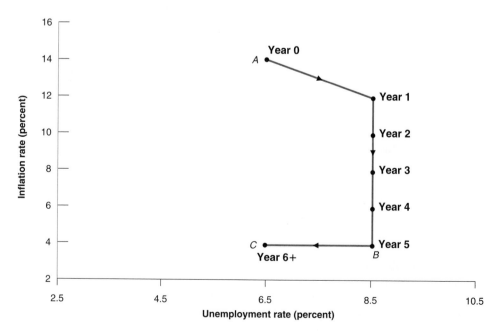

FIGURE 9–3

A Disinflation Path

Five years of unemployment above the natural rate lead to a permanent decrease in inflation.

rate is 14%. Years 1 to 5 are years of disinflation, during which the economy moves from *A* to *B*. Unemployment is higher than the natural rate, leading to a steady decline in inflation. Inflation decreases until it reaches 4%. From year 6 on, the economy remains at point *C*, with unemployment back down to its natural rate and an inflation rate of 4%. *In the medium run, money growth and inflation are lower, and the unemployment rate and output growth are back to normal; this is the neutrality result we obtained in section 9-2. But the transition to lower money growth and lower inflation is associated with a period of higher unemployment.*

The disinflation path drawn in Figure 9–3 is one of many possible paths. We could have looked instead at a path that front-loaded the increase in the unemployment rate and allowed it to return slowly to the natural rate, avoiding the awkward increase in money growth that takes place at the end of our scenario (year 6 in Table 9–1). Or we could have looked at a path where the central bank decreased the rate of money growth from 14% to 4% at once, letting inflation and unemployment adjust over time.[2] But all the paths we would draw would share one characteristic: The total unemployment cost—that is, the number of point-years of excess unemployment—would be the same. Put another way, *unemployment has to remain above the natural rate by a large enough amount, and/or long enough, to achieve disinflation.*

The analysis we have just developed is very much the type of analysis economists at the Fed were conducting in the late 1970s. The econometric model they used, as well as most econometric models in use at the time, shared our simple model's property that policy could change the timing, but not the number of point-years of excess unemployment. I shall call this the *traditional approach* in what follows. This traditional approach was challenged by two groups of academic economists. The next section presents their arguments, and the discussion that followed.

9-4 | Expectations, Credibility, and Nominal Contracts

The focus of both groups of economists was the role of expectations, and how changes in expectation formation might affect the unemployment cost of disinflation. But despite this common focus, they reached quite different conclusions.

Expectations and Credibility: The Lucas Critique

The conclusions of the first group were based on the work of Robert Lucas and Thomas Sargent, from the University of Chicago.

In what has become known as the **Lucas critique**, Lucas pointed out that when trying to predict the effects of a major change in policy—such as the change considered by the Fed at the time—it could be very misleading to take as given the relations estimated from past data.

In the case of the Phillips curve, taking equation (9.5) as given was equivalent to assuming that wage setters would keep expecting inflation in the future to be the same as in the past, that the way wage setters formed expectations would not change in response to the change in policy. This was an unwarranted assumption, Lucas argued. Why shouldn't wage setters take policy changes into account? If they believed that the Fed was committed to lower inflation, they might well expect inflation to be lower in the future than in the past. If

[2]**DIGGING DEEPER.** It would seem natural to look at a policy where the central bank permanently decreases the rate of money growth, say, from 14% to 4%. If you trace the effects of such a policy on output, unemployment, and inflation (solve for output, unemployment and inflation for time *t*, then for *t* + 1, and so on), you will find that it leads to a complicated path of inflation and unemployment, with inflation actually being lower than its new medium-run value for some time.

they lowered their expectations of inflation, then actual inflation would decline without the need for a protracted recession.

The logic of Lucas's argument can be seen by returning to equation (9.4),

$$\pi_t = \pi_t^e - \alpha(u_t - u_n)$$

If $\pi_t^e = \pi_{t-1}$, the Phillips curve is given by

$$\pi_t - \pi_{t-1} = -\alpha(u_t - u_n)$$

To achieve $\pi_t < \pi_{t-1}$, one must have $u_t > u_n$.

If wage setters kept forming expectations of inflation by looking at last year's inflation (if $\pi_t^e = \pi_{t-1}$), then the only way to decrease inflation would indeed be to accept higher unemployment for some time; we explored the implications of this assumption in the preceding section.

But if wage setters could be convinced that inflation was indeed going to be lower than in the past, they would decrease their expectations of inflation. This would in turn reduce actual inflation, without necessarily any change in the unemployment rate. For example, if wage setters were convinced that inflation, which had been running at 14% in the past, would be only 4% in the future, and if they formed expectations accordingly, then inflation would decrease to 4% *even if unemployment remained at the natural rate*

$$\pi_t = \pi_t^e - \alpha(u_t - u_n)$$
$$4\% = 4\% - \qquad 0\%$$

Money growth, inflation, and expected inflation could all be reduced without the need for a recession. Put another way, decreases in money growth could be neutral not only in the medium run, but also in the short run.

Lucas and Sargent did not believe that disinflation could really take place without some increase in unemployment. But Sargent, looking at the historical evidence on the end of several very high inflations, concluded that the increase in unemployment could be small. The sacrifice ratio—the amount of excess unemployment needed to achieve disinflation—might be much lower than suggested by the traditional approach. The essential ingredient of successful disinflation, he argued, was **credibility** of monetary policy—the belief by wage setters that the central bank was truly committed to reducing inflation. Only credibility would lead wage setters to change the way they formed expectations. Furthermore, he argued, a clear and quick disinflation program was much more likely to be credible than a protracted one that offered plenty of opportunities for reversal and political infighting along the way.

The credibility view: Fast disinflation is likely to be more credible than slow disinflation. Credibility decreases the unemployment cost of disinflation. Thus, the central bank should implement a fast disinflation.

Nominal Rigidities and Contracts

A contrary view was taken by Stanley Fischer, from MIT, and John Taylor, then at Columbia University. Both emphasized the presence of **nominal rigidities**, meaning that in modern economies, many wages and prices are set in nominal terms for some time and are typically not readjusted when there is a change in policy.

Fischer argued that even with credibility, too rapid a decrease in money growth would lead to higher unemployment. Even if the Fed fully convinced workers and firms that money growth was going to be lower, the wages set before the change in policy would reflect expectations of inflation prior to the change in policy. In effect, inflation would already be built into existing wage agreements, and could not be reduced costlessly and instantaneously. At the very least, Fischer said, a policy of disinflation should be announced sufficiently in advance of its actual implementation to allow wage setters to take it into account when setting wages.

Taylor's argument went one step further. An important characteristic of wage contracts, he argued, is that they are not all signed at the same time. Instead, they are staggered over time. He showed that this **staggering of wage decisions** imposed strong limits on how fast disinflation could proceed without triggering higher unemployment, even if the Fed's commitment to inflation was fully credible. Why the limits? If workers cared about relative wages—that is, cared about their wages relative to the wages of other workers—each wage contract would choose a wage not very different from wages in the other contracts in force at the time. Too rapid a decrease in nominal money growth would not lead to a proportional decrease in inflation. So, the real money stock would decrease, triggering a recession and an increase in the unemployment rate.

Taking into account the time pattern of wage contracts in the United States, Taylor then showed that under full credibility of monetary policy, there *was* a path of disinflation consistent with no increase in unemployment. This path is shown in Figure 9–4.

Disinflation starts in quarter 1 and lasts for 16 quarters. Once it is achieved, the inflation rate, which started at 10%, is 3%. The striking feature is how slowly disinflation proceeds at the beginning. One year (four quarters) after the announcement of the change in policy, inflation is still 9.9%. But then disinflation occurs faster. By the end of the third year inflation is down to 4%, and by the end of the fourth year the desired disinflation is achieved.

The reason for the slow decrease in inflation at the beginning—and, behind the scene, for the slow decrease in nominal money growth—is straightforward. Wages in force at the time of the policy change are the result of decisions made before the policy change, so that the path of inflation in the near future is largely predetermined. If nominal money growth were to decrease sharply, inflation could not decrease very much right away, and the result would be a decrease in real money and a recession. Thus, the best policy is for the Fed to proceed slowly at the beginning, while announcing it will proceed faster in the future. This announcement leads new wage settlements to take the new policy into account. When most wage decisions in the economy come from decisions made after the change in policy, disinflation can proceed much faster. This is what happens in the third year following the policy change.

Like Lucas and Sargent, Taylor did not believe that disinflation really could be implemented without increasing unemployment. For one thing, he realized that the path of disinflation drawn in Figure 9–4 might not be credible. The announcement this year that money growth will be decreased two years from now is likely to run into a serious credibility problem. Wage setters are likely to ask themselves: If the decision has been made to disinflate, why should the central bank wait two years? Without credibility, inflation expectations might not change, defeating the hope of disinflation without an increase in the unemployment rate. But Taylor's analysis had two clear messages. First, like Lucas and Sargent's analysis, it emphasized the role of expectations. Second, it suggested that a slow but credible disinflation might have a cost lower than that implied by the traditional approach.

The nominal rigidities view: Many wages are set in nominal terms, sometimes for many years. The way to decrease the unemployment cost of disinflation is to give wage setters time to take the change in policy into account. Thus, the central bank should implement a slow disinflation.

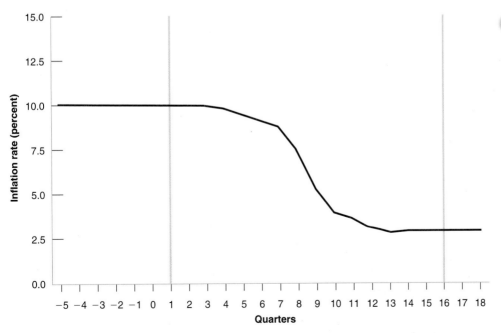

FIGURE 9–4

Disinflation Without Unemployment in the Taylor Model

With staggering of wage decisions, disinflation must be phased in slowly to avoid an increase in unemployment.

With this discussion in mind, let us end the chapter with a look at what happened in the United States from 1979 to 1985.

9-5 | The U.S. Disinflation, 1979 to 1985

In 1979, the U.S. unemployment rate was 5.8%. GDP growth was 2.5%. The inflation rate (using the CPI deflator) was a high 13.3%. The question the Federal Reserve faced was no longer whether it should reduce inflation, but how fast it should reduce it. In August 1979, President Carter appointed Paul Volcker chairman of the Federal Reserve Board. Volcker, who had served in the Nixon administration, was considered an extremely qualified chairman who could and would lead the fight against inflation.

In October 1979, the Fed announced several changes in its operating procedures. In particular, it indicated that it would shift from targeting a given level of the short-term interest rate to targeting the growth rate of nominal money.

This change would hardly seem to be the stuff of history books. The Fed made no announcement of a battle against inflation, nor of a targeted path of disinflation, nor of various other ambitious-sounding plans. Nevertheless, financial markets widely interpreted this technical change as a sign of a major change in monetary policy. In particular, the change was interpreted as indicating that the Fed was now committed to reducing inflation and, if needed, ready to let interest rates increase, perhaps to very high levels.

Recall from chapter 4 ▶ that the federal funds rate (the rate at which banks lend and borrow reserves overnight) is the rate most directly under the control of the Fed.

Over the following seven months, the Fed let the federal funds rate increase by more than 6 percentage points, from 11.4% in September 1979 to 17.6% in April 1980. But then there was a halt, followed by a rapid reversal. By July 1980, the rate was back down to 9%, an 8.6% drop in four months. This roller-coaster movement of the federal funds rate is shown in Figure 9–5, which plots the federal funds rate and the inflation rate, measured as the rate of change of the CPI over the previous 12 months, for the period January 1979 to December 1984.

The reason for the decrease in the federal funds rate in mid-1980 was the accumulation of signs that the economy was entering a sharp recession. In March 1980, believing that high consumer spending was one of the causes of inflation, the Carter administration had imposed controls on consumer credit—limits on how much consumers could borrow to buy some durable goods. The effect of these controls was much larger than the Carter administration had anticipated. The combination of the fear of a sharp recession and the political pressure

FIGURE 9–5

The Federal Funds Rate and Inflation, 1979–1984

A sharp increase in the interest rate from September 1979 to April 1980 was followed by a sharp decline in mid-1980, and then a second and sustained increase from January 1981 on, lasting for most of 1981 and 1982.

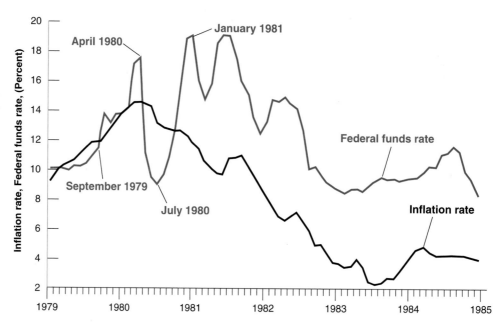

coming from the proximity of presidential elections was enough to lead the Fed to decrease interest rates sharply.

By the end of 1980, with the economy apparently in recovery, the Fed increased the federal funds rate sharply again. By January 1981, the rate was back up to 19%.

By the end of 1981, signs accumulated that the very high interest rates had triggered a second recession. The Fed decided not to repeat its mistake of 1980—the abandonment of its disinflation target in the face of a recession. In contrast to its actions in 1980, it kept interest rates high. The federal funds rate decreased to 12.3% in December 1981, but then increased back to 14.9% in April 1982.

I have gone through the events of 1979 to 1982 in some detail to show the practical difficulties of establishing "credibility." Paul Volcker had credibility when he came to office. However, the credibility of the Fed's disinflation stance was surely eroded by the Fed's behavior in 1980. Credibility was progressively reestablished in 1981 and 1982, especially when, despite clear indications that the economy was in recession, the Fed increased the federal funds rate in the spring of 1982.

Cumulative increases in the federal funds rate of 3 percentage points just before the election surely did not improve Carter's re-election prospects.

Did this credibility—to the extent that it was present—lead to a more favorable trade-off between unemployment and disinflation than implied by the traditional approach? Table 9–2 gives the relevant numbers. The upper half of the table makes it clear that there was no expectation miracle: Disinflation was associated with substantial unemployment. The average unemployment rate was above 9% in both 1982 and 1983, peaking at 10.8% in the month of December 1982.

The answer to whether the unemployment cost was lower than implied by the traditional approach is given in the bottom half of the table. Under the traditional approach, each point of disinflation is predicted to require about one point-year of excess unemployment. Line 4 computes the cumulative number of point-years of excess unemployment from 1980 on, assuming a natural rate of 6.5%. Line 5 computes cumulative disinflation—the decrease in inflation starting from its 1979 level. Line 6 gives the sacrifice ratio, the ratio of the cumulative point-years of unemployment above the natural rate to cumulative disinflation.

The table shows that there were no obvious "credibility gains". By 1982, the sacrifice ratio looked quite attractive: The cumulative decrease in inflation since 1979 was nearly 9.5%, at a cost of 4.9 point-years of unemployment—a sacrifice ratio of 0.51, relative to the sacrifice ratio of 1 predicted by the traditional approach. But by 1985, the sacrifice ratio had reached 1.02. A 10% disinflation had been achieved with close to 10 point-years of excess unemployment, very much the outcome predicted by the traditional approach.

In short, the U.S. disinflation of the early 1980s was associated with a substantial increase in unemployment. The Phillips curve relation between the change in inflation and the

TABLE 9–2 Inflation and Unemployment, 1979–1985

	1979	1980	1981	1982	1983	1984	1985
1. GDP growth (%)	2.5	−0.5	1.8	−2.2	3.9	6.2	3.2
2. Unemployment rate (%)	5.8	7.1	7.6	9.7	9.6	7.5	7.2
3. CPI inflation (%)	13.3	12.5	8.9	3.8	3.8	3.9	3.8
4. Cumulative unemployment		0.6	1.7	4.9	8.0	9.0	9.7
5. Cumulative disinflation		0.8	4.4	9.5	9.5	9.4	9.5
6. Sacrifice ratio		0.75	0.39	0.51	0.84	0.95	1.02

Cumulative unemployment is the sum of point-years of excess unemployment from 1980 on, assuming a natural rate of 6.5%.

Cumulative disinflation is the difference between inflation in a given year and inflation in 1979. The sacrifice ratio is the ratio of cumulative unemployment to cumulative disinflation.

deviation of the unemployment rate from the natural rate proved more robust than many economists anticipated. Was this outcome due to a lack of credibility of the change in monetary policy, or to the fact that credibility is not enough to reduce substantially the cost of disinflation? One way of learning more is to look at other disinflation episodes. This is the approach followed in a paper by Laurence Ball, from Johns Hopkins. Ball has estimated sacrifice ratios for 65 disinflation episodes in 19 OECD countries over the last 30 years. He reaches three main conclusions:

Laurence Ball, "What Determines the Sacrifice Ratio?" in N. Gregory Mankiw, ed., *Monetary Policy* (NBER and the University of Chicago, 1994), 155–194.

- Disinflations typically lead to higher unemployment for some time. Put another way, even if it is neutral in the medium run, a decrease in money growth leads to an increase in unemployment for some time.
- Faster disinflations are associated with smaller sacrifice ratios. This conclusion provides some evidence to support the expectation and credibility effects emphasized by Lucas and Sargent.
- Sacrifice ratios are smaller in countries that have shorter wage contracts. This provides some evidence to support Fischer and Taylor's emphasis on the importance of the structure of wage settlements.

SUMMARY

- There are three relations linking inflation, output, and unemployment:

  The first is Okun's law, which relates the change in the unemployment rate to the deviation of the rate of growth of output from the normal growth rate. In the United States today, output growth of 1% above normal for a year leads to a decrease in the unemployment rate of about 0.4%.

  The second is the Phillips curve, which relates the change in the inflation rate to the deviation of the actual unemployment rate from the natural rate. In the United States today, an unemployment rate 1% below the natural rate for a year leads to an increase in inflation of about 1%.

  The third is the aggregate demand relation, which relates the rate of growth of output to the rate of growth of the real money stock. The growth rate of output is equal to the growth rate of nominal money minus the rate of inflation. Given nominal money growth, higher inflation leads to a decrease in output growth.

- In the medium run, the unemployment rate is equal to the natural rate, and output grows at its normal growth rate. Money growth determines the inflation rate: A 1% increase in money growth leads to a 1% increase in the inflation rate. As Milton Friedman put it, inflation is always and everywhere a monetary phenomenon.

- In the short run, a decrease in money growth leads to a slowdown in growth and an increase in unemployment for some time. Thus, disinflation (a decrease in the in-

flation rate) can be achieved only at the cost of more unemployment. How much unemployment is required is a controversial issue.

- The traditional approach assumes that people do not change the way they form expectations when monetary policy changes, so that the relation between inflation and unemployment is unaffected by the change in policy. This approach implies that disinflation can be achieved by a short but large increase in unemployment, or by a longer and smaller increase in unemployment. But policy cannot affect the total number of point-years of excess unemployment.

- An alternative view is that if the change in monetary policy is credible, expectation formation may change, leading to a smaller increase in unemployment than predicted by the traditional approach. In its extreme form, this alternative view implies that if policy is fully credible, it can achieve disinflation at no cost in unemployment. A less extreme form recognizes that although expectation formation may change, the presence of nominal rigidities is likely to imply some increase in unemployment, although less than implied by the traditional answer.

- The U.S. disinflation of the early 1980s, during which inflation decreased by approximately 10%, was associated with a large recession. The unemployment cost was close to the predictions of the traditional approach.

- Okun's law, 168
- normal growth rate, 169
- labor hoarding, 169
- adjusted nominal money growth, 172
- disinflation, 173
- point-year of excess unemployment, 174
- sacrifice ratio, 174
- Lucas critique, 177
- credibility, 178
- nominal rigidities, 178
- staggering of wage decisions, 178

QUESTIONS & PROBLEMS

An asterisk denotes a harder problem.

1. TRUE/FALSE/UNCERTAIN

a. The U.S. unemployment rate will remain constant as long as output growth is positive.

b. Many firms prefer to keep workers around when demand is low (rather than lay them off) even if the workers are underutilized.

c. The behavior of Okun's law across countries and across decades is consistent with our knowledge of firm behavior and labor market regulations.

d. There is a reliable negative relation between the rate of inflation and the growth rate of output.

e. In the medium run, the rate of inflation is equal to the rate of nominal money growth.

f. According to the Phillips curve relation, the sacrifice ratio is independent of the speed of disinflation.

g. Contrary to the traditional Phillips curve analysis, Taylor's analysis of staggered wage contracts made a case for a slow approach to disinflation.

h. Ball's analysis of disinflation episodes provides some support for both the credibility effects of Lucas and Sargent and for the nominal wage-setting effects of Fischer and Taylor.

2. OKUN'S LAW

As shown by equation (9.2) the estimated Okun's law for the United States is given by:

$$u_t - u_{t-1} = -0.4(g_{yt} - 3\%)$$

a. What growth rate of output leads to an increase in the unemployment rate of 1% per year? How can the un-employment rate increase even though the growth rate of output is positive?

b. What rate of growth output do we need to decrease unemployment by two percentage points over the next four years?

c. Suppose that we experience a second baby boom. How do you expect Okun's law to change if the rate of growth of the labor force increases by two percentage points?

3. REDUCING THE INFLATION RATE

Suppose that the economy can be described by the following three equations:

$$u_t - u_{t-1} = -0.4(g_{yt} - 3\%) \qquad \text{Okun's law}$$
$$\pi_t - \pi_{t-1} = -(u_t - 5\%) \qquad \text{Phillips curve}$$
$$g_{yt} = g_{mt} - \pi_t \qquad \text{aggregate demand}$$

a. What is the natural rate of unemployment for this economy?

b. Suppose that the unemployment rate is equal to the natural rate, and that the inflation rate is 8%. What is the growth rate of output? What is the growth rate of the money supply?

c. Suppose that conditions are as in (b), when, in year t, the authorities use monetary policy to reduce the inflation rate to 4% in year t and keep it there. What must happen to the unemployment rate and output growth in years t, $t + 1$, and $t + 2$? What money growth rate in years t, $t + 1$, and $t + 2$ will accomplish this goal?

4. THE EFFECTS OF A PERMANENT DECREASE IN MONEY GROWTH

Suppose that the economy can be described by the following three equations:

$$u_t - u_{t-1} = -0.4(g_{yt} - 3\%) \qquad \text{Okun's law}$$

$$\pi_t - \pi_{t-1} = -(u_t - 5\%) \qquad \text{Phillips curve}$$

$$g_{yt} = g_{mt} - \pi_t \qquad \text{aggregate demand}$$

a. Reduce the three equations to two by substituting g_{yt} from the aggregate demand equation into Okun's law.

Assume initially that $u_t = u_{t-1} = 5\%$, $g_{mt} = 13\%$ and $\pi_t = 10\%$. Now suppose that this year's money growth is permanently reduced from 13% to 0%.

b. Compute the impact on unemployment and inflation this year and next year.

c. Compute the values of unemployment and inflation in the medium run.

5. POLICY RECOMMENDATIONS

Suppose that you are advising a government that wants to reduce its inflation rate. It is considering two options: a gradual reduction over several years and an immediate reduction.

a. Lay out the arguments for and against each option.

b. If the only criterion you were to consider was the sacrifice ratio, which option would you take? Why might you want to consider other criteria?

c. What particular features of the economy might you want to look at before giving your advice?

*6. DISINFLATION AND CREDIBILITY

Suppose that the Phillips curve is given by:

$$\pi_t = \pi_t^e + K - 2u_t$$

where K is a constant, and that

$$\pi_t^e = \pi_{t-1}$$

Suppose that initially unemployment is equal to the natural rate and $\pi = 12\%$. The authorities decide in year t that 12% inflation is too high and that they will maintain the unemployment rate one percentage point above the natural rate of unemployment until the inflation rate decreases to 2%.

a. Solve for the natural rate of unemployment as a function of the constant K. What is the sacrifice ratio? How does the sacrifice ratio depend on the natural rate of unemployment?

b. Compute the rate of inflation for years t and $t + 1$. (*Hint*: express the Phillips curve as a function of the difference between the current unemployment rate and the natural rate of unemployment.)

c. For how many years must the authorities keep the unemployment rate above the natural rate of unemployment? Is the implied sacrifice ratio consistent with your answer to (a)?

Now suppose that people know that the authorities want to lower inflation to 2%, but they are not sure of the authorities' willingness to accept an unemployment rate above the natural rate of unemployment. So, their expectation of inflation is a weighted average of the target of 2% and last year's inflation, that is,

$$\pi_t^e = b\,2\% + (1 - b)\pi_{t-1}$$

where b is the weight they put on the government's target of 2%.

d. Let $b = .25$. How long will it take before the inflation rate is no higher than 2%? What is the sacrifice ratio now?

e. Suppose that after the government's policy has been in effect for one year, people believe the authorities completely. So, they now set their expectations according to

$$\pi_t^e = 2\%$$

From what year onward can the authorities let the unemployment rate return to the natural rate?

f. What advice would you give to a policy maker interested in lowering the rate of inflation by increasing the rate of unemployment as little and for as short a time period as possible?

7. THE APPROPRIATE REACTION TO OIL SHOCKS

Suppose that the Phillips curve is given by

$$\pi_t - \pi_{t-1} = -(u_t - 5\%) + .1\mu$$

where μ is the markup.

Suppose that unemployment is initially at its natural rate. Suppose now that an oil shock increases μ, but that the monetary authority continues to keep the unemployment rate at its previous value.

a. What will happen to inflation?

b. What should the monetary authority do instead?

FURTHER READINGS

The Lucas critique was first presented by Robert Lucas in "Econometric Policy Evaluation: A Critique," in *The Phillips Curve and Labor Markets*, Carnegie Rochester Conference, Volume 1, 1976, 19–46.

The article by Stanley Fischer arguing that credibility would not be enough to achieve costless disinflation is "Long-Term Contracts, Rational Expectations, and the Optimal Money Supply Rule," *Journal of Political Economy*, 85, 1977, 163–190.

The article that derived the path of disinflation reproduced in Figure 9–4 is by John Taylor, "Union Wage Settle-ments," *American Economic Review*, December 1983, 981–993.

(All three preceding articles are relatively technical.)

A description of U.S. monetary policy in the 1980s is given by Michael Mussa in chapter 2 of Martin Feldstein, ed., *American Economic Policy in the 1980s* (University of Chicago Press and NBER, 1994), 81–164. One of the comments on the chapter is by Paul Volcker, who was chairman of the Fed from 1979 to 1987.

We invite you to visit the Blanchard page on the Prentice Hall Web site at:

http://www.prenhall.com/blanchard

for this chapter's World Wide Web exercises

THE **CORE**

The Long Run

The next four chapters focus on the long run. In the long run, what dominates is not fluctuations, but growth. The basic question is now, What determines growth?

CHAPTER 10

Chapter 10 looks at the facts of growth. Looking first at OECD countries over the past 50 years, it documents the large increase in output, the convergence of output per capita across countries, and the slowdown in growth that has taken place since the mid-1970s. Taking a wider look, both across time and space, it shows that on the scale of human history, growth is a recent phenomenon, and that convergence is not a worldwide phenomenon: Many countries are both poor and not growing.

CHAPTER 11

Chapter 11 focuses on the role of capital accumulation in growth. It shows that capital accumulation cannot by itself sustain output growth, but that it does affect the level of output. A higher saving rate typically leads to lower consumption initially, but more consumption in the long run.

CHAPTER 12

Chapter 12 turns to the role of technological progress. It shows how, in the long run, the growth rate of an economy is determined by the rate of technological progress. It then returns to the facts of growth presented in Chapter 10, and shows how to interpret them in the light of the theory we have developed.

CHAPTER 13

Chapter 13 (an optional chapter) shows how we can integrate the study of the long run with our previous study of short- and medium-run movements in output. It discusses in particular whether and when technological progress can cause unemployment, and whether technological progress should be blamed for the increase in wage inequality in the United States over the last 20 years.

CHAPTER 10

The Facts of Growth

Our perceptions of how the economy is doing tend to be dominated by year-to-year fluctuations in activity. A recession leads to gloom, an expansion to optimism. But if we step back to get a look at activity over longer periods of time—say, over the course of many decades—we see a different picture. Fluctuations fade in importance. **Growth**—the steady increase in aggregate output over time—dominates the picture.

Figure 10–1 shows the evolution of U.S. GDP (in 1992 dollars) since 1890. The years from 1929 to 1933 correspond to the large decrease in output during the Great Depression, and the years 1980 to 1982 correspond to the largest postwar recession. Note how small these two episodes appear compared to the steady increase in output over the last 100 years.

Our focus so far in the book has been on fluctuations. In this and the next three chapters, we focus instead on growth. Put another way, we turn from the study of the determination of output in the *short and medium run*—where fluctuations dominate—to the determination of output in the *long run*—where growth dominates.

This chapter presents the facts of growth, from the United States and elsewhere, from the recent as well as the not so recent past, and introduces the framework economists use to think about growth. The framework is developed in the next two chapters. Chapter 11 focuses on the role of capital accumulation in growth. Chapter 12 focuses on the role of technological progress. Chapter 13, an optional chapter, shows how we can integrate what have we learned about the determination of output in the short, the medium, and the long run. It does so by discussing the relation between technological progress, unemployment, and wages.

FIGURE 10-1

U.S. GDP, 1890–1998

Aggregate U.S. output has increased by a factor of 37 since 1890.
Source: 1890–1929: Historical Statistics of the United States; 1929–1998: National Income and Product Accounts.

The scale used to measure GDP on the vertical axis in Figure 10–1 is called a **logarithmic scale**. It differs from the standard, linear scale in the following way:

Take a variable that grows over time at a constant growth rate, say, 3% per year. Then, the larger the variable, the larger will be its increase from one year to the next. When GDP was $204 billion (in 1992 dollars) in 1890, a 3% increase meant an increase of $6.1 billion; in 1998, with GDP at $7552 billion (in 1992 dollars), a 3% increase meant an increase of $226 billion. If we were to plot GDP using a linear vertical scale, the increments would become larger and larger over time. Using a logarithmic scale, the same proportional increase is represented by the same vertical distance on the scale. Put another way, the behavior of a variable that grows at a constant rate is represented by a curve that becomes steeper and steeper when a linear scale is used, but is represented by a straight line when a logarithmic scale is used. The slope of the line is equal to the rate of growth: If a variable grows at 3% per year, the slope of the line is 0.03.

Even when a variable has a growth rate that varies from year to year—as is the case for GDP— the slope at any point in time still gives the growth rate of the variable at that point in time. The slope of the line between two points at two different dates gives the average growth rate from the first to the second date. This is the reason for using a logarithmic scale to plot variables that grow over time: By looking at the slope, we easily can see what is happening to the growth rate.

Check that you have understood how to use a logarithmic scale. Look at Figure 10–1. In which 10-year period was output growth highest? Has average growth since 1950 been lower or higher than average growth from 1890 to 1930?

The Organization for Economic Cooperation and Development (OECD) is an international organization that includes most of the world's rich economies. (See chapter 1)

Output: GDP

Output per capita: GDP divided by population

10-1 | Growth in Rich Countries Since 1950

Table 10–1 gives the evolution of **output per capita** (GDP divided by population) for France, Germany, Japan, the United Kingdom, and the United States since 1950. I have chosen these five countries not only because they are the world's major economic powers, but because their experience is broadly representative of that of advanced countries (the countries that are members of the OECD) over the last half century or so.

There are two reasons for looking here at the numbers for output *per capita* rather than the numbers for total output. The evolution of the standard of living is given by the evolution of output per capita, not total output. And, when comparing countries with different populations, output numbers must be adjusted to take into account these differences in population size. This is exactly what output per capita does.

	Annual Growth Rate Output per Capita (%)		Real Output per Capita (1992 dollars)		
	1950–1973	1973–1998	1950	1998	Ratio of Real Output Per Capita, 1998/1950
France	4.2	1.6	5,150	19,158	3.7
Germany	4.9	1.8	4,356	20,059	4.6
Japan	8.1	2.5	1,820	19,907	10.9
United Kingdom	2.5	1.9	6,870	19,005	2.8
United States	2.2	1.5	11,170	25,890	2.3
Average	4.4	1.9	5,872	20,804	3.5

Source: Robert Summers and Alan Heston, "The Penn World Table Mark 5: An Expanded Set of International Comparisons, 1950–1988," *Quarterly Journal of Economics*, 1991:2, 327–368.
   Note: Updated numbers for the period 1950–1992 are taken from the Web at http://www.nber.org/pwt56.html. Adjusted from 1985 dollars to 1992 dollars, by multiplying original numbers by 1.27, the ratio of the U.S. price level in 1992 relative to the price level in 1985.
   Extended from 1992 to 1998 by using rates of real GDP growth from *OECD Economic Outlook*, December 1998, Table A1, and population growth rates from the IMF International Financial Statistics (*IFS*), February 1999. The average in the last line is a simple (unweighted) average.

Before discussing the table, I must discuss the way the output numbers are constructed. So far, in constructing output numbers for countries other than the United States, I have used the straightforward method of taking that country's GDP expressed in that country's currency, then multiplying it by the current exchange rate to express it in terms of dollars (see chapter 1). But this simple computation will not do here, for two reasons.

First, exchange rates can vary a lot (more on this in chapters 18 to 21). The dollar increased and then decreased in the 1980s by roughly 50% vis-à-vis the currencies of its trading partners. But surely the standard of living in the United States did not increase by 50% and then decrease by 50% compared to the standard of living of its trading partners in the 1980s. Yet this is the conclusion we would reach if we compared GDP per capita using current exchange rates

The second reason goes beyond fluctuations in exchange rates. In 1997, GDP per capita in India, using the current exchange rate, was $362, compared to $29,800 in the United States. Surely nobody could live on $362 a year in the United States. But people live on it—admittedly, not very well—in India, where the prices of basic goods, those goods needed for subsistence, are much lower than in the United States. The level of consumption of the average consumer in India, who consumes mostly basic goods, is not 82 times smaller than that of his or her U.S. counterpart. This pattern applies to other countries besides the United States and India: In general, the lower a country's income, the lower the prices of food and basic services in that country.

Thus, when our focus is on comparing standards of living, either across time or across countries, we get more meaningful comparisons by correcting for the effects just discussed. This is what the numbers in Table 10–1 do. The details of construction are complicated, but the principle is simple: The numbers for GDP in Table 10–1 are constructed using a common set of prices for the goods and services produced in each economy. Such adjusted real GDP numbers, which you can think of as measures of **purchasing power** across time or across countries, are called **purchasing power parity (PPP)** numbers. Further discussion is given in the Focus box "The Construction of PPP Numbers."

The Asian crisis we saw in chapter 1 provides another example. When the currency of several Asian countries plunged against the dollar by 50% or more, these countries did not suddenly become poorer by 50% or more.

At this point, the "Penn World Tables" project (described in the accompanying Focus Box) has constructed PPP numbers only up to the early 1990s. In Table 10–1, I extended those numbers to 1998 for the five major OECD countries. When looking however at larger sets of countries later in this chapter, extending the numbers would be too much work. So we look at evolutions of output per capita only up to the latest year available in the data set (1992 for most countries).

The Construction of PPP Numbers

FOCUS

Let's consider two countries—say, the United States and Russia—but without attempting to fit the facts of these two countries very closely.

In the United States, annual consumption per capita equals $20,000. Individuals buy two goods. Every year, they buy a new car for $10,000, and spend the rest on food. The price of a yearly bundle of food is $10,000.

In Russia, annual consumption per capita equals 12,000 rubles. People keep their cars for 15 years. The price of a car is 60,000 rubles, so that individuals spend on average 4,000 rubles—60,000/15—a year on cars. They buy the same yearly bundle of food as their U.S. counterparts, at a price of 8,000 rubles.

Russian and U.S. cars are of identical quality, and so are Russian and U.S. food. (You may dispute the realism of these assumptions. Whether a car in country X is the same as a car in country Y is very much the type of problem confronting economists constructing PPP measures.) The exchange rate is such that 1 dollar is equal to 6 rubles. What is consumption per capita in Russia relative to consumption per capita in the United States?

One way to answer is by taking consumption per capita in Russia and converting it into dollars using the exchange rate. Using that method, Russian consumption per capita in dollars is $2,000 (12,000 rubles divided by the exchange rate, 6 rubles to the dollar), thus 10% of U.S. consumption.

Does this answer make sense? True, Russians are poorer, but food is relatively much cheaper in Russia. A U.S. consumer spending all of his $20,000 on food would buy ($20,000/$10,000) = 2 bundles of food. A Russian consumer spending all of his 12,000 rubles on food would buy (12,000 rubles/8,000 rubles) = 1.5 bundles of food. In terms of food bundles, the difference between U.S. and Russian consumption per capita looks much smaller. And given that one-half of consumption in the United States and two-thirds of consumption in Russia go to spending on food, this seems like a relevant computation.

Can we improve on our initial answer? Yes. One way is to use the same set of prices for both countries and then measure the quantities of each good consumed in each country using this common set of prices. Suppose we use U.S. prices. In terms of U.S. prices, annual consumption per capita in the United States is obviously still $20,000. What is it in Russia? Every year, the average Russian buys approximately 0.07 car (one car every 15 years) and one bundle of food. Using U.S. prices—specifically, $10,000 for a car and $10,000 for a bundle of food—gives Russian consumption per capita as [(0.07 × $10,000) + (1 × $10,000)] = ($700 + $10,000] = $10,700. This puts annual Russian consumption per capita at $10,700/$20,000 = 53.5% of annual U.S. consumption per capita, a better estimate of relative standards of living than we obtained using our first method (which gave only 10%).

This type of computation, namely the construction of variables across countries using a common set of prices, underlies PPP estimates. Rather than using U.S. dollar prices as in our example (why use U.S. rather than Russian, or for that matter, French prices?), these estimates use average prices across countries; these prices are called international dollar prices. The estimates we use in Table 10–1 and elsewhere in this chapter are the result of an ambitious project known as the "Penn World Tables." Led by three economists—Irving Kravis, Robert Summers, and Alan Heston—over more than 15 years, this project has constructed PPP series not only for consumption (as we just did in our example), but more generally for GDP and its components, going back to 1950, for most countries in the world.

Reference

For more on the construction of PPP numbers, read Robert Summers and Alan Heston, "The Penn World Table Mark 5: An Expanded Set of International Comparisons, 1950–1988," *Quarterly Journal of Economics*, 1991:2, 327–368.

The differences between PPP numbers and the numbers based on current exchange rates can be substantial. Take our comparison between India and the United States. Using PPP numbers, GDP per capita in the United States is roughly equal to 17 times GDP per capita in India. This is still a large difference, but less than the 82 times difference we derived using the current exchange rate. Or consider the ranking of rich countries by output per capita. In 1997, using current exchange rates, U.S. GDP per capita was only 90% of Japan's output per capita; using PPP numbers, it was 130%. Using PPP numbers, the United States still has the highest GDP per capita among the world's major countries.

Bottom line: When comparing standard of living across countries, use PPP numbers.

We can now turn to the numbers in Table 10–1. You should draw three main conclusions from the table:

(1) First and foremost is how strong growth has been in all five countries, how much the standard of living has improved since 1950. Growth from 1950 to 1998 has increased real

output per capita by a factor of 2.3 in the United States, by a factor of 4.6 in Germany, and by a factor of 10.9 in Japan.

These numbers show what is sometimes called the *force of compounding*. In a different context, you probably have heard how saving even a little while you are young will build to a large amount by the time you retire. For example, if the interest rate is 5.1% a year, an investment of one dollar, with the proceeds reinvested every year, leads to about 11 dollars 48 years later ($[1 + 0.051]^{48} = 10.9$ dollars). The same logic applies to the Japanese growth rate from 1950 to 1998. The average annual growth rate in Japan over the period was equal to 5.1% [(8.1% a year × 23 years + 2.5% a year × 25 years), divided by 48 years], leading to a nearly elevenfold increase in real output per capita. Clearly, a better understanding of growth, if it leads to the design of policies that stimulate growth, can have a very large effect on the standard of living. A policy measure that increased the growth rate from, say, 2% to 3%, would lead, after 40 years, to a standard of living 100% higher than it would have been without the policy.

Needless to say, policy measures with such magic results have proven difficult to discover.

(2) Growth rates have decreased since the mid-1970s.

The first two columns of Table 10–1 show growth rates of output per capita for both pre- and post-1973. Pinpointing the exact date of the decrease in growth is difficult; 1973, the date used to split the sample in the table, is as good as any date in the mid-1970s.

Growth has decreased in all five countries. The decrease has been stronger in the countries that were growing fast pre-1973, such as France, Germany, and especially Japan, with the result that the differences in growth rates across countries are smaller post-1973 than they were pre-1973.

If it continues, this decline in growth will have profound implications for the evolution of income per capita in the future. At a growth rate of 4.4% per year—the average growth rate across our five countries from 1950 to 1973—it takes only 16 years for the standard of living to double. At a growth rate of 1.9% per year—the average from 1973 to 1998—it takes 37 years, so more than twice as long. Expectations of fast growth in individual income that had developed in the 1950s and 1960s have had to confront the reality of lower growth since 1973. For some socioeconomic groups, lower growth of income per capita for the economy as a whole, together with a decline in their income relative to the average, has led to an absolute decline in their income. Those who have been affected the most have typically been the least-skilled workers. We explore this topic in more detail in chapter 13.

The "rule of 70": If a variable grows at x% a year, then it will take approximately $70/x$ years for the variable to double. If $x = 4.4$, it will take about 16 years (70/4.4) for the variable to double. If $x = 1.9$, it will take about 37 years (70/1.9).

(3) Levels of output per capita across the five countries have converged over time. Put another way, those countries that were behind have grown faster, reducing the gap between them and the United States.

In 1950, output per capita in the United States was around twice the level of output per capita in the United Kingdom, Germany, and France, and more than six times that of Japan. Looking from Japan and Europe, the United States was seen as the land of plenty, where everything was bigger and better. Today these perceptions have faded, and the numbers explain why. Using PPP numbers, U.S. output per capita is still the highest, but, in 1998, it was only 30% above output per capita in the other four countries, a much smaller difference than in the 1950s.

This **convergence** of levels of output per capita across countries extends to the set of OECD countries. This is shown in Figure 10–2, which plots the average annual growth rate of output per capita from 1950 to 1992 against the initial level of output per capita in 1950 for the set of countries that are members of the OECD today. There is a clear negative relation between the initial level of output per capita and the growth rate since 1950: Countries that were behind in 1950 have typically grown faster. The relation is not perfect: Turkey, which had roughly the same low level of output per capita as Japan in 1950, has had a growth rate equal to only about half that of Japan. But the relation is clearly there.

The issue of convergence of output per capita has been a hot topic of macroeconomic research over the past decade. Some have pointed to a potential flaw in graphs like Figure 10–2. By looking at the set of countries that are members of the OECD today, what we have

As explained earlier, at this time, 1992 (and, in some cases, 1991 or 1990) is the latest year for which we have PPP numbers for most countries in the world.

THE FACTS OF GROWTH

FIGURE 10-2

Growth Rate of GDP Per Capita Since 1950 versus GDP Per Capita in 1950; OECD Countries

Countries that had a lower level of output per capita in 1950 have typically grown faster.
Source: See Table 10–1.
Note: South Korea, the Czech Republic, Hungary, and Poland are not included because of missing data.

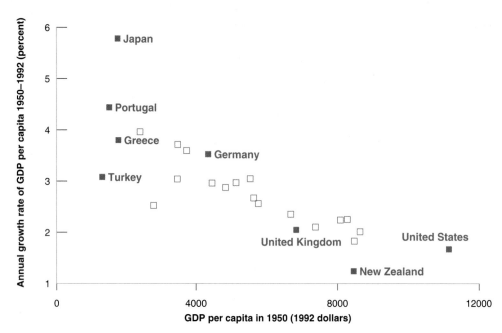

done in effect is to look at a club of economic winners: OECD membership is not officially based on economic success, but economic success is surely an important determinant of membership. But when you look at a club whose membership is based on economic success, you will find that those who came from behind had the fastest growth: This is precisely why they made it to the club. Thus, the finding of convergence could come in part from the way we selected the countries in the first place.

Thus, a better way of looking at convergence is to define the set of countries we look at not on the basis of where they are today—as we did in Figure 10–2 by looking at today's OECD members—but on the basis of where they were in, say, 1950. For example, we can look at all countries that had an output per capita of at least one fourth of U.S. output per capita in 1950, then look for convergence within that group. It turns out that most of the countries in that group have indeed converged, and therefore convergence is not solely an OECD phenomenon. However, a few countries—Uruguay, Argentina, and Venezuela among them—have not converged. Perhaps the most striking case is Argentina. Output per capita in Argentina, which was $5,120 (in 1992 dollars) in 1950—similar to France then—was only $5,976 (in 1992 dollars) in 1990, a meager 17% increase in 40 years, and far below the 1990 French level of $17,658.

1990 is the latest year for which PPP numbers are available for Argentina.

10-2 | A Broader Look Across Time and Space

The three basic facts we shall keep in mind and try to explain as we go along are:

● The large increase in the standard of living since 1950.
● The decrease in growth since the mid-1970s.
● The convergence of output per capita among rich countries.

Before we do so, however, it is useful to put them in a broader perspective. This is what we do in this section, by looking at the evidence both over a much longer time span and a wider set of countries.

Looking Across Two Millennia

Has output per capita in the currently rich economies always grown at growth rates similar to those in Table 10–1? The answer is no. To see why, you do not even need to look at history, just do a simple computation. Suppose that the annual growth rate in the five countries of Table 10–1 had been as small as 0.5% per year since year 0 of the Christian calendar (clearly an arbitrary date here). Working backward, this implies that output per capita in year 0 would have been 0.005% of output per capita today. This is an absurdly small number.

An examination of history confirms this conclusion. Estimates of growth are clearly harder to construct as we look further back in time. But there is agreement among economic historians about the main evolutions over the last 2,000 years.

From the end of the Roman Empire to roughly year 1500, there was essentially no growth of output per capita in Europe: Most workers were employed in agriculture, in which there was little technological progress. Because agriculture's share of output was so large, inventions with applications outside agriculture could contribute little to overall production and output. Although there was some output growth, it was reflected in a roughly proportional increase in population, leading to rough constancy of output per capita.

From about 1500 to 1700, growth of output per capita turned positive but small, around 0.1% per year, increasing to 0.2% per year from 1700 to 1820.

Even during the Industrial Revolution, growth rates were not high by current standards. The growth rate of output per capita from 1820 to 1950 in the United States was only 1.5% per year.

> If the growth rate had been 0.5% per year, output per capita today would be equal to $1.005^{1998} =$ approximately 20,000 times output per capita in year 0. Equivalently, output in year 0 would have been equal to approximately $1/20,000 = 0.005\%$ of output today.

The Reality of Growth: A Workingman's Budget in 1851

FOCUS

Data on GDP per capita does not fully convey the reality of growth and the accompanying increase in the standard of living. An examination of an annual "workingman's budget" in 1851 Philadelphia gives a much better sense of the improvement (Table 1).

Note how much a family consumed on food in 1851: 41% of expenditures. Today's corresponding share—as reflected in the composition of the consumption basket used to compute the consumer price index—is only 14%. And food at home—as opposed to food in restaurants—ac-

counts for only 8.6% of total consumption today. But perhaps more revealing is the composition of food consumption. Compare the food in the table to the richness and diversity of the food we eat today.

Source: William Baumol et al., *Productivity and American Leadership* (Cambridge, MA: MIT Press, 1989), Chapter 3, Table 3.2. The information on the composition of expenditures today comes from Table 712 (Average annual income and expenditures of all consumer units, 1995) in the *Statistical Abstract of the United States*, 1997.

TABLE 1   Annual workingman's budget, Philadelphia, 1851

Item of Expenditure	Amount (Dollars)	Percent of Total
Butcher's meat (2 lb a day)	72.80	13.5
Flour ($6\frac{1}{2}$ lb a year)	32.50	6.0
Butter (2 lb a week)	32.50	6.0
Potatoes (2 pk a week)	26.00	4.8
Sugar (4 lb a week)	16.64	3.0
Coffee and tea	13.00	2.4
Milk	7.28	1.4
Salt, pepper, vinegar, starch, soap, yeast, cheese, eggs	20.80	3.9
Total expenditures for food	221.52	41.0
Rent	156.00	29.0
Coal (3 tons a year)	15.00	2.8
Charcoal, chips, matches	5.00	0.9
Candles and oil	7.28	1.4
Household articles (wear, tear, and breakage)	13.00	2.4
Bedclothes and bedding	10.40	1.9
Wearing apparel	104.00	19.3
Newspapers	6.24	1.2
Total expenditures other than food	316.92	58.9

On the scale of human history, therefore, growth of output per capita is a recent phenomenon. In light of the growth record of the last 200 years or so, what appears unusual is the high growth rate achieved in the 1950s and the 1960s rather than the lower growth rate since 1973.

History also puts into context the convergence of OECD countries to the level of U.S. output per capita since 1950. The United States was not always the world's economic leader. History looks more like a long-distance race in which one country assumes leadership for some time, only to lose it to another and return to the pack or disappear from sight. For much of the first millennium, and until the fifteenth century, China probably had the world's highest level of output per capita. For a couple of centuries, leadership moved to the cities of northern Italy. It was then assumed by the Netherlands until around 1820, and then by the United Kingdom from 1820 to around 1870. Since then, the United States has been in the lead. Seen in this light, history looks more like **leapfrogging** (in which countries get close to the leader and then overtake it) than like convergence, (in which the race becomes closer and closer). If history is any guide, the United States will not remain in the lead forever.

Looking Across Countries

The numbers for 1950 are missing for too many countries to use 1950 as the initial year, as we did in Figure 10–2. Figure 10–3 includes all the countries for which PPP estimates of GDP per capita exist for both 1960 and 1992 (or, in some cases, 1990 or 1991). There are some notable absences, such as China and several Eastern European countries, for which the numbers for 1960 are not available.

We have seen how output per capita has converged among OECD countries. But what about the other countries? Are the poorest countries also growing faster? Are they converging toward the United States, even if they are still far behind?

The answer is given in Figure 10–3, which plots the annual growth rate of output per capita from 1960 to 1992 against output per capita for the year 1960, for 97 countries.

Figure 10–3 shows no clear pattern. Over the last 30 years, convergence has not been the rule. Countries that were relatively poorer in 1960 have not in general grown faster.

However, the cloud of points hides several interesting subpatterns, which appear when we put countries into different groups. We identify three groups in Figure 10–4. The diamonds represent the OECD countries we looked at earlier. The squares represent African countries. The triangles represent four Asian economies: Singapore, Taiwan, Hong Kong, and South Korea. Together, these three groups account for 59 countries. To avoid cluttering, Figure 10–4 leaves out all other countries; these show less obvious patterns.

FIGURE 10–3

Growth Rate of GDP per Capita 1960–1992, versus GDP per Capita in 1960; 97 Countries

There is no clear relation between the growth rate of output since 1960 and the level of output per capita in 1960.
Source: See Table 10–1.

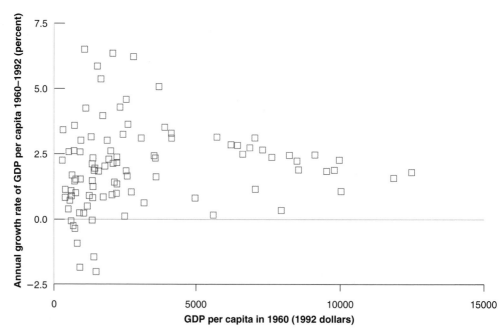

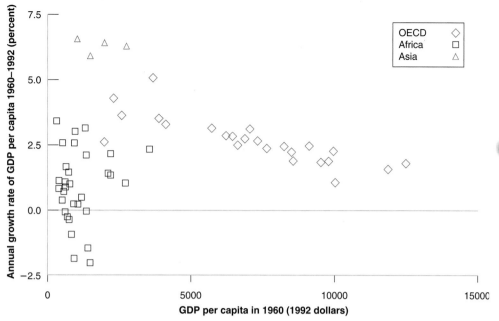

FIGURE 10-4

Growth Rate of GDP per Capita, 1960–1992, versus GDP per Capita in 1960: OECD, Africa, and Asia

Asian countries are converging to OECD levels. There is no evidence of convergence for African countries.
Source: See Table 10–1.

The figure yields three main conclusions:

1. The picture for OECD countries is much the same as in Figure 10–2, which looked at a slightly longer period of time (from 1950 on, rather than from 1960 on here). Nearly all start at relatively high levels of output per capita (say, at least one-third of the U.S. level in 1960), and there is clear evidence of convergence.

2. Convergence is also evident in the case of the four Asian economies. Whereas Japan (represented by a diamond as a member of the OECD) was the first of the Asian economies to grow rapidly and now has the highest level of output per capita in Asia, several other Asian economies are trailing it closely. Singapore, Taiwan, Hong Kong, and South Korea—sometimes called the **four tigers**—have had average annual growth rates of GDP per capita in excess of 6% over the last 30 years. In 1960, their average output per capita was about 16% of the U.S. number; by 1992, it had increased to 62% of U.S. output. Several other Asian countries, among them Indonesia, Malaysia, China, and Thailand (which are not included in the figure because of the lack of data for 1960), have recently grown at similar rates, and are also rapidly catching up.

3. The picture is very different for African countries. Convergence is certainly not the rule in Africa. Most African countries were very poor in 1960, and many have experienced negative growth of output per capita—an absolute decline in their standard of living—since then. Even in the absence of major wars, output per capita has declined at the rate of 1.3% annually in Chad and Madagascar since 1960; output per capita in these two countries stands at 67% of its 1960 level. Why so many African countries are not growing is one of the main questions facing development economists today.

We shall not take on the wider challenges raised by the facts presented in this section. Doing so would take us too far into economic history and development economics. But they put in perspective the three basic facts we discussed earlier for the OECD:

1. Growth is not a historical necessity. There was little growth for most of human history, and in many countries today growth remains elusive. Theories that explain growth in the OECD today must also in principle be able to explain the absence of growth in the past, and its absence in much of Africa today.

2. Convergence of OECD countries to the United States may well be the prelude to leapfrogging, a stage when economic leadership slips from one country to another.

These numbers cover only 1960 to 1992, and do not include recent years, and the decrease in growth due to the "Asian crisis" discussed in chapter 1. But including the lower growth numbers for the late 1990s would make no difference. Put another way, the current output decline in some Asian economies does not change the fact that they have done extremely well since 1960.

The distinction between *growth theory* and *development economics* is fuzzy. A rough distinction: Growth theory takes many institutions (for example, the legal system, the form of government) as given. Development economics asks what institutions are needed to sustain steady growth.

Theories that explain convergence must therefore also allow for the possibility that convergence will be followed by leapfrogging and the appearance of a new economic leader.

3. Finally, in a longer historical perspective, it is not so much the lower growth since 1973 in the OECD that is puzzling. More puzzling is the earlier period of exceptionally fast growth. Finding the explanation for lower growth today may come from understanding what factors contributed to fast growth post–World War II, and whether these factors have disappeared.

10-3 | Thinking About Growth: A Primer

How do we explain the facts we saw in sections 10-1 and 10-2? What determines growth? What is the role of capital accumulation? What is the role of technological progress? To think about and answer these questions, economists use a framework developed originally by Robert Solow, from MIT, in the late 1950s. The framework has proven sturdy and useful, and we shall use it here. This section provides an introduction. Chapters 11 and 12 provide a more detailed analysis, first of the role of capital accumulation and then of the role of technological progress in the process of growth.

Solow's article, "A Contribution to the Theory of Economic Growth," appeared in the *Quarterly Journal of Economics*, February 1956, 65–94. Solow received the Nobel prize in 1987 for his work on growth.

The Aggregate Production Function

The starting point of any theory of growth is the **aggregate production function**, the relation between aggregate output and the inputs in production.

The aggregate production function we introduced in chapter 6 to study the determination of output in the short and the medium run took a particularly simple form. Output was simply proportional to employment (equation [6.2]). This assumption was acceptable so long as our focus was on fluctuations in output and employment. But, now that our focus shifts to growth, it will no longer do: It implies that output per worker is constant, ruling out growth (or at least growth of output per worker) altogether.

It is time to relax it. So, from now on, we shall assume that aggregate output is produced using two inputs, capital and labor

$$Y = F(K,N) \tag{10.1}$$

As before, Y is aggregate output; K is capital—the sum of all the machines, plants, office buildings, and housing in the economy; N is labor—the number of workers in the economy. The function F, which tells us how much output is produced for given quantities of capital and labor, is the aggregate production function. This way of thinking about aggregate production is clearly an improvement on our treatment in chapter 6. It is still a drastic simplification of reality. Surely, machines and office buildings play very different roles in the production of aggregate output, and should be treated as separate inputs. Surely, workers with Ph.D.s are different from high-school dropouts; yet, by constructing the labor input as simply the *number* of workers in the economy, we treat all workers as identical. We shall relax some of these simplifications later. For the time being, equation (10.1), which emphasizes the role of both labor and capital in production, will do.

The aggregate production function is:

$$Y = F(K,N)$$

Aggregate output (Y) depends on the aggregate capital stock (K), and aggregate employment (N).

What does the aggregate production function F itself depend on? In other words, how much output can be produced for given quantities of capital and labor? This depends on the **state of technology**. A country with a more advanced technology will produce more output from the same quantities of capital and labor than will an economy with only a primitive technology.

The function F depends on the state of technology. The higher the state of technology, the higher $F(K,N)$ for a given K and a given N.

What do we mean by the state of technology? In a narrow sense, we can think of the state of technology as the list of blueprints defining both the range of products that can be produced in the economy as well as the techniques available to produce them. We can also think of the state of technology in a broader sense: How much output is produced in an economy also depends on how well firms are run, on the organization and sophistication of markets, on the system of laws and their enforcement, on the political environment, and so on. We shall think of the state of technology in the narrow sense for most of the next two chapters. I shall return at the end of chapter 12 to what we know about the role of the other factors, from the system of laws to the form of government.

Returns to Scale and Returns to Factors. Now that we have introduced the aggregate production function, what restrictions can we reasonably impose on this function?

Consider a thought experiment in which we doubled both the number of workers and the amount of capital in the economy. It is reasonable to guess that output would roughly double as well: In effect, we would have cloned the original economy, and the clone economy could produce output in the same way as the original economy. This property is called **constant returns to scale**: If the scale of operation is doubled—that is, if the quantities of capital and labor are doubled—then output will also double

$$2Y = F(2K, 2N)$$

Or more generally, for any number x

$$xY = F(xK, xN) \tag{10.2}$$

Constant returns to scale refers to what happens to production when *both* capital and labor are increased. What should we assume when only *one* input—say capital—is increased?

It is surely reasonable to assume that output will increase as well. It is also reasonable to assume that a given increase in capital will lead to smaller and smaller increases in output as the level of capital increases. Why? Think, for example, of a secretarial pool, composed of a given number of secretaries. Think of capital as computers. The introduction of just one computer will substantially increase the pool's production, as the computer assumes some of the more time-consuming tasks. As the number of computers increases and more secretaries in the pool get their own PCs, production will further increase, although by less per additional computer than was the case when the first one was introduced. Once each secretary has his own PC, increasing the number of computers further is unlikely to increase production very much, if at all. Additional computers may simply remain unused and left in their shipping boxes, and lead to no increase in output whatsoever.

We shall refer to the property that increases in capital lead to smaller and smaller increases in output as the level of capital increases as **decreasing returns to capital** (a property that will be familiar to those who have taken a course in microeconomics). A similar property holds for the other input, labor: Increases in labor, given capital, lead to smaller and smaller increases in output as the level of labor increases. (Return to our previous example, and think of what happens as you increase the number of secretaries for a given number of computers.) There are **decreasing returns to labor** as well.

Output and Capital Per Worker. The aggregate production function we have written and the two properties we have just assumed imply a simple relation between output per worker and capital per worker.

To derive the relation between output per worker and capital per worker, we let $x = 1/N$ in equation (10.2), so that

$$\frac{Y}{N} = F\left(\frac{K}{N}, 1\right) \tag{10.3}$$

Note that Y/N is output per worker, K/N is capital per worker. So equation (10.3) says that the amount of output per worker depends on the amount of capital per worker. This relation between output per worker and capital per worker is drawn in Figure 10–5.

Output per worker (Y/N) is measured on the vertical axis, capital per worker (K/N) on the horizontal axis. The relation between the two is given by the upward-sloping curve. As capital per worker increases, so does output per worker. But, because of decreasing returns to capital, increases in capital lead to smaller and smaller increases in output. At point A, where capital per worker is low, an increase in capital per worker equal to the distance AB

Following up on growth versus development economics: Think of growth theory as focusing on the role of technology in the narrow sense, and development economics as focusing on the role of technology in the broader sense.

You may question this assumption: Doubling the economy requires double the space. What about the fact that a country has a given size? This objection is right in theory, but not very important in practice, except for economies where agriculture plays a central role. For example, Hong Kong, with very little land, has a thriving economy. For modern economies, constant returns to scale seems to be a good approximation to reality.

Even under constant returns to scale, there are decreasing returns to each factor, keeping the other factor constant:

- Given labor, there are decreasing returns to capital: Increases in capital lead to smaller and smaller increases in output as the level of capital increases.
- Given capital, there are decreasing returns to labor: Increases in labor lead to smaller and smaller increases in output as the level of labor increases.

FIGURE 10-5

Output and Capital per Worker

Increases in capital per worker lead to smaller and smaller increases in output per worker.

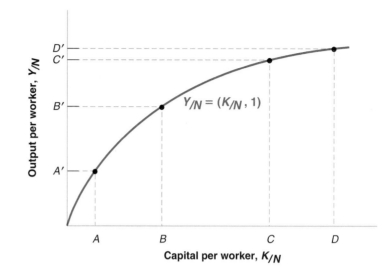

leads to an increase in output per worker of $A'B'$. At point C, where capital per worker is larger, the same increase in capital per worker, CD (the distance CD is equal to the distance AB), leads to a much smaller increase in output per worker, only $C'D'$. This is just as in our example of the secretarial pool, where additional computers led to less and less effect on total output.

Increases in capital per worker lead to smaller and smaller increases in output per worker as the level of capital per worker increases. ▶

The Sources of Growth

We are now ready to return to growth. Where does growth come from? Why does output per worker—or output per capita, if we assume the ratio of workers to the population as a whole remains roughly constant over time—go up over time? Equation (10.3) gives a simple answer:

Increases in capital per worker: Movements along the production function. ▶

- Increases in output per worker (Y/N) can come from increases in capital per worker (K/N). This is the relation we just looked at in Figure 10–5. As (K/N) increases—as we move to the right on the horizontal axis—(Y/N) increases.
- Or they can come from improvements in the state of technology, which shift the production function, F, and lead to more output per worker *given* capital per worker. This is shown in Figure 10–6. An improvement in the state of technology shifts the production

FIGURE 10-6

The Effects of an Improvement in the State of Technology

An improvement in the state of technology shifts the production function up, leading to an increase in output per worker for a given level of capital per worker.

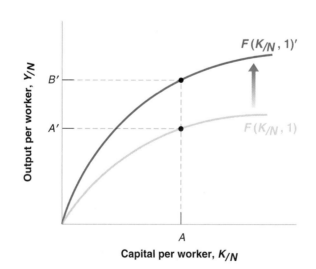

function from F to F'. For given level of capital per worker, the improvement in technology leads to an increase in output per worker. For example, for the level of capital per worker corresponding to point A, output per worker increases from A' to B'.

Improvements in the state of technology: Shifts of the production function.

Hence, we can think of growth as coming from **capital accumulation** and from **technological progress**—the improvement in the state of technology. We shall see, however, that these two factors play very different roles in the growth process:

- Capital accumulation by itself cannot sustain growth. A formal argument will have to wait until chapter 11. But we can derive the basic intuition for this answer from Figure 10–5. Because of decreasing returns to capital, sustaining a steady increase in output per worker would require larger and larger increases in the level of capital per worker. At some stage, society will not be willing to save and invest enough to further increase capital. At that stage, output per worker will stop growing.

    Does this mean that an economy's **saving rate**—the proportion of income that is saved—is irrelevant? No. It is true that a higher saving rate cannot permanently increase the *growth rate* of output. But it can sustain a higher *level* of output. Let me state this in a slightly different way. Take two economies that differ only in their saving rate. The two economies will grow at the same rate; but, at any point in time, the economy with the higher saving rate will have a higher level of output per capita than the other. How and how much the saving rate affects the level of output, and whether a country such as the United States (which has a very low saving rate) should try to increase its saving rate, will be one of the topics we take up in chapter 11.

- Sustained growth requires sustained technological progress. This really follows from the first proposition: Given that the two factors that can lead to an increase in output per capita are capital accumulation and technological progress, if capital accumulation cannot sustain growth forever, then technological progress must be key—and it is. We shall see in chapter 12 that the rate of growth of output per capita is eventually determined by the rate of technological progress.

    This has a strong implication. In the long run, an economy that sustains a higher rate of technological progress will eventually overtake all other economies. This raises the question of what determines the rate of technological progress. What we know about the determinants of technological progress—from the role of spending on fundamental and applied research, to the role of patent laws, to the role of education and training—will be one of the topics taken up in chapter 12.

SUMMARY

- Over long periods of time, fluctuations in output are dwarfed by growth, the steady increase of aggregate output over time.

- Looking at growth in five rich countries (France, Germany, Japan, the United Kingdom, and the United States) since 1950, three main facts emerge:

    1. All five countries have experienced strong growth and a large increase in the standard of living. Growth from 1950 to 1998 increased real output per capita by a factor of 2.3 in the United States, by a factor of 4.6 in Germany, and by a factor of 10.9 in Japan.
    2. Growth has decreased since the mid-1970s. The average growth rate of output per capita has gone

from 4.4% per year from 1950 to 1973 to 1.9% from 1973 to 1998.

    3. The levels of output per capita across the five countries have converged over time. Put another way, those countries that were behind have grown faster, reducing the gap between them and the current world economic leader, the United States.

- Looking at the evidence across a broader set of countries and a longer period of time, the following facts emerge:

    1. On the scale of human history, sustained output growth is a recent phenomenon. From the end of the Roman Empire to roughly year 1500, there was essentially no growth of output per capita in

Europe. Even during the Industrial Revolution, growth rates were not high by current standards. The growth rate of output per capita from 1820 to 1950 in the United States was 1.5%.

2. Convergence of levels of output per capita is not a worldwide phenomenon. Many Asian countries are rapidly catching up, but most African countries have both very low levels of output per capita and low growth rates.

- To think about growth, economists start from an aggregate production function relating aggregate output to two factors of production, capital and labor. How much output is produced given these inputs depends on the state of technology.

- Under the assumption of constant returns, the aggregate production function implies that increases in output per worker can come either from increases in capital per worker, or from improvements in the state of technology.

- Capital accumulation by itself cannot permanently sustain growth of output per capita. Nevertheless, how much a country saves is very important because the saving rate determines the *level* of output per capita, if not its growth rate.

- Sustained growth of output per capita is ultimately due to technological progress. Perhaps the most important question in growth theory is what the determinants of technological progress are.

QUESTIONS & PROBLEMS

An asterisk denotes a harder question. [Web] indicates that the question requires access to the Internet.

1. **TRUE/FALSE/UNCERTAIN**

a. Despite the Great Depression, U.S. output was higher in 1940 than in 1929.

b. On a log scale, a variable that increases at 5% a year will move along an upward-sloping line, with slope 0.05.

c. If Japan had continued to grow at the same rate during 1973 to 1998 as it had during 1950 to 1973, its output per capita in 1998 would have been roughly 3 times U.S. output per capita.

d. The price of food is higher in poor than in rich countries.

e. Output per capita in most countries in the world is converging to the level of output per capita in the United States.

f. Capital accumulation does not affect the level of output in the long run. Only technological progress does.

g. The aggregate production function is a relation between output, labor, and capital.

h. Because eventually we shall know everything, technological progress will end and growth will eventually end as well.

2. **THE DECREASE IN GROWTH SINCE 1973**

Use Table 10–1 to answer the following questions:

a. Compute what output per capita would have been in 1998 for each of the five countries if the growth rate from 1973 to 1998 for each country had remained the same as during 1950 to 1973.

b. What would have been the ratio of output per capita in Japan relative to output per capita in the United States?

c. Did convergence continue during the growth slowdown from 1973 to 1998?

3. PURCHASING POWER PARITY

Assume that the typical consumers in Mexico and the United States buy the quantities and pay the prices indicated in the accompanying table:

| | Bread | | Car Services | |
	Price	Quantity	Price	Quantity
Mexico	1 peso	400	7 pesos	300
U.S.	$1	1,000	$2	2,000

a. Compute U.S. consumption per capita in dollars.

b. Compute Mexican consumption per capita in pesos.

c. Suppose a peso is worth 20 cents ($0.20). Compute Mexican consumption per capita in dollars.

d. Using the purchasing power parity method and U.S. prices, compute Mexican consumption per capita in dollars.

e. Under each of the methods used in (c) and (d), how much smaller is the standard of living in Mexico than in the United States? Does the choice of method make a difference?

4. THE PRODUCTION FUNCTION AND CONSTANT RETURNS TO SCALE

Consider the production function $Y = \sqrt{K}\sqrt{N}$

a. Compute output when $K = 49$ and $N = 81$.

b. If both capital and labor double, what happens to output?

c. Is this production function characterized by constant returns to scale? Explain.

d. Write this production function as a relationship between output per worker and capital per worker.

e. Let $K/N = 4$. What is Y/N? Now double K/N to 8. Does Y/N more or less than double?

f. Does the relation between output per worker and capital per worker exhibit constant returns to scale?

g. Is your answer in (f) the same as your answer in (c)? Why or why not?

h. Plot the relation between output per worker and capital per worker. Does it have the same general shape as the relation in Figure 10–5? Explain.

5. GROWTH AND TECHNOLOGICAL PROGRESS

Between 1950 and 1973, France, Germany, and Japan all experienced growth rates that were at least 2 percentage points higher than those in the United States. Yet the most important technical advances of that period were made in the United States. How can this be?

6. CONVERGENCE OVER TIME [WEB]

In Table 10–1, we saw that the levels of output per capita in the United Kingdom, Germany, France, Japan, and the United States were much closer in 1998 than they were in 1950. Here we will examine convergence for another set of countries.

Go to <http://www.nber.org/pwt56.html>. It contains the Penn World Tables (see Table 10–1 and the Focus box "The Construction of PPP Numbers").

a. At the web site's menu, select GDP per capita (RGDPCH) for France, Belgium, Italy, and the United States, for 1950 to 1992.

b. Once the numbers appear on your web browser, save them as a text file and import them to your favorite spreadsheet program. Define for each country for each year the ratio of its real GDP to that of the United States for that year (so that this ratio will be equal to one for the United States for all years).

c. Graph the ratios for France, Belgium, and Italy over the period 1950 to 1992 (all in the same graph). Does your graph support the notion of convergence among the four countries listed in (a)?

d. Repeat the same exercise for Argentina, Venezuela, Chad, Madagascar, and the United States. Does your new graph support the notion of convergence among this group of countries?

FURTHER READINGS

A broad presentation of facts about growth is given by Angus Maddison in *Phases of Economic Development* (New York: Oxford University Press, 1982).

Chapter 3 in *Productivity and American Leadership* by

William Baumol, Sue Anne Batey Blackman, and Edward Wolff (Cambridge, MA: MIT Press 1989) gives a vivid description of how life has been transformed by growth in the United States since the mid-1880s.

CHAPTER 11

Saving, Capital Accumulation, and Output

Since 1950 the U.S. **saving rate**—the ratio of saving to GDP—has averaged only 18.6%, compared to 24.6% in Germany and 33.7% in Japan. Can this explain why the U.S. growth rate has been lower than in most OECD countries in the last 50 years? Would increasing the U.S. saving rate lead to sustained higher U.S. growth in the future?

I have already given the basic answer to these questions at the end of chapter 10: The answer is no. Over the long run (an important qualification to which we shall return), an economy's growth rate does not depend on its saving rate. Lower U.S. growth in the last 50 years is not due to the low saving rate. Nor should we expect that an increase in the saving rate would lead to sustained higher U.S. growth.

This conclusion does not imply, however, that we should not be concerned about the low U.S. saving rate. Even if the saving rate does not permanently affect the growth rate, it does affect the level of output and the standard of living. An increase in the saving rate would lead to higher growth for some time and eventually to a higher standard of living in the United States.

The effects of the saving rate on capital and output are the topics of this chapter. The first two sections look at the interactions between output and capital accumulation, and the effects of the saving rate. The third section plugs in numbers to give a better sense of the magnitudes involved. The fourth section extends the initial model to allow not only for physical capital but also for human capital.

To understand the determination of output in the long run, you must keep in mind two relations between output and capital.

- The amount of capital determines the amount of output being produced.
- The amount of output determines the amount of saving and investment, and thus the amount of capital being accumulated.

Together, these two relations, which are represented in Figure 11–1, determine the evolution of output and capital over time. We now look at each relation in turn.

The Effects of Capital on Output

We started discussing the first of these two relations, the effect of capital on output, in section 10-3. There, we introduced the aggregate production function and saw that, under the assumption of constant returns to scale, we can write the following relation between output and capital per worker

$$\frac{Y}{N} = F\left(\frac{K}{N}, 1\right)$$

Suppose the function F has the following "double square root" form:

$$F(K,N) = \sqrt{K}\sqrt{N}$$

Then

$$Y/N = F(K/N,1)$$
$$= \sqrt{K/N}\sqrt{N/N}$$
$$= \sqrt{K/N}$$

So the function f is simply the square root function:

$$f(K/N) = \sqrt{K/N}$$

Output per worker (Y/N) is an increasing function of capital per worker (K/N). Under the assumption of decreasing returns to capital, the effects of an increase in capital per worker become smaller, the larger the initial ratio of capital per worker. When capital per worker is already very high, further increases have only a small effect on output.

To simplify notation, we rewrite this relation between output and capital per worker simply as

$$\frac{Y}{N} = f\left(\frac{K}{N}\right)$$

where the function f represents the same relation between output and capital per worker as the function F

$$f(K/N) \equiv F(K/N,1)$$

In this chapter, in order to focus on the role of capital accumulation, we shall make two further assumptions:

Labor force (L) =
Population ×
Participation rate

Employment (N) =
Labor force (L) ×
[1 minus unemployment rate (u)]

If population, the participation rate, and the unemployment rate are constant, population, the labor force, and employment will be constant.

- The first is that employment, N, is constant. Let me be more specific here. Start with the relations we saw in chapter 2 (and again in chapter 6) among population, the labor force, and employment. Employment is equal to the labor force times 1 minus the unemployment rate. The labor force in turn is equal to population times the participation rate. In this chapter, we shall assume that population, the participation rate, and the unemployment rate are all constant. Constant population and a constant participation rate imply that the labor force is constant. A constant labor force and a constant unemployment rate imply that the level of employment, N, is constant. Note that, under these assumptions, output per worker (output divided by employment), output per capita (output divided by population), and output itself all move proportionately. Although I shall usually refer to movements in output or capital *per*

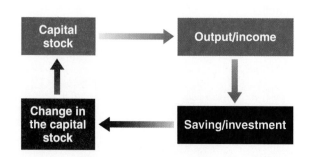

worker, to lighten the text I shall sometimes just talk about movements in output or capital, leaving out the "per worker" or "per capita" qualification, where it is completely obvious.

The reason for assuming that N is constant is to make it easier to focus on the role of capital accumulation in growth: If N is constant, the only factor of production that changes over time is capital. The assumption is not very realistic however, and we shall relax it in the next two chapters. In chapter 12, we shall allow for steady population and employment growth. And in chapter 13, we shall see how we can integrate our analysis of the long run, which ignores fluctuations in employment, with our earlier analysis of the short and medium run, which focused precisely on these fluctuations in employment (as well as output and unemployment). But both steps are better left for later chapters.

- The second assumption is that there is no technological progress, so the production function f (or, equivalently, F) does not change through time. Again, the reason for making this—obviously counterfactual—assumption is to focus on the role of capital accumulation. In chapter 12, we shall introduce technological progress and see that the basic conclusions we derive here about the role of capital in growth also hold when there is technological progress. Again, this step is better left for the next chapter.

With these two assumptions, our first relation between output and capital per worker, from the production side, can be written as

$$\frac{Y_t}{N} = f\left(\frac{K_t}{N}\right) \tag{11.1}$$

where I have introduced time indices for output and capital (but not for labor, N, which we assume to be constant and so does not need a time index). In short, higher capital per worker leads to higher output per worker.

The Effects of Output on Capital Accumulation

To derive the second relation, between output and capital accumulation, we proceed in two steps. First, we derive the relation between output and investment. Then we derive the relation between investment and capital accumulation.

Output and Investment. To derive the relation between output and investment, we make three assumptions:

- We continue to assume that the economy is closed. As we saw in chapter 3, this implies that investment is equal to saving, private and public.

$$I = S + (G - T)$$

- To focus on the behavior of private saving, we ignore both taxes and government spending, so $G = T = 0$, and by implication public saving $(G - T) = 0$. (We shall relax this assumption later when we focus on the implications of fiscal policy on growth.) Replacing in the equation above gives

$$I = S$$

Investment is equal to private saving.
- We assume that private saving is proportional to income, so

$$S = sY$$

The parameter s is the saving rate, and has a value between 0 and 1. This assumption captures two basic facts about saving. The saving rate does not appear systematically to increase or decrease as a country becomes richer. And richer countries do not appear to have systematically higher or lower saving rates than poorer ones.

Combining the two relations above, and introducing time indices gives

$$I_t = sY_t$$

Output per capita
$$= \frac{\text{Employment}}{\text{Population}}$$
$$\times \text{ Output per worker}$$

If the participation rate is 60% and the unemployment rate is 10%, then employment is 60% times $(1 - 0.10) = 54\%$ of the population. Output per capita is 54% of output per worker.

From the production side: The level of capital per worker determines the level of output per worker.

As we shall see in chapter 19, saving and investment need not be equal in an open economy. A country may save more than it invests, and lend the difference to the rest of the world. This has been the case for Japan, which has been running a large trade surplus, lending part of its saving to the rest of the world. I shall ignore this possibility here, and use saving and investment interchangeably.

You have now seen two specifications of saving behavior (equivalently consumption behavior): one for the short run in chapter 3, and one for the long run in this chapter. You may wonder how the two specifications relate to each other, and whether they are consistent. The answer is yes. A full discussion is given in chapter 16.

Investment is proportional to output: The higher the level of output, the higher the level of investment.

Investment and Capital Accumulation.
The second step relates investment, which is a flow (the new machines produced and new plants built during a given period), to capital, which is a stock (the existing machines and plants in the economy at a point in time).

Recall that flows are variables that have a time dimension (that is, they are defined per unit of time); stocks are variables that do not have a time dimension (they are defined at a point in time). Output, saving, and investment are flows. Employment and the capital stock are stocks.

Think of time as measured in years, so t denotes year t, $t + 1$ denotes year $t + 1$, and so on. Think of capital as being measured at the beginning of each year, so K_t refers to the capital stock at the beginning of year t, K_{t+1} to the capital stock at the beginning of year $t + 1$ and so on.

Assume that capital depreciates at rate δ (the lowercase Greek letter delta) per year: That is, from one year to the next, a proportion δ of the capital stock breaks down and becomes useless. The parameter δ is called the **depreciation rate**.

The evolution of the capital stock is then given by

$$K_{t+1} = (1 - \delta)K_t + I_t$$

The capital stock at the beginning of year $t + 1$, K_{t+1}, is equal to the capital stock at the beginning of year t, K_t, adjusted for depreciation—thus multiplied by $(1 - \delta)$—plus investment during year t, I_t.

We can now combine the relation between output and investment, and the relation between investment and capital accumulation to obtain the second relation we need to think about growth, namely, the relation between output and capital accumulation.

Replacing investment by saving in the previous equation, and dividing both sides by N (the number of workers in the economy) gives

$$\frac{K_{t+1}}{N} = (1 - \delta)\frac{K_t}{N} + s\frac{Y_t}{N}$$

In words: Capital per worker at the beginning of year $t + 1$ is equal to capital per worker at the beginning of year t, adjusted for depreciation, plus investment per worker during year t. Investment per worker is in turn equal to the saving rate times output per worker during year t.

Moving K_t/N to the left and reorganizing

From the saving side: The level of output per worker determines the change in the level of capital per worker over time.

$$\frac{K_{t+1}}{N} - \frac{K_t}{N} = s\frac{Y_t}{N} - \delta\frac{K_t}{N} \qquad (11.2)$$

In words: The change in the capital stock per worker—the term on the left—is equal to saving per worker (the first term on the right) minus depreciation (the second term on the right.) This equation gives us the second relation between output and capital per worker.

11-2 | Implications of Alternative Saving Rates

We have derived two relations. From the production side, equation (11.1) shows how capital determines output. From the saving side, equation (11.2) shows how output, in turn, determines capital accumulation. Let's now put them together and see what they imply for the behavior of output and capital over time.

Dynamics of Capital and Output

Replacing output per worker (Y_t/N) in equation (11.2) by its expression in terms of capital per worker from equation (11.1) gives

$$\underbrace{\frac{K_{t+1}}{N} - \frac{K_t}{N}}_{\substack{\text{change in capital} \\ \text{from year } t \text{ to year } t + 1}} = \underbrace{sf\left(\frac{K_t}{N}\right)}_{\substack{= \text{ investment} \\ \text{during year } t}} - \underbrace{\delta\frac{K_t}{N}}_{\substack{\text{depreciation} \\ \text{during year } t}} \qquad (11.3)$$

This relation describes what happens to capital per worker. The change in capital per worker from this year to next year depends on the difference between two terms:

- Investment per worker, the first term on the right. The level of capital per worker this year determines output per worker this year. Given the saving rate, output per worker determines the amount of saving per worker and thus of investment per worker this year.

- Depreciation per worker, the second term on the right. The capital stock per worker determines the amount of depreciation per worker this year.

$K_t/N \Rightarrow Y_t/N = f(K_t/N)$
$f(K_t/N) \Rightarrow sf(K_t/N)$

$K_t/N \Rightarrow \delta K_t/N$

If investment per worker exceeds depreciation per worker, the change in capital per worker is positive. Capital per worker increases. If investment per worker is less than depreciation per worker, the change in capital per worker is negative. Capital per worker decreases.

Given capital per worker, output per worker is then given by equation (11.1)

$$\frac{Y_t}{N} = f\left(\frac{K_t}{N}\right)$$

Equations (11.3) and (11.1) contain all the information we need to understand the dynamics of capital and output over time. The easiest way to interpret them is to use a graph. We do this in Figure 11–2, where output per worker is measured on the vertical axis, capital per worker on the horizontal axis.

In Figure 11–2, look first at the curve representing output per worker, $f(K_t/N)$, as a function of capital per worker. The relation is the same as in Figure 10–5. Output per worker increases with capital per worker, but the effect is smaller the higher the level of capital per worker.

Now look at the two curves representing the two components on the right of equation (11.3).

The relation representing investment per worker, $sf(K_t/N)$, has the same shape as the production function, except that it is lower by a factor s. At the level of capital per worker K_0/N, for example, output per worker is given by the distance AB, and investment per worker is given by the distance AC, which is equal to s times the distance AB. Thus, investment increases with capital, but by less and less as capital increases. When capital is already very high, the effect of a further increase in capital on output, and thus in turn on investment, is very small.

The relation representing depreciation per worker, $\delta K_t/N$ is represented by a line. Depreciation per worker increases in proportion to capital per worker so the relation is repre-

To make the graph easier to read, I have assumed an unrealistically high saving rate. (Can you tell roughly what value I have assumed for s? What would be a plausible value for s?)

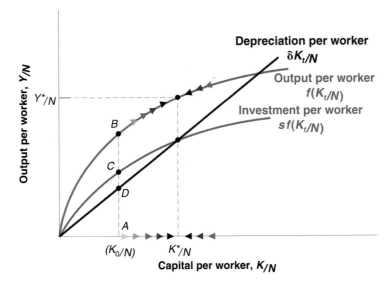

Capital per worker, K/N

FIGURE 11–2

Capital and Output Dynamics

When capital and output are low, investment exceeds depreciation, and capital increases. When capital and output are high, investment is less than depreciation and capital decreases.

sented by a straight line with slope equal to δ. At the level of capital per worker given by K_0/N, depreciation is given by the distance AD.

The change in capital per worker is given by the difference between investment per worker and depreciation per worker. At K_0/N, the difference is positive, and given by the distance $CD = AC - AD$. As we move to the right along the horizontal axis and look at higher and higher levels of capital per worker, investment increases by less and less, while depreciation keeps increasing in proportion to capital. For some level of capital per worker, K^*/N in Figure 11–2, investment is just enough to cover depreciation, and capital per worker remains constant. To the left of K^*/N, investment exceeds depreciation and capital per worker increases. This is indicated by the arrows pointing to the right along the curve representing the production function. To the right of K^*/N, depreciation exceeds investment, and capital per worker decreases. This is indicated by the arrows pointing to the left along the curve representing the production function.

▶ When capital per worker is low, capital per worker and output per worker increase over time. When capital per worker is high, capital per worker and output per worker decrease over time.

Characterizing the evolution of capital per worker and output per worker over time is now easy. Consider an economy that starts with a low level of capital per worker—say, K_0/N in Figure 11–2. Because investment exceeds depreciation, capital per worker increases. And because output moves with capital, output per worker increases as well. Capital per worker eventually reaches K^*/N, the level at which investment is equal to depreciation. Once the economy has reached the level of capital K^*/N, output and capital per worker remain constant at Y^*/N and K^*/N, their long-run equilibrium levels.

For example, think of a country that loses part of its capital stock, perhaps as a result of a war. The mechanism we have just seen suggests that if it has suffered much larger capital losses than population losses, it will come out of the war with a low level of capital per worker, so at a point to the left of K^*/N. It will then experience a large increase in both capital per worker and output per worker for some time. This appears to describe quite well what happened after World War II to countries that had proportionately larger destructions of capital than of human lives (see the Global Macro box "Capital Accumulation and Growth in France in the Aftermath of World War II").

▶ What does the model predict for postwar growth if a country suffers roughly proportional losses in population and in capital? Do you find this answer convincing? What elements may be missing from the model?

If a country starts instead from a high level of capital per worker, from a point to the right of K^*/N, then capital per worker and output per worker will decrease: The initial level of capital per worker is too high to be sustained given the saving rate. This decrease in capital per worker will continue until the economy again reaches the point where investment is equal to depreciation, where capital per worker is equal to K^*/N. From then on, capital and output per worker will remain constant.

Steady-State Capital and Output

Let us characterize the levels of output per worker and capital per worker to which the economy converges in the long run. This will be useful to us later. The state in which output per worker and capital per worker are no longer changing is called the **steady state** of the economy. Putting the left side of equation (11.3) equal to zero (in steady state, by definition, the change in capital per worker is zero), the steady-state value of capital per worker, K^*/N, is given by

$$sf\left(\frac{K^*}{N}\right) = \delta\frac{K^*}{N} \tag{11.4}$$

The steady-state value of capital per worker is such that the amount of saving (the left side) is just sufficient to cover depreciation of the existing capital stock (the right side).

Given steady-state capital per worker (K^*/N), the steady-state value of output per worker (Y^*/N), is given by the production function

$$\frac{Y^*}{N} = f\left(\frac{K^*}{N}\right) \tag{11.5}$$

We now have the elements we need to discuss the effects of the saving rate on output per worker, both over time and in steady state.

Capital Accumulation and Growth in France in the Aftermath of World War II

When World War II ended in 1945, France had suffered some of the heaviest losses of all European countries. The losses in lives were large; more than 550,000 people had died, out of a population of 42 million. The losses in capital were much larger. Estimates are that the French capital stock in 1945 was about 30% below its prewar value. A more vivid picture of the destruction of capital is provided by the numbers in Table 1.

The model of growth we have just seen makes a clear prediction about what will happen to a country that loses a large part of its capital stock: The country will experience fast capital accumulation and output growth for some time. In terms of Figure 11–2, a country with capital per worker initially far below K^*/N will grow rapidly as it converges to K^*/N and output converges to Y^*/N.

This prediction fares well in the case of postwar France. There is plenty of anecdotal evidence that small increases in capital led to large increases in output. Minor repairs to a major bridge would lead to the reopening of a bridge. Reopening the bridge would lead, in turn, to large reductions in the travel time between two cities, leading to a large reduction in transport costs. A large reduction in transport costs would then allow a plant to receive much needed inputs and increase production and so on.

The more convincing evidence, however, comes directly from the numbers on growth of aggregate output itself. From 1946 to 1950, the annual growth rate of French real GDP was a very high 9.6% per year, leading to an increase in real GDP of about 60% over five years.

Was all the increase in French GDP due to capital accumulation? The answer is no. There were other forces in addition to the mechanism in our model. Much of the remaining capital stock in 1945 was old. Investment had been low in the 1930s (a decade dominated by the Great Depression), and nearly nonexistent during the war. Much of the postwar capital accumulation was associated with the introduction of more modern capital and the use of more modern production techniques. This was another reason for the high growth rates of the postwar period.

Source: Gilles Saint-Paul, "Economic Reconstruction in France, 1945–1958," in Rudiger Dornbusch, Willem Nolling, and Richard Layard, eds., *Postwar Economic Reconstruction and Lessons for the East Today* (Cambridge, MA: MIT Press, 1993), 83–114.

TABLE 1	**Proportion of the french capital stock destroyed at the end of World War II**			
Railways			Rivers	
Tracks	6%		Waterways	86%
Stations	38%		Canal locks	11%
Engines	21%		Barges	80%
Hardware	60%		Buildings	
Roads			Dwellings	1,229,000
Cars	31%		Industrial	246,000
Trucks	40%			

Source: See source note for this box.

The Saving Rate and Output

We can now return to the question asked at the beginning of the chapter: What are the effects of the saving rate on the growth rate of output per worker? Our analysis leads to a three-part answer:

1. *The saving rate has no effect on the long run growth rate of output per worker, which is equal to zero.*

This result is rather obvious: We have seen that, eventually, the economy converges to a constant level of output per worker. In other words, in the long run, the growth rate of the economy is equal to zero, whatever the value of the saving rate.

There is, however, a way of thinking about this result that will be useful when we introduce technological progress in chapter 12. Think of what would be needed to sustain a constant positive growth rate of output per worker in the long run. Capital per worker would have to increase. And because of decreasing returns to capital, it would have to increase faster than output per worker. This implies that each year the economy would have to save a larger and larger fraction of output and put it toward capital accumulation. At some point, the fraction of output that it would need to save would be greater than one: This is clearly not possible. This is why it is impossible to sustain a constant positive growth rate forever. In the long run, capital per worker must be constant and so must be output per worker.

Some economists argue that the relatively high growth rate achieved by the Soviet Union from 1950 to 1990 was the result of such a steady increase in the saving rate over time, and so could not be sustained forever. Paul Krugman has used the term "Stalinist growth" to denote this type of growth—growth resulting from a higher and higher saving rate over time.

2. Nonetheless, *the saving rate determines the level of output per worker in the long run.* Other things being equal, countries with a higher saving rate will achieve higher output per worker in the long run.

Figure 11–3 illustrates this point. Consider two countries with the same production function, the same level of employment, and the same depreciation rate, but different saving rates, say, s_0 and $s_1 > s_0$. Figure 11–3 draws their common production function, $f(K_t/N)$, and the functions giving saving/investment as a function of capital for each of the two countries, $s_0 f(K_t/N)$ and $s_1 f(K_t/N)$. In the long run, the country with saving rate s_0 will reach the level of capital per worker K_0/N and output Y_0/N. The country with saving rate s_1 will reach the higher levels K_1/N and Y_1/N.

3. *An increase in the saving rate will lead to higher growth of output per worker for some time, but not forever.*

This conclusion follows from the two propositions we just discussed. From the first, we know that an increase in the saving rate does not affect the long-run *growth rate of output per worker*, which remains equal to zero. From the second, we know that an increase in the saving rate leads to an increase in the long-run *level of output per worker*. It follows that, as output per worker increases to its new higher level in response to the increase in the saving rate, the economy will go through a period of positive growth. This period of growth will come to an end when the economy reaches its new steady state.

We can use Figure 11–3 again to illustrate this point. Consider a country that has an initial saving rate of s_0. Assume that capital per worker is initially equal to K_0/N, with associated output per worker Y_0/N. Now consider the effects of an increase in the saving rate from s_0 to s_1. (You can think of this increase as coming from tax changes that make it more attractive to save or from reductions in the budget deficit; the origin of the increase in the saving rate does not matter here.) The function giving saving/investment per worker as a function of capital per worker shifts upwards from $s_0 f(K_t/N)$ to $s_1 f(K_t/N)$.

FIGURE 11-3

The Effects of Different Saving Rates

A country with a higher saving rate achieves a higher level of output in steady state.

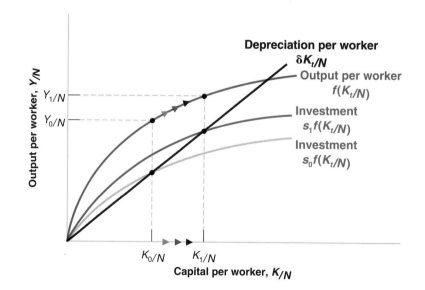

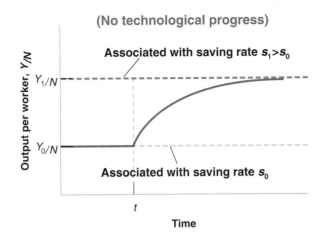

(No technological progress)

Output per worker, Y/N

Associated with saving rate $s_1 > s_0$

Y_1/N

Y_0/N

Associated with saving rate s_0

t

Time

FIGURE 11–4

The Effects of an Increase in the Saving Rate on Output per Worker

An increase in the saving rate leads to a period of positive growth until output reaches its new higher steady-state level.

At the initial level of capital per worker, K_0/N, investment now exceeds depreciation, so capital per worker increases. As capital per worker increases, so does output per worker, and the economy goes through a period of positive growth. When capital eventually reaches K_1/N, investment is again equal to depreciation and growth ends. The economy remains from then on at K_1/N, with associated output per worker Y_1/N. The movement of output per worker is plotted against time in Figure 11–4. Output per worker is initially constant at level Y_0/N. After the increase in the saving rate at, say, time t, output per worker increases for some time until it reaches the higher level Y_1/N and the growth rate returns to zero.

We have derived these three results under the assumption of no technological progress and thus no growth of output in the long run. But, as we shall see in chapter 12, the three results extend directly to an economy in which there is technological progress. Let me briefly indicate how.

An economy where there is technological progress has a positive growth rate of output per worker even in the long run. This growth rate is independent of the saving rate—the extension of the first result just discussed. The saving rate affects the level of output per worker, however—the extension of the second result. And an increase in the saving rate leads to growth greater than the steady-state growth rate for some time until the economy reaches its new higher path—the extension of our third result.

These three results are illustrated in Figure 11–5, which extends Figure 11–4 by plotting the effect of an increase in the saving rate in an economy with positive technological

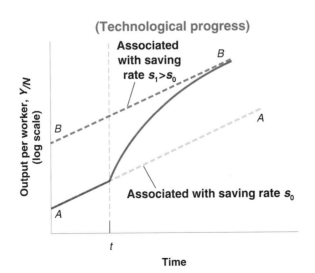

(Technological progress)

Output per worker, Y/N (log scale)

Associated with saving rate $s_1 > s_0$

B

B

A

A

Associated with saving rate s_0

t

Time

FIGURE 11–5

The Effects of an Increase in the Saving Rate on Output per Worker in an Economy with Technological Progress

An increase in the saving rate leads to a period of higher growth until output reaches a new, higher path.

See the sidebar on logarithmic scales in chapter 10.

progress. The figure uses a logarithmic scale to measure output per worker, so that an economy where output per worker grows at a constant rate is represented by a line with slope equal to that growth rate. At the initial saving rate, s_0, the economy moves along AA. If, at time t, the saving rate increases to s_1, the economy experiences higher growth for some time until, eventually, it reaches its new higher path, BB. On path BB, the growth rate is again the same as before the increase in the saving rate (that is, the slope of BB is the same as the slope of AA). But the level of output per worker is permanently higher than before.

The Saving Rate and the Golden Rule

Governments can use various instruments to affect the saving rate. They can run budget deficits or surpluses. They can give tax breaks to saving, making it more attractive for people to save. What saving rate should governments aim for? To think about this question, we must shift our focus from the behavior of *output* to the behavior of *consumption*. What matters to people is not output per se, but how much they consume.

Given the definition of K_t as the capital stock at the beginning of year t, investment this year does not affect the capital stock this year: I_t affects K_{t+1}, not K_t.

It is clear that an increase in saving must come initially at the expense of lower consumption. (Except when I think it helpful, I shall drop the "per worker" in this subsection and refer just to consumption rather than consumption per worker, capital rather than capital per worker, and so on.) A change in the saving rate this year has no effect on capital this year, and thus no effect on output and income *this year*. Therefore, an increase in saving comes initially with an equal decrease in consumption.[1]

Does an increase in saving lead to an increase in consumption in the long run? Not necessarily. Consumption may decrease, not only initially, but also in the long run. You may find this surprising. After all, we know from Figure 11–3 that an increase in the saving rate always leads to an increase in the level of *output* per worker. But output is not the same as consumption. To see why not, consider what happens for two extreme values of the saving rate:

- An economy in which the saving rate is (and has always been) zero is an economy in which capital is equal to zero. In this case, output is also equal to zero, and so is consumption. A saving rate equal to zero implies zero consumption in the long run.
- Now consider the opposite extreme: an economy in which the saving rate is equal to 1. People save all their income. The level of capital, and thus output, will be very high. But because people save all of their income, consumption is equal to zero. What happens is that the economy is carrying an excessive amount of capital: Simply maintaining that level requires that all output be devoted to replacing depreciation! A saving rate equal to 1 also implies zero consumption in the long run.

These two extreme cases suggest that there must be some value of the saving rate between 0 and 1 at which the steady-state level of consumption reaches a maximum value. Increases in the saving rate *below* this value lead to a decrease in consumption initially, but to an increase in consumption in the long run. Increases in the saving rate *beyond* this value decrease consumption not only initially, but also in the long run. This happens because the increase in capital associated with the increase in the saving rate leads to only a small increase in output, an increase that is too small to cover the increased depreciation: The economy carries too much capital. The level of capital associated with the value of the saving rate that yields the highest level of consumption in steady state is known as the **golden-rule level of capital**. Increases in capital beyond the golden-rule level reduce steady state consumption.

[1]**DIGGING DEEPER**. Because we assume that employment is constant, we are ignoring the short-run effect of an increase in the saving rate on output we focused on in chapter 3. In the short-run, not only does an increase in the saving rate reduce consumption given income, but it may also create a recession, and decrease income further. We shall return to a discussion of short- and long-run effects of changes in saving at various points in the book. See, for example, chapter 27.

Social Security, Social Security Reform, and Capital Accumulation in the United States

Social Security was introduced in the United States in 1935. Its goal was to make sure retirees would have enough income to live on. It has become the largest transfer program in the United States. Benefits paid to retirees now exceed 4% of GDP. For two-thirds of retirees, Social Security benefits account for more than 50% of their income.

One can think of two ways to set up and run a social security system:

- One is to tax workers and distribute the tax contributions as benefits to retirees. Such a system is called a **pay-as-you-go** system: The system pays benefits out "as it goes", that is, as it collects them in contributions.
- The other is to tax workers, invest the contributions in financial assets, and pay back the principal plus the interest to workers when they retire. Such a system is called **fully funded**: at any time, the system has funds equal to the accumulated contributions of workers, and from which it will be able to pay out benefits when those workers retire.

From the point of view of retirees, the two systems feel similar. Not quite identical: What the retirees receive in a pay-as-you-go system depends on demographics—the ratio of retirees to workers—and on the evolution of the tax rate set by the system; what they receive in a fully funded system depends on the rate of return on the financial assets held by the fund. But, in both cases, they pay contributions when they are employed, and receive benefits later.

From the point of view of the economy, the two systems are very different however: In a pay-as-you-go system, the contributions are redistributed, not invested; in a fully funded system, they are invested, leading to a higher capital stock. So, a fully funded social security system leads to a higher capital stock.

Most actual social security systems are somewhere between pay-as-you-go and fully funded systems. The U.S. system is close to a pay-as-you-go system. The initial intention was to partially fund it. But this did not happen. Contributions from workers were used to pay benefits to the retirees; for the first few decades of the system, retirees received benefits without having contributed, or without having contributed for very long. This gift to the initial retirees was widely perceived as fair: These were the generations that had suffered during the Great Depression and World War II. It also was not very costly: The number of eligible retirees was small at the beginning—only 7% of the population over 65 received benefits in 1940 (compared to 91% today)—so the Social Security tax rate required to finance benefits was low.

Social Security is now in trouble because of demographic changes. Life expectancy and the average length of retirement have steadily increased. The large baby-boom generations are approaching retirement. As a result, the ratio of workers to retirees has steadily decreased, and will continue to decrease over the next 50 years. Today, there are 3.3 workers for every retiree in the United States; projections are that this number will drop to 2 by 2050. At current benefit and tax rates, this means a growing imbalance between benefits and contributions.

In anticipation of these demographic evolutions, the Social Security tax rate already has been increased, and contributions have been higher than benefits for some time, leading to the accumulation of a **Social Security trust fund**. This does not mean the Social Security system is now fully funded; the fund is small relative to the benefits to be paid in the future. Under current rules, benefits are expected to start exceeding contributions by 2020, and the fund is expected to be depleted by 2030.

It is clear that something will have to be done to balance the system over the next century. This means either an increase in the tax rate, or a decrease in the benefit rate, or an increase in the retirement age. These measures can be implemented now, and used to accumulate a larger trust fund, or they can be implemented later. The longer the wait, the larger the needed adjustment: Suppose the adjustment takes place only through an increase in the tax rate. Computations suggest that the rate would have to increase today from 12.5% to about 15%. If we waited until 2030, the rate would have to increase to about 17%.

In this context, some economists and politicians have suggested that Social Security reform should do more than just balance the existing system. They argue that the goal should be a shift to a fully funded system. Their argument is that the U.S. saving rate is too low and that funding the Social Security system would increase it. Martin Feldstein, an advocate of such a shift, has concluded that it could lead to a 34% increase of the capital stock in the long run.

How should we think about such a proposal? It might have been a good idea to fully fund the system at the start: The United States would have a higher saving rate. The U.S. capital stock would be higher and output and consumption would also be higher. But we cannot rewrite history. The existing system has promised benefits to retirees and these promises have to be honored. This means that, if we wanted to shift to a fully funded system, current workers would have in effect to contribute twice: once to finance the benefits owed to retirees, and then again to fund the system and finance their own retirement. This would be good for the United States in the long run, but would impose a disproportionate cost on current workers. The practical implication is that, if it is to happen, the move to a fully funded system will have to be very slow, so that the burden of adjustment does not fall too much on one generation relative to the others.

Reference

A recent review of the history, the problems, and the choice facing the U.S. Social Security system is *Social Security Reform: Links to Saving, Investment, and Growth*, Federal Reserve Bank of Boston, Conference Series No. 41, June 1997.

FIGURE 11-6

The Effects of the Saving Rate on Consumption per Worker in Steady State

An increase in the saving rate leads to an increase, then to a decrease in consumption per worker in steady state.

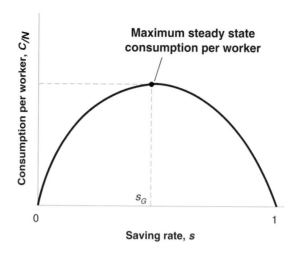

This argument is illustrated in Figure 11–6, which plots consumption per worker in steady state against alternative values of the saving rate. A saving rate equal to zero implies a capital stock per worker equal to zero, a level of output per worker equal to zero, and, by implication, a level of consumption per worker equal to zero. For s between 0 and s_G, (G for golden rule) higher values of the saving rate imply higher values for capital per worker, output per worker, and consumption per worker. For s larger than s_G, increases in the saving rate still lead to higher values of capital per worker and output per worker; but they lead to lower values of consumption per worker: This is because the increase in output is more than offset by the increase in depreciation due to the larger capital stock. For $s = 1$, consumption per worker is equal to zero. Capital per worker and output per worker are high, but all of output is used just to replace depreciation, leaving nothing for consumption.

If an economy already has so much capital that it is operating beyond the golden rule, then increasing saving further will decrease consumption not only now, but also later. Is this a relevant worry? Do some countries actually have too much capital? The empirical evidence indicates that most OECD countries are actually far below their golden-rule level of capital. If they were to increase the saving rate, it would lead to higher consumption in the future.

This conclusion implies that, in practice, governments face a trade-off: An increase in the saving rate implies lower consumption initially, higher consumption later. What should governments do? How close to the golden rule should they try to get? That depends on how much weight they put on the welfare of current generations—who are more likely to lose from policies aimed at increasing the saving rate—versus the welfare of future generations—who are more likely to gain. However, future generations do not vote. This implies that governments are unlikely to ask current generations for large sacrifices, which in turn means that capital is likely to stay far below its golden-rule level. These intergenerational issues are very much in evidence in the current debate on Social Security reform; this is explored in the In Depth box "Social Security, Social Security Reform, and Capital Accumulation in the United States."

11-3 | Getting a Sense of Magnitudes

How large is the effect of a change in the saving rate on output in the long run? For how long and by how much would an increase in the saving rate affect growth? How far is the United States from the golden-rule level of capital? To get a better sense of the answers to these questions, let us now make more specific assumptions, plug in some numbers, and see what comes out.

Assume the production function is

$$Y = \sqrt{K} \sqrt{N} \qquad (11.6)$$

Output equals the product of the square root of capital and the square root of labor. Note that this production function exhibits both constant returns to scale, and decreasing returns to either capital or labor.[2]

Dividing both sides by N (because we are interested in output per worker) gives

$$\frac{Y}{N} = \frac{\sqrt{K}\sqrt{N}}{N} = \frac{\sqrt{K}}{\sqrt{N}} = \sqrt{\frac{K}{N}}$$

◄ The second equality follows from the following steps:
$$\sqrt{N}/N = \sqrt{N}/(\sqrt{N}\sqrt{N})$$
$$= 1/\sqrt{N}$$

Output per worker equals the square root of capital per worker. Put another way, the production function f relating output per worker to capital per worker is given by $f(K_t/N) = \sqrt{K_t/N}$.

Now go back to equation (11.3), which is repeated here for convenience

$$\frac{K_{t+1}}{N} - \frac{K_t}{N} = sf\left(\frac{K_t}{N}\right) - \delta\frac{K_t}{N}$$

Replace $f(K_t/N)$ by $\sqrt{K_t/N}$

$$\frac{K_{t+1}}{N} - \frac{K_t}{N} = s\sqrt{\frac{K_t}{N}} - \delta\frac{K_t}{N} \tag{11.7}$$

This equation describes the evolution of capital per worker over time. Let's now look at what it implies.

The Effects of the Saving Rate on Steady-State Output

How large is the effect of an increase in the saving rate on the steady-state level of output per worker?

Start with equation (11.7). In steady state the amount of capital per worker is constant, so the left side of the equation equals zero. This implies

$$s\sqrt{\frac{K}{N}} = \delta\frac{K}{N}$$

(I have dropped time indexes, which are no longer needed because in steady state K/N is constant.) Square both sides

$$s^2\frac{K}{N} = \delta^2\left(\frac{K}{N}\right)^2$$

Divide both sides by (K/N) and reorganize

$$\frac{K}{N} = \left(\frac{s}{\delta}\right)^2 \tag{11.8}$$

---

[2]**DIGGING DEEPER.** A more general specification for the production function would be
$$Y = K^\alpha N^{1-\alpha}$$
where α is a number between 0 and 1.

The production function we use in the text assumes $\alpha = 0.5$, giving equal weights to capital and labor. (Taking the square root of a variable is the same as raising it to the power 0.5.) A more realistic production function would give more weight to labor and less to capital, for example $\alpha = 0.3$.

There are two reasons why I use $\alpha = 0.5$: The first is that it makes the algebra much simpler. The second is based on a broader interpretation of capital than just physical capital. As we shall see in section 11-4, we can think of the accumulation of skills, say, through education or on-the-job training, as a form of capital accumulation as well. Under this broader view of capital, a coefficient of 0.5 for capital is roughly appropriate.

This gives us an equation for steady-state capital per worker. From equations (11.6) and (11.8), steady-state output per worker is given by

$$\frac{Y}{N} = \sqrt{\frac{K}{N}} = \sqrt{\left(\frac{s}{\delta}\right)^2} = \frac{s}{\delta} \tag{11.9}$$

Output per worker is equal to the ratio of the saving rate to the depreciation rate; capital per worker is equal to the square of that ratio. A higher saving rate and a lower depreciation rate both lead to higher capital per worker and output per worker in the long run.

Suppose the depreciation rate is 10% per year, and take the saving rate to be 10% as well. Then, using equations (11.8) and (11.9), we see that capital per worker and output per worker in steady state are both equal to 1. Now suppose that the saving rate doubles, from 10% to 20%. It follows from equation (11.8) that in the new steady state, capital per worker increases from 1 to 4. And from equation (11.9), output per worker doubles, from 1 to 2. Thus doubling the saving rate leads, in the long run, to doubling output: This is a large effect.

The Dynamic Effects of an Increase in the Saving Rate

After an increase in the saving rate, how long does it take for the economy to reach the new higher level of output? Put another way, by how much and for how long does an increase in the saving rate affect the growth rate?

To answer these questions, we must use equation (11.7) and solve it for capital in year 0, year 1, and so on.

Suppose that the saving rate, which had always been equal to 0.1, increases in year 0 from 0.1 to 0.2 and remains at this higher value forever after. In year 0, nothing happens to the capital stock (recall that it takes one year for higher saving and higher investment to show up in higher capital). So, capital per worker remains equal to the steady-state value associated with a saving rate of 0.1. From equation (11.8), $K_0/N = (0.1/0.1)^2 = 1^2 = 1$.

In year 1, equation (11.7) gives

$$\frac{K_1}{N} - \frac{K_0}{N} = s\sqrt{\frac{K_0}{N}} - \delta\frac{K_0}{N}$$

With a depreciation rate equal to 0.1 and a saving rate now equal to 0.2, this equation implies that $(K_1/N) - 1 = [(0.2)(\sqrt{1})] - [(0.1)1]$ so that $K_1/N = 1.1$.

In the same way, we can solve for K_2/N, and so on. Once we have the values of capital per worker in year 0, year 1, and so on, we can then use equation (11.6) to solve for output per worker in year 0, year 1, and so on. The results of this computation are presented in Figure 11–7(a), which plots the *level* of output per worker against time. (Y/N) increases over time from its initial value of 1 in year 0 to its steady-state value of 2 in the long run. Figure 11–7(b) gives the same information in a different way, plotting instead the *growth rate* of output per worker against time. Growth of output per worker is highest at the beginning and then decreases over time. As the economy reaches its new steady state, growth of output per worker returns to zero.

Figure 11–7 clearly shows that the adjustment to the new, higher, long-run equilibrium takes a long time. It is only 40% complete after 10 years, 63% complete after 20 years. Put another way, the increase in the saving rate increases the growth rate of output per worker for a long time. The average annual growth rate is 3.1% for the first 10 years, 1.5% for the next 10. Although changes in the saving rate have no effect on growth in the long run, they do lead to higher growth for quite some time.

To return to the question raised at the beginning of the chapter, can the low saving/investment rate in the United States explain why the U.S. growth rate has been so low (relative to other OECD countries) since 1950? The answer would be yes if the United States had had a higher saving rate in the past, and *if this saving rate had decreased substantially in the last 50 years*. If this were the case, this could explain the period of lower growth in the United States in the last 50 years along the lines of the mechanism in Figure 11–7 (with the sign reversed, as we would be looking at a decrease, not an increase, in the saving rate). But this is

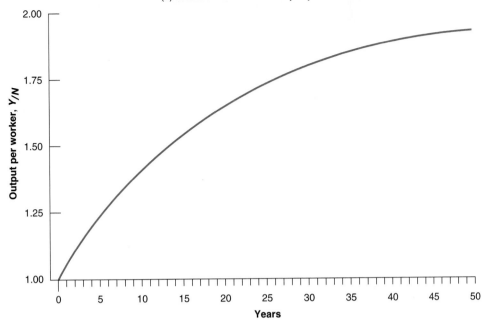

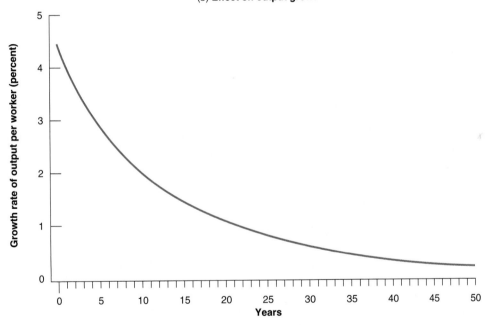

(b) **Effect on output growth**

FIGURE 11–7

Dynamic Effects of an Increase in the Saving Rate from 10% to 20% on the Level and the Growth Rate of Output per Worker

It takes a long time for output to adjust to its new higher level after an increase in the saving rate. Put another way, an increase in the saving rate leads to a long period of higher growth.

not the case: The U.S. saving rate has been low for a long time. Low saving cannot explain the poor U.S. growth performance over the last 50 years.

The U.S. Saving Rate and the Golden Rule

Let's now turn to the third question we asked at the beginning of this section. What is the saving rate that would maximize steady state consumption?

In steady state, consumption per worker is equal to output per worker minus depreciation per worker.

$$\frac{C}{N} = \frac{Y}{N} - \delta \frac{K}{N}$$

Saving Rate, s	Capital per Worker, K/N	Output per Worker, Y/N	Consumption per Worker, C/N
0.0	0.0	0.0	0.0
0.1	1.0	1.0	0.9
0.2	4.0	2.0	1.6
0.3	9.0	3.0	2.1
0.4	16.0	4.0	2.4
0.5	25.0	5.0	2.5
0.6	36.0	6.0	2.4
...	...	...	...
1.0	100.0	10.0	0.0

Using equations (11.8) and (11.9) for the steady-state values of output per worker and capital per worker, consumption per worker is thus given by

$$\frac{C}{N} = s/\delta - \delta(s/\delta)^2$$
$$= s(1 - s)/\delta$$

Using this equation together with equations (11.8) and (11.9), Table 11–1 gives the steady-state values of capital per worker, output per worker, and consumption per worker for different values of the saving rate (and for a depreciation rate equal to 10%).

Steady-state consumption is largest when $s(1 - s)$ is largest, so when s equals one-half: The golden-rule level of capital is associated with a saving rate of 50%. Below that level, increases in the saving rate lead to an increase in long-run consumption. Above that level, they lead to a decrease. Few economies in the world today have saving rates above 40%, and (as we saw at the beginning of the chapter) the U.S. saving rate is actually less than 20%. As rough as it is, our computation suggests that, in most economies, an increase in the saving rate would increase both output and consumption levels in the long run.

Check your understanding of the issues: Using the equations in this section, argue the pros and cons of policy measures aimed at increasing the U.S. saving rate from its current value of about 16% to, say, 20%.

11-4 | Physical versus Human Capital

We have concentrated so far on physical capital—on machines, plants, office buildings, and so on. But economies have another type of capital: the set of skills of the workers in the economy, what economists call **human capital**. An economy with many highly skilled workers is likely to be much more productive than an economy in which most workers cannot read or write.

The increase in human capital has been as dramatic as the increase in physical capital over the last two centuries. At the beginning of the Industrial Revolution, only 30% of the population knew how to read. Today, the literacy rate in OECD countries is above 95%. Schooling was not compulsory prior to the Industrial Revolution. Today it is, usually until the age of 16. Still, there are large differences across countries. Today, in OECD countries, nearly 100% of children get a primary education, 90% get a secondary education, and 38% get a higher education. The corresponding numbers in poor countries, countries with GDP per capita below $400 in 1985, are 95%, 32%, and 4%, respectively.

Even this comparison may be misleading. The quality of education may be quite different across countries.

How should we think about the effect of human capital on output? How does the introduction of human capital change our earlier conclusions? These are the questions we take up in this last section.

Extending the Production Function

The most natural way of extending our analysis to allow for human capital is to modify the production function relation (11.1) to read

$$\frac{Y}{N} = f\left(\frac{K}{N}, \frac{H}{N}\right)$$

(11.10)

$$(+, +)$$

The level of output per worker depends on both the level of physical capital per worker, K/N, and the level of human capital per worker, H/N. As before, an increase in capital per worker (K/N) leads to an increase in output per worker. And an increase in the average level of skill (H/N) also leads to more output per worker. More skilled workers can use more complex machines; they can deal more easily with unexpected complications; they can adapt faster to new tasks. All of these lead to higher output per worker.

Note that we are using the same symbol, H, to denote the monetary base in chapter 4, and human capital in this chapter. Both uses are traditional. Do not be confused.

We assumed earlier that increases in physical capital per worker increased output per worker, but that the effect became smaller as the level of capital per worker increased. The same assumption is likely to apply to human capital per worker. Think of increases in H/N as coming from increases in the number of years of education. The evidence is that the returns to increasing the proportion of children acquiring a primary education are very large. At the very least, the ability to read and write allows workers to use more sophisticated equipment. For rich countries, however, primary education—and, for that matter, secondary education—are no longer the relevant margins: Most children now get both. The relevant margin is higher education. The evidence here—and I am sure this will come as good news to most of you—is that higher education increases skills, at least as measured by the increase in wages for those who acquire it. But, to take an extreme example, it is not clear that forcing everybody to acquire a Ph.D. would increase aggregate output very much. Many people would end up overqualified and probably more frustrated rather than more productive.

We look at the relation between skills and relative wages in more detail in chapter 13.

How should we construct the measure for human capital, H? The answer is very much the same way we construct the measure for physical capital, K. In constructing K, we just add the values of the different pieces of capital, so that a machine that costs $2,000 gets twice the weight of a machine that costs $1,000. Similarly, we construct the measure of H such that workers who are paid twice as much get twice the weight.[3] Take, for example, an economy with 100 workers, half of them unskilled and half of them skilled. Suppose the relative wage of skilled workers is twice that of unskilled workers. We can then construct H as $[(50 \times 1) + (50 \times 2)] = 150$. Human capital per worker, H/N, is equal to $150/100 = 1.5$.

Human Capital, Physical Capital, and Output

How does the introduction of human capital change the analysis of the previous sections?

Our conclusions about *physical capital accumulation* remain valid: An increase in the saving rate increases steady-state physical capital per worker, and therefore increases output per worker. But our conclusions now extend to *human capital accumulation* as well. An

---

[3]**DIGGING DEEPER**. The logic for using relative wages as weights is that they are supposed to capture the relative marginal products of different workers, so that a worker who is paid three times as much as another has a marginal product that is three times higher.

This would be correct if labor markets were perfectly competitive: Recall from your microeconomics course that in a perfectly competitive labor market, each worker is paid a wage equal to his or her marginal product. But as we discussed in chapter 6, labor markets are not perfectly competitive, and you may question whether relative wages accurately reflect relative marginal products. To take one, very controversial, example: In the same job, with the same seniority, women still often earn less than men. Does this fact reflect that their marginal product is lower? Should they be given a lower weight than men in the construction of human capital?

increase in how much society "saves" in the form of human capital—through education and on-the-job training—increases steady-state human capital per worker, which leads to an increase in output per worker.

Our extended model gives us a richer picture of the determination of output per worker. In the long run, it tells us, output per worker depends both on how much society saves and on how much it spends on education.

What is the relative importance of human and physical capital in the determination of output per worker? To answer this question, we can start by comparing how much is spent on formal education and how much is invested in physical capital. In the United States, spending on formal education is about 6.5% of GDP. This number includes both government and private expenditures. This number is between one-third and one-half of the gross investment rate for physical capital (which is around 16%). But this comparison is only a first pass. Consider the following complications:

- Education, especially higher education, is partly consumption—done for its own sake—and partly investment. We should include only the investment part for our purposes. However, the 6.5% number in the preceding paragraph includes both.
- At least for post-secondary education, the opportunity cost of a person's education is also foregone wages while one is acquiring the education. Spending on education should include not only the actual cost of education but also the opportunity cost. The 6.5% number does not include the opportunity cost.

How large is your opportunity cost relative to your tuition? ▷

- Formal education is only part of education. Much of what we learn comes from on-the-job training, formal or informal. Both the actual costs and the opportunity costs of on-the-job training should also be included. The 6.5% number does not include either cost.
- We should compare investment rates net of depreciation. Depreciation of physical capital, especially of machines, is likely to be higher than depreciation of human capital. Skills deteriorate, but do so slowly. And, unlike physical capital, skills deteriorate more slowly the more they are used.

For all these reasons, it is difficult to come up with reliable numbers for investment in human capital. The bulk of the evidence from recent research suggests that increases in physical capital and increases in human capital may have played roughly equal roles in the increase in output per worker over time. The implication is clear: Countries that save more, and/or spend more on education, can achieve substantially higher steady-state levels of output per worker.

Endogenous Growth

Note what the conclusion we just reached did and did not say. It did say that a country that saves more or spends more on education will achieve a *higher level* of output per worker in steady state. It did not say that by saving or spending more on education a country can sustain permanent *higher growth* of output per worker.

We have mentioned Lucas once already, in connection with the Lucas critique in chapter 9. ▷

This conclusion, however, has been challenged in the past decade. Following the lead of Robert Lucas and Paul Romer, researchers have explored the possibility that the combination of physical and human capital accumulation may actually be enough to sustain growth. They have asked the following question: Given human capital, increases in physical capital will run into decreasing returns. And given physical capital, increases in human capital will also run into decreasing returns. But what if both physical and human capital increase in tandem? Can't an economy grow forever just by having steadily more capital and more skilled workers?

The models these researchers have explored are called **models of endogenous growth** to reflect the fact that in those models—in contrast to the model we saw in earlier sections of this chapter—growth depends, even in the long run, on variables such as the saving rate and the rate of spending on education. The verdict is still out, but the indications so far are that the conclusions we drew earlier need to be qualified but not abandoned. There is no evidence that countries can sustain higher growth just from capital accumulation and skill improvements.

To end this chapter, let us state our earlier conclusions, modified to take into account human capital: Output per worker depends on the level of both physical capital per worker and human capital per worker. Both forms of capital can be accumulated, one through physical investment, the other through education and training. Increasing either the saving rate or the fraction of output spent on education and training can lead to much higher levels of output per worker in the long run. However, for a given rate of technological progress, such measures are unlikely to lead to a permanently higher growth rate.

Note the qualifier in the last proposition: *for a given rate of technological progress*. But is technological progress unrelated to the level of human capital in the economy? Can't a better-educated labor force lead to a higher rate of technological progress? These questions take us to the topic of the next chapter, the sources and the effects of technological progress.

SUMMARY

- In the long run, the evolution of output is determined by two relations. (To make the reading of this summary easier, I shall omit "per worker" in what follows.) First, the level of output depends on the amount of existing capital. Second, capital accumulation depends in turn on the level of output, which determines saving and investment.

- These interactions between capital and output imply that, starting from any level of capital (and ignoring technological progress, the topic of chapter 12), an economy converges in the long run to a steady-state (constant) level of capital. Associated with this level of capital is a steady-state level of output.

- The steady-state level of capital, and thus the steady-state level of output depend positively on the saving rate. A higher saving rate leads to a higher steady-state level of output; during the transition to the new steady state, a higher saving rate leads to positive output growth. But (again ignoring technological progress) in the long run, the growth rate of output is equal to zero, and is thus independent of the saving rate.

- An increase in the saving rate requires an initial decrease in consumption. In the long run, the increase in the saving rate may lead to an increase or to a decrease in consumption, depending on whether the economy is below or above the golden-rule level of capital, the level of capital at which steady-state consumption is highest.

- Most countries appear to have a level of capital below the golden-rule level. Thus, an increase in the saving rate will lead to an initial decrease in consumption followed by an increase in the long run. In thinking about whether to take policy measures aimed at changing the saving rate, policy makers must decide how much weight to put on the welfare of current generations versus the welfare of future generations.

- Although most of the analysis of this chapter focuses on the effects of physical capital accumulation, output depends on the levels of both physical *and* human capital. Both forms of capital can be accumulated, one through investment, the other through education and training. Increasing the saving rate and/or the fraction of output spent on education and training can lead to large increases in output in the long run.

KEY TERMS

- saving rate, 205
- depreciation rate, 208
- steady state, 210
- golden-rule level of capital, 214
- pay-as-you-go social security system, 215
- fully funded social security system, 215
- Social Security trust fund, 215
- human capital, 220
- models of endogenous growth, 222

An asterisk denotes a harder problem.

1. TRUE/FALSE/UNCERTAIN

a. The saving rate is always equal to the investment rate.

b. A higher investment rate can sustain growth of output forever.

c. If capital never depreciated, growth could go on forever.

d. The higher the saving rate, the higher consumption in steady state.

e. Output per capita in the United States is roughly equal to 60% of output per worker.

f. We should fund Social Security. This would increase consumption, now and in the future.

g. The U.S. capital stock is far below the golden-rule level. The government should give tax breaks for saving.

2. THE GROWTH RATE AND THE SAVING RATE

"The Japanese growth rate of output per worker will remain higher than that of the United States for as long as the Japanese saving rate exceeds that of the United States." Do you agree with this statement? Why or why not?

3. THE PARADOX OF SAVING REVISITED

In chapter 3 we saw that an increase in the saving rate can lead to a recession in the short run. You now can examine the effects beyond the short run. If the saving rate increases permanently, what will be the effect on the growth rate after 1 year, 10 years, 50 years? Explain in words.

4. THE DETERMINANTS OF OUTPUT PER WORKER IN STEADY STATE

Discuss the likely impact of the following changes on the level of output per worker in the long run.

a. The right to exclude saving from income when paying the income tax

b. A higher rate of female participation (but constant population)

*5. GROWTH WITH A MORE GENERAL PRODUCTION FUNCTION. I

Suppose that the economy's production function is given by $Y = K^{\alpha}N^{1-\alpha}$. (This production function is called the Cobb Douglas production function.) In section 11-3, we took α to be 1/2. Assume now that $\alpha = 1/3$.

a. Is this production function characterized by constant returns to scale? Explain.

b. Are there decreasing returns to capital?

c. Are there decreasing returns to labor?

d. Transform the production function into a relation between output per worker and capital per worker.

e. For a given saving rate (s) and a depreciation rate (δ), give an expression for capital per worker in the steady state.

f. Give an expression for output per worker in the steady state.

g. Solve for the steady state level of output per worker when $\delta = 0.08$ and $s = 0.32$.

h. Suppose that the depreciation rate remains constant at $\delta = 0.08$, whereas the saving rate is reduced by half to $s = 0.16$. What happens to the steady state level of output per worker?

*6. GROWTH WITH A MORE GENERAL PRODUCTION FUNCTION. II

Suppose that the economy's production function is $Y = K^{1/3}N^{2/3}$, and that both the saving rate (s) and the depreciation rate (δ) are equal to 0.10.

a. What is the steady-state level of capital per worker?

b. What is the steady-state level of output per worker?

Suppose that the economy has reached its steady state in period t, and then, in period $t + 1$, the depreciation rate doubles to 0.20.

c. Solve for the new steady-state levels of capital per worker and output per worker.

d. Compute the path of capital per worker and output per worker over the first three periods after the change in the depreciation rate.

7. SEARCHING FOR THE GOLDEN RULE

Suppose that the production function is given by $Y = 0.5\sqrt{K}\sqrt{N}$.

a. Derive the steady-state levels of K/N and Y/N in terms of the saving rate (s) and the depreciation rate (δ).

b. Derive the equation for steady-state output per worker and steady-state consumption per worker in terms of s and δ.

c. Suppose that $\delta = 5\%$. With your favorite spreadsheet software, compute steady-state output per worker and steady state consumption per worker for $s = 0, 0.1, 0.2, \ldots, 1.0$. Explain.

d. Use your software to graph the steady-state level of output per worker and consumption per worker as a function of the saving rate (that is, measure the saving rate on the horizontal axis of your graph and the corresponding values of output per worker and consumption per worker on the vertical axis).

e. Does the graph show that there is a value of s that maximizes output per worker? Does the graph show that there is a value of s that maximizes consumption per worker? If so, what is this value?

FURTHER READINGS

The classic treatment of the relation between the saving rate and output is by Robert Solow, *Growth Theory: An Exposition* (New York: Oxford University Press, 1970).

An easy-to-read discussion of whether and how to increase saving and improve education in the United States is given in Memoranda 23 to 27 in *Memos to the President: A Guide through Macroeconomics for the Busy Policymaker*, by Charles Schultze [the chairman of the Council of Economic Advisers during the Carter administration] (Washington DC: Brookings Institution, 1992).

We invite you to visit the Blanchard page on the Prentice Hall Web site at:

http://www.prenhall.com/blanchard

for this chapter's World Wide Web exercises

CHAPTER 12

Technological Progress and Growth

Our conclusion in chapter 11 that capital accumulation cannot by itself sustain growth has a straightforward implication: Sustained growth *requires* technological progress. This chapter looks at the relation between technological progress and growth.

Section 12-1 looks at the respective role of technological progress and capital accumulation in growth. It shows how, in steady state, the rate of growth of output per capita in steady state is simply equal to the rate of technological progress. This does not mean however that the saving rate is irrelevant: The saving rate affects the level of output per capita, if not its rate of growth. Section 12-2 turns to the determinants of technological progress, focusing in particular to the role of research and development (R&D). Finally, section 12-3 returns to the facts of growth presented in chapter 10, and interprets them in the light of what we have learned in this and the preceding chapter.

In chapter 11, we assumed that technology did not change, only the amount of capital used in production. In this chapter, we take into account that technology itself changes over time, that there is technological progress.

The average number of items carried by a supermarket increased from 2,200 in 1950 to 17,500 in 1985. To get a sense of what this means, watch Robin Williams (who plays an immigrant from the Soviet Union) in the supermarket scene in the movie *Moscow on the Hudson.*

As we saw in the Focus box "Real GDP, Technological Progress, and the Price of Computers" in chapter 2, thinking of products as providing several underlying services is the method used to construct the price index for computers.

For simplicity, we shall ignore human capital here.

12-1 Technological Progress and the Rate of Growth

In an economy in which there is both capital accumulation and technological progress, at what rate will output grow? To answer this question, we need to extend the model developed in chapter 11 to allow for technological progress. To do so, we must first revisit the aggregate production function.

Technological Progress and the Production Function

Technological progress has many dimensions:

- It may mean larger quantities of output for given quantities of capital and labor. For example, think of a new type of lubricant that allows a machine to run at a higher speed.
- It may mean better products. For example, think of the steady improvement in car safety and comfort over time.
- It may mean new products. For example, think of the introduction of the CD player and the fax machine.
- It may mean a larger variety of products. For example, think of the steady increase in the number of breakfast cereals available at your local supermarket.

These dimensions are more similar than they may appear. If we think of consumers as caring not about the goods themselves, but about the services these goods provide, then all these examples have something in common. In each case, consumers receive more services. A better car provides more safety, a new product such as the fax machine provides more information services, and so on.

If we think of output as the set of underlying services provided by the goods produced in the economy, we can think of technological progress as leading to increases in output for given amounts of capital and labor. We can then think of the *state of technology* as a variable that tells us how much output can be produced from capital and labor at any time. Let's denote the state of technology by A and rewrite the production function as

$$Y = F(K, N, A)$$
$$(+, +, +)$$

This is our extended production function. Output depends on both capital and labor (K and N) and on the state of technology (A): Given capital and labor, an improvement in the state of technology, A, leads to an increase in output.

It will prove convenient to use a slightly more restrictive form of the preceding equation, namely,

$$Y = F(K, AN) \qquad (12.1)$$

This equation states that production depends on capital and on labor multiplied by the state of technology. This way of introducing the state of technology makes it easier to think about the effect of technological progress on the relation among output, capital, and labor.[1] Equation (12.1) implies we can think of technological progress in two equivalent ways:

1. Given the existing capital stock, technological progress reduces the number of workers needed to achieve a given amount of output. A doubling of A allows the economy to produce the same quantity of output with only half the original number of workers, N.

---

[1]**DIGGING DEEPER**. This way of writing the production function implies that technological progress is *labor augmenting*: It *augments* (that is, multiplies) labor in the production function. We could assume instead that technological progress is *capital augmenting* (that is, multiplies capital), or that it is both labor and capital augmenting. The justification for the assumption made here is convenience: It leads to a simpler characterization of growth in the long run.

2. Technological progress increases AN, the amount of **effective labor** in the economy. If the state of technology doubles, it is as if the economy had twice as many workers. In other words, we can can think of output being produced by two factors: capital (K) on the one hand, and effective labor (AN) on the other.

What restrictions should we impose on the extended production function, equation (12.1)? We can build directly here on our discussion in chapter 10.

It is again reasonable to assume constant returns to scale: *For a given state of technology* (A), doubling both the amount of capital (K) and the amount of labor (N) is likely to lead to a doubling of output

$$2Y = F(2K, 2AN)$$

More generally, for any number x,

$$xY = F(xK, xAN)$$

It is also reasonable to assume decreasing returns to each of the two factors, capital and effective labor. Given effective labor, an increase in capital is likely to increase output, but at a decreasing rate. Symmetrically, given capital, an increase in effective labor is likely to increase output, but at a decreasing rate.

It was convenient in chapter 11 to think in terms of output and capital *per worker*. That was because the steady state of the economy was a state where output and capital *per worker* were constant. It is convenient here to look at output and capital *per effective worker*. The reason is the same: As we shall soon see, in steady-state, output and capital *per effective worker* are constant.

To get a relation between output per effective worker and capital per effective worker, take $x = 1/AN$ in the preceding equation. This gives

$$\frac{Y}{AN} = F\left(\frac{K}{AN}, 1\right)$$

Or, if we define the function f so that $f(K/AN) \equiv F(K/AN, 1)$

$$\frac{Y}{AN} = f\left(\frac{K}{AN}\right) \tag{12.2}$$

  Output per effective worker   Capital per effective worker

Equation (12.2) gives us a relation between *output per effective worker* and *capital per effective worker*. Output per effective worker increases if and only if capital per effective worker increases. The relation between output per effective worker and capital per effective worker is drawn in Figure 12–1. It looks very much the same as the relation we drew in Figure 11–2 between output per worker and capital per worker in the absence of technological progress: Increases in K/AN lead to increases in Y/AN, but at a decreasing rate.

AN is also sometimes called **labor in efficiency units**. The use of "efficiency" for "efficiency units" here and of "efficiency wages" in chapter 6 is a coincidence: The two notions are unrelated.

Per worker: divided by the number of workers (N).

Per effective worker: divided by the number of effective workers (NA)—the number of workers, N, times the state of technology, A.

Suppose that F has the "double square root" form:

$$Y = F(K, AN) = \sqrt{K}\sqrt{AN}$$

Then,

$$Y/AN = \sqrt{K/AN}\sqrt{AN/AN}$$
$$= \sqrt{K/AN}$$

So the function f is simply the square root function:

$$f(K/AN) = \sqrt{K/AN}$$

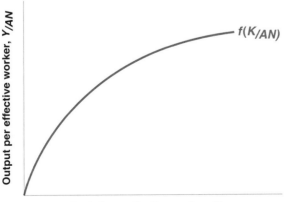

FIGURE 12–1

Output per Effective Worker versus Capital per Effective Worker

Increases in capital per effective worker lead to smaller and smaller increases in output per effective worker.

Interactions between Output and Capital

We now have the elements we need to think about the determinants of growth. Our analysis will parallel the analysis of chapter 11. There we looked at *output and capital per worker*. Here we look at the dynamics of *output and capital per effective worker*.

Here is the key to understanding the results in this chapter: The results we derived for *output per worker* in chapter 11 still hold in this chapter, but now for *output per effective worker*. For example, in chapter 11, we saw that output per worker was constant in steady state. In this chapter, we shall see that output per effective worker is constant in steady state.

In chapter 11, we characterized the dynamics of output and capital per worker using Figure 11–2. In that figure, we drew three relations:

- The relation between output per worker and capital per worker.

- The implied relation between investment per worker and capital per worker.

- The relation between depreciation per worker—the investment per worker needed to maintain a constant level of capital per worker—and capital per worker.

The dynamics of capital per worker and, by implication, of output per worker, were determined by the relation between investment per worker and depreciation per worker. Depending on whether investment per worker was greater or smaller than depreciation per worker, capital per worker increased or decreased over time, and so did output per worker.

We follow exactly the same approach here in building Figure 12–2. The difference is that we focus on output, capital, and investment per effective worker, rather than per worker.

(1) The relation between output per effective worker and capital per effective worker was derived in Figure 12–1. This relation is repeated in Figure 12–2. Output per effective worker increases with capital per effective worker, but at a decreasing rate.

(2) Under the same assumptions as in chapter 11—investment is equal to private saving, and the private saving rate is constant—investment is given by

$$I = S = sY$$

Divide both sides by the number of effective workers, AN, to get

$$\frac{I}{AN} = s\frac{Y}{AN}$$

Substituting output per effective worker Y/AN by its expression from equation (12.2) gives

$$\frac{I}{AN} = sf\left(\frac{K}{AN}\right)$$

The relation between investment per effective worker and capital per effective worker is drawn as the lower curve in Figure 12–2. It is equal to the upper curve—the relation between output per effective worker and capital per effective worker—multiplied by the saving rate, s (which is less than one).

In chapter 11, we were assuming both g_A and g_N were equal to zero. Our main focus in this chapter is on the implications of technological progress, $g_A > 0$. But, once we allow for technological progress, introducing population growth $g_N > 0$ is straightforward. Thus, I allow for both.

(3) Finally, we need to derive the level of investment per effective worker needed to maintain a given level of capital per effective worker.

In chapter 11, the answer was simple; for capital to be constant, investment had to be equal to the depreciation of the existing capital stock. Here, the answer is slightly more complicated. The reason is as follows: Now that we allow for technological progress, the number of effective workers (AN) is increasing over time. Thus, maintaining the same ratio of capital to effective workers (K/AN) requires an increase in the capital stock (K) proportional to the increase in the number of effective workers (AN). Let's look at this condition more closely.

Assume that population is growing at annual rate g_N. If we assume that the ratio of employment to the total population remains constant, the number of workers (N) also grows at annual rate g_N. Assume also that the rate of technological progress equals g_A. Together, these two assumptions imply that the growth rate of effective labor (AN) equals $g_A + g_N$. If the number of workers is growing at 1% per year and the rate of technological progress is 2% per year, then the growth rate of effective labor is equal to 3%.

The growth rate of the product of two variables is the sum of the growth rates of the two variables. See proposition 7 in appendix 2 at the end of the book.

Let δ be the depreciation rate of capital. Then the level of investment needed to maintain a given level of capital per effective worker is given by

$$\delta K + (g_A + g_N)K$$

An amount δK is needed just to keep the capital stock constant. If the depreciation rate is 10%, then investment must be equal to 10% of the capital stock just to maintain the same level of capital. And an additional amount $(g_A + g_N)K$ is needed to ensure that the capital stock increases at the same rate as effective labor. If effective labor increases at 3% a year, then capital must increase by 3% a year to maintain the same level of capital per effective worker. Putting δK and $(g_A + g_N)K$ together in this example, if the depreciation rate is 10% and the growth rate of effective labor is 3%, then investment must equal 13% of the capital stock to maintain a constant level of capital per effective worker.

Grouping the terms in K in the preceding expression and dividing by the number of effective workers to get the amount of investment per effective worker needed to maintain a constant level of capital per effective worker gives

$$(\delta + g_A + g_N)\frac{K}{AN}$$

The level of investment per effective worker needed to maintain a given level of capital per effective worker is represented by the upward-sloping line, "Required investment" in Figure 12–2. The slope of the line equals $\delta + g_A + g_N$.

Dynamics of Capital and Output

We can now give a graphical description of the dynamics of capital per effective worker and output per effective worker. Consider in Figure 12–2 a given level of capital per effective worker, say, $(K/AN)_0$. At that level, output per effective worker equals the distance AB. Investment per effective worker is equal to AC. The amount of investment required to maintain that level of capital per effective worker is equal to AD. Because actual investment exceeds the investment level required to maintain the existing level of capital per effective worker, K/AN increases.

Hence, starting from $(K/AN)_0$, the economy moves to the right, with the level of capital per effective worker increasing over time. This goes on until investment is just sufficient to

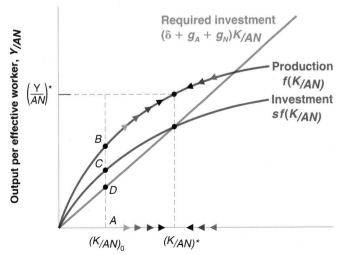

FIGURE 12–2

Dynamics of Capital and Output per Effective Worker

Capital and output per effective worker converge to constant values in the long run.

maintain the existing level of capital per effective worker, until capital per effective worker reaches $(K/AN)^*$. In the long run, capital per effective worker reaches a constant level, and so does output per effective worker. Put another way, the steady state of this economy is such that *capital per effective worker and output per effective worker are constant, and equal to $(K/AN)^*$ and $(Y/AN)^*$ respectively.*

If the number of effective workers is constant, then constant output per effective worker implies constant output. This was the case in chapter 11 where we assumed there was neither population growth nor technological progress. But this is not the case here.

Note what this conclusion implies: *In steady state, in this economy, what is constant is not output but rather output per effective worker.* This implies that in steady state, output (Y) is growing at the same rate as effective labor (AN) (so that the ratio of the two is indeed constant). Because effective labor grows at rate $(g_A + g_N)$, output growth in steady state must also equal $(g_A + g_N)$. The same reasoning applies to capital. Because capital per effective worker is constant in steady state, capital is also growing at rate $(g_A + g_N)$.

If Y/AN is constant, Y must grow at the same rate as AN. So, it must grow at rate $g_A + g_N$.

These conclusions give us our first important result. *In steady state, the growth rate of output equals the rate of population growth (g_N) plus the rate of technological progress, (g_A). By implication, the growth rate of output is independent of the saving rate.*

The best way to strengthen your intuition for this result is to go back to the argument we used in chapter 11 to show that without technological progress and population growth, the economy could not sustain positive growth forever. The argument went as follows: Suppose the economy tried to achieve positive output growth. Because of decreasing returns to capital, capital would have to grow faster than output. The economy would have to devote a larger and larger proportion of output to capital accumulation. At some point there would be no more output to devote to capital accumulation. And growth would come to an end.

Exactly the same logic is at work here. Effective labor grows at rate $(g_A + g_N)$. Suppose the economy tried to achieve output growth in excess of $(g_A + g_N)$. Because of decreasing returns to capital, capital would have to increase faster than output. The economy would have to devote a larger and larger proportion of output to capital accumulation. At some point this would prove impossible. Thus, the economy cannot permanently grow faster than $(g_A + g_N)$.

The standard of living is given by the level of output per worker (or, more accurately, the level of output per capita), not the level of output per effective worker.

We have focused on the behavior of aggregate output. To get a sense of what happens not to aggregate output, but rather to the standard of living over time, we must look instead at the behavior of output per worker (not output per *effective worker*). Because output grows at rate $(g_A + g_N)$ and the number of workers grows at rate g_N, output per worker grows at rate g_A. In other words, *in steady state, output per worker grows at the rate of technological progress.*

The growth rate of Y/N is equal to the growth rate of Y minus the growth rate of N (see proposition 8 in appendix 2 at the end of the book). So the growth rate of Y/N is given by $(g_Y - g_N) = (g_A + g_N) - g_N = g_A$

Because output, capital, and effective labor all grow at the same rate $(g_A + g_N)$ in steady state, the steady state of this economy is also called a state of **balanced growth**: In steady state, output and the two inputs, capital and effective labor, grow in balance (at the same rate). The characteristics of balanced growth will be helpful later in the chapter, and are summarized in Table 12-1.

TABLE	12-1	The Characteristics of Balanced Growth	
			Growth rate
1.		Capital per effective worker	0
2.		Output per effective worker	0
3.		Capital per worker	g_A
4.		Output per worker	g_A
5.		Labor	g_N
6.		Capital	$g_A + g_N$
7.		Output	$g_A + g_N$

On the balanced growth path (equivalently, in steady state; equivalently, in the long run):

- Capital per effective worker and output per effective worker are constant; this is the result we derived in Figure 12–2.
- Equivalently, capital per worker and output per worker are growing at the rate of technological progress, g_A.
- Or, in terms of labor, capital, and output: Labor is growing at the rate of population growth, g_N; capital and output are growing at a rate equal to the sum of population growth and the rate of technological progress, $(g_A + g_N)$.

The Effects of the Saving Rate

Note an important implication of our results so far: In steady state, the growth rate of output depends *only* on the rate of population growth and the rate of technological progress. Changes in the saving rate do not affect the steady-state growth rate. This does not mean however that the saving rate is irrelevant: Changes in the saving rate do affect the steady-state level of output per effective worker.

This result is best seen in Figure 12–3, which shows the effect of an increase in the saving rate from s_0 to s_1. The increase in the saving rate shifts the investment relation from $s_0 f(K/AN)$ to $s_1 f(K/AN)$. It follows that the steady-state level of capital per effective worker increases from $(K/AN)_0$ to $(K/AN)_1$, with a corresponding increase in the level of output per effective worker from $(Y/AN)_0$ to $(Y/AN)_1$.

Figure 12–4 is the same as Figure 11–5, which anticipated the derivation presented here.

Following the increase in the saving rate, capital per effective worker and output per effective worker increase for some time as they converge to their new higher level. Figure 12–4 plots the evolution of output and capital against time. Both output and capital are measured on logarithmic scales. The economy is initially on the balanced growth path AA: Capital and output are growing at rate $(g_A + g_N)$—the slope of AA is equal to $(g_A + g_N)$. After the increase in the saving rate at time t, output and capital grow faster for some time. Eventually, capital and output end up at higher levels than they would have without the increase in saving. But their growth rate returns to $g_A + g_N$. In the new steady state, the economy grows at the same rate, but on a higher growth path BB—BB, which is parallel to AA, also has a slope equal to $(g_A + g_N)$.

For a description of logarithmic scales, see the margin note in chapter 10.

To summarize: In an economy with technological progress and population growth, output grows over time. In steady state, output *per effective worker* and capital *per effective worker* are constant. Put another way, output *per worker* and capital *per worker* grow at the rate of technological progress. Put yet another way, output and capital grow at the same rate as effective labor, thus at a rate equal to the growth rate of the number of workers plus the rate of technological progress. When the economy is in steady state, it is said to be on a balanced growth path.

When a logarithmic scale is used, a variable growing at a constant rate moves along a straight line. The slope of the line is equal to the rate of growth of the variable.

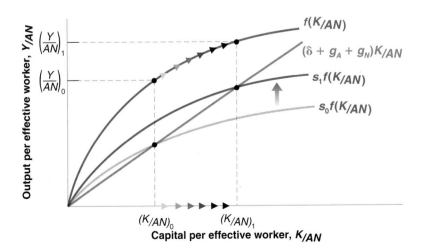

Capital per effective worker, K/AN

FIGURE 12–3

The Effects of an Increase in the Saving Rate: I

An increase in the saving rate leads to an increase in the steady-state levels of output and capital per effective worker.

TECHNOLOGICAL PROGRESS AND GROWTH

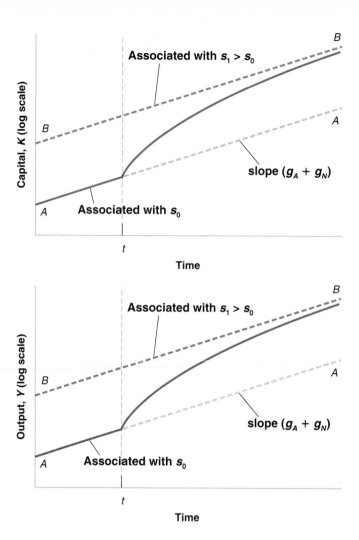

The rate of output growth in steady state is independent of the saving rate. The saving rate affects the steady-state level of output per effective worker, however. And increases in the saving rate lead, for some time, to an increase in the growth rate above the steady-state growth rate.

12-2 | The Determinants of Technological Progress

We have just seen that the growth rate of output per worker is ultimately determined by the rate of technological progress. But what in turn determines the rate of technological progress? This is the question we take up in this section.

Technological progress brings to mind images of major discoveries: the invention of the microchip, the discovery of the structure of DNA, and so on. These discoveries suggest a process driven largely by scientific research and chance rather than by economic forces. But the truth is that most technological progress in modern economies is the result of a humdrum process: the outcome of firms' **research and development (R&D)** activities. Industrial R&D expenditures account for between 2% and 3% of GDP in each of the five major rich countries we looked at in chapter 10 (the United States, France, Germany, Japan, and the United Kingdom). About 75% of the roughly one million U.S. scientists and researchers working in R&D are employed by firms. U.S. firms' R&D spending equals more than 20% of their spending on gross investment, and more than 60% of their spending on net investment.

Firms spend on R&D for the same reason they buy new machines or build new plants: to increase profits. By increasing spending on R&D, a firm increases the probability that it will discover and develop a new product. (I shall use "product" as a generic term to denote new goods or new techniques of production.) If the new product is successful, the firm's profits will increase. There is, however, an important difference between purchasing a machine and spending more on R&D. The difference is that the outcome of R&D is fundamentally ideas. And, unlike a machine, an idea potentially can be used by many firms at the same time. A firm that has just acquired a new machine does not have to worry that another firm will use that particular machine. A firm that has discovered and developed a new product can make no such assumption.

This last point implies that the level of R&D spending depends not only on the **fertility** of the research process, but also on the *appropriability* of research results. Let's look at each aspect in turn.

The Fertility of the Research Process

Fertility refers to how spending on R&D translates into new ideas and new products. If research is very fertile—if R&D spending leads to many new products—then, other things being equal, firms will have more incentives to do R&D; R&D and technological progress will be higher. The determinants of the fertility of research lie largely outside the realm of economics. Many factors interact here:

- The fertility of research depends on the successful interaction between basic research (the search for general principles and results) and applied research and development (the application of these results to specific uses, and the development of new products). Basic research does not lead, by itself, to technological progress. But the success of applied research and development depends ultimately on basic research. Much of the computer industry's development can be traced to a few breakthroughs, from the invention of the transistor to the invention of the microchip.

- Some countries appear more successful at basic research; others are more successful at applied research and development. Studies point to the relevance of the education system. For example, it is often argued that the French higher education system, with its strong emphasis on abstract thinking, produces researchers who are better at basic research than at applied research and development. Studies also point to the importance of a "culture of entrepreneurship," in which a big part of technological progress comes from the entrepreneurs' ability to organize the successful development and marketing of new products.

- It takes many years, and often many decades, for the full potential of major discoveries to be realized. The usual sequence is one in which a major discovery leads to the exploration of potential applications, then to the development of new products, then to the adoption of these new products. The Focus box "The Diffusion of New Technology: Hybrid Corn" shows the results of one of the first studies of this process of diffusion of ideas. Closer to us is the example of personal computers. Twenty years after the commercial introduction of personal computers, it often feels as if we have just started discovering their uses.

In chapter 11, we looked at the role of human capital as an input in production: More educated people can use more complex machines, or handle more complex tasks. Here, we see a second role of human capital: Better researchers and scientists and, by implication, a higher rate of technological progress.

An age-old worry is that most major discoveries have already been made and that technological progress will now slow down. This fear may come from thinking about mining, where high-grade mines were exploited first, and where we have had to turn to lower-and-lower-grade mines as resources are depleted. But this is only an analogy, and so far there is no evidence that it applies.

The Appropriability of Research Results

The second determinant of the level of R&D and of technological progress is the degree of **appropriability** of research results, the extent to which firms benefit from the results of their own R&D. If firms cannot appropriate the profits from the development of new products,

The Diffusion of New Technology: Hybrid Corn

New technologies are not developed or adopted overnight. One of the first studies of the diffusion of new technologies was carried out in 1957 by Zvi Griliches, who looked at the diffusion of hybrid corn in different states in the United States.

Hybrid corn is, in the words of Griliches, "the invention of a method of inventing." Producing hybrid corn entails crossing different strains of corn to develop a type of corn adapted to local conditions. Introduction of hybrid corn can increase the corn yield by up to 20%.

Although the idea was first developed at the beginning of the twentieth century, the first commercial application of hybridization on a substantial scale did not take place until the 1930s in the United States. Figure 1 shows the rate at which hybrid corn was adopted in five U.S. states from 1932 to 1956.

The figure shows two dynamic processes at work. One is the process through which appropriate hybrid corns were discovered for each state. Hybrid corn became available in southern states (Texas, Alabama) many years after it had become available in northern states (Iowa, Wisconsin, Kentucky). The other is the speed at which hybrid corn was adopted within each state. Within eight years of introduction, practically all corn in Iowa was hybrid corn. The process was much slower in the south. More than 10 years after its introduction, hybrid corn accounted for only 60% of total acreage in Alabama.

Why was the speed of adoption higher in Iowa than in the South? Griliches' article showed that the reason was an economic one: The speed of adoption in each state was a function of the profitability of introducing hybrid corn. And profitability was higher in Iowa than in the southern states.

Source: Zvi Griliches, "Hybrid Corn: An Exploration in the Economics of Technological Change," *Econometrica*, October 1957, 25-4.

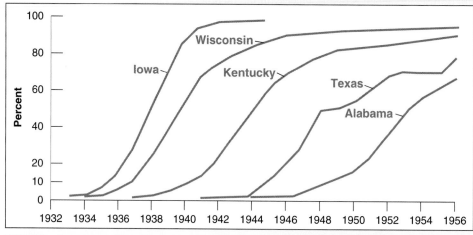

FIGURE 1   Percentage of Total Corn Acreage Planted with Hybrid Seed, Selected U.S. States, 1932–1956

Source: *See source note for this box.*

they will not engage in R&D and technological progress will be slow. Many factors are also at work here:

- One is the nature of the research process itself. For example, if it is widely believed that the discovery of a new product will quickly lead to the discovery of an even better product, there may be little payoff to being first. Thus, a highly fertile field of research may not generate high levels of R&D. This example is extreme, but revealing.
- Probably most important is the degree of protection given to new products by the law. Without legal protection, profits from developing a new product are likely to be small. Except in rare cases where the product is based on a trade secret (such as Coca Cola), it generally will not take long for other firms to produce the same product, eliminating any advantage the innovating firm may have had initially. This is why countries have patent laws. **Patents** give a firm that has discovered a new product—usually a new technique or

device—the right to exclude anyone else from the production or use of the new product for some time.

How should governments design patent laws? On the one hand, protection is needed to provide firms with the incentives to spend on R&D. On the other, once firms have discovered new products, it would be best for society if the knowledge embodied in those new products were made available to other firms and to people without restrictions. Take biogenetic research for example. The prospect of large profits is what leads bioengineering firms to embark on expensive research projects. Once a firm has found a new product, and this product can save many lives, it clearly would be best to make it available to all potential users at a price equal to the cost of production. But if such a policy was systematically followed, it would eliminate incentives for firms to do research in the first place. Patent law must strike a difficult balance: Too little protection will lead to little R&D. Too much protection will make it difficult for new R&D to build on the results of past R&D, and may also lead to little R&D.

This type of dilemma is known as "time inconsistency." We shall see other examples and discuss the issue at length in chapter 25.

Countries that are less technologically advanced often have poorer patent protection. For example, China is a country with poor enforcement of patent rights. Our discussion helps explain why. Poorer countries are typically users rather than producers of new technologies. Much of their improvement in productivity comes not from inventions within the country, but from the adaptation of foreign technologies. In this case, the costs of weak patent protection are small, because there would be few domestic inventions anyway. But the benefits of low patent protection are clear: They allow domestic firms to use and adapt foreign technology without having to pay royalties to the foreign firms that developed the technology.

12-3 | The Facts of Growth Revisited

In chapter 10, we looked at growth in five rich countries since 1950 and we identified three main facts:

- Sustained growth, especially from 1950 to the mid-1970s;
- A slowdown in growth since the mid-1970s;
- Convergence: Countries that were further behind now have been growing faster.

Let us now use the theory we have developed to see what light it sheds on these facts.

Capital Accumulation versus Technological Progress

Suppose we see an economy growing unusually fast—either in relation to its own growth in the past, or in relation to growth in other countries. Our theory suggests that this fast growth may be due to one of two causes:

- It may be due to a higher rate of technological progress, so that faster output growth reflects faster balanced growth. In other words, if g_A is higher, balanced output growth $(g_A + g_N)$ will also be higher.
- Or it may reflect the adjustment to a higher level of capital per effective worker, K/AN. As we saw in Figure 12–4, such an adjustment leads to a period of higher growth, even if the rate of technological progress has not increased.

How can we tell which is the cause? If high growth reflects high balanced growth, output per worker should be growing at a rate *equal* to the rate of technological progress (see Table 12–1, line 4). If high growth reflects instead the adjustment to a higher level of capital per effective worker, this adjustment should be reflected in a growth rate of output per worker that exceeds the rate of technological progress.

This discussion suggests a simple strategy, that of computing the growth rate of output per worker and the rate of technological progress for our five countries since 1950, then comparing the two numbers. Angus Maddison recently implemented this strategy; his results are summarized in Table 12–2. (What Maddison has computed, and thus what is reported in Table 12–2, is the growth rate of output *per capita* rather than the growth rate of output *per*

	Growth of Output per Capita			Rate of Technological Progress		
	1950–73 (1)	1973–87 (2)	Change (3)	1950–73 (4)	1973–87 (5)	Change (6)
France	4.0	1.8	−2.2	4.9	2.3	−2.6
Germany	4.9	2.1	−2.8	5.6	1.9	−3.7
Japan	8.0	3.1	−4.9	6.4	1.7	−4.7
United Kingdom	2.5	1.8	−0.7	2.3	1.7	−0.6
United States	2.2	1.6	−0.6	2.6	0.6	−2.0
Average	4.3	2.1	−2.2	4.4	1.6	−2.8

"Average" is a simple average of the growth rates in each column. Germany refers to West Germany only.

Source: Constructed from Tables 3–3, 5–3, 5–4 and 5–19 in Angus Maddison, *Dynamic Forces in Capitalist Development*, (New York: Oxford University Press, 1991).

worker. If the ratio of employment to population had remained constant, the growth rates of output per capita and of output per worker would be identical. They are not, but they are close, so we can ignore the difference here.)

In the United States, for example, the ratio of employment to population increased from 55% in 1950 to 62.5% in 1994. This represents an increase of 0.17% per year. Thus, in the United States, output per capita increased by 0.17% more per year than output per worker—a small difference, relative to the numbers in the table.

Columns 1 and 2 correspond to the first two columns of Table 10–1. (There are minor differences between the two tables, due to differences in sources and in time periods.) They give the average annual growth rates of output per capita during 1950 to 1973 and 1973 to 1987, respectively. Column 3 gives the change in the growth rate from the first to the second period.

Columns 4 and 5 give the average annual rates of technological progress during 1950 to 1973 and 1973 to 1987, respectively. Column 6 gives the change in the rate of technological progress from the first period to the second. (The method of construction of the rate of technological progress—which is not directly observable—is presented in the appendix at the end of this chapter.)

Let's now return to our three main facts. The table suggests the following conclusions:

(1) *The period of high growth of output per capita, from 1950 to 1973, was due to rapid technological progress, not to unusually high capital accumulation.*

Look at columns 1 and 4 of the table. In all five countries, the growth rate of output per capita from 1950 to 1973 was roughly equal to the rate of technological progress. This is what we would expect when countries are growing along their balanced growth path; the main source of high growth from 1950 to 1973 was a high rate of technological progress.

This is an important conclusion, because it rejects one hypothesis for why growth was so high from 1950 to 1973. The hypothesis is that fast growth was the result of the destruction of capital during World War II, leading to rapid rates of capital growth after the war. As we saw in the Global Macro box in chapter 11, this explanation does explain some of the high growth in the immediate postwar period in France, and probably in other countries as well. But it is not the reason for the sustained growth of the 1950s and 1960s in the five countries we are looking at.

(2) *The slowdown in growth of output per capita since 1973 has come from a decrease in the rate of technological progress, not from unusually low capital accumulation.*

This conclusion comes from looking at columns 3 and 6 of Table 12–2. If lower capital accumulation were to blame for the growth slowdown, we would see a larger decline in the growth rate of output per capita than in the rate of technological progress. But this is not what the table shows. In all five countries, the decrease in technological progress has been roughly equal to the decrease in the growth rate of output per capita.

Thus, contrary to some popular beliefs, the slowdown in growth since the mid-1970s is not due to a sharp drop in the saving rate, to the "disappearance of thrift." It is due to the decrease in the rate of technological progress, which declined from an average of 4.4% per year during 1950 to 1973 to only 1.6% per year from 1973 to 1987. This is potentially bad news for the future. In contrast to a decline in the saving rate—which, as we have seen, leads only to a temporary decline in growth—lower technological progress implies a permanently lower rate of growth.

(3) *Convergence of output per capita across countries has come from higher technological progress, rather than from faster capital accumulation, in the countries that started behind.*

Look at column 4 of Table 12–2. During 1950 to 1973, the annual rate of technological progress in Japan was 3.8% higher than that in the United States. The German rate was 3.0% higher, the French rate 2.3% higher. Only the U.K. rate was slightly below that of the United States. During 1973 to 1987, the differences narrowed to 1.1% for Japan, 1.3% for Germany, and 1.7% for France.

These facts yield an important conclusion: One can think in general of two sources of convergence between countries. The first is that the poorer countries are poorer because they have less capital to start with. Over time, they accumulate capital faster than the others, generating convergence. The second is that the poorer countries are poorer because they are less technologically advanced than the others. Thus, over time, they become more sophisticated, either by importing technology from advanced countries or developing their own. As technological levels converge, so does output per capita. The conclusion we can draw from Table 12–2 is that the more important source in this case has clearly been the second one. For example, Japan's output per worker has increased relative to that of the United States not so much because Japan has accumulated capital extremely quickly, but rather because the state of technology has improved very quickly in Japan over the last 40 years.

Why Has Technological Progress Slowed Since the Mid-1970s?

The conclusions we reached in the preceding section represent (intellectual) progress. But, by putting the focus on the role of technological progress in growth, they raise a new set of issues. One is *why* technological progress has slowed down since the mid-1970s. Much research has been devoted to answering this question. Several hypotheses have been suggested, from measurement error to the rise of the service sector to decreased spending on R&D. Let's look at each in turn.

Measurement Error. The first hypothesis is that there has been in fact no slowdown in technological progress, and that the measured slowdown is solely the result of measurement error.

That measurement error could be important is obvious to anybody who looks at how measures of output (such as GDP) are actually constructed. In several sectors, productivity is not easily measured: How do you measure the evolution of the productivity of doctors or lawyers over time? Due to the difficulties in measuring productivity in these sectors, the National Income and Product Accounts make simple assumptions about productivity growth in those sectors. And these assumptions may well be wrong. To take an example, technological progress in financial services is assumed equal to zero. But there is plenty of evidence that there has been substantial technological progress in financial services. In check processing, for example, the average number of checks processed per worker per hour increased from 265 in 1971 to 825 in 1986, an increase of 7.6% per year.

There is an interesting connection here between the measurement of inflation and the measurement of productivity growth. If an increase in the price of a good reflects in fact an increase in its quality, and if this quality increase is ignored by statisticians, what should be counted as productivity growth (the increase in quality) will be counted instead as inflation (an increase in prices.) A recent study of the U.S. CPI has concluded that the failure to fully adjust for quality improvements in the basket of goods underlying the index has led the

Bureau of Labor Statistics (which is in charge of constructing the CPI) to overstate CPI inflation by about 0.6% per year. If the conclusion of this study is correct, and if the findings extend to the GDP deflator, this implies that productivity growth has been understated by 0.6% per year.

There is no question that there is measurement error and that we may be systematically understating technological progress and output growth. This is an important point: Our standard of living may be increasing faster than the official statistics suggest. To explain the slowdown, however, one would have to show that the error has become larger since the mid-1970s, so technological progress is more understated now than it was earlier. There is so far little evidence that this is the case.

The Rise of the Service Sector. The second hypothesis is that the slowdown in technological progress reflects the fact that the United States, and the other rich countries, have become **post-industrial economies** in which manufacturing's share of GDP is steadily declining, and the share of services is steadily increasing. And, the argument goes, the scope for technological progress is much more limited in services than in manufacturing. How much technological progress can take place in haircuts?

This argument is plausible. However, the facts suggest that the shift toward services has played a limited role in the slowdown. We can see why in Figure 12–5, which plots the change in average annual labor productivity growth from 1948 to 1973 to 1973 to 1987, by sector. What is striking about Figure 12–5 is how the slowdown in productivity growth has affected nearly all sectors. Only farming and nonelectrical machinery (mainly computers) have seen increases in labor productivity growth from the first period to the second. The decline has been largest in mining (reflecting the depletion of the most easily available reserves) and in utilities (where it is in large part the result of more stringent environmental regulations). More directly relevant for our purposes here, the decline has been roughly the same in manufacturing sectors (goods production) as in service sectors (retail trade). Thus, the shift in composition toward services cannot account for the slowdown in overall productivity growth.

Decreased R&D Spending. The third hypothesis focuses on R&D. Because of the roughly equal decline in the productivity of the manufacturing and service sectors, the search for explanations must center on factors that can explain why there has been a slowdown in most sectors. A natural hypothesis is that there was a general decline in R&D, leading to a decline

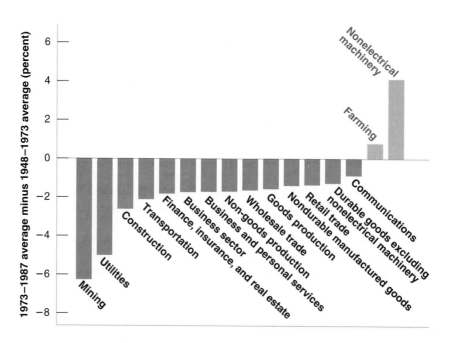

There are other problems of construction associated with the CPI, and the overall conclusion of the report is that CPI inflation exceeds true inflation by more than 1% a year. But these other problems are not related to the issues discussed in this chapter. For more on the conclusions of the report, and the debate it has triggered, look at the papers on "Measuring the CPI," *Journal of Economic Perspectives*, 1998-1, volume 12.

For reasons of data availability, the numbers in the figure refer to labor productivity growth—that is, the growth rate of output per worker $(g_Y - g_N)$—rather than to the rate of technological progress g_A. Based on what we know for specific industries, the results would be very similar if we used estimates of the rate of technological progress instead.

FIGURE 12–5

Changes in Average Annual Labor Productivity Growth, 1948–1973 to 1973–1987, by Sector

Most sectors of the U.S. economy have experienced a slowdown in productivity growth.
Source: Martin N. Baily and Robert Gordon, "The Productivity Slowdown, Measurement Issues, and the Explosion of Computer Power," *Brookings Papers on Economic Activity*, 1988: 2, 347–431.

TABLE 12–3 Spending on R&D as a Percentage of GDP

	1963	1975	1989
France	1.6	1.8	2.3
Germany	1.4	2.2	2.9
Japan	1.5	2.0	3.0
United Kingdom	2.3	2.0	2.3
United States	2.7	2.3	2.8

Source: Kumiharu Shigehara, "Causes of Declining Growth in Industrialized Countries," in *Policies for Long-Run Economic Growth*, Kansas City, MO: Kansas City Fed, 1993, Table 4, p. 22.

in technological progress. It turns out that the facts do not support this hypothesis. Table 12–3 shows the evolution of spending on R&D in each of our five countries. In all five countries, spending on R&D remained constant or increased as a percentage of GDP between 1963 and 1989.

The facts therefore suggest that the proximate reason for the decline in the rate of technological progress is a decline not in the amount but in the fertility of R&D. Although rich countries are spending as much as or more than they used to on R&D, measured technological progress has slowed down. This is unfortunately the extent of our knowledge at this point. Some economists argue that we are in a phase where there has not been a truly major discovery for some time. Others argue that different sectors have developed sector-specific technologies, with the result that discoveries affect a smaller number of sectors than in the past, leading to smaller spillovers of research across sectors. At this stage, these hypotheses are largely untested, and research goes on.

12-4 | Epilogue: The Secrets of Growth

Why the rate of technological progress has declined since the mid-1970s is not the only unanswered question in the economics of growth. Many questions remain.

We understand the basic mechanisms of growth in rich countries. But we are not very good at answering more specific questions, for example, what specific measures could be taken to increase growth. Are governments spending the right amount on basic research? Should patent laws be modified? Is there a case for an **industrial policy**, a policy aimed at helping specific sectors of the economy (for example, those sectors with the potential for high technological progress, and so the potential for large spillovers for the rest of the economy)? What can we expect in terms of additional growth from increasing the average number of years of education by another year?

Turning from growth in rich countries since 1950 to growth over a longer time span, or over a broader set of countries, our knowledge is even more limited. For example, consider the fact that many countries in the world have a level of output per worker equal to less than one-tenth the U.S. level of output per worker. The framework developed in this and the previous chapter gives us a way of approaching this fact. If we think of output per worker as depending on physical capital per worker, human capital per worker (the two factors emphasized in chapter 10), and on the state of technology (the factor emphasized in this chapter), we can ask: Are these countries poorer because they have less physical and human capital, or because the state of their technology is lower?

See Robert Hall and Charles Jones, "Why Do Some Countries Produce So Much More Output per Worker Than Others?" NBER working paper 6564, May 1998.

The answer turns out that much of the difference comes from differences in the measured level of technology across countries. Compare for example the United States and

Hong Kong and Singapore: A Tale of Two Cities

IN DEPTH

Between 1960 and 1985, the average growth rate of output in both Hong Kong and Singapore was 6.1% per year.* How did both Hong Kong and Singapore grow so fast? On close inspection, one is struck both by the similarities and by the differences in their economic evolutions.

The Similarities

Hong Kong and Singapore have much in common. Both are ex-British colonies. Both are essentially cities that served initially as trading ports with little manufacturing activity. The postwar population of both countries was composed primarily of immigrant Chinese from southern China. During the course of their rapid growth, they have gone through a similar sequence of industries, with Singapore starting later than Hong Kong by 10 to 15 years. The respective sequences are summarized in Table 1.

The Differences

A closer look shows, however, major differences in the way the two countries have grown.

Hong Kong has grown under a policy of minimal government intervention. For the most part, the government has limited its intervention to providing infrastructure and selling land as it became required for further growth. In contrast, growth in Singapore has been dominated by government intervention. Through budget surpluses, as well as forced saving through pension contributions, the government has achieved a very high national saving rate. Singapore's share of gross investment in GDP increased from 9% in 1960 to 43% in 1984, one of the highest investment rates in the world. The development of specific industries has been the result of systematic government targeting, implemented through large tax incentives for mostly foreign investors.

These differences in strategies are reflected in the relative roles of capital accumulation and technological progress. In Hong Kong, the annual growth rate of output per worker from 1970 to 1990 was 2.4%; the growth rate of technological progress over the same period was 2.3%. Using the interpretation provided by the model we developed in this chapter, growth in Hong Kong has been roughly balanced. In Singapore, the growth rate of output per worker from 1971 to 1990 was 1.5%. In the article on which this box is based, Alwyn Young, an economist at the University of Chicago, concludes that the rate of technological progress during that period was a surprisingly low 0.1%. If his computation is right (and, after an intense controversy triggered by his article, it appears to be largely so), this implies that Singapore has grown nearly entirely through unusually high capital accumulation, not through technological progress. Singapore's growth has been very much unbalanced.

Why has Singapore achieved so little technological progress? Alwyn Young argues that in effect Singapore has gone too fast from one industry to the next. By going so fast, it has not had time to learn how to produce any of them very efficiently. And, by relying largely on foreign investment, it has not allowed a class of domestic entrepreneurs to learn and replace foreign investment in the future.

If Alwyn Young is right, what lies in store for Singapore? The model we have developed in this chapter suggests that a slowdown in growth is inevitable. High saving and investment rates can lead to high growth only for a while. The numbers appear brighter for Hong Kong, which seems to be growing on a balanced growth path. But major changes are in store for Hong Kong as well: In 1997, Hong Kong again became part of China; whether this will help or hinder its growth remains to be seen.

*These numbers are computed using PPP measures of GDP, from Heston and Summers (see the Focus box on PPP measures in chapter 10).

Source: Alwyn Young, "A Tale of Two Cities: Factor Accumulation and Technical Change in Hong Kong and Singapore," *NBER Macroeconomics Annual*, 1992, 13–63.

TABLE	1	The sequence of activities in Hong Kong and Singapore since the early 1950s

Hong Kong		Singapore	
Early 1950s	Textiles	Early 1960s	Textiles
Early 1960s	Clothing, Plastics	Late 1960s	Electronics, Petroleum refining
Early 1970s	Electronics	Early 1970s	Electronics, Petroleum refining, Textiles, Clothing
1980s	Trade, Banking	1980s	Banking, Electronics

Source: See source note for this box.

China. GDP per worker (Y/N) is 16 times higher in the United States than in China. If this ratio reflected only differences in the level of physical capital and human capital per worker between the two countries, then we would find that adjusting for differences in physical and human capital, the two economies had the same value of A: The level of technology would be the same in both countries. Existing estimates imply that A is, in fact, 10 times higher in the United States than in China. In short, even if China suddenly acquired the same levels of physical capital and education per worker as the United States, output per worker would still be only a small fraction of what it is in the United States.

This answer is a useful first step, but it raises another question. Poor countries have access to most of the technological knowledge in the world. What prevents these countries from simply adapting much of the advanced countries' technology, quickly closing a good part of their **technology gap**? It is clear that the answer to that question requires us to take a broader interpretation of technology than we have so far in this chapter, and to look at many of the factors we left aside in thinking about the determinants of the production function in chapter 10. These include poorly established property rights, political instability, the lack of entrepreneurs, and poorly developed financial markets. The importance of these factors has been particularly obvious in the transition from central planning to a market economy in the countries of Eastern Europe during the 1990s. In many of these countries, poorly defined property rights, poorly enforced laws, and corruption of public officials have severely constrained the growth of new firms. The list is easy to make. But the specific role of each of these factors is hard to pinpoint. And solving these problems is not easy: Many of them are as much the result of low income as they are the cause of low income.

Looking at the poor countries that have grown rapidly in the last 20 years (such as the "four tigers": Hong Kong, Taiwan, Singapore, and South Korea) or at the even more recent fast growers (such as China, Indonesia, Malaysia, and Thailand) would seem the best way of uncovering the secrets of growth. But here again the lessons are not proving simple. In all these countries, growth has come with the rapid accumulation of both physical and human capital. And in all these countries growth has also come with an increase in the importance of foreign trade, an increase in exports and imports. But beyond these two factors, clear differences emerge. Some countries, such as Hong Kong, have relied mostly on free markets and limited government intervention. Others, such as Korea and Singapore, have relied instead on government intervention and an industrial policy aimed at fostering the growth of specific industries. (The cases of Hong Kong and Singapore are discussed in detail in the In Depth box "Hong Kong and Singapore: A Tale of Two Cities.") The bottom line is clear: We have not yet unraveled the secrets of growth.

Looking at these factors takes us from the realm of growth theory to the realm of development economics.

For more on transition, see chapter 24.

For example, political instability and ethnic conflicts are at the source of output stagnation in several African countries. And, in turn, output stagnation contributes to political instability and exacerbates ethnic conflicts.

SUMMARY

- When looking at the implications of technological progress for growth, it is useful to think of technological progress as increasing the amount of effective labor available in the economy (that is, labor multiplied by the state of technology). We can then think of output as being produced with capital and effective labor.

- In steady state, output *per effective worker* and capital *per effective worker* are constant. Put another way, output *per worker* and capital *per worker* grow at the rate of technological progress. Put yet another way, output and capital grow at the same rate as effective labor, thus at a rate equal to the growth rate of the number of workers plus the rate of technological progress. When the economy is in steady state, it is said to be on a balanced growth path.

- The rate of output growth in steady state is independent of the saving rate. However, the saving rate affects the steady-state level of output per effective worker. And increases in the saving rate lead, for some time, to an increase in the growth rate above the steady-state growth rate.

- Technological progress depends on both (1) the fertility of research and development and (2) the appropriability of the results of R&D (that is, the extent to which firms benefit from the results of their R&D).

- In designing patent laws, governments must trade off protection for future discoveries with a desire to make existing discoveries available to potential users without restrictions.

- Germany, France, Japan, the United Kingdom, and the United States have had roughly balanced growth since 1950. The slowdown in growth since the mid-1970s is the result of a decrease in the rate of technological progress. Convergence of output appears to have come primarily from a convergence in technology levels.

- There is no good explanation for the decline in the rate of technological progress since the mid-1970s. More generally, our understanding of the determinants of technological progress, and its relation to factors such as the legal system or the political system, remains limited.

- effective labor, or labor in efficiency units, 229
- balanced growth, 232
- research and development (R&D), 234
- fertility, 235
- appropriability, 235

- patents, 236
- post-industrial economies, 240
- industrial policy, 241
- technology gap, 243

QUESTIONS & PROBLEMS

An asterisk denotes a harder question. [Web] indicates that the question requires access to the Internet.

1. TRUE/FALSE/UNCERTAIN

a. Writing the production function in terms of capital and effective labor implies that as the level of technology increases by a certain percentage, the number of workers required to achieve the same level of output decreases by the same percentage.

b. Because our production function exhibits constant returns to capital and effective labor, output per effective worker also exhibits constant returns to capital per effective worker.

c. If the rate of technological progress increases, the investment rate (the ratio of investment to output) required to keep capital per effective worker constant must increase.

d. In steady state, output per effective worker grows at the rate of population growth.

e. In steady state, output per worker grows at the rate of technological progress.

f. A higher saving rate implies a higher level of capital per effective worker in the steady state, and thus a higher rate of growth of output per effective worker.

g. Even if the potential returns from R&D spending are identical to the potential returns from investing in a new machine, R&D spending is much riskier for firms than investing in new machines.

h. The fact that one cannot patent a theorem implies that private firms will not engage in basic research.

i. The slowdown in technological progress since the 1970s seems to be driven by the widespread decline in R&D spending in most industrialized countries.

2. R&D SPENDING

Why is the amount of R&D spending important for growth? How do the appropriability and fertility of research affect the amount of R&D spending?

For each of the following policy proposals, determine how the appropriability and fertility of research are affected and what you expect the long-run effect to be on R&D and on output:

a. An international treaty that ensures that each country's patents are legally protected all over the world.

b. Tax credits for each dollar of R&D spending.

c. A decrease in funding of government-sponsored conferences between universities and corporations.

d. The elimination of patents on breakthrough drugs, so the drugs can be sold at low cost as soon as they are available.

3. PATENTS AND GROWTH

Where does technological progress come from for the economic leaders of the world? Where does it come from in developing countries? Do you see any reasons why developing countries may choose to have poor patent protection? Are there any dangers in such a policy (for developing countries)?

4. DIFFUSION OF INVENTIONS

Use the medical and automobile industries to provide examples of technological advances that have not yet fully diffused in the economy. Can you think of some advances in those industries whose diffusion is relatively more important than others for society? Name a policy that would accelerate the diffusion process. Would such a policy also have disadvantages for society? Explain.

5. MEASUREMENT ERROR, INFLATION, AND PRODUCTIVITY GROWTH

Suppose that there are only two goods produced in the economy, haircuts and banking services. Over two years the prices, quantities, and number of workers occupied in the production of each good are given by:

	Year 1			Year 2		
	P1	Q1	N1	P2	Q2	N2
Haircuts	10	100	50	12	100	50
Banking	10	200	50	12	230	60

a. What is nominal GDP in each year?

b. Using Year 1 prices, what is real GDP in year 2? What is the growth rate of real GDP?

c. What is the rate of inflation using the GDP deflator?

d. Using Year 1 prices, what is real GDP per worker in Year 1 and Year 2? What is labor productivity growth between Year 1 and Year 2 for the whole economy?

Now suppose that banking services in Year 2 are not the same as banking services in Year 1 because they include telebanking, which Year 1 banking services did not include. The technology for telebanking was available in Year 1 but the price of banking services with telebanking in Year 1 was $13 and no one chose that package. However, in Year 2 the price of banking services with telebanking was $12 and everyone chose to have that package in Year 2 (that is, in Year 2 no one chose to have the Year 1 banking services package without telebanking).

e. Using Year 1 prices, what is real GDP for Year 2? What is the growth rate of real GDP?

f. What is the rate of inflation using the GDP deflator?

g. What is labor productivity growth between Year 1 and Year 2 for the whole economy?

h. If banking services were mismeasured by not taking into account the introduction of telebanking, what would have been the effect on our measures of productivity growth and inflation?

6. THE SLOWDOWN IN PRODUCTIVITY GROWTH

Consider the following two scenarios:

i. The rate of technological progress declines forever.

ii. The saving rate declines forever.

a. What is the impact of each of these scenarios on economic growth over the next five years?

b. Over the next five decades?

In both cases, make sure to consider the effects on both the growth rate and the level of output.

7. STEADY STATE OUTPUT AND TECHNOLOGICAL PROGRESS

Suppose that the economy's production function is:

$$Y = \sqrt{K}\sqrt{NA}$$

and that the saving rate (s) is equal to 16% and that the rate of depreciation (δ) is equal to 10%. Further, suppose that the number of workers grows at 2% per year and that the rate of technological progress is 4% per year.

a. Find the steady state values of
   The capital stock per effective worker.
   Output per effective worker.
   The growth rate of output per effective worker.
   The growth rate of output per worker.
   The growth rate of output.

b. Suppose that the rate of technological progress doubles to 8% per year. Recompute the answers to (a). Explain.

c. Now suppose that the rate of technological progress is still equal to 4% per year, but the number of workers now grows at 6% per year. Recompute the answers to (a). Are people better off in (a) or in (c)? Explain.

*8. GROWTH ACCOUNTING [Web]

In the appendix to this chapter, it is shown how data on output, capital, and labor can be used to construct estimates of the rate of growth of technological progress. Consider the following production function, which gives a good description of production in rich countries:

$$Y = K^{1/3}NA^{2/3}$$

Following the same steps as in the appendix, you can show that:

$$\text{Residual} = [g_Y - \tfrac{1}{3}g_K - \tfrac{2}{3}g_N]$$

or reorganizing:

$$\text{Residual} = [(g_Y - g_N) - \tfrac{1}{3}(g_K - g_N)]$$

The rate of technological progress is then obtained by dividing the residual by the share of labor, which, given the production function we have assumed, is equal to 2/3:

$$g_A = \text{Residual}/(2/3) = (3/2)\,\text{Residual}$$

Using the instructions provided in chapter 10, problem 6, download the series "Real GDP per worker" and "Nonresidential capital stock per worker" for both Japan and the United States for the period 1965 to 1992 from the Penn World Tables. (Unfortunately, the series on K/N is not available for years prior to 1965.)

Input the series into your favorite spreadsheet program.

a. Compute the growth rate of Y/N, $(g_Y - g_N)$, and K/N, $(g_K - g_N)$, for each year and for each country.

b. For each country, calculate the average growth rate of Y/N and K/N for the sub-periods 1965 to 1973 and 1974 to 1992.

c. Using the equations above, compute the rate of technological progress for both sub-periods for both countries.

d. Do you find evidence of a slowdown? For which period?

e. The U.S. was the technological leader in both periods. So why is it that Japan's growth rate of technological progress is so much higher than that of the U.S. in both periods? Why does the difference become smaller in the later sub-period?

f. Does the difference in g_A explain all the difference in $(g_Y - g_N)$? If not, where does the rest come from?

*9. THE SECRETS OF GROWTH

Discuss the potential role of the following factors on the steady-state level of output per worker. In each case, indicate whether the effect is through A, and/or through K or H.

a. Geographic location

b. Education

c. Protection of property rights

d. Openness to trade

e. Low tax rates

f. Good public infrastructure

g. Low population growth

FURTHER READINGS

Two classic books on the nature of invention and its role in growth are:

Joseph Schmookler, *Invention and Economic Growth* (Cambridge, MA: Harvard University Press, 1966), which looks at the precise nature of invention and inventions.

Joseph Schumpeter, *Capitalism, Socialism and Democracy* (New York: Harper & Row, 1942), which builds a general theory of fluctuations and growth, giving central roles to innovations and to entrepreneurs.

A thorough assessment of what we know about technological progress in rich countries is given in William Baumol, Sue Anne Batey Blackman, and Edward Wolff, *Productivity and American Leadership: The Long View* (Cambridge, MA: MIT Press, 1989).

For an issue we have not explored in the text, growth and the environment, read *Development and the Environment, World Development Report*, (Oxford: World Bank: Oxford University Press, 1992).

For more on the theory of growth, read Charles Jones, *Introduction to Economic Growth*, (New York, NY: Norton, 1998).

APPENDIX

CONSTRUCTING A MEASURE OF TECHNOLOGICAL PROGRESS

In 1957, Robert Solow suggested a way of constructing an estimate of the rate technological progress. The method, still used today, relies on one important assumption: Each factor of production is paid its marginal product.

Under this assumption, it is easy to compute the contribution of an increase in any factor of production to the increase in output. For example, if a worker is paid $30,000 a year, the assumption implies that her contribution to output is equal to $30,000. Now suppose that this worker increases the amount of hours she works by 10%.

The increase in output coming from the increase in her hours will therefore be equal to $30,000 × 10%, or $3,000.

Let us write this more formally. Denote output by Y, labor by N, and the real wage by W/P. Then, as we just established, the change in output is equal to the real wage multiplied by the change in labor.

$$\Delta Y = \frac{W}{P} \Delta N$$

Divide both sides of the equation by Y, divide and multiply the right side by N, and reorganize

$$\frac{\Delta Y}{Y} = \frac{WN}{PY} \frac{\Delta N}{N}$$

Note that the first term on the right (WN/PY) is equal to the share of labor in output—the total wage bill in dollars divided by the value of output in dollars. Denote this share by α. Note that $\Delta Y/Y$ is the rate of growth of output, and denote it by g_Y. Note similarly that $\Delta N/N$ is the rate of change of the labor input, and denote it by g_N. Then the previous relation can be written as

$$g_Y = \alpha g_N$$

More generally, this reasoning implies that the part of output growth attributable to growth of the labor input is equal to α times g_N.

Similarly, we can compute the part of output growth attributable to growth of the capital stock. As there are only two factors of production, labor and capital, and as the share of labor is equal to α, the share of capital in income must be equal to $(1 - \alpha)$. If the growth rate of capital is equal to g_K, then the increase in output attributable to growth of capital is equal to $(1 - \alpha)$ times g_K.

Putting the contributions of labor and capital together, the growth in output attributable to growth in both labor and capital is equal to $(\alpha g_N + (1 - \alpha)g_K)$.

We can then measure the effects of technological progress by computing what Solow called the residual, the excess of actual growth of output over the growth attributable to growth in labor and capital $(\alpha g_N + (1 - \alpha)g_K)$.

$$\underset{\substack{\text{actual} \\ \text{growth}}}{\text{residual} \equiv \quad g_Y} \quad - \quad \underset{\substack{\text{growth attributable to} \\ \text{growth of labor and capital}}}{([\alpha g_N + (1 - \alpha)g_K])}$$

This measure is called the **Solow residual**. It is easy to compute: All we need to know to compute it are the growth rates of output, labor, and capital, as well as the shares of labor and capital.

The Solow residual is sometimes called the **rate of growth of multifactor productivity**. This is to distinguish it from the *rate of growth of labor productivity*, which is defined as $(g_Y - g_N)$, the rate of output growth minus the rate of labor growth.

The Solow residual is related to the rate of technological progress in a simple way. The residual is equal to the share of labor times the rate of technological progress

$$\text{residual} = \alpha g_A$$

I shall not derive this result here. But the intuition for this relation comes from the fact that what matters in the production function $Y = F(K, AN)$ (equation [12.1]) is the product of labor times the state of technology, AN. We saw that to get the contribution of labor growth to output growth, we must multiply the growth rate of labor by its share. Because N and A enter in the same way in the production function, it is clear that to get the contribution of technological progress to output growth, we must also multiply it by the share of labor.

If the Solow residual is equal to zero, so is technological progress. To construct an estimate of g_A, one must construct the Solow residual and then divide it by the share of labor. This is how the estimates of g_A presented in the text are constructed.

Keep straight the definitions of productivity growth we have seen in this chapter. The two important ones are:

(1) labor productivity growth: $g_Y - g_N$

and

(2) rate of technological progress: g_A

In steady state, labor productivity growth $(g_Y - g_N)$ equals the rate of technological progress g_A. Outside of steady state, they need not be equal. An increase in the ratio of capital per effective worker, due, for example, to an increase in the saving rate, increases $g_Y - g_N$ over g_A for some time.

The rate of technological progress is not directly observable. To construct it, we start from:

(3) the Solow residual: $g_Y - (\alpha g_N + (1 - \alpha)g_K)$

The Solow residual is also called the rate of growth of total factor productivity. The rate of technological progress equals the Solow residual divided by the labor share: $g_A = \text{residual}/\alpha$.

Source: Robert Solow, "Technical Change and the Aggregate Production Function," *Review of Economics and Statistics*, 1957, 312–320.

KEY TERMS

- Solow residual, or rate of growth of multifactor productivity, 247

CHAPTER 13

Technological Progress, Wages, and Unemployment

We spent much of chapter 12 celebrating the merits of technological progress. In the long run, we argued, technological progress is the key to steady increases in output per capita, to increases in the standard of living.

Popular and political discussions of technological progress are often more ambivalent. Since the beginning of the Industrial Revolution, workers have worried that technological progress will eliminate their jobs and throw them into unemployment. In early nineteenth-century England, groups of workers in the textile industry, known as the Luddites, destroyed the new machines that they saw as a direct threat to their jobs. Similar movements took place in other countries as well. The word *saboteur* comes from one of the ways French workers destroyed machines: by putting their sabots (their heavy wooden shoes) in the machinery.

The theme of **technological unemployment** typically resurfaces whenever unemployment is high. During the Great Depression, adherents to a movement called the *technocracy movement* argued that high unemployment came from the introduction of new machines, and that things would only get worse if technological progress were allowed to continue. Today in Europe—where unemployment is also very high—there is widespread support in many countries for a shorter workweek, down to 35 or even 30 hours. Because of technological progress, the argument goes, there is no longer enough work for all workers to have full-time jobs. The solution is to have each worker work fewer hours so that more workers can be employed.

In its crudest form, the argument that technological progress must lead to unemployment is obviously false. The very large improvements in the standard of living that advanced countries have enjoyed over the twentieth century have been associated with large *increases* in employment and no systematic increase in the unemployment rate. (Steady growth of income has been associated with a steady decrease in the number of hours worked. In rich countries, the average annual number of hours worked per worker has decreased from around 2600 hours (50 hours a week × 52 weeks) in 1900 to 1700 hours (35 hours a week × 48 weeks) today. Technological progress has led people to consume both more goods and more leisure. But it has not led to a steady increase in unemployment.) In the United States, output per capita has increased by a factor of 6 since 1900 and, far from declining, employment has increased by a factor of 5 (reflecting a parallel increase in the size of the U.S. population). Nor, looking across countries, is there any evidence of a systematic positive relation between the unemployment rate and the level of productivity. Japan and the United States, two of the countries with the highest levels of productivity, have two of the lowest unemployment rates among OECD countries.

Do these facts mean that the fears reflected in popular perceptions are groundless? No, or at least not necessarily. To organize the discussion here, it is useful to distinguish between two related but separate dimensions of technological progress:

- Technological progress allows for the production of larger quantities of goods using the same number of workers.
- Technological progress leads to the production of new goods and the disappearance of old ones.

Consider the first dimension and note that the effect of technological progress on the relation between output and the number of workers can be stated in two ways:

- An optimistic one: Technological progress allows the economy to produce *more and more* output with the *same* number of workers.

- A pessimistic one: Technological progress implies that the economy can produce the *same* amount of output with *fewer and fewer workers*.

Those who emphasize the role of technological progress in increasing output and the standard of living think in terms of the first. Those who worry about technological unemployment think in terms of the second.

The evidence we saw in previous chapters clearly shows that, in the long run, the adjustment to technological progress is through increases in output, not increased unemployment. But how much time does this adjustment take? Does output increase quickly enough in response to an increase in productivity to avoid a prolonged period of unemployment? By assuming in chapter 12 that employment remained constant—or grew at a constant rate—we assumed away the issue. We now take it up. In section 13-1, we look at the short-run response of output and unemployment to increases in productivity. In section 13-2, we look at their medium-run responses. As we shall see, neither theory nor evidence supports the fear that faster technological progress leads to more unemployment. If anything, the effect seems to go the other way: Productivity growth slowdowns, not increases, appear to be associated with more unemployment for some time.

Consider now the second dimension. With technological progress comes a complex process of job creation and job destruction. This theme was central to the work of Joseph Schumpeter, a Harvard economist who in the 1930s emphasized that the process of growth was fundamentally a process of **creative destruction**. For those who lose their jobs and have to find new ones, or for those who have skills that are no longer in demand, technological progress can be a curse, not a blessing. As consumers, they benefit from the availability of new goods. As workers, however, they may suffer from prolonged unemployment and settle for lower wages when taking a new job. This concern is of particular relevance in the United States today. The last 20 years have been

characterized by a decline, both relative and absolute, in the wages of unskilled workers. Many signs point to technological progress as the main cause. The distribution effects of technological progress, and in particular the change in the structure of wages, are the topics taken up in section 13-3.

In chapter 12, we represented technological progress as an increase in A, the *state of technology*, in the production function

$$Y = F(K, AN)$$

Technological progress, not capital accumulation, is central to the issues we shall be discussing here. So, for simplicity, we shall ignore capital altogether here and assume that output is produced according to the following production function:

$$Y = AN \qquad (13.1)$$

Output is produced using only labor, N, and each worker produces A units of output. Increases in A represent technological progress. Note that A has two interpretations here. The first is indeed as the state of technology. The second, which follows from the fact that $Y/N = A$, is as labor productivity (output per worker). So, when referring to increases in A, I shall use *technological progress* or (labor) *productivity growth* interchangeably.

Rewrite equation (13.1) as

$$N = Y/A \qquad (13.2)$$

Employment is equal to output divided by productivity. Given output, the higher the level of productivity, the lower the level of employment. This naturally leads to the following question: When productivity increases, does output increase enough to avoid a decrease in employment—equivalently, an increase in unemployment? In this section we look at the short-run responses of output, employment, and unemployment. In the next, we look at their medium-run responses and, in particular, at the relation between the natural rate of unemployment and the rate of technological progress.

> "Output per worker" and "the state of technology" are in general not the same. Recall from chapter 12 that an increase in output per worker may come from an increase in capital per worker, even if the state of technology has not changed. They are the same here because, in writing the production function as equation (13.1), I have ignored the role of capital in production.

Technological Progress, Aggregate Supply, and Aggregate Demand

The right model to use when thinking about the short- and medium-run response of output to a change in productivity in the short run is the model of aggregate supply and aggregate demand that we developed in chapter 7. Recall its basic structure:

Output is determined by the intersection of the aggregate supply curve and the aggregate demand curve. The *aggregate supply* relation captures the effects of output on the price level. The aggregate supply curve is upward sloping: An increase in the level of output leads to an increase in the price level. Behind the scenes, the mechanism is the following: An increase in output leads to a decrease in unemployment. The decrease in unemployment leads to an increase in wages, which leads to an increase in prices—an increase in the price level.

The *aggregate demand* relation captures the effects of the price level on output. The aggregate demand curve is downward sloping: An increase in the price level leads to a decrease in the demand for output. Behind the scenes, the mechanism is the following: An increase in the price level leads to a decrease in the real money stock. The decrease in real money leads in turn to an increase in the interest rate. The increase in the interest rate leads to a decrease in the demand for goods, decreasing output.

> Aggregate supply curve: Given P^e,
> $$Y\uparrow \Rightarrow u\downarrow \Rightarrow W\uparrow \Rightarrow P\uparrow$$

Aggregate supply is drawn as AS in Figure 13–1. Aggregate demand is drawn as AD. Their intersection gives the level of output Y consistent with equilibrium in labor, goods, and financial markets. Given output, the level of employment is determined by $N = Y/A$.

> Aggregate demand curve:
> $$P\uparrow \Rightarrow \frac{M}{P}\downarrow \Rightarrow i\uparrow \Rightarrow Y\downarrow$$

Suppose that the level of productivity increases from A to A'. What happens to output, and to employment and unemployment? The answer depends on how the increase in productivity shifts the aggregate supply curve and the aggregate demand curve.

> A and A' refer to levels of productivity, not points on the graph. (To avoid confusion, points in the graph are denoted by B and B'.)

Take aggregate supply first. The effect of an increase in productivity is to decrease the amount of labor needed to produce a unit of output, reducing cost for firms. This leads firms to reduce the price they charge at any level of output. Aggregate supply shifts down, from AS to AS' in Figure 13–2.

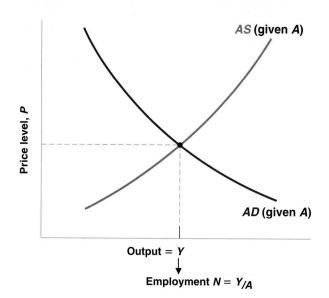

FIGURE 13-1

Aggregate Supply and Aggregate Demand for a Given Level of Productivity

Aggregate supply is upward sloping: An increase in output leads to an increase in the price level. Aggregate demand is downward sloping: An increase in the price level leads to a decrease in output.

Now take aggregate demand. Does an increase in productivity increase or decrease the demand for goods at a given price level? The answer is that there is no general answer. The reason is that productivity increases do not appear in a vacuum, and what happens to aggregate demand depends on what triggered the increase in productivity in the first place:

- Take the case where productivity increases come from the widespread implementation of a major technological breakthrough. It is easy to see how this change may be associated with an increase in demand at a given price level. The prospect of higher growth in the future leads consumers to feel more optimistic about the future, and thus to increase their consumption, given current income. The prospect of higher profits in the future, as well as the need to put the new technology in place, may also lead to a boom in investment. In this case, the demand for goods increases at a given price level; the aggregate demand curve shifts to the right.

- Now take the case where productivity growth comes not from the introduction of new technologies but from the more efficient use of existing technologies. One of the implications of increased international trade has been an increase in foreign competition. This competition has forced many firms to cut costs by reorganizing production and eliminat-

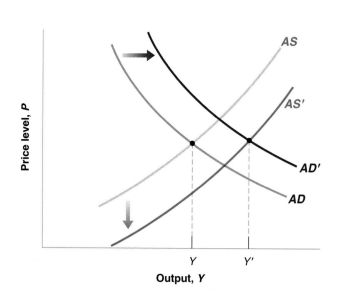

FIGURE 13-2

The Effects of an Increase in Productivity on Output in the Short Run

An increase in productivity shifts the aggregate supply curve down. It has an ambiguous effect on the aggregate demand curve, which may shift to the left or to the right. In this figure, we assume a shift to the right.

ACTIVE GRAPH

ing jobs (a process referred to as "downsizing"). When such reorganizations are the source of productivity growth, there is no presumption that aggregate demand will increase: Reorganization of production may require little or no new investment. Increased uncertainty and worries about job security may well lead workers to want to save more, and thus reduce consumption spending. In this case, aggregate demand may shift to the left rather than to the right.

Let's assume the most favorable case (most favorable from the point of view of output and employment), namely the case where aggregate demand shifts to the right. The effects of the increase in productivity are thus to shift the aggregate supply curve from AS to AS', and the aggregate demand curve from AD to AD'. These shifts are drawn in Figure 13–2. Both shifts contribute to an increase in equilibrium output, from Y to Y'. In this case, the increase in productivity unambiguously leads to an increase in output.

Without more information however, we cannot tell what happens to employment. To see why, note that equation (13.2) implies the following relation:

% change in employment = % change in output − % change in productivity

Thus, what happens to employment depends on whether output increases proportionately more or less than productivity. For example, if productivity increases by 2%, it takes an increase in output of at least 2% to avoid a decrease in employment—that is, to avoid an increase in unemployment. And without a lot more information about the slopes and the size of the shifts of the two curves, we just cannot tell whether this condition is satisfied in Figure 13–2. In the short run, increases in productivity may or may not lead to an increase in unemployment. Theory alone cannot settle the issue.

The Empirical Evidence

Can empirical evidence help us reach a conclusion? At first glance, it would seem to. Look at Figure 13–3, which plots the behavior of labor productivity and the behavior of output for the U.S. business sector from 1960 to 1998. The figure shows a strong positive relation between output growth and productivity growth. Furthermore, the movements in output are typically larger than the movements in productivity. This would seem to imply that, when

Start from the production function $Y = AN$. From proposition 7 in Appendix 2, this relation implies that $g_Y = g_A + g_N$. Or equivalently, $g_N = g_Y - g_A$.

This discussion has assumed that monetary policy was given. But it can clearly affect the outcome. Suppose you were in charge of monetary policy in this economy: What level of output would you try to achieve?

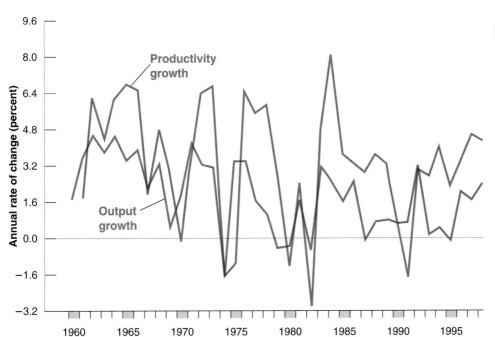

FIGURE 13–3

Labor Productivity and Output Growth: U.S. Business Sector, 1960–1998

There is a strong positive relation between output growth and productivity growth. But the causality runs from output growth to productivity growth, not the other way around.
Source: U.S. Department of Labor, Bureau of Labor Statistics.

productivity growth is high, output increases by enough to avoid any adverse effect on employment. But this conclusion would be wrong. The reason is that the causal relation runs mostly the other way, from output growth to productivity growth. That is, high output growth leads to high productivity growth, not the other way around.

Here is another example ▶ of the difference between correlation and causality. If we see a positive correlation between output growth and productivity growth, should we conclude that high productivity growth leads to high output growth? Or should we conclude that high output growth leads to high productivity growth?

We saw why when we discussed Okun's law in chapter 9: In bad times, firms hoard labor—that is, they keep more workers than is absolutely necessary for production. When the demand for goods increases for any reason, firms respond partly by increasing employment and partly by having currently employed workers work harder. This is why increases in output lead to increases in productivity. And this is what we see in Figure 13–3: High output growth leads to higher productivity growth. This is not the relation we are after. Rather, we want to know what happens to output and unemployment when there is an *exogenous* change in productivity—a change in productivity that comes from a change in technology, not from the response of firms to movements in output. Figure 13–3 does not help us here. And the conclusion from the research that has looked at the effects of exogenous movements in productivity growth on output is that the data give an answer just as ambiguous as the answer given by the theory:

- Sometimes increases in productivity lead to increases in output sufficient to maintain or even increase employment in the short run.
- Sometimes they do not, and unemployment increases in the short run.

13-2 | Productivity and the Natural Rate of Unemployment

We have looked so far at the *short-run* effects of a change in productivity on output, employment, and unemployment. In the medium run, we know that the economy returns to the natural level of output, the level of output consistent with the natural rate of unemployment. Now we must ask: Is the natural rate of unemployment itself affected by changes in productivity?

Recall from chapter 6 that the natural rate of unemployment is determined by two relations, price setting and wage setting. Our first step must be to think about how changes in productivity affect each of these two relations.

Price Setting and Wage Setting Revisited

Consider price setting first. Recall from equation (13.1) that each worker produces A units of output; equivalently, producing 1 unit of output requires $1/A$ workers. If the nominal wage is equal to W, the cost of producing 1 unit of output equals $(1/A)W = W/A$. Assuming that firms set prices as a markup over cost, μ, the price level is given by

$$\text{Price setting: } P = (1 + \mu)\frac{W}{A} \qquad (13.3)$$

The only difference between this equation and equation (6.3) is the presence of the productivity term, A (which we had implicitly set to 1 in chapter 6). An increase in productivity decreases cost, which decreases the price level given the nominal wage.

Turn now to wage setting. The evidence suggests that other things being equal, wages are typically set to reflect the increase in productivity over time. If productivity has been growing at 3% a year on average for some time, then wage contracts will build in a wage increase of 3% a year. This suggests the following extension of our earlier wage-setting equation:

$$\text{Wage setting: } W = A^e P^e F(u,z) \qquad (13.4)$$

Look at the three terms on the right of equation (13.4).

P^e and $F(u,z)$ are familiar from equation (6.1). Workers care about real wages, not nominal wages. So wages depend on the (expected) price level, P^e. Wages depend on the unemployment rate, u, and on institutional factors captured by the variable z.

The new term is A^e: Wages now also depend on the expected level of productivity, A^e. If workers and firms expect productivity to increase, they incorporate those expectations into the wages set in bargaining.[2]

The Natural Rate of Unemployment

Let's now characterize the natural rate graphically. Recall that the natural rate of unemployment is determined by the price-setting and wage-setting relations, and the additional condition that expectations be correct. In this case, this condition requires that expectations of *both* prices and productivity be correct.

The price-setting equation determines the real wage paid by firms. Reorganizing equation (13.3), we can write

$$\frac{W}{P} = \frac{A}{1 + \mu} \qquad (13.5)$$

The real wage paid by firms, W/P, depends on both the level of productivity and the markup. The higher the level of productivity, the lower the price set by firms given the nominal wage, and therefore the higher the real wage paid by firms. The real wage is measured on the vertical axis in Figure 13–4. The unemployment rate is measured on the horizontal axis. Equation (13.5) is represented by the gray horizontal line at $A/(1 + \mu)$: The real wage implied by price setting is independent of the unemployment rate.

Turn to the wage-setting equation. Under the condition that expectations are correct—so both $P^e = P$ and $A^e = A$—the wage-setting equation (13.4) becomes

$$\frac{W}{P} = A\,F(u,z) \qquad (13.6)$$

The real wage implied by wage bargaining depends on both the level of productivity and the unemployment rate. The higher the level of productivity, the higher the real wage. The higher the unemployment rate, the lower the real wage. For a given level of productivity,

Go back to equation (13.3): $P = (1 + \mu)W/A$.

Given W

$$A\uparrow \Rightarrow P\downarrow$$

This implies $(W/P)\uparrow$

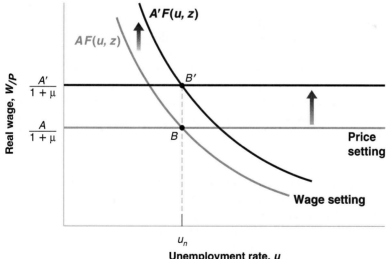

FIGURE 13–4

The Effects of an Increase in Productivity on the Natural Rate of Unemployment

An increase in productivity shifts both the wage and the price-setting curves in the same proportion and thus has no effect on the natural rate of unemployment.

---

[2]**DIGGING DEEPER**. We can think of workers and firms setting the wage to divide (expected) output between workers and firms according to their relative bargaining power. If both sides expect higher productivity and thus higher output, this will be reflected in the bargained wage. How productivity affects wage setting is one of the main questions examined in the book by Edmund Phelps, *Structural Slumps* (Cambridge, MA: Harvard University Press, 1994).

equation (13.6) is represented by the red downward-sloping curve in Figure 13−4: The real wage implied by wage setting is a decreasing function of the unemployment rate.

Equilibrium in the labor market is given by point B, and the natural rate of unemployment is u_n. Let's now ask what happens to the natural rate in response to an increase in productivity. Suppose that A increases by 5%, so the new level of productivity A' equals 1.05 times A.

From equation (13.5) we see that the real wage implied by price setting is now higher by 5%. The price-setting curve shifts up. From equation (13.6), we see that at a given unemployment rate, the real wage implied by wage setting is also higher by 5%. The wage-setting curve shifts up.

Note that, at the initial unemployment rate u_n, both curves shift up by the same amount, namely 5% of the initial real wage. That is why the new equilibrium is at B', directly above B: The real wage is higher by 5%, and the natural rate remains the same.

The intuition for this result is straightforward. A 5% increase in productivity leads firms to reduce prices by 5% given wages, leading to a 5% increase in real wages. This increase exactly matches the increase in real wages from wage bargaining at the initial unemployment rate. Real wages increase by 5%, and the natural unemployment rate remains the same.

We have looked at a one-time increase in productivity, but the argument we have developed also applies to productivity growth. Suppose that productivity steadily increases, so that each year A increases by 5%. Then, each year, real wages will increase by 5%, and the natural rate will remain unchanged.

The Empirical Evidence

We have derived two strong results: The natural rate of unemployment should depend neither on the level of productivity nor on the rate of productivity growth. How do these two results fit the facts?

An obvious difficulty in answering this question is that we do not observe the natural rate of unemployment. But we can work around this problem by looking at the relation between average productivity growth and the average unemployment rate across decades. Because the actual unemployment rate moves around the natural rate, looking at the average unemployment rate over a decade should give us a good estimate of the natural rate for that decade. Looking at average productivity growth over a decade also takes care of another problem we discussed earlier: Whereas changes in labor hoarding can have a large effect on yearly changes in labor productivity, these changes in labor hoarding are unlikely to make much difference when we look at average productivity growth over a decade.

Figure 13−5 plots average U.S. labor productivity growth and the average unemployment rate during each decade since 1890. At first glance, there seems to be little relation between the two variables. One may argue, however, that the decade of the Great Depression is so different that it should be left aside. If we do so, then a relation—although, admittedly, not a very strong one—emerges between productivity growth and the unemployment rate. Surprisingly, it is the opposite of the relation predicted by those who believe in technological unemployment. Periods of *high productivity growth*, such as the 1940s to the 1960s, were associated with *a lower unemployment rate*. Periods of *low productivity growth*, such as the United States saw in the 1970s and 1980s, have been associated with *a higher unemployment rate*.

The inverse relation between productivity growth and unemployment is even stronger when we look at Europe, where the large slowdown in productivity growth since the mid-1970s has been associated with a large increase in unemployment. (See chapter 22 for further discussion.)

Can the theory we have developed be extended to explain this inverse relation between productivity growth and unemployment? The answer is yes. To do so, we must look more closely at the formation of expectations of productivity in wage setting.

We have looked at the rate of unemployment that prevails when *both* price expectations *and* expectations of productivity are correct. However, one of the lessons of the 1970s and 1980s is that it takes a very long time for expectations of productivity to adjust to the reality of lower productivity growth. When productivity growth slows down for any reason, it takes a long time for society in general, and workers in particular, to adjust their expectations. In the meantime, workers keep asking for wage increases that are no longer consistent with the new lower rate of productivity growth.

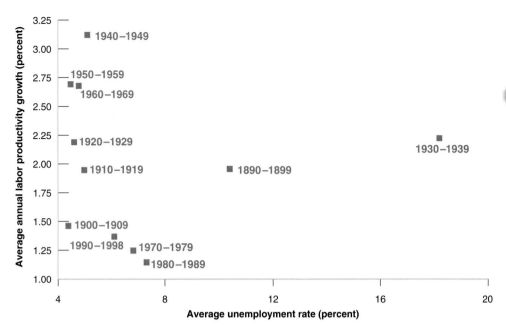

FIGURE 13-5

Productivity Growth and Unemployment: Averages by Decade, 1890–1998

There is little relation between the 10-year averages of productivity growth and the 10-year averages of the unemployment rate. If anything, higher productivity growth is associated with lower unemployment.
Source: U.S. Bureau of the Census, *Historical Statistics of the United States*.

To see what this implies, let's look at what happens to the unemployment rate when price expectations are correct (that is, $P^e = P$), but expectations of productivity (A^e) are not. In this case, the relations implied by price setting and wage setting become

$$\text{Price setting: } \frac{W}{P} = \frac{A}{1 + \mu}$$

$$\text{Wage setting: } \frac{W}{P} = A^e \, F(u,z)$$

If expectations of productivity growth adjust slowly, then A^e will keep increasing by more than A when productivity growth declines. What will happen to unemployment is shown in Figure 13–6. If A^e increases by more than A, the wage-setting relation will shift up by more than the price-setting relation. The equilibrium will move from B to B', and the natural rate of unemployment will increase from u_n to u'_n. The natural rate will remain higher until expectations of productivity have adjusted to the new reality, until A^e and A are again equal.

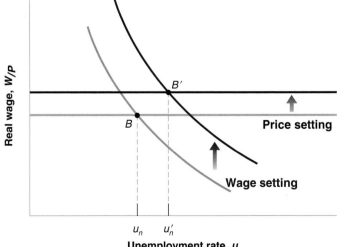

FIGURE 13-6

The Effects of a Decrease in Productivity Growth on the Unemployment Rate When Expectations of Productivity Growth Adjust Slowly

If it takes time for workers to adjust their expectations of productivity growth, a slow-down in productivity growth will lead to an increase in the natural rate of unemployment for some time.

Let's summarize what we have learned in this and the preceding section. Put simply, we have not found much support, either in theory or in the data, for the idea that faster technological progress leads to higher unemployment. In the short run, there is no reason to expect, nor does there appear to be, a systematic relation between movements in productivity and movements in unemployment. If there is a relation between the two in the medium run, it appears to be an inverse relation: Lower productivity growth appears to lead to higher unemployment, and higher productivity growth appears to lead to lower unemployment. One plausible explanation is that high unemployment is what it takes to reconcile workers' wage aspirations with lower productivity growth until those aspirations have adjusted to this new reality.

So, where do the fears of technological unemployment come from? They are likely to come from the dimension of technological progress we have neglected so far, structural change. And for some workers, those with skills no longer in demand, structural change may indeed mean unemployment and lower wages.

13-3 | Technological Progress and Distribution Effects

Technological progress is a process of structural change. New goods are developed, making old ones obsolete. New techniques of production appear, requiring new skills and making some old skills less useful. The essence of this **churning** process is nicely reflected in the following quote from the president of the Federal Reserve Bank of Dallas in his introduction to a report entitled *The Churn*:

> *My grandfather was a blacksmith, as was his father. My dad, however, was part of the evolutionary process of the churn. After quitting school in the seventh grade to work for the sawmill, he got the entrepreneurial itch. He rented a shed and opened a filling station to service the cars that had put his dad out of business. My dad was successful, so he bought some land on the top of a hill, and built a truck stop. Our truck stop was extremely successful until a new interstate went through 20 miles to the west. The churn replaced US 411 with Interstate 75, and my visions of the good life faded.*

Many professions, from blacksmiths to harness makers, have indeed vanished forever. There were more than 11 million farm workers in the United States at the beginning of the twentieth century; because of very high productivity growth in agriculture, there are fewer than 1 million today. But there are now more than 3 million truck, bus, and taxi drivers in the United States; there were none in 1900. There are more than 1 million computer programmers; there were practically none in 1960. The Focus box "Fastest-Growing and Fastest-Declining U.S. Occupations, 1990–2005" lists the occupations that are expected to grow fastest and those that are expected to decline the fastest in the United States between 1990 and 2005.

The Increase in Wage Inequality

For those in growing sectors or those with the right skills, technological progress leads to new opportunities and higher wages. But for those in declining sectors, or those with skills that are no longer in demand, technological progress can mean the loss of a job, a period of unemployment, and possibly much lower wages. The last 20 years in the United States have seen a large increase in wage inequality. Most economists believe that one of the main culprits is technological progress.

Table 13–1 shows the evolution of real wages for various groups of workers, by education level and sex. The table is based on data from the CPS from 1963 to 1995.

The Churn: The Paradox of Progress (Dallas, TX: Federal Reserve Bank of Dallas, 1993).

We described the CPS survey in chapter 6.

FOCUS

The U.S. Department of Labor regularly makes projections of the future number of workers in different occupations. Table 1 gives the 10 occupations that are forecast to have the highest growth rate from 1990 to 2005.* Table 2 gives the 10 occupations that are forecast to have the highest rate of decline during the same period.

Technological progress is surely the main force behind the rise of systems analysts and computer analysts, the decline in the number of farmers, and the demise of switch-board operators. But both tables clearly show that there are other forces at work:

- Trade is important. The decline in the number of textile operators and electrical and electronic assemblers reflects the fact that these activities are moving to low-wage countries.

- Increases in income and the aging of the U.S. population, both of which change the structure of demand, are also important. Note that six of the fastest-growing occupations are related to health care, and one (travel agents) is related, at least in part, to leisure.

- The presence of "correction officers" in the list of the 10 fastest-growing occupations is a reflection on the larger problems confronting the United States.

*A warning: These are the occupations expected to have the highest growth rate, not the largest absolute increase in employment. The largest absolute increases are forecast to be for salespersons, registered nurses, and cashiers.

TABLE 1 Fastest-growing occupations

	1990 (thousands)	2005 (thousands)	Change (%)
Home health aides	287	550	+92%
Systems analysts and computer scientists	463	829	+79%
Personal and home care aides	103	183	+77%
Medical assistants	165	287	+74%
Human services workers	145	249	+71%
Radiologic technologists and technicians	149	252	+70%
Medical secretaries	232	390	+68%
Psychologists	125	204	+64%
Travel agents	132	214	+62%
Correction officers	230	342	+61%

Source: Statistical Abstract of the United States, 1993, table 645.

TABLE 2 Fastest-declining occupations

	1990 (thousands)	2005 (thousands)	Change (%)
Electrical/electronic precision assemblers	171	90	−48%
Electrical/electronic assemblers	232	128	−45%
Child-care workers, private household	314	190	−40%
Textile draw-out and winding machine operators	199	138	−31%
Telephone/cable/TV line installers and repairers	133	92	−30%
Machine tool cutting operators and tenders	145	104	−29%
Cleaners and servants, private households	411	310	−25%
Switchboard operators	246	189	−25%
Farmers	1074	822	−21%
Sewing machine operators, garment	585	368	−20%

Source: Statistical Abstract of the United States, 1993, table 645.

TABLE	**13-1**	Real Wage Changes for Full-Time Workers, 1963–1995 (percent)	

	1963–1979	1979–1995
All workers	17.7	−11.2
By education (years of schooling)		
0–11 (less than high school)	17.2	−20.2
12 (high school)	18.8	−13.4
13–15 (less than 4 years of college)	17.7	−12.4
16+ (4 years of college or more)	18.9	3.5
18+ (graduate degree)	25.8	14.0
By sex		
Men	18.3	−17.4
Women	16.8	−1.5

Source: Lawrence Katz and David Autor, "Changes in the Wage Structure and Earnings Inequality," in Orley Ashenfelter and David Card, eds., *Handbook of Labor Economics* (1999, forthcoming).

The table's first striking fact is that, since 1979, the annual growth rate of the average real wage (for all workers) has been *negative*. How can this be? Based on what we saw in section 13-2, we would expect real wages to increase roughly at the same rate as labor productivity; and, since 1979, labor productivity has grown at about 1% a year. So why have real wages declined? There are two main reasons:

For more on this topic, read Barry Bosworth and George Perry, "Productivity and Real Wages: Is There a Puzzle?" *Brookings Papers on Economic Activity*, 1994:1, 317–343.

- The first is that the wage measure used in Table 13–1 does not include various benefits received by workers, from health care to pensions. And benefits have increased faster than wages. Hence, the growth of total compensation—wages and benefits—has been higher than that of wages.
- The second is subtle but important. Based on section 13-2, we would expect the real wage, defined as the wage *in terms of output*, to go up with productivity. But the real wage in Table 13–1, and the real wage relevant to workers, is the wage *in terms of consumption*—that is, the nominal wage divided by the CPI. What has happened over the last two decades is that the CPI (the price of consumption goods) has increased a bit faster on average—about 0.6% faster per year—than the GDP deflator (the price of output). The real wage in terms of consumption has done worse than the real wage in terms of output, and thus worse than productivity.

This explanation raises the question of why the CPI (the price index for consumption) has increased faster than the GDP deflator (the price index for aggregate output). One factor has been a steady decline in the relative price of investment goods (machines) relative to consumption goods: The price of investment goods is a component of the GDP deflator, not of the CPI. Another factor has been an increase in the relative price of foreign goods: The price of imported foreign consumption goods is a component of the CPI, not of the GDP deflator.

The poor performance of the average real wage goes a long way toward explaining why, despite the long expansion of the 1990s, some workers still feel that the U.S. economy is not doing well. But now look at the rest of the table, which gives the evolution of real wages for workers by level of education and sex.

- The lower the level of education, the larger has been the wage decline. Since 1979, the real wage of workers who have not completed high school has gone down by 20.2%. In contrast, the real wage of workers who have four years of college or more has gone up by 3.5%; the real wage of workers with a graduate degree has gone up by 14%.
- The wage decline has been much larger for men than for women. Since 1979, the real wages of women—which were lower to start with than those of men—have increased by more than 16% relative to men.
- As a result of these changes in the wage distribution, some groups of workers have experienced large decreases in real wages. For example, the real wages of men with only a high school diploma and with less than five years' experience have decreased by about 40% since 1979.

The Causes of Increased Wage Inequality

What are the causes of this increase in wage inequality?

There is general agreement that the main factor behind the increase in the relative wage of skilled versus unskilled workers is a steady increase in the relative demand for skilled workers. This trend in relative demand is not new; it was already present to some extent in the 1960s and 1970s. But it was offset then by a steady increase in the relative supply of skilled workers: A larger and larger proportion of the population finished high school, went to college, finished college, and so on. Since the early 1980s, relative supply has continued to increase, but not fast enough to match the continuing increase in relative demand. The result has been a steady increase in the relative wage of skilled workers versus unskilled workers.

There is less agreement, however, on the factors behind this steady shift in relative demand. Most economists believe that two main forces are at work:

- One is international trade. Those U.S. firms that employ higher proportions of unskilled workers, the argument goes, are increasingly driven out of markets by imports from similar firms in low-wage countries. Alternatively, to remain competitive, firms must relocate some of their production to low-wage countries. In both cases, the result is a steady decrease in the relative demand for unskilled workers in the United States. There are clear similarities between the effects of trade and the effects of technological progress: Although both are good for the economy as a whole, they both lead to structural change, and leave some workers worse off.

  There is no question that trade is partly responsible for increased wage inequality. The presence of two occupations in the textile industry in the list of the 10 fastest-declining occupations in the United States (see the Focus box earlier) is testimony to this fact: The U.S. textile industry has largely moved to low-wage countries. But a closer examination shows that trade accounts for only part of the shift in relative demand. The most telling fact against explanations based solely on trade is that the shift in relative demand toward skilled workers appears to be present even in those sectors that are not exposed to foreign competition.

- The other is **skill-biased technological progress**. New machines and new methods of production, the argument goes, require skilled workers, more so today than in the past. The development of computers requires workers to be increasingly computer literate. The new methods of production require workers to be more flexible, better able to adapt to new tasks. Greater flexibility in turn requires more skills and more education. Unlike explanations based on trade, skill-biased technological progress can explain why the shift in relative demand appears to be present in all sectors of the economy. At this point, most economists believe that it has indeed been the dominant factor in explaining the increase in wage dispersion.

Does all this mean that the United States is condemned to steadily increasing wage inequality? Not necessarily. There are three reasons for at least some optimism:

1. The trend in relative demand may simply slow down. For example, it is likely that computers will become easier and easier to use in the future, even by unskilled workers. Computers may even replace skilled workers, those whose skills involve primarily the ability to compute or to memorize. Paul Krugman, from MIT, has argued—only partly tongue in cheek—that accountants, lawyers, and doctors may be next on the list of professions to be replaced by computers.

2. Technological progress is not exogenous: This is a theme we explored in chapter 12. How much firms spend on R&D and in what directions they direct their research depend on expected profits. The low relative wage of unskilled workers may lead firms to explore new technologies that take advantage of unskilled, low-wage workers. In other words, market forces may lead technological progress to become less skill biased in the future.

> Pursuing the effects of international trade would take us too far. For a more thorough discussion of who gains and who loses from trade, look at the textbook by Paul Krugman and Maurice Obstfeld, *International Economics*, 4th ed. (New York: HarperCollins, 1996).

One reason the relative wages of unskilled workers have increased in the late 1990s has been an increase in the (legislated) minimum wage. More than that must have been at work, however: If the minimum wage had increased but the demand for unskilled workers had continued to decrease, we would have observed an increase in the unemployment rate of unskilled workers. This has not been the case. (See Lawrence Katz and Alan Krueger, *The High Pressure U.S. Labor Market of the 1990s*, Brookings Papers on Economic Activity, 1999:1.)

3. The relative supply of skilled versus unskilled workers is also not exogenous. The large increase in the relative wage of more educated workers implies that the returns to acquiring more education and training are higher than they were one or two decades ago. Higher returns to training and education can increase the relative supply of skilled workers and, as a result, work to stabilize relative wages. Many economists believe that policy has an important role to play here, making sure that the quality of primary and secondary education for the children of low-wage workers does not further deteriorate, and that those who want to acquire more education can borrow to pay for it.

Backing these theoretical considerations, the evidence is that since 1996, U.S. wage inequality has not increased further. The relative wage of unskilled workers has increased, not enough to undo the cumulated decrease since the late 1970s, but enough to suggest that maybe the underlying trends have changed. Only time will tell.

SUMMARY

- Popular discussions often reflect fears that technological progress destroys jobs and leads to higher unemployment. Such fears were present during the Great Depression. They have reemerged in Europe today, where there is widespread support for a shorter workweek to allow more workers to have jobs. Theory and evidence suggest these fears are largely unfounded. There is not much support, either in theory or in the data, for the idea that faster technological progress leads to higher unemployment.

- In the short run, there is no reason to expect, nor does there appear to be, a systematic relation between changes in productivity and movements in unemployment.

- If there is a relation between changes in productivity and movements in unemployment in the medium run, it appears to be an inverse relation: Lower productivity growth appears to lead to higher unemployment; higher productivity growth appears to lead to lower un-

employment. One plausible explanation is that it takes high unemployment to reconcile workers' wage aspirations with lower productivity growth.

- Technological progress is not a smooth process in which all workers are winners. Rather, it is a process of churning, of structural change. Even if most people benefit from the increase in the average standard of living, there are losers as well. As new goods and new techniques of production are developed, old goods and old techniques of production become obsolete. Some workers find their skills in higher demand; they benefit from technological progress. Some find their skills in lower demand; they suffer reductions in relative wages and/or employment.

- Wage inequality has increased in the past 20 years in the United States. The real wage of unskilled workers has declined not only relative to that of skilled workers, but also in absolute terms. The two main causes are international trade and skill-biased technological progress.

KEY TERMS

- technological unemployment, 249
- creative destruction, 250
- churning, 258
- skill-biased technological progress, 261

An asterisk denotes a harder problem.

1. TRUE/FALSE/UNCERTAIN

a. The change in employment and output per capita in the United States since 1900 lends support to the argument that technological progress is consistent with a steady increase in employment.

b. Workers and consumers benefit equally from the process of creative destruction.

c. In the last two decades, the real wages of unskilled U.S. workers have declined in both a relative and an absolute sense.

d. Technological progress leads to a decrease in employment if and only if the increase in output is smaller than the increase in productivity.

e. Studies of exogenous increases in productivity have found that they sometimes lead to unemployment in the short run.

f. Higher productivity growth can lead to a decrease in the natural rate of unemployment for some time.

g. In the medium run, higher productivity growth appears to lead to lower unemployment.

h. In the United States in the past two decades, the largest decrease in real wages has been experienced by workers with the lowest level of education.

i. Economists have no explanation for the recent increase in U.S. wage inequality.

2. PRODUCTIVITY AND THE NATURAL RATE OF UNEMPLOYMENT

Suppose an economy is characterized by the following equations:

$$\text{price setting: } P = (1 + \mu)\frac{W}{A}$$
$$\text{wage setting: } W = A^e P^e(1 - u)$$

a. Solve for the unemployment rate if $P^e = P$, but A^e is not necessarily equal to A. Explain the effects of (A^e/A) on the unemployment rate.

Now suppose that expectations of both prices and productivity are accurate.

b. Solve for the natural rate of unemployment if the markup is equal to 5%.

c. Does the natural rate of unemployment depend on productivity? Provide some intuition for your answer.

*3. THE AGGREGATE SUPPLY CURVE WITH CHANGES IN PRODUCTIVITY

Consider an economy where production is given by

$$Y = AN$$

Assume that price setting and wage setting are given by:

$$\text{Price setting: } P = (1 + \mu)\frac{W}{A}$$
$$\text{Wage setting: } W = A^e P^e(1 - u)$$

Recall that the relation between employment (N), the labor force (L), and the unemployment rate (u) is given by

$$N = (1 - u)L$$

a. Derive the aggregate supply curve (that is, the relation between the price level and the level of output given the markup, the actual and the expected level of productivity, the labor force, and the expected price level. Explain the role of each variable.)

b. Show the effect of an increase in both actual productivity, A, and expected productivity, A^e (so $[A^e/A]$ remains equal to one) on the position of the aggregate supply curve. Explain.

c. Suppose instead that actual productivity, A, increases but expected productivity, A^e, does not change. Compare to the conclusions in (b). Explain the difference.

4. LABOR PRODUCTIVITY

"Higher labor productivity allows firms to produce more goods with the same number of workers, and thus sell the goods at the same or even lower prices. That's why increases in labor productivity can permanently decrease the rate of unemployment without causing inflation." Discuss.

5. THE WAGE GAP BETWEEN SKILLED AND UNSKILLED WORKERS

How might each of the following changes affect the wage gap between skilled and unskilled workers in the United States?

a. Increased spending on computers in public schools.

b. Limits on the numbers of foreign temporary farm workers allowed to enter the United States.

c. Increasing the number of public colleges.

d. Tax credits in Central America for U.S. firms.

6. TRENDS IN THE LABOR MARKET

Examine Table 2 in the Focus box on page 259. What factors might be responsible for the projected decline in:

a. sewing machine operators?

b. child care workers in private households?

c. switchboard operators?

7. AGRICULTURE AND TECHNOLOGICAL UNEMPLOYMENT

"Those who argue that technological progress does not decrease employment should look at agriculture. At the start of the twentieth century, farm population was 29 million—44% of the total population. In 1990, it was down to 4 million—2% of the total population. If all sectors start having the productivity growth that has taken place in agriculture, nobody will be employed a century from now." Discuss.

FURTHER READINGS

For more on the process of reallocation that characterizes modern economies, read *The Churn: The Paradox of Progress*, a report by the Federal Reserve Bank of Dallas, 1993.

For more on increasing wage inequality in the United States, read David Brauer and Susan Hickok, "Explaining the Growing Gap between Low Skilled and High Skilled Wages," *Symposium on U.S. Wage Trends*, Federal Reserve Bank of New York, 1994.

We invite you to visit the Blanchard page on the Prentice Hall Web site at:

http://www.prenhall.com/blanchard

for this chapter's World Wide Web exercises

EXTENSIONS

Expectations

The next four chapters represent the first major extension of the core. They look at the role of expectations in fluctuations.

CHAPTER 14

Chapter 14 introduces two important tools. The first is the distinction between the real interest rate and the nominal interest rate. The second is the concept of expected present discounted value. The chapter ends by deriving and discussing the "Fisher hypothesis," the proposition that, in the medium run, nominal interest rates fully reflect inflation and money growth.

CHAPTER 15

Chapter 15 focuses on the role of expectations in financial markets. It first looks at the determination of bond prices and bond yields. It shows how we can learn about the course of expected future interest rates by looking at the yield curve. It then turns to stock prices, and shows how they depend on expected future dividends and interest rates. Finally, it discusses whether stock prices always reflect fundamentals, or may instead contain bubbles or fads.

CHAPTER 16

Chapter 16 focuses on the role of expectations in consumption and investment decisions. It argues that consumption depends partly on current income, and partly on wealth defined as the sum of financial, housing, and human wealth—the expected present value of labor income. It argues that investment depends partly on current cash flow, and partly on the expected present value of future profits.

CHAPTER 17

Chapter 17 puts the pieces together and looks at the role of expectations in fluctuations. It modifies our previous description of goods market equilibrium (the *IS* relation) to reflect the effect of expectations on spending. It then revisits the effects of monetary and fiscal policy on output. It shows in particular, that, in contrast to the results derived in the core, a fiscal contraction may increase output, even in the short run.

CHAPTER 14

Expectations: The Basic Tools

The consumer considering whether to buy a new car must ask: Can I safely take a new car loan? How much of a wage raise can I expect over the next few years? How safe is my job?

The manager who observes an increase in current sales must ask: Is this a temporary boom that I should meet with the existing production capacity? Or does this upswing reflect a permanent increase in sales, in which case I should order new machines? How much additional profit can I expect if I buy a new machine?

The pension fund manager who observes a boom in the stock market must ask: Are stock prices going to increase further, or is the boom likely to fizzle? Does this increase in prices reflect expectations of higher profits by firms in the future? Do I share those expectations? Should I reallocate some of my funds between stocks and bonds?

These examples make clear that many economic decisions depend not only on what is happening today but also on expectations of what will happen in the future. Indeed, some decisions should depend very little on what is happening today. For example, why should an increase in sales today, if that increase is not accompanied by expectations of higher sales in the future, lead a firm to alter its investment plans? The new machines may not be in operation before sales have returned to normal. By then, they might sit idle, gathering dust.

Until now, we have not paid much attention to the role of expectations in goods and financial markets. We have ignored them in our construction of both the *IS-LM* model, and the aggregate demand component of the *AS–AD* model that builds on the *IS-LM*. When looking at the goods market, we assumed that consumption depended on current income and that investment depended on current sales. When looking at financial markets, we lumped assets together and called them "bonds"; we then focused on the choice between bonds and money, and ignored the choice between bonds and stocks, short-term bonds and long-term bonds, and so on. We introduced these simplifications to build the intuition for the basic mechanisms at work. It is now time to think about the role and the determination of expectations in fluctuations. This is our task in this and the next three chapters.

In this chapter, I lay the groundwork by introducing two key concepts: The first is the distinction between the *nominal* and the *real* interest rate. The second is the concept of *expected present discounted value*. I then show, in the last two sections of the chapter, how the distinction between real and nominal interest rates sheds light on the relation between interest rates and inflation in the short and the medium run. The next three chapters build on this groundwork. Chapter 15 looks at the role of expectations in financial markets. It looks in particular at the determination of the term structure of interest rates, and the determination of stock prices. Chapter 16 looks at the role of expectations in consumption and investment decisions. Chapter 17 puts the pieces together: It extends the analysis of the *IS-LM* model we developed in the core to allow for the presence of expectations. It then takes another look at the role and the limits of policy in an economy in which expectations play a major role in affecting decisions.

14-1 | Nominal versus Real Interest Rates

In January 1981, the *one-year T-bill rate*—the interest rate on one-year government bonds—was 12.6%. In January 1999, the one-year T-bill rate was only 4.5%. Although most of us cannot borrow at the same interest rate as the government, the interest rates we face as consumers were also substantially lower in 1999 than in 1981. Borrowing was clearly much cheaper in 1999 than it was in 1981.

Or was it? In 1981, inflation was around 12%. In 1999, inflation was around 2%. This information would seem very relevant: The interest rate tells us how many dollars we shall have to pay in the future in exchange for having one more dollar today. But we do not consume dollars; we consume goods. When we borrow, what we really want to know is how many goods we shall have to give up in the future in exchange for the goods we get today. Likewise, when we lend, we want to know how many goods—not how many dollars—we shall get in the future for the goods we give up today. The presence of inflation makes the distinction important. What is the point of receiving high interest payments in the future if inflation between now and then is so high that we are able to buy only a few goods with the proceeds?

To examine this further, let's introduce two definitions. Let us refer to interest rates in terms of dollars (or, more generally, in units of the national currency) as **nominal interest rates**. The interest rates printed in the financial pages of newspapers are nominal interest rates. For example, when we say that the one-year T-bill rate is 4.5%, we mean that for every dollar the government borrows by issuing one-year T-bills, it promises to pay 1.045 dollars a year from now. More generally, if the nominal interest rate for year t is i_t, borrowing 1 dollar this year requires you to pay $1 + i_t$ dollars next year. This relation is represented in Figure 14–1(a): 1 dollar this year corresponds to $1 + i_t$ dollars next year.

Let us refer to interest rates expressed *in terms of a basket of goods* as **real interest rates**. Thus, if we denote the real interest rate for year t by r_t, then, by definition, borrowing the equivalent of one basket of goods this year requires you to pay the equivalent of $1 + r_t$ baskets of goods next year. This relation is represented in Figure 14–1(b): 1 basket of goods this year corresponds to $1 + r_t$ baskets of goods next year.

Nominal interest rate: the interest rate in terms of dollars.

I shall use interchangeably "this year" for "today" and "next year" for "one year from today."

Real interest rate: the interest rate in terms of a basket of goods.

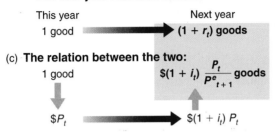

(a) Definition:
The one-year nominal interest rate

This year | Next year
$1 $\longrightarrow$ $\$(1 + i_t)$

(b) Definition:
The one-year real interest rate

This year | Next year
1 good $\longrightarrow$ **$(1 + r_t)$ goods**

(c) **The relation between the two:**

1 good $\quad$ $\$(1 + i_t)\dfrac{P_t}{P^e_{t+1}}$ **goods**

$\$P_t \longrightarrow \$(1 + i_t)\,P_t$

FIGURE 14–1

Nominal and Real
Interest Rates

Computing the Real Interest Rate

Let's look at the relation between the nominal and the real interest rates. Suppose the nominal interest rate is i_t. What is the real interest rate r_t, and how can we construct it? To start, assume there is only one good in the economy, say, bread (we shall add jam and other goods later). If you borrow enough to eat one more pound of bread this year, how much will you have to repay, in terms of pounds of bread, next year?

Figure 14–1(c) helps us derive the answer.

- If the price of a pound of bread this year is P_t dollars, to eat one more pound of bread, you must borrow P_t dollars. This is represented by the arrow pointing down in Figure 14–1(c).
- Let i_t be the one-year nominal interest rate, the interest rate in terms of dollars. If you borrow P_t dollars, you will have to repay $(1 + i_t)P_t$ dollars next year. This is represented by the arrow from left to right at the bottom of Figure 14–1(c).
- What you care about is not dollars, but pounds of bread. Thus, the last step involves converting dollars to pounds of bread next year. Let P^e_{t+1} be the price of bread you expect for next year (The superscript "e" indicates this is an expectation: You do not know yet what the price of bread will be next year.) How much you expect to repay next year, in terms of pounds of bread, is therefore equal to $(1 + i_t)P_t/P^e_{t+1}$. This is represented by the arrow pointing up in Figure 14–1(c).

Putting together parts (b) and (c) of Figure 14–1, it follows that one plus the one-year real interest rate, r_t, is defined by

$$1 + r_t \equiv (1 + i_t)\frac{P_t}{P^e_{t+1}} \tag{14.1}$$

This looks intimidating. Two simple manipulations make it look friendlier:

Denote expected inflation by π^e_t. Given there is only one good—bread—the expected rate of inflation equals the expected change in the dollar price of bread between this year and next year, divided by the dollar price of bread this year

$$\pi^e_t \equiv \frac{(P^e_{t+1} - P_t)}{P_t} \tag{14.2}$$

Using equation (14.2), rewrite P_t/P^e_{t+1} in equation (14.1) as $1/(1 + \pi^e_t)$. Replace in (14.1) to get

$$(1 + r_t) = \frac{1 + i_t}{1 + \pi^e_t} \tag{14.3}$$

Add 1 to both sides in equation (14.2)

$$1 + \pi^e_t = 1 + \frac{(P^e_{t+1} - P_t)}{P_t}$$

Reorganize

$$1 + \pi^e_t = \frac{P^e_{t+1}}{P_t}$$

Take the inverse on both sides:

$$\frac{1}{1 + \pi^e_t} = \frac{P_t}{P^e_{t+1}}$$

Replace in (14.1):

$$1 + r_t \equiv \frac{1 + i_t}{1 + \pi^e_t}$$

One plus the real interest rate equals the ratio of one plus the nominal interest rate, divided by one plus the expected rate of inflation.

Equation (14.3) gives us the *exact* definition of the real interest rate. However, when the nominal rate and expected inflation are not too large—say, less than 20% per year—a close approximation to this equation is given by the simpler relation

$$r_t \approx i_t - \pi_t^e \tag{14.4}$$

This approximation is derived in proposition 6, appendix 2. To see how close the approximation is, suppose the nominal interest rate is 10% and expected inflation is 5%. Using the exact formula (14.3) gives $r_t = 4.8\%$. The approximation given by equation (14.4) is 5%, which is close enough. The approximation is not nearly as good when nominal interest rates and expected inflation are very high, say, equal to 100% and 80% respectively—the exact formula gives a real interest rate of 11%, whereas the approximation yields 20%.

Equation (14.4) is simple, and you should remember it. It says that *the real interest rate is (approximately) equal to the nominal interest rate minus expected inflation*. It has several implications:

- When expected inflation equals zero, the nominal and the real interest rates are equal.
- Because expected inflation is typically positive, the real interest rate is typically lower than the nominal interest rate.
- For a given nominal interest rate, the higher the expected rate of inflation, the lower the real interest rate.

The case where expected inflation happens to be equal to the nominal rate is worth looking at more closely. Suppose the nominal interest rate and expected inflation both equal 10%, and you are the borrower. For every dollar you borrow, you will have to repay 1.10 dollars next year, but dollars will be worth 10% less in terms of goods next year. Thus, if you borrow the equivalent of one good, you will have to repay the equivalent of one good next year: The real cost of borrowing—the real interest rate—is equal to zero. Now suppose you are the lender: For every dollar you lend, you will receive 1.10 dollars next year. This looks attractive, but dollars next year will be worth 10% less in terms of goods. If you lend the equivalent of one good, you will get the equivalent of one good next year: Despite a 10% nominal interest rate, the real interest rate is equal to zero.

We have assumed so far that there was only one good, bread. But what we have done generalizes easily. All we need to do is to substitute the *price level*—the price of a basket of goods—for the price of bread. If we use the consumer price index (the CPI) to measure the price level, the real interest rate tells us how much consumption we must give up next year in order to consume more today.

Nominal and Real Interest Rates in the United States Since 1978

The real interest rate $(i - \pi^e)$ is based on expected inflation, not actual inflation. If actual inflation turns out to be different from expected inflation, the realized real interest rate $(i - \pi)$ will turn out to be different from the real interest rate.

To reflect this distinction, the real interest rate is sometimes called the *ex-ante* real interest rate ("*ex-ante*" means "before the fact"; here, before inflation is known), and the realized real interest rate is called the *ex-post* real interest rate ("ex-post" means "after the fact"; here, after inflation is known).

Let us return to the question with which we started this section. We can now restate it as follows: Was the *real interest rate* lower in 1999 than it was in 1981? More generally, what has happened to the real interest rate in the United States since the early 1980s?

The answer is given in Figure 14–2, which plots both nominal and real interest rates since 1978. For each year, the nominal interest rate is the one-year T-bill rate at the beginning of the year. To construct the real interest rate, we need a measure for expected inflation—more precisely, the rate of inflation expected as of the beginning of each year. We use, for each year, the commercial forecast of CPI inflation for that year published at the end of the previous year by Data Resources Incorporated, a firm specializing in economic forecasting. For example, the forecast of inflation used in constructing the real interest rate for 1999 is the forecast of inflation published by DRI in December 1998—2.0%.

Figure 14–2 shows the importance of adjusting for inflation. Whereas the nominal interest was much lower in 1999 than it was in 1981, the real interest rate was actually *higher* in 1999 than it was in 1981: 2.5% in 1999 versus 0.8% in 1981. This follows from the fact that inflation (and with it expected inflation) has steadily declined since the early 1980s.

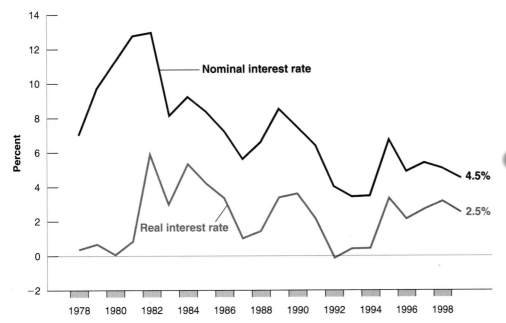

FIGURE 14-2

Nominal and Real One-Year T-bill Rates in the United States, 1978–1999.

Although the nominal interest rate has declined considerably since the early 1980s, the real interest rate is actually higher in 1999 than it was then.

14-2 | Expected Present Discounted Values

Let's now turn to the second key concept we introduce in this chapter, that of expected present discounted value.

To see why this concept is helpful, let's return to the example of the manager considering whether to buy a new machine. On the one hand, buying and installing the machine involves a cost today. On the other, the machine allows for higher production, higher sales, and thus higher profits in the future. The question facing the manager is whether the value of these expected profits is higher than the cost of buying and installing the machine. This is where the concept of expected present discounted value comes in handy: The **expected present discounted value** of a sequence of future payments is the value today of this expected sequence of payments. Once the manager has computed the expected present discounted value of the sequence of profits, her problem becomes simple. If this value exceeds the initial cost, she should go ahead and buy the machine. If it does not, she should not.

As in the case of the real interest rate in section 14–1, the practical problem is that expected present discounted values are not directly observable. They must be constructed from information on the sequence of expected payments and interest rates. Let's first look at the mechanics of construction.

Computing Expected Present Discounted Values

If the one-year nominal interest rate is i_t, *lending one dollar this year yields $1 + i_t$ dollars next year.* Equivalently, borrowing one dollar this year implies paying back $1 + i_t$ dollars next year. In that sense, one dollar this year is worth $1 + i_t$ dollars next year. This relation is represented graphically in Figure 14–3(a).

Turn the argument around and ask: One dollar *next year* is worth how many dollars this year? The answer, shown in Figure 14–3(b), is $1/(1 + i_t)$ dollars. Think of it this way: If you lend $1/(1 + i_t)$ dollars this year, you will receive $1/(1 + i_t) \times (1 + i_t) = 1$ dollar next year. Equivalently, if you borrow $1/(1 + i_t)$ dollars this year, you will have to repay exactly one dollar next year.

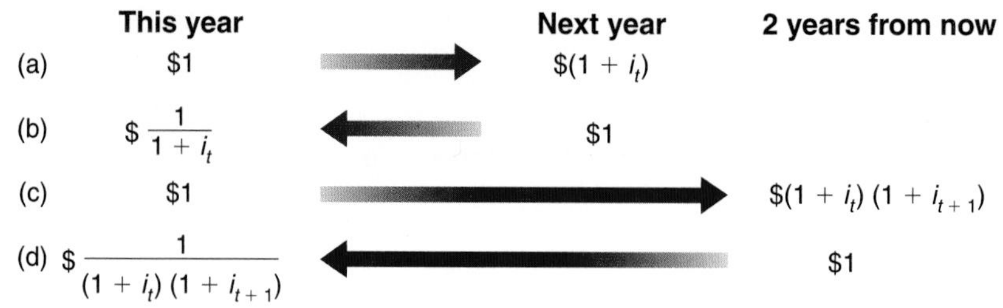

FIGURE 14-3

Computing Present Discounted Values

	This year	Next year	2 years from now
(a)	$1	$(1 + i_t)	
(b)	$\dfrac{1}{1 + i_t}$	$1	
(c)	$1		$(1 + i_t)(1 + i_{t+1})$
(d)	$\dfrac{1}{(1 + i_t)(1 + i_{t+1})}$		$1

Thus, one dollar next year is worth $1/(1 + i_t)$ dollars this year. More formally, we say that $1/(1 + i_t)$ is the *present discounted value* of one dollar next year. The term "present" comes from the fact that we are looking at the value of a payment next year in terms of dollars *today*. The term "discounted" comes from the fact that the value next year is discounted, with $1/(1 + i_t)$ being the **discount factor** (the one-year nominal interest rate, i_t, is sometimes called the **discount rate**). Note that because the nominal interest rate is always positive, the discount factor is always less than 1: A dollar next year is worth less than a dollar this year. The higher the nominal interest rate, the lower the value this year of a dollar next year. If $i = 5\%$, the value this year of a dollar next year is $1/1.05 \approx 95$ cents. If $i = 10\%$, the value this year of a dollar next year is $1/1.10 \approx 91$ cents.

> **Discount rate:** i_t
> **Discount factor:** $1/(1 + i_t)$
>
> If the discount rate goes up, the discount factor goes down.

Now apply the same logic to the value this year of a dollar two years from now. For the moment, assume that current and future one-year nominal interest rates are known with certainty. Let i_t be the nominal interest rate for this year, and i_{t+1} be the one-year nominal interest rate next year.

If you lend one dollar for two years, you will get $(1 + i_t)(1 + i_{t+1})$ dollars two years from now. Put another way, one dollar this year is worth $(1 + i_t)(1 + i_{t+1})$ dollars two years from now. This relation is represented in Figure 14-3(c).

What is one dollar two years from now worth this year? By the same logic as before, the answer is $1/(1 + i_t)(1 + i_{t+1})$ dollars: If you lend $1/[(1 + i_t)(1 + i_{t+1})]$ dollars this year, you will get exactly one dollar in two years. More formally, the *present discounted value of a dollar two years from now* is equal to $1/(1 + i_t)(1 + i_{t+1})$ dollars. This relation is shown in Figure 14-3(d). If, for example, the one-year nominal interest rate is the same this year and next, and equal to 5%, so $i_t = i_{t+1} = 5\%$, then the present value of a dollar in two years is equal to $1/(1.05)^2$ or about 91 cents this year.

A General Formula. Having gone through these steps, it is easy to derive the present discounted value for the general case.

Consider a sequence of payments in dollars, now and in the future. Assume for the moment that these future payments are known with certainty. Denote the current payment by $\$z_t$, the payment next year by $\$z_{t+1}$, the payment two years from now by $\$z_{t+2}$, and so on.

The present discounted value of this sequence of payments—the value in this year's dollars of the sequence of payments, which we shall call $\$V_t$—is given by

$$\$V_t = \$z_t + \frac{1}{(1 + i_t)}\$z_{t+1} + \frac{1}{(1 + i_t)(1 + i_{t+1})}\$z_{t+2} + \cdots$$

Each payment in the future is multiplied by its respective discount factor. The more distant the payment, the smaller the discount factor, and thus the smaller the value of the payment this year. In other words, future payments are discounted more heavily, so their present value is lower.

We have assumed so far that both future payments and future interest rates were known with certainty. Actual decisions, however, have to be based on expectations of future payments rather than on actual values for these payments. In our earlier example, the manager cannot be sure of how much profit the new machine will actually bring; nor can she be sure of what interest rates will be. The best she can do is to get the best forecasts she can, and then compute the *expected present discounted value* of profits, based on these forecasts.

How do we compute the expected present discounted value when future payments or interest rates are uncertain? Basically in the same way as before, but replacing the *known* future payments and *known* interest rates in the expression above by *expected* future payments and *expected* interest rates.[1] Formally, denote expected payments next year by $\$z_{t+1}^e$, expected payments two years from now by $\$z_{t+2}^e$, and so on. Similarly, denote the expected one-year nominal interest rate next year by i_{t+1}^e, and so on (the one-year nominal interest rate this year, i_t, is known today, so it does not need a superscript "*e*"). The expected present discounted value of this expected sequence of payments is given by

$$\$V_t = \$z_t + \frac{1}{(1 + i_t)}\$z_{t+1}^e + \frac{1}{(1 + i_t)(1 + i_{t+1}^e)}\$z_{t+2}^e + \cdots \tag{14.5}$$

"Expected present discounted value" is a heavy expression to carry; I shall often use, for short, just **present value**. Also, it will be convenient to have a shorthand way of writing expressions such as equation (14.5). To denote the present value of an expected sequence for $\$z$, I shall write $V(\$z_t)$, or just $V(\$z)$.

Using Present Values: Examples

Equation (14.5) has two important implications:

- The present value depends positively on current and expected future payments. An increase in either $\$z$ or any future $\$z^e$ leads to an increase in the present value.
- The present value depends negatively on current and expected future interest rates. An increase in either i or in any future i^e leads to a decrease in the present value.

$\$z$ or future $\$z^e \uparrow \Rightarrow V \uparrow$

i or future $i^e \uparrow \Rightarrow V \downarrow$

Equation (14.5) is not simple however, and intuition for these effects is best built by going through some examples.

Constant Interest Rates. To focus on the effects of the sequence of payments on the present value, assume that interest rates are expected to be constant over time, so that $i_t = i_{t+1}^e = \ldots$, and denote their common value by i. The present value formula—equation (14.5)—becomes

$$\$V_t = \$z_t + \frac{1}{(1 + i)}\$z_{t+1}^e + \frac{1}{(1 + i)^2}\$z_{t+2}^e + \cdots \tag{14.6}$$

In this case, the present value is a *weighted sum* of current and expected future payments: The weights decline *geometrically* through time. The weight on a payment this year is one, the weight on the payment n years from now is $[1/(1 + i)]^n$. With a positive interest rate, the weights get closer and closer to zero as we look further and further into the future.

The weights correspond to the terms of a geometric series. See geometric series in appendix 2.

[1] **DIGGING DEEPER.** This statement glosses over a difficult issue. If people dislike risk, the value of a risky payment, now or in the future, will be lower than that of a riskless payment, even if both have the same expected value. I shall ignore this effect here, assuming implicitly that people in the economy are **risk neutral** (they are indifferent to risk). Studying what happens when people are **risk averse** (when they dislike risk) would take us too far afield. It would require a whole course, namely a course in finance theory.

For example, with an interest rate equal to 10%, the weight on a payment in 10 years is equal to $1/(1 + 0.10)^{10} = 0.386$, so that a payment of \$1,000 in 10 years is worth \$386 this year; the weight on a payment in 30 years is $1/(1 + 0.10)^{30} = 0.057$, so that a payment of \$1,000 in 30 years is worth only \$57 this year!

Constant Interest Rates and Payments. In some cases, the sequence of payments for which we want to compute the present value is simple. For example, a typical fixed-rate 30-year mortgage requires constant dollar payments over 30 years. Consider a sequence of equal payments—call them \$z without a time index—over n years including the current year. In this case, the present value formula in equation (14.6) simplifies to

$$\$V_t = \$z \left[1 + \frac{1}{(1 + i)} + \cdots + \frac{1}{(1 + i)^{n-1}} \right]$$

Because the terms in the expression in brackets represent a geometric series, we can

By now, geometric series should not hold any secret, and you should have no problem deriving this relation. But if you do, see appendix 2.

compute the sum of the series, and get

$$\$V_t = \$z \frac{1 - [1/(1 + i)^n]}{1 - [1/(1 + i)]}$$

Suppose you have just won a million dollars from your state lottery and have been presented with a 6-foot \$1,000,000 check on TV. Afterward, you are told that to protect you from your worst spending instincts as well as from your many new "friends," the state will pay you the million dollars in equal yearly installments of \$50,000 over the next 20 years. What is the present value of your prize? Taking, for example, an interest rate of 6%, the equation above gives $V = \$50,000 \, (0.688)/(0.057) =$ or about \$608,000. Not bad, but winning the prize did not make you a millionaire.

What is the present value if i equals 4%? 8%? (Answers: \$706,000; \$530,000)

Constant Interest Rates and Payments, Going on Forever. Let's go one step further and assume that payments are not only constant, but go on forever. Real world examples are harder to come by for this case, but one comes from nineteenth-century England, when the government issued *consols*, bonds paying a fixed yearly amount forever. Let \$z be the constant payment. Assume that payments start next year, rather than right away as in the previous example (this makes for simpler algebra). From equation (14.6), we have

Many consols were bought back by the British government at the end of the nineteenth and early twentieth centuries. But some are still around.

$$\$V_t = \frac{1}{(1 + i)} \$z + \frac{1}{(1 + i)^2} \$z + \cdots$$

$$= \frac{1}{(1 + i)} \left[1 + \frac{1}{(1 + i)} + \cdots \right] \$z$$

where the second line follows by factoring out $1/(1 + i)$. The reason for factoring out $1/(1 + i)$ should be clear from looking at the term in brackets: It is an infinite geometric sum, so we can use the property of geometric sums to rewrite the present value as

$$\$V_t = \frac{1}{1 + i} \frac{1}{(1 - [1/(1 + i)])} \$z$$

Or, simplifying (the steps are given in the application of proposition 2 in appendix 2)

$$\$V_t = \frac{\$z}{i}$$

The present value of a constant sequence of payments $z is equal to the ratio of $z to the interest rate i. If, for example, the interest rate is expected to be 5% forever, the present value of a consol that promises $10 per year forever equals $10/0.05 = $200. If the interest rate increases and is now expected to be 10% forever, the present value of the consol decreases to $10/0.10 = $100.

Zero Interest Rates. Because of discounting, computing present discounted values typically requires the use of a calculator. There is, however, a special case worth keeping in mind where computations simplify. This is the case where the interest rate is equal to zero. Because the interest rate is in fact positive, this is only an approximation, but it is a very useful one for back-of-the-envelope computations. The reason is obvious from equation (14.6): If $i = 0$, then $1/(1 + i)$ equals one, and so does $1/(1 + i)^n$ for any power n. For that reason, the present discounted value of a sequence of expected payments at zero interest rate is then just the *sum* of those expected payments.

Nominal versus Real Interest Rates, and Present Values

We have so far computed the present value of a sequence of dollar payments by using interest rates in terms of dollars—nominal interest rates. Specifically, we have written equation (14.5)

$$\$V_t = \$z_t + \frac{1}{(1 + i_t)} \$z_{t+1}^e + \frac{1}{(1 + i_t)(1 + i_{t+1}^e)} \$z_{t+2}^e + \cdots$$

where i_t, i_{t+1}^e, . . . is the sequence of current and expected future nominal interest rates, and $\$z_t$, $\$z_{t+1}^e$, $\$z_{t+2}^e$, . . . is the sequence of current and expected future dollar payments.

Suppose we want to compute instead the present value of a sequence of *real* payments, that is, payments in terms of a basket of goods rather than in terms of dollars. Following the same logic as before, what we need to do is to use the right interest rates for this case, namely interest rates in terms of the basket of goods—*real interest rates*. Specifically, we can write the present value of a sequence of real payments as

$$V_t = z_t + \frac{1}{(1 + r_t)} z_{t+1}^e + \frac{1}{(1 + r_t)(1 + r_{t+1}^e)} z_{t+2}^e + \cdots \qquad (14.7)$$

where r_t, r_{t+1}^e, . . . is the sequence of current and expected future real interest rates, z_t, z_{t+1}^e, z_{t+2}^e, . . . is the sequence of current and expected future real payments, and $V_t \equiv \$V_t/P_t$ is the real present value of future payments.

These two ways of writing the present value are equivalent. That is, we can compute the present value as (1) the present value of the sequence of payments expressed in dollars, discounted using nominal interest rates, or (2) the present value of payments expressed in real terms, discounted using real interest rates.

Do we need both formulas? Yes. Which one is more helpful depends on the context. Take bonds, for example. Bonds typically are claims to a sequence of nominal payments over a period of years. For example, a 10-year bond may promise $50 a year for 10 years, plus a final payment of $1,000 in the last year. So when we look at the pricing of bonds in chapter 15, we shall rely on equation (14.5) rather than on equation (14.7).

But sometimes, we have a better sense of future expected real values than of future expected dollar values. You may have little idea of what your dollar income will be in 20 years: Its value depends very much on what happens to inflation between now and then. But you may be confident that your nominal income will increase at least as much as inflation—equivalently, that your real income will not decrease. In this case,

How bad an approximation it is depends on how far the interest rate is from zero. Go back to the lottery example. The sum of payments is $1,000,000, If the interest rate is 1%, the present value of payments is $911,000. The approximation is not too bad. If the interest rate is 2%, the expected present value is $834,000. The approximation quickly gets worse.

The proof that they are equivalent is given in the appendix to this chapter. Go through it to test your understanding of the two tools introduced in this chapter: real versus nominal rates, and expected present values.

using equation (14.5), which requires you to form expectations of future dollar income, may be difficult; using equation (14.7), which requires you to form expectations of future real income, will be easier. For that reason, when we discuss consumption and investment decisions in chapter 16, we shall rely on equation (14.7) rather than on equation (14.5).

14-3 | Nominal and Real Interest Rates, and the *IS-LM* Model

We shall spend the next three chapters using the tools we have just developed to explore the role of expectations in determining activity. In the rest of this chapter we take a first step, introducing the distinction between real and nominal interest rates in the *IS-LM* model, and then exploring the relation between money growth, inflation, real and nominal interest rates.

In the *IS-LM* model we developed in the core (chapter 5), the interest rate entered in two places: It affected investment in the *IS* relation, and affected the choice between money and bonds in the *LM* relation. Which interest rate — nominal or real — were we talking about in each case?

Take the *IS* relation first. Our discussion earlier in this chapter should make it clear that in deciding how much investment to undertake, firms care about the *real interest rate*: Firms produce goods. They want to know how much they will have to repay, not in terms of dollars but in terms of goods. So what belongs in the *IS* relation is the real interest rate. Let r denote the real interest rate. The IS relation therefore must be rewritten as

I shall ignore time subscripts here; they are not needed for the rest of the chapter.

$$Y = C(Y - T) + I(Y, r) + G$$

Investment spending, and thus the demand for goods, depends on the real interest rate.

Now turn to the *LM* relation. In deriving the *LM* relation, we argued that the demand for money depends on the interest rate. Were we referring to the nominal interest rate or the real interest rate?

The answer is the *nominal interest rate*. Remember why the interest rate affects the demand for money. When thinking about whether to hold money or bonds, people take into account the opportunity cost of holding money rather than bonds — what they give up by holding money rather than bonds. Money pays a zero nominal interest rate. Bonds pay a nominal interest rate of i. Hence, the opportunity cost of holding money is equal to the difference between the two interest rates, $i - 0 = i$, which is just the nominal interest rate. Therefore, the *LM* relation is still given by

$$\frac{M}{P} = YL(i)$$

Collecting the two equations and the relation between the real and the nominal interest rates, the extended *IS-LM* model is given by

$$\begin{aligned} IS: &\quad Y = C(Y - T) + I(Y, r) + G \\ LM: &\quad M/P = Y L(i) \\ \text{Real interest rate:} &\quad r \approx i - \pi^e \end{aligned}$$

Interest rate in the *IS* relation: Real interest rate, *r*

Interest rate in the *LM* relation: Nominal interest rate, *i*

Note an immediate implication of these three equations. The interest rate directly affected by monetary policy (the interest rate that enters the *LM* equation) is the nominal interest rate. The interest rate that affects spending and output (the rate that enters the *IS* relation) is the real interest rate. The effects of monetary policy on output depend therefore on the relation between the movements in the nominal interest rate and the real interest rate. To explore this implication further, the next section looks at the effects of an increase in money growth on the nominal interest rate and the real interest rate, both in the short run and in the medium run.

14-4 | Money Growth, Inflation, and Nominal and Real Interest Rates

The Fed's decision to allow for higher money growth is the main factor behind the decline in interest rates in the last six months. (imaginary quote, circa 1991)

The nomination to the Board of the Federal Reserve of two left-leaning economists, both perceived to be soft on inflation, has led financial markets to worry about higher money growth, higher inflation, and higher interest rates in the future. (Imaginary quote, circa May 1994)

These two quotes are made up, but they are composites of what was written at the time. Which one is correct? Does higher money growth lead to lower interest rates, or does it lead to higher interest rates? The answer is: Both! There are two keys to this answer. The first is the distinction we just introduced between the real and the nominal interest rate. The second is the distinction we developed in the core between the short run and the medium run. As we shall see, the full answer is that:

- Higher money growth leads to lower nominal interest rates in the short run, but to higher nominal interest rates in the medium run.
- Higher money growth leads to lower real interest rates in the short run, but has no effect on real interest rates in the medium run.

The purpose of this section is to develop this answer, and draw its implications.

◀ Effects of higher money growth:

	Short Run	Medium Run
i	↓	↑
r	↓	→

Nominal and Real Interest Rates in the Short Run

To look at the short run, it is convenient to reduce the three equations we derived in the last section—the *IS* relation, the *LM* relation, and the relation between the real and the nominal interest rate—to two, by replacing the real interest rate in the *IS* relation by the nominal interest rate minus expected inflation. This gives

$$IS: \quad Y = C(Y - T) + I(Y, i - \pi^e) + G$$
$$LM: \quad M/P = Y L(i)$$

These two equations are the same as in chapter 5, with just one difference: Spending in the *IS* relation depends on the real interest rate, which is equal to the nominal interest rate minus expected inflation.

The associated *IS* and *LM* curves are drawn in Figure 14–4, for given values of P, M, π^e, G, and T.

- For a given expected rate of inflation (π^e), the nominal interest rate and the real interest rate move together. Hence, a decrease in the nominal interest rate implies an equal decrease in the real interest rate, leading to an increase in spending and in output: The *IS* curve is downward sloping.
- The *LM* curve is upward sloping: An increase in output leads to an increase in the demand for money, putting pressure on the nominal interest rate.
- The equilibrium is at the intersection of the *IS* and *LM* curves, point A, with output level Y_A, nominal interest rate i_A. Given the nominal interest rate i_A the real interest rate r_A is given by $r_A = i_A - \pi^e$.

Assume the economy initially is at the natural level of output, so $Y_A = Y_n$. Now suppose that the central bank increases the rate of growth of money. What happens to output, to the nominal interest rate, and to the real interest rate in the short run?

◀ We could eliminate the nominal interest rate and keep the real interest rate. r would enter the *IS* relation; $(r + \pi^e)$ would enter the *LM* relation. The graphical analysis would look a bit different, but the conclusions would be the same.

◀ If $r = i - \pi^e$, then
$$\Delta r = \Delta i - \Delta \pi^e.$$
If π^e is constant,
$$\Delta \pi^e = 0,$$
so
$$\Delta r = \Delta i.$$

EXPECTATIONS: THE BASIC TOOLS

FIGURE 14–4

The equilibrium level of output and the equilibrium nominal interest rate are given by the intersection of the *IS* and the *LM* curve. The real interest rate equals the nominal interest rate minus expected inflation.

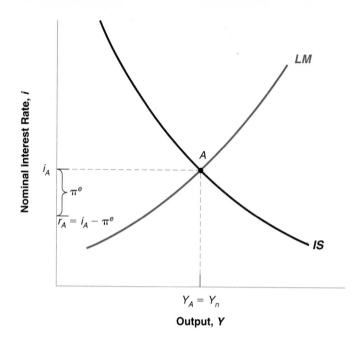

One of the lessons from our analysis of monetary policy in the core is that, in the short run, the faster increase in nominal money will not be matched by an equal increase in the price level. In other words, the higher rate of growth of nominal money will lead, in the short run, to an increase in the real money stock, (M/P). This is all we need to know for our purposes. What happens to output and to interest rates in the short run is shown in Figure 14–5.

The increase in the real money stock leads to a downward shift in the *LM* curve, from *LM* to *LM′*: For a given level of output, the increase in the real money stock leads to a de-

FIGURE 14–5

The Short-Run Effects of an Increase in Money Growth

An increase in money growth increases the real money stock in the short run. This increase in real money leads to an increase in output and a decrease in both the nominal and the real interest rate.

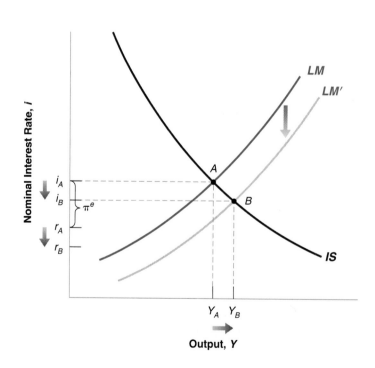

crease in the nominal interest rate. The *IS* curve does not shift: Given expected inflation, a given nominal interest rate corresponds to the same real interest rate and to the same level of spending and output. The equilibrium moves from *A* to *B*: Output is higher. The nominal interest rate is lower, and given expected inflation, so is the real interest rate.

To summarize. In the short run, the increase in nominal money growth leads to an increase in the real money stock. This increase in real money leads to an increase in output, and to a decrease in both the nominal and the real interest rate.[2] Return to our first quote: The goal of the Fed, circa 1991, was precisely to achieve this outcome. Worried that the recession might get worse, the Fed increased money growth in order to decrease the real interest rate and increase output.

In the short run, when the rate of money growth increases, M/P increases. Both i and r decrease

Nominal and Real Interest Rates in the Medium Run

Turn now to the medium run. Suppose the central bank increases the rate of money growth permanently. What will happen to output, nominal, and real interest rates in the medium run?

To answer that question, we rely on two of the central propositions we derived in the core. The two propositions were derived in a model that did not make a distinction between real and nominal rates, but they still hold here:

- In the medium run, output returns to its natural level.

    As we saw in chapter 6, this is because, in the medium run, the unemployment rate must return to the natural unemployment rate. The natural level of output is simply the level of output associated with the natural unemployment rate.

    Although we spent chapters 10 to 13 looking at growth of output over time, we shall, for simplicity, ignore output growth here. Thus, we shall assume that Y_n, the natural level of output, is constant over time.

In the medium run: $Y = Y_n$

- In the medium run, the rate of inflation is equal to the rate of money growth minus the rate of growth of output.

    We derived this conclusion in chapter 9. The intuition for it is simple: A growing level of output implies a growing level of transactions and thus a growing demand for real money. If output is growing at 3%, the real money stock must also grow at 3% per year. If the nominal money stock grows at a rate different from 3%, the difference must show up in inflation (or deflation). For example, if nominal money growth is 10%, then inflation must be equal to 7%.

    If, as we assume here, output growth is equal to zero, this proposition takes an even simpler form: In the medium run, the rate of inflation is equal to the rate of nominal money growth.

In the medium run (if $g_y = 0$): $\pi = g_m$

The implications of these two propositions for the behavior of the real and the nominal interest rate in the medium run are then straightforward:

- Take the real interest rate first. For convenience, let me rewrite the *IS* equation

$$Y = C(Y - T) + I(Y, r) + G$$

One way of thinking about the *IS* relation is that it tells us, for given values of *G* and *T*, what real interest rate *r* is needed to sustain a given level of spending, and so a given

---

[2]**DIGGING DEEPER**. Even in the short run, there may be a second effect at work—in addition to the increase in M/P. As money growth increases, so does inflation—although, initially, by less than money growth. As inflation increases, expected inflation may also increase. The implications of an increase in expected inflation are explored in problem 8 at the end of the chapter. In short, the increase in expected inflation leads to an even larger decrease in the real interest rate in the short run.

level of output Y. If, for example, output is equal to its natural level Y_n, then, for given values of G and T, the real interest rate must be such that

$$Y_n = C(Y_n - T) + I(Y_n, r) + G$$

By analogy with our use of the word "natural" to denote the level of output in the medium run, call this value of the real interest rate the *natural real interest rate*, and denote it by r_n. Then, our earlier proposition that in the medium run, output returns to its natural level Y_n, has a direct implication: For given G and T, in the medium run, the real interest rate returns to the natural interest rate, r_n. In other words, in the medium run, both output *and* the real interest rate are unaffected by the rate of money growth.

- Turn to the nominal interest rate. Recall the relation between the nominal and the real interest rate

$$i = r + \pi^e$$

We have just seen that in the medium run, the real interest rate equals the natural interest rate, r_n. This means

$$i = r_n + \pi^e$$

In the medium run, expected inflation is equal to actual inflation (people do not have incorrect expectations of inflation forever), so

$$i = r_n + \pi$$

In the medium run, inflation is equal to money growth (recall we are assuming that the rate of growth of output equals zero), so

$$i = r_n + g_m$$

In words: In the medium run, an increase in money growth leads to an equal increase in the nominal interest rate.

To summarize. In the medium run, money growth does not affect the real interest rate, but affects both inflation and the nominal interest rate one for one. A permanent increase in nominal money growth of, say, 10%, is eventually reflected in a 10% increase in the inflation rate, and a 10% increase in the nominal interest rate—leaving the real interest rate unchanged.

Irving Fisher, *The Rate of Interest* (New York: Macmillan 1906).

The result that in the medium run, nominal interest rates increase one for one with inflation is known as the **Fisher effect**, or the **Fisher hypothesis**, after Irving Fisher, an economist at Yale University who first stated it at the beginning of the twentieth century. This result underlies the second quote at the beginning of the section: If financial investors were indeed worried that the appointment of certain new Board members at the Fed might lead to higher money growth, they were right to expect higher nominal interest rates in the future.

In this case, their fears turned out to be unfounded. The Fed remained committed to low inflation throughout the 1990s.

From the Short to the Medium Run

We have now shown how to reconcile the two quotes at the beginning of the section: An increase in monetary growth (a monetary expansion) is likely to lead to a *decrease* in nominal interest rates in the short run, but to an *increase* in nominal interest rates in the medium run.

What happens between the short run and the medium run? A complete characterization of the movements of real and nominal interest rates over time would take us beyond what we can do here. But the basic features of the adjustment process are easy to describe.

In the short run, real and nominal interest rates go down. Why don't they stay down forever? As long as the real interest rate is below the natural real interest rate (the value corresponding to the natural level of output), output is higher than the natural level. Equivalently, unemployment is below the natural rate. From the Phillips curve relation, we know that as long as unemployment is below the natural rate, inflation increases.

In the short run: $i \downarrow \, r \downarrow$

$r < r_n \Rightarrow Y > Y_n$
$Y > Y_n \Rightarrow u < u_n$
$u < u_n \Rightarrow \pi \uparrow$

As inflation increases, it eventually becomes higher than nominal money growth, leading to negative real money growth. When real money growth turns negative, the nominal interest rate starts increasing. And, given expected inflation, so does the real interest rate.

In the medium run, the real interest rate increases back to its initial value. Output is then back to its natural level, unemployment is back to its natural rate, and inflation is no longer changing. As the real interest rate converges back to its initial value, the nominal interest rate converges to a new higher value, equal to the real interest rate plus the new, higher rate of nominal money growth.

Figure 14–6 summarizes these results by showing the adjustment over time of the real and the nominal interest rates to an increase in nominal money growth from, say, 0% to 10%, starting at time t. Before time t, both interest rates are constant and equal to each other. The real interest rate is equal to r_n. The nominal interest rate is also equal to r_n (as inflation and expected inflation are equal to zero).

At time t, the rate of money growth increases from 0% to 10%. The increase in the rate of nominal money growth leads, for some time, to an increase in real money, and to a decrease in the nominal interest rate. As expected inflation increases, the decrease in the real interest rate is larger than the decrease of the nominal interest rate.

Eventually, the nominal and the real interest rates start increasing. In the medium run, the real interest rate returns to its initial value. Inflation and expected inflation converge to the new rate of money growth, thus 10%. The nominal interest rate converges to a value equal to the real interest rate plus 10%.

Over time: $\pi \uparrow$
Eventually $\pi > g'_m$
$g'_m - \pi < 0 \Rightarrow i \uparrow$

In the medium run:
$$r = r_n$$
$$Y = Y_n,$$
$$u = u_n, \ \pi \text{ constant}$$
$$\pi = g'_m$$
$$i = r_n + g'_m$$

Evidence on the Fisher Hypothesis

There is plenty of evidence that a monetary expansion decreases nominal interest rates in the short run (see, for example, section 5–5). But how much evidence is there for the Fisher hypothesis, the proposition that in the medium run, increases in inflation lead to one-for-one increases in nominal interest rates?

Economists have tried to answer this question by looking at two types of evidence. The first is the relation between nominal interest rates and inflation *across countries*. Because the relation holds only in the medium run, we should not expect inflation and nominal interest rates to be close to each other in any one country at any one time, but the relation should hold on average. This approach is explored further in the Global Macro box "Nominal

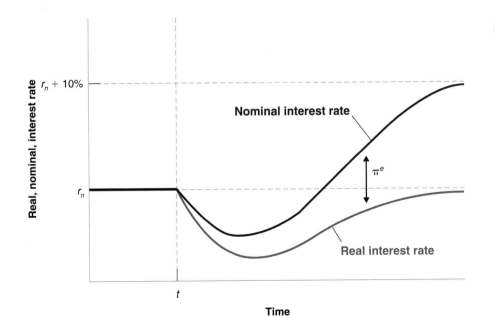

FIGURE 14–6

The Adjustment of the Real and the Nominal Interest Rates to an Increase in Money Growth From 0% to 10%

An increase in money growth leads initially to a decrease in both the real and the nominal interest rate. Over time, the real interest rate returns to its initial value. The nominal interest rate converges to a new higher value. This new higher value is equal to the initial value plus the increase in money growth.

Nominal Interest Rates and Inflation Across Latin America

Figure 1 plots nominal interest rates and inflation for eight Latin American countries (Argentina, Bolivia, Chile, Ecuador, Mexico, Peru, Uruguay, and Venezuela) for both 1992 and 1993. (Because the Brazilian numbers would dwarf those from other countries, they are not included here. In 1992, Brazil's inflation rate was 1,008% and its nominal interest rate was 1,560%. In 1993, inflation was 2,140% and the nominal interest rate was 3,240%.) The numbers for inflation refer to the rate of change of the consumer price index. The numbers for nominal interest rates refer to the "lending rate." The exact definition of this term varies with each country, but you can think of it as corresponding to the prime interest rate in the United States—the rate charged to borrowers with the best credit rating.

Note the wide range of inflation rates, from 10% to about 100%. This is precisely why I have chosen to pre-

sent numbers from Latin America in the early 1990s. With this much variation in inflation, we can learn a lot about the relation between nominal interest rates and inflation. And Figure 1 indeed shows a clear relation between inflation and nominal interest rates. The line drawn in the figure plots what the nominal interest rate should be under the Fisher hypothesis, assuming an underlying real interest rate of 10%, so that $i = 10\% + \pi$. The slope of the line is one: Under the Fisher hypothesis, a 1% increase in inflation should be reflected in a 1% increase in the nominal interest rate.

As you can see, the line fits well; roughly half of the points are above the line, the other half below. The Fisher hypothesis appears roughly consistent with the evidence from Latin America in the early 1990s.

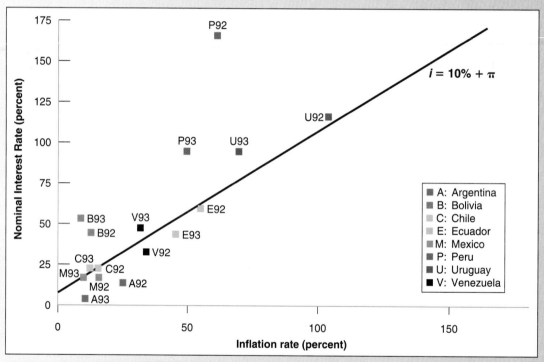

FIGURE 1   **Nominal Interest Rates and Inflation: Latin America, 1992 and 1993**

Brazil is not shown; its four-digit nominal interest rate and inflation rate would be way off the scale.

Interest Rates and Inflation Across Latin America," which looks at Latin American countries in the early 1990s and finds substantial support for the Fisher hypothesis.

The second type of evidence is the relation between the nominal interest rate and inflation over time for one country. Again, the Fisher hypothesis does not suggest that the two should move together from year to year. But it does suggest that the long swings in inflation should eventually be reflected in similar swings in the nominal interest rate. To see these

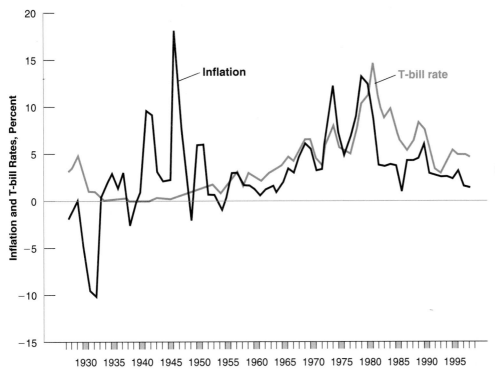

FIGURE 14-7

The Three-Month Treasury Bill Rate and Inflation, 1927–1998

The increase in inflation from the early 1960s to the early 1980s was associated with an increase in the nominal interest rate. The decrease in inflation since the mid-1980s has been associated with a decrease in the nominal interest rate.

long swings, we need to look at as long a period of time as we can. Figure 14–7 looks at the nominal interest rate and inflation in the United States since 1927. The nominal interest rate is the three-month Treasury bill rate, and the inflation rate is the rate of change of the CPI.

Figure 14–7 has several interesting features.

- The steady increase in inflation from the early 1960s to the early 1980s was associated with a roughly parallel increase in the nominal interest rate. The decrease in inflation since the mid-1980s has been associated with a decrease in the nominal interest rate. These evolutions support the Fisher hypothesis.
- Evidence of the short-run effects that we discussed earlier is also easy to see. The nominal interest rate lagged behind the increase in inflation in the 1970s, whereas the disinflation of the early 1980s was associated with an initial *increase* in the nominal rate, followed by a much slower decline in the nominal interest rate than in inflation.
- The other episode of inflation, during and after World War II, underlines the importance of the "medium run" qualifier in the Fisher hypothesis. During that period, inflation was high but short-lived. And it disappeared before it had time to be reflected in a higher nominal interest rate. The nominal interest rate remained very low throughout the 1940s.

This low nominal interest rate was the result of a deliberate policy by the Fed aimed at reducing interest payments on the large government debt created during the war.

More careful studies confirm our basic conclusion. The Fisher hypothesis that in the medium run increases in inflation are reflected in a higher nominal interest rate appears to fit the data quite well. But the adjustment takes a long time. The data confirm the speculation by Milton Friedman, which we quoted in chapter 8, that it typically takes a "couple of decades" for nominal interest rates to reflect the higher inflation rate.

- The nominal interest rate tells us how many dollars one has to repay in the future in exchange for one dollar today.

- The real interest rate tells us how many goods one has to repay in the future in exchange for one good today.

- The real interest rate is approximately equal to the nominal interest rate minus expected inflation.

- The expected present discounted value of a sequence of payments is the value this year of the expected sequence of payments. It depends positively on current and future expected payments. It depends negatively on current and future expected interest rates.

- In discounting a sequence of current and expected future nominal payments, one should use current and expected future nominal interest rates. In discounting a sequence of current and expected future real payments, one should use current and expected future real interest rates.

- Investment decisions depend on the real interest rate. The choice between money and bonds depends on the nominal interest rate. Thus, the real interest rate enters the *IS* relation, whereas the nominal interest rate enters the *LM* relation.

- In the short run, an increase in money growth typically leads to a decrease of both the nominal interest rate and the real interest rate. In the medium run, an increase in money growth has no effect on the real interest rate, and increases the nominal interest rate one for one.

- The proposition that in the medium run, changes in inflation are reflected one for one in changes in the nominal interest rate is known as the Fisher effect, or the Fisher hypothesis. The empirical evidence suggests that although it takes a long time, changes in inflation are eventually reflected in changes in the nominal interest rate.

- nominal interest rate, 269
- real interest rate, 269
- expected present discounted value, present discounted value (present value), 272
- discount factor, 272

- discount rate, 272
- risk neutral, 273
- risk averse, 273
- Fisher effect, Fisher hypothesis, 280

An asterisk denotes a harder problem.

1. TRUE/FALSE/UNCERTAIN

a. As long as inflation remains roughly constant, the movements in the real interest rate are equal to the movements in the nominal interest rate.

b. If inflation turns out to be higher than expected, then the realized real cost of borrowing turns out to be lower than expected.

c. Looking across countries, the real interest rate is likely to vary much less than the nominal interest rate.

d. The real interest rate is equal to the nominal interest rate divided by the price level.

e. In the medium run, the real interest rate is not affected by money growth.

f. The Fischer effect states that in the medium run, the nominal interest rate is not affected by money growth.

g. The experience of Latin American countries in the early 1990s supports the Fischer hypothesis.

h. The value today of a nominal payment in the future cannot be greater than the nominal payment itself.

i. The real value today of a real payment in the future cannot be greater than the real payment itself.

2. REAL AND NOMINAL INTEREST RATES. I

For each of the following problems would you use real payments and real interest rates or nominal payments and nominal interest rates to compute the expected present discounted value? In each case, explain why.

a. Estimating the present discounted value of the profits from purchasing a new machine.

b. Estimating the present value of a 20-year U.S. government bond.

c. Deciding whether to lease or buy a car.

3. REAL AND NOMINAL INTEREST RATES. II

For each of the following, compute the real interest rate using the exact formula and the approximation formula.

a. $i = 4\%; \pi^e = 2\%$

b. $i = 15\%; \pi^e = 11\%$

c. $i = 54\%; \pi^e = 46\%$

4. REAL AND NOMINAL INTEREST RATES. III

a. Can the nominal interest rate ever be negative? Explain.

b. Can the real interest rate ever be negative? Under what circumstances? If so, why not just hold cash instead?

c. What are the effects of a negative real interest rate on borrowing and lending?

d. Find a recent issue of *The Economist* and look at the tables in the back ("Economic Indicators" and "Financial Indicators"). Use the three-month money-market rate as the nominal interest rate and the most recent three-month rate of change in consumer prices as the expected rate of inflation (both are in annual terms). Which countries have the lowest nominal interest rates? Which countries have the lowest real interest rates? Are some of these real interest rates negative?

5. EARLY VERSUS LATE TAX CREDITS

You want to save $2,000 today for retirement in 40 years. You have to choose between two plans:

i. Pay no taxes today, put the money in an interest-yielding account, and pay taxes equal to 25% of the total amount withdrawn at retirement. (In the United States, such an account is known as a regular individual retirement account, or IRA.)

ii. Pay taxes equivalent to 20% of the investment amount today, put the remainder in an interest-yielding account, and pay no taxes when you withdraw your funds at retirement. (In the United States, this is known as a Roth IRA.)

a. What is the expected present discounted value of each of these options if the interest rate is 1%? 10%?

b. Which alternative would you pick in each case? Under what circumstances would you pick the other policy? (*Hint:* Think of the tax rates.)

6. CONSOLS

The present value of an infinite stream of dollar payments of $z (that starts next year) is $z/i when the nominal interest rate i is constant. This formula gives the price of a consol. It also is a good approximation for the present discounted value of a stream of constant payments over long but not infinite periods. Let's examine how close the approximation is. Suppose that $i = 10\%$.

a. Let $z = 100$. What is the present value of the consol?

b. What is the expected present discounted value for a bond that pays $z over the next 10 years? 20 years? 30 years? 60 years? (*Hint:* Use the formula from Chapter 14 but remember to adjust for the first payment.)

c. Repeat the exercise with $i = 2\%$ and $i = 5\%$.

7. THE FISHER HYPOTHESIS

a. What is the Fisher hypothesis?

b. Does the experience of Latin American countries in the 1990s support or refute the Fisher hypothesis? Explain.

c. Look at the figure in the Global Macro box on Latin America. Note that the line drawn through the scatter of points does not go through the origin. Does the Fisher effect suggest that it should go through the origin? Explain.

d. "If the Fisher hypothesis is true, then changes in the growth rate of the money stock translate one for one into changes in i and the real interest rate is left unchanged. Thus, there is no room for monetary policy to affect activity." Discuss.

*8. THE SHORT-RUN EFFECTS OF AN INCREASE IN MONEY GROWTH REVISITED

When looking at the short run in section 14-4, we concentrated on the effects of higher nominal money growth on the real money stock. We saw how this led to higher output and lower nominal and real interest rates.

Starting from the analysis in the text (as summarized in Figure 14–5), assume that as a result of higher money growth, expected inflation increases by $\Delta\pi^e$.

a. Show the effect of the increase in π^e on the *IS* curve. Explain in words.

b. Show the effect of the increase in π^e on the *LM* curve. Explain in words.

c. Show the combined effects of the increase in the real money stock and of the increase in expected inflation on output and on the nominal interest rate. Could the nominal interest rate end up higher, not lower, than before the change in money growth? Why?

d. Even if what happens to the nominal interest rate is ambiguous, can you tell what happens to the real interest rate? (*Hint:* What happens to output? What does this imply for what happens to the real interest rate?)

DERIVING THE EXPECTED PRESENT DISCOUNTED VALUE USING REAL OR NOMINAL INTEREST RATES

This appendix shows that the two ways of expressing present discounted values, equations (14.5) and (14.7), are equivalent.

Let's first rewrite these two equations.

Equation (14.5) gives the present value as the sum of current and future expected *nominal payments*, discounted using current and future expected *nominal interest rates*

$$\$V_t = \$z_t + \frac{1}{1+i_t}\$z_{t+1}^e$$
$$+ \frac{1}{(1+i_t)(1+i_{t+1}^e)}\$z_{t+2}^e + \cdots \quad (14.5)$$

Equation (14.7) gives the present value as the sum of current and future expected *real payments*, discounted using current and future expected *real interest rates*

$$V_t = z_t + \frac{1}{1+r_t}z_{t+1}^e$$
$$+ \frac{1}{(1+r_t)(1+r_{t+1}^e)}z_{t+2}^e + \cdots \quad (14.7)$$

Divide both sides of equation (14.5) by the current price level, P_t. The left side becomes $\$V_t/P_t = V_t$, the real present discounted value, the same as the left-hand side of equation (14.7).

Now consider each term on the right of equation (14.5):

- The first becomes $\$z_t/P_t = z_t$, the current payment in real terms. This term is the same as the first term on the right of equation (14.7).

- The second is given by $[1/(1+i_t)](\$z_{t+1}^e/P_t)$. Multiplying the numerator and the denominator by P_{t+1}^e, the price level expected for next year, gives

$$\frac{1}{1+i_t}\ \frac{P_{t+1}^e}{P_t}\ \frac{\$z_{t+1}^e}{P_{t+1}^e}$$

The third fraction, $\$z_{t+1}^e/P_{t+1}^e$, is the expected real payment at time $t+1$. Consider the second fraction. Note that P_{t+1}^e/P_t can be rewritten as $1 + [(P_{t+1}^e - P_t)/P_t]$, thus, using the definition of expected inflation, as $(1 + \pi_t^e)$. This gives

$$\frac{(1+\pi_t^e)}{(1+i_t)}z_{t+1}^e$$

Finally, using the definition of the real interest rate in equation (14.3) $[1 + r_t = (1+i_t)/(1+\pi_t^e)]$ gives

$$\frac{1}{(1+r_t)}z_{t+1}^e$$

This is the same as the second term on the right-hand side of equation (14.7).

- The same method applies to the other terms; make sure that you can derive the next one.

It follows that equations (14.5) and (14.7) are equivalent ways of stating and deriving the expected present discounted value of a sequence of payments.

We invite you to visit the Blanchard page on the Prentice Hall Web site at:

http://www.prenhall.com/blanchard

for this chapter's World Wide Web exercises

CHAPTER 15

Financial Markets and Expectations

In our first look at financial markets in the core (back in chapter 4), I assumed there were only two assets, money and just one type of bond—so we could easily focus on the choice between money and all other assets. We are now ready to relax this assumption. In this chapter, we look at the choices among non-money assets—between short-term and long-term bonds, between bonds and stocks, and so on.

Section 15-1 looks at the determination of bond prices and the yield curve. It shows in particular how we can use the yield curve to infer what financial markets expect to happen to short-term interest rates in the future. Section 15-2 looks at the determination of stock prices. It shows how stock prices depend on current and expected future profits, as well as on current and expected future interest rates. It then discusses the relation between movements in stock prices and movements in economic activity. Finally, section 15-3 looks at fads and bubbles in the stock market—episodes when stock prices appear to move for reasons unrelated to either profits or interest rates—and discusses their macroeconomic implications.

Bonds differ in two basic dimensions:

- **Default risk**, the risk that the issuer of the bond will not pay back the full amount promised by the bond, and
- **Maturity**, the length of time over which it promises to make payments to the holder. A bond that promises to make one payment of $1,000 in six months has a maturity of six months; a bond that promises $100 per year for the next 20 years and a final payment of $1,000 at the end of those 20 years has a maturity of 20 years. Maturity is the more important dimension for our purposes and we shall focus on it here.

Term structure ⇔
Yield curve ▸

Bonds of different maturities each have a price and an associated interest rate called the *yield to maturity*, or simply the *yield*. By looking on any given day at the yields on bonds of different maturities, we can graphically trace the relation between yields and maturity. This relation is called the **yield curve**, or the **term structure of interest rates** (the word "term" is synonymous with maturity).

To find out what the term structure is at the time you read this chapter, look for "Treasury Bonds, Notes and Bills" in the "Money & Investing" section of *The Wall Street Journal.*

Figure 15–1 gives the term structure on U.S. government bonds on January 1, 1993, and on July 22, 1998. The choice of the two dates is not accidental; why I chose them will be clear shortly.

Note how steep the yield curve was in January 1993. The three-month rate (the interest rate on a three-month T-bill) was only 3%, whereas the 30-year rate (the interest rate on a 30-year bond) was 7.34%. Note how much flatter the yield curve was in July 1998. The three-month rate was 2% higher than it was in January 1993, and the 30-year rate was 1.5% lower, leading to a much smaller difference between the three-month and 30-year rates.

Two steps: (1) the determination of bond prices and (2) the determination of bond yields.

Why was the yield curve so steep in early 1993, and why was it nearly flat in mid-1998? What does a steep yield curve tell us about expectations in financial markets? To answer these questions, we proceed in two steps. First, we look at the relation between the *prices of bonds* of different maturities. Second, we show the relation between *yields of bonds* of different maturities, and examine the determinants of the shape of the yield curve.

Bond Prices as Present Values

Note both bonds are *discount bonds* (see the Focus box).

Consider two bonds: a one-year bond that promises one payment of $100 in one year, and a two-year bond that promises one payment of $100 in two years. Let their prices today be P_{1t} and P_{2t}, respectively. How will these two prices be determined?

U.S. Yield Curves: January 1993 and July 1998

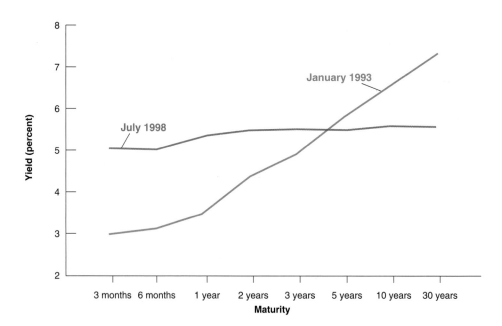

The Vocabulary of Bond Markets

Understanding the basic vocabulary of financial markets will help make them less mysterious. Here is a basic vocabulary review.

- Bonds are issued by the government to finance its deficit, or by firms to finance their investment. If issued by the government or government agencies the bonds are called **government bonds**. If issued by firms, they are called **corporate bonds**.

- In the United States, bonds are rated for their default risk (the risk they will not be repaid) by two private firms, the Standard and Poor's Corporation (S&P) and Moody's Investors Service. Moody's **bond ratings** range from *Aaa* for bonds with nearly no risk of default, such as U.S government bonds, to *C* for bonds whose default risk is high. A lower rating typically implies that the bond has to pay a higher interest rate. The difference between the interest rate paid on a bond and the interest rate paid on the bond with the highest (best) rating is called the **risk premium**.

  Bonds with high default risk are known as **junk bonds**. Because they promised a very high interest rate, they became very popular with financial investors in the 1980s. After a few well-publicized defaults, they have become less popular today.

- Bonds that promise a single payment at maturity are called **discount bonds**. The single payment is called the **face value** of the bond.

- Bonds that promise multiple payments before maturity and one payment at maturity are called **coupon bonds**. The payments before maturity are called **coupon payments**. The final payment is called the face value of the bond. The ratio of coupon payments to the face value is called the **coupon rate**. The **current yield** is the ratio of the coupon payment to the price of the bond.

  For example, a bond with coupon payments of $5 each year, a face value of $100, and a price of $80 has a coupon rate of 5% and a current yield of 6.25%. From an economic viewpoint, neither the coupon rate nor the current yield are interesting measures. The

correct measure of the interest rate on a bond is its *yield to maturity*, or simply *yield*; you can think of it as roughly the average annual interest rate paid by the bond over its life (we shall define it more precisely later in this chapter).

- **Short-term**, **medium-term**, and **long-term bonds** typically refer to bonds with maturity of one year or less, one to ten years, and ten years or more, respectively.

- U.S. government bonds range in maturity from a few days to 30 years. Bonds with a maturity of up to a year when they are issued are called **Treasury bills**, or **T-bills**. They are discount bonds, making only one payment at maturity. Bonds with a maturity of one to 10 years when they are issued are called **Treasury notes**. Bonds with a maturity of 10 or more years when they are issued are called **Treasury bonds**. Treasury notes and bonds are coupon bonds.

- Bonds are typically nominal bonds: They promise a sequence of fixed nominal payments—payments in terms of domestic currency. However, there are other types of bonds. Among them are **indexed bonds**, bonds that promise not fixed nominal payments but rather payments adjusted for inflation. Instead of promising to pay, say, 100 dollars in a year, a one-year indexed bond promises to pay $100 (1 + \pi)$ dollars, where π is the rate of inflation that will take place over the coming year. Because they protect bondholders against the risk of inflation, indexed bonds are popular in many countries. They play a particularly important role in the United Kingdom, where, over the last 20 years, people have increasingly used them to save for retirement. By holding long-term indexed bonds, they can make sure that the payments they receive when they retire will be protected from inflation. Indexed bonds (called *inflation-indexed bonds*) were introduced in the United States in 1997. They account for only a small proportion of U.S. government bonds at this point, but their role will surely increase in the future.

Take the *one-year bond* first. Let the current one-year nominal interest rate be i_{1t}. Note that I now denote the one-year interest rate in year t by i_{1t} rather than simply by i_t as I did in earlier chapters. This is to make it easier to remember that it is the *one-year* interest rate.

The price of the one-year bond today is the present value of $100 next year. So,

$$\$P_{1t} = \frac{\$100}{1 + i_{1t}} \tag{15.1}$$

The price of a one-year bond varies inversely with the current one-year nominal interest rate. We already saw this relation in chapter 4. Indeed, we saw that what actually is determined in the bond market is the price of one-year bonds, and the one-year interest rate is then inferred from the price according to equation (15.1). Reorganizing equation (15.1), it follows that if the price of one-year bonds is $\$P_{1t}$, then the current one-year interest rate equals $(\$100 - \$P_{1t})/\$P_{1t}$.

Turn now to the *two-year bond*. Its price is the present value of $100 in two years:

$$\$P_{2t} = \frac{\$100}{(1 + i_{1t})(1 + i_{t+1}^e)} \qquad (15.2)$$

where i_{1t} denotes the one-year interest rate this year and i_{t+1}^e denotes the one-year rate expected by financial markets for next year. The price of a two-year bond depends on both the current one-year rate and the one-year rate expected for next year.

In the same way, we could write the price of an *n*-year bond—a bond that promises to pay, say, $100 in *n* years—as depending on the sequence of one-year rates expected by financial markets over the next *n* years.

Before exploring further the implications of equations (15.1) and (15.2), let's look at an alternative derivation of equation (15.2) based on the notion of *arbitrage*. This alternative derivation will prove useful at many points in the book.

Arbitrage and Bond Prices

Suppose you have the choice between holding one-year bonds or two-year bonds. You care about how much you will have one year from now. Which bonds should you hold?

- For every dollar you put in one-year bonds, you will get $(1 + i_{1t})$ dollars next year. This relation is represented in the first line of Figure 15–2.
- Because the price of a two-year bond is $\$P_{2t}$, every dollar you put in two-year bonds buys you $\$1/\$P_{2t}$ bonds today. When next year comes, the bond will have only one more year before maturity, and thus will have become a one-year bond. Therefore, the price at which you can expect to sell it next year is $\$P_{1t+1}^e$, the expected price of a one-year bond next year. Thus, for every dollar you put in two-year bonds, you can expect to receive $(\$P_{1t+1}^e/\$P_{2t})$ dollars next year. This is represented in the second line of Figure 15–2.

Which bonds should you hold? Suppose that you, and other financial investors, care *only* about the expected return and choose to hold only the bond with the higher expected return.[1]

Under this assumption, and if there are positive amounts of one-year and two-year bonds in the economy, it follows that the two bonds must offer the same expected one-year return. To see why, suppose this condition were not satisfied. For example, suppose that the one-year return on one-year bonds were lower than the expected one-year return on two-year

FIGURE 15–2

Returns from Holding One-Year and Two-Year Bonds for One Year

	Year t	**Year t + 1**
One-year bonds	$1	$1 $(1 + i_{1t})$
Two-year bonds	$1	$1 $\dfrac{\$P_{1t+1}^e}{\$P_{2t}}$

[1]**DIGGING DEEPER**. The return from holding one-year bonds for one year is known with certainty. The return from holding two-year bonds for one year depends on the price of one-year bonds next year and is therefore uncertain. The assumption that financial investors care only about expected return is another way of saying they are indifferent to risk—in other words, they are risk neutral. This is the same assumption we made to derive expected present discounted values in chapter 14. In the context of the choice between bonds of different maturities, it is called the **expectations hypothesis**—to capture the notion that the choice only depends on expected returns.

bonds. Nobody would want to hold the existing supply of one-year bonds, and the market for one-year bonds would not be in equilibrium. Only if the expected one-year return is the same will financial investors be willing to hold both one-year bonds and two-year bonds.

If the two bonds offer the same expected one-year return, it follows from Figure 15–2 that

$$1 + i_{1t} = \frac{\$P^e_{1t+1}}{\$P_{2t}} \tag{15.3}$$

The left side gives the return per dollar from holding a one-year bond for one year; the right side gives the expected return per dollar from holding a two-year bond for one year. I shall call equations such as (15.3)—equations that state that the expected returns on two assets have to be equal—**arbitrage** relations.

Rewrite equation (15.3) as

$$\$P_{2t} = \frac{\$P^e_{1t+1}}{1 + i_{1t}} \tag{15.4}$$

I use "arbitrage" to denote the proposition that the expected returns on two assets must be equal. Some economists reserve "arbitrage" for the narrower proposition that *riskless* profit opportunities do not go unexploited.

Arbitrage implies that the price of a two-year bond today is the present value of the expected price of the bond next year. This raises the question: What does the expected price of one-year bonds next year ($\$P^e_{1t+1}$) depend on?

The answer is straightforward. Just as the price of a one-year bond this year depends on this year's one-year interest rate, the price of a one-year bond next year will depend on the one-year interest rate next year. Writing equation (15.1) for next year (year $t + 1$) and denoting expectations in the usual way

$$\$P^e_{1t+1} = \frac{\$100}{(1 + i^e_{1t+1})}$$

The price of the bond next year is expected to equal the final payment, $100, discounted by the one-year rate expected for next year.

Replacing $\$P^e_{1t+1}$ in equation (15.4) gives

$$\$P_{2t} = \frac{\$100}{(1 + i_{1t})(1 + i^e_{1t+1})} \tag{15.5}$$

This expression is the same as equation (15.2). What we have shown is that *arbitrage* between one- and two-year bonds implies that the price of the two-year bond is the *present value* of the payment in two years, namely $100, discounted using current and next year's expected one-year rates. We could have used the same approach to derive the price of three-year bonds and so on; you may want to make sure you can do it. The relation between arbitrage and present value is important; we shall use it again in this and later chapters.

The relation between arbitrage and present values: Arbitrage between bonds of different maturities implies that bond prices are equal to the expected present values of payments on these bonds.

From Bond Prices to Bond Yields

We have derived bond prices. We now move to bond yields.

To begin, we need a definition of the yield to maturity. The **yield to maturity** on an n-year bond, or equivalently the **n-year interest rate**, is defined as that constant annual interest rate that makes the bond price today equal to the present value of future payments on the bond.

This definition is simpler than it sounds. For example, take the two-year bond we introduced earlier. Denote its yield by i_{2t}, where the subscript 2 reminds us that this is the yield to maturity on a two-year bond, or equivalently the two-year interest rate. This yield is defined as the constant annual interest rate that would make the present value of $100 in two years equal to the price of the bond today

$$\$P_{2t} = \frac{\$100}{(1 + i_{2t})^2} \tag{15.6}$$

$$\$90 = \frac{\$100}{(1 + i_{2t})^2} \implies$$

$$(1 + i_{2t})^2 = \frac{\$100}{\$90} \implies$$

$$(1 + i_{2t}) = \sqrt{\frac{\$100}{\$90}} \implies$$

$$i_{2t} = 5.4\%$$

Suppose the bond sells for $90 today. Then, the two-year rate i_{2t} is given by $\sqrt{100/90} - 1$, or 5.4%. In other words, holding the bond for two years—until maturity—yields an interest rate of 5.4% per year.

What is the relation of the two-year rate to the current one-year rate and the expected one-year rate? To answer this question, we simply compare equation (15.6) with equation (15.5). Eliminating $\$P_{2t}$ between the two gives:

$$\frac{\$100}{(1 + i_{2t})^2} = \frac{\$100}{(1 + i_{1t})(1 + i^e_{1t+1})}$$

Rearranging

$$(1 + i_{2t})^2 = (1 + i_{1t})(1 + i^e_{1t+1})$$

This gives the exact relation between the two-year rate and the current and expected one-year rates. A useful approximation to this relation is given by

> We used a similar approximation when we looked at the relation between nominal and real interest rates in chapter 14. See proposition 3 in appendix 2.

$$i_{2t} \approx \frac{1}{2}(i_{1t} + i^e_{1t+1}) \tag{15.7}$$

Equation (15.7) is intuitive and important. It says that the two-year rate is (approximately) the average of the current one-year rate and next year's expected one-year rate. The relation extends to interest rates on bonds of higher maturity. *The n-year rate is (approximately) equal to the average of current and expected one-year rates over this and the next (n − 1) years*

$$i_{nt} \approx \frac{1}{n}(i_{1t} + i^e_{1t+1} + \cdots + i^e_{1t+n-1})$$

These relations give us the key we need to interpret the yield curve. *An upward-sloping yield curve tells us that financial markets expect short-term rates to increase in the future. A downward-sloping yield curve tells us that financial markets expect short-term interest rates to decrease in the future.*

An example will make this clear. Return to the January 1993 yield curve in Figure 15–1. We can infer from it what financial markets expected the one-year interest rate to be one year hence—namely, in January 1994. To do so, multiply both sides of equation (15.7) by 2, and reorganize to get

$$i^e_{1t+1} = 2i_{2t} - i_{1t} \tag{15.8}$$

In January 1993 i_{1t}, (the one-year rate, the interest rate for 1993) was 3.5%. The two-year rate was 4.4%. The expected one-year rate for January 1994 was therefore equal to $(2 \times 4.4\%) - 3.5\% = 5.3\%$, thus 1.8% above the January 1993 one-year rate.[2]

The Yield Curve and Economic Activity

Why was the yield curve so steep in early 1993? Equivalently, why did financial markets expect short-term interest rates to increase in the near future? The short answer is because the U.S. economy was growing out of a recession. To see why, let's use the *IS-LM* we developed in the core (chapter 5). Also, to concentrate on the difference between interest rates of differ-

[2]**DIGGING DEEPER**. Back to risk: Bonds of higher maturity are more risky to hold because, if they are sold before maturity, variations in their price can lead to large gains or losses. Contrary to our assumption that people are indifferent to risk, participants in bond markets are in fact risk averse and require a risk premium for bonds of higher maturity. Thus, a mildly upward-sloping yield curve—such as the yield curve in July 1998—is more likely to reflect a risk premium that increases with maturity rather than expectations of higher short-term rates in the future. The computation in the text does not take this risk premium into account.

ent maturities, let's leave aside the distinction between nominal and real interest rates we introduced in chapter 14. More specifically, let's assume that expected inflation is equal to zero, so that real and nominal rates are the same.

Go back to the recession of 1990–1991. We argued in chapter 4 that this recession was due in large part to a decrease in consumer confidence, which triggered a decrease in demand and in output. This is represented in Figure 15–3(a): The recession was due to a shift

In chapter 17, we shall extend the *IS-LM* model to take explicitly into account what we have learned about the effects of expectations on decisions. For the moment, the basic *IS-LM* will do.

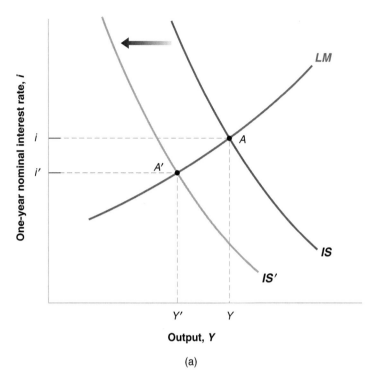

(a)

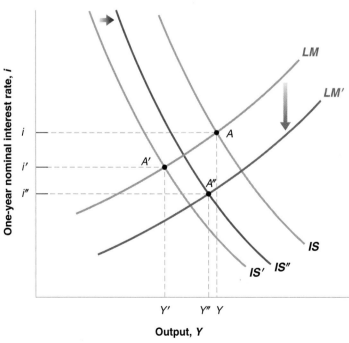

(b)

FIGURE 15–3

The Recession of 1990–1991 and the Following Recovery

(a) 1990–1991. The decrease in consumer confidence decreases spending and output. The *IS* curve shifts to the left. (b) After 1991. Households and firms slowly regain confidence. The *IS* curve slowly shifts to the right. The Fed increases the money supply and the *LM* curve shifts down.

of the *IS* curve to the left, from *IS* to *IS'*, leading to a movement in the equilibrium from *A* to *A'*, a decrease in output from *Y* to *Y'*, and a decrease in the interest rate from *i* to *i'*.

From 1991 on, the economy then slowly recovered. There were two main reasons. One was a slow shift of the *IS* curve to the right, from *IS'* to *IS"*, as households and firms slowly regained confidence and increased spending. The other was a downward shift of the *LM* curve—from *LM* to *LM'*—as the Fed decided to help the economy recover by increasing the money supply and allowing the short-term interest rate to decline even further. The short-term interest rate declined from above 6% in early 1991 to 3.5% in early 1993. Both shifts are shown in Figure 15–3(b). In early 1993, the economy was at *A"*, with output above *Y"*, and the short term interest rate at *i"*.

Now turn to Figure 15–4. Point *A"* in Figure 15–4 corresponds to point *A"* in Figure 15–3(b) and describes where the economy was as of early 1993. Financial markets expected two things to happen over the following years:

- They expected consumer confidence and spending to keep increasing, shifting the *IS* curve farther to the right.
- They also anticipated that the Fed might worry about the pace of recovery becoming too strong, and shift to a more contractionary monetary policy, leading to an upward shift in the *LM* curve.

For both reasons, they expected short-term interest rates to be higher in the future, as the economy went from *A"* to a point such as *A"'*, with interest rate *i"'*. This is why the yield curve was upward sloping in early 1993: It signaled the belief of financial markets that either because of strong spending, or because of the reaction of the Fed to the recovery, interest rates were likely to start increasing soon.

With the benefit of hindsight, we can ask: Were financial markets right? The answer is no, they had the timing wrong. The recovery in 1993 was slower than they (and most economists) had anticipated, and there was no increase in short-term interest rates in 1993. In January 1994, the one-year rate was still 3.5%, contrary to the forecasts implicit in the yield curve of early 1993. However, what financial markets had predicted did happen one year later. From 1994 on, the recovery was stronger, leading the Fed to increase short-term interest rates, and leading to a higher and flatter yield curve.

FIGURE 15–4

The Expected Path of Recovery, as of Early 1993

In early 1993, financial markets expect both stronger demand and a tighter monetary policy to lead to higher short-term interest rates in the future.

ACTIVE GRAPH

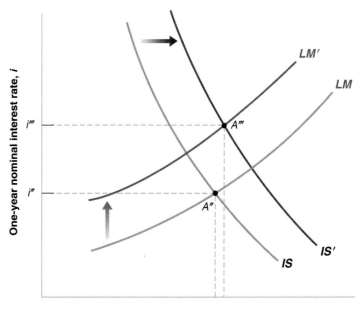

Our discussion suggests a more general proposition: When short-term interest rates move, whether down (as in the 1990 to 1991 recession) or up, long-term interest rates are likely to move in the same direction, but by less. They move by less because financial markets are likely to believe that part of the movement in short-term interest rates will not last. Figure 15–5 shows how well this proposition characterizes movements in U.S. short- and long-term interest rates.

Figure 15–5 plots quarterly changes in the three-month interest rate against changes in the 10-year interest rate, since 1960. Changes in the three-month interest rate are plotted on the horizontal axis; changes in the 10-year rate are plotted on the vertical axis. The figure has three main features:

- The long-term rate varies indeed less than the short-term interest rate. Quarterly changes in the short-term interest rate range from −4% to +5%. Quarterly changes in the long-term interest rate range only from −2.5% to +1.5%.
- Most of the points lie in the northeast and the southwest quadrants of the diagram: Most of the time, short- and long-term interest rates move in the same direction.
- Third, the typical response of movements in the long-term interest rate to movements in the short-term interest rate is positive but less than one for one. The diagram plots the regression line. The equation associated with this regression is

$$\Delta i_L = 0.00 + 0.42\Delta i_S$$

where i_L (L for long) denotes the 10-year rate and i_S (S for short) denotes the 3-month rate, and Δ denotes the change in a rate from one quarter to the next. This equation tells us that an increase in the short-term interest rate of 1% is typically associated with an increase in the long-term interest rate of only 0.42%.

To summarize:

- Arbitrage between bonds of different maturities implies that the price of a bond is the present value of the payments on the bond, discounted using current and expected one-year interest rates. Thus, higher current or expected one-year interest rates lead to lower bond prices.
- The yield to maturity on a bond with a maturity of n years (or equivalently, the n-year rate) is approximately equal to the average of current and expected future one-year interest rates.

Here are two examples: From January 1, 1980, to April 1, 1980, the three-month rate declined from 13.3% to 9.6% (a decrease of 3.7%); the 10-year rate went down from 12.0% to 10.5% (a decrease of only 1.5%).

From July 1, 1980, to October 1, 1980, the three-month rate increased from 9.1% to 13.6% (an increase of 4.5%); the 10-year rate increased from 10.9% to 12.4% (an increase of only 1.5%).

For more on why the short-term rate moved so much (both up and down) in 1980, go back to the discussion of disinflation in the United States in section 9-5.

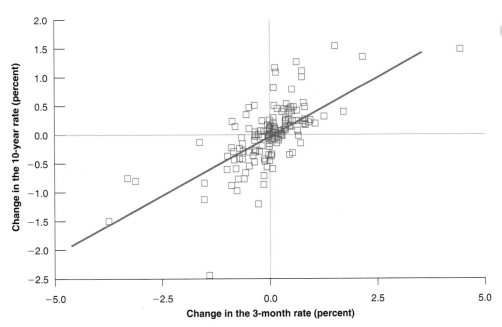

FIGURE 15–5

Quarterly Changes in the U.S. Three-Month and 10-Year Interest Rates, 1960–1998

Movements in the short-term interest rate are typically associated with smaller movements in the long-term interest rate in the same direction.

● The slope of the yield curve tells us what financial markets expect to happen to short-term rates in the future. A downward-sloping yield curve implies that the markets expect a decrease in short-term rates in the future; an upward-sloping yield curve implies that the markets expect an increase in short-term rates in the future.

15-2 | The Stock Market and Movements in Stock Prices

We have so far focused on bonds. But while the government finances itself primarily by issuing bonds, the same is not true of firms. Firms raise funds in two ways: through **debt finance**—bonds and loans; and through **equity finance**, through issues of **shares**—or **stocks**, as shares are also called. Instead of paying predetermined amounts as bonds do, stocks pay **dividends** in an amount decided by the firm. Dividends are paid from the firm's profits. They are typically less than profits, as firms retain some of their profits to finance their investment. But dividends move with profits: When profits increase, so do dividends.

Our focus in this section is on the determination of stock prices. As a way of introducing the issues, Figure 15–6 shows the behavior of an index of U.S. stock prices, the *Standard & Poor's 500 Composite Index* (or the S&P index, for short) from 1960 to 1998. Movements in the S&P index measure movements in the average stock price of 500 large companies. (Another and better-known index is the *Dow Jones Industrial Index*, an index of stocks of industrial firms only, and therefore less representative of the average price of stocks than the S&P index. Similar indexes exist for other countries. The *Nikkei Index* reflects movements in stock prices in Tokyo, and the *FT* and *CAC* indexes reflect stock-price movements in London and Paris, respectively.)

Figure 15–6 plots two lines. The purple line gives the evolution of the index as it was published in newspapers or flashed on the evening news. The index shows near constancy until 1980, and a rapid increase since. It rose from 120 in 1980 to more than 330 in 1990, and to 1190 in December 1998 (the value given in Figure 15–6 for 1998, 1085, is the average value for the year, which is lower than the December value).

This index, however, is nominal—that is, it gives the evolution of stock prices in terms of dollars. Of more interest to us is the evolution of the index in real terms (that is, adjusted for inflation). The evolution of that index, constructed by dividing the nominal index by the CPI for each year, is shown by the blue line in Figure 15–6. By construction, the CPI is equal to 1.0 in January 1980, so the nominal and real indexes are equal by construction in January 1980.

▶ The S&P index is defined so that its average value for the period 1941 to 1943 is equal to 10. (Do not ask why this particular normalization was chosen. No one seems to know.)

FIGURE 15–6

Standard and Poor's Index, in Nominal and Real Terms, 1960–1998

Nominal stock prices have increased more than 19-fold since 1960. Real stock prices have increased by a factor of only 3. Real stock prices went through a slump in the late 1960s and the 1970s. Only since then have they grown rapidly.

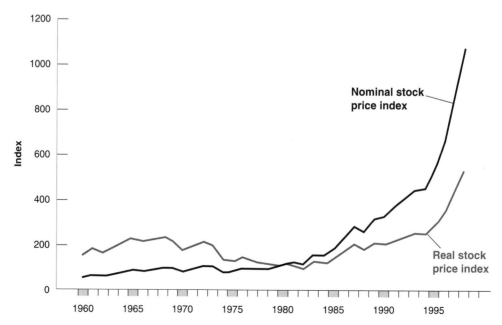

The plot of the real index shows a somewhat different picture. It shows how dismal the stock market's performance was in the late 1960s and 1970s. Roughly constant nominal stock prices and a steadily increasing price level implied steadily decreasing real stock prices. And although real stock prices have increased since about 1980, it took until 1992 for them to reach their level of the mid-1960s. Since then however, they have increased a lot more. In December 1998, the real index stood at 597, about 2.5 times its value of 240 in 1992 (the value given in Figure 15–6 for 1998 is the average value for the year, which is lower than the December value).

Why did the stock market do so badly for so long? Why did it rebound in the early 1980s? Why has it increased so much in the 1990s? More generally, how do stock prices respond to changes in the economic environment and in macroeconomic policy? This is the question we take up in the rest of this section.

Stock Prices as Present Values

What determines the price of a stock that promises a sequence of dividends in the future? By now, I am sure the material in chapter 14 has become second nature, and you already know the answer: The stock price must equal the present value of future expected dividends.

Let $\$Q_t$ be the price of the stock. Let $\$D_t$ denote the dividend this year, $\$D_{t+1}^e$ the dividend expected for next year, $\$D_{t+2}^e$ the dividend expected for two years from now, and so on.

Suppose we look at the price of the stock just after the dividend has been paid this year — this price is known as the *ex-dividend price* — so that the first dividend to be paid after the purchase of the stock is next year's dividend. (This is just a matter of convention; alternatively, we could look at the price before this year's dividend has been paid.) The price of the stock is then given by

$$\$Q_t = \frac{\$D_{t+1}^e}{1 + i_{1t}} + \frac{\$D_{t+2}^e}{(1 + i_{1t})(1 + i_{1t+1}^e)} + \cdots \tag{15.9}$$

The price of the stock is equal to the present value of the dividend next year, discounted using the current one-year interest rate, plus the present value of the dividend two years from now, discounted using both this year's one-year interest rate and next year's expected one-year interest rate, and so on.

As in the case of long-term bonds, the present value relation in equation (15.9) can be derived from arbitrage, from the assumption that the expected return per dollar from holding a stock for one year must be equal to the return from holding a one-year bond. The derivation is given in the appendix to this chapter. (Going through it will improve your understanding of the relation between arbitrage and present value, but it can be skipped without harm.)[3]

Equation (15.9) gives the stock price as the present value of *nominal* dividends, discounted by *nominal* interest rates. From chapter 14, we know we can rewrite it to get the *real* stock price as the present value of *real* dividends, discounted by *real* interest rates. So we can rewrite the real stock price as:

$$Q_t = \frac{D_{t+1}^e}{(1 + r_{1t})} + \frac{D_{t+2}^e}{(1 + r_{1t})(1 + r_{1t+1}^e)} + \cdots \tag{15.10}$$

[3]**DIGGING DEEPER**. Two complications: (1) The assumption we have maintained throughout this and the previous chapter that financial investors are risk neutral and require equal expected rates of returns on all assets is definitely not right here. Holding stocks for one year is much more risky than holding one-year bonds for one year, and historically financial investors have required a *risk premium*—a higher expected rate of return—for holding stocks relative to bonds. How to modify both the arbitrage equation and the present value formula to take account of a risk premium is discussed in the appendix. (2) That arbitrage implies that the price of a stock is the present value of dividends is true except in the presence of speculative bubbles, which we discuss in section 15-3.

The two equivalent ways
of writing the stock price:
The (nominal) stock price
equals the expected pre-
sent discounted value of
future nominal dividends,
discounted by current and
future nominal interest
rates. The (real) stock
price equals the expected
present discounted value
of future real dividends,
discounted by current and
future real interest rates.

Q_t and D_t, without a dollar sign, denote the real price and real dividends at time t. *The real stock price is the expected present value of future real dividends, discounted by the sequence of one-year real interest rates.*

This relation has two important implications. Higher expected future real dividends lead to a higher stock price. Higher current and expected future one-year real interest rates lead to a lower stock price. Let's now see what light this relation sheds on movements in the stock market.

The Stock Market and Economic Activity

Figure 15–6 showed the large movements in stock prices over the last 39 years. It is not unusual for the index to go up or down by 15% within a year. In 1974, the stock market went down by 30% (in real terms); in 1983, it went up by 30%. Daily movements of 2% or more also are not unusual. What causes these movements?

The first point to be made is that these movements are for the most part unpredictable. The reason is best understood by thinking in terms of the choice people have between stocks and bonds. If it were widely believed that, a year from now, the price of a stock was going to be 20% higher than today's price, holding the stock for a year would be unusually attractive, much more attractive than holding short-term bonds. There would be a very large demand for the stock. Its price would increase *today* to the point where the expected return from holding the stock was back in line with the expected return on other assets. In other words, the expectation of a high stock price next year would lead to a high stock price today.

You may have heard the
proposition that stock
prices follow a **random
walk**. This is a technical
term, but with a simple interpretation: Something—
it can be a molecule,
or the price of an asset—
follows a random walk if
each step it takes is as
likely to be up as it is to be
down. Its movements are
therefore unpredictable.

There is indeed a saying in economics that it is a sign of a well-functioning stock market that movements in stock prices are unpredictable. The saying is too extreme: A few financial investors may indeed have better information or simply be better at reading the future. If they are only a few, they may not buy enough of the stock to bid its price all the way up today. Thus, they may get large expected returns. But the basic idea is nevertheless right. The financial market gurus who regularly predict large imminent movements in the stock market over the next few months are quacks. Major movements in stock prices cannot be predicted.

If movements in the stock market cannot be predicted, if they are the result of news, where does this leave us? We can still do two things:

- We can do Monday-morning quarterbacking, looking back and identifying the news to which the market reacted.
- We can ask "what if" questions. For example, What would happen to the stock market if the Fed was going to embark on a more expansionary policy, or if consumers were to become more optimistic and increase spending?

Let us look at two "what if" questions. To do so, let us use the *IS-LM* model. To simplify things, let's assume, as we did earlier, that expected inflation equals zero, so that real and nominal interest rates are equal.

On September 30, 1998,
the Fed lowered the target
federal funds rate by
0.5%. This decrease was
expected by financial markets. The Dow Jones index
remained roughly un-
changed (actually, going
down 28 points for the
day).
    Less than a month
later, on October 15,
1998, the Fed lowered
the target federal funds
rate again, that time by
0.25%. In contrast to the
September cut, that move
by the Fed came as a
complete surprise to fi-
nancial markets. The Dow
Jones index increased by
330 points on that day, an
increase of more than 3%.

A Monetary Expansion and the Stock Market. Suppose the economy is in a recession (output is below its natural level) and the Fed decides to adopt a more expansionary monetary policy. The increase in money shifts the *LM* curve down in Figure 15–7. Equilibrium output moves from A to A'. How will the stock market react? The answer depends on what the stock market expected monetary policy to be before the Fed's move.

If the stock market fully anticipated the expansionary policy, then the stock market will not react: Neither its expectations of future dividends nor its expectations of future interest rates are affected by a move it had already anticipated. Thus, in equation (15.9) nothing changes, and stock prices will remain the same.

Suppose instead that the Fed's move is at least partly unexpected. In that case, stock prices will increase. There are two reasons for this. First, a more expansionary monetary policy implies lower interest rates for some time. Second, a more expansionary monetary policy also implies higher output for some time (until the economy returns to the natural level of output), and so higher dividends. As equation (15.9) tells us, both lower interest rates and higher dividends, current and expected, will lead to an increase in stock prices.

FIGURE 15-7

An Expansionary Monetary Policy and the Stock Market

A monetary expansion decreases the interest rate and increases output. What it does to the stock market depends on whether financial markets anticipated the monetary expansion.

ACTIVE GRAPH

An Increase in Consumer Spending and the Stock Market. Now consider an unexpected shift of the *IS* curve to the right, resulting, for example, from stronger-than-expected consumer spending. As a result of the shift, equilibrium output in Figure 15–8(a) increases from *A* to *B*. Will stock prices go up? One is tempted to say yes: A stronger economy means higher profits and higher dividends for some time. But this answer is incomplete, for at least two reasons.

First, it ignores the effect of higher activity on interest rates: The movement along the *LM* curve from *A* to *B* also implies an increase in interest rates. Higher interest rates decrease stock prices. Which of the two effects, higher profits or higher interest rates, dominates? The answer depends on the slope of the *LM* curve. As drawn in Figure 15–8(b), a very steep *LM* curve implies large increases in interest rates, small increases in output, and so a fall in stock prices. As drawn in Figure 15–8(c), a very flat *LM* curve leads to small increases in interest rates, large increases in output, and so an increase in stock prices.

Second, it ignores the effect of the shift in the *IS* curve on the Fed's behavior. In practice, this is the effect that financial investors often care about the most. When receiving the news of unexpectedly strong economic activity, the main question on Wall Street is: How will the Fed react?

FOCUS

Making (Some) Sense of (Apparent) Nonsense: Why the Stock Market Moved Yesterday, and Other Stories

Here are several quotes from *The Wall Street Journal* from May 1993 to July 1993. See whether you can make sense of them, using what you've just learned.

● May 1993. Good news on the economy leading to a decline in stock prices:

Stocks ended mixed after interest rates shot up amid signs that the employment picture is brightening. . . . The good economic news sparked a sell-off in bonds, which generally tend to weaken in the face of a pickup in business. Stocks also fell, pressured by the rise in interest rates.

● May 1993. Bad news on the economy leading to a decline in stock prices:

Nagging concerns about the economy's strength overshadowed another positive reading on inflation, dragging stock prices mostly lower.

● July 1993. Bad news on the economy leading to an increase in stock prices:

The Dow Jones Industrial Average climbed to within a point of a record as investors cast aside downbeat economic news and concentrated on a rally in bonds. . . . The rally came despite a series of disappointing developments yesterday morning. The Commerce Department estimated gross domestic product grew at an annual rate of 1.6% in the second quarter, short of the 2.2% pace analysts had largely forecast.

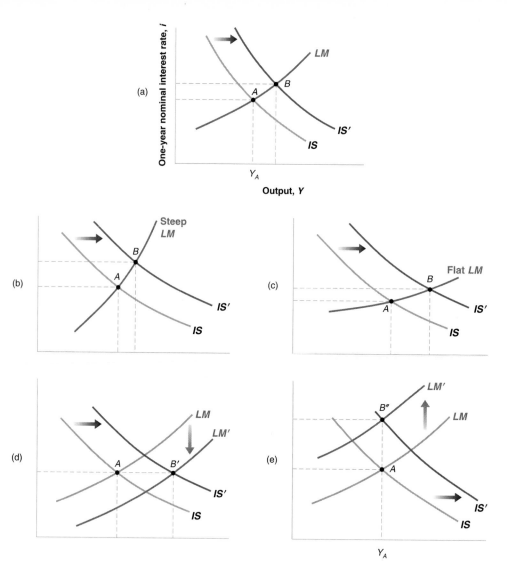

FIGURE 15–8

An Increase in Consumption Spending, and the Stock Market

(a) The increase in consumption spending leads to a higher interest rate and a higher level of output. What happens to the stock market depends on the slope of the *LM* curve and on the Fed's behavior. (b) Steep *LM* curve: The interest rate increases a lot, and output increases little. Stock prices go down. (c) Flat *LM* curve: The interest rate increases little, and output increases a lot. Stock prices go up. (d) The Fed accommodates: The interest rate does not increase, but output does. Stock prices go up. (e) The Fed decides to keep output constant: The interest rate increases, but output does not. Stock prices go down.

- Will the Fed **accommodate** the shift in the *IS* curve—that is, increase the money supply in line with money demand to avoid an increase in the interest rate? This case is shown in Figure 15–8(d). Accommodation corresponds to a downward shift of the *LM* curve, from *LM* to *LM'*. In this case, the economy will go from point *A* to point *B'*. Stock prices will increase: Output is expected to be higher, and interest rates are not expected to increase.
- Will the Fed instead keep the same monetary policy, leaving the *LM* curve unchanged? This is the case we saw in Figure 15–8(a), the economy will go from *A* to *B*. As we saw earlier, what happens to stock prices is ambiguous. The economy will have higher profits, but the interest rate will be higher as well.
- Or will the Fed worry that an increase in output above Y_A may lead to an increase in inflation? This will be the case if the economy is already close to the natural level of output, if Y_A is close to Y_n. This case is shown in Figure 15–8(e). In this case, a further increase in output would lead to an increase in inflation, something that the Fed wants to avoid. The Fed decides to counteract the rightward shift of the *IS* curve with a monetary contraction, an upward shift of the *LM* curve from *LM* to *LM'*, so that output does not change. In that case, stock prices will surely go down: There is no change in expected profits, but the interest rate is now likely to be higher for some time.

To summarize: Changes in output may or may not be associated with changes in stock prices in the same direction. Whether they are depends on (1) what the market expected in the first place, (2) the source of the shocks, and (3) how the market expects the central bank to react to the output change.

15-3 | Bubbles, Fads, and Stock Prices

Do all movements in stock prices come from news about future dividends or interest rates? Many economists doubt it. They point to times such as Black October in 1929, when the U.S. stock market fell by 23% in two days, or to October 19, 1987, when the Dow Jones index fell by 22.6% in a single day. They point to the amazing rise of Japanese stock prices in the 1980s, followed by a sharp fall in the 1990s. As we saw in chapter 1 (Figure 1–6), the Nikkei increased from around 13,000 in 1985 to around 35,000 in 1989, only to decline to around 16,000 in 1992. In each case, they point to the lack of obvious news, or at least news important enough to justify such enormous movements.

They argue that stock prices are not always equal to their **fundamental value**, defined as the present value of expected dividends given in equation (15.10), and that stocks are sometimes underpriced or overpriced. Overpricing eventually ends, sometimes with a crash as in October 1987, or with a long slide as has occurred in Japan.

Under what conditions can such mispricing occur? The surprising answer is that it can occur even when investors are rational, and when arbitrage holds. To see why, consider the case of a truly worthless stock (that is, a stock of a company that all financial investors know will never make profits and will never pay dividends). Putting D^e_{t+1}, D^e_{t+2}, and so on, equal to zero in equation (15.10) yields a simple and unsurprising answer: The fundamental value of such a stock is equal to zero.

Might you nevertheless be willing to pay a positive price for such a stock? Yes. You might if you expect the price at which you can sell the stock next year to be higher than this year's price. And the same applies to a buyer next year: She may be willing to buy at a high price if she expects to sell at an even higher price in the following year. This process suggests that stock prices may increase just because investors expect them to increase. Such movements in stock prices are called **rational speculative bubbles**. Financial investors may be behaving rationally as the bubble inflates. Even those investors who hold the stock at the time of the crash, and therefore sustain a large loss, may also have been rational. They may have realized there was a chance of a crash, but also a chance that the bubble would keep growing, and they could sell at an even higher price.

> In a speculative bubble, the price of a stock is higher than its fundamental value. Investors are willing to pay a high price for the stock, in anticipation of being able to resell the stock at an even higher price.

To make things simple, our example assumed the stock to be fundamentally worthless. But the argument is general and applies to stocks with a positive fundamental value as well. People might be willing to pay more than the fundamental value of a stock if they expect its price to increase more in the future. And the same argument applies to other assets, such as housing, gold, and paintings. Two such bubbles are described in the Global Macro box, "Famous Bubbles: From Tulipmania in Seventeenth-Century Holland to Russia in 1994".

Are all deviations from fundamental values in financial markets rational bubbles? Probably not. Many financial investors are not rational. An increase in stock prices in the past, say, due to a succession of good news, often creates excessive optimism. If investors simply extrapolate from past returns to predict future returns, a stock may become "hot" (high priced) for no reason other than the fact that its price has increased in the past. Such deviations of stock prices from their fundamental value are called **fads**. We are all aware of the existence of fads outside of the stock market; there are good reasons to believe that they exist in the stock market as well.

> In the context of the U.S. stock market, Alan Greenspan has called it "irrational exuberance."

How much of the movement in stock prices is due to movements in the fundamental value of stocks, and how much to fads and bubbles? At the time of this writing, the question is very much on the minds of many economists and financial investors. They are wondering whether the large increase in the U.S. stock market since the early 1990s is not, in part, a

Famous Bubbles: From Tulipmania in 17th-Century Holland to Russia in 1994

Tulipmania in Holland

In the seventeenth century, tulips became increasingly popular in western European gardens. A market developed in Holland for both rare and common forms of tulip bulbs.

The episode called the "tulip bubble" took place from 1634 to 1637. In 1634, the price of rare bulbs started increasing. The market went into a frenzy, with speculators buying tulip bulbs in anticipation of even higher prices later. The price of a bulb called "Admiral Van de Eyck," for example, increased from 1,500 guineas in 1634 to 7,500 guineas in 1637, the equivalent of the price of a house at the time. There are stories about a sailor mistakenly eating bulbs, only to realize the cost of his "meal" later. In early 1637, prices increased faster. Even the price of more common bulbs exploded, rising by a factor of up to 20 in January. But, in February 1637, prices collapsed. A few years later, bulbs were trading for roughly 10% of their value at the peak of the bubble.

The MMM Pyramid in Russia

In 1994 a Russian "financier," Sergei Mavrody, created a company called MMM and proceeded to sell shares, promising shareholders a rate of return of at least 3,000% per year!

The company was an instant success. The share price increased from 1,600 rubles (then $1) in February to 105,000 rubles ($51) in July. And by July, according to company claims, the number of shareholders had increased to 10 million.

The trouble was that the company was not involved in any type of production and held no assets, except for its 140 offices in Russia. The shares were intrinsically worthless. The company's initial success was based on a standard pyramid scheme: MMM used the funds from the sale of new shares to pay the promised returns on the old shares. Despite repeated warnings by government officials, including Boris Yeltsin, that MMM was a scam and that the increase in the price of shares was a bubble, the promised returns were just too attractive to many Russian people, especially in the midst of a deep economic recession.

The scheme could work only as long as the number of new shareholders—and thus new funds to be distributed to existing shareholders—increased fast enough. By the end of July 1994, the company could no longer make good on its promises and the scheme collapsed. The company closed. Mavrody tried to blackmail the government into paying the shareholders, claiming that not doing so would trigger a revolution or a civil war. The government refused, leading many shareholders to be angry at the government rather than at Mavrody. Later that year, Mavrody actually ran for Parliament, as a self-appointed defender of the shareholders who had lost their savings. He won!

Source: The account of "Tulipmania in Holland" is taken from Peter Garber, "Tulipmania," *Journal of Political Economy*, June 1989, 535–560.

Anthony Claesz (1592–1635), *Tulips, Lilies, Irises & Roses.* Around the time this painting was painted, some tulip bulbs in Holland were selling for the same price as a house.

bubble. The In Depth box "Is the U.S. Stock Market Overvalued?" looks at the evidence, and concludes that the current level of the stock market seems indeed high relative to fundamentals. The general question of what determines stock prices—fundamentals only, or also fads and bubbles—is an important question, not only for finance but also for macroeconomics. The stock market is more than just a sideshow: As we shall see in the next two chapters, not only are stock prices affected by economic activity, but they also affect it through their effect on both consumption and investment spending. Many economists believe the stock market crash of 1929 was one of the sources of the Great Depression. And, as we saw in chapter 7, the long and large decline of the Nikkei after what was probably in large part a speculative bubble in the 1980s is one of the causes of the slump in Japan since the early 1990s.

See chapter 22.

Is the U.S. Stock Market Overvalued?*

At the end of 1998, U.S. stock prices stood in real terms at nearly three times their 1990 level. This large increase has led a number of economists, financial investors, and policy makers to worry that the stock market might be overvalued, and that a large market correction (as large declines in stock prices are euphemistically called) may be in store.

That stock prices have increased in the 1990s is not by itself a puzzle. Since the 1990 to 1991 recession, the U.S. economy has undergone a long expansion, one lasting much longer than most economists and financial investors had anticipated. With the long expansion have come high profits and high dividends—higher than could have been expected in 1990. These higher-than-expected dividends should have led to higher-than-expected stock prices—and indeed they have!

The question is whether the strong performance of stock prices can be fully explained by the strong performance of dividends. The evidence here suggests that it cannot. If higher dividends fully accounted for higher prices, stock prices should have increased roughly in line with dividends. Put another way, the dividend-price ratio (also called the dividend yield) should have remained roughly constant. Figure 1 plots the evolution of the dividend-price ratio for the stocks in the S&P index since 1990. The message is clear: the dividend-price ratio has declined a lot, from 3.6% in 1990 to 1.4% in 1998—a historical low. Prices have increased much more than dividends.

That stock prices are high relative to current dividends does not prove the stock market is overvalued, for at least three reasons:

- High stock prices may reflect anticipations of much higher dividends in the future. Return to equation (15.10): The higher the future expected dividends, the higher the stock price, even given the current dividend.

- High stock prices may reflect a decrease in real interest rates since 1990. Again, return to equation (15.10): Given current and expected dividends, the lower current and future expected real interest rates, the higher the stock price.

- High stock prices may reflect a factor we have ignored in this chapter, a decrease in the risk premium associated with stocks relative to bonds. To the extent that investors perceive stocks as less risky than before, they may be willing to pay a higher price for stocks than before. (The appendix shows how a decrease in the risk premium leads to an increase in the stock price.)

Whether these factors together can explain the full increase in stock prices is the subject of much current research and is far from settled. In a recent article, John Campbell, from Harvard, and Robert Shiller, from Yale, have shown that based on historical evidence, there are good reasons to worry. Whenever the dividend-price ratio has been low in the past, stock prices have done poorly over the following 10 years, leading to a much lower return on holding stocks than holding bonds.

To reach this conclusion, Campbell and Shiller compute two variables for each year from 1927 to 1987: (1) the dividend-price ratio and (2) the rate of change of real stock prices over the following 10 years. They then plot the rate of change of real stock prices against the dividend-price ratio. The scatter plot they obtain is shown in Figure 2.

The plot clearly shows that historically a low dividend-price ratio has been followed by a poor performance of the stock market over the following 10 years. (For example, on the eve of the stock market crash of 1929, the dividend-price ratio was the lowest it had been in decades; the rate

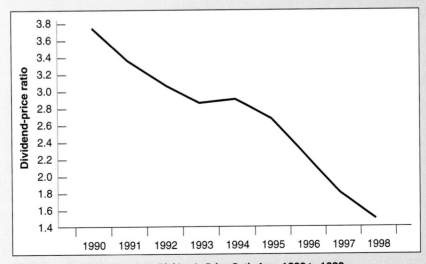

FIGURE 1   The Evolution of the Dividend–Price Ratio from 1990 to 1998

of return over the next 10 years, 1929 to 1938, was a dismal −46%.) The figure plots the regression line, the line that fits the scatter of points best. According to this line, a dividend-price ratio of 1.4% (the value of the ratio in 1998) is followed on average by a decrease in real stock prices of more than 50% over the following 10 years! The relation is not very tight and things well may be different this time; but it is a serious warning nevertheless.

Reference

John Campbell and Robert Shiller, "Valuation Ratios and the Long-Run Stock Market Outlook," *Journal of Portfolio Management*, Winter 1998, 11–26.

*This was written in mid-1999. As you read it and have the benefit of hindsight, see how it has stood the test of time.

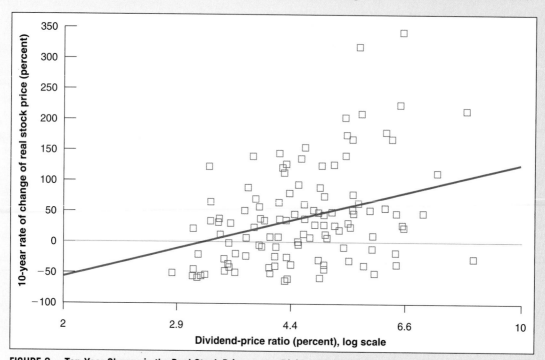

FIGURE 2   Ten-Year Change in the Real Stock Price versus Dividend Price Ratio, 1872–1987

SUMMARY

- Arbitrage between bonds of different maturities implies that the price of a bond is the present value of the payments on the bond, discounted using current and expected short-term interest rates. Hence, higher current or expected short-term interest rates lead to lower bond prices.

- The yield to maturity on a bond with a maturity of n years (or equivalently, the n-year interest rate) is approximately equal to the average of current and expected future one-year interest rates over this and the next $n − 1$ years.

- The slope of the yield curve (equivalently, the term structure) tells us what financial markets expect to happen to short-term interest rates in the future. A downward-sloping yield curve implies that the markets

expect a decrease in short-term rates; an upward-sloping yield curve implies that the markets expect an increase in short-term rates.

- The fundamental value of a stock is the present value of expected future real dividends, discounted using current and future expected one-year real interest rates. In the absence of bubbles or fads, the price of a stock is equal to its fundamental value.

- An increase in expected dividends leads to an increase in the fundamental value of stocks; an increase in current and expected one-year interest rates leads to a decrease in the fundamental value.

- Changes in output may or may not be associated with changes in stock prices in the same direction. Whether they are depends on (1) what the markets expected in the first place, (2) the source of the shocks, and (3) how the markets expect the central bank to react to the output change.

- Stock prices can be subject to bubbles or fads that lead a stock price to differ from its fundamental value. Bubbles are episodes when financial investors buy a stock for a price higher than its fundamental value in anticipation of reselling the stock at an even higher price. "Fad" is a general term for times when, for reasons of fashion or overoptimism, financial investors are willing to pay more than the fundamental value of the stock.

QUESTIONS & PROBLEMS

An asterisk denotes a harder problem.

1. TRUE/FALSE/UNCERTAIN

a. Junk bonds are bonds nobody wants to hold.

b. The price of a one-year bond decreases when the nominal one-year interest rate increases.

c. Given the Fisher hypothesis (see chapter 14), an upward-sloping yield curve may indicate that financial markets are worried about inflation in the future.

d. Long-term interest rates typically move more than short-term interest rates.

e. An equal increase in expected inflation and nominal interest rates at all maturities should have no effect on the stock market.

f. A monetary expansion will lead to an upward-sloping yield curve.

g. A rational investor should never pay a positive price for a stock that will never pay dividends.

h. The strong performance of the U.S. stock market of the 1990s reflects the strong performance of the U.S. economy.

2. THE YIELD TO MATURITY

Determine the yield to maturity of each of the following bonds:

a. A discount bond with a face value of $1,000, a maturity of three years, and a price of $800.

b. A discount bond with a face value of $1,000, a maturity of four years, and a price of $800.

c. A discount bond with a face value of $1,000, a maturity of four years, and a price of $850.

3. THE YIELD CURVE

Suppose that the interest rate this year is 5% and financial markets expect the interest rate to increase by 0.5% each year for the following three years. Determine the yield to maturity on a

a. one-year bond.

b. two-year bond.

c. three-year bond.

*4. THE EQUITY PREMIUM, DIVIDENDS, AND STOCK PRICES

A share is expected to pay a dividend of $1,000 next year, and the real value of dividend payments is expected to increase by 3% per year forever after. Determine the current price of the stock if the real interest rate is expected to remain constant at

a. 5%.

b. 8%.

Now suppose that people require a risk premium to hold stocks (as described in the appendix to this chapter).

c. Repeat (a) and (b) with the required risk premium at 8%.

d. Repeat (a) and (b) with the required risk premium at 4%.

e. What happens to stock prices if the risk premium decreases? Explain in words.

5. MACROECONOMICS AND STOCK PRICES

Using the *IS-LM* model, determine the impact of each of the following on stock prices. If the effect is ambiguous, explain what additional information would be needed to reach a conclusion.

a. An unexpected expansionary monetary policy with no change in fiscal policy.

b. A fully expected expansionary monetary policy with no change in fiscal policy.

c. A fully expected expansionary monetary policy with expansionary fiscal policy.

6. EXPANSIONARY MONETARY POLICY AND THE YIELD CURVE

In the previous chapter, we examined the effects of an increase in the growth rate of money on interest rates and inflation.

a. Draw the path of the nominal interest rate following an increase in growth rate of money.

Suppose that the lowest point in the path is reached after one year and that the long-run value is achieved after three years.

b. Draw the yield curve, just after the increase in the growth rate of money, one year later, three years later.

7. MOVEMENTS IN THE STOCK MARKET

Discuss the following cartoon:

Cartoon by Wasserman, The Boston Globe, *April 9, 1994; by permission of LA Times Syndicated.*

FURTHER READINGS

There are many bad books written about the stock market. A good one, and one that is fun to read is Burton Malkiel, *A Random Walk Down Wall Street*, 6th ed. (New York: Norton, 1995).

An account of historical bubbles is given by Peter Garber in "Famous First Bubbles," *Journal of Economic Perspectives*, Spring 1990, 35–54.

APPENDIX

ARBITRAGE AND STOCK PRICES

This appendix shows that, in the absence of rational speculative bubbles, arbitrage between stocks and bonds implies that the price of a stock is equal to the expected present value of dividends.

Suppose you face the choice of investing either in one-year bonds or in stocks for a year. What should you choose?

Suppose you decide to hold one-year bonds. Then, for every dollar you put in one-year bonds, you will get $(1 + i_{1t})$ dollars next year. This payoff is represented in the upper line of Figure 15A–1.

Suppose instead you decide to hold stocks for a year. This implies buying a stock today, receiving a dividend next year, and then selling the stock. As the price of a stock is $\$Q_t$, every dollar you put in stocks buys you $\$1/\$Q_t$ stocks. And for each stock you buy, you expect to receive $(\$D_{t+1}^e + \$Q_{t+1}^e)$, the sum of the expected dividend and the stock price next year. So, for every dollar you put in stocks, you expect to receive $(\$D_{t+1}^e + \$Q_{t+1}^e)/\$Q_t$ dollars next year. This payoff is represented in the lower line of Figure 15A–1.

Let's use the same arbitrage argument we used for bonds earlier. If financial investors care only about expected rates of return, then equilibrium requires that the expected rate of return from holding stocks for one year be the same as the rate of return on one-year bonds:

$$\frac{(\$D_{t+1}^e + \$Q_{t+1}^e)}{\$Q_t} = 1 + i_{1t}$$

Rewrite this equation as

$$\$Q_t = \frac{\$D_{t+1}^e}{(1 + i_{1t})} + \frac{\$Q_{t+1}^e}{(1 + i_{1t})} \tag{15A.1}$$

Arbitrage implies that the price of the stock today must be equal to the present value of the expected dividend plus the present value of the expected stock price next year.

The next step is to think about what determines $\$Q_{t+1}^e$, the expected stock price next year. Next year, financial investors will again face the choice between stocks and one-year bonds. Thus, the same arbitrage relation will hold. Writing the previous equation, but now for time $t + 1$, and taking expectations into account gives:

$$\$Q_{t+1}^e = \frac{\$D_{t+2}^e}{(1 + i_{1t+1}^e)} + \frac{\$Q_{t+2}^e}{(1 + i_{1t+1}^e)}$$

The expected price next year is simply the present value next year of the sum of the expected dividend and price two years from now. Replacing the expected price $\$Q_{t+1}^e$ in equation (15A.1) gives:

$$\$Q_t = \frac{\$D_{t+1}^e}{(1 + i_{1t})} + \frac{\$D_{t+2}^e}{(1 + i_{1t})(1 + i_{1t+1}^e)}$$

$$+ \frac{\$Q_{t+2}^e}{(1 + i_{1t})(1 + i_{1t+1}^e)}$$

The stock price is the present value of the expected dividend next year, plus the present value of the expected divi-

	Year *t*		Year *t* + 1
One-year bonds	$1	⟹	$1 $(1 + i_{1t})$
Stocks	$1	⟹	$1 $\dfrac{\$D_{t+1}^e + \$Q_{t+1}^e}{\$Q_t}$

dend two years from now, plus the expected price two years from now.

If we replace the expected price in two years as the present value of the expected price and dividends in three years, and so on for n years, we get

$$\$Q_t = \frac{\$D^e_{t+1}}{(1 + i_{1t})} + \cdots + \frac{\$D^e_{t+n}}{(1 + i_{1t}) \cdots (1 + i^e_{1t+n-1})}$$
$$+ \frac{\$Q^e_{t+n}}{(1 + i_{1t}) \cdots (1 + i^e_{1t+n-1})}$$

Look at the last term, which is the present value of the expected price in n years. As long as people do not expect the stock price to explode in the future, then, as we keep replacing Q^e_{t+n}, and n increases, this term will go to zero. To see why, suppose the interest rate is constant and equal to i, and people expect the price of the stock to converge to some value, call it $\$\overline{Q}$ in the far future. Then, the last term becomes $\$\overline{Q}/(1 + i)^n$. If the interest rate is positive, the term goes to zero as n becomes large.* The previous expression reduces to equation (15.9) in the text: The price today is the present value of expected future dividends.

An Extension to the Present Value Formula to Take Risk into Account

If people perceive stocks as more risky than bonds, and people dislike risk, they will require a risk premium to hold stocks rather than bonds. In the case of shares, this risk premium is called the **equity premium**. Denote it by θ (the Greek lowercase letter theta). If θ is, for example, 5%, then people will hold stocks only if the expected rate of return on stocks exceeds the expected rate of return on short-term bonds by 5% a year.

In that case, the arbitrage equation between stocks and bonds becomes

$$\frac{\$D^e_{t+1} + \$Q^e_{t+1}}{\$Q_t} = 1 + i_{1t} + \theta$$

The only change is the presence of θ on the right side of the equation. Going through the same steps as above, the stock price equals

$$\$Q_t = \frac{\$D^e_{t+1}}{(1 + i_{1t} + \theta)} + \cdots$$
$$+ \frac{\$D^e_{t+n}}{(1 + i_{1t} + \theta) \cdots (1 + i^e_{1t+n-1} + \theta)} + \cdots$$

The stock price is still equal to the present value of expected future dividends. But the discount rate here equals the interest rate plus the equity premium. Note that the higher the premium, the lower the stock price. Over the last 100 years in the United States the average equity premium has been equal to roughly 5%. But (in contrast to our assumption above) it is not constant. The equity premium appears, for example, to have decreased since the early 1950s, from around 7% to less than 3% today. Variations in the equity premium are another source of fluctuations in stock prices.

---

*DIGGING DEEPER. When prices are subject to rational bubbles as discussed in section 15-3, the condition that the expected stock price does not explode is not satisfied. When there are bubbles, the stock price need not be equal to the present value of expected dividends.

KEY TERMS

- equity premium, 308

We invite you to visit the Blanchard page on the Prentice Hall Web site at:

http://www.prenhall.com/blanchard

for this chapter's World Wide Web exercises

CHAPTER 16

Expectations, Consumption, and Investment

Having looked at the role of expectations in financial markets, we now turn to their role in determining the two main components of spending—consumption and investment. This description of consumption and investment will be the main building block of the expanded *IS-LM* model we shall develop in chapter 17.

Section 16-1 looks at consumption, and shows how consumption decisions depend not only on current income but also on expected future income as well as on financial wealth. Section 16-2 turns to investment and shows how investment decisions depend on current and expected profits and current and expected interest rates. Finally, section 16-3 looks at the movements of consumption and investment over time and shows how we can interpret them in the light of the theories developed in this chapter.

16-1 | Consumption

How do people decide how much to consume and how much to save? In our first pass at the answer in the core (chapter 3), we made the simple assumption that consumption and saving depended on current income. By now, you do not need to be convinced that they depend on much more, particularly on expectations of the future. We now explore how those expectations affect the consumption decision.

The theory of consumption on which this section is based was developed independently in the 1950s by Milton Friedman of the University of Chicago, who called it the **permanent income theory of consumption**, and by Franco Modigliani, of MIT, who called it the **life cycle theory of consumption**. Each chose his label carefully. Friedman's "permanent income" emphasized that consumers look beyond current income. Modigliani's "life cycle" emphasized that consumers' natural planning horizon is their entire lifetime.

> Friedman received the Nobel prize in economics in 1976; Modigliani in 1985.

The behavior of aggregate consumption has remained a hot area of research ever since, for two reasons. The first is simply the sheer size of consumption in GDP, and therefore the need to understand movements in consumption. The second is the increasing availability of large surveys of individual consumers, such as the Panel Study of Income Dynamics described in the Focus box "Up Close and Personal: Learning from Panel Data Sets." These surveys, which were not available when Friedman and Modigliani developed their theories, have allowed economists to steadily improve their understanding of how consumers actually behave. What follows summarizes what we know today.

The Very Foresighted Consumer

> With a slight abuse of language, I shall use "housing wealth" to refer not only to housing but also to the other goods that the consumer may own, from cars to paintings and so on.

Let's start with an assumption that will surely—and rightly—strike you as extreme, but will serve as a convenient benchmark. We'll call it the theory of the *very foresighted consumer*. How would a very foresighted consumer decide how much to consume? He would proceed in two steps.

- First, he would add up the value of the stocks and bonds he owns, the value of his checking and savings accounts, the value of the house he owns minus the mortgage still due, and so on. This would give him a notion of his **financial wealth** and his **housing wealth**.

Up Close and Personal: Learning from Panel Data Sets

Panel data sets are data sets that give the value of one or more variables for many individuals or many firms over time. I described one such survey, the *Current Population Survey* (or CPS), in chapter 6. Another is the Panel Study of Income Dynamics, or PSID.

The PSID was started in 1968, with approximately 4,800 families. Interviews of these families have been conducted every year since, and are still continuing. The survey has grown as new individuals have joined the original families, either by marriage or by birth. Each year, the survey asks people about their income, wage rate, number of hours worked, health, and food consumption. (The focus on food consumption is because one of the survey's initial aims was to better understand the living conditions of poor families. The survey would be more useful if it asked about all of consumption rather than food consumption. Unfortunately, it does not.)

By giving 30 years of information about individuals and about extended families, the survey has allowed economists

to ask and answer questions for which there was previously only anecdotal evidence. Among the many questions for which the PSID has been used in the recent past are the following:

- How much does (food) consumption respond to transitory movements in income? For example, to the loss of income from becoming unemployed?

- How much risk-sharing is there within families? For example, when a family member becomes sick or unemployed, how much help does he or she get from other family members?

- How much do people care about staying geographically close to their families? When somebody becomes unemployed, for example, how does the probability that he will migrate to another city depend on how many family members live in the city in which he currently lives?

He would also estimate what his after-tax labor income was likely to be over his working life, and compute the present value of expected after-tax labor income. This would give him an estimate of what economists call his **human wealth**—to contrast it with his **nonhuman wealth**, defined as the sum of financial and housing wealth.

- Adding his human and nonhuman wealth, he would have an estimate of his **total wealth**. He would then decide how much to spend out of this total wealth. A reasonable assumption is that he would decide to spend a proportion of total wealth such as to maintain roughly the same level of consumption each year throughout his life. If that level of consumption was higher than his current income, he would then borrow the difference. If it was lower than his current income, he would instead save the difference.

Human wealth (= Present value of expected after-tax labor income) + Nonhuman wealth (= Housing wealth + Financial wealth) = Total wealth

Let's write this formally. What we have described is a consumption decision of the form

$$C_t = C(\text{total wealth}_t) \tag{16.1}$$

where C_t is consumption, and (total wealth)$_t$ is the sum of nonhuman wealth (financial plus housing wealth) and human wealth (the expected present value of after-tax labor income).

This description contains much truth: Like the foresighted consumer, we surely do think about our wealth and our expected future labor income in deciding how much to consume today. But one cannot help thinking that it assumes too much computation and foresight on the part of the typical consumer.

To get a better sense of what the description implies and what is wrong with it, let's apply this decision process to the problem facing a typical U.S. college student.

Because each of us is a consumer, we can use introspection as a way of checking on the plausibility of a particular theory. Alas, introspection is not without potential pitfalls: Economists perhaps do not think like other people. . . .

An Example

Let's assume you are 21 years old, with three more years of college before you take your first job. Some of you may be in debt today, having borrowed to go to college; some of you may own a car and a few other worldly possessions. For simplicity, let's assume your debt and your possessions roughly offset each other, so that your nonhuman wealth is equal to zero. Your only wealth is your human wealth, the present value of your expected after-tax labor income.

You are welcome to use your own numbers, and see where the computation takes you.

Based on what we know today, you can expect your starting salary in three years to be around $40,000 (in year 2000 dollars) and to increase by an average of 3% a year in real terms, until your retirement at age 60. About 25% of your income will go to taxes.

Building on what we saw in chapter 14, let's compute the present value of your labor income as the value of *real* expected after-tax labor income, discounted using *real* interest rates (equation [14.7]). Let Y_{Lt} denote real labor income in year t. Let T_t denote real taxes (net of transfers). Let $V(Y_{Lt}^e - T_t^e)$ denote your human wealth, that is, the expected present value of your after-tax labor income. To make the computation simple, assume the real interest rate equals zero—so the expected present value is simply the sum of expected after-tax labor income over your working life and is therefore given by

$$V(Y_{Lt}^e - T_t^e) = 0.75[1 + (1.03) + (1.03)^2 + \cdots + (1.03)^{36}](\$40,000)$$

The first term (0.75) comes from the fact that because of taxes you keep only 75% of what you earn. The second term $[1 + (1.03) + (1.03)^2 + \cdots + (1.03)^{36}]$ reflects the fact that you expect your real income to increase by 3% a year for 37 years (you will start earning income at age 24, and work until age 60). The third term ($40,000) is the initial level of labor income, in year 2000 dollars. Using the properties of geometric series to solve for the sum in brackets gives

$$V(Y_{Lt}^e - T_t^e) = 0.75(66.2)(\$40,000) = \$1,986,000$$

Your wealth today, the expected value of your lifetime after-tax labor income, is around $2 million.

How much should you consume? You can expect to live about 16 years after retirement, so your expected remaining life today is 56 years. If you want to consume the same amount every year, the constant level of consumption that you can afford equals your total wealth divided by your expected remaining life, or $1,986,000/56 = $35,464 a year. Given that your

The computation of what consumption level you can sustain is made easier by our assumption that the real interest rate equals zero. In this case, if you consume one fewer good today, you can consume exactly one more good next year, and the condition you must satisfy is simply that the sum of consumption over your lifetime is equal to your wealth. If you want to consume a constant amount each year, then, to find how much you can consume each year you need to divide your wealth by the remaining number of years in your life.

income until you get your first job is equal to zero, this implies borrowing $35,464 a year for the next three years, and starting to save when you get your first job.

Toward a More Realistic Description

Your first reaction to this computation may be that this is a stark and slightly sinister way of summarizing your life prospects. Your second reaction may be that while you agree with most of the ingredients that went into the computation, you surely do not intend to borrow $35,464 \times 3 = $106,392 over the next three years.

1. You may not want to plan for constant consumption over your lifetime and may be quite happy with deferring higher consumption until later. Student life usually does not leave much time for expensive activities. You may want to defer memberships in golf clubs and trips to the Galapágos islands to later in life. You also have to think about the additional expenses that will come with having children, sending them to nursery school, summer camp, college, and so on.

How Much Do Expectations Matter? Looking for Natural Experiments

How much does consumption depend on current income versus expected future income? This is not an easy question to answer because, most of the time, expectations of future income move very much with current income. If we get promoted and receive a raise, not only does our current income go up, but typically so does the income we can expect to receive in future years. Whether or not we are very foresighted, our consumption will typically move closely with our current income.

What can economists do to disentangle the effects of current versus future income? They must look for times and events where current income and expected future income move in different ways, and then look at what happens to consumption. Such events are called **natural experiments**. "Experiments" in the sense that like laboratory experiments, these events allow us to test a theory or to get a better estimate of an important parameter. "Natural" meaning that, unlike researchers in the physical sciences, economists typically cannot run experiments themselves. They must rely on experiments given by nature—or, as we shall see in our second example below, created by policy makers.

Here are two examples from recent research on consumption:

(1) Retirement

Retirement implies a large, predictable change in labor income: Labor income drops to zero. By looking at how people save for retirement, we can in principle find out whether, when, and by how much people take into account the predictable decline in their future labor income.

A recent study, based on a panel data set called the *Survey of Income and Program Participation*, sheds some light on retirement behavior. Table 1, taken from the study, shows the mean level and the composition of total wealth for people between 65 and 69 years in 1991.

A mean wealth of $313,807 is substantial (U.S. per capita personal disposable income was $16,205 in 1991), suggesting an image of forward-looking individuals making careful saving decisions and retiring with enough wealth to enjoy a comfortable retirement.

A closer look at the table, and at differences between individuals, suggests two caveats.

- The largest component of wealth is the present value of Social Security benefits, an amount over which workers have no control. Indeed, one of the main motivations behind the introduction of the Social Security program in the United States was to make sure people contributed to their retirement, whether or not they would have done so on their own. The third largest component is an employer-provided pension—another component over which workers have limited control. The only components that clearly reflect individual saving decisions (personal retirement assets + other financial assets) account only for $53,010, or about 17% of total wealth. Thus, one also can read the evidence as suggesting that people save enough for retirement because they are forced to, through social security and other contributions.

- The numbers in the table are averages and hide substantial differences across individuals. The same study shows that most people retire with little more than their Social Security pensions. More generally, studies of retirement saving give the following picture: Most people appear to give little thought to retirement saving until some time during their 40s. At that point, many start saving for retirement. But many also save little and rely mostly on Social Security benefits when they retire.

(2) Announced Tax Cuts

In 1981 the Reagan administration designed a fiscal package with phased-in tax cuts over 1981 to 1983. Income tax rates were to be reduced in three steps: 5% in 1981, 10% in 1982, and 8% in 1983, implying a cumulative reduction of 23%, a very large amount indeed. Congress passed the package in July 1981 and it became law in August 1981.

This period of U.S. history provides us with a natural experiment. The experiment is a change in expected future after-tax labor income coming from an anticipated decrease in taxes. And the question we want to answer is simple: Did consumers react in 1981 to the expected decrease in taxes in 1982 and 1983, and if so, by how much?

This is exactly the question asked by James Poterba, from MIT, in a 1988 article. Using econometrics, Poterba looked for evidence of an unusual increase in consumption, given disposable income, in the summer of 1981 (the time when Congress passed the package). He found no evidence of such an increase.

Is this conclusive evidence that consumers do not take into account changes in expected future income in their consumption decision? Not necessarily. There are at least two alternative interpretations of the facts. People may have believed that Congress would change its mind, leading them to take a wait-and-see attitude and wait for the actual decreases in taxes to adjust their consumption. Or maybe people do not take into account expected changes in taxes, but take into account other expected changes in their income (say, an expected promotion or the coming of retirement). These arguments cannot be dismissed. But what can be safely said is that the evidence from that particular natural experiment does not provide evidence for a strong effect of expected future tax changes on consumption.

References

On retirement: Steven Venti and David Wise, "The Wealth of Cohorts: Retirement and Saving and the Changing Assets of Older Americans," mimeo, Kennedy School, Harvard University, October 1993.

On the Reagan tax cuts: James Poterba, "Are Consumers Forward Looking? Evidence from Fiscal Experiments," *American Economic Review*, May 1988, 413–418.

TABLE 1	Mean wealth of people, age 65–69, in 1991 (in current dollars)
Social Security pension	$ 99,682
Employer-provided pension	62,305
Personal retirement assets	10,992
Other financial assets	42,018
Home equity	64,955
Other equity	33,855
Total	$313,807

Source: Venti and Wise, Table A1. (The first two items are expected present values of future payments.)

2. You may find that the amount of computation and foresight involved in the computation we just went through far exceeds the amount you use in your own decisions. You may never have thought until now about exactly how much income you are going to make, and for how many years. You may feel that most consumption decisions are made in a simpler, less forward-looking fashion.

3. The computation of total wealth is based on forecasts of what can reasonably be expected to happen. But things can turn out better or worse. What happens if you are unlucky, and you become unemployed or sick? How will you pay back what you borrowed? You may well want to be prudent, making sure that you can adequately survive even the worst outcomes, and thus borrow much less than $106,392.

4. Even if you decided to borrow $106,392, you are likely to find the bank from which you try to borrow that amount to be unreceptive. Why? The bank may worry that you are taking on a commitment you will not be able to afford if times turn bad, and that you may not be able or willing to repay the loan.

These reasons, all good ones, imply that to characterize consumers' actual behavior, we must modify the description we gave earlier. The last three reasons in particular suggest consumption depends not only on total wealth but also on current income.

Take the second reason. You may, because it is a simple rule, decide to let your consumption follow your income and not think about what your wealth might be. In that case, consumption will depend on current income, not on your wealth. Now take the third reason. It implies that a safe rule may be to consume no more than your current income. This way, you do not run the risk of accumulating debt that you could not repay if times were to turn bad. Or take the fourth reason. It implies that you may have little choice anyway. Even if you wanted to consume more than your current income, you may be unable to do so, because no bank will make you a loan.

If we want to allow for a direct effect of current income on consumption, what measure of current income should we use? A convenient variable is after-tax labor income, introduced earlier when defining human wealth. This leads to a consumption function of the form

$$C_t = C(\text{Total wealth}_t, Y_{Lt} - T_t) \qquad (16.2)$$
$$(\quad + \quad, \quad + \quad)$$

The plus sign under "Total wealth" indicates that an increase in total wealth increases consumption. The same holds for $Y_{Lt} - T_t$.

In words: *Consumption is an increasing function of total wealth and of current after-tax labor income. Total wealth is the sum of nonhuman wealth—financial wealth plus housing wealth—and of human wealth—the present value of expected after-tax labor income.*

The practical issue then becomes how much consumption depends on total wealth (and thus on expectations of future income) and how much on current income. Some consumers, especially those who have temporarily low income and poor access to credit, are likely to consume their current income, regardless of what they expect will happen to them in the future. A worker who becomes unemployed and has no financial wealth may have a hard time borrowing to maintain her level of consumption, even if she is fairly confident that she will soon find another job. Consumers who are richer and have easier access to credit are more likely to give more weight to the expected future and to try to maintain roughly constant consumption through time.

The relative importance of wealth and income on consumption can be settled only by looking at the empirical evidence. This is not easy to do, and the In Depth box "How Much Do Expectations Matter? Looking for Natural Experiments" explains why. But even if some details still need to be filled in, the basic evidence is clear and unsurprising: Both total wealth and current income affect consumption.

Putting Things Together: Current Income, Expectations, and Consumption

Let's go back to what motivates this chapter, the importance of expectations in the determination of spending. Note first that with consumption behavior described by equation (16.2), expectations affect consumption in two ways:

They affect it directly through human wealth: To compute their human wealth, consumers have to form their own expectations of future labor income, real interest rates, and taxes.

They affect it indirectly, through nonhuman wealth—stocks, bonds, housing. Consumers do not need to do any computation here, and can take the value of these assets as given. But as we saw in chapter 15, the computation is in effect done for them by financial markets. The price of their stocks, for example, depends itself on expectations of future dividends and interest rates.

This dependence of consumption on expectations has in turn two main implications.

First, *consumption is likely to respond less than one for one to fluctuations in current income.* In thinking about how much they should consume, consumers look at more than current income. If they conclude that a decrease in income is permanent, they may decrease consumption one for one with the decrease in income. But if they conclude that the decrease in current income is transitory, they will adjust their consumption by less. In a recession, consumption adjusts less than one for one to decreases in income. This is because consumers know that recessions typically do not last for more than a few quarters, and that the economy will eventually return to its natural output level. The same is true during expansions. Faced with an un-

How expectations of higher output in the future affect consumption today:

Future output ↑ ⇒
Future labor income ↑ ⇒
Human wealth ↑ ⇒
Consumption today ↑

Future output ↑ ⇒
Future dividends ↑ ⇒
Stock prices ↑ ⇒
Non human wealth ↑ ⇒
Consumption today ↑

Go back to the two consumption functions we used in the core:

Looking at the short run (chapter 3), we assumed $C = c_0 + c_1 Y$. (Ignore taxes for simplicity here.) This implied that when output increased, consumption increased less than proportionately (C/Y goes down). This was appropriate, as our focus was on output fluctuations, on transitory movements in output.

Looking at the long run (chapter 10), we assumed $S = sY$, or, equivalently, $C = (1 - s)Y$. This implied that, when output increases, consumption increases proportionately (C/Y is constant). This was appropriate, as our focus was on permanent—long run—movements in output.

usually rapid increase in income, consumers are unlikely to increase consumption by as much. They are likely to assume that the boom is transitory, and that things will return to normal.

What does this suggest happens to the saving rate in a recession?

Second, *consumption may move even if current income does not change.* The election of a charismatic president who articulates the vision of an exciting future may lead people to become more optimistic about the future in general, and about their own future income in particular, leading them to increase consumption even if their current income does not change. We saw in chapter 3 that the U.S. recession of 1990–1991 was caused in large part by a large decrease in consumption, caused in turn by a large decrease in consumer confidence. Even today, economists are not sure why people became suddenly so pessimistic. But they did, and their expectations of the future turned somber. Consumer pessimism was one of the main causes of the 1990–1991 recession.

16-2 | Investment

How do firms make investment decisions? In our first pass at the answer in the core (chapter 5), we took investment to depend on the current interest rate and the current level of sales. We improved on that answer in chapter 14 by pointing out that what mattered was the real interest rate, not the nominal interest rate. It is clear that these answers underplayed the role of expectations. We shall now look at their role more closely.

Think of the decision by a firm whether to buy a new machine. What will matter is the present value of profits the firm expects from having this machine, compared to the cost of buying the machine. If the present value exceeds the cost, the firm should buy the machine, that is, invest; if the present value is less than the cost, then the firm should not buy the machine, that is, not invest. This, in a nutshell, is the theory of investment. Let's look at it in more detail.

Investment and Expectations of Profit

Let's go through the steps a firm must take to determine whether to buy a new machine. (Although I refer to a machine, the same reasoning applies to the other components of investment, the building of a new factory, the renovation of an office complex, and so on.)

(1) To compute the present value of expected profits, the firm first must estimate how long the machine will last. Most machines are like cars. They can last nearly forever; but as time passes they become more and more expensive to maintain and less and less reliable.

Let's assume a machine loses its usefulness at rate δ (the Greek lowercase letter delta) per year. A machine that is new this year is worth only $(1 - \delta)$ machines next year, $(1 - \delta)^2$ machines in two years, and so on. The *depreciation rate*, δ, measures how much usefulness the machine loses from one year to the next. What are reasonable values for δ? This is a question that the statisticians in charge of computing how the U.S. capital stock changes over time have had to answer. Based on their studies of depreciation of specific machines and buildings, they use numbers between 4% and 15% per year for machines, and between 2% and 4% per year for buildings and factories.

If the firm has a large number of machines, we can think of δ as the proportion of machines that die every year. If the firm starts the year with K working machines and does not buy new ones, it has only $K(1 - \delta)$ machines left one year later, and so on.

(2) The firm must then compute the present value of expected profits. To capture the fact that it takes some time to put machines in place (and even more time to build a factory or an office building), let's assume that a machine bought in year t becomes operational—and starts depreciating—only one year later, in year $t + 1$.

Denote profit per machine in real terms by Π (this is an uppercase pi as opposed to the lowercase pi, which we use to denote inflation). If the firm purchases a machine in year t, the machine generates its first expected profit in year $t + 1$; denote this expected profit by Π^e_{t+1}. The present value, in year t, of this expected profit in year $t + 1$, is given by

$$\frac{1}{1 + r_t} \Pi^e_{t+1}$$

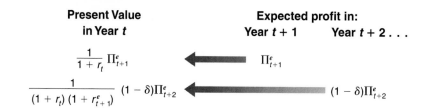

Present Value in Year t	Expected profit in:	
	Year $t + 1$	Year $t + 2$ . . .
$\dfrac{1}{1 + r_t}\Pi^e_{t+1}$	Π^e_{t+1}	
$\dfrac{1}{(1 + r_t)(1 + r^e_{t+1})}(1 - \delta)\Pi^e_{t+2}$		$(1 - \delta)\Pi^e_{t+2}$

FIGURE 16–1

Computing the Present Value of Expected Profits

This computation is represented by the arrow pointing left in the upper line of Figure 16–1. Because we are measuring profit in real terms, we are using real interest rates to discount future profits. This is one of the lessons we learned in chapter 14.

Denote expected profit per machine in year $t + 2$ by Π^e_{t+2}. Because of depreciation, only $(1 - \delta)$ of the machine bought in year t is left in year $t + 2$, so the expected profit from the machine is equal to $(1 - \delta)\Pi^e_{t+2}$. The present value of this expected profit as of year t is equal to

$$\frac{1}{(1 + r_t)(1 + r^e_{t+1})}(1 - \delta)\Pi^e_{t+2}$$

This computation is represented by the arrow pointing left in the lower line of Figure 16–1.

The same reasoning applies to expected profit in following years. Putting the pieces together gives us *the present value of expected profits* from buying the machine in year t, call it $V(\Pi_t^e)$

$$V(\Pi_t^e) = \frac{1}{1 + r_t}\Pi^e_{t+1} + \frac{1}{(1 + r_t)(1 + r^e_{t+1})}(1 - \delta)\Pi^e_{t+2} + \cdots \tag{16.3}$$

The expected present value is equal to the discounted value of expected profit next year, plus the discounted value of expected profit two years from now (taking into account the depreciation of the machine), and so on.

(3) The firm must then decide whether to buy the machine. This decision depends on the relation between the present value of expected profits and the price of the machine. To simplify notation, let's assume that the real price of a machine—that is, the machine's price in terms of the basket of goods produced in the economy—equals 1. What the firm must then do is compare the present value of profits to one.

If the present value is less than 1, the firm should not buy the machine: If it did, it would be paying more for the machine than it expects to get back in profits later. If the present value exceeds 1, the firm has an incentive to buy the new machine.

Let's now jump from this one-firm, one-machine example to investment in the economy as a whole. Let I_t denote aggregate investment. Denote profit per machine, or more generally profit per unit of capital (where capital includes machines, factories, office buildings, and so on), for the economy as a whole by Π_t. Denote the expected present value of profit per unit of capital by $V(\Pi_t^e)$, defined as in equation (16.3). Our discussion suggests an investment function of the form

$$I_t = I(V(\Pi_t^e)) \tag{16.4}$$
$$(\ + \ )$$

In words: Investment depends positively on the expected present value of future profits (per unit of capital). The higher current or expected profits, the higher the expected present value and the higher the level of investment. The higher current or expected real interest rates, the lower the expected present value, and thus the lower the level of investment.

If the present value computation the firm has to make strikes you as quite similar to the present value computation we saw in chapter 15 for the fundamental value of a stock, you are right. This relation was first explored by James Tobin, from Yale University, who argued that there indeed should be a tight relation between investment and the value of the stock market. His argument and the evidence are presented in the Focus box "Investment and the Stock Market."

Tobin received the Nobel prize in economics in 1981.

Investment and the Stock Market

Suppose a firm has 100 machines and 100 shares outstanding—one share per machine. Suppose the price per share is $2, and the purchase price of a machine is only $1. Obviously the firm should invest—buy a new machine and finance it by issuing a share. Each machine costs the firm $1 to purchase, but stock market participants are willing to pay $2 for a share corresponding to this machine when it is installed in the firm.

This is an example of a more general argument made by James Tobin: There should be a tight relation between the stock market and investment. In deciding whether to invest, he argued, firms may not need to follow a complicated computation such as we saw in the text. In effect, the stock price tells firms how much the stock market values each unit of capital already in place. The firm then has a simple problem: Compare the purchase price of an additional unit of capital to the price the stock market is willing to pay for it. If the stock market value exceeds the purchase price, the firm should buy the machine; otherwise, it should not.

Tobin then constructed a variable corresponding to the value of a unit of capital in place relative to its purchase price, and looked at how closely it moved with investment. He used the letter "q" to denote the variable, and the variable has become known as **Tobin's q**. Its construction is as follows:

(1) Take the total value of U.S. corporations, as assessed by financial markets. That is, compute the sum of their stock market value (the price of a share times the number of shares). Also compute the total value of their bonds outstanding (firms finance themselves not only through stocks but also through bonds). Add together the value of stocks and bonds.

(2) Divide this total value by the value of the capital stock of U.S. corporations at replacement cost (the price firms would have to pay to replace their machines, their plants, and so on).

The ratio gives us in effect the value of a unit of capital in place relative to its current purchase price. This ratio is Tobin's q. Intuitively, the higher q, the higher the value of capital relative to its current purchase price, and the higher should be investment. (In the example at the start of this box, Tobin's q is equal to 2; the firm should definitely invest.)

How tight is the relation between Tobin's q and investment? The answer is given in Figure 1, which plots the two variables for each year from 1947 to 1990 for the United States.

Measured on the left vertical axis is the rate of change of the ratio of investment to capital. Measured on the right vertical axis is the rate of change of Tobin's q. This variable is lagged once. For 1987, for example, the figure shows the rate of change of investment to capital for 1987, and the rate of change of Tobin's q for 1986—that is, a year earlier. The reason for presenting the two variables this way is that the strongest relation in the data is between investment *this* year and Tobin's q *last* year. Put another way, movements in investment are more closely associated with movements in the stock market last year rather than this year; this may be because it takes time for firms to make investment decisions, build new factories, and so on.

The message from the figure is clear: There is a strong relation between Tobin's q and investment. This is probably not because firms follow blindly the signals from the stock market, but because investment decisions and stock market prices depend very much on the same factors—future expected profits and future expected interest rates.

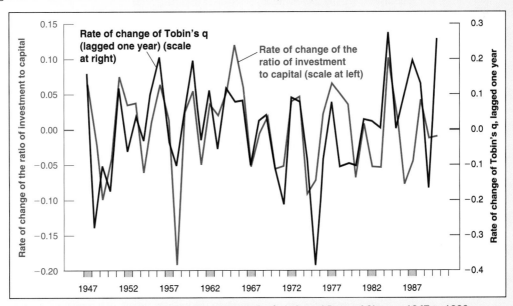

FIGURE 1   Tobin's q versus the Ratio of Investment to Capital. Annual Rates of Change, 1947 to 1990

A Convenient Special Case

Before exploring further implications and extensions of equation (16.4), it is useful to go through a special case where the relation between investment, profit, and interest rates becomes very simple.

Suppose firms expect both future profits (per unit of capital) and future interest rates to remain at the same level as today, so that $\Pi_{t+1}^e = \Pi_{t+2}^e = \cdots = \Pi_t$, and $r_{t+1}^e = r_{t+2}^e = \cdots = r_t$. Under these assumptions, equation (16.3) becomes

$$V(\Pi_t^e) = \frac{\Pi_t}{r_t + \delta} \qquad (16.5)$$

(The derivation is given in the appendix to this chapter.) The present value of expected profits is simply the ratio of profit to the sum of the real interest rate and the depreciation rate.

Replacing (16.5) in equation (16.4), investment is

$$I_t = I\left(\frac{\Pi_t}{r_t + \delta}\right) \qquad (16.6)$$

Look more closely at the fraction in parentheses. The denominator—the sum of the real interest rate and the depreciation rate—is called the **user cost** or the **rental cost of capital**. To see why, suppose the firm, instead of buying the machine, rented it by the year from a rental agency. How much would the rental agency charge? Even if the machine did not depreciate, the agency would have to charge an interest rate equal to r_t times the price of the machine (we have assumed the price of a machine to be 1 in real terms, so r_t times 1 is just r_t): The agency has to get at least as much from buying and then renting the machine as it would from, say, buying bonds. In addition, the rental agency would have to charge for depreciation, δ times the price of the machine, 1. The rental price would therefore be equal to $(r_t + \delta)$. Even though firms typically do not rent their machines, $(r_t + \delta)$ still captures the implicit cost—sometimes called the *shadow cost*—to the firm of using the machine for one year.

The investment function given by equation (16.6) then has a simple interpretation: *Investment depends on the ratio of profit to the user cost.* The higher the profit compared to the user cost, the higher the level of investment. The higher the real interest rate, the higher the user cost, the lower the level of investment.

This relation between profit, the real interest rate, and investment relies on a strong simplifying assumption: The future is expected to be the same as the present. It is nevertheless a useful relation to remember, and a relation macroeconomists keep handy in their toolbox.

Current versus Expected Profit

Let's now return to the general case. Equations (16.3) and (16.4) imply that investment should be forward looking, and depend primarily on *expected future profits*. (Under our assumption that new capital starts being operational only one year after purchase, current profit does not even appear in equation [16.3].) One striking empirical fact about investment, however, is how strongly it moves with fluctuations in *current profit*.

This relation is shown in Figure 16–2, which plots yearly changes in investment and profit since 1960 for the U.S. economy. Investment is measured as *fixed nonresidential investment* in 1992 dollars. Profit is constructed as the ratio of the sum of *after-tax profits plus interest payments paid by U.S corporations*, divided by their capital stock. The average value of this ratio is equal to approximately 6% a year; put another way, one dollar of capital generates on average 6 cents of profit a year. The shaded areas in the figure represent years in which there was a recession—a decline in output for at least two consecutive quarters of the year.

The positive relation between changes in investment and changes in current profit is clear in Figure 16–2. Is this relation inconsistent with the theory we have just developed, which

Such arrangements exist: Many firms lease cars and trucks from leasing companies.

If the future is expected to be the same as the present, investment depends on the ratio of profit to the user cost—the sum of the real interest rate and the depreciation rate.

Profit ↑ ⟹ investment ↑

Real interest rate ↑ ⟹ investment ↓

For definitions of all these terms, see Appendix 1 on national income accounts at the end of the book.

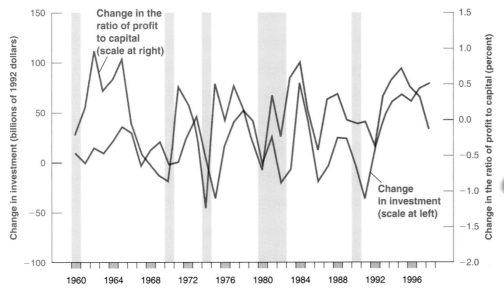

holds that investment should be related to the present value of expected future profits rather than to current profit? It need not be: If firms expect future profits to move very much like current profit, then the present value of profits will move very much like current profit, and so will investment.

Economists who have looked at the question more closely have concluded, however, that the effect of current profit on investment is stronger than the theory we have developed so far would predict. (How they have gathered some of the evidence is described in the Focus box "Profitability versus Cash Flow.") On the one hand, some firms with highly profitable investment projects but low current profits appear to be investing too little. On the other hand, some firms that have high current profit sometimes appear to invest in projects of doubtful profitability. In short, current profit appears to affect investment, even after controlling for the expected present value of profits.

Why does current profit play a role in the investment decision? The answer lurks in our discussion in section 16-1 of why consumption also depends directly on current income: Many of the reasons we used to explain the behavior of consumers also apply to firms:

1. If its current profit is low, a firm that wants to buy new machines can get the funds it needs only by borrowing. It may be reluctant to borrow: Although expected profits may look good, things may turn bad, leaving the firm unable to repay the debt. But if current profit is high, the firm may be able to finance its investment by retaining some of its earnings and without having to borrow. The bottom line is that higher current profit may lead the firm to invest more.

2. Even if the firm wants to invest, it may find it difficult to borrow. Potential lenders may not be convinced the project is as good as the firm says, and they may worry the firm will be unable to repay. If the firm has large current profits, it does not have to borrow and so does not need to convince potential lenders. It can proceed and invest as it pleases, and is more likely to do so.

In summary, to fit the investment behavior we observe, the investment equation is better written as

$$I_t = I(V(\Pi_t^e), \Pi_t) \qquad (16.7)$$
$$(\quad + \ , +)$$

Investment depends both on the expected present value of profits and on the current level of profit.

How much does investment depend on the expected present value of profits, and how much does it depend on current profit? Economists often refer to the question as the relative importance of **profitability** (the expected present discounted value of profits) versus **cash flow** (current profit, the net flow of cash the firm is receiving) in investment decisions.

The difficulty in answering this question is similar to the problem of identifying the relative importance of current and expected future income on consumption—a problem we discussed in the first Focus box in this chapter: Most of the time, cash flow and profitability are likely to move together. Firms that do well typically have both large cash flows and good future prospects. Firms that suffer losses often also have poor future prospects.

As in the case for consumption, the best way to isolate the effects of cash flow and profitability is to identify times or events when cash flow and profitability move in different directions, and then look at what happens to investment. This is the approach taken by Owen Lamont, an economist at the University of Chicago. An example will help you understand Lamont's strategy:

Think of two firms, A and B. A is involved only in steel production. B is composed of two parts, one part steel production, the other part petroleum exploration.

Suppose there is a sharp drop in the price of oil, leading to losses in oil exploration. This shock decreases firm B's cash flow. If the losses in oil exploration are large enough to offset the profits from steel production, firm B may show an overall loss.

The question we can now ask is: As a result of the decrease in the price of oil, will firm B invest less in its steel operation than firm A does? If only *profitability* in steel production matters, there is no reason for firm B to invest less in its steel operation than firm A. But if current *cash flow* also matters, the fact that firm B has a lower cash flow may prevent it from investing as much as firm A in its steel operation. Looking at investment in the steel operations of the two firms can tell us how much investment depends on cash flow versus profitability.

This is the empirical strategy followed by Lamont. He focuses on what happened in 1986 when the price of oil in the United States dropped by 50%, leading to large losses in oil-related activities. He then looks at whether firms that had substantial oil activities cut investment in their non-oil activities relatively more than other firms in the same non-oil activities. He concludes that they did. He finds that for every $1 decrease in cash flow due to the decrease in the price of oil, investment spending in non-oil activities was reduced by 10 to 20 cents. In short, current cash flow matters.

References

Owen Lamont, "Cash Flow and Investment: Evidence from Internal Capital Markets," *Journal of Finance*, March 1997.

A general review of studies along these lines is given by R. Glenn Hubbard "Capital-market Imperfections and Investment," *Journal of Economic Literature*, 1995.

Profit and Sales

We have argued that investment depends on both current and expected profit. One last step is to ask: What in turn determines profit? The answer is primarily two factors: (1) the level of sales, and (2) the existing capital stock. If sales are low relative to the capital stock, profits per unit of capital are likely to be depressed as well.

Let's write this more formally. Ignore the distinction between sales and output, and let Y_t denote output or, equivalently, sales. Let K_t denote the capital stock at time t. Our discussion suggests the following relation:

$$\Pi_t = \Pi \left(\frac{Y_t}{K_t} \right)$$

$$(\; + \;)$$

(16.8)

Profit per unit of capital is an increasing function of the ratio of sales to the capital stock. Given the capital stock, the higher the sales, the higher profit. Given sales, the higher the capital stock, the lower profit.

How does this relation hold in practice? Figure 16–3 plots yearly changes in profit per unit of capital and changes in the ratio of output to capital for the United States since 1960. As in Figure 16–2, profit per unit of capital is defined as the sum of after-tax profits plus interest payments paid by U.S. corporations, divided by their capital stock, measured at replacement cost. The ratio of output to capital is constructed as the ratio of GDP to the aggregate capital stock.

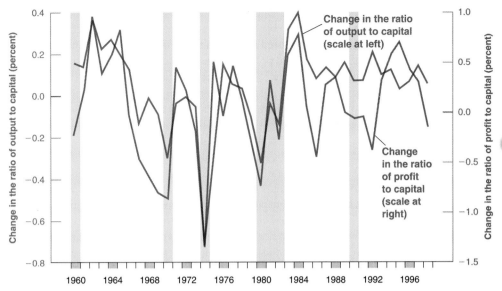

FIGURE 16-3

Changes in the Ratio of Profit to Capital and Changes in the Ratio of Output to Capital in the United States, 1960–1998

Profit and the ratio of output to capital move largely together.

The figure shows a clear relation between changes in profit and changes in the ratio of output to capital. Given that most of the year-to-year changes in the ratio of output to capital come from movements in output (capital moves slowly over time; even large swings in investment lead to slow changes in capital), we can state the relation as follows: Profit decreases in recessions, and increases in expansions.

Why is this relation between output and profit relevant here? Because it implies a link between *current output* and *expected output* on the one hand, and *investment* on the other. For example, the anticipation of a long, sustained economic expansion leads firms to expect high profits, now and for some time in the future. These expectations in turn lead to higher investment. The effect of current and expected output on investment, together with the effect ◄ of investment back on demand and output, will play a crucial role when we return to the determination of output in chapter 17.

High expected output $\Rightarrow$ High expected profit $\Rightarrow$ High investment today.

16-3 | The Volatility of Consumption and Investment

You surely will have noticed the similarities between our treatment of consumption and of investment behavior in sections 16-1 and 16-2:

- Whether consumers perceive current movements in income to be transitory or permanent affects their consumption decisions.
- In the same way, whether firms perceive current movements in sales to be transitory or permanent affects their investment decisions. The less they expect a current increase in sales to last, the less they revise their assessment of the present value of profits, and thus the less likely they are to buy new machines or build new factories. This is why, for example, the boom in sales that happens every year between Thanksgiving and Christmas does not lead to a boom in investment every year in December. Firms understand that this ◄ boom is transitory.

But there are also important differences between consumption and investment decisions:

- The theory of consumption we developed implies that when faced with an increase in income consumers perceive as permanent, they respond with *at most* an equal increase in consumption. The permanent nature of the increase in income implies that they can afford to increase consumption now and in the future by the same amount as the increase in

In the United States, retail sales are 24% higher on average in December than in other months. In France and Italy, sales are 60% higher in December. (These numbers and other facts about such seasonal cycles come from J. Joseph Beaulieu and Jeffrey Miron, "A Cross Country Comparison of Seasonal Cycles and Business Cycles," *Economic Journal*, July 1992, 772–778.)

income. Increasing consumption more than one for one would require cuts in consumption later, and there is no reason for consumers to want to plan consumption this way.

- Now consider the behavior of firms faced with an increase in sales they believe to be permanent. The present value of expected profits increases, leading to an increase in investment. In contrast to consumption, there is no implication that the increase in investment should be no greater than the increase in sales. Rather, once a firm has decided that an increase in sales justifies the purchase of a new machine or the building of a new factory, it may want to proceed quickly, leading to a large but short-lived increase in investment spending. This increase may exceed the increase in sales.

  More concretely, take a firm that has a ratio of capital to its annual sales of, say, 3. An increase in sales of $10 million this year, if expected to be permanent, requires the firm to spend $30 million on additional capital if it wants to maintain the same ratio of capital to output. If the firm buys the additional capital right away, the increase in investment spending this year will be equal to *three times* the increase in sales. Once the capital stock has adjusted, the firm will return to its normal pattern of investment. This example is extreme, because firms are unlikely to adjust their capital stock right away. But even if they do adjust their capital stock more slowly, say, over a few years, the increase in investment may still exceed the increase in sales for a while.

  We can tell the same story in terms of equation (16.8). As we make no distinction here between output and sales, the initial increase in sales leads to an equal increase in output, Y, so that Y/K (the ratio of the firm's output to its existing capital stock) also increases. The result is higher profit, which leads the firm to undertake more investment. Over time, the higher level of investment leads to a higher capital stock, K, so that Y/K decreases, returning to normal. Profit per unit of capital returns to normal, and so does investment. Thus, in response to a permanent increase in sales, investment may increase a lot initially, and then return to normal over time.

These differences suggest that investment should be more volatile than consumption. How much more volatile? The answer from the data is given in Figure 16–4, which plots yearly rates of change in U.S. consumption and investment since 1960. The shaded areas are again years during which the U.S. economy was in recession. To make the figure easier to interpret, both rates of change are plotted as deviations from the average rate of change, so that they are on average equal to zero.

FIGURE 16–4

Rates of Change of Consumption and Investment in the United States, 1960–1998

Relative movements in investment are much larger than relative movements in consumption.

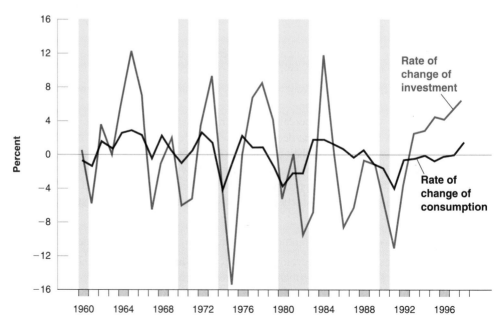

You can see two things in the figure:

- Consumption and investment usually move together: Recessions, for example, are typically associated with decreases in *both* investment and consumption. Given our discussion, which has emphasized that consumption and investment depend largely on the same determinants, this should not come as a surprise.
- Investment is indeed much more volatile than consumption. Relative movements in investment range from −15% to +12%, whereas relative movements in consumption range only from −4% to +4%.
- Another way of stating the same fact is that whereas the level of investment is much smaller than the level of consumption (recall, investment accounts for 14% of GDP, vs 68% for consumption) the range of changes in the level of investment from one year to the next is roughly the same as the range of changes in the level of consumption from one year to the next. Both components contribute roughly equally to fluctuations in output over time.

SUMMARY

- Consumption depends on both current income and wealth. Wealth is the sum of nonhuman wealth (financial and housing wealth) and human wealth (the present value of expected after-tax labor income).

- The response of consumption to changes in income depends on whether consumers perceive these changes as transitory or permanent.

- Consumption is likely to respond less than one for one to movements in income, and consumption may move even if current income does not change.

- Investment depends on both current profit and the present value of expected future profits.

- Under the simplifying assumption that firms expect future profits and interest rates to be the same in the future as they are today, we can think of investment as depending on the ratio of profit to the user cost of capital, where the user cost is the sum of the real interest rate and the depreciation rate.

- Movements in profit are closely related to movements in output. Hence, we can think of investment as depending indirectly on current and future expected output movements. Firms that anticipate a long output expansion, and thus a long sequence of high profits, will invest. Movements in output that are not expected to last will have a small effect on investment.

- Investment is much more volatile than consumption.

KEY TERMS

- permanent income theory of consumption, 310
- life cycle theory of consumption, 310
- panel data sets, 310
- financial wealth, 310
- housing wealth, 310
- human wealth, 311
- nonhuman wealth, 311

- total wealth, 311
- natural experiment, 312
- Tobin's q, 317
- user cost or rental cost of capital, 318
- profitability, 320
- cash flow, 320

An asterisk denotes a harder question. [Web] indicates that the question requires access to the Internet.

1. TRUE/FALSE/UNCERTAIN

a. For the typical college student, human wealth and non-human wealth are approximately equal.

b. Natural experiments, such as retirement and announced tax cuts, do not suggest that expectations of future income are major factors affecting consumption.

c. Buildings and factories depreciate much faster than machines do.

d. A high value for Tobin's q indicates the stock market believes that capital is overvalued and thus investment should be lower.

e. Economists have found that the effect of current profit on investment can be fully explained by the effect of current profit on expectations of future profits.

f. Data from the past three decades in the United States suggest that corporate profits are closely tied to the business cycle.

g. Changes in consumption and investment are typically of the same sign and are roughly of the same magnitude.

2. PDV COMPUTATIONS AND RETIREMENT

A consumer has nonhuman wealth equal to $100,000. She earns $40,000 this year, and expects her salary to rise by 5% in real terms each year for the following two years. She will then retire. The real interest rate is equal to 0% and is expected to remain at 0% in the future. Labor income is taxed at the rate of 25%.

a. What is this consumer's human wealth?

b. What is her total wealth?

c. If she expects to live for another seven years after retirement and wants her consumption to remain the same (in real terms) every year from now on, how much can she consume this year?

d. If she were given a bonus of $20,000 in the current year only, with all future salary payments remaining as stated earlier, by how much could she increase consumption now and in the future?

e. Suppose now that at retirement Social Security will start paying each year benefits equal to 60% of the consumer's earnings during her last working year. (Assume benefits are not taxed.) How much can she consume this year (and still maintain constant consumption)?

3. INVESTMENT DECISIONS IN THE PRETZEL INDUSTRY

A pretzel manufacturer is considering buying a pretzel-making machine that costs $100,000. The machine will depreciate by 8% per year. It will generate real profits equal to $18,000 next year, $18,000(1−8%) two years from now (that is, the same real profits, but adjusted for depreciation), $18,000(1−8%)^2 three years from now, and so on. Determine whether the manufacturer should buy the machine if the real interest rate is assumed to remain constant at

a. 5%.

b. 10%.

c. 15%.

4. INVESTING IN EDUCATION

Suppose that at age 22 you have just finished college and have been offered a starting salary of $40,000. Your salary will remain constant in real terms. However, you have also been admitted to a professional school. The school takes two years to complete and upon graduation you expect your starting salary to be 10% higher in real terms, and remain constant in real terms thereafter. The tax rate on labor income is 40%.

a. If the real interest rate is zero and you expect to retire at age 60 (that is, if you do not go to professional school, you expect to work for 38 years total), what is the maximum you should be willing to pay in tuition to attend this professional school?

b. What should you pay in tuition for professional school if you expect to pay 30% of your income in taxes?

*5. WEALTH ACCUMULATION

Suppose that every consumer is born with zero financial wealth and lives for three periods: youth, middle age, and retirement age. Consumers work in the first two periods and retire in the last one. Their income is $5 in the first period, $25 in the second, and $0 in the last one. Inflation and expected inflation are zero, and the real interest rate is also zero.

a. What is the present discounted value of future labor income at the beginning of life? What is the highest sustainable level of consumption such that consumption is equal in all three periods?

b. For each age group, what is the amount of saving that allows consumers to maintain the constant level of consumption you found in (a)? (*Hint*: Saving can be a negative number, if the consumer needs to borrow in order to maintain a certain level of consumption.)

c. Suppose there are *N* people born each period. What is total saving? (*Hint*: Compute the total amount saved by the generations that save and subtract the total amount dissaved by the generations that dissave.) Explain.

d. What is total financial wealth in the economy? (*Hint*: Compute the financial wealth of people at the beginning of the first period of life, of the second period of life, of the third period of life. Remember that people can be in debt, so financial wealth can be negative. Add them up.)

Suppose now that restrictions on borrowing do not allow young consumers to borrow. At each age group, consumers once again compute their total wealth and then determine their desired level of consumption as the highest level that allows their consumption to be equal in all three periods. However, if that is greater than their income plus their financial wealth, then they are constrained to consuming exactly their income plus their financial wealth.

e. Derive consumption in each period of life. Explain the difference from your answer to (a).

f. Derive total saving. Explain the difference, if any, from your answer to (c).

g. Derive total financial wealth. Explain the difference from your answer to (d).

h. "Financial liberalization may be good for people, but it is bad for overall capital accumulation." Discuss.

6. MOVEMENTS IN CONSUMPTION AND INVESTMENT [Web]

For this exercise, you will need annual data on consumption and investment. Go to the NIPA web page provided by the University of Virginia at www.lib.virginia.edu/socsci/nipa.

Follow the link sequence "Personal Income and Outlays," "Personal Consumption Expenditures (Table 2.2)." Then click on the box for annual series, and then click on the box titled "Submit Query." On the next page, click on "Personal Consumption Expenditures," for the years 1959 to 1997. Then click "submit query." In the bottom of the next page, click on the link "FTP these data." Save the file as text and import it into your favorite spreadsheet program.

Return to the NIPA home page and repeat the same procedure for "Saving and Investment," "Gross Saving and Investment (Table 5.1)." On the resulting screen, scroll down the first table and select "Gross Investment" from 1959 to 1997. Then click "submit query" and follow the same steps as above.

Similarly, obtain the time series for the GDP deflator by following "Quantity and Price Indexes," "Quantity and Price Indexes (Table 7.1)," and "Implicit price deflator for GDP." Download the data for 1959 to 1997.

a. Use the GDP deflator to turn the consumption and investment series into real consumption and investment in terms of 1992 prices.

b. On average, how much bigger is consumption than investment?

c. Compute the change in the levels of consumption and investment from one year to the next, and graph them for the period 1959 to 1997. Are the year-to-year changes in consumption and investment of the same magnitude?

d. What do your answers in (b) and (c) imply about the volatility of consumption and investment? Is this implication consistent with Figure 16–4?

e. Use Figure 16–4 to identify the years for the last two recessions. Using your graph from part (c), which component played the largest role in each of these recessions, consumption or investment? Is this consistent with what we have learned so far about these recessions?

DERIVATION OF THE EXPECTED PRESENT VALUE OF PROFITS WHEN FUTURE PROFITS AND INTEREST RATES ARE EXPECTED TO BE THE SAME AS TODAY

We saw that the expected present value of profits is given by

$$V(\Pi_t^e) = \frac{1}{1 + r_t} \Pi_{t+1}^e$$

$$+ \frac{1}{(1 + r_t)(1 + r_{t+1}^e)} (1 - \delta)\Pi_{t+2}^e + \cdots \quad (16.3)$$

If firms expect both future profits (per unit of capital) and future interest rates to remain at the same level as today, so that $\Pi_{t+1}^e = \Pi_{t+2}^e = \cdots = \Pi_t$, and $r_{t+1}^e = r_{t+2}^e = \cdots = r_t$, the equation becomes

$$V(\Pi_t^e) = \frac{1}{1 + r_t} \Pi_t + \frac{1}{(1 + r_t)^2} (1 - \delta)\Pi_t + \cdots$$

Factoring out $[1/(1 + r_t)]\Pi_t$,

$$V(\Pi_t^e) = \frac{1}{1 + r_t} \Pi_t \left(1 + \frac{1 - \delta}{1 + r_t} + \cdots \right)$$

The term in parentheses in this equation is a geometric series, a series of the form $1 + x + x^2 + \cdots$ where x equals $(1 - \delta)/(1 + r_t)$. Thus, its sum is given by $1/(1 - x) = (1 + r_t)/(r_t + \delta)$. Replacing it in the equation above, we get

$$V(\Pi_t^e) = \frac{1}{1 + r_t} \frac{1 + r_t}{r_t + \delta} \Pi_t$$

Simplifying gives the equation we use in the text

$$V(\Pi_t^e) = \frac{\Pi_t}{(r_t + \delta)} \quad (16.5)$$

We invite you to visit the Blanchard page on the Prentice Hall Web site at:

http://www.prenhall.com/blanchard

for this chapter's World Wide Web exercises

CHAPTER 17

Expectations, Output, and Policy

In chapter 15, we saw how expectations affected the determination of bond and stock prices. In chapter 16, we saw how expectations affected consumption and investment decisions. Now, in this chapter, we put the pieces together and take another look at the effects of monetary and fiscal policy.

Section 17-1 draws the major implication of what we have learned, namely that expectations of both future income and future interest rates affect current spending and therefore affect current output. Section 17-2 looks at monetary policy. It shows how the effects of monetary policy depend crucially on how expectations respond to policy: Monetary policy affects only the current interest rate. What happens to spending and output then depends on how changes in the current interest rate lead people and firms to change their expectations of future interest rates and of future income, and, by implication, lead them to change their investment and consumption decisions. Section 17-3 turns to fiscal policy. It shows that, in sharp contrast to the simple model we saw back in the core, a fiscal contraction may, under the right circumstances, lead to an increase in output, even in the short run. Again, how expectations respond to policy are at the center of the story.

Let's start by reviewing what we have learned, and discuss how we should modify the characterization of goods and financial markets—the *IS-LM* model—we developed in the core.

Expectations and the IS Relation

The theme of chapter 16 was that both consumption and investment decisions very much depend on expectations of future income and interest rates. The channels through which expectations affect consumption and investment spending are summarized in Table 17–1.

A model that gave a detailed treatment of consumption and investment along the lines shown in Table 17–1 could be very complicated, and although this can be done—and indeed is done in the large empirical models that macroeconomists build to understand the economy and analyze policy—this is not the place to try. We want to capture the essence of what we have learned so far—the dependence of consumption and investment on expectations of the future—without getting lost in the details.

To do so, we make a major simplification. We reduce the present and the future to only two periods: (1) a *current* period, which you can think of as the current year, and (2) a *future* period, which you can think of as all future years lumped together. This way we do not have to keep track of expectations about each future year.

Having made this assumption, how should we then write the *IS* relation for the current period? Let's go back to the *IS* relation we wrote down before thinking about the role of expectations in consumption and investment decisions:

$$Y = C(Y - T) + I(Y,r) + G$$

Goods-market equilibrium requires that output be equal to aggregate spending—the sum of consumption spending, investment spending, and government spending. Before we introduce expectations into this equation, it will prove convenient to rewrite it in more compact form, but without changing its content. Let's define

$$A(Y, T, r) \equiv C(Y - T) + I(Y,r)$$

where *A* stands for **aggregate private spending**, or, simply, ***private spending***. With this notation we can rewrite the *IS* relation as

$$Y = A(Y, T, r) + G \qquad (17.1)$$
$$(+, -, -)$$

The properties of aggregate private spending, *A*, follow from the properties of consumption and investment that we laid down in earlier chapters:

> This way of dividing time between "today" and "later" is the way many of us organize our own life: Think of "things to do today" versus "things that can wait."

> This is the equation we saw in chapter 14, where we introduced the distinction between real and nominal interest rates.

> The reason for doing so is to regroup the two components of demand, *C* and *I*, which both depend on expectations. We continue to treat *G*, government spending, as exogenous—unexplained within our model.

TABLE 17–1 Spending and Expectations: The Channels

	Depends on:	Which in Turn Depends on Expectations of:
Consumption	• Current after-tax labor income	
	• Human wealth	• Future after-tax labor income
		• Future real interest rates
	• Nonhuman wealth	
	• Stocks	• Future real dividends
		• Future real interest rates
	• Bonds	• Future nominal interest rates
Investment	• Current cash flow	
	• Present value of after-tax profits	• Future after-tax profits
		• Future real interest rates

- Aggregate private spending is an increasing function of income, Y: Higher income (equivalently, output) increases consumption and investment.
- It is a decreasing function of taxes, T: Higher taxes decrease consumption.
- It is a decreasing function of the real interest rate, r: A higher real interest rate decreases investment.

All we have done so far is simplify notation. Now we need to extend equation (17.1) to reflect the role of expectations. The natural extension is to allow spending to depend not only on current variables but also on their expected values in the future period, thus

$$Y = A(Y, T, r, Y'^e, T'^e, r'^e) + G \qquad (17.2)$$
$$(+, -, -, +, -, -)$$

Notation: Primes stand for values of the variables in the future period. The superscript e stands for "expected."

Primes denote future values and the superscript e denotes an expectation, so Y'^e, T'^e, and r'^e denote expected future income, expected future taxes, and the expected future real interest rate respectively. The notation is a bit heavy, but what it captures is straightforward:

- Increases in either current or expected future income increase private spending.
- Increases in either current or expected future taxes decrease private spending.
- Increases in either the current or expected future real interest rate decrease private spending.

Y or $Y'^e \uparrow \Rightarrow A \uparrow$
T or $T'^e \uparrow \Rightarrow A \downarrow$
r or $r'^e \uparrow \Rightarrow A \downarrow$

With goods-market equilibrium now given by equation (17.2), Figure 17–1 shows the new IS curve. As usual, to draw the curve, we take all variables other than current output, Y, and the current real interest rate, r, as given. Thus, the IS curve is drawn for given values of current and future expected taxes, T and T'^e, for given values of expected future output, Y'^e, and for given values of the expected future real interest rate, r'^e.

The new IS curve is still downward sloping, and the reason is the same as before: A decrease in the current real interest rate leads to an increase in spending, which leads, through a multiplier effect, to an increase in output. We can say more, however: The new IS curve is much steeper than the IS curve we drew in earlier chapters. Put another way, a large decrease in the current interest rate is likely to have only a small effect on equilibrium output.

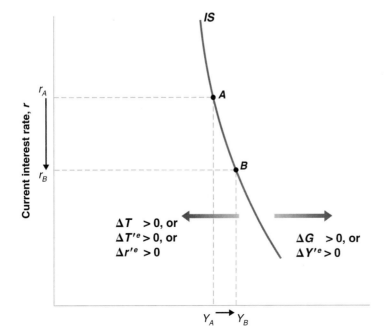

FIGURE 17–1

The New *IS* Curve

Given expectations, a decrease in the real interest rate leads to a small increase in output. Increases in government spending, or in expected future output, shift the *IS* curve to the right. Increases in taxes, or in expected future taxes, or in the expected future real interest rate shift the *IS* curve to the left.

To see why, take point A on the IS curve in Figure 17–1, and consider the effects of a decrease in the real interest rate. The effect of the decrease in the real interest rate on output depends on the strength of two effects: (1) the effect of the real interest rate on spending given income and (2) the size of the multiplier. Let's examine each one.

In terms of derivatives, A_r is small (in absolute value).

- A decrease in the current real interest rate, *given unchanged expectations of the future real interest rate*, does not have much effect on spending. We saw why in the previous chapters: A change in only the current real interest rate does not lead to large changes in present values, and so does not lead to large changes in spending. For example, firms are not likely to change their investment plans very much in response to a decrease in the current real interest rate if they do not expect future real interest rates to be lower as well.

In terms of derivatives, A_Y is small.

- The multiplier is likely to be small. Recall that the size of the multiplier depends on the size of the effect of a change in current income (output) on spending. But a change in current income, *given unchanged expectations of future income*, is unlikely to have a large effect on spending. The reason is that changes in income that are not expected to last have only a limited effect on both consumption and investment. Consumers who expect their income to be higher only for a year will increase consumption, but by much less than the increase in income. Firms expecting sales to be higher only for a year are unlikely to change their investment plans very much.

Putting things together, a large decrease in the current real interest rate, from r_A to r_B in Figure 17–1, leads to only a small increase in output, from Y_A to Y_B. The IS curve, which goes through points A and B, is steeply downward sloping.

Changes in current taxes (T) or in government spending (G) shift the IS curve. An increase in current government spending increases spending at a given interest rate, shifting the IS curve to the right; an increase in taxes shifts the IS curve to the left. These shifts are represented in Figure 17–1.

Changes in expected future variables also shift the IS curve. An increase in expected future output, Y'^e, shifts the IS curve to the right: Higher expected future income leads consumers to feel wealthier and consume more. Higher expected future output implies higher expected profits, leading firms to invest more. By a similar argument, an increase in expected future taxes leads consumers to decrease current spending, and shifts the IS curve to the left. And an increase in the expected future real interest rate decreases current spending, shifting the IS curve to the left. These shifts are also represented in Figure 17–1.

The LM Relation Revisited

The LM relation we derived in chapter 4 and have used until now was given by

$$\frac{M}{P} = Y L(i) \tag{17.3}$$

where M/P is the supply of money and $Y L(i)$ is the demand for money. Equilibrium in financial markets requires that the supply of money be equal to the demand for money. The demand for money depends on real income and on the short-term nominal interest rate—the opportunity cost of holding money. We derived this demand for money before thinking about expectations. Now that we have, the question is: Should we modify equation (17.3)? The answer—I am sure this will be good news—is: No.

Think of your own demand for money. How much money you want to hold today depends on your *current* level of transactions, not on the level of transactions you expect next year or the year after; there will be time to adjust your money balances to your transaction level if it changes in the future. And the opportunity cost of holding money today depends on the *current* nominal interest rate, not on the expected nominal interest rate next year or the year after. If short-term interest rates were to increase in the future, increasing the opportunity cost of holding money, the time to reduce your money balances would be, not now.

So, in contrast to the consumption decision, the decision about how much money to hold is myopic, depending primarily on current income and the current short-term nominal interest rate. We can still think of the demand for money as depending on the current level of output and the current nominal interest rate, and use equation (17.3) to describe the determination of the nominal interest rate in the current period.

To summarize: We have seen that expectations about the future play a major role in spending decisions. This implies that expectations enter the *IS* relation: Private spending depends not only on current output and the current real interest rate, but also on expected future output, and the expected future real interest rate. In contrast, the decision about how much money to hold is largely myopic: The two variables entering the *LM* relation are still current income and the current nominal interest rate.

17-2 | Monetary Policy, Expectations, and Output

In the basic *IS-LM* model, there was only one interest rate, *i*, which entered both the *IS* relation and the *LM* relation. When the Fed expanded the money supply, "the" interest rate went down, and spending increased. From the previous three chapters, we have learned that there are in fact many interest rates, and that we must keep two distinctions in mind:

- The distinction between the nominal interest rate and the real interest rate.
- The distinction between current and expected future interest rates.

The interest rate that enters the *LM* relation, and thus the interest rate that the Fed affects directly, is the *current nominal interest rate*. In contrast, spending in the *IS* relation depends on both *current and expected future real interest rates*. Economists sometimes state this distinction even more starkly by saying that, although the Fed controls the *short-term nominal interest rate*, what matters for spending and output is the *long-term real interest rate*.

Let's look at this more closely. Recall from chapter 14 that the real interest rate is approximately equal to the nominal interest rate minus expected current inflation—inflation expected, as of today, for the current period.

$$r = i - \pi^e$$

Similarly, the expected future real interest rate is approximately equal to the expected future nominal interest rate minus expected future inflation—inflation expected, as of today, for the future period.

$$r'^e = i'^e - \pi'^e$$

When the Fed increases the money supply, therefore decreasing the current nominal interest rate *i*, the effect on the current and the expected future real interest rates depends on two factors:

- Whether the increase in the money supply leads financial markets to revise their expectations of the future nominal interest rate, i'^e, as well.
- Whether the increase in the money supply leads financial markets to revise their expectations of current and future inflation, π^e and π'^e. If for example, the change in money leads them to expect more inflation in the future, the expected future real interest rate, r'^e will decrease by more than the expected future nominal interest rate, i'^e.

I shall leave aside here the second factor, the role of changing expectations of inflation, and focus on the first, the role of changing expectations of the future nominal interest rate. Thus, I shall assume that expected current and future inflation are both equal to zero. In this case, we need not distinguish between the nominal and the real interest rate, as they are equal, and we can use the same letter to denote both.

We explored the role of changing expectations of inflation on the relation between the nominal interest rate and the real interest rate in chapter 14. Leaving changes in expected inflation aside will keep the analysis simpler here. You have, however, all the elements you need to think through what would happen if we also allowed expectations of current inflation and future inflation to adjust in response to an increase in the money supply. How would these expectations adjust? Would this lead to a larger or a smaller effect on output in the current period?

The *IS* relation is unchanged. The *LM* relation is now in terms of the real interest rate, which, here, is equal to the nominal interest rate.

Let r and r'^e denote the current and expected future real (and nominal) interest rates. With this simplification we can rewrite the *IS* and *LM* relations in equations (17.2) and (17.3) as

$$IS: \quad Y = A(Y, T, r, Y'^e, T'^e, r'^e) + G \qquad (17.4)$$

$$LM: \quad \frac{M}{P} = Y L(r) \qquad (17.5)$$

The corresponding *IS* and *LM* curves are drawn in Figure 17–2(a). The vertical axis measures the current interest rate r; the horizontal axis measures current output Y. The *IS* curve is downward sloping, and steep. We saw the reason earlier: For given expectations, a change in the current interest rate has a limited effect on spending, and the multiplier is small. The *LM* is upward sloping. An increase in income leads to an increase in the demand for money; given the supply of money, the result is an increase in the interest rate.

Now suppose that, at point A, the economy is in a recession, and the Fed decides to increase the money supply. Assume for the moment this expansionary monetary policy does not change expectations of either the future interest rate or future output. In Figure

There is no need to distinguish here between real and nominal interest rates: Given zero expected inflation, they are the same.

FIGURE 17–2

The Effects of an Expansionary Monetary Policy

(a) The equilibrium is determined by the intersection of the *IS* and the *LM* curves. (b) The effects of monetary policy on output depend very much on whether and how monetary policy affects expectations.

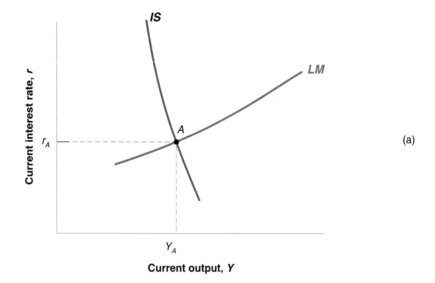

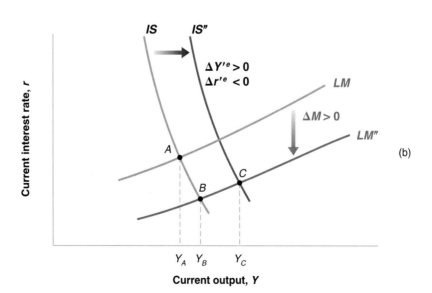

17–2(b), the *LM* shifts down, from *LM* to *LM″*. (Because I already use primes to denote future values of the variables, I shall use double primes (such as in *LM″*) to denote shifts in curves in this chapter.) The equilibrium moves from point *A* to point *B*, with higher output and a lower interest rate. The steep *IS* curve, however, implies that the increase in money has only a small effect on output: Changes in the current interest rate, unaccompanied by changes in expectations, have only a small effect on spending, and in turn on output.

But is it reasonable to assume that expectations are unaffected by an expansionary monetary policy? Isn't it likely that as the Fed decreases the current interest rate, financial markets anticipate lower interest rates in the future as well, along with higher future output stimulated by this lower future interest rate? What happens if they do? At a given current interest rate, prospects of a lower future interest rate and of higher future output both increase spending and output; they shift the *IS* curve to the right, from *IS* to *IS″*. The new equilibrium is given by point *C*. Thus, although the direct effect of the expansion in money on output is limited, the full effect, once changes in expectations are taken into account, is much larger.

Given expectations, an increase in money leads to a shift in the *LM*, and a movement down the steep *IS*. This leads to a large decrease in *r*, a small increase in *Y*.

If the increase in money leads to an increase in Y^e and a decrease in r^e, the *IS* curve shifts to the right, leading to a larger increase in *Y*.

FOCUS

Rational Expectations

Most macroeconomists today routinely solve their models under the assumption of rational expectations. But this was not always the case. Indeed, the last 25 years in macroeconomic research are often called the "rational expectations" revolution.

The importance of expectations is an old theme in macroeconomics. But until the early 1970s, macroeconomists thought of expectations in one of two ways:

1. One was as **animal spirits** (from an expression Keynes introduced in the *General Theory* to refer to movements in investment that could not be explained by movements in current variables): Shifts in expectations were taken as important but largely unexplained.

2. The other was as simple, backward-looking rules. For example, people were often assumed to have **adaptive expectations**, to assume that if their income had grown fast in the past it would continue to do so in the future, to revise their expectations of future inflation upwards if they had underpredicted in the past, and so on.

In the early 1970s, a group of macroeconomists led by Robert Lucas and Thomas Sargent argued that these assumptions did not do justice to the way people form expectations. (Robert Lucas received the Nobel prize in 1995 for his work on expectations.) They argued that in thinking about the effects of alternative policies, economists should assume that people have rational expectations, that people look to the future and do the best job they can in predicting it. This is not the same as assuming that people know the future, but rather that they use the information they have in the best possible way.

Using the popular macroeconomic models of the time, Lucas and Sargent showed how replacing traditional assumptions about expectations formation by the assumption of rational expectations could fundamentally alter the results. We saw, for example, in chapter 9 how Lucas challenged the notion that disinflation necessarily required an increase in unemployment for some time. Under rational expectations, he argued, a credible disinflation policy might decrease inflation without any increase in unemployment. More generally, Lucas and Sargent's research showed the need for a complete rethinking of macroeconomic models under the assumption of rational expectations, and this is what has happened since.

Most macroeconomists today use the assumption of rational expectations as a working assumption in their models and in their analyses of policy. This is not because they believe that people always have rational expectations. Surely there are times when people, firms, or financial market participants lose sight of reality and become too optimistic or too pessimistic. But these are more the exception than the rule, and it is not clear that economists can say much about those times anyway. In thinking about the likely effects of a particular economic policy, the best assumption to make seems to be that financial markets, people, and firms will do the best they can to work out its implications. Designing a policy on the assumption that people will make systematic mistakes in responding to it is unwise.

So why did it take until the 1970s for rational expectations to become a standard assumption in macroeconomics? Largely because of technical problems. Under rational expectations, what happens today depends on expectations of what will happen in the future. But what happens in the future depends on what happens today. The success of Lucas and Sargent in convincing most macroeconomists to use rational expectations comes not only from the strength of their case, but also from showing how it could actually be done. Much progress has been made since in developing solution methods for larger and larger models. Today, several large macroeconometric models are solved under rational expectations. (I presented a simulation from such a model in chapter 7. We shall see another example in chapter 25.)

To summarize: We have just learned an important lesson. The effects of monetary policy (of any type of macroeconomic policy for that matter) depend crucially on their effect on expectations. If a monetary expansion leads financial investors, firms, and consumers to revise their expectations of future interest rates and output, then the effects of the monetary expansion on output may be very large. But if expectations remain unchanged, the effects of the monetary expansion on output will be small.

Saying that the effect of policy depends on its effect on expectations is not the same as saying that anything can happen. Expectations are not arbitrary. A fund manager deciding whether to invest in stocks or bonds, a firm thinking about whether to build a new plant, a consumer thinking about how much he should save for retirement—all give a lot of thought to what may happen in the future. We can think of them as forming expectations about the future by assessing the likely course of future policy and then working out the implications for future activity. If they do not do it themselves—surely most of us do not spend our time solving macroeconomic models before making decisions—they do so indirectly by watching TV and reading newsletters and newspapers, which themselves rely on the forecasts of public and private forecasters. Economists refer to expectations formed in this forward-looking manner as **rational expectations**. The introduction of the assumption of rational expectations is one of the most important developments in macroeconomics in the last 25 years, and is discussed further in the Focus box "Rational Expectations" on page 333.

We could go back and think about the implications of rational expectations in the case of the monetary expansion we have just studied. It will be more fun to do this in the context of a change in fiscal policy, and this is what we now turn to.

17-3 | Deficit Reduction, Expectations, and Output

See section 7-5 for the analysis of short and medium run effects, and section 11-2 for the analysis of long run effects—through the effect on the saving rate and, in turn, on capital accumulation.

Recall the conclusions we reached in the core about the effects of a budget deficit reduction:

- In the medium and the long run, a budget deficit reduction is likely to be beneficial for the economy. In the medium run, a lower budget deficit leads to higher investment. In the long run, higher investment translates into higher output.
- In the short run, however, unless it is offset by a monetary expansion, a reduction of the budget deficit leads to a reduction in spending, and so to a contraction in output.

It is this adverse short-run effect that—in addition to the unpopularity of increases in taxes or reductions in transfers or in other government programs—has often deterred governments from tackling their budget deficit: Why take the risk of a recession now for benefits that will accrue only in the future?

In the past 10 years, however, several economists have questioned this conclusion, and have argued that a deficit reduction may actually increase output even in the *short run*. Their basic argument is simple: If people take into account the future beneficial effects of deficit reduction, their expectations about the future may improve enough to lead to an increase rather than a decrease in current spending, and so an increase in current output. This section presents their argument more formally. The Global box "Can a Budget Deficit Reduction Lead to an Output Expansion? The Example of Ireland in the 1980s" reviews some of the supporting evidence.

Assume the economy is described by equation (17.4) for the *IS* relation and equation (17.5) for the *LM* relation. Now suppose the government announces a program to reduce the deficit, through decreases both in current spending, G, and in future spending, G'^e. What will happen to output *this period*?

The Role of Expectations About the Future

Suppose first that expectations of future output (Y'^e) and of the future interest rate (r'^e) do not change. In this case, the decrease in government spending in the current period leads to a shift in the *IS* curve to the left, and thus to a decrease in equilibrium output. The crucial question is therefore: What happens to expectations? To answer, let us go back to what we learned in the core about the effects of a deficit reduction in the medium and the long run:

- In the medium run, a deficit reduction has no effect on output. It leads, however, to a lower interest rate, and to higher investment. These were two of the main lessons of chapter 7. Let's review the logic behind each one:

  Recall that when we look at the medium run, we ignore the effects of capital accumulation on output. Thus, in the medium run, the natural level of output depends on the level of productivity (taken as given) and on the natural level of employment. The natural level of employment depends on the natural rate of unemployment. If spending by the government on goods and services does not affect the natural rate of unemployment—and there is no obvious reason why it should—then changes in spending will not affect the natural level of output. Thus, deficit reduction has no effect on the level of output in the medium run.

  Now recall that output must be equal to spending, which itself is the sum of public and private spending. Given that output is unchanged and that public spending is lower, private spending must be higher. This requires a lower interest rate: A lower interest rate leads to higher investment, and thus to higher private spending, which offsets the decrease in public spending and leaves output unchanged.

In the medium run: Y does not change, $I\uparrow$

- In the long run—that is, taking into account the effects of capital accumulation on output—higher investment leads to a higher capital stock, and thus a higher level of output. This was the main lesson of chapter 11. The higher the proportion of output saved (or invested; the two must be equal for the goods market to be in equilibrium), the higher the capital stock, and thus the higher the level of output in the long run.

In the long run, $I\uparrow \Rightarrow K\uparrow \Rightarrow Y\uparrow$

If people, firms, and financial market participants have rational expectations, then, in response to the announcement of a deficit reduction, they will expect these developments to take place in the future. Thus, they will revise their expectation of future output (Y'^e) up, and their expectation of the future interest rate (r'^e) down.

Back to the Current Period

We can now return to the question of what happens *this period* in response to the announcement and start of the deficit reduction program. Figure 17–3 draws the *IS* and *LM* curves for the current period. In response to the announcement of the deficit reduction, there are now three factors shifting the *IS* curve:

- Current government spending (G) goes down, leading to a shift of the *IS* curve to the left. At a given interest rate, the decrease in government spending leads to a decrease in spending and in output.

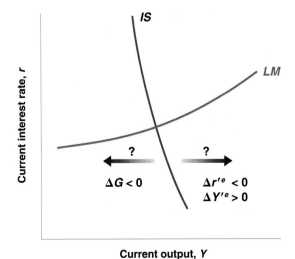

FIGURE 17–3

The Effects of Deficit Reduction on Current Output

When account is taken of its effect on expectations, the decrease in government spending need not lead to a decrease in output.

ACTIVE GRAPH

- Expected future output (Y'^e) goes up, leading to a shift of the *IS* curve to the right. At a given interest rate, the increase in expected future output leads to an increase in private spending, increasing output.
- The expected future interest rate goes down, leading to a shift of the *IS* curve to the right. At a given current interest rate, a decrease in the expected future interest rate stimulates spending and increases output.

What is the net effect of these three shifts in the *IS* curve? Can the effect of expectations on consumption and investment spending offset the decrease in government spending? Without much more information about the exact form of the *IS* and *LM* relations and about the details of the deficit reduction program, we cannot tell which shifts will dominate, and whether output will go up or down. But our analysis tells us that both cases are possible, that output may go up in response to the deficit reduction. And it gives us a few hints about when this might happen:

Note that the smaller the decrease in current government spending (G), the smaller the adverse effect on spending today. Note also that the larger the decrease in expected future

GLOBAL MACRO

Can a Budget Deficit Reduction Lead to an Output Expansion? The Example of Ireland in the 1980s

Ireland underwent two major deficit reduction programs in the 1980s.

- The first program began in 1982. In 1981, the budget deficit had reached a very high 13.0% of GDP. Government debt, the result of the accumulation of current and past deficits, stood at 77% of GDP, also a very high level. The government clearly had to regain control of its finances. Over the next three years, it embarked on a program of deficit reduction, based mostly on tax increases. This was an ambitious program: Had output continued to grow at its normal rate, the program would have reduced the deficit by 5% of GDP.

  The results were dismal. As shown in line 2 of Table 1 output growth was low in 1982, and negative in 1983. Low growth was associated with a major increase in unemployment, from 9.5% in 1981 to 15% in 1984 (line 3). Because of low output growth, tax revenues, which depend on the level of activity, were lower than anticipated. The actual deficit reduction, shown in line 1, was only 3.5% of GDP. And the result of continuing high deficits and low GDP growth was a further increase in the ratio of debt to GDP to 97% in 1984.

- A second attempt was made starting in February 1987. The economy was still in very bad shape. The 1986 deficit was 10.7% of GDP; debt stood at 116% of GDP, a record high in Europe at the time. This new program of deficit reduction was different from the first. The focus was more on a reduction of the role of government and a decrease in government spending, rather than on an increase in taxes. The tax increases in the pro-

gram were achieved through a tax reform widening the tax base, and without an increase in the marginal tax rate (the highest tax rate) on income. The program was again very ambitious: Had output grown at its normal rate, the reduction in the deficit would have been 6.4% of GDP.

The results could not have been more different from those of the first program. The years 1987 to 1989 marked a period of strong growth, with average GDP growth exceeding 5%. The unemployment rate was reduced by 2%. Because of strong output growth, tax revenues were stronger than anticipated, and the deficit was reduced by nearly 9% of GDP.

Several economists have argued that the striking difference between the results of the two programs can be traced to the different reaction of expectations in each case. The first package, they argue, focused on tax increases and did not change what many saw as too large a role of government in the economy. The second, with its focus on cuts in spending and on tax reform, had a much more positive impact on expectations and thus on output.

Are they right? One variable, the household saving rate (defined as disposable income minus consumption, divided by disposable income) strongly suggests that expectations are indeed an important part of the story. To interpret the behavior of the saving rate, recall the lessons from chapter 16 about consumption behavior. When disposable income grows unusually slowly or goes down—as it does in a recession—consumption typically slows down or declines by less than disposable income, as people expect things to improve in the future. Put another way, when the growth of disposable income is unusually low or negative, the saving rate typically comes down. Now look in line 4 of the table at what happened from 1981 to 1984: Despite low growth throughout the period and a recession in 1983, the household saving rate actually increased a little. Put another way, people reduced their consumption by more than the reduction in disposable income. To do so, they must have been very pessimistic about the future.

Now turn to 1986 to 1989. During that period, the economy was growing unusually strongly. By the same argument as in the previous paragraph, we would have expected consumption to increase less strongly, and thus the saving rate to increase. Instead, it decreased very strongly, from 15.7% in 1986 to 12.6% in 1989. Consumers must have become much more optimistic about the future to increase their consumption by more than the increase in disposable income in such a way.

Can this difference in the adjustment of expectations over the two episodes be fully attributed to the differences in the two fiscal programs? The answer is it almost surely can not. Monetary policy was not identical during the two episodes. More importantly, Ireland was changing in many ways at the time of the second fiscal program. Productivity was increasing much faster than real wages, reducing the cost of labor for firms. Attracted by tax breaks, low labor costs, and an educated labor force, many foreign firms were coming to Ireland to create new plants: These factors played a major role in the expansion of the late 1980s. Irish growth has been very strong ever since, with average output growth exceeding 6% since 1990. Surely, this long expansion is due to other factors besides fiscal policy. Nevertheless, the change in fiscal policy in 1987 probably played a role in convincing people, firms (including foreign firms), and financial markets that the government was regaining control of its finances. In any case, the fact remains that the substantial deficit reduction of 1987 to 1989 was accompanied by a strong output expansion, not by the recession predicted by the basic *IS-LM* model.

References

For a more detailed discussion, look at Francesco Giavazzi and Marco Pagano, "Can Severe Fiscal Contractions be Expansionary? Tales of Two Small European Countries," *NBER Macroeconomics Annual*, 1990, 75–110.

A recent survey of what we have learned by looking at programs of deficit reduction around the world is given in John McDermott and Robert Wescott, "An Empirical Analysis of Fiscal Adjustments," IMF working paper, June 1996.

TABLE 1	Fiscal and other macroeconomic indicators, Ireland, 1981–1984, and 1986–1989							
	1981	**1982**	**1983**	**1984**	**1986**	**1987**	**1988**	**1989**
1. Budget deficit (% of GDP)	−13.0	−13.4	−11.4	−9.5	−10.7	−8.6	−4.5	−1.8
2. Output growth rate (%)	3.3	2.3	−0.2	4.4	−0.4	4.7	5.2	5.8
3. Unemployment rate (%)	9.5	11.0	13.5	15.0	17.1	16.9	16.3	15.1
4. Household saving rate (% of disposable income)	17.9	19.6	18.1	18.4	15.7	12.9	11.0	12.6

Source: OECD Economic Outlook, June 1998.

government spending (G'^e), the larger the effect on expected future output and interest rates, thus the larger the favorable effect on spending today. This suggests that *backloading* (the tilting of the deficit reduction toward the future), with small cuts today and larger cuts in the future, is more likely to lead to an increase in output.

On the other hand, backloading raises other issues. If the government announces the need for painful cuts in spending, but then defers the required measures to some time in the future, its **credibility**—the perceived probability that the government will actually do what it has promised—may well decrease. The government must play a delicate balancing act: There have to be enough cuts in the current period to show a commitment to deficit reduction and enough cuts left to the future to reduce the adverse effects on the economy in the short run.

More generally, our analysis suggests that anything in a deficit reduction program that improves expectations of how the future will look is likely to make the short-run effects of deficit reduction less painful. Let me give two examples.

Measures which are perceived by firms and financial markets as reducing some of the existing distortions in the economy may improve expectations, and make it more likely that output increases in the short run. Take, for example, unemployment benefits. We saw in chapter 6 that lower unemployment benefits lead to a decline in the natural rate of unemployment, and thus a higher natural level of output. Thus, a reform of the social insurance system, which includes a reduction in the generosity of unemployment benefits, is likely to have two effects on spending and thus on output in the short run. The first is the adverse effect on the consumption of the unemployed: Lower unemployment benefits will reduce their income and their consumption. The second is a positive effect on spending through expectations: The anticipation of a lower unemployment rate and of a higher level of output in the future may lead to both higher consumption and higher investment. If the second effect dominates, the effect may be an increase in overall spending, increasing output not only in the medium run but also in the short run.

Another example is that of an economy where the government has in effect lost control of its budget: Government spending is high, tax revenues are low, and the deficit is very large. In such an environment, a credible deficit reduction program is also more likely to increase output in the short run. Before the annoucement of the program, people may have expected major political and economic trouble in the future. The announcement of a program of deficit reduction may well reassure people that the government has regained control, and that the future is less bleak than they anticipated. This decrease in pessimism about the future may lead to an increase in spending and output, even if taxes are increased as part of the deficit reduction program.

To summarize: A program of deficit reduction may increase output even in the short run. Whether it does depends on many factors, in particular:

- The credibility of the program: Will spending be cut or taxes increased in the future as announced?
- The timing of the program: How large are spending cuts in the future relative to current spending cuts?
- The composition of the program: Does the program remove some of the distortions in the economy?
- The state of government finances in the first place: How large is the initial deficit? Is this a "last chance" program? What will happen if it fails?

This gives you a sense of both the importance of expectations in determining the outcome, and of the difficulty of predicting the effects of fiscal policy in such a context.

SUMMARY

- Spending in the goods market depends on current and expected future output and on the current and the expected future real interest rate. Changes in expected future output or in the expected future real interest rate lead to changes in spending and in output today.

- By implication, the effects of any policy on spending and output depend on whether and how policy affects expectations of future output and the real interest rate.

- The assumption of rational expectations is that people, firms, and participants in financial markets form expectations of the future by assessing the course of future expected policy and then working out the implications for future output, interest rates, and so on. Although it is clear that most people do not go through this exercise themselves, we can think of them doing

so indirectly by watching TV and reading newspapers, which themselves rely on the predictions of public and private forecasters.

- Although there surely are cases where people, firms, or financial investors do not have rational expectations, the assumption seems to be the best benchmark to evaluate the potential effects of alternative policies. Designing a policy on the assumption that people will make systematic mistakes in responding to it is surely unwise.

- Changes in the money supply affect the short-term nominal interest rate. Spending, however, depends on the current and the expected future real interest rate. Thus, the effect of monetary policy on activity depends crucially on whether and how changes in the short-term nominal interest rate lead to changes in the current and the expected future real interest rate.

- When account is taken of its effect on expectations, a budget deficit reduction may lead to an increase rather than a decrease in output. This is because expectations of higher output and lower interest rates may more than offset the direct effect of the deficit reduction on spending.

KEY TERMS

- aggregate private spending, 328
- animal spirits, 333
- adaptive expectations, 333

- rational expectations, 334
- credibility, 337

QUESTIONS & PROBLEMS

An asterisk denotes a harder question. [Web] indicates that the question requires access to the Internet.

1. TRUE/FALSE/UNCERTAIN

a. Changes in expected future one-year real interest rates have a much larger effect on spending than changes in the current one-year real interest rate.

b. The introduction of expectations implies that the *IS* curve is still downward sloping but is now much flatter.

c. Current real money demand is inversely related to the future nominal interest rate.

d. The rational expectations assumption implies that consumers take into account the effects of future fiscal policy on output.

e. Future monetary policy affects future economic activity but not current economic activity.

f. Depending on its effect on expectations, a fiscal contraction may actually lead to an economic expansion.

g. The very different effects of Ireland's deficit reduction programs in 1982 and in 1987 provide little support for a single theory of expectations.

2. POLICY EXPERIMENTS

For each of the following, determine whether the *IS* curve, the *LM* curve, both curves, or neither shift. In each case, assume that expected current and future inflation are equal to zero, and that no other exogenous variable is changing.

a. A decrease in the expected future real interest rate.

b. A steeper yield curve.

c. An increase in the current money supply.

d. An increase in the expected future money supply.

e. An increase in expected future taxes.

f. A decrease in expected future income.

3. RATIONAL EXPECTATIONS

"The rational expectations assumption is unrealistic, because it essentially amounts to the assumption that every consumer has perfect knowledge of the economy." Discuss this statement.

4. FISCAL POLICY

A new president, who promised during her campaign that she would cut taxes, has just been elected. People trust that she will keep her promise, but that the tax cuts will be implemented only in the future. Determine the impact of the election on current output, the current interest rate, and current private spending under each of the following assumptions. (In each case, indicate what you think will happen to Y'^e, r'^e, and T'^e, and then how these changes in expectations affect output today.)

a. The Fed will not change its policy.

b. The Fed will act to prevent any change in future output.

c. The Fed will act to prevent any increase in the future interest rate.

5. THE CLINTON DEFICIT REDUCTION PACKAGE

In 1992, the U.S. deficit was $290 billion. During the presidential campaign, the large deficit emerged as a major issue. So when President Clinton won the election, deficit reduction was one of the first items on the new administration's agenda.

a. What does deficit reduction imply for output in the medium run and the long run? What are the advantages of reducing the deficit?

In the final version passed by Congress in August 1993, the deficit reduction package included a reduction of $20 billion in its first year, increasing gradually to $131 billion four years later.

b. Why was the deficit reduction package backloaded? Are there any advantages/disadvantages to this approach?

In February 1993, Clinton presented the budget in his "State of the Union" address. He asked Alan Greenspan, the Fed chairman at the time, to sit next to First Lady Hillary Clinton during the delivery of the address.

c. What was the purpose of this symbolic gesture? How can the Fed's decision to use expansionary monetary policy in the future affect the short run response of the economy?

6. THE CLINTON DEFICIT REDUCTION PACKAGE (continued) [Web]

Following the instructions in chapter 15, problem 7, go to the web page for the Federal Reserve Bank of St. Louis and download the following three series:

i. "Three-Month Treasury Constant Maturity Rate"

ii. "Three-Year Treasury Constant Maturity Rate"

iii. "Thirty-Year Treasury Constant Maturity Rate"

a. Using these three interest rates, plot the yield curve for November 1992 (the election month) and for August 1993 (the month that the deficit reduction plan was passed). What can you tell from the change in the yield curve about the financial markets' expectation of the Fed's stance?

Following the instructions of chapter 16, problem 6, download the "Current Surplus or Deficit, National Income and Products Account" series for the 1990s. You will find it under "Government Receipts and Current Expenditures (Table 3.1)." Also, download nominal and real GDP for the 1990s. You will find them under "National Product and Income."

b. Did the economy go into a recession following the passing of the deficit reduction package in 1993? Is this consistent with your answer to (a)?

c. Was the deficit reduced (as a percentage of GDP)?

*d. Are there any reasons to think that factors other than the deficit reduction package may have helped reduce the deficit in the 1990s? (*Hint*: Look at the growth rate of real GDP in the 1990s.)

We invite you to visit the Blanchard page on the Prentice Hall Web site at:

http://www.prenhall.com/blanchard

for this chapter's World Wide Web exercises

EXTENSIONS

The Open Economy

The next four chapters represent the second major extension of the core. They look at the implications of openness, the fact that most economies trade both goods and assets with the rest of the world.

CHAPTER 18

Chapter 18 discusses the implications of openness in goods and financial markets. Openness in goods markets allows people to choose between domestic and foreign goods. An important determinant of their decisions is the real exchange rate—the relative price of foreign goods in terms of domestic goods. Openness in financial markets allows people to choose between domestic and foreign assets. This imposes a tight relation between the exchange rate, current and expected, and domestic and foreign interest rates. This is known as the interest parity condition.

CHAPTER 19

Chapter 19 focuses on goods market equilibrium in an open economy. It shows how the demand for domestic goods now depends also on the real exchange rate. It shows how fiscal policy affects both output and the trade balance. It discusses the conditions under which a real depreciation improves the trade balance, and increases output.

CHAPTER 20

Chapter 20 characterizes goods and financial market equilibrium in an open economy. In other words, it gives an open economy version of the *IS-LM* model we saw in the core. It shows how, under flexible exchange rates, monetary policy affects output not only through its effect on the interest rate but also through its effect on the exchange rate. It shows how fixing the exchange rate implies giving up the ability to change the interest rate.

CHAPTER 21

Chapter 21 focuses on the implications of fixed and flexible exchange rates. It shows how, in the medium run, the real exchange rate can adjust even under a fixed exchange rate regime. It looks at what triggers exchange rate crises and how governments should react. It ends by discussing the pros and cons of various exchange rate regimes, including the adoption of a common currency.

CHAPTER 18

Openness in Goods and Financial Markets

W e have assumed so far that the economy was *closed*—that it did not interact with the rest of the world. We had to start this way, to keep things simple and build up your intuition for the basic macroeconomic mechanisms. We are now ready to open the economy. Understanding the macroeconomic implications of openness will occupy us for this and the next three chapters. "Openness" has three distinct dimensions:

1. **Openness in goods markets**: the opportunity for consumers and firms to choose between domestic and foreign goods. In no country is this choice completely free of restrictions: Even the countries most committed to free trade have tariffs and quotas on at least some foreign goods. (**Tariffs** are taxes on imported goods; **quotas** are restrictions on the quantities of goods that can be imported.) At the same time, in most countries average tariffs are low and getting lower.

2. **Openness in financial markets**: the opportunity for financial investors to choose between domestic and foreign financial assets. Until recently even some of the richest countries, such as France and Italy, had **capital controls**, tight restrictions on the foreign assets their domestic residents could hold as well as on the domestic assets foreigners could hold. These restrictions are rapidly disappearing. As a result, world financial markets are becoming more and more closely integrated.

3. **Openness in factor markets**: the opportunity for firms to choose where to locate production, and for workers to choose where to work and whether or not to migrate. Here also trends are clear. More and more companies move their operations around the world to take advantage of low costs. Much of the debate about the **North American Free Trade Agreement (NAFTA)**, signed in 1993 by the United States, Canada, and Mexico centered on its implications for the relocation of U.S. firms to Mexico. Immigration from low-wage countries to high-wage countries is a hot political issue in countries ranging from Germany to the United States.

In the short run and the medium run—the focus of this and the next three chapters—openness in factor markets plays much less of a role than openness in either goods or financial markets. Thus, I shall ignore openness in factor markets, and focus only on the first two dimensions of openness here. Section 18-1 looks at the implications of openness in the goods market. Section 18-2 looks at the implications of openness in financial markets.

Figure 18–1 plots the evolution of U.S. exports and imports, as ratios to GDP, since 1929. ("U.S. exports" means exports *from* the United States; "U.S. imports" means imports *to* the United States.) What is striking is how these ratios have increased over time. Exports and imports, which were equal to 5% of GDP as recently as the 1960s, now stand around 12% of GDP (11.2% for exports, 13% for imports). The United States trades substantially more with the rest of the world than it did just 30 years ago.

A closer look at Figure 18–1 reveals two other interesting features.

● The first is the sharp decline in both exports and imports between 1929 and 1936. This decline was due in large part to the now-infamous *Smoot–Hawley Act of 1930*. In a misguided attempt to help the U.S. economy recover from the Great Depression, Smoot–Hawley sharply increased tariffs in the hope of increasing the demand for domestic goods. The results were retaliation by other countries (in the form of higher tariffs on U.S. goods) and a sharp decrease in world trade.

● The second is that while imports and exports have broadly followed the same trend, they have also diverged for long periods, generating sustained trade surpluses or trade deficits. Two episodes stand out: the large trade surpluses in the late 1940s and the large trade deficits in the 1980s. The surpluses of the late 1940s were due to the post–World War II reconstruction effort in Europe, leading to large exports from the United States to Europe. The trade deficits of the mid-1980s were due to the U.S. fiscal–monetary policy mix. We shall examine this episode at length in chapter 20.

Given the constant media talk about *globalization*, a volume of trade (measured by the ratio of exports or imports to GDP) around 12% of GDP may strike you as small. However, the volume of trade is not necessarily a good measure of openness. Many sectors can be exposed to foreign competition without the effects of this competition showing up in high imports: By being competitive and keeping their prices low enough, these sectors can retain their domestic market share and keep imports out. This suggests that a better index of openness than export or import ratios is the proportion of aggregate output composed of **tradable goods** — goods that compete with foreign goods in either domestic or foreign markets. Estimates are that tradable goods represent around 60% of aggregate output in the United States today.

Mr. Smoot and Mr. Hawley had a moment of renewed fame during a TV debate on NAFTA in 1993, when U.S. Vice President Albert Gore presented their picture to H. Ross Perot as a way of reminding Americans of the dangers of opposing free trade. ▷

Recall from chapter 3 that ▷ the trade balance is equal to the difference between exports and imports. If exports are larger than imports, then there is a trade surplus (equivalently, a positive trade balance). If exports are smaller than imports, then there is a trade deficit (equivalently, a negative trade balance).

Tradable goods: Cars, computers, . . . Nontradable ▷ goods: Housing, medical services, haircuts, ...

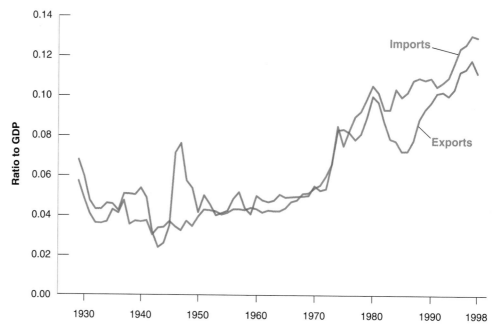

FIGURE 18–1

U.S. Exports and Imports as Ratios of GDP, 1929–1998

Exports and imports, which were equal to 5% of GDP as recently as the 1960s, now stand around 12% of GDP.

TABLE 18-1 Ratios of Exports to GDP for Selected OECD Countries, 1997

Country	Export Ratio (%)	Country	Export Ratio (%)
United States	12	Switzerland	40
Japan	10	Austria	38
Germany	23	Belgium	73
United Kingdom	29	Luxembourg	91

Source: *International Financial Statistics*, IMF, April 1999.

It remains true that with exports around 12% of GDP, the United States has one of the smallest ratios of exports to GDP among the rich countries of the world. Table 18–1 gives ratios for eight OECD countries.

The United States and Japan are at the low end of the range of export ratios. The large European countries, such as Germany and the United Kingdom, have ratios that are two to three times larger. And the smaller European countries have even larger ratios, from 40% in Switzerland, to 73% in Belgium, to 91% in Luxembourg! (Luxembourg's 91% ratio of exports to GDP raises an odd possibility: Could a country have exports larger than its GDP, an export ratio greater than one? The answer is yes. The reason is given in the Focus box: "Can Exports Exceed GDP?")

Do these numbers indicate that the United States has more trade barriers than, say, the United Kingdom or Luxembourg? No. The main factors behind these differences are geography and size. Distance from other markets explains a good part of the low Japanese ratio. Size also matters: The smaller the country, the more it must specialize in only a few products, produce and export them, and rely on imports for the others. Luxembourg can hardly afford to produce the range of goods produced by the United States, a country with a GDP more than 300 times larger.

> For more on the OECD and for the list of member countries, see chapter 1.

> Iceland is both isolated and small. What would you expect its export ratio to be? (Answer: 36%)

The Choice between Domestic and Foreign Goods

How does openness in goods markets force us to rethink the way we look at equilibrium in the *goods* market? When thinking about consumers' decisions in the goods market, we have focused so far on their decision to save or to consume. But when goods markets are open, domestic consumers face another decision: whether to buy domestic goods or foreign goods. Other

Can Exports Exceed GDP?

Can a country have exports larger than its GDP—an export ratio greater than one?

At first it would seem that countries cannot export more than they produce, so that the export ratio must be less than one. Not so. The trick is to realize that exports and imports may include exports and imports of intermediate goods.

For example, take a country that imports intermediate goods for $1 billion. Suppose it transforms them into final goods using only labor. Say that total wages equal $200 million and there are no profits. The value of final goods is thus equal to $1,200 million. Assume that $1 billion worth of final goods is exported and the rest is consumed domestically.

Exports and imports therefore both equal $1 billion. What is GDP in this economy? Remember that GDP is value added *in* the economy (see chapter 2). So, in this example, GDP equals $200 million, and the ratio of exports to GDP equals $1,000/$200 = 5.

Hence, exports can exceed GDP. This is indeed the case for many small countries where most economic activity is organized around a harbor and import–export activities. This is even the case for other small countries, such as Singapore, where manufacturing plays an important role. In 1997, the ratio of exports to GDP in Singapore was 180%. (For more on Singapore, look at the Focus box in chapter 12.)

domestic buyers (firms, the government) and foreign buyers also face this decision. If they decide to buy more domestic goods, the demand for domestic goods increases, and so does domestic output. If they decide to buy more foreign goods, then foreign output increases instead.

Central to consumers' and firms' decisions to buy foreign or domestic goods is the price of foreign goods in terms of domestic goods. We call this relative price the **real exchange rate**. The real exchange rate is not directly observable, and you will not find it in the newspapers. What you will find there are *nominal exchange rates*, the relative prices of currencies. Let's start by looking at nominal exchange rates, then see how we can use them to construct real exchange rates.

Nominal Exchange Rates

Nominal exchange rates between two currencies are quoted in two ways: (1) the price of the domestic currency in terms of the foreign currency, or (2) the price of the foreign currency in terms of the domestic currency. In December 1998, for example, the nominal exchange rate between the dollar and the German currency, the Deutsche Mark (DM) was quoted either as the price of a dollar in terms of DM (1 dollar = 1.67 DM), or as the price of a DM in terms of dollars (1 DM = 0.60 dollars).

In this book, we shall define the **nominal exchange rate** as *the price of foreign currency in terms of domestic currency*, and denote it by E. When, for example, looking at the exchange rate between Germany and the United States (from the viewpoint of the United States, so the dollar is the domestic currency), E will denote the price of a DM in terms of dollars—so, as of December 1998, this is 0.60.

Exchange rates between foreign currencies and the dollar change every day, every minute of the day. These changes are called *nominal appreciations* or *nominal depreciations*—appreciations or depreciations for short. An **appreciation** of the domestic currency is an increase in the price of the domestic currency in terms of a foreign currency. Given our definition of the exchange rate as the price of the foreign currency in terms of domestic currency, an appreciation of the domestic currency corresponds to a *decrease* in the exchange rate, E.

This is more intuitive than it seems: Consider the dollar and the DM (from the viewpoint of the United States). An *appreciation* of the dollar (also called a *dollar appreciation*) means the price of the dollar in terms of DM goes up. Equivalently, the price of DM in terms of dollars goes down, the same as saying the exchange rate has decreased. A *depreciation* of the dollar (a *dollar depreciation*) means the price of the dollar in terms of DM goes down. Equivalently, the price of DM in terms of dollars goes up, the same as saying the exchange rate has increased.

That an appreciation corresponds to a decrease in the exchange rate, and a depreciation to an increase in the exchange rate, will almost surely be confusing to you at first—indeed, it confuses many professional economists—but it will eventually become second nature as your understanding of open-economy macroeconomics deepens. Until then, consult Figure 18–2, which summarizes the terminology. (You may have encountered two other words for movements in exchange rates: "revaluations" and "devaluations." These two terms are used when countries operate under **fixed exchange rates**—a system in which two or more countries maintain an unchanging exchange rate between their currencies. Under such a system, decreases in the exchange rate—infrequent, by definition—are called **revaluations** (rather than appreciations). Increases in the exchange rate are called **devaluations** (rather than depreciations). We discuss fixed exchange rates in chapter 20.)

Keep in mind these definitions as we move on to Figure 18–3, which plots the nominal exchange rate between the DM and the dollar since 1975. The figure has two important features:

1. *The trend increase in the exchange rate*. In 1975, a DM was worth 40 cents. In the last quarter of 1998—the last observation in the figure—it was worth 60 cents, 1.5 times its value in 1970. Put another way, there has been a steady depreciation of the dollar vis-à-vis the DM since 1975.

2. *The large fluctuations in the exchange rate*. In the space of five years in the early 1980s, the value of the DM dropped from 57 cents to only 30 cents. This drop was fully reversed during the following three years, with the value of the DM increasing to 60 cents

From the point of view of United States looking at Germany

Nominal exchange rate *E*
Price of DM in terms of dollars

Appreciation of the dollar
Price of dollars in DM increases
equivalently:
Price of DM in dollars decreases
equivalently:
Exchange rate decreases: E↓

Depreciation of the dollar
Price of dollars in DM decreases
equivalently:
Price of DM in dollars increases
equivalently:
Exchange rate increases: E↑

FIGURE 18–2

The Nominal Exchange Rate, Appreciation, and Depreciation: Germany and the United States (from the Point of View of the United States)

by the end of 1987. Put another way, there was a large appreciation of the dollar in the first half of the 1980s, followed by an equally large depreciation during the following three years.

Figure 18–3 tells us only about movements in the relative price of the two currencies. To German tourists thinking of visiting the United States, the question is not, however, how many dollars they can get for their DM, but also how many goods a dollar will buy. It does them little good to get more dollars per DM if the dollar prices of goods have increased in roughly the same proportion. This takes us closer to where we want to go—to the construction of real exchange rates.

Real Exchange Rates

How do we construct the real exchange rate between Germany and the United States—the price of German goods in terms of U.S. goods?

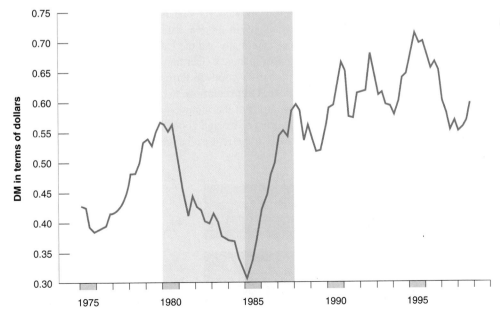

FIGURE 18–3

The Nominal Exchange Rate between the DM and the Dollar, 1975–1998

A sharp dollar appreciation in the first half of the 1980s was followed by an equally sharp dollar depreciation in the second half of the 1980s.

Suppose Germany produced only one good, a Mercedes SL-class car (this is one of those completely counterfactual "Suppose" statements, but we shall become more realistic shortly), and the United States also produced only one good, say, a Cadillac Seville.

Constructing the real exchange rate, the price of this one German good in terms of that one U.S. good, would be straightforward.

Computing the relative price of Mercedes in terms of Cadillacs:

Mercedes:
DM 100,000 × 0.60
           = $60,000

Cadillac: = $40,000

Relative price of Mercedes in terms of Cadillacs:

$$\frac{\$60,000}{\$40,000} = 1.5$$

- The first step would be to take the price of a Mercedes in DM and convert it to a price in dollars. Suppose the price of a Mercedes in Germany is 100,000 DM. Suppose a DM is worth 0.60 dollars. So the price of a Mercedes in dollars is 100,000 × 0.60 = $60,000.
- The second step would be to compute the ratio of the price of the Mercedes in dollars to the price of the Cadillac in dollars. The price of a Cadillac in the United States is $40,000. Thus, the price of a Mercedes in terms of Cadillacs—that is, the real exchange rate between the United States and Germany—would be $60,000/$40,000 = 1.5.

But Germany and the United States produce more than Mercedes and Cadillacs, and we want to construct a real exchange rate that reflects the relative price of *all* the goods produced in Germany in terms of *all* the goods produced in the United States. The computation we just went through tells us how to proceed. Rather than use the DM price of a Mercedes and the dollar price of a Cadillac, we must use a DM price index for all goods produced in Germany and a dollar price index for all goods produced in the United States. This is exactly what the GDP deflators we introduced in chapter 2 do: They are by definition price indexes for the set of final goods and services produced in the economy.

Another definition to remember: ϵ is the real exchange rate or the price of foreign goods in terms of domestic goods. (For example, from the point of view of the U.S., it is the price of German goods in terms of U.S. goods.)

So let P be the GDP deflator for the United States, P^* be the GDP deflator for Germany (as a rule, I shall denote foreign variables by an asterisk), and E be the DM–dollar nominal exchange rate. Figure 18–4 shows the steps needed to construct the real exchange rate.

- The price of German goods in DM is P^*. Multiplying it by the exchange rate, E (the price of DM in terms of dollars) gives us the price of German goods in dollars, EP^*.
- The price of U.S. goods in dollars is P. The real exchange rate, the price of German goods in terms of U.S. goods, which we shall call ϵ (the greek lowercase epsilon), is thus given by

$$\epsilon = \frac{EP^*}{P} \qquad (18.1)$$

Note that unlike the price of Mercedes in terms of Cadillacs, the real exchange rate is an index number: That is, its level is arbitrary, and thus uninformative. This is because the GDP deflators used in the construction of the real exchange rate are themselves index numbers; as we saw in chapter 2, they are equal to 1 (or 100) in whatever year is chosen as the base year. But while its level is uninformative, relative changes in the real exchange rate are informative: If for example, the real exchange rate between Germany and the United States increases by 10%, this tells us U.S. goods are now 10% cheaper relative to German goods than they were before.

An increase in the relative price of domestic goods in terms of foreign goods is called a **real appreciation**; a decrease is called a **real depreciation**. *Real* indicates that we are referring to changes in the relative price of *goods*, not the relative price of currencies. Given our definition of the real exchange rate as the price of foreign goods in terms of domestic goods, a real appreciation corresponds to a *decrease* in the real exchange rate, ϵ. Similarly, a real de-

FIGURE 18–4

The Construction of the Real Exchange Rate

**From the point of view of United States
Looking at Germany**

Real exchange rate ϵ Price of German goods in terms of U.S. goods

Real appreciation
Price of U.S. goods in terms of German goods increases equivalently: Price of German goods in terms of U.S. goods decreases equivalently: Real exchange rate decreases: ϵ↓

Real depreciation
Price of U.S. goods in terms of German goods decreases equivalently: Price of German goods in terms of U.S. goods increases equivalently: Real exchange rate decreases: ϵ↑

FIGURE 18–5

The Real Exchange Rate, Real Appreciation, and Real Depreciation: Germany and the United States (from the Viewpoint of the United States)

preciation corresponds to an *increase* in ϵ. These definitions are summarized in Figure 18–5, which does for the real exchange rate what Figure 18–2 did for the nominal exchange rate.

Figure 18–6 plots the evolution of the real exchange rate between Germany and the United States from 1975 to 1998. For convenience, it also reproduces the evolution of the nominal exchange rate from Figure 18–3. The GDP deflators have both been set equal to 1 in 1992, so that in that year the nominal and real exchange rates are equal by construction.

Figure 18–6 has two major features:

- In 1998, the real exchange rate was equal to 0.60, nearly the same value as in 1975. In other words, the relative price of German goods was roughly the same in 1998 as in 1975.

  How can it be, given the increase in the nominal exchange rate over the period, that the real exchange rate has remained roughly the same? The answer is that although the DM has increased vis-à-vis the dollar, the price level in the United States has increased

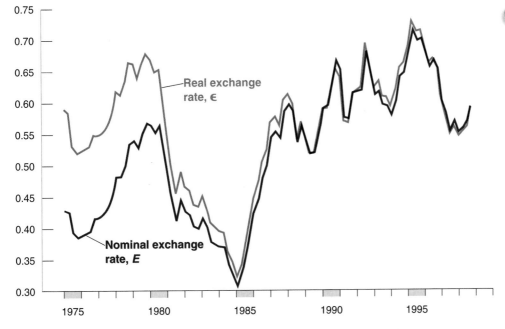

FIGURE 18–6

Real and Nominal Exchange Rates Between Germany and the United States, 1975–1998

Except for a difference in trend, the nominal and the real exchange rates have moved very much together since 1970.

more than the price level in Germany. To see this more clearly, return to the definition of the real exchange rate

$$\epsilon = E \frac{P*}{P}$$

Two things have happened since 1975. First, E has gone up: The DM has gone up in terms of dollars—this is the nominal depreciation we saw earlier. Second, inflation has been higher in the United States than in Germany, leading to a larger increase in the U.S. price level, P, than in the German price level, $P*$. This has led to a decrease in $P*/P$. The increase in E and the decrease in $P*/P$ have roughly cancelled out, leading to an unchanged real exchange rate.

To make this more concrete, return to our German tourists thinking of visiting the United States. They can buy 50% more dollars per DM than in 1975. Does this imply their trip will be 50% cheaper? No. When they arrive in the United States, they will discover that the prices of goods in the United States have increased by 50% more than the prices of goods in Germany, roughly cancelling the increase in the value of the DM in terms of dollars. Their trip will be no cheaper than it would have been in 1975.

Can there be a real appreciation with no nominal appreciation? Can there be a nominal appreciation with no real appreciation?

There is a general lesson here. Over long periods of time, depending on differences in inflation rates across countries, nominal and real exchange rates can move quite differently. We shall return to this issue in chapter 20.

- The large swings in the nominal exchange rate during the 1980s we saw in Figure 18–3 also show up in the real exchange rate. The reason is not hard to find: As inflation rates have not been very different in Germany and the United States, year-to-year movements in the price ratio $P*/P$ have been small compared to the often sharp movements in the nominal exchange rate, E. Thus, from year to year, or even over a few years, movements in the real exchange rate (ϵ) have been driven mostly by movements in the nominal exchange rate E. Note that since the mid-1980s, the nominal and the real exchange rates have moved nearly together; this reflects the fact that since the mid-1980s, inflation rates have been very similar in both countries.

Since 1975, the difference between the German inflation rate and the U.S. inflation rate has never been more than 5% in a given year. In other words, the change in $P*/P$ from one year to the next has never been more than 5%. In contrast, there have been several years when the nominal exchange rate has changed by more than 20% within the year.

We have one last step to take. So far, we have concentrated on the nominal and real exchange rates between the United States and Germany. But the United States trades with many countries besides Germany. Table 18–2 gives the geographic composition of U.S. trade for both exports and imports. The numbers refer only to **merchandise trade**—exports and imports of goods; they do not include exports and imports of services, such as travel services and tourism, for which the decomposition by country is not available.

TABLE 18–2 The Country Composition of U.S. Merchandise Trade, 1998

Countries	Exports to		Imports from	
	$ Billions	Percent	$ Billions	Percent
Canada	156	23	177	19
Western Europe	159	24	193	21
Japan	57	8	121	13
Mexico	78	12	95	11
Asia*	126	19	247	27
OPEC**	15	2	19	2
Others	80	11	67	7
Total	671	100	919	100

*Not including Japan.
**OPEC: Organization of Petroleum Exporting Countries.
Source: Survey of Current Business, April 1999.

Canada and Western Europe account for 40% to 47% (depending on whether one looks at imports or exports) of U.S. merchandise trade. But trade with Japan and the rest of Asia accounts for a steadily increasing proportion of U.S. merchandise trade. Interestingly, trade is much more unbalanced with Japan and the rest of Asia than with Canada and Western Europe: In 1998, the dollar volume of U.S. exports of goods to Japan was equal to roughly half the dollar volume of U.S. imports of goods from Japan. This merchandise trade deficit with Japan has been a major source of tension between the two countries for some time.

How do we go from **bilateral real exchange rates**, such as the real exchange rate between the United States and Germany, to **multilateral real exchange rates**? The answer is straightforward. If we want to measure the average price of goods of U.S. trading partners relative to the average price of U.S. goods, we should use the U.S. share of trade with each country as the weight for that country. Using export shares we can construct an "export" real exchange rate, and using import shares we can construct an "import" real exchange rate. Because economists usually do not want to keep track of two different exchange rates, they typically use an exchange rate that takes an average of export and import shares. This variable is called the **multilateral real U.S. exchange rate**, or the U.S. real exchange rate, for short.

Figure 18–7 shows the evolution of this multilateral real exchange rate, the average price of foreign goods relative to U.S. goods from 1975 to 1998. Like the bilateral real exchange rates we saw earlier, it is an index number. Thus, its level is arbitrary; here it is set equal to 1 in 1992.

In this figure, you can see that in the 1980s the movement in the multilateral exchange rate was similar to the movement in the German–U.S. real exchange rate shown in Figure 18–6. Foreign goods were substantially less expensive compared to U.S. goods in the mid-1980s than they were either at the beginning or the end of the decade. In other words, there was a large real appreciation in the first half of the 1980s, followed by an almost equally large real depreciation in the second half. This large swing, which, as we have seen, has its origins in the movement of the nominal exchange rate, is so striking that it has been given many names, from the "dollar cycle" to the more graphic "dance of the dollar." It is tempting to think of it as one of the causes of the large U.S. trade deficits that also characterized much of the 1980s. In the coming chapters we will look at where this swing came from and what effects these movements in the real exchange rate had on the trade deficit and on economic activity.

> *Bi-* means two. *Multi-* means many.

> The multilateral real U.S. exchange rate is also called the U.S. **trade-weighted real exchange rate**, and the U.S. **effective real exchange rate**.

> Increase in the real exchange rate ⇔ Real depreciation.
>
> Decrease in the real exchange rate ⇔ Real appreciation.

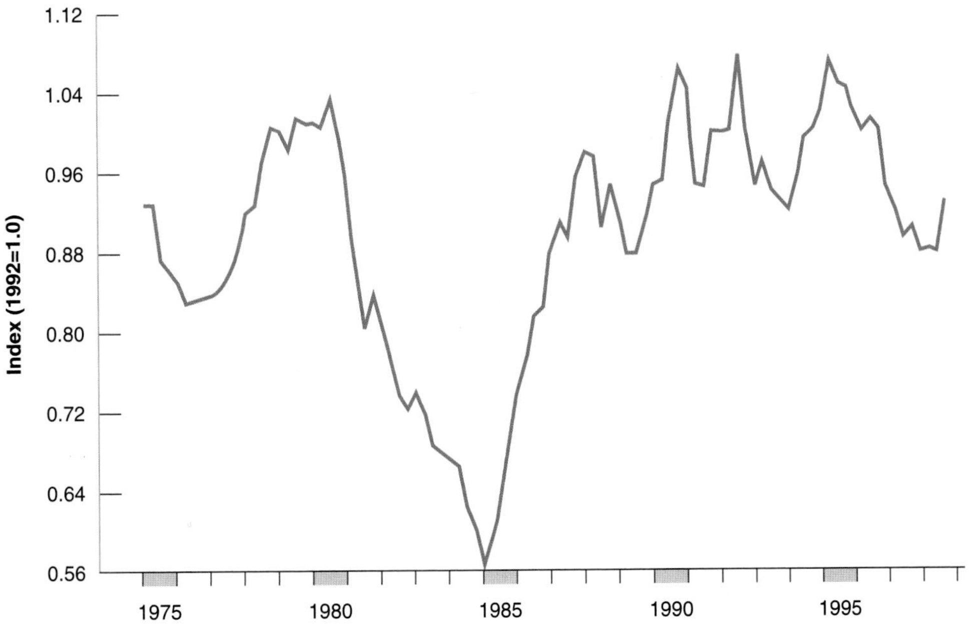

FIGURE 18–7

The U.S. Multilateral Real Exchange Rate, 1975–1998

The large real appreciation in the first half of the 1980s was followed by an equally large real depreciation in the second half of the 1980s. These large swings are sometimes called the "dance of the dollar."

18-2 | Openness in Financial Markets

Openness in financial markets allows financial investors to hold both domestic and foreign assets, to diversify their portfolios, to speculate on movements in foreign versus domestic interest rates, exchange rates, and so on. And diversify and speculate they do. Given that buying or selling foreign assets implies, as part of the operation, buying or selling foreign currency (sometimes called **foreign exchange**) the size of transactions in foreign-exchange markets gives a sense of the importance of international financial transactions. In 1997, the recorded *daily* volume of foreign-exchange transactions in the world was $2.5 trillion, of which 80%—about $2.0 trillion—involved dollars on one side of the transaction.

To get a sense of the magnitude of these numbers, the sum of U.S. exports and imports in 1997 totaled $1.8 trillion for the year, or about $6 billion a day. If the only dollar transactions in foreign-exchange markets had been on one side by U.S. exporters selling their foreign currency earnings, and on the other side by U.S. importers buying the foreign currency they needed to buy foreign goods, the volume of transactions would have been $6 billion a day, or about 0.3% of the actual daily volume of dollar transactions ($2.0 trillion) involving dollars in foreign-exchange markets. This computation yields a simple conclusion: Most of the transactions are associated not with trade, but with purchases and sales of financial assets. The volume of transactions in foreign-exchange markets is not only high but also increasing rapidly. The volume of foreign-exchange transactions in New York is now more than 20 times what it was in 1980. Again, this activity reflects an increase in financial transactions rather than an increase in trade over the last 15 years.

For a country as a whole, openness in financial markets has an important implication. It allows the country to run trade surpluses and trade deficits. A country running a trade deficit is buying more from the rest of the world than it is selling to the rest of the world, and must borrow the difference. It borrows by making it attractive for foreign financial investors to increase their holdings of domestic assets—in effect, to lend to the country. Let's now look at the relation between trade and financial flows more closely.

> Daily volume of foreign exchange transactions with dollars on one side of the transaction: $2.0 trillion. Daily volume of trade of the United States with the rest of the world: $6 billion (0.3% of the volume of foreign exchange transactions).

The Balance of Payments

A country's transactions with the rest of the world are summarized by a set of accounts called the **balance of payments**. Table 18–3 presents the U.S. balance of payments for 1998.

The table has two parts, separated by a line. Transactions are referred to as either **above the line** or **below the line**.

The Current Account. The transactions above the line all record payments to and from the rest of the world. These are called **current account** transactions.

The first two lines record exports and imports of goods and services. Exports lead to payments from the rest of the world, imports to payments to the rest of the world. In 1998, imports exceeded exports, leading to a U.S. trade deficit of $169 billion. (Note that the numbers for exports and imports are different from those in Table 18–2; this is because the numbers in Table 18–2 refer only to goods and the numbers here include both goods *and* services.)

Exports and imports are not the only sources of payments to and from the rest of the world. U.S. residents receive **investment income** on their holdings of foreign assets, and foreign residents receive investment income on their holdings of U.S. assets. In 1998, investment income received from the rest of the world was $242 billion and investment income paid to foreigners was $265 million, for a net balance of −$23 billion.

Finally, countries give and receive foreign aid; the net value of these payments is recorded as **net transfers received**. In 1998, these amounted to −$41 billion. This negative amount reflects the fact that the United States has traditionally been a net donor of foreign aid.

Adding all payments to and from the rest of the world, net payments were equal to −$169 − $23 − $41 = −$233 billion. This total is the *current account balance*. So,

Current Account		
Exports	931	
Imports	1100	
Trade balance (deficit = −) (1)		− 169
Investment income received	242	
Investment income paid	265	
Net investment income (2)		− 23
Net transfers received (3)		− 41
Current account balance (deficit = −) (1) + (2) + (3)		− 233
Capital Account		
Increase in foreign holdings of U.S. assets	542	
Increase in U.S. holdings of foreign assets	305	
Net increase in foreign holdings/(net capital flows to the U.S.)		237
Statistical discrepancy		4

Source: *Survey of Current Business*, April 1999. All numbers in billions of dollars.

in 1998, the United States ran a current account deficit of $233 billion, or just under 3% of its GDP.

The Capital Account. The fact that the United States had a current account deficit of $233 billion in 1998 implies that it had to borrow $233 billion from the rest of the world—equivalently, net foreign holdings of U.S. assets had to increase by $233 billion. The numbers below the line describe the way this result was achieved. Transactions below the line are called **capital account** transactions.

The increase in U.S holdings of foreign assets in 1998 was $305 billion. But at the same time, the increase in foreign holdings of U.S. assets was $542 billion. So the net increase in U.S foreign indebtedness, which is also called **net capital flows** to the United States, was $542 − $305 = $237 billion.

Shouldn't net capital flows be equal to the current account deficit? Yes. But the numbers for current and capital account transactions come from different sources; although they should give the same answers, they typically do not. In 1998, the difference between the two, the **statistical discrepancy**, was small, less than $4 billion. But in 1997, for example, the difference was $98 billion—more than 1% of GDP. Keep this example as a reminder that even for the United States, the data are far from perfect.

Now that we have looked at the current account, we can return to an issue we touched on in chapter 2, the difference between GDP, the measure of output we have used so far, and GNP, another measure of aggregate output. This is done in the Global Macro box "GDP versus GNP: The Example of Kuwait."

The Choice between Domestic and Foreign Assets

Why were foreign investors willing, in 1998, to increase their holdings of U.S. assets by $542 billion? To answer this question, we must look at the choice investors face between holding domestic versus foreign assets.

It might appear that we have to think about at least two new decisions, the choice of holding domestic versus foreign *money*, and the choice of holding domestic versus foreign *interest-paying assets*. But remember why people hold money: to engage in transactions. For somebody who lives in the United States whose transactions are thus in dollars, there is little point in holding foreign currency: It cannot be used for transactions, and if the goal is to

Can a country have a trade deficit and no current account deficit? A current account deficit and no trade deficit?

Here is another statistical problem: The sum of the current account deficits of all countries should be equal to zero: One country's deficit should show up as a surplus for the other countries taken as a whole. This is not, however, the case in the data: If we add the published current account deficits of all the countries in the world, it would appear that the world is running a large current account deficit. Some economists speculate that the explanation is unrecorded trade with the Martians. Most others believe that mismeasurement is the explanation.

GDP versus GNP: The Example of Kuwait

Should value added in an open economy be defined as:

- The value added domestically (that is, within the country)

or

- The value added by domestically owned factors of production?

The two definitions need not give the same result. Some domestic output may be produced by capital owned by foreigners, whereas some foreign output may be produced by capital owned by domestic residents.

The answer is that either definition is fine, and economists use both. **Gross domestic product (GDP)**, the measure we have used so far, corresponds to value added domestically. **Gross national product (GNP)** corresponds to the value added by domestically owned factors of production. GNP is equal to GDP plus net factor payments from the rest of the world (factor payments from the rest of the world minus factor payments to the rest of the world). Although GDP is now the measure most commonly mentioned, GNP was widely used until a few years ago, and you will still often encounter it in newspapers and academic publications.

For most countries, the difference between GNP and GDP is typically small, because factor payments to and from the rest of the world roughly cancel. For the United States in 1998, the difference between GDP and GNP was $21 billion, less than 0.3% of GDP.

But there are a few exceptions. One is Kuwait. When oil was discovered in Kuwait, Kuwait's government decided that a portion of oil revenues would be saved and invested abroad rather than spent, so as to provide future Kuwaiti generations with investment income when oil revenues came to an end. As a result, Kuwait accumulated large foreign assets, and now receives substantial investment income from the rest of the world. Table 1 gives GDP, GNP, and net factor payments for Kuwait from 1989 to 1994.

Note how much larger GNP is compared to GDP throughout the period. But note also how net factor payments have decreased since 1989. This is because Kuwait has had to pay its allies for part of the cost of the 1990–1991 Gulf War and to pay for reconstruction after the war. It has done this by running a current account deficit—equivalently, by decreasing its net holdings of foreign assets. This in turn has led to a decrease in the income from foreign assets, and by implication, in net factor payments.

TABLE 1 — GDP, GNP, and net factor payments in Kuwait, 1989–1994

Year	GDP	GNP	Net Factor Payments
1989	7143	9616	2473
1990	5328	7560	2232
1991	3131	4669	1538
1992	5826	7364	1538
1993	7231	8314	1083
1994	7380	8207	827

All numbers are in millions of Kuwaiti dinars. 1 dinar = $3.3 (1998).

Source: *International Financial Statistics*, IMF, Yearbook 1997.

There are two qualifications to this statement: Foreigners involved in illegal activities often hold dollars, because dollars can be exchanged easily and cannot be traced. Also, in times of very high inflation, people sometimes switch to the use of a foreign currency, often the dollar, even for some domestic transactions. This is known

hold foreign assets, holding foreign currency is clearly less desirable than holding foreign bonds, which, at least, pay interest. Thus, the only new choice we have to think about is the choice between domestic and foreign interest-paying assets.

Let's think of them for now as domestic and foreign one-year bonds, and consider the choice between U.S. and German one-year bonds.

- Suppose you decide to hold U.S. bonds. Let i_t be the one-year U.S. nominal interest rate. Then, as Figure 18–8 shows, for every dollar you put in U.S. bonds, you will get $(1 + i_t)$ dollars next year.
- Suppose you decide instead to hold German bonds. To buy German bonds, you must first buy DM. Let E_t be the nominal exchange rate between the dollar and the DM. For every dollar, you get $(1/E_t)$ DM.

Let i_t^* denote the one-year nominal interest rate on German bonds (in DM). When next year comes, you will have $(1/E_t)(1 + i_t^*)$ DM. You will then have to convert your

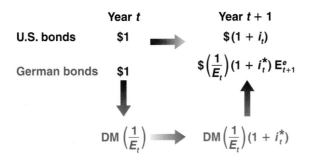

DM back into dollars. If you expect the nominal exchange rate next year to be E^e_{t+1}, you can expect to have $(1/E_t)(1 + i^*_t)E^e_{t+1}$ dollars next year for every dollar you invested. This set of steps is represented in the lower part of Figure 18–8. We shall look at the expression we just derived in more detail soon. But note already its basic implication: In assessing the attractiveness of German bonds, you cannot look just at the German and U.S. interest rates; you must also assess what you think will happen to the dollar/DM exchange rate between this year and next.

as the *dollarization* of an economy (see chapter 23). As we saw in chapter 4, recent estimates suggest that more than half of the U.S. currency stock is held abroad. We shall ignore this aspect of reality here.

Let's now make the same assumption we made in chapter 14 when discussing the choice between short- and long-term bonds, or between bonds and stocks. Let's assume that you and other financial investors want to hold only the asset with the highest rate of return. In that case, if both German and U.S bonds are to be held, they must have the same expected rate of return, so that the following *arbitrage relation* must hold.

$$1 + i_t = \left(\frac{1}{E_t}\right)(1 + i^*_t)(E^e_{t+1})$$

Or, reorganizing slightly,

$$1 + i_t = (1 + i^*_t)\left(\frac{E^e_{t+1}}{E_t}\right) \tag{18.2}$$

Equation (18.2) is called the **uncovered interest parity relation,** or simply the **interest parity condition**.[1]

The assumption that financial investors will hold only the bonds with the highest expected rate of return is obviously too strong, for two reasons:

- It ignores transaction costs: Going in and out of German bonds requires three separate transactions, each with a transaction cost.
- It ignores risk: The exchange rate a year from now is uncertain; that means that holding German bonds is more risky, in terms of dollars, than holding U.S. bonds.[2]

[1]**DIGGING DEEPER**. The word "uncovered" is to distinguish this relation from another relation called the *covered interest parity* condition. That condition is derived by looking at the following choice: Buy and hold U.S. bonds for one year. Or buy DM today, buy one-year German bonds with the proceeds, and agree to sell the DM for dollars a year ahead at a predetermined price, called the *forward exchange rate*. The rate of return to these two alternatives, which can both be realized at *no risk today*, must be the same. The covered interest parity condition is a *riskless arbitrage condition*.

[2]**DIGGING DEEPER**. Whether holding German or U.S. bonds is more risky depends on which investors we are looking at. Holding German bonds is more risky from the point of view of U.S. investors. Holding U.S. bonds is more risky from the point of view of German investors. (Why?)

But as a characterization of capital movements among the major world financial markets (New York, Frankfurt, London, and Tokyo), it is not far off. Small changes in interest rates and rumors of impending appreciation or depreciation can lead to movements of tens of billions of dollars within minutes. For the rich countries of the world, the arbitrage assumption in equation (18.2) is a good approximation of reality. Other countries, whose capital markets are smaller and less developed, or that have various forms of capital control, have more leeway in choosing their domestic interest rate than is implied by equation (18.2). We shall return to this issue at the end of chapter 20.

To get a better sense of what arbitrage implies, rewrite equation (18.2) as

$$1 + i_t = (1 + i_t^*)\left(1 + \frac{E_{t+1}^e - E_t}{E_t}\right) \tag{18.3}$$

This follows from proposition 3 in appendix 2.

This gives a relation between the domestic nominal interest rate, the foreign nominal interest rate, and the expected rate of depreciation. Remember that an increase in E is a depreciation, so that $(E_{t+1}^e - E_t)/E_t$ is the expected rate of depreciation of the domestic currency. (If the domestic currency is expected to appreciate, then this term is negative.) As long as interest rates or the expected rate of depreciation are not too large (say, below 20% a year) a good approximation to this equation is given by

$$i_t \approx i_t^* + \frac{E_{t+1}^e - E_t}{E_t} \tag{18.4}$$

This is the relation you must remember: Arbitrage implies that *the domestic interest rate must be (approximately) equal to the foreign interest rate plus the expected depreciation rate of the domestic currency.*

An important relation to remember: Under the uncovered interest parity condition, the domestic interest rate must approximately equal the foreign interest rate plus the expected depreciation of the domestic currency.

Let's apply this equation to U.S. versus German bonds. Suppose the one-year nominal interest rate is 4.0% in the United States, 2.5% in Germany. Should you hold German or U.S. bonds? It depends whether you expect the dollar to depreciate vis-à-vis the DM by more or less than $4.0\% - 2.5\% = 1.5\%$ over the coming year. If you expect the dollar to depreciate by more than 1.5%, then, despite the fact that the interest rate is lower in Germany than in the United States, investing in German bonds is more attractive than investing in U.S. bonds. By holding German bonds, you will get fewer DM a year from now, but the DM will also be worth more in terms of dollars a year from now, making investing in German bonds more attractive than investing in U.S. bonds. However, if you expect the dollar to depreciate by less than 1.5% or even to appreciate, then the reverse holds, and U.S bonds are more attractive than German bonds.

In other words, the uncovered interest parity condition tells us that financial investors must be expecting on average a depreciation of the dollar with respect to the DM of about 1.5% over the coming year, and this is why they are willing to hold German bonds despite their lower interest rate. (Another example is provided in the Global Macro box "Buying Brazilian Bonds".)

The arbitrage relation between interest rates and exchange rates in equation (18.4) will play a central role in the following chapters. It suggests that unless financial markets expect large depreciations or appreciations, domestic and foreign interest rates are likely to move very much together. Take the extreme case of two countries that commit to maintaining their bilateral exchange rates at a fixed value. If markets have faith in this commitment, they will expect the exchange rate to remain constant, and the expected depreciation will be zero. In that case, the arbitrage condition implies that interest rates in the two countries will have to move together exactly. Most of the time, as we shall see, governments do not make such absolute commitments, but they often do try to avoid large movements in the exchange rate. This puts sharp limits on how much they can allow their interest rate to deviate from interest rates elsewhere in the world.

How much do nominal interest rates actually move together between major countries? Figure 18–9 plots one-year nominal interest rates in the United States and Germany since

Buying Brazilian Bonds

Put yourself back in September 1993 (the very high interest rate in Brazil at the time helps make the point I want to get across here). Brazilian bonds are paying a *monthly* interest rate of 36.9%. This seems very attractive compared to the *annual* rate of 3% on U.S. bonds—corresponding to a *monthly* interest rate of about 0.2%. Shouldn't you buy Brazilian bonds?

The discussion in this chapter tells you that to decide, you need one more crucial element, the expected rate of appreciation of the dollar vis-à-vis the cruzeiro (the name of the Brazilian currency at the time; the currency is now called the real). You need this information because (as Figure 18–8 makes clear) the return in dollars from investing in Brazilian bonds for a month is

$$(1 + i_t^*) \frac{E_{t+1}^e}{E_t} = (1.369) \frac{E_{t+1}^e}{E_t}$$

What rate of cruzeiro depreciation should you expect over the coming month? Assume that the rate of depreciation

next month will be equal to the rate of depreciation last month. You know that 100,000 cruzeiros, worth $1.01 at the end of July 1993, were worth only $0.75 at the end of August 1993. If depreciation continues at the same rate, the return from investing in Brazilian bonds for a month is

$$(1 + i_t^*) \frac{E_{t+1}^e}{E_t} = (1.369)\left(\frac{0.75}{1.01}\right) = 1.016$$

The expected rate of return in dollars from holding Brazilian bonds is only $(1.016 - 1) = 1.6\%$ per month, not the 36.9% per month that looked so attractive. Note that 1.6% per month is still much higher than the monthly interest rate on U.S. bonds (about 0.2%.) But think of the risk and the transaction costs—all the elements we ignored when we wrote the arbitrage condition. When these are taken into account, you may well decide to keep your funds out of Brazil.

1975. The impression is indeed one of closely related but not identical movements. Interest rates were high (by historical standards) in both countries in the mid-1970s, low in the late 1970s, and very high in the early 1980s. They generally have been decreasing since then in both countries. At the same time, differences between the two are sometimes large. In 1984, the German interest rate was nearly 5% below the U.S. interest rate. In 1992, by contrast, the German interest rate was nearly 6% above the U.S. interest rate. In the coming chapters, we shall return to why these differences emerged, and what their implications were.

Meanwhile, do the following: Look at the back pages of a recent issue of The *Economist* for short-term interest rates in different countries relative to the United States. Which are the currencies against which the dollar is expected to depreciate?

FIGURE 18–9

U.S. and German One-Year Nominal Interest Rates, 1975–1998

U.S. and German nominal interest rates have largely moved together over the last 25 years.

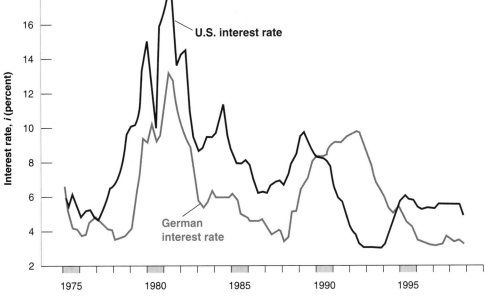

We have now set the stage for the study of the open economy. Openness in goods markets allows a choice between domestic and foreign goods. This choice depends primarily on the *real exchange rate*—the relative price of foreign goods in terms of domestic goods.

Openness in financial markets allows a choice between domestic and foreign assets. This choice depends primarily on their relative rates of return, which depend in turn on domestic and foreign interest rates, and on the expected rate of depreciation of the domestic currency.

In the next chapter, chapter 19, we look at the implications of openness in goods markets. Chapter 20 brings in openness in financial markets. In chapter 21, we look at the medium run in an open economy, and we discuss the pros and cons of different exchange rate regimes.

SUMMARY

- Openness in goods markets allows people and firms to choose between domestic and foreign goods. Openness in financial markets allows financial investors to choose between domestic or foreign financial assets.

- The nominal exchange rate is the price of foreign currency in terms of domestic currency. From the viewpoint of the United States, the nominal exchange rate between the United States and Germany is the price of DM in terms of dollars.

- A nominal appreciation (an appreciation, for short) is an increase in the price of the domestic currency in terms of foreign currency; given the definition of the exchange rate, it corresponds to a decrease in the exchange rate. A nominal depreciation (a depreciation, for short) is a decrease in the price of the domestic currency in terms of foreign currency; it corresponds to an increase in the exchange rate.

- The real exchange rate is the relative price of foreign goods in terms of domestic goods. It is equal to the nominal exchange rate times the foreign price level divided by the domestic price level.

- A real appreciation is an increase in the relative price of domestic goods in terms of foreign goods; it corresponds to a decrease in the real exchange rate. A real depreciation is a decrease in the relative price of domestic goods; it corresponds to an increase in the real exchange rate.

- The multilateral real exchange rate, or real exchange rate, for short, is a weighted average of bilateral real exchange rates, with weights equal to trade shares.

- The balance of payments records a country's transactions with the rest of the world. The current account balance is equal to the sum of the trade balance, net investment income, and net transfers received from the rest of the world. The capital account balance is equal to capital flows from the rest of the world, minus capital flows to the rest of the world.

- The current account and the capital account are mirror images of each other. A current account deficit is financed by net capital flows from the rest of the world, thus by a capital account surplus. Similarly, a current account surplus corresponds to a capital account deficit.

- Uncovered interest parity, or interest parity, for short, is an arbitrage condition stating that the expected rates of return in terms of domestic currency on domestic and foreign bonds must be equal. Interest parity implies that the domestic interest rate approximately equals the foreign interest rate plus the expected depreciation rate of the domestic currency.

KEY TERMS

- openness in goods markets, 343
- tariffs, 343
- quotas, 343
- openness in financial markets, 343
- capital controls, 343
- openness in factor markets, 343

QUESTIONS & PROBLEMS

An asterisk denotes a harder question. [Web] indicates that the question requires access to the Internet.

1. TRUE/FALSE/UNCERTAIN

a. Countries with net capital inflows must be running current account deficits.

b. Although the export ratio can be larger than one (as it is in Singapore), the same cannot be true of the ratio of imports to GDP.

c. That a rich country such as Japan has such a small ratio of imports to GDP is clear evidence of an unfair playing field for U.S. exporters.

d. Uncovered interest parity implies that real interest rates must be the same across countries.

e. If the nominal exchange rate between the DM and the dollar is 0.70, it means that one DM is worth 70 cents.

f. If the real exchange rate between Germany and the United States is 2, this means that goods are twice as expensive in Germany as in the United States.

2. FRANCE AND GERMANY [Web]

Retrieve the nominal exchange rates between Germany and France from the Internet. A useful and free Canadian site that allows you to construct graphs on-line is located at http://pacific.commerce.ubc.ca/xr/

Plot the DM versus the franc since 1979, and compare this graph with that of the DM versus the dollar in the text. In particular, how are the trend and volatility of the two series different in the 1980s? For the exchange rate between the DM and the franc, discuss the differences in the behavior of the exchange rate across time periods 1979 to 1987, 1988 to 1991, and 1992 to 1998. When did the franc depreciate or appreciate vis-à-vis the DM?

3. BALANCE OF PAYMENTS

Consider two fictional economies, one the "domestic country" and the other the "foreign country." Construct a balance of payments for each country given the following list of transactions:

The domestic country purchased $100 in oil from the foreign country.

Foreign tourists spent $25 on domestic ski slopes.

Domestic residents purchased $45 in life insurance in the foreign country.

Domestic residents purchased $5 in illegal substances from foreigners.

Foreign investors were paid $15 in dividends from their holdings of domestic equities.

Domestic residents sent $25 to foreign charities.

Foreign businessmen spent $35 in bribes to domestic government officials.

Domestic businesses borrowed $65 from foreign banks.

Foreign investors purchased $15 in domestic junk bonds.

Domestic investors sold off $50 in holdings of foreign government bonds.

*4. THE REAGAN YEARS

When Ronald Reagan was president, the U.S. trade deficit increased substantially. Democrats pointed to the trade deficit as a sign that the U.S. economy was no longer competitive. Ronald Reagan pointed to the large net capital inflows instead as a sign that the U.S. economy had become a very attractive place for foreign investors. Who was right? Can you tell?

5. UNCOVERED INTEREST PARITY

Consider the following prices for government bonds and foreign exchange in the United States and Germany. Assume that both government securities are one-year bonds, paying the face value of the bond one year from now. The exchange rate E stands at 1 DM = 0.95 dollars.

The face values and prices on the two bonds are given by

		Face Value	Price
United States	1-year bond	$10,000	$9615.38
Germany	1-year bond	DM 13,333	DM 12698.10

a. Compute the nominal interest rate on each of the bonds.

b. Compute the expected exchange rate next year consistent with uncovered interest parity.

c. If you expect the dollar to depreciate relative to the DM, which bond should you buy?

d. Assume you are a U.S. investor. You exchange dollars for DM and purchase the German bond. One year from now it turns out E is actually 0.90 (1 DM = 0.90 dollars). What is your realized return in dollars compared to the realized return you would have made had you held the U.S. bond?

e. Are the differences in returns in (d) consistent with the uncovered interest parity condition? Why or why not?

*6. COVERED INTEREST PARITY

Assume that there exists a market for buying and selling foreign exchange one year in the future, at a price determined today. This price is called the forward exchange rate. Denote the forward price of 1 DM in terms of dollars by F. In other words, you can enter into a contract today to sell 1 DM for F dollars one year in the future.

a. Derive the following approximation to covered interest parity where i denotes expected nominal return and an asterisk denotes foreign variables:

$$i = i^* + \frac{F - E}{E}$$

b. Given the two government bonds and exchange rate from the previous problem, find the forward exchange rate of 1 DM consistent with covered interest parity.

c. What should you do if the forward exchange rate is different from the value you just derived?

d. Suppose the forward exchange rate is as you computed it in (b). You buy DM today, buy the German bond today, and enter into a contract today to sell the DM you will receive in a year, at the forward exchange rate. Does a surprise in the exchange rate between now and next year affect the returns on your investment? Why or why not?

FURTHER READINGS

If you want to learn more about international trade and international economics, read the textbook by Paul Krugman and Maurice Obstfeld, *International Economics, Theory and Policy*, 4th ed. (New York: HarperCollins, 1996).

If you want to know current exchange rates between nearly any pair of currencies in the world, look at the "currency converter" at www.oanda.com.

We invite you to visit the Blanchard page on the Prentice Hall Web site at:

http://www.prenhall.com/blanchard

for this chapter's World Wide Web exercises

CHAPTER 19

The Goods Market in an Open Economy

When, after three years of little or no growth, the U.S. recovery became stronger in 1993, countries around the world cheered. Not for the United States, but for themselves. They saw higher U.S. output as implying higher demand not only for U.S. goods but for foreign goods as well. To them, higher demand meant higher exports to the United States, an improvement in their trade position, an increase in their output, and a chance to grow more quickly out of their own recessions.

Can a foreign expansion really lift a country out of a recession? If there are such strong interactions between countries, shouldn't macroeconomic policies be coordinated between countries? If so, why does it seem so difficult to achieve such coordination? To answer these questions, we must expand our treatment of the goods market in the core (chapter 3), taking into account openness in goods markets. This is what we do in this chapter.

When we were assuming the economy was closed to trade, there was no need to distinguish between the domestic demand for goods and the demand for domestic goods: They were clearly the same. Now, we must distinguish between the two: Some domestic demand falls on foreign goods, and some of the demand for domestic goods comes from foreigners. Let's look at this distinction more closely.

The terms "the domestic demand for goods" and "the demand for domestic goods" may sound close. But, in an open economy, they need not be equal.

The Demand for Domestic Goods

In an open economy, the **demand for domestic goods** is given by

$$Z \equiv C + I + G - \epsilon Q + X \tag{19.1}$$

The first three terms—consumption (C), investment (I), and government spending (G)—constitute the **domestic demand for goods**. If the economy were closed, $C + I + G$ would also be the demand for domestic goods. This is why, until now, we looked only at $C + I + G$. But now we have to make two adjustments.

In chapter 3, I ignored this and subtracted Q. This was wrong, but I did not want to have to talk about the real exchange rate and complicate matters so early in the book.

- First, we must subtract imports, that part of domestic demand that falls on foreign goods. We must be careful here. Foreign goods are different from domestic goods, so we cannot just subtract the quantity of imports, Q; if we were to do so, we would be subtracting apples (foreign goods) from oranges (domestic goods). We must first express the value of imports in terms of domestic goods. This is what ϵQ in equation (19.1) stands for: As we saw in chapter 18, ϵ is the real exchange rate, the price of foreign goods in terms of domestic goods. Thus, ϵQ (the price times the quantity of imports) is the value of imports in terms of domestic goods.
- Second, we must add exports, the demand for domestic goods that comes from abroad. This is captured by the term X in equation (19.1).

The Determinants of the Demand for Domestic Goods

Domestic demand for goods ($C + I - G$)
 − domestic demand for foreign goods (imports, ϵQ)
 + foreign demand for domestic goods (exports, X)
 = Demand for domestic goods ($C + I + G - \epsilon Q + X$)

Having listed the five components of demand, our next task is to specify their determinants. Let's start with the first three: C, I, and G.

The Determinants of C, I, and G. Now that we are assuming the economy is open, how should we modify our earlier descriptions of consumption, investment, and government spending? The answer is not very much, if at all. How much consumers decide to spend still depends on their income and their wealth. Although the real exchange rate surely affects the *composition* of consumption spending between domestic and foreign goods, there is no obvious reason why it should affect the overall *level* of consumption. The same is true of investment: The real exchange rate may affect whether firms buy domestic or foreign machines, but it should not affect total investment.

This is good news because it implies that we can use the descriptions of consumption, investment, and government spending that we developed earlier. Therefore,

$$\text{Domestic demand:} \quad C + I + G = C(Y - T) + I(Y, r) + G$$
$$(\quad + \quad) \quad (+, -)$$

We assume that consumption depends positively on disposable income ($Y - T$), and that investment depends positively on production (Y) and negatively on the real interest rate (r). We continue to take government spending (G) as given. We leave aside for the moment the refinements introduced in chapters 14 to 17, where we looked at the role of expectations in affecting spending. The point is to take things one step at a time to understand the effects of opening the economy; we shall reintroduce some of those refinements later.

Domestic demand ($C + I + G$) depends on income (Y), the interest rate (r), taxes (T), and the level of government spending (G).

The Determinants of Imports. What does the quantity of imports, Q, depend on? Primarily on the overall level of domestic demand: The higher the level of domestic demand, the higher the demand for all goods, both domestic and foreign. This is what the paragraph that started the chapter said: In 1993, the rest of the world wanted a U.S. recovery because a U.S. recovery would lead to higher U.S. imports. But Q also clearly depends on the real exchange rate: The higher the price of foreign goods relative to domestic goods, the lower the relative domestic demand for foreign goods, and the lower the quantity of imports.

Thus, we write imports as

$$Q = Q(Y, \epsilon) \qquad (19.2)$$
$$(+,-)$$

Imports depend on income (or, equivalently, output—the two are still the same in an open economy), Y: Higher income leads to higher imports.[1] Imports also depend on the real exchange rate. Recall that the real exchange rate, ϵ, is defined as the price of foreign goods in terms of domestic goods. A higher real exchange rate means that foreign goods are relatively more expensive, leading to a decrease in the quantity of imports, Q. This negative effect of the real exchange rate on imports is captured by the negative sign under ϵ in the import equation.

The Determinants of Exports. The export of one country is, by definition, the import of another. In thinking about what determines U.S. exports, we can ask, equivalently, what determines foreign imports. From our discussion of the determinants of imports in the preceding paragraph, we know that foreign imports are likely to depend on foreign activity, and on the relative price of foreign goods. Thus, we can write exports as

$$X = X(Y^*, \epsilon) \qquad (19.3)$$
$$(+,+)$$

Y^* is income in the rest of the world, or simply *foreign* income (equivalently foreign output). An increase in foreign income leads to an increase in the foreign demand for all goods, some of which falls on U.S. goods, leading to higher U.S. exports. An increase in epsilon—an increase in the relative price of foreign goods in terms of U.S. goods—makes U.S. goods relatively more attractive, leading to an increase in exports.

We can represent what we have learned so far in Figure 19–1, which plots the various components of demand against output, keeping constant all other variables that affect demand (the interest rate, taxes, government spending, foreign output, and the real exchange rate).

In Figure 19–1(a), the line DD plots *domestic demand*, $C + I + G$, as a function of output, Y. This relation between demand and output is familiar from the core. Under our standard assumptions, the slope of the relation between demand and output is positive but less than 1: An increase in output (equivalently, in income) increases demand but less than one for one. (In the absence of good reasons to the contrary, I draw the relation between demand and output, and the other relations in this chapter, as lines rather than curves. This is purely for convenience, and none of the discussions that follow depend on that assumption.)

To arrive at the *demand for domestic goods*, we must first subtract imports. This is done in Figure 19–1(b) and gives us the line AA: The distance between DD and AA equals the value of imports, ϵQ. Because the quantity of imports increases with income, the distance between the two lines increases with income. We can establish two facts about line AA, which will be useful later in the chapter:

1. AA is flatter than DD: As income increases, some of the additional domestic demand falls on foreign goods rather than on domestic goods. As income increases, the domestic demand for domestic goods increases less than total domestic demand.

As ϵ goes up while Q goes down, what happens to ϵQ, the value of imports in terms of domestic goods, is ambiguous. We return to this point later.

The volume of imports (Q) depends on the level of output (Y), and the real exchange rate (ϵ).

Recall that asterisks refer to foreign variables.

Exports depend on the level of foreign income (Y^*), and the real exchange rate (ϵ).

For a given real exchange rate ϵ, ϵQ (the value of imports in terms of domestic goods) moves exactly with Q (the volume of imports).

---

[1]**DIGGING DEEPER**. We cheat a bit here. Our discussion suggests that we should be using domestic demand, $C + I + G$, instead of income, Y. You might also dispute the assumption that imports depend on the sum of domestic demand and not on its composition: It may well be that the proportion of imports in investment differs from that of imports in consumption. For example, many poor countries import most of their capital equipment but consume mostly domestic goods. In that case, the composition of demand would matter for imports. I leave these complications aside. You may want to explore them on your own.

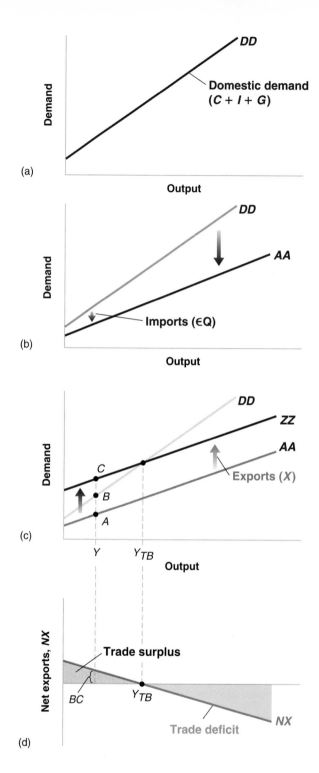

The Demand for Domestic Goods and Net Exports

The domestic demand for goods is an increasing function of income. The demand for domestic goods is obtained by subtracting the value of imports from domestic demand, and then adding exports. The trade balance is a decreasing function of output.

2. As long as some of the additional demand falls on domestic goods, *AA* has a positive slope: An increase in income leads to some increase in the demand for domestic goods.

Finally, we must add exports. This is done in Figure 19–1(c) and gives us the line *ZZ*, which is above *AA*. The distance between *ZZ* and *AA* equals exports. Because exports do not depend on domestic output, the distance between *ZZ* and *AA* is constant, so the two lines are parallel. Because *AA* is flatter than *DD*, *ZZ* is flatter than *DD* as well.

From the information in Figure 19–1(c) we can characterize the behavior of net exports—the difference between exports and imports $(X - \epsilon Q)$—as a function of output. At output level Y for example, exports are given by the distance AC and imports by the distance AB, so net exports are given by the distance BC.

This relation between net exports and output is represented as the line denoted NX (for Net eXports) in Figure 19–1(d). Net exports are a decreasing function of output: As output increases, imports increase and exports are unaffected, leading to lower net exports. Call Y_{TB} (TB for trade balance) the level of output at which the value of imports is just equal to exports, so that net exports are equal to zero. Levels of output above Y_{TB} lead to higher imports, leading to a trade deficit. Levels of output below Y_{TB} lead to lower imports, and to a trade surplus.

Recall that *net exports* is synonymous with trade balance. Positive net exports correspond to a trade surplus, negative net exports to a trade deficit.

19-2 | Equilibrium Output and the Trade Balance

The goods market is in equilibrium when domestic output equals the demand for domestic goods

$$Y = Z$$

Equilibrium in the goods market requires that domestic output be equal to the demand for domestic goods.

Collecting the relations we derived for the components of the demand for domestic goods, Z,

$$Y = C(Y - T) + I(Y, r) + G - \epsilon Q(Y, \epsilon) + X(Y^*, \epsilon) \qquad (19.4)$$

This equilibrium condition determines output as a function of all the variables we take as given, from taxes, to the real exchange rate to foreign output. This is not a simple relation; Figure 19–2 represents it in a more user-friendly way. In Figure 19–2(a), demand is measured on the vertical axis, output (equivalently, income) on the horizontal axis. The line ZZ

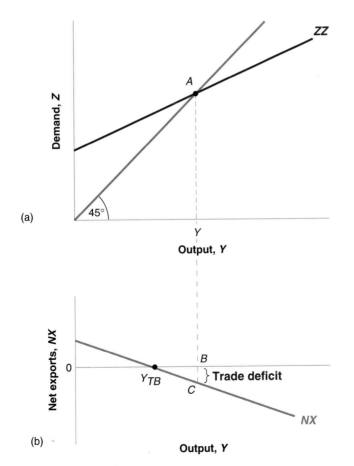

(a)

(b)

FIGURE 19-2

Equilibrium Output and Net Exports

The goods market is in equilibrium when production is equal to the demand for domestic goods. At the equilibrium level of output, the trade balance may show a deficit or a surplus.

plots demand as a function of output; this line just replicates the line ZZ in Figure 19–1; ZZ is upward sloping, but with slope less than 1.

Equilibrium output is at the point where demand equals output, at the intersection of the line ZZ and the 45-degree line, so at point A in the figure, with associated output level Y.

Figure 19–2(b) replicates Figure 19–1(d), drawing net exports as a decreasing function of output. There is in general no reason why the equilibrium level of output, Y, should be the same as the level of output at which trade is balanced, Y_{TB}. As I have drawn the figure, equilibrium output is associated with a trade deficit, equal to the distance BC.

The equilibrium level of output is given by the condition $Y = Z$. The level of output at which there is trade balance is given by the condition $\epsilon Q = Y$. These are two different conditions.

We now have the tools needed to answer the questions we asked at the beginning of this chapter.

19-3 | Increases in Demand, Domestic or Foreign

How do changes in demand affect output in an open economy? Let's start with a variation of what is by now an old favorite, an increase in government spending, and then turn to a new exercise, the effects of an increase in foreign activity.

Increases in Domestic Demand

Suppose the economy is in recession and the government decides to increase government spending to increase domestic demand and output. What will be the effects on output and on the trade balance?

As in the core, we start by ignoring all other markets than the goods market; the conclusions we derive here will still apply when we introduce financial and labor markets later on.

The answer is given in Figure 19–3. Before the increase in government spending, demand is given by ZZ in Figure 19–3(a), and the equilibrium is at point A, where output equals Y. Let's assume (though, as we have seen, there is no reason why this should be true in general) that trade is initially balanced, so, in Figure 19–3(b), $Y = Y_{TB}$.

What happens if the government increases spending by ΔG? At any level of output, demand is higher by ΔG, shifting the demand relation up by ΔG from ZZ to ZZ'. The equilibrium point moves from A to A', and output increases from Y to Y'. The increase in output is larger than the increase in government spending: There is a multiplier effect.

So far, the story sounds like what happened in the closed economy earlier (see chapter 3). However, let's look more closely: There is now an effect on the trade balance. Because government spending enters neither the exports relation nor the imports relation directly, the relation between net exports and output in Figure 19–3(b) does not shift. Thus, the increase in output from Y to Y' leads to a trade deficit equal to BC.

Starting from trade balance, an increase in government spending leads to a trade deficit.

Not only does government spending now generate a trade deficit, but its effect on output is smaller than in the closed economy. Recall from chapter 3 that the smaller the slope of the demand relation, the smaller the multiplier (for example, if ZZ were horizontal, the multiplier would be 1). And recall from Figure 19–1 that the demand relation, ZZ, is flatter than the demand relation in the closed economy, DD. That means the multiplier is smaller in the open economy.

The trade deficit and the smaller multiplier arise from the same cause: An increase in demand now falls not only on domestic goods, but also on foreign goods. Thus, when income increases, the effect on the demand for domestic goods is smaller than it would be in a closed economy, leading to a smaller multiplier. And, because some of the increase in de-

The smaller multiplier and the trade deficit have the same underlying cause: Some domestic demand falls on foreign goods, not domestic goods.

mand falls on imports—and exports are unchanged—the result is a trade deficit.

These two implications are important. In an open economy, an increase in domestic demand has a smaller effect on output than in a closed economy, as well as an adverse effect on the trade balance. Indeed, the more open the economy, the smaller the effect on output and the larger the adverse effect on the trade balance. For example, take Belgium, which has a ratio of imports to GDP close to 70%. This implies that when demand increases in Belgium, roughly 70% of this increased demand goes to higher imports, and only 30% to an increase in the demand for domestic goods. The effect of an increase in government spend-

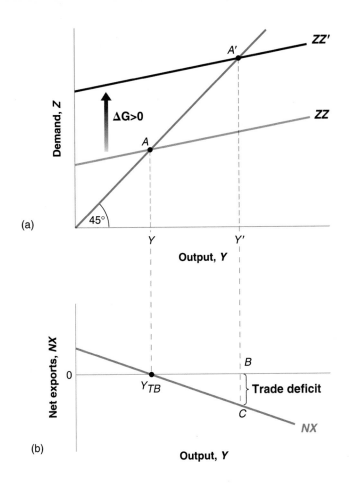

(a)

(b)

FIGURE 19-3

The Effects of Higher Government Spending

An increase in government spending leads to an increase in output and a trade deficit.

ing is thus likely to be a large increase in Belgium's trade deficit and only a small increase in its output, making domestic demand expansion a rather unattractive policy for Belgium. Even for the United States, which has an import ratio of only 13%, an increase in demand will be associated with some deterioration in the trade position. (This conclusion is discussed further in the Focus box "Multipliers: Belgium versus the United States.")

Increases in Foreign Demand

Consider now an increase in foreign activity, an increase in Y^*. This could be due to an increase in foreign government spending, G^*—the policy change we just analyzed, but now taking place abroad. But we do not need to know where the increase comes from to analyze the effects on the U.S. economy.

Figure 19–4 shows the effects of an increase in foreign activity on domestic output and the trade balance. The initial demand for domestic goods is given by ZZ in Figure 19–4(a). The equilibrium is at point A, with output level Y. Let's assume trade is balanced, so that in Figure 19–4(b) the net exports associated with Y equal zero.

It will be useful to refer to the line that gives the domestic demand for goods $C + I + G$ as a function of income. This line is drawn as DD. Recall from Figure 19–1 that DD is steeper than ZZ. The difference between ZZ and DD equals net exports, so that if trade is balanced at point A, then ZZ and DD intersect at point A.

Now consider the effects of an increase in foreign output, ΔY^*. Higher foreign output means higher foreign demand, including higher foreign demand for U.S. goods. So the direct effect of the increase in foreign output is to increase U.S. exports by some amount, call it ΔX. For a given level of output, this increase in exports leads to an increase in the demand

DD is the domestic demand for goods. ZZ is the demand for domestic goods.

$Y^* \uparrow \Rightarrow X = X(Y^*, \epsilon) \uparrow$

Multipliers: Belgium versus the United States

If we assume that the various relations in equation (19.4) are linear, we can compute the effects of government spending, foreign output, and so forth on both output and the trade balance. In this box we look at the differences between the effects of government spending in a large country such as the United States and in a small country such as Belgium.

Assume consumption and investment are given by

$$C = c_0 + c_1(Y - T)$$
$$I = d_0 + d_1 Y - d_2 r$$

Consumption increases with disposable income; investment increases with output and decreases with the real interest rate.

For simplicity, ignore movements in the real exchange rate and assume $\epsilon = 1$. Assume imports and exports are given by

$$Q = q_1 Y$$
$$X = x_1 Y^*$$

Imports are proportional to domestic output, and exports are proportional to foreign output. In the same way we referred to c_1 as the marginal propensity to consume, q_1 is the **marginal propensity to import**.

The equilibrium condition is that output equals the demand for domestic goods

$$Y = C + I + G - Q + X$$

(Recall that we are assuming that ϵ equals 1, so $\epsilon Q = Q$.) Replace C, I, G, Q, and X by their expressions from above

$$Y = [c_0 + c_1(Y - T)] + (d_0 + d_1 Y - d_2 r) + G - q_1 Y + x_1 Y^*$$

Regroup terms

$$Y = (c_1 + d_1 - q_1)Y$$
$$+ (c_0 + d_0 - c_1 T - d_2 r + G + x_1 Y^*)$$

Bring the terms in output together, and solve for output

$$Y = \frac{1}{1 - (c_1 + d_1 - q_1)}$$
$$\times (c_0 + d_0 - c_1 T - d_2 r + G + x_1 Y^*)$$

Output equals the multiplier times the term in parentheses—which captures the effect of all the variables we take as given in explaining output.

Consider the multiplier. Specifically, consider $(c_1 + d_1 - q_1)$ in the denominator. As in the closed economy, $(c_1 + d_1)$ gives the effects of an increase in output on consumption and investment demand; $(-q_1)$ captures the fact that some of the increased demand falls not on domestic goods but on foreign goods. In the extreme case where all the additional demand falls on foreign goods—when $q_1 = c_1 + d_1$—an increase in output has no effect on the demand for domestic goods; in that case, the multiplier equals 1. In general, q_1 is less than $(c_1 + d_1)$, so the multi-

plier is larger than 1. But it is smaller than it would be in a closed economy.

Using this equation, we can easily characterize the effects of an increase in government spending of ΔG. The increase in output is equal to the multiplier times the change in government spending

$$\Delta Y = \frac{1}{1 - (c_1 + d_1 - q_1)} \Delta G$$

And the increase in imports that follows from the increase in output implies the following change in net exports

$$\Delta NX = -q_1 \Delta Y$$
$$= -\frac{q_1}{1 - (c_1 + d_1 - q_1)} \Delta G$$

Let's see what these formulas imply by choosing numerical values for the parameters. Take $c_1 + d_1$ equal to 0.6. What value should we choose for q_1? We saw in chapter 18 that, in general, the larger the country, the more self-sufficient it is, and the less it imports. So let's choose two values of q_1—a small value, say, 0.1, for a large country such as the United States, and a larger one, say, 0.4, for a small country such as Belgium. Note that the proportion of an increase in demand that falls on imports is given by $q_1/(c_1 + d_1)$. (An increase in output of 1 dollar leads to an increase in spending of $[c_1 + d_1]$ dollars, of which q_1 dollars is spent on foreign goods.) So an equivalent way of stating our choice of q_1 is that in the large country, 1/6 (0.1 divided by 0.6) of demand falls on imports, versus 4/6 (0.4 divided by 0.6) in the small country.

Now return to the expressions for output and the trade balance. For the large country, the effects on output and the trade balance are given by

$$\Delta Y = \frac{1}{1 - (0.6 - 0.1)} \Delta G = 2.0 \, \Delta G$$

and

$$\Delta NX = -0.1 \, \Delta Y = \frac{-0.1}{1 - (0.6 - 0.1)} \Delta G = -0.2 \, \Delta G$$

For the small country, the effects are given by

$$\Delta Y = \frac{1}{1 - (0.6 - 0.4)} \Delta G = 1.25 \, \Delta G$$

and

$$\Delta NX = -0.4 \, \Delta Y = \frac{-0.4}{1 - (0.6 - 0.4)} \Delta G = -0.5 \, \Delta G$$

These computations show how different the trade-offs faced by both countries are.

● In the large country, the effect of an increase in G on output is large and the effect on the trade balance is small.

THE OPEN ECONOMY

- In the small country, the effect on output is small, and the deterioration of the trade balance is equal to half of the increase in government spending.

   This example shows how openness makes it more difficult to use fiscal policy to affect output, especially in small countries. The more open the economy, the smaller the effect of fiscal policy on output and the larger the effect on the trade position. We shall see more examples of this proposition as we go along.

for U.S. goods by ΔX, so the line giving the demand for domestic goods as a function of output shifts up by ΔX, from ZZ to ZZ'. As exports increase by ΔX at a given level of output, the line giving net exports as a function of output in Figure 19–4(b) also shifts up by ΔX, from NX to NX'.

   The new equilibrium is at point A', with output level Y'. The increase in foreign output leads to an increase in domestic output. The reason is clear: Higher foreign output leads to higher exports of domestic goods, which increases domestic output and the domestic demand for goods through the multiplier.

   What happens to the trade balance? We know that exports go up. But could it be that the increase in domestic output leads to such a large increase in imports that the trade balance actually deteriorates? The answer is: No, the trade balance must improve. To see why, note that when foreign demand increases, the demand for domestic goods shifts up from ZZ to ZZ'; but the line DD, which gives domestic demand for goods as a function of output, does not shift. At the new equilibrium level of output Y', domestic demand is given by the dis-

Y^* directly affects exports and so enters the relation between the demand for domestic goods and output. An increase in Y^* leads to a shift in ZZ.

   Y^* does not affect consumption, investment, or government spending directly, and so does not enter the relation between the domestic demand for goods and output. An increase in Y^* does not lead to a shift in DD.

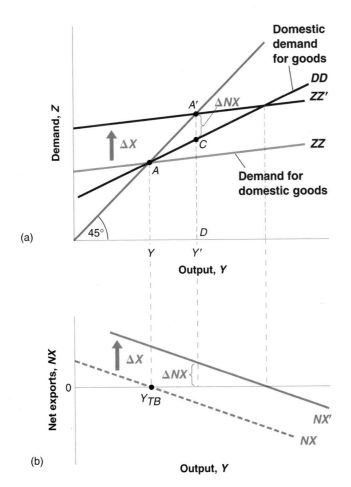

(a)

(b)

tance DC, and the demand for domestic goods is given by DA'. Net exports are thus given by the distance CA'—which, because DD is necessarily below ZZ', is necessarily positive. Thus, although imports increase, the increase does not offset the increase in exports, and the trade balance improves.

Games That Countries Play

We have derived two basic results so far:

- An increase in domestic demand leads to an increase in output, but also to a trade deficit. (We looked at an increase in government spending, but the results would have been the same for a decrease in taxes, or for an increase in consumer spending, and so on.)
- An increase in foreign demand (which could come from the same types of changes taking place abroad) leads to an increase in domestic output and a trade surplus.

Governments do not like trade deficits, and for good reasons. The main reason is that a country that runs a trade deficit accumulates debt vis-à-vis the rest of the world, and therefore has to pay higher interest payments to the rest of the world. Thus, it is no wonder that countries prefer increases in foreign demand (which lead to an improvement in the trade balance) to increases in domestic demand (which lead to a deterioration in the trade balance).

These preferences may have disastrous implications. Consider a group of countries, all trading a lot with each other, so that an increase in demand in any one country falls largely on the goods produced in the other countries. Suppose all these countries are in recession and each has roughly balanced trade to start. Each country may be very reluctant to increase domestic demand: The result would be a small increase in output but also a large trade deficit. Each country may just wait for others to increase their own demand. But if they all wait, nothing happens and the recession may endure.

Is there a way out of this situation? Yes, at least in theory. If all countries coordinate their macroeconomic policies to increase domestic demand simultaneously, each can expand without increasing its trade deficit (vis-à-vis the others; their combined trade deficit with respect to the rest of the world will still increase). The reason is clear: The coordinated increase in demand leads to increases in both exports and imports in each country. It is still true that domestic demand expansion leads to larger imports; but this increase in imports is offset by the increase in exports, which comes from the foreign demand expansions.

Coordination is a word that governments often invoke. The seven major countries of the world—the so-called **G-7** (the United States, Japan, France, Germany, the United Kingdom, Italy, and Canada)—meet regularly to discuss their economic situations; the communiqué at the end of the meeting rarely fails to mention coordination. But the evidence is that there is in fact very limited macrocoordination among countries. Here are some reasons why:

Coordination may imply that some countries have to do more than others. They may not want to do so:

- Suppose, in our example, that only some countries are in recession. Countries that are not in a recession will be reluctant to increase their own demand; but if they do not, the countries that expand will run a trade deficit vis-à-vis countries that do not.
- Suppose instead that some countries are already running a large budget deficit. These countries will not want to cut taxes or increase spending further, and will ask other countries to take on more of the adjustment. Those other countries may be reluctant to do so.

Another reason is that countries have a strong incentive to promise to coordinate, and then not deliver on that promise. Once all countries have agreed, say, to an increase in spending, each country has an incentive not to deliver, in order to benefit from the increase in demand elsewhere and thereby improve its trade position. But if each country cheats, or does not do everything it promised, there will be insufficient demand expansion to get out of the recession.

These are far from abstract concerns. Countries in the European Union, which are highly integrated with one another, have in the past 30 years often suffered from such coordination problems. In the late 1970s, a bungled attempt at coordination left most countries weary of trying again. In the early 1980s, an attempt by the French socialists to go at it alone led to a large French trade deficit, and eventually to a change in policy (this is described in the Global Macro box "The French Socialist Expansion: 1981 to 1983"). Thereafter, most countries decided that it was better to wait for an increase in foreign demand than to increase their own demand. There has been very little coordination of fiscal policy since then in Europe.

> What happened in the late 1970s is that European countries embarked on fiscal expansion "too late." By the time they increased spending, their economies were already recovering, and there was no longer a need for higher government spending.

GLOBAL MACRO

The French Socialist Expansion: 1981 to 1983

In May 1981, the Socialist party won the elections in France. Faced with an economy suffering from more than 7% unemployment, the Socialists offered a program aimed at increasing demand through more generous social policies and subsidies to job creation. Welfare benefits and pensions were increased. Public jobs were created, as were new training programs for the young and the unemployed. Table 1 summarizes the macroeconomic results of the policy.

The fiscal expansion is visible in the data: The budget, which was balanced in 1980, was in deficit by 2.8% of GDP in 1982. The effects on growth are equally visible. Average growth in 1981 to 1982 was 1.85%—not an impressive growth rate, but still much above the EU's dismal 0.45% average growth rate over the same two years.

Nevertheless, the Socialists abandoned their policy in March 1983. The last line of Table 1 tells why. As France was expanding faster than its trading partners, it experienced a sharp increase in its trade deficit. Although the government may have tolerated those trade deficits, financial markets—which were very nervous about the Socialists in the first place—forced three devaluations of

the franc in 18 months. (Recall from chapter 18 that when countries try to maintain a fixed exchange rate—as was the case for France at the time—depreciations are called devaluations. We shall see the mechanisms that lead to such devaluations in the next two chapters.) The first was in October 1981, by 8.5% against the DM; the second in June 1982, by 10% against the DM; and the third in March 1983, by 8% against the DM. In March 1983, unwilling to face further attacks on the franc and worried about the trade deficits, the French government gave up its attempt to use demand policies to decrease unemployment and shifted to a new policy of "austerity"—a policy aimed at achieving low inflation, budget and trade balance, and no further devaluations. This policy has been maintained by the various French governments, from both the left and the right, to this day.

Reference

For more on French economic policy in the 1980s, read Pierre-Alain Muet and Alain Fonteneau, *Reflation and Austerity: Economic Policy under Mitterand* (New York: Berg, 1990).

TABLE 1	Macroeconomic aggregates, France: 1980–1983			
	1980	**1981**	**1982**	**1983**
GDP growth (%)	1.6	1.2	2.5	0.7
EU growth (%)	1.4	0.2	0.7	1.6
Budget surplus	0.0	−1.9	−2.8	−3.2
Current account surplus	−0.6	−0.8	−2.2	−0.9

Budget surplus and current account surplus are measured as ratios to GDP, in percent. A minus sign indicates a deficit. EU growth refers to the average growth rate for the countries of the European Union.

Source: OECD Economic Outlook, December 1993.

Suppose the U.S. government takes policy measures that lead to a depreciation of the dollar. (We shall see in chapter 20 how it can do so using monetary policy; for the moment we assume the government can simply choose the exchange rate).

Recall that the real exchange rate is given by

$$\epsilon \equiv \frac{EP^*}{P}$$

The real exchange rate, ϵ (the price of foreign goods in terms of domestic goods) equals the nominal exchange rate, E (the price of foreign currency in terms of domestic currency) times the foreign price level, P^*, divided by the domestic price level, P. Under our maintained assumption that the price levels are given, a nominal depreciation is thus reflected one for one in a real depreciation. More concretely, if the dollar depreciates vis-à-vis the yen by 10% (a 10% nominal depreciation), and if the price levels in Japan and the United States do not change, U.S. goods will be 10% cheaper compared to Japanese goods (a 10% real depreciation).

Let's now ask what the effects of this real depreciation will be on the U.S. trade balance and on U.S. output.

Depreciation and the Trade Balance: The Marshall–Lerner Condition

Return to the definition of net exports

$$NX \equiv X - \epsilon Q$$

Replace X and Q by their expressions from equations (19.2) and (19.3)

$$NX = X(Y^*, \epsilon) - \epsilon Q(Y, \epsilon)$$

As the real exchange rate ϵ enters in three places, this equation makes clear that the real depreciation—an increase in ϵ—affects the trade balance through three channels.

1. *X increases.* The real depreciation makes U.S. goods relatively cheaper abroad, leading to an increase in foreign demand for U.S. goods—an increase in U.S. exports.
2. *Q decreases.* The real depreciation makes foreign goods relatively more expensive in the United States, leading to a shift in domestic demand toward domestic goods, to a decrease in the quantity of imports.
3. *The relative price of foreign goods, ϵ, increases.* This tends to increase the import bill, ϵQ. The same quantity of imports now costs more to buy (in terms of domestic goods).

For the trade balance to improve following a depreciation, exports must increase enough and imports must decrease enough to compensate for the increase in the price of imports. The condition under which a real depreciation leads to an increase in net exports is known as the **Marshall–Lerner condition**. (The condition is named for the two economists, Alfred Marshall and Abba Lerner, who stated it first.) It is derived formally in this chapter's appendix. It turns out—with a caveat we shall state when we introduce dynamics later in this chapter—that this condition is satisfied in reality. So, for the rest of this book, we shall assume that an increase in ϵ, a real depreciation, leads to an increase in net exports.

The Effects of a Depreciation

We have looked so far only at the *direct* effects of a depreciation on the trade balance, that is, the effects *given U.S. and foreign output*. But the effects do not end there. The change in net exports changes domestic output, which affects net exports further.

Because the effects of a real depreciation are very much like those of an increase in foreign output, we can use Figure 19–4, the same figure that we used to show the effects of an increase in foreign output earlier.

Margin notes:

A look ahead: In chapter 21, when we allow the price level to adjust, we shall have a second look at the effects of a nominal depreciation. We shall see that a nominal depreciation leads to a real depreciation in the short run, but not in the medium run.

If the dollar depreciates vis-à-vis the yen by 10% U.S. goods will be cheaper in Japan, leading to a larger volume of U.S. exports to Japan.

Japanese goods will be more expensive in the U.S., leading to a smaller volume of imports of Japanese goods to the U.S.

Japanese goods will be more expensive, leading to a higher import bill for a given volume of imports of Japanese goods to the United States.

Just like an increase in foreign output, a depreciation leads to an increase in net exports (assuming, as we do, that the Marshall–Lerner condition holds), at any level of output. Both the demand relation (ZZ in Figure 19–4a) and the net exports relation (NX in Figure 19–4b) shift up. The equilibrium moves from A to A′; output increases from Y to Y′. By the same argument we used earlier, the trade balance improves: The increase in imports induced by the increase in output is smaller than the direct improvement in the trade balance induced by the depreciation.

To summarize: the depreciation leads to a shift in demand, both foreign and domestic, toward domestic goods. This leads in turn both to an increase in domestic output and to an improvement in the trade position.

Although a depreciation and an increase in foreign output each have the same effect on domestic output and the trade balance, there is a subtle but important difference between the two. A depreciation works by making foreign goods relatively more expensive. But this means that given their income, people—who now have to pay more to buy foreign goods because of the depreciation—are worse off. This mechanism is strongly felt in countries that undergo a major depreciation. Governments that try to achieve a major depreciation often find themselves with strikes and riots in the streets, as people react to the much higher prices of imported goods. This was the case in Mexico, where the large depreciation of the peso in 1994 to 1995 (from 3.44 pesos per dollar in November 1994 to 5.88 pesos per dollar in May 1995) led to a large decline in workers' living standards, and strong social tensions. A more recent example is that of Indonesia in 1998.[2]

Combining Exchange-Rate and Fiscal Policies

Suppose a government wants to reduce the trade deficit without changing the level of output. A depreciation alone will not do: It will reduce the trade deficit, but it also will increase output. Nor will a fiscal contraction do: It will reduce the trade deficit, but it will decrease output. What should the government do? The answer is to use the right combination of depreciation and fiscal contraction. Figure 19–5 shows what this combination should be.

The initial equilibrium in Figure 19–5(a) is at A, associated with output Y. The trade deficit is given by the distance BC in Figure 19–5(b). If the government wants to eliminate the trade deficit without changing output, it must do two things:

- First, it must achieve a depreciation sufficient to eliminate the trade deficit at the initial level of output. So, the depreciation must shift the net exports relation from NX to NX′ in Figure 19–5(b). But this depreciation, and the associated increase in net exports, also shifts the demand relation in Figure 19–5(a) from ZZ to ZZ′. In the absence of other measures, the equilibrium would move from A to A′, and output would increase from Y to Y′.

- Second, to avoid the increase in output, the government must reduce government spending so as to shift ZZ′ back to ZZ. This combination of a depreciation and a fiscal contraction leads to the same level of output and an improved trade balance.

There is a general point behind this example. To the extent that governments care about *both* the level of output and the trade balance, they have to use *both* fiscal and exchange-rate policies. We just saw one such combination. Table 19–1 shows others, depending on the initial output and trade situation. Take, for example, the case represented in the top right corner of the table. Initial output is too low (put another way, unemployment is too high), and the economy has a trade deficit. A depreciation will help on both the trade and the output fronts:

A general lesson: If you want to achieve two targets (here, output and trade balance), you better have two instruments (here, fiscal policy and the exchange rate).

[2]**DIGGING DEEPER**. There is an alternative to strikes and riots: asking for and obtaining an increase in wages. But, if wages increase, presumably the prices of domestic goods will increase as well, leading to a smaller real depreciation. To discuss this mechanism, we need to look at the supply side in more detail than we have done so far. We return to the dynamics of depreciation, wage movements, and price movements in chapter 21.

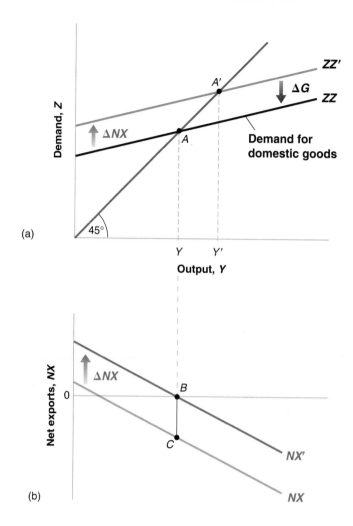

(a)

(b)

FIGURE 19-5

Reducing the Trade Deficit Without Changing Output

To reduce the trade deficit without changing output, the government must achieve a depreciation and decrease government spending.

It reduces the trade deficit and increases output. But there is no reason for the depreciation to achieve both the right increase in output and the elimination of the trade deficit. Depending on the initial situation and the relative effects of the depreciation on output and the trade balance, the government may need to complement the depreciation with either an increase or a decrease in government spending. This ambiguity is captured by the question mark in the box. Make sure that you understand the logic behind each of the other three cases.

TABLE 19-1	Exchange-Rate and Fiscal Policy Combinations	
Initial Conditions	**Trade Surplus**	**Trade Deficit**
Low output	ϵ? $G\uparrow$	$\epsilon\uparrow$ G?
High output	$\epsilon\downarrow$ G?	ϵ? $G\downarrow$

19-5 | Looking at Dynamics: The J-Curve

We have ignored dynamics so far in this chapter. It is time to reintroduce them. The dynamics of consumption, investment, sales, and production we discussed in chapter 3 are as relevant to the open economy as they were to the closed economy. But there are additional dynamic effects as well, which come from the dynamics of exports and imports. I focus on these effects here.

Return to the effects of the exchange rate on the trade balance. I argued earlier that a depreciation leads to an increase in exports and to a decrease in imports. But these effects do not happen overnight. Think of the dynamic effects of, say, a 10% dollar depreciation. In the first few months following the depreciation, the effect of the depreciation is likely to be reflected much more in prices than in quantities. The price of imports in the United States goes up, the price of U.S. exports abroad goes down.[3] But the quantity of imports and exports is likely to adjust slowly: It takes a while for consumers to realize that relative prices have changed, it takes a while for firms to shift to cheaper suppliers, and so on. Thus, a depreciation well may lead to an initial deterioration of the trade balance; ϵ increases, but neither X nor Q adjusts very much initially, leading to a decline in net exports $(X - \epsilon Q)$.

As time passes, the effects of the change in the relative prices of both exports and imports become stronger. Exports increase, imports decrease. If the Marshall–Lerner condition eventually holds—and we have argued that it does—the response of exports and imports eventually becomes stronger than the adverse price effect, and the eventual effect of the depreciation is to improve the trade balance.

Figure 19–6 captures this adjustment by plotting the evolution of the trade balance against time in response to a real depreciation. The trade deficit before the depreciation is OA. The depreciation initially *increases* the trade deficit to OB: ϵ goes up, but neither Q nor X changes right away. Over time, exports increase and imports decrease, reducing the trade deficit. Eventually the trade balance improves beyond its initial level; this is what happens from point C on in the figure. Economists refer to this adjustment process as the **J-curve**, because—admittedly, with a bit of imagination—the curve in the figure resembles a "J": first down, then up.

The importance of the dynamic effects of the real exchange rate on the trade balance can be seen from the evidence from the United States in the mid-1980s: Figure 19–7 plots the U.S. trade balance against the U.S. real exchange rate in the 1980s. As we saw in the last chapter, the period from 1980 to 1985 was one of sharp real appreciation and the period

The response of the trade balance to the real exchange rate:

Initially:
(X,Q) unchanged, $\epsilon \uparrow \Rightarrow$
$(X - \epsilon Q) \downarrow$

Eventually:
$(X \uparrow, Q \downarrow, \epsilon \uparrow) \Rightarrow$
$(X - \epsilon Q) \uparrow$

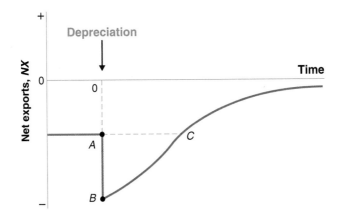

FIGURE 19-6

The J-Curve

A real depreciation leads initially to a deterioration, then to an improvement of the trade balance.

[3]**DIGGING DEEPER**. The price of imported goods may not go up by 10%, however. The price would go up 10% if importers adjusted their dollar price fully for the dollar depreciation. To keep their market share, or because they are committed under previous contracts to deliver at a given dollar price, importers may decide instead to pass along only part of the dollar depreciation and take a reduction in their profit margins. This is what we observe in practice: Whereas import prices respond to a depreciation, they respond less than one for one. The same logic applies to the prices of exports. We abstract from these complications here.

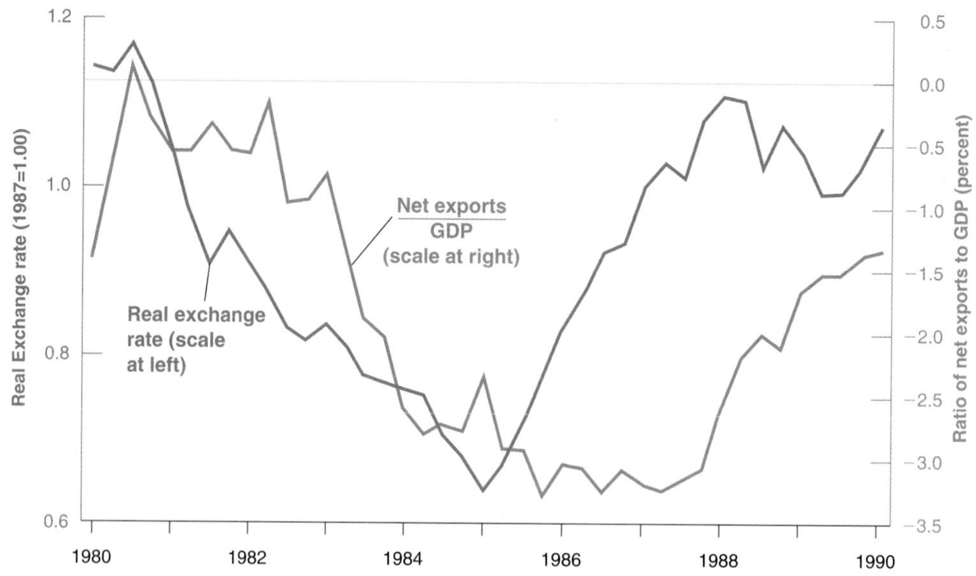

FIGURE 19-7

The Real Exchange Rate and the Ratio of Net Exports to GDP: United States, 1980–1990

The real appreciation and the depreciation of the dollar in the 1980s were reflected in increasing, then decreasing trade deficits. There were, however, substantial lags in the effects of the real exchange rate on the trade balance.

from 1985 to 1988 one of sharp real depreciation. Turning to the trade balance, which is expressed as a proportion of GDP, two facts are clear:

1. Movements in the real exchange rate were reflected in parallel movements in net exports. The appreciation was associated with a large deterioration of the trade balance, and the later depreciation was associated with a large improvement in the trade balance.

2. However, there were substantial lags in the response of the trade balance to changes in the real exchange rate. Note how from 1981 to 1983, the trade deficit remained small while the dollar was appreciating. And note how the steady depreciation of the dollar from 1985 on was not reflected in an improvement in the trade balance before 1987: The J-curve was very much at work in both episodes.

In general, the econometric evidence on the dynamic relation between exports, imports, and the real exchange rate suggests that in rich countries, a real depreciation eventually leads to a trade balance improvement. But it also suggests that this process takes some time, typically between six months and a year. These lags have implications not only for the effects of a depreciation on the trade balance but also for the effects of a depreciation on output. If a depreciation initially decreases net exports, it also initially exerts a contractionary effect on output. Thus, if a government relies on a depreciation to both improve the trade balance and expand domestic output, the effects will go the "wrong" way for a while.

> The delays in 1985 to 1988 were unusually long, prompting some economists at the time to question whether there was still a relation between the real exchange rate and the trade balance. In retrospect, the relation was still very much there—the delays were just longer than usual.

19-6 | Saving, Investment, and Trade Deficits

We saw in chapter 3 how we could rewrite the condition for equilibrium in the goods market as the condition that investment equals saving, private and public. We now derive the corresponding condition for the open economy. Start from our equilibrium condition

$$Y = C + I + G - \epsilon Q + X$$

Subtract $C + T$ from both sides, and use the fact that private saving is given by $S = Y - C - T$, to get

$$S = I + G - T - \epsilon Q + X$$

Using the definition of net exports $NX \equiv X - \epsilon Q$, and reorganizing gives

$$NX = S + (T - G) - I \tag{19.5}$$

This condition says that in equilibrium, the trade balance (NX) must equal saving—private (S) and public ($T - G$)—minus investment (I). It follows that a trade surplus must correspond to an excess of saving over investment; a trade deficit must correspond to an excess of investment over saving.

One way of getting more intuition for this relation is to go back to the discussion of the current and capital accounts in chapter 18. There we saw that a trade surplus implies net lending to the rest of the world, and a trade deficit implies net borrowing from the rest of the world. Consider a country that invests more than it saves, so that $S + (T - G) - I$ is negative. That country must be borrowing the difference from the rest of the world; it must therefore be running a trade deficit.

Note some of the things that equation (19.5) says:

- An increase in investment must be reflected either in an increase in private or public saving, or in a deterioration of the trade balance (a smaller trade surplus, or a larger trade deficit.)
- An increase in the budget deficit must be reflected in an increase in private saving, or a decrease in investment, or a deterioration of the trade balance.
- A country with a high saving rate, private and public, must have either a high investment rate or a large trade surplus.

Note also, however, what equation (19.5) does *not* say. It does not say, for example, whether and under what conditions a budget deficit will be reflected in a trade deficit, or in an increase in private saving, or in a decrease in investment. To answer that question, we must explicitly solve for what happens to output and its components using the assumptions that we have made about consumption, investment, exports, and imports. We can do so using either equation (19.1) (as we have done throughout this chapter) or equation (19.5), as the two are equivalent. However, let me strongly recommend that you use equation (19.1). Using (19.5) can, if you are not careful, be very misleading. Consider, for example, the following argument (which is so common that you may have read it in some form in newspapers):

> It is clear that a country cannot reduce its trade deficit through a depreciation. Look at equation (19.5). It shows that the trade deficit is equal to investment minus saving, private and public. Why should a depreciation affect either saving or investment? Thus, how can a depreciation affect the trade deficit?

The argument may sound convincing, but we know it is wrong. We showed earlier that a depreciation leads (if the Marshall–Lerner condition holds) to an increase in output and an improvement in the trade position. So what is wrong with it? A depreciation actually affects saving and investment: It does so by affecting the demand for domestic goods, thereby increasing output. Higher output leads to an increase in saving over investment, or, equivalently, to a decrease in the trade deficit.

A good way of making sure that you understand the material in this chapter is to go back and look at the various cases we have considered, from changes in government spending, to changes in foreign output, to combinations of depreciation and fiscal contraction, and so on. Trace what happens in each case to each of the four components of equation (19.5): private saving, public saving (equivalently, the budget surplus), investment, and the trade balance. Make sure, as always, that you can tell the story in words. If you can, you are ready to go on to chapter 20.

Show, for example, that an increase in foreign demand leads to:

- An increase in private saving.
- An increase in investment (but by less than private saving).
- No change in the budget deficit.
- An improvement in the trade balance.

- In an open economy, the demand for domestic goods is equal to the domestic demand for goods (consumption, plus investment, plus government spending) minus imports, plus exports.

- An increase in domestic demand leads to a smaller increase in output in an open economy than in a closed economy because some of the additional demand falls on imports. It also leads to a deterioration of the trade balance.

- An increase in foreign demand leads, as a result of increased exports, to an increase in domestic output and an improvement in the trade balance.

- Because increases in foreign demand improve the trade balance and increases in domestic demand worsen it, countries may be tempted to wait for increases in foreign demand to move them out of a re-

cession. When a group of countries is in recession, coordination can help them get out of it.

- If the Marshall–Lerner condition is satisfied—and econometric evidence suggests that it is—a real depreciation leads to an improvement in net exports.

- The typical response of the trade balance to a real depreciation is first a deterioration, and then an improvement. This adjustment process is known as the J-curve.

- The condition for equilibrium in the goods market can be rewritten as the condition that saving (public and private) minus investment must be equal to the trade balance. A trade surplus corresponds to an excess of saving over investment, a trade deficit to an excess of investment over saving.

KEY TERMS

- demand for domestic goods, 362
- domestic demand for goods, 362
- marginal propensity to import, 368
- coordination, 370

- G-7, 370
- Marshall–Lerner condition, 372
- J-curve, 375

QUESTIONS & PROBLEMS

An asterisk denotes a harder problem.

1. TRUE/FALSE/UNCERTAIN

a. Trade deficits generally reflect high investment.

b. Budget deficits cause trade deficits.

c. It is much easier for the government of a small open economy to maintain output at a given level than for the government of a large closed economy.

d. The only way a country can eliminate a trade surplus is through an appreciation of its currency.

e. A small open economy can reduce its trade deficit through fiscal contraction at a smaller cost in output than a large economy.

f. If the trade deficit is equal to zero, the domestic demand for goods and the demand for domestic goods are the same.

2. REAL EXCHANGE RATES AND THE BALANCE OF TRADE

a. Using the definition of the real exchange rate, verify that the following is true (you may want to use propositions 7 and 8 of Appendix 2 at the end of the book):

$$\frac{\Delta \epsilon}{\epsilon} = \frac{\Delta E}{E} + \frac{\Delta P^*}{P^*} - \frac{\Delta P}{P}$$

b. If domestic inflation is higher than foreign inflation, but the domestic country has a fixed exchange rate, what happens to net exports over time? Assume the Marshall–Lerner condition holds. Explain in words.

*3. COORDINATION AND FISCAL POLICY

Consider the following open economy. The real exchange rate is fixed and equal to one. Consumption, investment, government spending, and taxes are given by

$$C = 10 + 0.8(Y - T) \quad I = 10 \quad G = 10 \quad T = 10$$

Imports and exports are given by

$$Q = 0.3Y \quad X = 0.3Y^*$$

where an asterisk denotes a foreign variable.

a. Solve for equilibrium income in the domestic economy, given Y^*. What is the multiplier in this economy? If we were to close the economy (so exports and imports were equal to zero) what would the multiplier be? Why are the two multipliers different?

b. Assume the foreign economy has the same equations as the domestic economy (remove the asterisk from all the variables with an asterisk, and add an asterisk to all the variables without an asterisk). Use the two sets of equations to solve for the equilibrium income of each country. What is the multiplier for each country now? Why is it different from the open economy multiplier above?

c. Assume both countries have a target level of output of 125. What is the increase in G necessary in either of these countries, assuming the other country does not change G, to achieve target output? Solve for net exports and the budget deficit in each country.

d. What is the common increase in G necessary to achieve target output?

e. Why is fiscal coordination (such as the common increase in G in [d]) difficult to achieve in practice?

*4. TARIFFS

Consider two open *IS-LM* economies.

a. Consider a domestic tax, at rate τ, on imports of foreign goods. How does this affect the import relation? The export relation?

b. What are the consequences of the tax on equilibrium output and net exports in the domestic country?

c. What are the consequences of the tax on equilibrium output and net exports in the foreign country?

d. Suppose that the foreign country retaliates by putting a tax on its imports. What is the additional effect of this foreign retaliation on equilibrium output in the domestic country and on the volume of trade? Assume identical economies and a foreign tax equal to the domestic one.

5. JAPAN'S RECESSION AND THE U.S. ECONOMY

a. The share of Japanese spending on U.S. goods is about 10% of U.S. exports, which are themselves equal to about 10% of GDP. What is the share of Japanese spending on U.S. goods relative to U.S. GDP?

b. Assume the multiplier in the United States is 2, and that a recession in Japan has reduced output by 5% (relative to its natural level). What is the impact of the Japanese slowdown on U.S. GDP?

c. If the Japanese recession also leads to a slowdown of the other economies which import goods from the United States, the effect could be larger. Assume exports fall by 5% (of themselves). What is the impact on U.S. GDP?

d. Comment on the following statement from an economist on television: "Unless Japan recovers from recession quickly, growth will grind to a halt in the rest of the world."

6. DYNAMICS OF A DEPRECIATION

Consider an economy with a fixed exchange rate. Assume that the price level is fixed.

a. What is the effect on equilibrium income and trade balance of a depreciation in the first six months after the depreciation?

b. What is the effect on equilibrium income and trade balance of the depreciation after the first six months?

*7. EXPORT RATIOS

Look at a recent issue of the *International Financial Statistics*, published monthly by the IMF. Find the list of countries in the table of contents. Make a list of five countries you would expect to have high ratios of exports to GDP. Then, go to the page corresponding to each country, and find the numbers for exports and for GDP for the most recent year available. (Make sure that you are comparing exports and GDP measured in the same units— either domestic currency or dollars. If one variable is in domestic currency and the other variable is in dollars, use the exchange rate to convert the two to the same currency.) Compute the export ratios. How good were your guesses?

A good discussion of the relation among the trade deficit, the budget deficit, private saving, and investment is given in Barry Bosworth's *Saving and Investment in a Global Economy* (Washington, DC: Brookings Institution, 1993).

APPENDIX

DERIVATION OF THE MARSHALL–LERNER CONDITION

Start from the definition of net exports, $NX \equiv X - \epsilon Q$, and assume trade to be initially balanced, so that $X = \epsilon Q$. The Marshall–Lerner condition is the condition under which a real depreciation, an increase in ϵ, leads to an increase in net exports.

To derive this condition, consider an increase in the real exchange rate of $\Delta \epsilon$. The change in the trade balance thus is given by

$$\Delta NX = \Delta X - \epsilon \Delta Q - Q \Delta \epsilon$$

The first term on the right (ΔX) gives the change in exports, the second ($\epsilon \Delta Q$) the real exchange rate times the change in the quantity of imports, and the third ($Q \Delta \epsilon$) the quantity of imports times the change in the real exchange rate.

Divide both sides of the equation by X to get

$$\frac{\Delta NX}{X} = \frac{\Delta X}{X} - \epsilon \frac{\Delta Q}{X} - \frac{Q \Delta \epsilon}{X}$$

Use the fact that $\epsilon Q = X$ to replace ϵ/X by $1/Q$ in the second term on the right, and to replace Q/X by $1/\epsilon$ in the third term on the right. This substitution gives

$$\frac{\Delta NX}{X} = \frac{\Delta X}{X} - \frac{\Delta Q}{Q} - \frac{\Delta \epsilon}{\epsilon}$$

This equation says that the change in the trade balance in response to a real depreciation, normalized by exports, is equal to the sum of three terms. The first is the proportional change in exports, $\Delta X/X$, induced by the real depreciation. The second term is equal to minus the proportional change in imports, $-\Delta Q/Q$, induced by the real depreciation. The third term is equal to minus the proportional change in the real exchange rate, $-\Delta \epsilon/\epsilon$, or equivalently, minus the rate of real depreciation.

The Marshall–Lerner condition is the condition that the sum of these three terms be positive. If it is satisfied, a real depreciation leads to an improvement in the trade balance.

A numerical example will help here. Suppose that a 1% depreciation leads to a relative increase in exports of 0.9% and to a relative decrease in imports of 0.8%. (Econometric evidence on the relation of exports and imports to the real exchange rates suggest that these are indeed reasonable numbers.) In that case, the right-hand side of the equation is equal to 0.9% − (−0.8%) − 1% = 0.7%. Thus, the trade balance improves: The Marshall–Lerner condition is satisfied.

We invite you to visit the Blanchard page on the Prentice Hall Web site at:

http://www.prenhall.com/blanchard

for this chapter's World Wide Web exercises

CHAPTER 20

Output, the Interest Rate, and the Exchange Rate

In chapter 19, we treated the exchange rate as one of the policy instruments available to the government. But the exchange rate is not a policy instrument. Rather, it is determined in the foreign-exchange market—a market where, as we saw in chapter 18, there is an enormous amount of trading. This fact raises two obvious questions: What determines the exchange rate? How can the government affect it?

These are the questions that motivate this chapter. More generally, we examine the implications of equilibrium in both the goods market and financial markets, including the foreign exchange market. This allows us to characterize the joint movements of output, the interest rate, and the exchange rate in an open economy. The model we develop is an extension to the open economy of the *IS-LM* model we saw in chapter 5, and is known as the **Mundell–Fleming model**, after the two economists Robert Mundell and Marcus Fleming, who first put it together in the 1960s. (The model presented here keeps the spirit but differs in its details from the original Mundell–Fleming model.)

Sections 20-1 and 20-2 look at equilibrium in the goods and the financial markets, respectively. Section 20-3 puts the two equilibrium conditions together, and looks at the determination of output, the interest rate, and the exchange rate. Section 20-4 looks at the role of policy under flexible exchange rates, and section 20-5 does the same under fixed exchange rates.

Equilibrium in the goods market was the focus of chapter 19, where we derived the following equilibrium condition

$$Y = C(Y - T) + I(Y, r) + G - \epsilon Q(Y, \epsilon) + X(Y^*, \epsilon)$$
$$(\ +\ )\qquad (+,-)\qquad\qquad (+,-)\qquad (+,+)$$

For the goods market to be in equilibrium, output (the left side of the equation) must be equal to the demand for domestic goods (the right side of the equation).

Demand in turn is equal to consumption plus investment plus government spending minus imports plus exports. Consumption depends positively on disposable income. Investment depends positively on output and negatively on the real interest rate. Government spending is taken as given. The volume of imports depends positively on output, negatively on the real exchange rate. Exports depend positively on foreign output and positively on the real exchange rate.

It will be convenient in what follows to regroup the last two terms under "net exports," defined as exports minus imports, $X - \epsilon Q$

$$NX(Y, Y^*, \epsilon) \equiv X(Y^*, \epsilon) - \epsilon Q(Y, \epsilon)$$

It follows from our assumptions about imports and exports that net exports depend on domestic output, foreign output, and the real exchange rate. An increase in domestic output increases imports and thus decreases net exports. An increase in foreign output increases exports, thus increases net exports. An increase in ϵ—a real depreciation—leads (under the Marshall–Lerner condition, which I shall assume to hold throughout this chapter) to an increase in net exports.

Using this definition of net exports, we can rewrite the equilibrium condition as

$$Y = C(Y - T) + I(Y, r) + G + NX(Y, Y^*, \epsilon) \qquad (20.1)$$
$$(\ +\ )\qquad (+,-)\qquad\qquad (-,+,+)$$

For our purposes the essential implication of equation (20.1) is the dependence of demand, and so of equilibrium output, on both the real interest rate and the real exchange rate:

- An increase in the real interest rate leads to a decrease in investment spending, and so to a decrease in the demand for domestic goods. This leads, through the multiplier, to a decrease in output.
- An increase in the real exchange rate—a real depreciation—leads to a shift in demand toward domestic goods, and thus an increase in net exports. The increase in net exports increases demand and output.

For the remainder of the chapter, I shall simplify equation (20.1) in two ways:

- Given our focus on the short run, we assumed in our previous treatment of the *IS-LM* model that the (domestic) price level was given. I shall extend this assumption to the foreign price level, so the real exchange rate ($\epsilon \equiv EP^*/P$) and the nominal exchange rate (E) move together. A nominal depreciation leads, one for one, to a real depreciation. If, for notational convenience, we choose P and P^* so that $P = P^* = 1$ (and we can do so because they are index numbers), then $\epsilon = E$ and we can replace ϵ by E in equation (20.1).
- As we take the domestic price level as given, there is no inflation, actual or expected. Thus, the nominal and the real interest rates are the same, and we can replace the real interest rate, r, in equation (20.1) by the nominal interest rate, i.

With these simplifications, equation (20.1) becomes

$$Y = C(Y - T) + I(Y, i) + G + NX(Y, Y^*, E) \qquad (20.2)$$
$$(\ +\ )\qquad (+,-)\qquad\qquad (-,+,+)$$

Output depends on both the nominal interest rate and the nominal exchange rate.

Side notes (left margin):

Goods–market equilibrium condition (*IS*): Output = Demand for domestic goods.

A reminder: A real depreciation is represented by an increase in the real exchange rate—an increase in the price of foreign goods in terms of domestic goods.

Simplification (1):
$P = P^* = 1$, so $\epsilon = E$

Simplification (2):
$\pi^e = 0$, so $r = i$

When we looked at financial markets in the *IS-LM* model, we assumed that people chose between only two financial assets, money and bonds. Now that we look at a financially open economy, we must allow for a second choice—the choice between domestic bonds and foreign bonds. Let's consider each choice in turn.

We leave aside the other choices—between short-term and long-term bonds, and between short-term bonds and stocks—we looked at in chapter 15.

Money versus Bonds

When looking at the determination of the interest rate in the *IS-LM* model, we wrote the condition that the supply of money be equal to the demand for money as

$$\frac{M}{P} = Y L(i) \tag{20.3}$$

We took the real supply of money (the left side of equation [20.3]) as given. We assumed that the real demand for money (the right side of equation [20.3]) depended on the level of transactions in the economy, measured by real output (Y), and on the opportunity cost of holding money rather than bonds, the nominal interest rate on bonds (i).

How should we change this characterization now that the economy is open? The answer is not very much, if at all.

In an open economy, the demand for domestic money is still mostly a demand by domestic residents. There is not much reason for, say, Germans to hold U.S. currency or dollar-denominated demand deposits. They cannot use them for transactions in Germany—which require payment in German money. If they want to hold dollar-denominated assets, they are better off holding U.S. bonds, which at least pay a positive interest rate. And the demand for money by domestic residents still depends on the same factors as before: their level of transactions, that we proxy by domestic real output, and the opportunity cost of holding money, the nominal interest rate on bonds.[1]

Two qualifications from chapter 18: (1) dollars used for illegal transactions abroad, and (2) dollarization, dollars used as money in countries with very high inflation. I shall ignore both qualifications here.

Therefore, we can still use equation (20.3) to think about the determination of the nominal interest rate in an open economy. The interest rate must be such that the supply and the demand for money are equal. An increase in the money supply leads to a decrease in the interest rate. An increase in money demand, say, as a result of an increase in output, leads to an increase in the interest rate.

Domestic Bonds versus Foreign Bonds

In looking at the choice between domestic bonds and foreign bonds, we shall rely on the assumption we introduced in chapter 18: Financial investors, domestic or foreign, go for the highest expected rate of return. This implies that, in equilibrium, both domestic bonds and foreign bonds must have the same expected rate of return; otherwise, investors would be willing to hold only one or the other, but not both, and this could not be an equilibrium.

As we saw in chapter 18, this assumption implies that the following arbitrage relation— the *interest parity condition*—must hold

$$i_t = i_t^* + \frac{E_{t+1}^e - E_t}{E_t}$$

The domestic interest rate i_t must be equal to the foreign interest rate i_t^* plus the expected rate of depreciation of the domestic currency $(E_{t+1}^e - E_t)/E_t$.

Recall from chapter 18 that this is only an approximation (but a good one). For notational convenience, I replace the earlier approximation symbol ($\approx$) by an equal sign ($=$).

---

[1]**DIGGING DEEPER.** Given that domestic residents can now hold both domestic and foreign bonds, the demand for money should depend on the expected rates of return on both domestic and foreign bonds. But our next assumption—interest parity—implies that these two expected rates of return are equal, so that we can write the demand for money directly as we did in equation (20.3).

For now, we shall take the expected future exchange rate as given and denote it as $\overline{E}^e$ (we shall relax this assumption in chapter 21).[2] Under this assumption, and dropping time indexes, the interest parity condition becomes

$$i = i* + \frac{\overline{E}^e - E}{E} \tag{20.4}$$

Multiplying both sides by E, bringing the terms in E to the left side, and dividing both sides by $(1 + i - i*)$ gives the current exchange rate as a function of the expected future exchange rate and the domestic and foreign interest rates

$$E = \frac{\overline{E}^e}{1 + i - i*} \tag{20.5}$$

Equation (20.5) implies a negative relation between the domestic interest rate and the exchange rate. Given the expected future exchange rate and the foreign interest rate, *an increase in the domestic interest rate leads to a decrease in the exchange rate—equivalently, to an appreciation of the domestic currency. A decrease in the domestic interest rate leads to an increase in the exchange rate—to a depreciation.*

> An increase in the domestic interest rate leads to an appreciation of the domestic currency. An increase in the foreign interest rate leads to a depreciation of the domestic currency.

This relation between the exchange rate and the domestic interest rate plays a central role in the real world, and will play a central role in the rest of this chapter. To understand it further, think about the sequence of events that takes place in financial and foreign exchange markets after an increase in the U.S. interest rate above, say, the German interest rate:

- Suppose that, to start with, the U.S. and German interest rates are equal, so that $i = i*$. This implies, from equation (20.5), that the current \$/DM exchange rate equals the expected future exchange rate: $E = E^e$.
- Suppose, as a result of a U.S. monetary contraction, the U.S. interest rate increases. At an unchanged exchange rate, U.S. bonds become more attractive, so financial investors want to shift out of German bonds and into U.S. bonds. To do so, they must sell German bonds for DM, then sell DM for dollars, then use the dollars to buy U.S. bonds. As investors sell DM and buy dollars, the dollar appreciates.
- That an increase in the U.S. interest rate leads to an appreciation of the dollar is intuitively straightforward: An increase in the demand for dollars leads to an increase in the price of dollars. What is less intuitive is *by how much* the dollar must appreciate. The important point here is if financial investors do not change their expectation of the future exchange rate, then *the more the dollar appreciates today*, the more investors expect it to *depreciate in the future* (as they expect it to return to the same value in the future). Other things being equal, this expectation makes German bonds more attractive: When the dollar is expected to depreciate, a given rate of return in DM means a higher rate of return in dollars.
- This gives us the answer: The initial dollar appreciation must be such that the expected future depreciation compensates for the increase in the U.S. interest rate. When this is the case, investors are again indifferent and equilibrium prevails.

A numerical example will help. Assume one-year U.S. and German interest rates are both equal to 4%. Suppose the U.S. interest rate now increases to 10%. The dollar will ap-

---

[2]**DIGGING DEEPER.** All that is needed for our purposes is that the future expected exchange rate responds less than one for one to movements in the current exchange rate. Check, for example, how the results of this chapter are modified if you assume that the expected future exchange rate is given by $E^e = \lambda E + (1 - \lambda)\overline{E}$, with λ between 0 and 1. The assumption we use in the text corresponds to the case where λ is 0. But all the qualitative results we derive below still hold when λ is between 0 and 1.

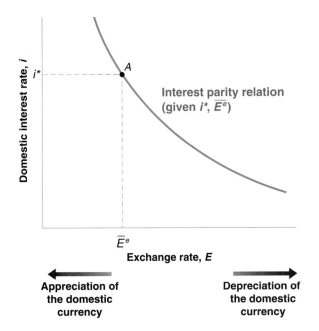

FIGURE 20–1

The Relation Between the Interest Rate and the Exchange Rate Implied by Interest Parity

A lower domestic interest rate leads to a higher exchange rate—to a depreciation of the domestic currency. A higher domestic interest rate leads to a lower exchange rate—to an appreciation of the domestic currency.

preciate by 6% today. Why? Because if the dollar appreciates by 6% today and investors do not change their expectation of the exchange rate one year ahead, the dollar is now expected to depreciate by 6% over the coming year. Put the other way, the DM is expected to appreciate by 6% relative to the dollar over the coming year, so that holding German bonds yields an expected rate of return of 10%—the 4% rate of return in DM, plus the expected 6% appreciation of the DM. Holding U.S. bonds or holding German bonds both yield an expected rate of return of 10% in dollars. Financial investors are willing to hold either one, so there is equilibrium in the foreign exchange market. In terms of equation (20.4),

$$i = i* + \frac{\bar{E}^e - E}{E}$$

$$10\% = 4\% + 6\%$$

The rate of return from holding U.S. bonds (the left side) is equal to 10%. The expected rate of return from holding German bonds, expressed in dollars, (the right side) is equal to the German interest rate, 4%, plus the expected depreciation of the dollar, 6%.

Figure 20–1 plots the relation between the (domestic) interest rate and the exchange rate implied by equation (20.5)—the interest parity relation. It is drawn for a given expected future exchange rate, $\bar{E}^e$, and a given foreign interest rate, $i*$. The lower the interest rate, the higher the exchange rate: The relation is thus drawn as a downward-sloping curve. Equation (20.5) also implies that when the domestic interest rate is equal to the foreign interest rate, the exchange rate is equal to the expected future exchange rate: When $i = i*$, then $E = \bar{E}^e$. This point is denoted A in the figure.[3]

Make sure you understand the three steps in the argument: (1) The one-year interest rate on U.S. bonds increases by 6%. Investors then buy U.S. bonds and dollars. (2) The dollar appreciates until it is expected to depreciate by 6% during the coming year. (3) This happens when the dollar has appreciated today by 6%.

What happens to the curve if $i*$ increases? if $\bar{E}^e$ increases?

[3]**DIGGING DEEPER.** The argument in the text relies heavily on the assumption that when the interest rate changes, the expected exchange rate remains unchanged. This implies that an appreciation today (a decrease in the current exchange rate) leads to an expected depreciation in the future (as the exchange rate is expected to return to the same, unchanged, value). We shall relax the assumption that the future exchange rate is fixed in chapter 21. But the two basic conclusions will remain: (1) An increase in the domestic interest rate leads to an appreciation. (2) An increase in the foreign interest rate leads to a depreciation.

We now have all the elements we need to understand the movements of output, the interest rate, and the exchange rate.

Goods-market equilibrium implies that output depends, among other factors, on the interest rate and the exchange rate

$$Y = C(Y - T) + I(Y, i) + G + NX(Y, Y^*, E)$$

The interest rate is determined by the equality of money supply and money demand

$$\frac{M}{P} = Y L(i)$$

And the interest parity condition implies a negative relation between the domestic interest rate and the exchange rate

$$E = \frac{\overline{E}^e}{1 + i - i^*}$$

Together, these three relations determine output, the interest rate, and the exchange rate. Working with three relations is not very easy. But we can easily reduce them to two by using the interest parity condition to eliminate the exchange rate in the goods–market equilibrium relation. Doing this gives us the following two equations, the open-economy versions of our old *IS* and *LM* relations:

$$LS: \qquad Y = C(Y - T) + I(Y, i) + G + NX\left(Y, Y^*, \frac{\overline{E}^e}{1 + i - i^*}\right)$$

$$LM: \qquad \frac{M}{P} = Y L(i)$$

Take the *IS* relation first, and consider the effects of an increase in the interest rate on output. An increase in the interest rate now has two effects:

● The first, which was already present in a closed economy, is the direct effect on investment. A higher interest rate leads to a decrease in investment, so to a decrease in the demand for domestic goods and a decrease in output.
● The second, which is present only in the open economy, is the effect through the exchange rate. An increase in the domestic interest rate leads to an appreciation of the domestic currency. The appreciation, which makes domestic goods more expensive relative to foreign goods, leads to a decrease in net exports, thus to a decrease in the demand for domestic goods and a decrease in output.

Both effects work in the same direction: An increase in the interest rate decreases demand directly, and indirectly—through the adverse effect of the appreciation. Note that the multiplier is smaller than in the closed economy. This is because part of demand falls on foreign goods rather than all on domestic goods.

The *IS* relation between the interest rate and output is drawn in Figure 20–2(a) for given values of all the other variables in the relation—namely T, G, Y^*, i^*, and $\overline{E}^e$. The *IS* curve is downward sloping: An increase in the interest rate leads to a decrease in output. It looks very much the same as in the closed economy, but it hides a more complex relation than before: The interest rate affects output not only directly, but also indirectly through the exchange rate.

▶ *An increase in the interest rate leads, both directly and indirectly (through the exchange rate), to a decrease in output.*

The *LM* relation is exactly the same as in the closed economy. The *LM* curve is upward sloping. For a given value of the real money stock, (M/P), an increase in output leads to an increase in the demand for money, and to an increase in the equilibrium interest rate.

Equilibrium in the goods and financial markets is attained at point A in Figure 20–2(a), with output level Y and interest rate i. The equilibrium value of the exchange rate cannot be

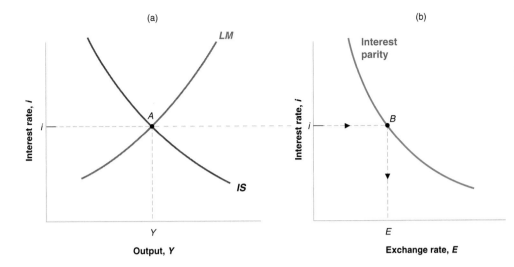

(a)

(b)

FIGURE 20–2

The *IS-LM* Model in the Open Economy

An increase in the interest rate reduces output both directly and indirectly (through the exchange rate): The *IS* curve is downward sloping. Given the real money stock, an increase in income increases the interest rate: The *LM* curve is upward sloping.

read directly from the graph. But it is easily obtained from Figure 20–2(b), which replicates Figure 20–1, and gives the exchange rate associated with a given interest rate. The exchange rate associated with the equilibrium interest rate i is equal to E.

To summarize: We have derived the *IS* and the *LM* relations for an open economy. The *IS* curve is downward sloping: An increase in the interest rate leads directly, and indirectly through the exchange rate, to a decrease in demand and a decrease in output. The *LM* curve is upward sloping: An increase in income increases the demand for money, requiring an increase in the equilibrium interest rate. Equilibrium output and the equilibrium interest rate are given by the intersection of the *IS* and the *LM* curves. Given the foreign interest rate and the expected future exchange rate, the equilibrium interest rate determines the equilibrium exchange rate.

20-4 | The Effects of Policy in an Open Economy

Having derived the *IS-LM* model for the open economy, we can now put it to use and look at the effects of policy.

The Effects of Fiscal Policy in an Open Economy

Let's look again at a change in government spending. Suppose that starting from budget balance, the government decides to increase defense spending and thus to run a budget deficit. What happens to the level of output and to its composition? To the interest rate? To the exchange rate?

The answers are given in Figure 20–3(a): The economy is initially at point A. An increase in government spending from G to G' increases output at a given interest rate, shifting the *IS* curve to the right, from *IS* to *IS'*. Because government spending does not enter the *LM* relation, the *LM* curve does not shift. The new equilibrium is at point A', with a higher level of output and a higher interest rate. As shown in Figure 20–3(b), the higher interest rate leads to a decrease in the exchange rate—an appreciation of the domestic currency. Thus, *an increase in government spending leads to an increase in output, an increase in the interest rate, and an appreciation.*

In words: An increase in government spending leads to an increase in demand, leading to an increase in output. As output increases, so does the demand for money, leading to upward pressure on the interest rate. The increase in the interest rate, which makes domestic bonds more attractive, also leads to an appreciation of the domestic currency. Both the higher interest rate and the appreciation decrease the domestic demand for goods, offsetting some of the effect of government spending on demand and output.

An increase in government spending shifts the *IS* curve to the right. It shifts neither the *LM* curve nor the interest parity curve.

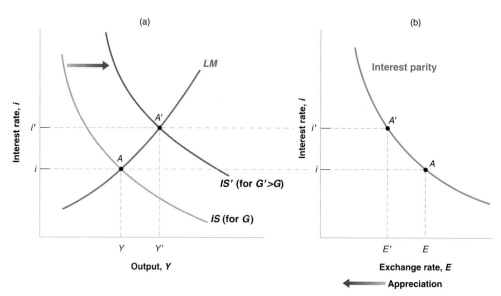

(a)

(b)

FIGURE 20-3

The Effects of an Increase in Government Spending

An increase in government spending leads to an increase in output, an increase in the interest rate, and an appreciation.

Can we tell what happens to the various components of demand?

- Clearly both consumption and government spending go up—consumption goes up because of the increase in income, government spending goes up by assumption.

The effect of a change in government spending on investment was ambiguous in the closed economy; it remains ambiguous in the open economy.

- What happens to investment is ambiguous. Recall that investment depends on both output and the interest rate: $I = I(Y, i)$. On the one hand, output goes up, leading to an increase in investment. But on the other, the interest rate also goes up, leading to a decrease in investment. Depending on which of these two effects dominates, investment can go up or down.

Note: Although an increase in the budget deficit increases the trade deficit, the effect is far from mechanical. It works through the effect of the budget deficit on output and on the exchange rate.

- Recall that net exports depend on domestic output, foreign output, and the exchange rate: $NX = NX(Y, Y^*, E)$. Thus, both the appreciation and the increase in output combine to decrease net exports: The appreciation decreases exports and increases imports, and the increase in output increases imports further. The budget deficit leads to a deterioration of the trade balance. If trade is balanced to start, then the budget deficit leads to a trade deficit.

The Effects of Monetary Policy in an Open Economy

A monetary contraction shifts the LM curve up. It shifts neither the IS curve nor the interest parity curve.

The effects of our other favorite policy experiment, a monetary contraction, are shown in Figure 20-4. At a given level of output, a decrease in the money stock, from M/P to M'/P leads to an increase in the interest rate: The *LM* curve in Figure 20-4(a) therefore shifts up, from *LM* to *LM'*. Because money does not directly enter the *IS* relation, the *IS* curve does not shift. The equilibrium moves from point *A* to point *A'*. The increase in the interest rate leads to an appreciation of the domestic currency (Fig. 20-4b).

Can you tell what happens to consumption, investment, and net exports?

Thus, *a monetary contraction leads to a decrease in output, an increase in the interest rate, and an appreciation.* The story is easy to tell. A monetary contraction leads to an increase in the interest rate, making domestic bonds more attractive and triggering an appreciation. The higher interest rate and the appreciation both decrease demand and output. As output decreases, money demand decreases, leading to a decrease in the interest rate, offsetting some of the initial increase in the interest rate and some of the initial appreciation.

That these experiments were instructive for economists does not imply they were good for the U.S. economy. How costly the large budget deficits have turned out to be is taken up in chapter 27.

How well do the implications of this model fit the facts? To answer, one could hardly design a better experiment than the sharp monetary and fiscal policy changes the U.S. economy went through in the late 1970s and early 1980s. This is the topic taken up in the In Depth box "Monetary Contraction and Fiscal Expansion: The United States in the Early 1980s." The Mundell–Fleming model and its predictions pass with flying colors.

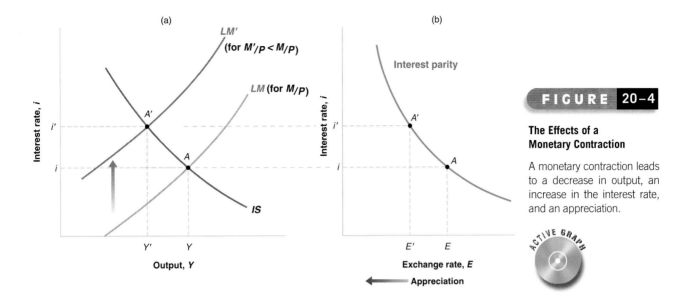

(a)

LM'
(for M'/P < M/P)

LM (for M/P)

IS

Interest rate, i

i'

i

A'

A

Y' Y

Output, Y

(b)

Interest parity

Interest rate, i

i'

i

A'

A

E' E

Exchange rate, E

← Appreciation

FIGURE 20-4

The Effects of a Monetary Contraction

A monetary contraction leads to a decrease in output, an increase in the interest rate, and an appreciation.

IN DEPTH

Monetary Contraction and Fiscal Expansion: The United States in the Early 1980s

The early 1980s in the United States were dominated by sharp changes in both monetary policy and fiscal policy.

We have already discussed the origins of the change in monetary policy in chapter 9 in the core. By the late 1970s, the chairman of the Fed, Paul Volcker, concluded that U.S. inflation was too high and had to be reduced. Starting in late 1979, Volker embarked on a path of sharp monetary contraction, realizing this might lead to a recession in the short run, but would lead to lower inflation in the medium run.

The change in fiscal policy was triggered by the election of Ronald Reagan in 1980. Reagan was elected on the promise of more conservative policies, namely a scaling down of taxation and of the government's role in economic activity. This commitment was the inspiration for the *Economic Recovery Act* of August 1981. Personal income taxes were cut by a total of 23%, in three installments from 1981 to 1983. Corporate taxes were also reduced. These tax cuts were not, however, accompanied by correspond-ing decreases in government spending, and the result was a steady increase in budget deficits, which reached a peak in 1983 at 5.6% of GDP. This is shown in Table 1 which gives spending and revenue numbers for 1980 to 1984.

What were the Reagan administration's motivations for cutting taxes without implementing corresponding cuts in spending? These are still being debated today, but there is agreement that there were two main motivations.

One motivation came from the beliefs of a fringe, but influential, group of economists called the **supply siders**, who argued that a cut in tax rates would lead people and firms to work much harder and more productively, and that the resulting increase in activity would lead to an in-crease, not a decrease, in tax revenues. Whatever the merits of the argument appeared to be then, it proved wrong after the fact: Even if some people did work harder and more productively after the tax cuts, tax revenues de-creased and the fiscal deficit increased.

(continued on page 390)

TABLE 1 The emergence of large U.S. budget deficits, 1980–1984

	1980	1981	1982	1983	1984
Spending	22.0	22.8	24.0	25.0	23.7
Revenues	20.2	20.8	20.5	19.4	19.2
Personal taxes	9.4	9.6	9.9	8.8	8.2
Corporate taxes	2.6	2.3	1.6	1.6	2.0
Budget surplus (−: deficit)	−1.8	−2.0	−3.5	−5.6	−4.5

Numbers are for fiscal years, which start in October of the previous calendar year. All numbers are ex-pressed as a percentage of GDP.

Source: Historical tables, Office of Management and Budget.

The other was the hope that the cut in taxes, and the resulting increase in deficits, would scare Congress into cutting spending, or, at the very least, into not increasing spending further. This motivation turned out to be partly right. Congress found itself under enormous pressure not to increase spending, and the growth of spending in the 1980s was surely lower than it would have been otherwise. Nonetheless, this decrease in spending was not enough to offset the shortfall in taxes and avoid the rapid increase in deficits.

Whatever the reason for the deficits, the effects of the monetary contraction and fiscal expansion were in line with what the Mundell–Fleming model predicts. Table 2 gives the evolution of the main macroeconomic variables from 1980 to 1984.

From 1980 to 1982, the evolution of the economy was dominated by the effects of the monetary contraction. Interest rates, both nominal and real, increased sharply, leading both to a large dollar appreciation (a decrease in the exchange rate) and a recession. The goal of lowering inflation was achieved, although not right away; by 1982, inflation was down to about 4%. Lower output and dollar appreciation had opposing effects on the trade balance (lower output leading to lower imports and an improvement in the trade balance, the appreciation of the dollar leading to a deterioration in the trade balance), resulting in little change in the trade deficit until 1983.

From 1982 on, the evolution of the economy was dominated by the effects of the fiscal expansion. As our model predicts, these effects were strong output growth, high interest rates, and further dollar appreciation. The effects of high output growth and dollar appreciation were an increase in the trade deficit to 2.7% of GDP by 1984. By the mid-1980s, the main macroeconomic policy issue had become that of the **twin deficits**, the budget deficit and the trade deficit. It was to remain one of the central macroeconomic issues throughout the 1980s and through much of the 1990s.

TABLE 2	Major U.S. macroeconomic variables, 1980–1984				
	1980	**1981**	**1982**	**1983**	**1984**
GDP growth (%)	−0.5	1.8	−2.2	3.9	6.2
Unemployment rate (%)	7.1	7.6	9.7	9.6	7.5
Inflation rate (CPI) (%)	12.5	8.9	3.8	3.8	3.9
Interest rate: Nominal (%)	11.5	14.0	10.6	8.6	9.6
Real (%)	2.5	4.9	6.0	5.1	5.9
Real exchange rate	117	99	89	85	77
Trade surplus (−: deficit) (% of GDP)	−0.5	−0.4	−0.6	−1.5	−2.7

The inflation rate is the rate of change of the CPI. The *nominal interest rate* is the three-month T-bill rate. The *real interest rate* is equal to the nominal rate minus the forecast of inflation by DRI, a private forecasting firm. The *real exchange rate* is the trade-weighted real exchange rate, normalized so that 1973 = 100.

20-5 | Fixed Exchange Rates

We have assumed so far that the central bank chose the money supply and let the exchange rate adjust in whatever manner was implied by equilibrium in the foreign-exchange market. In most countries, this assumption does not reflect reality: Central banks act under implicit or explicit exchange-rate targets and use monetary policy to achieve those targets. The targets are sometimes implicit, sometimes explicit; they are sometimes specific values, sometimes bands or ranges. These exchange-rate arrangements come under many names. Let's first see what these various names mean.

Pegs, Crawling Pegs, Bands, the EMS, and the Euro

At one end of the spectrum, there are countries with flexible exchange rates such as the United States and Japan. These countries have no explicit exchange-rate targets. Although their central banks surely do not ignore movements in the exchange rate, they have shown themselves quite willing to let their exchange rates fluctuate considerably.

At the other end, there are countries that operate under fixed exchange rates. These countries maintain a fixed exchange rate in terms of some foreign currency. Some **peg** their currency to the dollar: The list ranges from the Bahamas to Oman. Others peg their currency to

Like the "dance of the dollar" in the 1980s (chapter 18), there has been a "dance of the yen" in 1990s, with the yen appreciating by more than 50% vis-à-vis the dollar from 1990 to 1995, and depreciating steadily since then.

the French franc; most of these are former French colonies in Africa. Others peg to a basket of currencies, with the weights reflecting the composition of their trade. The label "fixed" is a bit misleading: It is not the case that the exchange rate in countries with fixed exchange rates actually never changes. But changes are rare. An extreme case is that of the African countries pegged to the French franc. When their exchange rates were readjusted in January 1994, this was the first adjustment in 45 years. Because these changes are rare, economists use specific words to distinguish them from the daily changes that occur under flexible exchange rates. They refer to an increase in the exchange rate under a fixed exchange rate regime as a *devaluation* rather than a depreciation, and to a decrease in the exchange rate under a fixed exchange rate regime as a *revaluation* rather than an appreciation.

Between these extremes are the countries with various degrees of commitment to an exchange rate target. For example, some countries operate under a **crawling peg**. The name describes it well: These countries often have inflation rates that exceed the U.S. inflation rate. If they were to peg their nominal exchange rate against the dollar, the more rapid increase in their domestic price level over the U.S. price level would lead to a steady real appreciation and rapidly make their goods noncompetitive. To avoid this effect, these countries choose a predetermined rate of depreciation against the dollar. They choose to "crawl" (move slowly) vis-à-vis the dollar.

> Recall the definition of the real exchange rate $\epsilon = EP^*/P$. If domestic inflation is higher than foreign inflation: P increases faster than P^*. Equivalently, P^*/P decreases. If the nominal exchange rate E is fixed, EP^*/P decreases: there is a steady real appreciation, and domestic goods become steadily more expensive relative to foreign goods.

Yet another arrangement is for a group of countries to maintain their bilateral exchange rates (the exchange rate between each pair of countries) within some bands. The most prominent example is the **European Monetary System (EMS)**—which determined the movements of exchange rates within the European Union from 1978 to 1998. Under the rules of this **exchange rate mechanism**, or **ERM**, member countries agreed to maintain their exchange rate vis-à-vis the other currencies in the system within narrow limits or **bands** around a **central parity**. Changes in the central parity and devaluations or revaluations of specific currencies could occur, but only by common agreement among member countries. After a major crisis in 1992, which forced several countries to drop out of the EMS altogether, exchange rate adjustments became more and more infrequent, leading several countries to move one step further and adopt a common currency, the *Euro*. Conversion from domestic currencies to the Euro started in earnest on January 1, 1999. If everything goes according to plan, full conversion will be achieved by the year 2002. We shall return to the implications of the move to the Euro in chapter 21.

> We look at the 1992 crisis in chapter 21.

> You can think of countries adopting a common currency as adopting an extreme form of fixed exchange rates: Their "exchange rate" is fixed at one-to-one between any pair of countries.

We shall discuss the pros and cons of different exchange regimes in the next chapter. But first, we must understand how pegging the exchange rate affects the scope for and the effects of monetary and fiscal policy. This is what we do in the rest of this section.

Pegging the Exchange Rate, and Monetary Control

> Until now, we looked at macroeconomic policy under flexible exchange rates. We now look at policy under fixed exchange rates.

Suppose a country decides to peg its exchange rate at some chosen value, call it $\overline{E}$. How does it actually achieve this? It cannot just announce the value of the exchange rate and just stand there and do nothing. Rather, it must take measures so that the chosen exchange rate will prevail in the foreign-exchange market. Let's look at the implications and mechanics of pegging.

Pegging or no pegging, under the assumption of perfect capital mobility, the exchange rate and the nominal interest rate must satisfy the interest parity condition:

$$i_t = i_t^* + \frac{E_{t+1}^e - E_t}{E_t}$$

Now suppose the country pegs the exchange rate at $\overline{E}$, so the current exchange rate $E_t = \overline{E}$. If financial and foreign exchange markets believe that the exchange rate will remain pegged at this value in the future, their expectation of the future exchange rate, E_{t+1}^e, is also equal to $\overline{E}$, and the interest parity relation becomes

$$i_t = i_t^* + \frac{\overline{E} - \overline{E}}{\overline{E}} = i_t^*$$

In words: If financial investors expect the exchange rate to remain fixed, they will require the same nominal interest rate in both countries. *Under a fixed exchange rate and perfect capital mobility, the domestic interest rate must be equal to the foreign interest rate.*

Under perfect capital mobility, fixing the exchange rate means giving up the freedom to choose the interest rate (which must equal the foreign interest rate).

This condition has one further important implication. Return to the equilibrium condition that the supply of money and demand for money be equal. Now that $i = i^*$, this condition becomes

$$\frac{M}{P} = Y L(i^*) \tag{20.6}$$

Suppose an increase in domestic output increases the demand for money. In a closed economy, the central bank could leave the money stock unchanged, leading to an increase in the equilibrium interest rate. In an open economy, and under flexible exchange rates, the central bank can still do the same: The result will be both an increase in the interest rate and an appreciation of the domestic currency. But under a fixed exchange rate, the central bank cannot keep the money stock unchanged. If it did, the domestic interest rate would increase above the foreign interest rate, leading to an appreciation of the domestic currency. To maintain the exchange rate, it must increase the supply of money in line with the increase in the demand for money so the equilibrium interest rate does not change. Given the price level, P, nominal money M must adjust so that equation (20.6) holds.

To summarize: *Under fixed exchange rates, the central bank gives up monetary policy as a policy instrument.* A fixed exchange rate implies a domestic interest rate equal to the foreign rate. And the money supply must adjust to maintain that interest rate.

These results depend very much on the assumption of perfect capital mobility. The case of fixed exchange rates with imperfect capital mobility, which is more relevant for middle-income countries such as in Latin America or Asia, is treated in the appendix to this chapter.

Fiscal Policy under Fixed Exchange Rates

If monetary policy can no longer be used under fixed exchange rates, what about fiscal policy? To answer, we use Figure 20–5.

Figure 20–5 starts by replicating Figure 20–3(a), which we used earlier to analyze the effects of fiscal policy under flexible exchange rates. In that case, we saw that a fiscal expansion shifted the *IS* curve to the right from *IS* to *IS′*. Under flexible exchange rates, the money stock remained unchanged, leading to a movement in the equilibrium from *A* to *B*, with an increase in output from Y_A to Y_B, an increase in the interest rate, and a decrease in the exchange rate—an appreciation of the domestic currency.

FIGURE 20–5

The Effects of a Fiscal Expansion Under Fixed Exchange Rates

Under flexible exchange rates, a fiscal expansion increases output from Y_A to Y_B. Under fixed exchange rates, output increases from Y_A to Y_C.

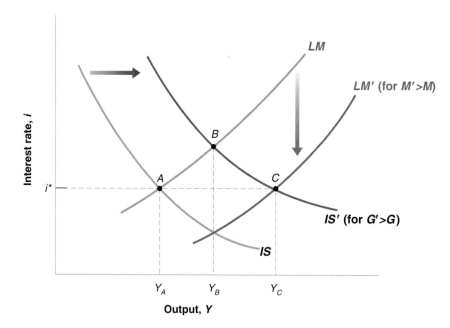

However, under fixed exchange rates the central bank cannot allow the currency to appreciate. As the increase in output leads to an increase in the demand for money, the central bank must accommodate this increased demand for money by increasing the money supply. In terms of Figure 20–5, the central bank must shift the *LM* curve down as the *IS* curve shifts to the right, so that the interest rate, and, by implication, the exchange rate, do not change. Therefore, the equilibrium moves from *A* to *C*, with higher output Y_C and unchanged interest and exchange rates. Thus, under fixed exchange rates, fiscal policy is more powerful than it is under flexible exchange rates. This is because fiscal policy triggers monetary accommodation.

As this chapter comes to an end, a question should have started to form in your mind. Why would a country choose to fix its exchange rate? We have seen several reasons why this appears to be a bad idea:

1. By fixing the exchange rate, a country gives up a powerful tool for correcting trade imbalances or changing the level of economic activity.

2. By committing to a particular exchange rate, a country also gives up control of its interest rate. Not only that, it must match movements in the foreign interest rate, at the risk of unwanted effects on its own activity. This is what happened in the early 1990s in Europe. Because of the increase in demand due to reunification, Germany felt it had to increase its interest rate. To maintain their parity with the DM, other countries in the European Monetary System (EMS) also were forced to increase their interest rate, something that they would rather have avoided. (This is the topic of the Global Macro box "German Unification, Interest Rates, and the EMS.") This tension was the cause of a major exchange rate crisis within the EMS in 1992, which we shall study in the next chapter.

3. While the country retains control of fiscal policy, one policy instrument is not enough. As we saw in chapter 19, for example, a fiscal expansion can help the economy get out of a recession, but only at the cost of a larger trade deficit. And a country that wants to decrease its budget deficit cannot, under fixed exchange rates, use monetary policy to offset the contractionary effect of its fiscal policy on output.

◄ Is the effect of fiscal policy stronger in a closed economy or in an open economy with fixed exchange rates? (*Hint*: The answer is ambiguous.)

GLOBAL MACRO

German Unification, Interest Rates, and the EMS

Under a system of fixed exchange rates such as the EMS (let's ignore here the degree of flexibility afforded by the bands), no individual country can change its interest rate if the others do not change theirs as well. So, how do interest rates actually change? Two arrangements are possible. One is for the member countries to coordinate all changes in their interest rates. Another is for one of the countries to take the lead and for the other countries to follow—this is what happened in the EMS, with Germany as the leader.

During the 1980s, most European central banks shared similar goals and were happy to let the Bundesbank (the German central bank) take the lead. But in 1990, German unification led to a sharp divergence in goals between the Bundesbank and the other EMS nations' central banks. Recall the macroeconomic implications of unification from chapter 5: Both the need for large transfers to eastern Germany and an investment boom led to a large increase in demand in Germany. The Bundesbank's fear that this shift would generate too strong an increase in activity led it to adopt a restrictive monetary policy. The result was, as we saw, strong growth in Germany together with a large increase in interest rates.

This may have been the right policy mix for Germany. But for other countries, the effects of German unification were less appealing. The other countries had not experienced the same increase in demand, but to stay in the EMS, they had to match German interest rates. The net result was a sharp decrease in demand and in output in the other countries. These results are presented in Table 1, which gives nominal and real interest rates, inflation rates, and GDP growth from 1990 to 1992 for Germany and for two of its EMS partners, France and Belgium.

Note first how the high German nominal interest rates were matched by both France and Belgium. Nominal interest rates were actually higher in France than in Germany in all three years! This is because France needed higher interest rates than Germany to maintain the DM/franc parity; the reason for this is financial markets were not sure that France would actually keep the parity of the franc vis-à-vis the DM. Worried about a possible devaluation of the franc, they asked for a higher interest rate on French bonds than on German bonds.

(*continued on page 394*)

Although they had to match—or, as we have just seen, more than match—German nominal rates, France and Belgium had less inflation than Germany. The result was very high real interest rates, higher than in Germany. In both France and Belgium, average real interest rates from 1990 to 1992 were close to 7%. And in both countries, the period 1990 to 1992 was characterized by slow growth and rising unemployment. Unemployment in France in 1992 was 10.4%, up from 8.9% in 1990. Unemployment in Belgium in 1992 was 12.1%, up from 8.7%.

Although we have looked at only two of Germany's EMS partners, a similar story was unfolding for the others. Average unemployment in the European Union, which stood at 8.7% in 1990, had increased to 10.3% in 1992. The effects of high real interest rates on spending were not the only source of this slowdown, but they were the main one.

By 1992, an increasing number of countries were wondering whether to keep defending their EMS parity or to give it up and lower their interest rates. Worried about the risk of devaluations, financial markets started to ask for higher interest rates in those countries where they thought devaluation was more likely. The result was two major exchange rate crises, one in the fall of 1992 and the other in the summer of 1993. By the end of these two crises, two countries, Italy and the United Kingdom, had left the EMS. We look at these crises, their origins and their implications, in chapter 21.

TABLE 1	German unification, interest rates, and output growth: Germany, France, and Belgium, 1990–1992					
	Nominal Interest Rates			**Inflation**		
	1990	**1991**	**1992**	**1990**	**1991**	**1992**
Germany	8.5	9.2	9.5	2.7	3.7	4.7
France	10.3	9.6	10.3	2.9	3.0	2.4
Belgium	9.6	9.4	9.4	2.9	2.7	2.4
	Real Interest Rates			**GDP Growth**		
	1990	**1991**	**1992**	**1990**	**1991**	**1992**
Germany	5.7	5.5	4.8	5.7	4.5	2.1
France	7.4	6.6	7.9	2.5	0.7	1.4
Belgium	6.7	6.7	7.0	3.3	2.1	0.8

The *nominal interest rate* is the short-term nominal interest rate. The *real interest rate* is the realized real interest rate over the year—that is, the nominal interest rate minus actual inflation over the year. All rates are annual.

Source: OECD Economic Outlook.

So why do some countries fix their exchange rate? Why have eleven European countries just adopted a common currency? To answer these questions, we must do some more work. We must look at what happens not only in the short run—which is what we did in this chapter—but also in the medium run, when the price level can adjust. We must look at the nature of exchange rate crises. Once we have done this, we shall then be able to give an assessment of the pros and cons of exchange rate regimes. These are the topics we take up in chapter 21.

SUMMARY

- In an open economy, the demand for goods depends on both the interest rate and the exchange rate. A decrease in the interest rate increases the demand for goods. An increase in the exchange rate—a depreciation—also increases the demand for goods.

- The interest rate is determined by the equality of money demand and money supply. The exchange rate is determined by the interest parity condition, which states that the domestic interest rate must equal the foreign interest rate plus the expected rate of depreciation.

- Given the expected future exchange rate and the foreign interest rate, increases in the domestic interest rate lead to a decrease in the exchange rate (an appreciation) and decreases in the domestic interest rate lead to an increase in the exchange rate (a depreciation).

- Under flexible exchange rates, an expansionary fiscal policy leads to an increase in output, an increase in the interest rate, and an appreciation. A contractionary monetary policy leads to a decrease in output, an increase in the interest rate, and an appreciation.

There are many types of exchange-rate arrangements. They range from fully flexible exchange rates to crawling pegs, to pegs, to fixed exchange rates, to the adoption of a common currency. Under fixed exchange rates, a country maintains a fixed exchange rate in terms of a foreign currency or a basket of currencies.

Under fixed exchange rates and perfect capital mobility, a country must maintain an interest rate equal to the foreign interest rate. Thus, the central bank loses the use of monetary policy as a policy instrument. Fiscal policy becomes more powerful, however, because fiscal policy triggers monetary accommodation and thus does not lead to offsetting changes in the domestic interest rate and exchange rate.

KEY TERMS

- Mundell–Fleming model, 381
- supply siders, 389
- twin deficits, 390
- peg, 390
- crawling peg, 391
- European Monetary System (EMS), 391
- exchange rate mechanism (ERM), 391
- bands, 391
- central parity, 391

QUESTIONS & PROBLEMS

1. TRUE/FALSE/UNCERTAIN

a. Because the multiplier is smaller in an open economy than in a closed economy, fiscal policy is more effective in an open economy than in a closed economy.

b. Monetary policy is more effective in a closed economy than in an open economy with flexible exchange rates.

c. If financial investors expect the exchange rate to be higher next year, interest parity implies that it will be higher today.

d. If financial investors expect the dollar to depreciate vis-à-vis the yen over the coming year, one-year interest rates will be higher in the United States than in Japan.

e. If the Japanese interest rate is equal to zero, foreigners will not want to hold Japanese bonds.

f. Under fixed exchange rates, the money stock must be constant.

2. A CURRENCY CRISIS

a. Consider an economy with fixed exchange rates. Suppose that the government devalues unexpectedly and that investors believe that there will be no further devaluation. What will be the effects of the devaluation on output and on the interest rate?

b. Suppose instead that, after the devaluation, investors believe that another devaluation is likely to come soon. What will be the effects of the initial devaluation on output and on the interest rate?

3. FIXED EXCHANGE RATES AND MONETARY POLICY

Consider a group of open economies with perfect capital mobility between them.

a. Assume there is a Leader country. All other countries (referred to as the Follower countries) fix their exchange rates to the Leader country. Discuss the effectiveness of monetary policy in the Follower countries.

b. If all countries fix their exchange rate vis-à-vis the Leader country, isn't the Leader country's exchange rate also fixed? What does this imply for the effectiveness of the Leader country's monetary policy?

c. If the Leader country reduces its money supply to fight inflation, what must the Follower countries do to enforce their fixed exchange rates? What is the effect on their economy? What would happen if Follower countries did nothing?

4. THE EFFECTS OF CHANGES IN FOREIGN VARIABLES

Consider the *IS* and *LM* equations in section 20-3.

a. Show the effect of a decrease in foreign output Y^* on domestic output Y. Explain in words.

b. Show the effect of an increase in the foreign interest rate i^* on domestic output Y. Explain in words.

c. "A monetary contraction abroad is likely to lead to a recession at home." Discuss this statement.

5. ELIMINATING A TRADE DEFICIT UNDER FIXED EXCHANGE RATES

Consider a small open *IS-LM* economy with a fixed exchange rate, where output is at its natural level, but there is a trade deficit. What is the appropriate fiscal-monetary policy mix?

6. MONETARY POLICY AND THE COMPONENTS OF GDP

Consider a monetary expansion in an economy operating under flexible exchange rates. Discuss the effects on consumption, investment, and net exports.

FURTHER READINGS

A fascinating account of the politics behind fiscal policy under the Reagan administration is given by David Stockman (who was then the director of the Office of Management and Budget) *The Triumph of Politics: Why the Reagan Revolution Failed* (New York: Harper & Row, 1986).

A good book on the evolution of exchange rate arrangements in Europe is Daniel Gros and Niels Thygesen, *European Monetary Integration: From the European Monetary System to Economic and Monetary Union*, 2nd ed., (New York: Addison-Wesley-Longman, 1998).

APPENDIX

FIXED EXCHANGE RATES, INTEREST RATES, AND CAPITAL MOBILITY

The assumption of perfect capital mobility is a good approximation to what happens in countries with highly developed financial markets and few capital controls, such as the United States, the United Kingdom, and Japan. But the assumption is more questionable in countries that have less developed financial markets or have a battery of capital controls in place. There, domestic financial investors may have neither the savvy nor the legal right to move easily into foreign bonds when domestic interest rates are low. The central bank may then be able both to decrease interest rates and to maintain a given exchange rate.

To look at these issues, let us start with the balance sheet of the central bank. In chapter 4, we assumed the only asset held by the central bank was domestic bonds. In an open economy, the central bank actually holds two types of assets: (1) domestic bonds and (2) **foreign-exchange reserves**, which we shall think of as foreign currency, although they also take the form of foreign bonds or foreign interest-paying assets. The balance sheet of the central bank is represented in Figure 20A–1. On the asset side are bonds and foreign currency reserves, and on the liability side is the monetary base. There are now two ways in which the central bank can change the monetary base: either by purchases or sales of bonds in the bond market, or by purchases or sales of foreign currency in the foreign-exchange market.*

FIGURE 20A–1

Balance Sheet of the Central Bank

Assets	Liabilities
Bonds Foreign exchange reserves	Monetary base

> *****DIGGING DEEPER**. If you have not read section 4-3 in chapter 4, replace "monetary base" by "money supply," and you will get the sense of the argument. If you have read that section, recall that the money supply is equal to the monetary base times the money multiplier. Take the money multiplier as given, and our conclusions about the monetary base extend straightforwardly to the money supply.

Perfect Capital Mobility and Fixed Exchange Rates

Consider first the effects of an open market operation under the assumptions of perfect capital mobility and fixed exchange rates (the assumptions we made in the last section of this chapter).

- Assume the domestic and foreign nominal interest rates are initially equal, so that $i = i^*$. Suppose the central bank embarks on an expansionary open-market operation, buying bonds in the bond market in amount ΔB, and creating money—increasing the monetary base—in exchange. This purchase of bonds leads to a decrease in the domestic interest rate, i. This is, however, only the beginning of the story:

- Now that the domestic interest rate is lower than the foreign interest rate, financial investors prefer to hold foreign bonds. To buy foreign bonds, they must first buy foreign currency. They go to the foreign exchange market and sell domestic currency for foreign currency.

- If the central bank did nothing, the price of domestic currency would fall, and the result would be a depreciation. Under its commitment to a fixed exchange rate, the central bank cannot allow the currency to depreciate. Thus, it must intervene in the foreign-exchange market and sell foreign currency for domestic currency. As it buys domestic money, the monetary base decreases.

- How much foreign currency must the central bank sell? It must keep selling until the monetary base is back to its pre-open market operation level, so the domestic interest rate is again equal to the foreign interest rate. Only then are financial investors willing to hold domestic bonds.

How long do all these steps take? Under perfect capital mobility, all this may happen within minutes or so of the original open market operation. After these steps, the balance sheet of the central bank looks as in Figure 20A–2. Bond holdings are up by ΔB, reserves of foreign currency are down by ΔB, and the monetary base is unchanged, having gone up by ΔB in the open market operation and down by ΔB as a result of the sale of foreign currency in the foreign exchange market.

To summarize: Under fixed exchange rates and perfect capital mobility, the only effect of the initial open market operation is to change the *composition* of the central bank's balance sheet but not the monetary base.

Imperfect Capital Mobility and Fixed Exchange Rates

Let's now move away from the assumption of perfect capital mobility. Suppose it takes some time for financial investors to shift between domestic and foreign bonds.

An expansionary open market operation can now initially bring the domestic interest rate below the foreign interest rate. But over time, investors shift to foreign bonds, leading to an increase in the demand for foreign currency in the foreign-exchange market. To avoid a depreciation of the domestic currency, the bank must again stand ready to sell foreign currency and buy domestic currency. Eventually, the central bank buys enough domestic currency to offset the effects of the initial open market operation. The monetary base is back to its pre-open market operation level, and so is the interest rate. The central bank holds more bonds and smaller reserves of foreign currency.

The difference between this case and the preceding one is that by accepting a loss in foreign exchange reserves, the central bank is now able to decrease interest rates *for some time*. If it takes just a few days for financial investors to adjust, the trade-off is rather unattractive—as many countries have discovered. But, if the central bank can affect the domestic interest rate for a few weeks or months, it may, in some circumstances, be willing to do so.

Now let's move further from perfect capital mobility. Suppose, in response to a decrease in the domestic interest rate, financial investors are either unwilling or unable to move much of their portfolio into foreign bonds. This is the relevant case for many middle-income countries, from Latin America to Eastern Europe to Asia. After an expansionary open market operation, the domestic interest rate decreases, making domestic bonds less attractive. Some domestic investors move into foreign bonds, selling domestic currency for foreign currency. To maintain the exchange rate, the central bank must buy domestic currency and supply foreign currency. However, the foreign-exchange intervention may now be small compared to the initial open market operation. And if capital controls truly

Assets		Liabilities	
Bonds:	ΔB	Monetary base $\Delta B - \Delta B$	
Reserves:	$-\Delta B$		$= 0$

FIGURE 20A–2

Balance Sheet of the Central Bank After an Open Market Operation, and the Induced Intervention in the Foreign-Exchange Market

prevent investors from moving into foreign bonds at all, there may be no need at all for such an intervention.

Even leaving this extreme case aside, the net effect is likely to be an increase in the monetary base, a decrease in the domestic interest rate, an increase in the central bank's bond holdings, and some (but smaller) loss in reserves of foreign currency. With imperfect capital mobility, a country has some freedom to move the domestic interest rate while maintaining its exchange rate. Its freedom to do so depends primarily on three factors:

- The degree of development of its financial markets, and how willing domestic and foreign investors are to shift between domestic and foreign assets.
- The degree of capital controls it is able to impose on both domestic and foreign investors.
- The amount of foreign exchange reserves it holds: The higher the amount, the more it can afford the loss in reserves it is likely to sustain if it decreases the interest rate at a given exchange rate.

KEY TERMS

- foreign-exchange reserves, 396

We invite you to visit the Blanchard page on the Prentice Hall Web site at:

http://www.prenhall.com/blanchard

for this chapter's World Wide Web exercises

CHAPTER 21

Exchange Rates: Adjustments, Crises, and Regimes

In July 1944, representatives of 44 countries met at Bretton Woods in New Hampshire to design a new international monetary and exchange rate system. The system they adopted was based on fixed exchange rates, with all member countries (other than the United States) pegging the price of their currency in terms of the dollar. (The Bretton Woods agreement also created both the International Monetary Fund (IMF) to oversee the new international monetary system and the World Bank to help war countries and their ex-colonies rebuild after the war. In chapter 24, we look at their role today.) In 1973, a series of exchange rate crises brought an abrupt end to the system—and an end to what is now called "the Bretton Woods period." Since then, the world has been characterized by many exchange rate arrangements. Some countries operate under flexible exchange rates; some operate under fixed exchange rates; some go back and forth between regimes. Which exchange rate regime is best for a country is one of the most debated issues in macroeconomics, and the issue I focus on in this chapter. To do so, I proceed in three steps.

In section 21-1, I extend the analysis of chapter 20 to look not only at the short run but also at the medium run in an open economy under fixed exchange rates. The reason for doing so is the following: A fixed exchange rate regime means a fixed *nominal* exchange rate. In the short run, both the domestic and foreign price levels are fixed, so a fixed nominal exchange rate implies a fixed real exchange rate as well. But in the medium run, price levels can adjust, and so can the real exchange rate—even if the nominal exchange rate is fixed. This opens the possibility that in the medium run, a fixed nominal exchange rate may be consistent with any real exchange rate. As we shall see, this is indeed the case: In the medium run, the real exchange rate does not depend on the exchange rate regime. But the adjustment process to the "right" exchange rate, and the path of output along the way, is quite different depending on whether the nominal exchange rate or the price level does the adjustment.

In section 21-2, I turn to exchange rate crises. Countries that fix their exchange rate often face serious crises. This was the case in 1973 for the countries operating under the Bretton Woods

The Asian crisis is discussed in Chapter 24.

agreement. It was the case in Europe in 1992 for the countries operating within the European Monetary System (EMS). It was again the case for many Asian countries in 1997 and 1998. Exchange rate crises typically start when participants in financial markets conclude that the current exchange rate is not sustainable, and that the country may soon devalue. To compensate investors for the perceived risk of devaluation, the central bank must increase the domestic interest rate, often to very high levels. The country is faced with a tough choice: Maintain the interest rate at a very high level, decreasing the demand for goods and triggering a recession; or give up the parity and devalue. Understanding such crises helps us assess one of the main problems associated with fixed exchange rates.

Building on what we have seen, the chapter closes, in section 21-3, with a discussion of the pros and cons of flexible and fixed exchange rates regimes.

21-1 | Fixed Exchange Rates and The Adjustment of the Real Exchange Rate

Remember that under fixed exchange rates, a change in the exchange rate is called a devaluation (not a depreciation), or a revaluation (not an appreciation).

Take a country operating under a fixed exchange rate regime. Suppose its currency is *overvalued*: At the real exchange rate implied by the fixed nominal exchange rate and the domestic and foreign price levels, domestic goods are very expensive relative to foreign goods. As a result, the demand for domestic goods is low, and so is output: The country is in a recession.

To get out of the recession, the country has several options. Among them:

To explore the short-run and the medium-run properties of an economy under both fixed and flexible exchange rates would take us too far. Thus, we only look at the case of fixed exchange rates here.

- Devalue: By making domestic goods cheaper relative to foreign goods, a devaluation leads to an increase in the demand for domestic goods, and thus to an increase in output and an improvement in the trade balance.
- Do nothing: Keep the nominal exchange rate fixed, and rely instead on the adjustment of the price level over time.

In this section, we compare the macro implications of these two options, both in the short run and in the medium run. To begin, we must derive the aggregate demand and aggregate supply relations for an open economy under fixed exchange rates.

Aggregate Demand Under Fixed Exchange Rates

Warning: The next paragraphs rely on what you learned in earlier chapters. Make sure you remember the definitions of the real interest rate (chapter 14), the real exchange rate (chapter 18), and the interest rate parity condition (chapter 18).

Go back to the condition for goods-market equilibrium we derived in chapter 20, equation (20.1)

$$Y = C(Y - T) + I(Y, r) + G + NX(Y, Y^*, \epsilon) \tag{21.1}$$

For the goods market to be in equilibrium, output must be equal to the demand for domestic goods—the sum of consumption, investment, government spending, and net exports.

Recall that the real interest rate equals the nominal interest rate minus expected inflation

$$r \equiv i - \pi^e$$

Recall that the real exchange rate ϵ is defined as

$$\epsilon = \frac{EP^*}{P}$$

Recall that, under fixed exchange rates, the nominal exchange rate is fixed. Denote by $\overline{E}$ the value at which it is fixed, so that

$$E = \overline{E}$$

Recall, finally, that under fixed exchange rates and perfect capital mobility, the domestic interest rate must be equal to the foreign interest rate

$$i = i*$$

Use these four relations to rewrite equation (21.1)

$$Y = C(Y - T) + I(Y, i* - \pi^e) + G + NX\left(Y, Y*, \frac{\overline{E}P*}{P}\right)$$

This is a rich—if complicated—equilibrium condition. It tells us that in an open economy with fixed exchange rates equilibrium output (or, more precisely, the level of output implied by equilibrium in the goods, financial, and foreign exchange markets) depends on the following variables:

- Government spending (G) and taxes (T). An increase in government spending increases output, as does a decrease in taxes.
- The domestic real interest rate, which is equal to the foreign nominal interest rate ($i*$) minus expected inflation (π^e). An increase in the domestic real interest rate, coming either from an increase in the foreign interest rate or from a decrease in expected inflation, decreases output.
- Foreign output ($Y*$). An increase in foreign output increases exports, and increases domestic output.
- The real exchange rate, equal to the fixed nominal exchange rate ($\overline{E}$) times the foreign price level ($P*$) divided by the domestic price level (P). An increase in the real exchange rate, equivalently a real depreciation, leads to an increase in net exports, increasing output.

I shall focus here on the effects of only three of these variables: the real exchange rate, government spending, and taxes. It will be convenient to write the relation between these three variables and output simply as

$$Y = Y\left(\frac{\overline{E}P*}{P}, G, T\right) \qquad (21.2)$$
$$= \quad (\ +\ , +, -)$$

An increase in the real exchange rate—a real depreciation—increases output. So does an increase in government spending, or a decrease in taxes. All the other variables that affect output in (21.1) are taken as given and, to simplify notation, I simply omit them from (21.2).

Equation (21.2) gives us our *aggregate demand relation*, the relation between output and the price level implied by equilibrium in the goods market and in financial markets. As in the closed economy, this aggregate demand relation implies a negative relation between the price level and output: Given the fixed nominal exchange rate ($\overline{E}$) and the foreign price level ($P*$), an increase in the domestic price level (P) leads to a decrease in the real exchange rate $\overline{E}P*/P$—equivalently, a real appreciation. This real appreciation leads to a decrease in net exports, and a decrease in Y.

In words, an increase in the price level makes domestic goods more expensive, decreasing the demand for domestic goods, and in turn decreasing output.

Although the sign of the effect of the price level on output is the same as in the closed economy, the channel is quite different. In a closed economy, the price level affects output through its effect on the real money stock and in turn on the interest rate. In an open economy under fixed exchange rates, the interest rate is fixed—pinned down by the foreign interest rate. The way the price level affects output is instead through its effect on the real exchange rate.

Aggregate Demand and Aggregate Supply

Rewrite the aggregate demand relation, equation (21.2), with time indices—which will be needed as we look at dynamics later

$$Y_t = Y\left(\frac{\overline{E}P^*}{P_t}, G, T\right) \tag{21.3}$$

In a closed economy:

$P\uparrow \Rightarrow M/P\downarrow \Rightarrow i\uparrow \Rightarrow Y\downarrow$

In an open economy with fixed exchange rates:

$P\uparrow \Rightarrow \overline{E}P^*/P\downarrow$
$\qquad \Rightarrow NX\downarrow \Rightarrow Y\downarrow$

Note that I have put time indices only on output and the price level. Given our assumption that the country operates under fixed exchange rates, the nominal exchange rate is fixed and does not need a time index. And, for convenience, I assume the foreign price level, and government spending and taxes, are constant as well.

The aggregate demand curve implied by equation (21.3) is drawn as the *AD* curve in Figure 21–1. The aggregate demand curve is downward sloping: An increase in the price level decreases output. As always, the relation is drawn for given values of all other variables, in particular for a given value of the nominal exchange rate.

Turn now to aggregate supply and the determination of the price level. Recall from chapter 7 that the aggregate supply relation is the relation between the price level and output implied by equilibrium in the labor market. I shall rely here on the version of the *aggregate supply relation* we derived in chapter 7, equation (7.1)

$$P_t = P_{t-1}(1 + \mu)\, F\left(1 - \frac{Y_t}{L}, z\right) \tag{21.4}$$

This equation was derived in chapter 7 assuming that expected prices are equal to last year's prices. While we refined the assumption in later chapters, this assumption will do here.

The price level depends on the price level last year, and on the level of output (this year). Recall the mechanisms at work:

- Last year's price level matters because it affects expectations of the price level this year, which affect nominal wages this year, which affect the price level this year.

FIGURE 21–1

Aggregate Demand and Aggregate Supply in an Open Economy Under Fixed Exchange Rates

An increase in the price level leads to a real appreciation and a decrease in output: The aggregate demand curve is downward sloping. An increase in output leads to an increase in the price level: The aggregate supply curve is upward sloping.

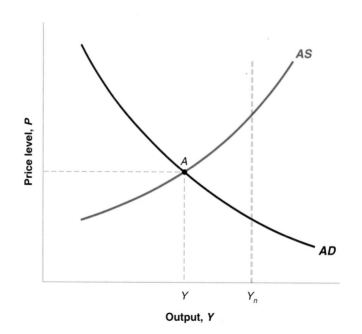

- Higher output matters because it leads to higher employment, which leads to lower unemployment, which leads to higher wages, which lead to a higher price level.

The aggregate supply curve is drawn as the *AS* curve in Figure 21–1, for a given value of last year's price level. It is upward sloping: Higher output leads to a higher price level.

The short-run equilibrium is given by the intersection of the aggregate demand curve and the aggregate supply curve, point *A* in Figure 21–1. Assume that at *A*, output is below the natural level of output, Y_n. The economy is in a recession. The rationale for looking at such a situation was given at the beginning of the section: We want to understand what will happen over time if the government either decides to maintain the exchange rate, or decides instead to devalue.

Adjustment Without a Devaluation. Suppose first the government does not devalue. What will happen over time is shown in Figure 21–2.

Recall that as long as output is below its natural level, the aggregate supply curve keeps shifting down. That is, at a given level of output, the price level in a given year will be below the price level the year before. In the absence of a change in the nominal ex- <inline-margin>Need a refresher? Reread chapter 7, section 7–1.</inline-margin> change rate, the aggregate demand curve does not shift. Thus, starting from *A*, the economy will move over time along the aggregate demand curve, until it reaches *B*. At *B*, output is equal to its natural level. The price level is lower; by implication the real exchange rate is higher.

In words, the steady decrease in the price level over time will lead to a steady real depreciation. This real depreciation will lead to an increase in output until output has returned to its natural level.

This is an important conclusion. In the medium run, despite the fact that the nominal exchange rate is fixed, the economy achieves the real depreciation needed to return output to its natural level. This is an important qualification to the conclusions we reached in the previous chapter—where we were focusing only on the short run:

- In the short run, a fixed nominal exchange rate implies a fixed real exchange rate.
- In the medium run, a fixed nominal exchange rate is consistent with an adjustment of the real exchange rate. The adjustment is achieved through movements in the price level.[1]

Adjustment with a Devaluation. Now suppose, instead of letting the economy adjust over time along the path *AB*, the government decides to give up the existing parity and devalue.

For a given price level, a devaluation (an increase in the nominal exchange rate) leads to a real depreciation (an increase in the real exchange rate), and thus to an increase in output. In other words, a devaluation shifts the aggregate demand curve to the right: Output is higher at a given price level.

This has a straightforward implication. A devaluation of the right size can take the economy directly back to the natural level of output. In terms of Figure 21–3, the right size

[1]**DIGGING DEEPER**. Note that along the path of adjustment, the price level *decreases*. This would seem implausible, as we rarely observe countries going through deflation. (Japan in the late 1990s is a recent exception.) But this is the result of our assumption that the foreign price level is constant, so that for domestic goods to become relatively cheaper, the domestic price level must *decrease*. If instead we had assumed that the foreign price level was increasing through time, the domestic price level would have to increase by less than the foreign price level or, put another way, domestic inflation would have to be lower than foreign inflation for some time.

FIGURE 21–2

Adjustment Without a Devaluation

The aggregate supply shifts down, leading to a decrease in the price level, a real depreciation, and an increase in output over time. The process ends when output has returned to its natural level.

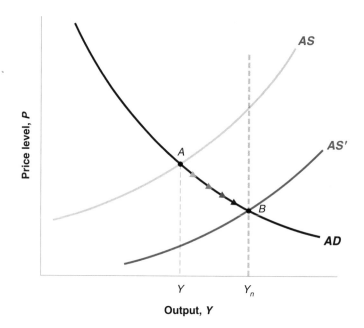

revaluation can take the economy from point A to point C. The economy is initially at A, the same point A as in Figure 21–1. The right size depreciation shifts the aggregate demand curve from AD to AD', moving the equilibrium from A to C. At C, output is equal to its natural level Y_n. The real exchange rate is the same as at B. (We know this because output is the same at points B and C. From equation [21.3], and without changes in G or T, this implies that the real exchange rate must also be the same.)

That the "right size" devaluation can return output to its natural level right away—rather than over time, as was the case without the devaluation—sounds too good to be true, and, in practice, it is. Achieving the "right size" devaluation—the devaluation that takes output to Y_n right away—is easier to achieve in a graph than in the real world:

FIGURE 21–3

Adjustment with a Devaluation

The right size devaluation can shift aggregate demand to the right, moving the economy from point A to point C. At point C, output is back at its natural level.

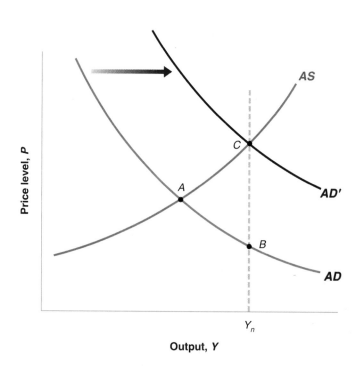

- In contrast to our simple aggregate demand relation (21.3), the effects of a real depreciation on output do not happen right away: Indeed, as we saw in chapter 19, the initial effects of a depreciation on output may be contractionary, as people pay more for imports, and the quantities of imports and exports have not yet adjusted.

See section 19–5 on the J-curve.

- Also, in contrast to our simple aggregate supply relation (21.4), there is likely to be a direct effect of the devaluation on the price level: As the price of imported goods increases, the price of a consumption basket increases. This is likely to lead workers to ask for higher nominal wages, forcing firms to increase their prices as well.

But these complications do not affect the basic conclusion: Allowing the nominal exchange rate to adjust can help output return to its natural level, if not right away, at least much faster than without a devaluation.

To summarize: We have learned that we must qualify some of the conclusions we had reached in chapter 20. Even under fixed *nominal* exchange rates, countries can adjust their *real* exchange rate in the medium run. They can do so by relying on adjustments in the price level. Nevertheless, the adjustment may be long and painful.

Thus, whenever an exchange rate appears overvalued—be it because output is too low, or the trade deficit too large—there is sure to be a debate about whether the country should devalue or instead stick to the existing parity.

- Those who want faster adjustment argue for devaluation. Perhaps the most forceful presentation of this view was made more than 70 years ago by Keynes, who argued against Winston Churchill's 1925 decision to return the English pound to its pre–World War I parity. His arguments are presented in the Global Macro box "The Return of Britain to the Gold Standard: Keynes versus Churchill." Most economic historians believe that history proved Keynes right, and that overvaluation of the pound was one of the main reasons for Britain's poor economic performance after World War I.
- Those who oppose a devaluation argue that there are good reasons to choose fixed exchange rates, and that too much willingness to devalue defeats the purpose of adopting a

GLOBAL MACRO

The Return of Britain to the Gold Standard: Keynes versus Churchill

In 1925, Britain decided to return to the **gold standard**. The gold standard was a system in which each country fixed the price of its currency in terms of gold and stood ready to exchange gold for currency at the stated parity. This system implied fixed nominal exchange rates between countries.

The gold standard had been in place from 1870 until World War I. Because of the need to finance the war, and to do so in part by money creation, Britain had suspended the gold standard in 1914. In 1925, Winston Churchill, then Britain's Chancellor of the Exchequer (the English equivalent of Secretary of the Treasury in the United States), decided to return to the gold standard, and to do so at the prewar parity—that is, at the prewar value of the pound in terms of gold. But, because prices had increased faster in Britain than in many of its trading partners, returning to the prewar parity implied a large real appreciation: At the same nominal exchange rate as before the war, British goods were now more expensive relative to foreign goods.

Keynes severely criticized the decision to return to the pre-war parity. In *The Economic Consequences of Mr.*

Churchill, a book he published in 1925, Keynes argued as follows: If Britain was going to return to the gold standard, it should have done so at a higher price of gold in terms of currency, at a nominal exchange rate higher than the prewar nominal exchange rate. In a newspaper article, he articulated his views as follows:

There remains, however, the objection to which I have never ceased to attach importance, against the return to gold in actual present conditions, in view of the possible consequences on the state of trade and employment. I believe that our price level is too high, if it is converted to gold at the par of exchange, in relation to gold prices elsewhere; and if we consider the prices of those articles only which are not the subject of international trade, and of services, i.e. wages, we shall find that these are materially too high—not less than 5 per cent, and probably 10 per cent. Thus, unless the situation is saved by a rise of prices

(continued on page 406)

elsewhere, the Chancellor is committing us to a policy of forcing down money wages by perhaps 2 shillings in the Pound.

I do not believe that this can be achieved without the gravest danger to industrial profits and industrial peace. I would much rather leave the gold value of our currency where it was some months ago than embark on a struggle with every trade union in the country to reduce money wages. It seems wiser and simpler and saner to leave the currency to find its own level for some time longer rather than force a situation where employers are faced with the alternative of closing down or of lowering wages, cost what the struggle may.

For this reason, I remain of the opinion that the Chancellor of the Exchequer has done an ill-judged thing—ill judged because we are running the risk for no adequate reward if all goes well.

Keynes's prediction turned out to be right. While other countries were growing, Britain was in a recession for the rest of the decade. Most economic historians attribute a good part of the blame to the initial overvaluation.

Source: The Nation and Athenaeum, May 2, 1925.

---

fixed exchange rate regime in the first place. They also argue that too much willingness on the part of governments to consider a devaluation may lead to an increased likelihood of exchange rate crises. To understand their arguments, we now turn to these crises: what triggers them and what their implications might be.

21-2 | Exchange Rate Crises

Take a country operating under fixed exchange rates. Suppose participants in financial markets start believing there may soon be an exchange rate adjustment—either a devaluation or a shift to a flexible exchange rate regime accompanied by a depreciation. Why might this be the case?

- The domestic currency may be overvalued. A real depreciation is called for. While this can be achieved without a devaluation, financial investors may conclude that the government will take the quickest way out, and devalue. Such an overvaluation often happens in countries that fix the nominal exchange rate while having an inflation rate higher than the inflation rate in the country they are pegging to. Higher relative inflation implies a steadily increasing price of domestic goods relative to foreign goods, a steady real appreciation, and so a steady worsening of the trade position. As time passes, the need for an adjustment of the real exchange rate steadily increases, and financial investors become more and more nervous.
- Internal conditions may call for a decrease in the domestic interest rate. A decrease in the domestic interest rate cannot be achieved under fixed exchange rates. But it can be achieved if the country is willing to shift to a flexible exchange rate regime. If a country lets the exchange rate float and then decreases its domestic interest rate, we know from chapter 20 that this will trigger an increase in the nominal exchange rate—a nominal depreciation.

Whatever the reason, suppose financial markets believe a devaluation may be imminent. For the central bank to maintain the exchange rate requires an increase, often a large one, in the domestic interest rate. To see this, return to the interest parity condition we derived in chapter 18:

$$i_t = i_t^* + \frac{(E_{t+1}^e - E_t)}{E_t} \tag{21.5}$$

In chapter 18, we interpreted this equation as a relation between the *one-year* domestic and foreign nominal interest rates, the current exchange rate and the expected exchange rate a year hence. But the choice of one year as the period was arbitrary. The relation holds over a day, a week, a month. If financial markets expect the exchange rate to be 2% higher a month from now, they will hold domestic bonds only if the one-month domestic interest rate exceeds the one-month foreign interest rate by 2% (or, if we express interest rates at an annual rate, if the domestic interest rate exceeds the foreign interest rate by $2\% \times 12 = 24\%$).

Under fixed exchange rates, the current exchange rate E_t is fixed at some level, say, $\bar{E}$. If markets expect the parity will be maintained over the period, then $E_{t+1}^e = \bar{E}$, and the interest parity condition simply states that the domestic and the foreign interest rates must be equal.

Suppose, however, that participants in financial markets start anticipating a devaluation—an increase in the exchange rate. Suppose they believe that over the coming month, there is a 50% chance the parity will be maintained and a 50% chance there will be a 10% devaluation. Thus, the term $(E_{t+1}^e - E_t)/E_t$ in the interest parity equation (21.5), which we assumed equal to zero earlier, now equals $0.5 \times 0\% + 0.5 \times 10\%$ (a 50% chance of no change plus a 50% chance of a devaluation of 10%), thus equals 5%.

This implies that if the central bank wants to maintain the existing parity, it must now offer a monthly interest rate 5% higher—that is, $12 \times 5\% = 60\%$ higher at an annual rate! Sixty percent is the interest differential needed to convince investors to hold domestic bonds in view of the risk of a devaluation!

What, then, are the choices confronting the government and the central bank?

- First, the government and the central bank can try to convince markets they have no intention of devaluing. This is always the first line of defense: Communiqués are issued, and prime ministers appear on TV to reiterate their absolute commitment to the existing parity. But words are cheap, and they rarely convince financial markets.

In most countries, the government is formally in charge of choosing the parity, the central bank formally in charge of defending it. In practice, choosing and defending the parity are joint responsibilities of the government and the central bank.

- Second, the central bank can increase the interest rate, but by less than needed to satisfy equation (21.5)—in our example, by less than 60%. Although domestic interest rates are high, they are not high enough to fully compensate for the perceived risk of devaluation. This action typically leads to a large capital outflow, as financial investors still see foreign bonds are more attractive. To maintain the parity, the central bank must buy domestic currency and sell foreign currency in the foreign exchange market. In doing so, it often loses most of its reserves of foreign currency. (The mechanics of central bank intervention were described in the appendix to chapter 20.)

In the summer of 1998, Boris Yeltsin announced that the Russian government had no intention of devaluing the ruble. Two weeks later, the ruble collapsed.

- Eventually—after a few hours or a few months—the choice for the central bank becomes either to increase the interest rate enough to satisfy equation (21.5) or to validate the market's expectations and devalue. Setting a very high short-term domestic interest rate can have a devastating effect on demand and on output. This course of action makes sense only if (1) the perceived probability of a devaluation is small, so the interest rate does not have to be too high, and (2) the government believes markets will soon become convinced that no devaluation is coming, allowing domestic interest rates to decrease. Otherwise, the only option is to devalue.

To summarize: Expectations that a devaluation may be on the way can trigger an exchange rate crisis. Faced with such expectations, the government has two options: (1) give in and devalue, or (2) fight and maintain the parity, at the cost of very high interest rates and a potential recession. Fighting may not work anyway: The recession may force the government to change policy later on, or force the government out of office.

An interesting twist here is that a devaluation may occur even if the belief that a devaluation was imminent was initially groundless. Even if the government initially had no intention of devaluing, it may be forced to devalue if financial markets believe that it will devalue: The cost of maintaining the parity would be a long period of high interest rates and a recession; so the government prefers to devalue instead. Some economists believe that the exchange rate crises that hit many Asian countries in 1997 had such a self-fulfilling element; we shall return to this issue in chapter 24. In the rest of the section, I focus on the exchange rate crisis which shook the European Monetary System in the early 1990s.

Crises in the European Monetary System

At the start of the 1990s, the European Monetary System (EMS) appeared to work well. Started in 1979, it was an exchange rate system based on fixed parities with bands: Each member country (among them, France, Germany, Italy, and (starting in 1990) the United Kingdom) had to maintain its exchange rate vis-à-vis all other member countries within narrow bands. The first few years had been rocky, with many **realignments**—adjustment of parities—among member countries, but, from 1987 to 1992, there were only two realignments. There was increasing talk about narrowing the bands further and even moving to the next stage—to a common currency.

See the Global Macro box in chapter 5 on "German Reunification and the German Monetary-Fiscal Tug-of-War" and the Global Macro Box in chapter 20 on "German Unification, Interest Rates, and the EMS."

In 1992, however, financial markets became increasingly convinced that more realignments were soon to come. The reason was one we have seen already, namely, the implications of German reunification. Because of the pressure on demand coming from reunification, the Bundesbank was maintaining high interest rates to try to avoid too large an increase in output and an increase in inflation in Germany. Although Germany's trading partners needed lower interest rates to reduce a growing unemployment problem, they had to match the German interest rates to maintain their EMS parities. To financial markets, the position of Germany's partners looked increasingly untenable. Lower interest rates outside Germany, and thus devaluations of many currencies vis-à-vis the DM, appeared increasingly likely.

Throughout 1992, the perceived probability of a devaluation forced several of Germany's trading partners to maintain higher nominal interest rates than Germany. But the first major crisis did not come until September 1992. The day-by-day story is told in the Global Macro box "Anatomy of a Crisis: The September 1992 EMS Crisis." The belief, in early September, that a number of countries were soon going to devalue led to speculative attacks on several currencies, with financial investors selling in anticipation of an oncoming devaluation. All the lines of defense described earlier were used. First, solemn communiqués were issued, but

---

GLOBAL MACRO

Anatomy of a Crisis: The September 1992 EMS Crisis

- **September 5–6**. The Ministers of Finance of the European Union meet in Bath, England. The official communiqué at the end of the meeting reaffirms their commitment to maintaining existing parities within the exchange rate mechanism (ERM) of the European Monetary System (EMS).

- **September 8: The first attack**. The attack comes not against one of the currencies in the EMS, but rather against the currencies of Scandinavian countries, which are also pegged to the DM. The Finnish authorities give in and decide to let their currency, the markka, **float**—that is, be determined in the foreign exchange market without central bank intervention. The markka depreciates by 13% vis-à-vis the DM. Sweden decides to maintain its parity and increases its overnight interest rate to 24% (at an annual rate). Two days later, it increases it further to 75%.

- **September 10–11: The second attack**. The Bank of Italy intervenes heavily to maintain the parity of the lira, leading the bank to sustain large losses of foreign exchange reserves. But on September 13, the lira is devalued by 7% vis-à-vis the DM.

- **September 16–17: The third and major attack**. Speculation starts against the English pound, leading to large losses in reserves by the Bank of England. The Bank of England increases its overnight rate from 10% to 15%. However, speculation continues against both the pound and (despite the previous devaluation) against the lira. Both England and Italy announce they are temporarily suspending their participation in the ERM. Over the following weeks, both currencies depreciate by roughly 15% vis-à-vis the DM.

- **September 16–17**. With the pound and the lira out of the ERM, the attack turns against the other currencies. To maintain its parity, Sweden increases its overnight rate to 500%! Ireland increases its overnight rate to 300%. Spain decides to stay in the ERM, but to devalue by 5%.

- **September 20**. French voters narrowly approve the Maastricht treaty (the treaty that sets the timing for the transition to a common currency) in a referendum. A negative vote would surely have amplified the crisis. The narrow, but positive, vote is seen as the sign that the worst may be over, and that the treaty will eventually be accepted by all EU members.
- **September 23–28**. Speculation against the franc forces the Banque de France to increase its short-term interest rate by 2½%. To defend their parity without

having to resort to very high short-term interest rates, both Ireland and Spain reintroduce capital controls.
- **End of September**. The crisis ends. Two countries, the United Kingdom and Italy, have left the ERM and let their currency depreciate. Spain remains within the ERM, but only after a devaluation. The other countries have maintained their parity, but, for some of them, at the cost of large reserve losses.

Source: *World Economic Outlook*, October 1993.

with no discernible effect. Then, interest rates were increased, up to 500% for the **overnight interest rate** (the rate for lending and borrowing overnight) in Sweden (expressed at an annual rate). But they were not increased enough to prevent capital outflows and large losses of foreign exchange reserves by the central banks under pressure. Next, different courses of action were followed in different countries: Spain devalued its exchange rate, Italy and the United Kingdom suspended their participation in the EMS, and France decided to tough it out through higher interest rates until the storm was over.

By the end of September, financial markets believed no further devaluations were imminent. Some countries were no longer in the EMS, others had devalued but remained in the EMS, and those that had maintained their parity had shown their determination to stay in the EMS, even if this meant very high interest rates. But the underlying problem—the high German interest rates—was still there, and it was only a matter of time until the next crisis. In November 1992, further speculation forced a devaluation of the Spanish peseta, the Portuguese escudo, and the Swedish krona. The peseta and the escudo were further devalued in May 1993. In July 1993, after yet another large speculative attack, EMS countries decided to adopt large bands of fluctuations (plus or minus 15%) around central parities, in effect moving to a system that allowed for very large exchange rate fluctuations. This system with wider bands was kept until the introduction of the Euro in January 1999.

21-3 | Choosing Between Exchange Rate Regimes

Let us return to the questions that started the chapter: Should countries choose flexible or fixed exchange rates? Are there circumstances when flexible rates dominate and others when fixed rates dominate?

On macroeconomic grounds, everything we have seen so far would seem to favor flexible exchange rates. True, in the medium run, real exchange rates can adjust even if the nominal exchange rate is fixed. But governments also care about what happens in the short run, and, in the short run, flexible exchange rates clearly dominate: Under fixed exchange rates, a country gives up control not only of its exchange rate but also—at least under perfect capital mobility—of its interest rate. How can it ever be a good idea to give up not one but two macro instruments?

The argument would appear convincing. Then how is it that many economists still favor fixed exchange rates? There are three reasons:

- Flexible exchange rates are not without their own problems.
- In some cases, the costs of fixed exchange rates may not be that high.
- In some cases, the benefits of fixed exchange rates may be large.

Let us look at each of these arguments.

The Problems of Flexible Exchange Rates

See Figure 20–1.

In the model we developed in chapter 20, there was a simple relation between the interest rate and the exchange rate: the lower the interest rate, the higher the exchange rate. This implied that a country that wanted to maintain a stable exchange rate simply had to maintain its interest rate close to the foreign interest rate. A country that wanted to achieve a given depreciation simply had to decrease its interest rate by the right amount.

In the real world, the relation between the interest rate and the exchange rate is not so simple. Exchange rates often move even in the absence of movements in interest rates. The size of the effect of a given decrease in the interest rate on the exchange rate is often hard to predict, making it much harder for monetary policy to achieve its desired outcome. To see why, let us go back to the interest parity condition (equation 18.2)

$$1 + i_t = \left(\frac{1}{E_t}\right)(1 + i_t^*)(E_{t+1}^e)$$

Rewrite it as

$$E_t = \frac{1 + i_t^*}{1 + i_t} E_{t+1}^e \tag{21.6}$$

Think of the time period as one year. The exchange rate this year depends on the domestic interest rate, the foreign interest rate, and the exchange rate expected for next year. We assumed in chapter 20 that the expected exchange rate next year (E_{t+1}^e) was constant. But this was a simplification. The exchange rate expected one year hence is not constant. Using equation (21.6), but now for next year, it is clear that the exchange rate one year hence will depend on the domestic and foreign interest rates expected for next year, on the expected exchange rate two years from now, and so on. Thus, any change in expectations of *current and future* domestic and foreign interest rates, as well as changes in the expected exchange rate in the far future, will affect the exchange rate today. This argument is explored in the appendix to this chapter, which focuses on exchange rate movements under flexible exchange rates. But, if the details are better left to the appendix, the two basic conclusions are simple:

Note the similarity with stock prices: The stock price depends on the current dividend and interest rate, and on the expected stock price next year. The expected price next year depends on next year's expected dividend and interest rate, as well as on the expected stock price two years from now. And so on. This similarity is no coincidence: Exchange rates, like stock prices, depend on current and expected future conditions.

- The exchange rate can move for many other reasons than changes in the current domestic interest rate.
- The effect of a change in the current domestic interest rate on the exchange rate depends very much on how this change in the interest rate affects expectations of future interest rates.

In short, under flexible exchange rates, the exchange rate may move for many reasons, creating large changes in the real exchange rate and large fluctuations in output. Stabilizing the exchange rate may require large movements in the interest rate; these large interest movements may themselves lead to large fluctuations in output. Thus, controlling the economy under flexible exchange rates is much harder than we made it look in chapter 20. Put another way, the benefits of a flexible exchange rate regime may be smaller than our previous arguments suggested.

The Limited Costs of Fixed Exchange Rates

The costs of a fixed exchange rate regime may also be smaller than our previous arguments suggested. True, countries that operate under a fixed exchange rate regime are constrained to have the same interest rate. But how costly is that constraint? If they face roughly the same macroeconomic problems and the same shocks, they would have chosen similar policies in the first place. Forcing them to have the same monetary policy may not be much of a constraint.

This argument was explored by Robert Mundell, who looked at the conditions under which a set of countries might want to operate under fixed exchange rates, or even adopt a common currency. For countries to constitute an **optimal currency area**, Mundell argued, they need to satisfy one of two conditions:

This is the same Mundell who put together the Mundell–Fleming model we saw in chapter 20.

- They have to experience similar shocks. We just saw the rationale for this: If they have similar shocks, then they would have chosen roughly the same policy anyway.
- Or, if they experience different shocks, they must have high factor mobility. For example, if workers are willing to move from countries doing poorly to countries doing well, factor mobility rather than macroeconomic policy can allow countries to adjust to shocks. The exchange rate is not needed.

Following Mundell's analysis, most economists believe that the common currency area composed of the 50 states of the United States is close to an optimal currency area. True, the first condition is not satisfied: Individual states suffer from different shocks. California is much more affected by shifts in demand from Asia than the rest of the United States; Texas is much more affected by what happens to the price of oil; and so on. But the second condition is largely satisfied. There is considerable labor mobility across states in the United States. When a state does poorly, workers leave the state. When it does well, workers come to the state. State unemployment rates quickly return to normal, not because of state-level macroeconomic policy, but because of labor mobility.

Each state could have its own currency that freely floated against other state currencies. But this is not the case: The United States is a common currency area, with one currency, the U.S. dollar.

The Benefits of Fixed Exchange Rates

Finally, fixed exchange rate systems have several potential benefits:

- First, operating under fixed exchange rates simplifies the life of firms. They can think about where to locate plants and how to increase sales without having to worry about potentially large fluctuations in the exchange rate. These advantages are very clear when countries decide not only to fix their bilateral exchange rates, but to go all the way and adopt a common currency. The benefits of having a common currency for all states within the United States for firms and consumers are obvious; think of how complicated life would be if you had to change currency every time you crossed a state line.

  This is true also of the major new common currency area, the Euro zone. (The Global Macro box "The Euro: A Short History" gives you a short history of the Euro, and a look ahead at things to come.) A report by the European Commission estimates that the adoption of the Euro, which will eliminate foreign exchange transactions within the Euro zone, will save 0.5% of the combined GDP of these countries. The benefits of the Euro in terms of improved efficiency are likely to be much larger than just lower transaction costs. When prices are quoted in the same currency, it becomes much easier for buyers to compare prices, and competition between firms increases, benefiting consumers. There is already some evidence that this is happening in Europe. When shopping for cars, for example, European consumers now are looking for the lowest price anywhere in the Euro zone. This already has led to a decline in the price of cars in several countries.

- Second, there may be cases where a country may actually want to limit its ability to use monetary policy. We shall look at this argument in more detail in chapter 23—where we look at the dynamics of hyperinflation—and in chapter 26—where we look at monetary policy in general—but the essence of the argument is simple:

  Take a country that has had very high inflation in the recent past. This may be, for example, because it was unable to finance its budget deficit by any other means than through money creation, resulting in high money growth and high inflation. Suppose the country decides to reduce money growth and inflation. One way of convincing financial markets that it is serious about reducing money growth is to fix its exchange rate: The need to use the money supply to maintain the parity then constrains the monetary authority. To the extent that financial markets expect the parity to be main-

The Euro: A Short History

- As the European Union celebrates its 30th birthday in 1988, several governments conclude that the time has come to plan a move to a common currency. They ask Jacques Delors, the president of the European Union, to prepare a report, which he presents in June 1989.

  The report suggests moving to a European Monetary Union (EMU) in three stages: Stage I includes the abolition of capital controls. Stage II is to fix the parities, except for "exceptional circumstances." Stage III is the adoption of a single currency.

- Stage I is implemented in July 1990. Stage II starts in 1994, after the exchange rate crises of 1992 to 1993 have subsided. A new institution, the European Monetary Institute (EMI), is created to work out both the details of the transition and the rules of the new regime. A minor but symbolic decision involves choosing the name of the new common currency. The French would like "Ecu" (European currency unit), which is also the name of an old French currency. But its partners prefer **Euro**, and the name is adopted in 1995.

- In parallel, EU countries hold referendums on whether they should adopt the **Maastricht treaty**. The treaty, negotiated in 1991, sets the conditions for joining the EMU. The three main ones are low inflation, a budget deficit below 3%, and a public debt below 60%. The treaty is not very popular and, in many countries, the outcome of the popular vote is close. In France, the treaty passes with only 51% of the votes. In Denmark, the treaty is rejected.

- In 1996 to 1997, it looks as if few European countries will satisfy the Maastricht conditions. But several countries take drastic measures to reduce their budget deficit. When the time comes to decide in May 1998 which countries will be members of the Euro, eleven countries make the cut: Austria, Belgium, Finland, France, Germany, Italy, Ireland, Luxembourg, the Netherlands, Portugal, and Spain. The United Kingdom, Denmark, and Sweden decide not to join, at least at the beginning. Greece does not qualify.

- Stage III starts in January 1999. Parities between the 11 currencies and the Euro are "irrevocably" fixed. The new **European Central Bank (ECB)**, based in Frankfurt, becomes responsible for monetary policy for the Euro zone. The plan is to take three years from 1999 to achieve the full transition to the Euro. Although the Euro already exists as a unit of account, Euro coins and bank notes will not be introduced before January 2002. National currencies and the Euro will circulate together until July 2002 at the latest, at which point national currencies will be taken out of circulation. Europe will then truly be a common currency area.

tained, they will stop worrying about money growth being used to finance the budget deficit.

Note the qualifier *to the extent that financial markets expect the parity to be maintained*. Fixing the exchange rate is not a magic solution. The country needs to convince participants in financial markets that not only is the exchange rate fixed today, it will remain fixed in the future. This has two implications:

Fixing the exchange rate must be part of a more general macroeconomic package. Fixing the exchange rate while continuing to run a large budget deficit will only convince financial markets that money growth will start again, and that a devaluation is soon to come.

This is what happened in ▷ Russia in 1998. (More on this in chapter 24.)

Making it symbolically or technically harder to change the parity may also be useful. With this aim, several countries have adopted an exchange rate regime known as a **currency board**. Under a currency board, a central bank stands ready to buy or sell foreign currency at the official exchange rate; furthermore, it cannot engage in open market operations, that is, buy or sell government bonds. Currency boards have been quite popular in the 1990s. Since 1991, Argentina, for example, has run a currency board, with a highly symbolic parity of one dollar for one Argentinian peso. Giving up the currency board and changing the parity would be seen as a major defeat for any government, making it less likely that governments will be tempted to devalue.

To summarize:

- For countries that are highly integrated, adopting fixed exchange rates can yield large benefits. If so, it makes sense for these countries to go all the way and adopt a common currency. Not only does it increase the benefits of fixed exchange rates, but it also eliminates the risk of exchange rate crises. Remember, however, if Mundell's conditions are not satisfied, the macroeconomic costs may be large.

  This is why not all economists are convinced that the Euro is such a good idea for Europe. The potential benefits are very large. So are the potential costs. This is because neither of the Mundell conditions appears to be satisfied. Although the future may be different, European countries have experienced very different shocks in the past; recall German reunification, and how differently it has affected Germany and the other European countries. And labor mobility is very low in Europe, and likely to remain low. Workers move much less *within* European countries than within the United States. Given the language and cultural differences between European countries, mobility *between* countries is likely to be even lower.

- For countries that have to establish or reestablish a reputation for responsible macroeconomic policy, a fixed exchange rate regime may also be useful. In this case, it may make sense to use a highly symbolic regime such as the currency board.

- For other countries, it probably makes more sense to float. This does not imply ignoring the exchange rate altogether in the setting of monetary policy. But it means being willing to let the exchange rate move over time, and to use the interest rate and the exchange rate to reduce output fluctuations.

SUMMARY

- Even under a fixed exchange rate regime, countries can adjust their *real* exchange rate in the medium run by relying on adjustments in the price level. Nevertheless, the adjustment may be long and painful. Nominal exchange rate adjustments can in principle allow the economy to adjust faster, and reduce the pain.

- Exchange rate crises typically start when participants in financial markets believe a currency may soon be devalued. Defending the parity then requires very high interest rates, with potentially large adverse macroeconomic effects. These adverse effects may force the country to devalue, even if there were no plans for such a devaluation in the first place.

- In thinking about flexible versus fixed exchange rates, you must keep in mind four sets of arguments:
  1. Flexible exchange rates allow the central bank to use both the interest rate and the exchange rate for macroeconomic purposes. Fixed exchange rates and perfect capital mobility eliminate the scope for using either the exchange rate or the interest rate.

  2. Flexible exchange rates are often associated with large fluctuations in the exchange rate, making it difficult for the central bank to stabilize the economy.

  3. Fixed exchange rates may not be very costly if one of two conditions is satisfied: The countries that are pegging their exchange rate face largely the same shocks. Or there is high labor mobility between them.

  4. Fixed exchange rates also have benefits. They reduce transaction costs and improve efficiency. These benefits are even larger if countries adopt not only fixed exchange rates but a common currency. Fixed exchange rates may also help governments establish or reestablish their reputation for responsible macroeconomic policy.

- gold standard, 405
- realignments, 408
- float, 408
- overnight interest rate, 409
- optimal currency area, 411

- currency board, 412
- Euro, 412
- Maastricht treaty, 412
- European Central Bank (ECB), 412

QUESTIONS & PROBLEMS

1. TRUE/FALSE/UNCERTAIN

a. Britain's return to the gold standard caused years of high unemployment.

b. If, in a country committed to a fixed exchange rate, investors suddenly fear a severe devaluation, they may well trigger an exchange rate crisis.

c. Because speculative behavior by foreign investors can cause currency crises, small countries would be better off not allowing foreigners to hold domestic assets.

d. The countries of Southeast Asia should form a common currency area as they produce similar goods, and are subject to largely similar shocks.

e. The large number of immigrants from Mexico to the United States every year indicates there is substantial labor mobility between the two countries, and thus they constitute an optimal currency area.

2. A CLOSER LOOK AT AGGREGATE DEMAND

Consider the specification of the aggregate demand relation in an open economy with fixed exchange rates given in the text:

$$Y = C(Y - T) + I(Y, i^* - \pi^e) + G + NX\left(Y, Y^*, \frac{\overline{E}P^*}{P}\right)$$

a. Discuss the effects on output, given the domestic price level, of an increase in the foreign price level.

b. Discuss the effects on output, given the domestic price level, of an increase in expected inflation.

c. Why do economists say inflation is bad? High inflation abroad and high expected inflation at home both increase output. Discuss.

3. SHORT-RUN AND MEDIUM-RUN EFFECTS OF CHANGES IN GOVERNMENT SPENDING

Consider a country operating under fixed exchange rates, with aggregate demand and aggregate supply given by:

$$Y_t = Y\left(\frac{\overline{E}P^*}{P_t}, G, T\right)$$

$$P_t = P_{t-1}(1 + \mu) F\left(1 - \frac{Y_t}{L}, z\right)$$

Assume the economy is initially in medium-run equilibrium, with constant prices and output equal to its natural level.

a. Describe the short-run and the medium-run effects of an increase in government spending on output, the real exchange rate, and the interest rate.

b. Describe the short-run and medium-run effects of an increase in government spending on the components of spending: consumption, investment, and net exports.

c. Budget deficits lead to trade deficits. Discuss.

4. EAST GERMANY AND REUNIFICATION

When East and West Germany were reunited in 1990, the exchange rate between the two countries was irrevocably fixed. In a symbolic gesture of equality between the two countries, it was decreed that one East German Mark would be worth the same as one West German Mark, even though the currency of the East was in reality worth much less.

a. Think of East Germany as the domestic economy. Suppose East Germany is initially in medium-run equilibrium before reunification (obviously a counterfactual assumption here, but one has to start somewhere . . .) and suppose that the exchange rate (vis-à-vis West Germany) is set much too low. Discuss the impact of that decision on equilibrium output and unemployment using *AS–AD* analysis.

b. What happens over time?

c. Suppose that prices in Western Germany are constant—there is no inflation. What has to happen to prices and wages in Eastern Germany?

5. THE BRAZILIAN DEVALUATION OF JANUARY 1999

In January 1999 Brazil was forced to devalue its currency, the Real, by 8% against the dollar despite receiving a multibillion-dollar package from the IMF in November 1998 to defend the currency. In the week before the devaluation, Brazilian stock prices decreased by nearly half. But after the devaluation was announced, the stock market indexes returned to their pre-crisis levels.

Can you explain these movements in stock prices, assuming arbitrage in financial markets.

(To learn more about events leading up to the crisis, you may want to read an editorial by Rudiger Dornbusch, from MIT, written in November at the time of the IMF package. You can find it at url:http://web.mit.edu/rudi/Editorials.html. In order to read more about the crisis itself, check out the January 16–22, 1999 issue of *The Economist*.)

APPENDIX

EXCHANGE RATE MOVEMENTS

We saw in chapter 18 how the interest parity condition led to a relation between the short-term domestic nominal interest rate and the foreign nominal interest rate on the one hand, and the current nominal exchange rate and the expected future nominal exchange rate on the other.

The same condition can be used to derive a relation between the long-term domestic real interest rate and the long-term foreign real interest rate on the one hand, and the current real exchange rate and the expected future real exchange rate on the other. This seems like a mouthful, but do not worry: It is simpler than it sounds. And this relation will provide us with a way of thinking about movements of the exchange rate.

Real Interest Rates and the Real Exchange Rate

Consider, as in chapter 18, the choice between one-year U.S. and one-year German bonds. But instead of expressing the two rates of return in dollars as we did there, let's express both of them in terms of U.S. goods. Suppose you decide to invest the equivalent of one U.S. good, to "invest one U.S. good," for short, in what follows.

● Suppose you decide to hold U.S. bonds. Let r_t be the one-year U.S. real interest rate, the interest rate on one-year U.S. bonds in terms of U.S. goods. By the definition of the real interest rate, you will get $(1 + r_t)$ U.S. goods next year. This is represented by the top line in Figure 21A–1.

● Suppose you decide instead to hold German bonds. This involves exchanging dollars for DMs, holding German bonds for a year, and selling DMs for dollars a year from now.

Let ϵ_t be the real exchange rate, the relative price of German goods in terms of U.S. goods. A real exchange rate of ϵ_t means you get $(1/\epsilon_t)$ German goods for every U.S. good you invest.

Let r_t^* be the one-year German real interest rate, the interest rate on one-year German bonds in terms of German goods. Let the expected real exchange rate a

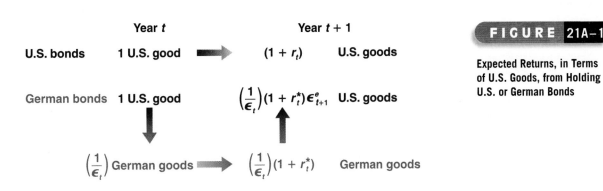

	Year *t*		Year *t* + 1	
U.S. bonds	1 U.S. good	→	$(1 + r_t)$	U.S. goods
German bonds	1 U.S. good		$\left(\frac{1}{\epsilon_t}\right)(1 + r_t^*)\epsilon_{t+1}^e$	U.S. goods
	$\left(\frac{1}{\epsilon_t}\right)$ German goods	→	$\left(\frac{1}{\epsilon_t}\right)(1 + r_t^*)$	German goods

FIGURE 21A–1

Expected Returns, in Terms of U.S. Goods, from Holding U.S. or German Bonds

year from now be ϵ^e_{t+1}. Then, for every U.S. good you invest in one-year German bonds, you can expect to get $(1/\epsilon_t)(1 + r^*_t)\,\epsilon^e_{t+1}$ U.S. goods next year. The three steps involved in the transaction are represented in the bottom part of Figure 21A–1.

If we assume that expected returns expressed in the same units (here U.S. goods) must be equal in equilibrium (the interest parity condition), the following condition must hold:

$$(1 + r_t) = \left(\frac{1}{\epsilon_t}\right)(1 + r^*_t)(\epsilon^e_{t+1}) \qquad (21A.1)$$

This equation gives us a relation between the domestic and the foreign real interest rates on the one hand, and the current and expected future real exchange rates on the other.

You may wonder whether this differs from the condition derived in terms of nominal interest rates and nominal exchange rates, equation (18.2). The answer is no. The two conditions are equivalent and one can derive one from the other. (It is presented as an exercise at the end of this appendix. The derivation is not much fun but it is good practice, and a useful way of brushing up on the relation between nominal and real interest rates, and nominal and real exchange rates.)

The basic reason why they are equivalent is that the interest parity condition states that the expected returns *when expressed in common units*—whatever these units are, as long as they are common—must be equal. Until now, we took the common unit to be the dollar. Here, we take the common unit to be a U.S. good.

Long-Term Real Interest Rates and the Real Exchange Rate

We have just looked at the choice of holding domestic versus foreign bonds *for one year*. But we can apply the same logic to the choice of holding domestic and foreign bonds *for many years*. Suppose you decide to invest the equivalent of one U.S. good—to invest one U.S. good, for short—for n years in either n-year U.S. bonds or n-year German bonds (think of n as, say, 10 years).

- Suppose you decide to hold n-year U.S. bonds. Let r_{nt} be the n-year U.S. real interest rate. Recall from chapter 15 that by the definition of an n-year interest rate, r_{nt} is the average annual interest rate you can expect to get if you hold the n-year bond for n years. So, by the definition of the n-year real interest rate, you can expect to get $(1 + r_{nt})^n$ goods in n years. This is represented in the top line of Figure 21A–2.
- Now suppose you decide to hold n-year German bonds instead. Let ϵ_t be the real exchange rate. Let r^*_{nt} be the n-year German real interest rate. Let the expected real exchange rate n years from now be ϵ^e_{t+n}. Then, for every U.S. good you invest in n-year German bonds, you can expect to get $(1/\epsilon_t)(1 + r^*_{nt})^n\epsilon^e_{t+n}$ U.S. goods in n years. This set of steps is represented in the bottom part of Figure 21A–2.

If we assume again that expected returns have to be the same, then the following condition must hold:

$$(1 + r_{nt})^n = \left(\frac{1}{\epsilon_t}\right)(1 + r^*_{nt})^n(\epsilon^e_{t+n}) \qquad (21A.2)$$

A good approximation (derived as an application of proposition 5 in appendix 2 at the end of the book) is given by:

$$n\,r_{nt} = n\,r^*_{nt} + \frac{(\epsilon^e_{t+n} - \epsilon_t)}{\epsilon_t}$$

Rewriting the equation so that the current exchange rate is on the left:

$$\epsilon_t = \frac{\epsilon^e_{t+n}}{1 + n(r_{nt} - r^*_{nt})} \qquad (21A.3)$$

This relation says that the real exchange rate today depends on the expected future real exchange rate n years from now, and on the differential between n-year domestic and foreign real interest rates. Let's look at it more closely.

The Real Exchange Rate, Trade, and Interest Rate Differentials

The first determinant of the current real exchange rate in equation (21A.3) is the expected future real exchange rate, ϵ^e_{t+n}. If we take the number of years, n, to be large we can

---

FIGURE 21A–2

Expected Returns, in Terms of U.S. Goods, From Holding n-year U.S. or German Bonds for n Years

	Year t	Year $t + n$
U.S. bonds	1 U.S. good ➡	$(1 + r_{nt})^n$ U.S. goods
German bonds	1 U.S. good	$\left(\frac{1}{\epsilon_t}\right)(1 + r^*_{nt})^n\epsilon^e_{t+n}$ U.S. goods
	$\left(\frac{1}{\epsilon_t}\right)$ German goods ➡	$\left(\frac{1}{\epsilon_t}\right)(1 + r^*_{nt})^n$ German goods

think of ϵ^e_{t+n} as the exchange rate that financial market participants expect to prevail in the *medium* or the *long run*. For simplicity, I shall now call it the *long-run real exchange rate*.

How should we think of the long-run real exchange rate? In the long run, we can assume that trade will be roughly balanced. No country can run trade deficits forever, and no country wants to run trade surpluses forever.[2] If trade is balanced in the long run, the long-run exchange rate must ensure trade balance. Thus, we can think of the expected future real exchange rate as that exchange rate consistent with trade balance in the long run.

The second determinant of the current real exchange rate is the difference between domestic and foreign long-term real interest rates. *An increase in the domestic long-term real interest rate over the foreign long-term real interest rate leads to a decrease in the real exchange rate—a real appreciation.* We focused on this mechanism when discussing a similar relation between the nominal interest rate and the nominal exchange rate in chapter 20. Let's go through its logic again.

Suppose the long-term domestic real interest rate goes up, making domestic bonds more attractive than foreign bonds. As investors try to shift out of foreign bonds into domestic bonds, they sell foreign currency and buy domestic currency, so that the domestic currency appreciates. Because the exchange rate is expected to return eventually to its long-run value, the more the domestic currency appreciates today, the more it is expected to depreciate in the future. Therefore, the domestic currency appreciates today to the point at which the expected future depreciation exactly offsets the fact that the long-term domestic real interest rate is higher than the long-term foreign real interest rate. At that point, financial investors are again indifferent to holding domestic bonds or holding foreign bonds.

We now have a way of thinking about exchange rate movements. Let's use this approach, first to look at the movements of the dollar in the 1980s, and then, more generally, to look at the effects of monetary policy and the relation between interest rates and exchange rates.

The Dance of the Dollar in the 1980s

Remember the large movements in the dollar in the 1980s we saw in chapters 18 and 19, the sharp real appreciation during the first half of the 1980s, and the sharp real depreciation during the second half? In light of the theory we just developed, we can ask: Were these movements due more to movements in long-term real interest rates in the United States relative to other countries, or more to movements in the long-run real exchange rate?

Note from equation (21A.3) that, if the long-run real exchange rate were constant, there would be an exact negative relation between the difference between the domestic and the foreign long-term real interest rates ($r_{nt} - r^*_{nt}$), and the real exchange rate, ϵ_t. Equivalently—this way of stating it will be more convenient to set up Figure 21A−3—there would be an exact positive relation between the difference between the foreign and the domestic real interest rates ($r^*_{nt} - r_{nt}$), and the real exchange rate, ϵ_t.

This statement suggests the following approach to interpreting movements in the real exchange rate: Construct for each year the difference between the long-term foreign real interest rate and the domestic long-term real interest rate. Then, plot the real exchange rate against this difference. If the two series move closely together, differences in long-term real interest rates must be the dominant factor in explaining movements in the real exchange rate. If they do not, changes in the long-run real exchange rate must play an important role.

Figure 21A−3 implements this approach. It focuses on the bilateral real exchange rate between the United States and Germany from 1980 to 1990. As we saw in chapter 18, movements in this bilateral real exchange rate are representative of movements in the multilateral U.S. real exchange rate during that period.

The real exchange rate is defined and constructed in the same way as in Figure 18−6. It is given by $(E_t P^*_t / P_t)$, where E_t is the Dollar/DM exchange rate, and P_t and P^*_t are the GDP deflators in the United States and Germany respectively. The evolution of the real exchange rate is given by the purple line in the figure. It is normalized to 100 in 1987, and is measured on the scale at the left of the figure.

The long-term U.S. real interest rate for each year is constructed as the nominal interest rate on a 10-year U.S. bond minus average expected inflation over the following 10 years. As a measure of expected inflation in each year, I use commercial forecasts (from DRI, a firm specializing in economic forecasting) of future inflation over the following 10 years. Thus, for 1985, for example, I use forecasts as of December 1984 of inflation for 1985 to 1994, and

---

[2] **DIGGING DEEPER**. This statement is not quite right. What must be balanced in the medium run is the current account. (For a refresher on the difference between the trade balance and the current account, see chapter 18.) A country that is a net creditor vis-à-vis the rest of the world can, even in the medium run, run a trade deficit equal to interest payments on its net holdings of foreign assets. I ignore the difference between trade and current account balance here.

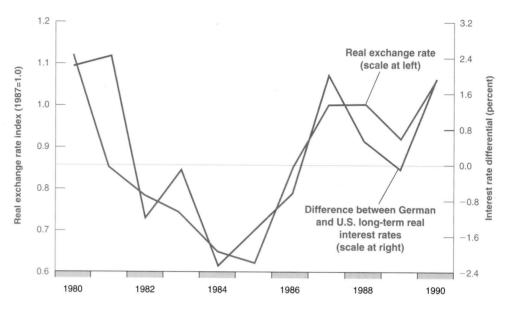

The Real Exchange Rate and the Difference Between 10-Year German and U.S. Real Interest Rates, 1980–1990

There is a close relation between movements in the real exchange rate, and movements in the difference between long-term German and U.S. real interest rates in the 1980s

construct a measure of average expected inflation over 1985 to 1994, which I then subtract from the nominal interest rate. The long-term German real interest rate is constructed in similar fashion. The blue line in the figure plots the difference between the German and the U.S. real interest rates. This difference is measured in percent on the scale at the right of the figure.

The fit between the two series in Figure 21A–3 is strikingly good, yielding a simple conclusion: *Most of the movements in the dollar in the 1980s can be traced to large movements in the difference between U.S. and foreign real interest rates.* The main reason why the dollar was so high in the mid-1980s was because long-term U.S. real interest rates were very attractive in the mid-1980s. The main reason why the dollar went down is that U.S. real interest rates became less attractive.

Where, in turn, did these movements in long-term real interest rates come from? The main reason lies in the monetary and fiscal policy mix followed by the United States in the 1980s. The first half of the 1980s in the United States was characterized by both tight money (the "Volcker disinflation") and fiscal expansion (the "Reagan deficits"), both leading to high nominal and high real interest rates. (See the In Depth box "Monetary Contraction and Fiscal Expansion: The United States in the Early 1980s" in chapter 20.) In the second half of the 1980s, monetary policy turned less restrictive in the United States, leading to a decline in U.S. long-term real interest rates.

Monetary Policy, Interest Rates, and Exchange Rates

Let us now return to how monetary policy works in an open economy with flexible exchange rates. Let us start with a blatantly unrealistic case. It is easier to analyze, yet it provides a good base on which to build a more realistic discussion.

Assume there is no inflation, here or abroad, current or expected, so we do not need to distinguish between nominal and real interest rates, or between nominal and real exchange rates. Suppose further that, initially, domestic and foreign interest rates are expected to be constant and equal to each other.

Now suppose the central bank unexpectedly announces that in order to increase output, it has decided to decrease interest rates. The central bank announces that one-year interest rates will be 2% lower for each of the next five years, after which they will return to normal. Financial markets fully believe this announcement.

What happens at the time of the announcement? Short-term interest rates go down by 2%, and so do rates on bonds with maturities less than or equal to five years. Yields on bonds with longer maturity go down, but by less.

What is the effect on the exchange rate today? To answer, work backward in time.

● Start five years in the future. The exchange rate five years from now depends on what is expected to happen to interest rates thereafter, as well as on the long-run exchange rate. Because the announcement does not change expectations of interest rates beyond the first five years, and presumably does not change the long-run exchange rate either, there is no change in the expected real exchange rate five years from now.

● What happens between today and five years hence? The interest parity condition tells us that for each of the next five years, there must be an expected appreciation of the domestic currency of 2% per year, so that the expected rates of return on holding domestic and foreign bonds are equal. That means there must be an expected cumulative appreciation of $5 \times 2\% = 10\%$ over the next five years.

- As the expected exchange rate five years hence is unchanged, to generate the expected appreciation of 10% over the next five years, there must therefore be a depreciation today of 10%. In other words, if the domestic currency *depreciates by 10% today* and then is expected to *appreciate by 2% a year for the next five years*, financial investors will be willing to hold domestic bonds although the domestic interest rate is 2% lower than the foreign interest rate.

The expected paths of one-year interest rates and the exchange rate are shown in Figure 21A–4. Before the announcement, the domestic interest rate is expected to be the same as the foreign interest rate forever. After the announcement, the domestic interest rate is expected to be 2% lower than the foreign interest rate for five years. The effect of the announcement is an increase in the exchange rate of 10% at the time of the announcement (a 10% depreciation), followed by a decrease of 2% a year (an expected appreciation of 2% a year) over the next five years. Note how much the exchange rate initially moves and overshoots its long-run value—increasing first, only to de-

crease back to its initial value five years later. For that reason, this exchange rate adjustment is often referred to as **overshooting**.

This result is an important one. When, in the early 1970s, countries moved from fixed to flexible exchange rates, the large fluctuations in exchange rates that followed came as a surprise to most economists. For a long time, these fluctuations were thought to be the result of irrational speculation in foreign exchange markets. It was not until the mid-1970s that economists realized that these large movements could be explained, as we have done here, by the rational reaction of financial markets to differences in future interest rates.

Policy and Expectations

In the example we just looked at, we dismissed many complications. We assumed in particular that the central bank announced what it was going to do over the next five years, and that financial markets fully believed the announcement. In practice, this is not the way things happen.

When the central bank cuts interest rates, financial markets have to assess whether this action signals a major shift in monetary policy and is just the first of many such cuts, or

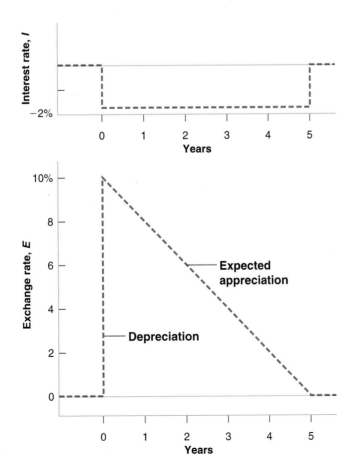

FIGURE 21A–4

The Effects of Monetary Policy on the Interest Rate and the Exchange Rate

A decrease in interest rates expected to last for five years leads to a depreciation today, followed by expected appreciation over the next five years.

whether this cut is just a temporary movement in interest rates. Announcements by the central bank itself may not be very useful: The central bank itself may not know what it will do in the future. Typically, it will be reacting to early signals, which may be reversed later. Financial markets also have to assess how foreign central banks will react, whether they will stay put or follow suit and cut their interest rates.

To summarize: How a change in the short-term interest rate affects the exchange rate is more complex than it appeared in chapter 20. The response of the exchange rate depends very much on the effect of the change in the interest rate on expectations of future domestic and foreign interest rates. Sometimes a small decrease in short-term interest rates may convince markets that monetary policy has substantially changed, resulting in a large decrease in long-term interest rates and a large depreciation. But if markets anticipated a large cut and the central bank announces a smaller cut than was anticipated, the effect may actually be an appreciation, not a depreciation. The reaction of foreign exchange, stock, and bond markets to policy news is the topic of the Focus box "News and Movements in Foreign Exchange, Stock, and Bond Markets."

- The real exchange rate today depends both on the long-run real exchange rate, and on the difference between domestic and foreign long-term real interest rates. An increase in the domestic long-term real interest rate over the corresponding foreign interest rate leads to a real appreciation, a decrease to a real depreciation.

- Movements in U.S. interest rates relative to foreign interest rates explain most of the movements in the U.S.

real exchange rate ("the dance of the dollar") in the 1980s.

- When account is taken of expectations, changes in monetary policy may lead to large variations in the exchange rate. An increase in interest rates leads to a large initial appreciation, followed by a slow depreciation over time. This large initial movement of the exchange rate is known as overshooting.

- overshooting, 419

1. DERIVING THE INTEREST PARITY CONDITION IN TERMS OF REAL INTEREST RATES

This problem helps you derive (21A.1) in the text. Start from the interest parity condition:

$$(1 + i_t) = (1 + i_t^*) \frac{E_{t+1}^e}{E_t}$$

Recall the definition of the (domestic) real interest rate,

$$(1 + r_t) = \frac{1 + i_t}{1 + \pi_t^e}$$

where $\pi_t^e = (P_{t+1}^e - P_t)/P_t$ is the expected rate of inflation. Similarly, the foreign real interest rate is given by:

$$(1 + r_t^*) = \frac{1 + i_t^*}{1 + \pi_t^{*e}}$$

where $\pi_t^{*e} = (P_{t+1}^{*e} - P_t^*)/P_t^*$ is the expected foreign rate of inflation. Recall that the real exchange rate is defined as:

$$\epsilon_t = E_t P_t^*/P_t$$

So the expected real exchange rate is given by

$$\epsilon_{t+1}^e = E_{t+1} P_{t+1}^{*e}/P_{t+1}^e$$

Derive condition (21A.1) in the text. (*Hint*: Use the two interest rate relations to eliminate nominal interest rates in the interest parity condition. Then, rewrite to get from nominal exchange rates to real exchange rates.)

2. EXPECTED NOMINAL AND REAL DEPRECIATIONS

Assume that the nominal interest rate on 10-year bonds is 10% at home and 6% abroad. Further, assume inflation is expected to be 6% at home and 3% abroad.

a. What is the expected annual real depreciation consistent with interest parity?

b. What is the expected annual nominal depreciation consistent with interest parity?

c. If you expected a nominal appreciation of the currency over the next ten years, which bond would you purchase?

We invite you to visit the Blanchard page on the Prentice Hall Web site at:

http://www.prenhall.com/blanchard

for this chapter's World Wide Web exercises

EXTENSIONS

Pathologies

Sometimes, (macroeconomic) things go very wrong: There is a sharp drop in output. Or unemployment remains high for very long. Or inflation increases to very high levels. These pathologies are the focus of the next three chapters.

CHAPTER 22

Chapter 22 looks at high unemployment. It first looks at the Great Depression, what triggered it, what made it so bad, and what eventually led to the recovery. It then turns to Europe today and examines the role of aggregate demand and aggregate supply factors in explaining high European unemployment.

CHAPTER 23

Chapter 23 looks at episodes of high or hyperinflation. It shows the role of both fiscal and monetary policy in generating high inflation. Budget deficits lead to high money growth, and high money growth leads to high inflation. It then looks at how high inflations end, and at the role and the nature of stabilization programs.

CHAPTER 24

Chapter 24 looks at two of the major macroeconomic events of the 1990s. It looks first at the transition of Eastern European countries from central planning to a market economy. It analyzes the sources of the initial output decline, why some countries have recovered and others have not. It then looks at the Asian crisis of the late 1990s. It focuses on the sources of the crisis, on the role of fundamentals versus self-fulfilling expectations, and on the size of the output decline.

CHAPTER 22 | Pathologies I: High Unemployment

A major theme of this book so far has been that, although economies undergo short-run fluctuations, they tend to return to normal over time.

Most of the time, this is what actually happens. But once in a while, things go wrong. There is a large and sudden drop in output, from which the economy takes many years to recover. Or the unemployment rate remains very high for very long. Or inflation increases to extraordinarily high levels, until drastic policy measures are taken to lower it.

These episodes raise obvious questions. Are they the result of unusually large adverse shocks? Are they the result of misguided policy responses? Or are they the result of a breakdown of the usual adjustment mechanisms that typically return the economy to normal? These are the questions we take up in this and the next two chapters.

- In this chapter we look at two episodes of high unemployment, the Great Depression in the United States, and high unemployment in Western Europe today.

- In chapter 23, we examine episodes of high inflation, from the German hyperinflation of the 1920s to the bouts of high inflation in Latin America in the late 1980s.

- In chapter 24, we examine two of the major macroeconomic events of the 1990s: the transition from central planning to capitalism in Eastern Europe, and the crisis in Asia.

22-1 | The Great Depression

In 1929, the U.S. unemployment rate was 3.2%. By 1933, it had increased to 24.9%. It was not until 10 years later, in 1942, that it was back down to 4.7%. This **Great Depression** (although there is no agreed-upon precise definition, economists use the word **depression** to describe a deep and long-lasting recession) was worldwide. The average unemployment rate from 1930 to 1938 was 15.4% in the United Kingdom, 10.2% in France, and 21.2% in Germany. In this chapter, I focus on what happened in the United States, and take up two questions: What shocks increased the unemployment rate by so much so quickly? And why did it take more than 10 years—and World War II—for the U.S. economy to return to low unemployment?

Table 22–1 gives the evolution of the U.S. unemployment rate, growth rate of output, consumer price index, and money stock from 1929 to 1942. Focusing only on unemployment and output for the moment, two facts stand out:

- The size and the speed of the initial output decline. The average annual growth rate from 1929 to 1932 was an astounding −8.6%, leading to an increase in the unemployment rate of more than 20 percentage points in four years.
- The length of the recovery. The average annual growth rate from 1933 to 1941 was a high 7.7%. But in 1941, at the eve of the United States' entry into World War II, the unemployment rate still stood at 9.9%. (There is no contradiction here, just an application of Okun's law: A long period of high growth was needed to steadily decrease the high unemployment rate.)

The Fall in Spending

Popular accounts often say the Great Depression was caused by the stock market crash of 1929. This is an overstatement. A recession had started before the crash, and other factors played a central role later in the Depression.

Warning: The quality of unemployment data is much lower pre–World War II than post–World War II. Cross-country comparisons are particularly perilous.

For a look at other countries, read Peter Temin's *Lessons from the Great Depression* (Cambridge, MA: MIT Press, 1989).

From section 9-1: Okun's law relates the change in the unemployment rate to the deviation of output growth from normal. In the United States today, output growth 1% above normal for a year leads to a decrease in the unemployment rate of about 0.4%. Using Table 22–1, find out how this quantitative relation fits the relation between output growth and unemployment from 1933 to 1941.

TABLE 22–1 U.S. Unemployment, Output Growth, Prices, and Money, 1929–1942

Year	Unemployment Rate (%)	Output Growth Rate (%)	Price Level	Nominal Money Stock
1929	3.2	−9.8	100.0	26.4
1930	8.7	−7.6	97.4	25.4
1931	15.9	−14.7	88.8	23.6
1932	23.6	−1.8	79.7	19.4
1933	24.9	9.1	75.6	21.5
1934	21.7	9.9	78.1	25.5
1935	20.1	13.9	80.1	29.2
1936	16.9	5.3	80.9	30.3
1937	14.3	−5.0	83.8	30.0
1938	19.0	8.6	82.2	30.0
1939	17.2	8.5	81.0	33.6
1940	14.6	16.1	81.8	39.6
1941	9.9	12.9	85.9	46.5
1942	4.7	13.2	95.1	55.3

Sources: Unemployment rate: Series D85–86; output growth: GNP growth (in 1958 prices), Series F31; price level: CPI (1929 = 100), Series E135; money stock: M1 (in billions of dollars), Series X414. *Historical Statistics of the United States*, U.S. Department of Commerce.

Nevertheless, the crash was important. The stock market had boomed from 1921 to 1929. Stock market prices had increased much faster than the dividends paid by firms—and as a result the dividend/price ratio had decreased from 6.5% in 1921 to 3.5% in 1929. On October 28, 1929, the stock market price index dropped from 298 to 260. The next day, it dropped further to 230. This was a fall of 23% in two days, and a drop of 40% from the peak of early September. By November the index was down to 198. A stock market recovery in early 1930 was followed by further declines in stock prices as the depth of the depression became increasingly clear to the market participants.

Note the parallel between the evolution of stock prices during the 1920s and during the 1990s. The dividend/price ratio was 3.2% in 1991 and 1.4% at the end of 1998. (See chapter 15)

Was the October crash caused by the sudden realization that a depression was coming? The answer is no. There is no evidence of major news in October. The source of the crash was almost surely the end of a speculative bubble. Stockholders who had purchased stocks at high prices in the anticipation of further increases in prices got scared and attempted to sell their stocks. The result was a large drop in prices.

Revisit the discussion of dividends and prices, and bubbles and crashes in section 15-3.

The crash not only decreased consumers' wealth, but it also increased their uncertainty. Unsettled by the crash and feeling uncertain about the future, consumers and firms decided to see how things evolved and to postpone purchases of durable goods and investment goods. There was, for example, a large decrease in car sales—the type of purchase that can easily be deferred—in the months just following the crash. Industrial production, which had declined by 1.8% from August to October 1929, declined by 9.8% from October to December, and by another 24% from December 1929 to December 1930. In terms of the *IS-LM* model in Figure 22–1, the crash shifted the *IS* curve to the left, from *IS* to *IS'*, leading to a sharp decrease in output from *Y* to *Y'*.

The Contraction in Nominal Money

When we described the effects of a decrease in the demand for goods in chapter 7, we showed how the economy would, after the initial recession, return to the natural level of output in the medium run. The mechanism was the following:

The focus in section 7-5 was on the effects of a reduction in government spending. The conclusions would have been the same had we looked instead at the effects of a reduction in consumption, due to a drop in wealth or in consumer confidence.

- Low output led to high unemployment.
- High unemployment led to lower wages.
- Lower wages led to lower prices.
- Lower prices led to an increase in the real money stock.
- Higher real money led to a steady shift in the *LM* curve downwards, and an increase in output.

This went on until output returned to its natural level.

Was this mechanism at work after 1929? You can see from Table 22–1 that low output did lead to lower prices in the years following 1929. The consumer price index decreased

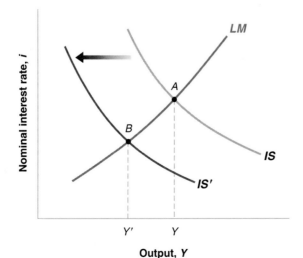

FIGURE 22–1

The Great Depression and the *IS-LM*: I

The effect of the stock market crash was to decrease wealth and increase uncertainty, leading the *IS* curve to shift to the left.

ACTIVE GRAPH

from 100.0 in 1929 to 75.6 in 1933, a 24% decrease in the price level in four years. But the rest of the mechanism failed, for two reasons: (1) There was a large decrease in nominal money, leaving real money roughly unchanged; and (2), the deflation itself had perverse effects, leading to a deeper decline in output.

Let's focus on the decrease in nominal money first. Table 22–2 gives the evolution of nominal money—both the nominal money stock (measured by $M1$) and the monetary base (H)—from 1929 to 1933. It also shows the evolution of the money multiplier ($M1/H$) and of the real money stock ($M1/P$) where P is the consumer price index.

From 1929 to 1933, nominal money, $M1$, *decreased* from $26.4 million to $19.4 million, a decrease of 27%. To understand what happened, recall the basic mechanics of money creation:

See section 4-3.

Nominal money, $M1$ (the sum of currency in circulation and checkable deposits), is equal to the monetary base, H (currency plus banks' reserves)—which is directly under the control of the Fed—times the money multiplier

$$M1 = H \times \text{money multiplier}$$

The money multiplier in turn depends both on how much reserves banks keep in proportion to their deposits, and what proportion of money people hold as currency.

Note that from 1929 to 1933, the monetary base, H, increased from $7.1 to $8.2 billion. That means the decrease in $M1$ did not come from a decrease in the monetary base. Rather, it came from a decrease in the money multiplier, $M1/H$, which fell from 3.7 in 1929 to 2.4 in 1933.

The classic treatment is by Milton Friedman and Anna Schwartz, *A Monetary History of the United States, 1867–1960* (Princeton, NJ: Princeton University Press, 1963).

This decrease in the multiplier was the result of bank failures. With the large decline in output, more and more borrowers found themselves unable to repay their loans to banks, and more and more banks became insolvent and closed down. Bank failures increased steadily from 1929 until 1933, when the number of failures reached a peak of 4,000, out of about 20,000 banks in operation at the time.

Bank failures had a direct effect on the money supply: Checkable deposits at the failed banks became worthless. But the major effect on the money supply was indirect: Worried that their bank might also fail, many people shifted from deposits to currency. The increase led to a decrease in the money multiplier, and thus to a decrease in the money supply. Think of the mechanism this way: If people had liquidated *all* their deposits and asked banks for currency in exchange, the multiplier would have decreased all the way down to 1: Nominal money, $M1$, would have been just equal to the monetary base. The actual shift was less dramatic; nevertheless, the multiplier dropped from 3.7 in 1929 to 2.4 in 1933, leading to a decrease in the money supply despite an increase in the monetary base. (Some economists have argued that the shift from checkable deposits to currency had implications that went beyond the effect on the money multiplier. See the Focus box "Money versus Bank Credit.")

TABLE 22–2 Money, Nominal and Real, 1929–1933

Year	Nominal Money Stock ($M1$)	Monetary Base (H)	Money Multiplier ($M1/H$)	Real Money Stock ($M1/P$)
1929	26.4	7.1	3.7	26.4
1930	25.4	6.9	3.7	26.0
1931	23.6	7.3	3.2	26.5
1932	20.6	7.8	2.6	25.8
1933	19.4	8.2	2.4	25.6

Source: $M1$: Series X414; H: Series X422 plus Series X423; P: Series E135. *Historical Statistics of the United States*, U.S. Department of Commerce.

We have focused in the text on the effects on the money multiplier of the shift from checkable deposits to currency. Many economists argue that this shift had implications beyond its effects on the money multiplier. Faced with a decrease in deposits, banks had to call in existing loans. Those who had borrowed from the banks were unable to find other sources of borrowing, and this was a further source of output contraction.

The argument has been developed by Ben Bernanke, from Princeton University. He starts with the observation that banks play a special role in credit markets. Banks make loans to borrowers who are typically too small, or not well-known enough, to be able to issue bonds. When making a loan to a firm, a bank acquires knowledge about the firm, and once the loan has been made, monitors the firm's decisions closely. If, for whatever reason, a bank stops lending to a firm, that firm may not be able to borrow elsewhere. Other banks do not have the specialized knowledge of the original bank, and neither do bond markets. Thus, the firm may be forced to cancel investment plans, curtail production, or close altogether. [Note that in writing the investment equation as $I = I(r, Y)$ so far in the book, we have implicitly assumed that firms could borrow as much as they wanted at the given interest rate r; we have therefore implicitly excluded the effect we are looking at now.]

By putting together many pieces of evidence, Bernanke builds a strong case that this **credit channel** was important in first deepening, and then prolonging, the Great Depression. One citation, from a report based on a large survey of firms carried out in 1934 to 1935, is very suggestive:

> [We find that there is] a genuine unsatisfied demand for credit by solvent borrowers, many of whom could make economically sound use of capital. The total amount of this unsatisfied demand for credit is a significant factor, among many others, in retarding business recovery.

References

Ben Bernanke, "Nonmonetary Effects of the Financial Crisis in the Propagation of the Great Depression," *American Economic Review*, 1983, 257–276.

For more on the role of banks and the credit channel of monetary policy, read Anil Kashyap and Jeremy Stein, "Monetary Policy and Bank Lending," in N. Gregory Mankiw, ed., *Monetary Policy*, (Chicago: University of Chicago Press and NBER, 1994), 221–262.

With the decrease in the nominal money supply from 1929 to 1933 roughly proportional to the decrease in prices, the real money stock remained roughly constant, eliminating one of the mechanisms that could have led to a recovery. In other words, the *LM* curve remained roughly unchanged—it did not shift down as it would have done if the nominal money stock had remained constant, implying an increase in the real money stock. This has led Milton Friedman and Anna Schwartz to argue that the Fed was responsible for the depth of the Depression, that it should have expanded the monetary base even more than it did to offset the decrease in the money multiplier.

The Adverse Effects of Deflation

In addition to the decrease in nominal money, deflation (the decrease in the price level) itself was a further source of decline in output during the Great Depression. We can use the *IS-LM* diagram to see why, keeping in mind the distinction between the real interest rate and the nominal interest rate we introduced in chapter 14.

◄ See section 14-3.

In Figure 22–2, think of the pre-crash equilibrium as given by point *A*. We argued earlier that the effect of the crash was, through its effects on wealth and uncertainty, to shift the *IS* curve to *IS'*, taking the economy from *A* to *B*. We then argued that from 1929 to 1933, the combined effects of the decrease in prices and the decrease in nominal money was to leave the *LM* curve roughly unchanged.

Now consider the effects of deflation on the difference between nominal and real interest rates. Recall that the real interest rate is equal to the nominal interest rate minus the expected rate of inflation (equivalently, plus the expected rate of deflation). By 1931, the rate of deflation exceeded 10% a year, and by then, the evidence is that people expected deflation to continue. This expectation implied that even low nominal interest rates—in 1931, the three-month Treasury bill rate stood at only 1.4%—implied high real interest rates. When expected deflation is 10%, even a nominal rate of 0% implies a real interest rate of $0\% - (-10\%) = 10\%$!

FIGURE 22–2

The Great Depression and the *IS-LM*: II

The effect of expected deflation was to shift the *IS* curve further to the left, leading to a further decline in output.

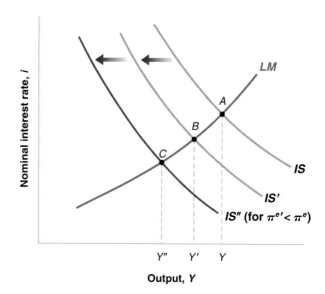

Given *i*,

$$\pi^e \downarrow \Rightarrow r \, (\equiv i - \pi^e) \uparrow$$
$$\Rightarrow Y \downarrow$$

The *IS* curve shifts left.

In terms of Figure 22–2, the effect of the increase in expected deflation was to shift the *IS* curve further to the left. At a given nominal interest rate, higher expected deflation means a higher real interest rate, lower demand and so lower output. The result of this shift from *IS'* to *IS"* was to move the economy from point *B* to point *C*, to further decrease output and deepen the depression.

People often ask whether the Great Depression could happen today. Until a few years ago, the answer would have been a clear no: We had learned from our mistakes, monetary and fiscal policy would be used much more aggressively than they were from 1929 to 1933. Recently, however, several economists have become worried. They have pointed out that Japan in the 1990s looks in some ways like the United States in the early 1930s. Few believe that Japan will suffer from a "great depression." But economists no longer feel the same assurance. (What is happening to Japan is explored in the Global Macro box, "Could the Great Depression Happen Again? Japan at the Crossroads.")

The Recovery

The recovery started in 1933. Except for another sharp decrease in the growth rate of output in 1937 (see Table 22–1), growth was consistently high, running at an average annual rate of 7.7% from 1933 to 1941. Macroeconomists and economic historians have studied the recovery much less than they studied the initial decline. And many questions remain.

One of the factors that contributed to the recovery is clear. Following the election of Franklin Roosevelt to the U.S. presidency in 1932, there was a change in monetary policy and a dramatic increase in nominal money growth. From 1933 to 1941, the nominal money stock increased by 140%, the real money stock by 100%. These increases were due to increases in the monetary base, not in the money multiplier. In a recent controversial article, Christina Romer (from U.C. Berkeley), has argued that if monetary policy had been unchanged from 1933 on, output would have been 25% lower than it actually was in 1937, and

Christina Romer, "What Ended the Great Depression?" *Journal of Economic History*, December 1992, 757–784.

50% lower than it was in 1942. These are very large numbers. Even if we believe these numbers overestimate the effect of monetary policy, the conclusion that money played an important role in the recovery is still surely warranted.

The role of other factors, from budget deficits to the **New Deal**—the set of programs put in place by the Roosevelt administration to get the U.S. economy out of the Great Depression—is much less clear.

One New Deal program was aimed at improving the functioning of banks by creating the *Federal Deposit Insurance Corporation (FDIC)* to insure demand deposits and to avoid bank runs and bank failures. And, indeed, there were few bank failures after 1933.

Other programs included relief and public works programs for the unemployed, and a program administered by the **National Recovery Administration (NRA)** to establish "orderly competition" in industry. Economists generally agree that these programs had few direct effects on the recovery. But some argue that their indirect effects—particularly the perception of the government's commitment to getting the economy out of the depression—were important in changing expectations in 1933 and after. We saw in earlier chapters how such expectational effects of policy can be important. However, establishing their importance in 1933 and after is difficult and remains largely undone.

The recovery also presents us with a puzzle. In 1933, deflation stopped. The rest of the decade was characterized by small but positive inflation. The CPI stood at 81.8 in 1940, compared to 75.6 in 1933. The end of deflation probably helped the recovery. The shift from deflation to small positive inflation implied much lower real interest rates than had been the case from 1929 until 1933. (In terms of Figure 22–2, the change from expected deflation to expected price stability undid the earlier adverse shift in the IS curve from IS' to IS''.) The puzzle is *why* deflation ended in 1933.

With a large deflation in 1932 and unemployment at an all-time high, the theory of wage determination we developed in previous chapters implies that there should have been further large wage cuts and further deflation. This is not what happened. As we saw in the Phillips curve diagram constructed for the United States by Samuelson and Solow (Fig. 8–1), the years 1933 to 1939 are clear outliers.

Why did deflation stop? One proximate cause is the set of measures taken by the Roosevelt administration. The **National Industrial Recovery Act (NIRA)**, signed in June 1933, asked industries to sign codes of behavior, to establish minimum wages, and not to take advantage of the high unemployment rate to impose further wage cuts on workers.

GLOBAL MACRO

Could the Great Depression Happen Again? Japan at the Crossroads

We saw in chapter 7 (Global Macro box "Why Has Japan Done So Poorly in the 1990s?") how a stock market collapse in Japan in the early 1990s led to a long period of low growth in the 1990s. In 1998, things took a turn for the worse. Growth turned from low to negative, with a decrease in GDP of 2.6%. Low inflation turned to deflation, with a decline in the GDP deflator close to 1% for the year.

Why isn't the Japanese government using monetary and fiscal policy more aggressively to increase demand and output? The answer to this question has two parts:

• The Japanese government has been, and still is, using monetary policy. The short-term nominal interest rate was kept nearly equal to zero (under 0.5%) throughout 1998. Monetary policy cannot do more. If it tried to decrease the nominal interest rate on bonds below zero, nobody would want to hold bonds, and everybody would want to hold money instead. Keynes refered to this lower limit as the **liquidity trap**: Japan has clearly fallen into the trap.

If inflation were positive in Japan, a zero nominal interest rate would imply a negative real interest rate. This negative real rate might be enough to stimulate investment demand and increase output. But, with the appearance of deflation in 1998 and a forecast of more deflation in 1999, zero nominal interest rates imply positive real interest rates. This is what reminds economists of the Great Depression: It is easy to think of a scenario in which low activity leads to more deflation; where more deflation leads to higher real interest rates; where higher real interest rates further decrease activity; and so on. This is the scenario under which Japan could see a repeat of what happened in the Great Depression.

• Even if monetary policy cannot be used, there is still fiscal policy. Large budget deficits can in principle increase demand and output. Until recently, the Japanese government was reluctant to run very large deficits. It was worried that financial markets might see the deficits as a sign of an irresponsible fiscal policy, and that the adverse effect on expectations may actually offset the positive direct effects of lower taxes or higher spending. (See chapter 17 for a discussion of potentially adverse effects of a fiscal expansion.) In the recent past, however, it has decided to increase the budget deficit, which is now forecast to reach 8% in 1999—a very large number. Only time will tell whether this is enough to turn Japan around.

Economists are usually doubtful that such admonitions to firms have much effect. But the NIRA offered firms a carrot in exchange, in effect a decrease in competition in goods markets under the guise of "orderly competition," and thus the potential for higher profits if they complied. The evidence suggests that the NIRA did have an effect on wage setting.

Another reason deflation stopped is that although unemployment was still high, output growth was high as well. As a result, there were bottlenecks in production, leading firms to increase their prices given wages. Because of the sharp increase in demand, the price of raw materials was also bid up, increasing costs, and again forcing firms to increase their prices given wages. In short, and in contrast to our simple specification of price setting where we assumed that prices depended only on wages, the effect of fast growth was to increase prices given wages, thereby reducing the deflationary pressure of unemployment.

A relevant fact in this discussion is that deflation ended in the mid-1930s in most countries, even those that did not have programs similar to the New Deal and did not have the same fast growth rates after 1933 as the United States. This fact suggests there may be general factors at work such that when unemployment has been high for a long time, the downward pressure of unemployment on wages decreases or disappears altogether. Europe today appears to be in a similar predicament, having high unemployment and roughly stable inflation (but not high growth). This naturally takes us to the next section, high unemployment in Europe today.

22-2 | Unemployment in Europe

European Union membership has expanded from 6 countries in 1957 to 15 countries in 1995. Whenever I refer to the EU unemployment rate, I mean the unemployment rate, now or in the past, for the group of 15 countries that compose the EU today. See Table 22-3 for a list of EU members.

Although far smaller than it was during the Great Depression, European unemployment is nevertheless very high. In 1998, the average unemployment rate in the European Union (EU) was 10.6%, down slightly from its 1996 postwar high of 11.4%.

Until 1970, the unemployment rate had been much lower in Europe than in the United States. But Figure 22–3, which gives unemployment rates in the European Union and the United States since 1970, shows that European unemployment began increasing steadily in the 1970s. By 1979, EU and U.S. unemployment rates were roughly similar, at around 6%. In both the European Union and the United States there was a further large increase in the early 1980s. But from 1982 on, as the U.S. rate decreased steadily, the European rate remained very high. A decrease in European unemployment in the late 1980s was reversed by

FIGURE 22–3

Unemployment Rates in the European Union and the United States, 1970–1998

The EU unemployment rate, which was lower than the U.S. unemployment rate until the late 1970s, is now much higher.

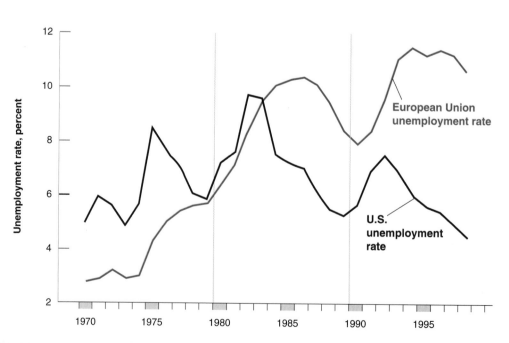

the recession of the early 1990s, and, in 1998, the European unemployment rate stood at about 6% above the U.S. unemployment rate.

Turn now to the joint behavior of inflation and unemployment in the European Union. Figure 22–4 plots the EU unemployment and inflation rates since 1970. There are at least four important facts in the figure:

1. The *increase* in unemployment in the 1970s was associated with an *increase* in inflation. This is suggestive of aggregate supply shocks: Recall from chapter 7 that aggregate demand shocks move unemployment and inflation in opposite directions, but that aggregate supply shocks move them in the same direction. There are several strong suspects here: labor unrest, which led workers to ask for higher wages in the late 1960s; the slowdown in productivity growth from the mid-1970s on; and the two large increases in OPEC oil prices in the mid- and late-1970s.
2. Just as in the United States, the further *increase* in European unemployment in the early 1980s was associated with a large *decrease* in inflation. Building on our study of disinflation in chapter 9, this suggests the increase in unemployment in the 1980s was due in large part to a shift in monetary policy aimed at decreasing inflation by lowering money growth.
3. Inflation started increasing again in 1987, despite the fact that the unemployment rate was still very high, around 10%. Building on our discussion of the natural rate of unemployment in chapters 6 and 8, this suggests that in 1987, the natural unemployment rate in the European Union was not far from 10%, thus clearly much higher than in the 1970s.
4. In the 1990s, unemployment has again climbed above 10%. Inflation has decreased for most of the decade, reaching 1.8% in 1998. By the end of the decade, inflation is still decreasing slowly. This suggests that the natural rate of unemployment in the European Union today is somewhat lower than the actual rate—which is around 10%.

Before trying to explain the evolution of unemployment and inflation in Figure 22–4, one must ask: Does it make sense to talk about *the* high European unemployment rate, or are there substantial differences across countries? In answer, Table 22–3 gives the unemployment numbers for each of the countries of the European Union, as well as for a few non-European countries in 1998.

An adverse supply shock increases inflation and decreases output. The decrease in output increases unemployment. Thus, an adverse supply shock increases both inflation and unemployment.

Revisit the effects of an increase in the price of oil on activity and the price level in section 7–6. See also chapter 13 for a discussion of a decrease in productivity growth on unemployment.

Recall from chapter 8 that we can think of the natural unemployment rate as the unemployment rate at which inflation remains constant. If inflation is decreasing, then we know that current unemployment is above the natural rate. If inflation is increasing, then we know that current unemployment is below the natural rate.

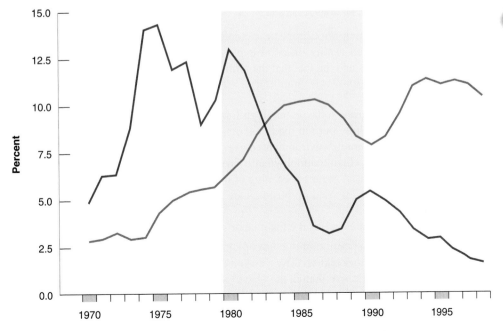

FIGURE 22–4

EU Unemployment and Inflation, 1970–1998

Although unemployment is very high today in Europe, inflation is decreasing only slowly.

TABLE	22-3	Unemployment Rates Across Countries, 1998 (percent of labor force)

European Union		European Union (*continued*)	
Austria	6.1	Portugal	5.1
Belgium	11.8	Spain	19.1
Denmark	6.5	Sweden	6.5
Finland	10.9	United Kingdom	6.5
France	11.8		
Germany	11.2		
Greece	10.0	**Other, non-European, Countries**	
Ireland	9.1	Australia	8.2
Italy	12.2	Canada	8.4
Luxembourg	3.1	New Zealand	8.3
Netherlands	4.1	United States	4.6

Source: OECD Economic Outlook, December 1998.

The table suggests three conclusions:

- Unemployment rates are indeed high in many European countries, including four of the largest five European economies—France, Germany, Italy, and Spain. (Unemployment in Spain is the subject of the In Depth box "Spanish Unemployment: Diagnosis and Policy Options.")
- There are, however, several European countries with relatively low unemployment at the end of the 1990s. The United Kingdom has an unemployment rate of only 6.5%—down from 10% in 1993. Other countries, such as Austria and Luxembourg, have maintained low unemployment throughout the last 30 years. Also look at Portugal, whose economy in many ways resembles that of Spain but has an unemployment rate of only 5.1%, compared to 19.1% in Spain.
- High unemployment is not limited to Europe. Canada has high unemployment. On the other side of the world, so does Australia.

Thus, one can talk about *the* European unemployment problem. At the same time, it is important, especially when testing different explanations, to keep in mind the differences across European countries and the fact that the problem is not limited to Europe.

Labor Market Rigidities

The dominant view in Europe today is that high European unemployment is the result of **labor market rigidities**. These put too many restrictions on firms, prevent them from adjusting to changes in the economic environment, make the cost of doing business too high, and, the argument goes, lead to high unemployment. The word **Eurosclerosis** has been coined to denote this view. ("Sclerosis" means hardening of the tissues—see chapter 6. The argument is that the many rigidities imposed on business are leading to the sclerosis of the economic structure.)

Here is a list of what are seen as the main labor market rigidities in Europe today:

- Wages represent only a fraction of the cost of labor. To these wages must be added employers' contributions to social security, pensions, and so on. Employers' contributions are typically larger in Europe than in the United States.
- Firms that want to lay off workers face large firing costs. These costs include large **severance payments** (payments that must be paid to laid-off workers) and/or a complex

and lengthy legal process to obtain the authorization to lay them off in the first place. These large costs not only make it hard to lay off unneeded workers, increasing the cost of doing business, but they also make firms think twice about hiring workers in the first place.

- Unions are more powerful in Europe than they are in the United States. They push for higher wages and, by imposing restrictions on the organization of work within firms, limit the flexibility of firms to adapt to changes, again increasing costs.
- Unemployment benefits are more generous in Europe than in the United States, representing a larger proportion of wages. They are also easier to qualify for and last longer, providing reduced incentives for the unemployed to find work.
- In many European countries, minimum wages are high in proportion to the average wage. Together with high nonwage labor costs, they often make it unprofitable to hire low-skill workers. Thus, low-skill workers remain unemployed. They also lose the opportunity for on-the-job training and thus lose the opportunity to become more skilled.

How do these factors lead to a high natural rate of unemployment? To answer, recall our discussion of the determinants of the natural rate in chapter 6. We can think of the natural rate as determined by two relations:

See section 6-5.

The first is the wage-setting relation

$$\frac{W}{P} = F(u, z)$$

This relation follows from our description of wage setting, together with the assumption that the expected price level is equal to the actual price level. The real wage is a decreasing function of the unemployment rate, u, and an increasing function of all the other factors that affect wage setting (captured by z). It is represented as the downward-sloping curve WS (for wage setting) in Figure 22-5.

The second relation is the price-setting relation, which implies

$$\frac{W}{P} = \frac{1}{(1 + \mu)}$$

where μ is the markup of prices over wages. It is represented by the horizontal line PS (for price setting) in Figure 22-5. Equilibrium is given by point A and the natural rate of unemployment is u_n.

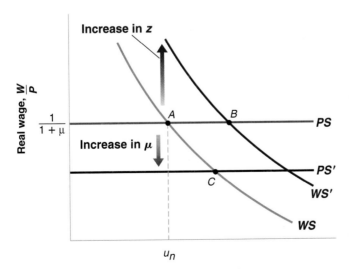

FIGURE 22-5

The Determinants of the Natural Rate of Unemployment

Increases in z and increases in μ both increase the natural rate of unemployment.

Although unemployment is higher at *B* than at *A*, real wages are unchanged. Thus, factors that increase the bargained wage at a given unemployment rate (increases in *z*) do not show up in higher wages, just in higher unemployment. In effect, higher unemployment forces wages back to their initial level.

Increases in z, which increase the real wage at a given unemployment rate, shift the *WS* curve up, moving the equilibrium from *A* to *B* and leading to an increase in the natural rate of unemployment.

Increases in μ shift the *PS* curve down, moving the equilibrium from *A* to *C*, and thus also leading to an increase in the natural rate of unemployment.

The list of factors we just presented links high unemployment in Europe to factors that increase either z or μ:

- High indirect or hidden labor costs lead to higher costs, and so to a higher μ, a higher markup of prices over wages.
- Unions decrease the flexibility firms need to operate efficiently, leading to higher costs and thus to a higher μ.
- By increasing workers' bargaining power, unions also lead to higher wages, increasing z, and so increasing the wage at a given unemployment rate.[1]
- By decreasing the cost of being unemployed, unemployment benefits strengthen the hand of workers in wage bargaining, leading also to an increase in z, to an increase in the wage at a given unemployment rate.

Evaluating the Eurosclerosis View. How convincing is the Eurosclerosis view of European unemployment? One main problem with the view is that although it is true that European labor markets indeed offer workers more job security than do their U.S. counterparts, this is not a new development: Many of the rules were already in place in the 1960s, when European unemployment was very low. Although some rigidities became stronger in the 1970s and early 1980s, the movement since has been in the direction of making labor markets more flexible. Many of these "rigidities" are in fact weaker today than they were a decade ago.

For example, the power of unions is clearly declining. **Union density**, the proportion of the workforce that is unionized, has decreased in most European countries since the early 1980s. Many countries have also passed legislation making it easier for firms to rely on part-time employment or to offer limited-time employment contracts, contracts that allow firms to lay off workers at the end of their contract at no cost.

Thus, to validate the argument that labor market rigidities are responsible for the *increase* in European unemployment, one has to argue that while the institutions have not gotten worse, their effect on unemployment is stronger than it was a few decades ago. This is not necessarily an implausible argument: The economic environment has changed a lot since the 1960s. Growth has slowed down, structural change is more rapid, and competition between firms has become more intense. In this new environment, rigidities may matter more than they used to. For example, for a firm that faces stable and growing demand and never needs to lay off workers, restrictions on firing are irrelevant. But in an environment where demand becomes more variable, and where the firm must adapt faster to survive, such restrictions become much more relevant indeed. The same restrictions may have been costless in the 1960s, but are very costly today.

"Structural change" means change in the economic structure, with some sectors growing while others are shrinking, new firms entering while old firms are closing, and so on.

Is there evidence that European economies are undergoing more rapid structural change than in earlier decades? Given the talk of increased international competition and the rapid development of new high-tech service sectors, you may be surprised to learn that economists

[1] **DIGGING DEEPER**. If asking for higher wages at a given unemployment rate only results in higher unemployment and unchanged wages, why would unions do it? Here are some of the answers:
- Competition between unions may force each one to ask for higher wages, even if they know that in the aggregate, the average real wage will be unchanged.
- Even if the average real wage is unchanged, unions can try to increase the wage of some workers relative to others.
- Our model may be too simple. Asking for higher wages may lead to higher wages, at least for some time. (In other words, the *PS* line may not be horizontal, but downward sloping.)

have found little hard evidence that the pace of European structural change is higher now than it was earlier.

One measure of "structural change" that economists have constructed is the dispersion of rates of change in employment across sectors. If all sectors grow at roughly the same rate, the dispersion will be small, indicating that the economy is undergoing little structural change. If some sectors are growing rapidly while others are shrinking, the dispersion will be large, indicating large underlying structural change. Dispersion measures constructed for each European country and each year show no consistent movement across countries and time. They are typically no higher today than they were in the 1960s or the 1970s. According to this measure, structural change in Europe is no higher now than it was in previous decades.

Change in the sectoral composition of employment is, however, only one of the dimensions of structural change. There is one dimension in which the last 20 years appear different from earlier decades. In both Europe and the United States, the demand for unskilled workers appears to have declined compared to the demand for skilled workers. Some economists argue that the labor market response to this shift has been different in the United States and in Europe. In the United States, the decrease in demand for unskilled workers has led to a decrease in their real wage. As a result, unskilled workers have remained employed, although at a lower wage. In Europe, the real wages of the unskilled have not declined, leading instead to an increase in the unemployment rate of unskilled workers.

See section 13-3.

How well does this last hypothesis fit the facts? Table 22-4 gives the change in the relative wage and the relative unemployment rate of unskilled workers from the late 1970s to the early 1990s for the United States and four European countries. The table suggests the following conclusions:

- The relative wage of unskilled workers has decreased more in the United States than in three of the four European countries.
- In contrast, the relative unemployment rate of the unskilled has increased substantially in all four European countries, whereas it has remained roughly constant in the United States.
- These two facts are consistent with the hypothesis that because of more wage rigidity in Europe, the adverse shift in the demand for unskilled workers has led to more unemployment in Europe.
- Looking within Europe, however, the hypothesis does not hold as well. Relative real wages have increased in France, Germany, and Italy. But they have decreased in the United Kingdom and, despite the large decrease, the relative unemployment rate of unskilled workers has still risen substantially.

TABLE 22-4 Changes in the Relative Wage and the Relative Unemployment Rate of Unskilled Workers

Country	Change in the Relative Wage of Unskilled Workers (1980–1995, %)	Relative Unemployment Rate of Unskilled Workers to Skilled Workers	
		(late 1970s)	(early 1990s)
United States	−13	3.5	3.5
France	3	1.5	2.9
Germany	8	2.1	2.6
Italy	1	0.4	1.1
United Kingdom	−14	3.1	5.3

First column: Change in the wage of male workers in the bottom decile of the overall earnings distribution relative to the wage of workers in the middle decile. *Second and third columns*: Ratio of the unemployment rate for the bottom quartile of the labor force, ranked by educational qualifications, to the unemployment rate for the top quartile.

Source: *World Employment 1996/1997*, ILO, 1996.

Thus, the evidence in support of the hypothesis is mixed at best. There in fact may be an alternative explanation for the large European increase in relative unemployment among unskilled workers—an explanation that has little to do with relative wages. When overall unemployment increases, as it has in Europe, the unemployment rate of unskilled workers always goes up by more than the unemployment rate of skilled workers. Firms get rid of their less skilled workers first and, when they need to hire, choose the more skilled workers from among the unemployed. Thus, the increase in the relative unemployment rate of the unskilled in Europe may reflect, in large part, the general increase in the unemployment rate, rather than problems of adjustment of relative wages.

Hysteresis

The weaknesses of the Eurosclerosis case have led several macroeconomists, including myself, to explore another line of explanation known as **hysteresis**. The argument is as follows:

In the late 1960s and then again in the 1970s, European countries were hit by a series of aggregate supply shocks: labor unrest in the late 1960s, a large decrease in productivity growth starting in the mid-1970s, and two large increases in oil prices, first in the mid-1970s, then in the late 1970s. The result was, very much as in the United States, stagflation—high unemployment and high inflation.

In the early 1980s, European countries decided to reduce inflation via monetary contraction. As in the United States, the result was disinflation and a sharp increase in unemployment.

See the In Depth box "Monetary Contraction and Fiscal Expansion: The United States in the Early 1980s" in chapter 20.

In the United States, monetary contraction was quickly followed by a fiscal expansion and the very large deficits of the Reagan administration. The result was a rapid output expansion from 1982 on. But because both European monetary and fiscal policies have remained tight to this day, unemployment has remained much higher there than in the United States.

This analysis raises, however, an obvious question: If unemployment in Europe is the result of tight macroeconomic policies that have increased the unemployment rate far above the natural rate, we should be observing a rapid decrease in inflation. But, as Figure 22–4 clearly shows, this is not the case. Inflation is low in Europe, but it is no longer decreasing, at least not very much.

Hysteresis comes from physics, where it describes the delay in the response of the magnetization of ferromagnetic substances to a varying magnetic field. More generally, the word is used to describe any system whose equilibrium position depends on the history of the system.

This is where hysteresis comes in. The natural unemployment rate, the argument goes, is not independent of actual unemployment—as we have assumed until now. Instead, the "natural rate" itself depends in part on the history of actual unemployment. In particular, a long period of high unemployment leads to an increase in the natural rate. Thus, persistently high unemployment is likely to be associated with less and less downward pressure on inflation. This is why inflation is no longer decreasing much in Europe. To return to our discussion of the Great Depression, hysteresis may also explain why, from 1933 on, deflation stopped in the United States despite very high unemployment.

The Role of Long-Term Unemployment. Why should actual unemployment affect the natural rate over time? Research has focused here on the role of **long-term unemployment**. High persistent unemployment leads to an increase in long-term unemployment. In 1998, the proportion of unemployed workers who had been unemployed for more than a year exceeded 30% for the European Union as a whole. The number was above 60% in Ireland, Belgium, and Italy (compared to only 9% for the United States).

There are two good reasons to worry about long-term unemployment:

- The human cost. It is one thing to be unemployed for a few months; it is another to be unemployed for a year or more. The evidence is that many of those who become long-term unemployed end up losing skills and work habits—or not acquiring them, in the case of youth unemployment, which is also very high in many European countries. The result is a vicious cycle in which employers become reluctant to hire the long-term unemployed, who then give up searching for jobs. The final result can be the permanent loss of employment, the loss of self-esteem, and psychological depression.

- The macroeconomic implications. The emergence of long-term unemployment leads to an increase in the natural rate of unemployment. Take the extreme case in which the long-term unemployed become, for the reasons we just saw, simply unemployable. They then become completely irrelevant to the process of wage determination: Employers cannot credibly threaten to hire the long-term unemployed to extract wage concessions from their current workers. Currently employed workers, were they to find themselves unemployed, do not have to worry about competing with the long-term unemployed.

If the long-term unemployed play no role in wage determination, then it follows that the higher the proportion of long-term unemployed in total unemployment, the less pressure a given unemployment rate exerts on wages, thus the higher the wage set in wage setting. In terms of Figure 22–6, an increase in the proportion of long-term unemployed shifts the wage-setting relation upward, from WS to WS'. This shift results in a higher natural unemployment rate, an increase from u_n to u'_n.

This increase in the natural rate can explain why an economy that has had high unemployment for a long time, and therefore has a high proportion of long-term unemployed, may have both high unemployment and roughly constant inflation. Take an economy in which the unemployment rate is 15%, with 10% long-term unemployed, and 5% short-term unemployed. Under our maintained assumption that the long-term unemployed workers are unemployable and therefore irrelevant to the process of wage determination, the unemployment rate relevant for wage determination (the unemployment rate taking into account only those workers who are employable) is only 5%. From the point of view of both employers and employed workers, the labor market is in effect tight, and there may well be wage pressure and increasing inflation.

The case we have just looked at is too extreme. Many of the long-term unemployed are employable, and long-term unemployment exerts some pressure on wages in wage determination. But the basic lesson is general. Prolonged high unemployment leads to an increase in the proportion of long-term unemployed. As the long-term unemployed become less employable, the same rate of unemployment exerts less downward pressure on wages, and thus less downward pressure on inflation.

Implications of Hysteresis. The theory of hysteresis has two important implications.

Disinflation may be more costly than we concluded in chapter 9 (where we assumed that the natural rate remained constant throughout). The increase in unemployment needed to

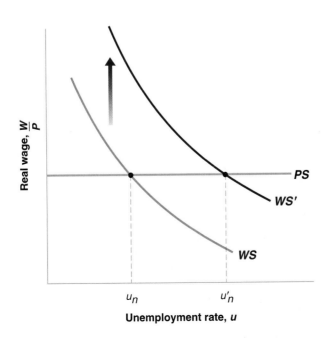

FIGURE 22–6

The Effects of an Increase in the Proportion of Long-Term Unemployed on the Natural Unemployment Rate

An increase in the proportion of long-term unemployed increases the natural rate of unemployment.

Spanish Unemployment: Diagnosis and Policy Options

In 1975, Francisco Franco died, ending nearly 40 years of dictatorship in Spain. Labor relations, which had been tightly controlled by the state, broke down. In an attempt to establish a constituency in the new democratic regime, socialist and communist unions competed in their demands for higher wages. The result was a rapid increase in wages, leading to a rapid increase in prices, leading to further increases in wages, and so on. With money growth accommodating these increases in prices and wages, inflation reached 25% in Spain in 1977. (Figure 1 shows the behavior of inflation and unemployment in Spain since 1971.)

Macroeconomic developments during the following 10 years (these years are shaded in the figure) were dominated by the fight against inflation. From 1978 on, the Bank of Spain maintained a policy of tight money; real interest rates, which had been negative in the mid-1970s (with expected inflation far exceeding nominal interest rates), turned positive, averaging 6% in the first half of the 1980s. By 1987, inflation was down to 5%. But the unemployment rate had increased to 20%, an increase of 15 percentage points in 10 years.

There was then a brief decrease in the unemployment rate at the end of the 1980s, reflecting a general economic expansion in Europe. But the unemployment rate rose again in the early 1990s, reaching 23.7% in 1994. It has decreased since then and, at the end of 1998, stood at just under 19%.

One's first reaction, when confronted with such high unemployment numbers, is to question whether the numbers can be trusted. In the case of Spain, a natural question is whether high measured unemployment actually hides a large underground economy. We already discussed this issue in the In Depth box on Spanish unemployment in chapter 2, and the answer is: No, most measured unemployment is real.

Does high unemployment reflect a high natural rate, or a large deviation from the natural rate? Recall that if high unemployment reflects a large positive deviation from the natural rate, it should be associated with a large decrease in inflation. But inflation is declining only slowly in Spain at this point. This suggests that the current unemployment rate is not far from the natural rate.

Where does this high natural rate come from? Economists have pointed to several potential culprits.

● Some have pointed to high firing costs. One of the legacies of the Franco period was a high degree of job protection: Workers could be dismissed only under limited conditions, and dismissals sometimes involved substantial severance payments. The OECD has computed an index of employment protection. Using that index, Spain has the second-highest level of protection among all OECD countries.

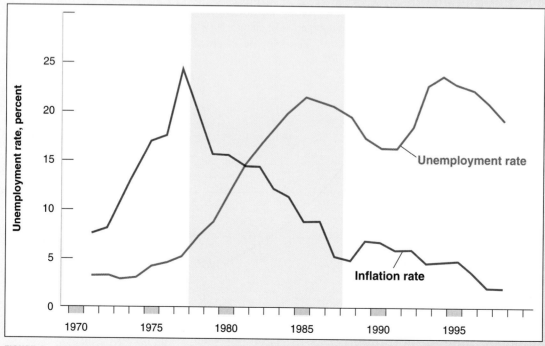

FIGURE 1   **Unemployment and Inflation in Spain, 1971–1995**

One problem with this explanation is that firing restrictions have substantially decreased since the mid-1980s. Since 1984, in particular, Spanish firms have been allowed to offer fixed-term contracts, contracts that allow firms to lay off workers at the expiration of the contract at no cost. As a result, the proportion of employment under fixed-term contracts has increased from 10% in 1984 to more than 35% today. How is it, then, that the unemployment rate has not decreased?

To answer this question, some economists have argued that the movement toward fixed-term employment contracts may have actually *decreased* the pressure of unemployment on wages, further increasing the natural rate of unemployment. Their argument is as follows: Now that firms can adjust employment through the use of workers under fixed-term contracts, workers with permanent contracts are even more protected from the risk of unemployment than they were before. If these workers, who are typically more senior, dominate wage negotiations, this may explain why the movement towards fixed-term employment has led to less rather than more downward pressure of unemployment on wages, and so to an increase rather than the intended decrease in the natural rate of unemployment.

● Others have pointed to hysteresis. They argue that, just as elsewhere in Europe, the increase in unemployment was initially due to tight money and the fight against inflation. But, they argue, the high actual unemployment rate has led over time to a high natural rate. The reason is that high unemployment has led to changes in the labor market. These changes have decreased the human cost of unemployment, but, at the same time, they have decreased the effect of high unemployment on wage determination, leading to an increase in the natural rate.

One such change is the increase in unemployment benefits. It is clear, for example, that the increase in unemployment has put pressure on politicians to increase the generosity of unemployment benefits. This surely has contributed in turn to an increase in the natural rate.

Unemployment benefits are not, however, so generous today that they can explain a 20% unemployment rate. In 1995, unemployment benefits in Spain were equal on average to 32% of the corresponding wage, a level higher than in the United States, but similar to the level in France or in Germany. And the generosity of unemployment benefits has decreased since the late 1980s.

A more important element may be the way in which families themselves have provided income to those who are unemployed. A striking characteristic of the increase in unemployment in Spain is how much it has been concentrated among the young, who typically can survive the loss of income more easily by staying home and relying on family income. The unemployment rate of Spanish people age 16 to 19 was an amazing 50% in 1994, and it remains very high today. More generally, most of the unemployed live in a household where somebody is working. At the end of 1993, although close to 25% of workers were unemployed, only 10% of households had no one employed in the household, and only 5% had no one employed and no one receiving unemployment benefits. Help from the family is probably why high unemployment has not led to extreme poverty and to riots. But it is also why the downward pressure of unemployment on wage determination has been weaker than one would have expected given the very high rate of unemployment.

What policy measures should be taken to reduce Spanish unemployment? The answer clearly depends on one's view of the sources of unemployment. But there is wide agreement that three sets of measures will be needed to decrease unemployment to much lower levels:

● A sustained increase in aggregate demand, leading to high growth in Spain for some time, and an associated decrease in the actual unemployment rate.
● Further reforms of the labor market to make sure that the natural unemployment rate decreases in line with the actual rate. To avoid some of the perverse effects we discussed earlier, further reform should take the form of an across-the-board reduction in firing costs, rather than the creation of two classes of workers, some with employment protection, and some (on fixed-duration contracts) without.
● The re-enfranchising of the long-term unemployed, through training programs or subsidies.

The figure shows that during the expansion of the late 1980s, the decrease in the actual unemployment rate was associated with an increase in inflation. Interestingly, the current expansion, which started in 1995, has so far not been associated with an increase in inflation, suggesting that the natural rate has decreased in tandem with actual unemployment. The challenge facing Spain is to continue along the same path until unemployment has reached a much lower level.

Reference

For more on the facts and policy options, read "Spanish Unemployment: Is There a Solution?", *Report of the CEPR Group on Spanish Unemployment*, CEPR, 1995.

decrease inflation may lead to an increase in the natural rate, and thus to long-lasting unemployment costs.

Turning to Europe today, there may be room for unemployment to decrease without fundamental changes in the organization of the labor market—regardless of the desirability of such reforms on other grounds. How fast and how much unemployment can decrease depends on how fast the hysteresis mechanisms can work in reverse, as unemployment decreases rather than increases. For example, can the long-term unemployed be "reenfranchised," and if so, how quickly? Will those who have given up searching for jobs start searching again if labor market conditions improve? Will those who have lost their skills be able to reacquire them quickly, or should specific training programs be put in place?

Eurosclerosis or Hysteresis?

I have presented so far the Eurosclerosis view and the hysteresis view as alternatives. In the recent past, a consensus has emerged that the two views are probably more complementary than opposite, and that a full answer needs to include elements of both. Here is an assessment of where current research stands:

There is no question that labor market institutions are very different in Europe and in the United States. Unemployment benefits are typically more generous, employment protection is typically higher, and unions are typically stronger in Europe than in the United States.

There is also no question that these differences in labor market institutions date back many decades, and so cannot by themselves explain why unemployment, which used to be lower in Europe than in the United States, is now so much higher.

Differences in labor market institutions may, however, be able to explain why hysteresis has played a more important role in Europe than in the United States. To understand why, consider, for example, two countries which differ in their unemployment benefit systems. In the first (think of the United States), unemployment benefits are paid only during the first six months of unemployment. In the second country (think of a European country), unemployment benefits are paid as long as somebody is unemployed. In the first country, somebody who is reaching the end of the period of unemployment benefits clearly has a strong incentive to find and take a job—any job. The proportion of long-term unemployed in total unemployment will be very low, so there will be little scope for hysteresis. In the second country, the proportion of long-term unemployed will be higher, and there will be more scope for hysteresis. Faced with the same adverse shocks, the two economies will react differently: In the first, high unemployment will lead to little long-term unemployment, and high unemployment will keep putting pressure on wages until unemployment has returned to normal. In the second, high unemployment will lead to a high proportion of long-term unemployment, and so may put little pressure on wages; the adjustment back to lower unemployment may take a much longer time.

This example suggests a more general proposition: It is the interaction between adverse shocks and bad labor market institutions that explains why European unemployment has remained so high for so long. This proposition is currently the subject of much research. If it is confirmed, we may at last have a convincing explanation for high European unemployment.

22-3 | Conclusions

It is not clear that there is a unique "high unemployment pathology." The two major episodes of high unemployment in the twentieth century appear quite different, both in their causes and in their symptoms:

The Great Depression was a case of a sharp decrease in activity followed by a long period of recovery. The decline in activity clearly had its origin on the demand side. Once the economy reached bottom, recovery was strong, largely because of an increase in the money supply and the resulting demand expansion.

High unemployment in Europe seems more like a long illness, with prospects only for a slow recovery. European unemployment crept up in the 1970s, before increasing faster in the early 1980s. There is no agreement about its sources. Some attribute it primarily to labor market rigidities, and to sclerosis. Others point to tight macroeconomic policies, and to hysteresis. As of 1998, the strong growth rates that accompanied the recovery from the Great Depression are nowhere to be seen.

SUMMARY

On the Great Depression in the United States:

- The unemployment rate increased from 3.2% in 1929 to 24.9% in 1933.

- The initial cause of this increase in unemployment was a large adverse shift in demand, brought about by the stock market crash of 1929 and the resulting increase in uncertainty.

- The result of high unemployment was a large deflation from 1929 to 1933.

- The favorable effect of deflation on real money balances was offset, however, by a roughly equal decrease in nominal money. This decrease was due to bank failures and a decrease in the money multiplier. Another perverse effect of deflation was to increase real interest rates, leading to a further decrease in demand and output.

- Recovery started in 1933. Average growth was high, 7.7% per year, from 1933 to 1941. But given its high 1933 value, the unemployment rate was still equal to 9.9% in 1941. In contrast to the predictions of the Phillips curve, deflation turned to inflation from 1934 on, despite a very high unemployment rate.

- Many questions remain about the recovery. It is clear, however, that high nominal money growth, leading to high real money growth, was an important factor in the recovery.

On European unemployment:

- The European unemployment rate was much lower than the U.S. rate until the early 1970s. Both increased in the 1970s and the early 1980s. Since then, however, the U.S. rate has declined while the European rate has remained very high. In 1998, the unemployment rate in the European Union was close to 11%.

- Although the increase in European unemployment in the 1980s was associated with a large decline in inflation, inflation is now roughly constant in Europe. This suggests that the current unemployment rate is close to the natural rate.

- One line of explanation for the high unemployment rate in Europe holds that high unemployment reflects rigidities in European labor markets, ranging from excessive employment protection to too-generous a system of unemployment benefits, to high minimum wages that price unskilled workers out of the labor market.

- An alternative line of explanation, called *hysteresis*, holds that high unemployment initially was due to disinflation policies, but that the high actual rate of unemployment has led to a high natural rate of unemployment. It argues in particular that high unemployment leads to a high proportion of long-term unemployed, and that the long-term unemployed have little effect on wage determination.

KEY TERMS

- Great Depression, 426
- depression, 426
- credit channel, 429
- New Deal, 430
- National Recovery Administration (NRA), 431
- National Industrial Recovery Act (NIRA), 431
- liquidity trap, 431

- labor market rigidities, 434
- Eurosclerosis, 434
- severance payments, 434
- union density, 436
- hysteresis, 438
- long-term unemployment, 438

An asterisk denotes a harder problem.

1. TRUE/FALSE/UNCERTAIN

a. The stock market crash of 1929 reflected the realization by financial investors that the Great Depression was coming.

b. The Fed could have done more—if not to prevent, then at least to limit the scope of the Great Depression.

c. We have learned how to use fiscal and monetary policy to avoid another Great Depression.

d. Because both firing costs and the rate of unemployment are much higher in Europe than in the United States, the solution to high European unemployment is simple: Eliminate firing costs.

e. Hysteresis implies that disinflation may lead to higher unemployment even in the medium run.

*2. THE LIQUIDITY TRAP AND ROLE OF POLICY

Consider an economy in a recession and with a nominal interest rate very close to zero. (Think of Japan in 1998.) Assume that there are only two relevant periods for economic decision making, corresponding to the current and the future period.

a. Draw the *IS-LM* for the current period. (Draw it so that the equilibrium interest rate is very close to zero.)

b. Can current monetary policy increase current output? (*Hint*: Can the *LM* curve cross the horizontal axis?)

c. Can expected future monetary policy increase current output? How? Under what conditions?

d. If you were the central bank, how would you convince people, firms, and financial investors that you will implement this monetary policy in the future?

(For more discussion in the context of Japan, look at Krugman's discussion at http://web.mit.edu/krugman/www/)

3. LONG-TERM UNEMPLOYMENT AND THE NATURAL RATE

Suppose that price setting is given by

$$\frac{W}{P} = \frac{1}{1 + 0.1}$$

And wage setting is given by

$$\frac{W}{P} = 1 - (u_s + 0.5u_L)$$

where u_S is the ratio of the number of short-term unemployed to the labor force and u_L is the ratio of the number of long-term unemployed to the labor force. Suppose further that the proportion of unemployed who are long-term unemployed is equal to β so $u_L = \beta u$, and $u_S = (1 - \beta)u$.

a. According to the wage-setting equation, which type of unemployment has a greater impact on wages—long term or short term? Explain.

b. Derive the natural rate (*Hint*: Substitute $u_L = \beta u$ and $u_S = (1 - \beta)u$ in the wage-setting equation. The natural rate will depend on β.)

c. Compute the natural rate if $\beta = 0.0$; 0.4; 0.8. Explain.

4. LONG-TERM UNEMPLOYMENT AND DISINFLATION

Recall equation (8.4) in chapter 8:

$$\pi - \pi_{t-1} = (\mu + z) - \alpha u$$

a. Interpret the equation. Why does higher unemployment lead to lower inflation given past inflation? Draw the change in inflation against the unemployment rate.

Write the overall unemployment rate u as $u = u_S + u_L$, with u_S the short-term unemployment rate (the ratio of the short-term unemployed to the labor force), and u_L the long-term unemployment rate (the ratio of the long-term unemployed to the labor force).

b. Now assume that the long-term unemployed have no effect on wage bargaining. Show how the equation above should be modified.

c. Suppose the proportion of long-term unemployed in unemployment increases (for a given u, u_L increases, and u_S decreases). Show what happens to the curve relating the change in inflation to the overall unemployment rate.

d. "Disinflation may lead to high unemployment for some time. High unemployment leads to a higher proportion of long-term unemployed. If the long-term unemployed play no role in bargaining, the unemployment cost of disinflation will be higher than the cost derived in chapter 8." Discuss.

5. EUROSCLEROSIS AND THE UNEMPLOYMENT RATE

"Unemployment benefits may sound attractive. But, in fact, all they do is lead to a higher natural unemployment rate, and so to more misery. They should be simply eliminated." Discuss.

For more on the Great Depression; Lester Chandler, *America's Greatest Depression* (New York: Harper and Row, 1970) gives the basic facts. So does the book by John A. Garraty, *The Great Depression* (New York: Harcourt Brace Jovanovich, 1986).

Peter Temin, *Did Monetary Forces Cause the Great Depression?* (New York: W.W. Norton, 1976) looks more specifically at the macroeconomic issues. So do the articles in a symposium on the Great Depression in the *Journal of Economic Perspectives*, Spring 1993.

A description of the Great Depression through the eyes of those who suffered through it is given in Studs Terkel, *Hard Times: An Oral History of the Great Depression in America* (New York, Pantheon Books, 1970).

The view that high European unemployment is due primarily to labor market rigidities is presented in the *OECD Jobs Study*, published in 1994. The report comes in three parts: a short report, and two longer volumes, Parts I and II, that give a detailed and useful description of labor markets in each OECD country. There have been several updates describing developments in policy and outcomes.

Discussions of European unemployment are given by Charles Bean in "European Unemployment: A Survey," *Journal of Economic Literature*, June 1994, 573–619; and Steve Nickell, "Unemployment and Labor Market Rigidities: Europe versus North America," *Journal of Economic Perspectives*, Summer 1997, 55–74.

We invite you to visit the Blanchard page on the Prentice Hall Web site at:

http://www.prenhall.com/blanchard

for this chapter's World Wide Web exercises

CHAPTER 23

Pathologies II: High Inflation

In 1913, the value of all currency circulating in Germany was 6 billion marks. Ten years later, in October 1923, 6 billion marks was barely enough to buy a one-kilo loaf of rye bread in Berlin. A month later, the price had increased to 428 billion marks.

The German hyperinflation of the early 1920s is probably the most famous hyperinflation. (**Hyperinflation** simply means very high inflation.) But it is not the only one. Table 23–1 summarizes the seven major hyperinflations that followed World War I and World War II. They share several features. They were all short (lasting for a year or so) but intense, with monthly inflation running at about 50% or more. In all, the increase in the price level was staggering. As you can

TABLE 23–1 Seven Hyperinflations of the 1920s and 1940s

Country	Beginning	End	P_T/P_0	Average Monthly Inflation rate (%)	Average Monthly Money Growth (%)
Austria	Oct. 1921	Aug. 1922	70	47	31
Germany	Aug. 1922	Nov. 1923	1.0×10^{10}	322	314
Greece	Nov. 1943	Nov. 1944	4.7×10^6	365	220
Hungary I	Mar. 1923	Feb. 1924	44	46	33
Hungary II	Aug. 1945	Jul. 1946	3.8×10^{27}	19,800	12,200
Poland	Jan. 1923	Jan. 1924	699	82	72
Russia	Dec. 1921	Jan. 1924	1.2×10^5	57	49

P_T/P_0: Price level in the last month of hyperinflation divided by the price level in the first month.

Source: Philip Cagan, "The Monetary Dynamics of Hyperinflation," in Milton Friedman ed., *Studies in the Quantity Theory of Money* (Chicago: University of Chicago Press, 1956), Table 1.

see, the largest price increase was actually not reached during the German hyperinflation, but in Hungary after World War II. What cost one Hungarian pengö in August 1945 cost 3,800 trillions of trillions of pengös less than a year later.

Such rates of inflation had not been seen before nor have they been seen since. The closest case in the recent past occurred in Bolivia. From January 1984 to September 1985, Bolivian inflation averaged 40% per month, implying a roughly 1,000-fold increase in the price level over 21 months. But many countries, especially in Latin America, have struggled with prolonged bouts of high inflation. Table 23–2 gives average *monthly* inflation rates for four Latin American countries since 1976. All four experienced at least five years of average monthly inflation running above 20%. Both Argentina and Brazil had monthly inflation rates in excess of 10% for more than a decade. All four countries have now returned to low inflation—nearly zero inflation, in the case of Argentina.

What causes hyperinflations? We saw in chapter 9 that *inflation ultimately comes from money growth.* This relation between money growth and inflation is confirmed by the last two columns of Table 23–1: Note how, in each country, high inflation was associated with correspondingly high nominal money growth. This raises the next question: *Why* was money growth so high? The answer turns out to be common to all hyperinflations: Money growth is high because the budget deficit is high. The budget deficit is high because the economy is affected by major shocks that make it difficult or impossible for the government to finance its expenditures. In this chapter, we look at this answer in more detail, relying on examples from various hyperinflations.

> With an inflation rate of 40% per month, the price level at the end of 21 months is $(1 + 0.4)^{21} = 1,171$ times the price level at the beginning.

TABLE 23–2 High Inflation in Latin America, 1976–1998

	Average Monthly Inflation Rate (%)				
	1976–1980	**1981–1985**	**1986–1990**	**1991–1995**	**1996–1998**
Argentina	9.3	12.7	20.0	2.3	0.1
Brazil	3.4	7.9	20.7	19.0	0.6
Nicaragua	1.4	3.6	35.6	8.5	—
Peru	3.4	6.0	23.7	4.8	0.8

Source: International Financial Statistics, IMF, various issues.

23-1 | Budget Deficits and Money Creation

A government can finance its deficit in one of two ways:

- It can borrow, the way you or I would. We would take a loan. Governments borrow by issuing bonds.
- It can do something that neither you nor I can do. It can, in effect, finance the deficit by creating money. I say "in effect" because, as you will remember from chapter 4, governments do not create money; the central bank does. But with the central bank's cooperation, the government can, in effect, finance itself by money creation: It can issue bonds

and ask the central bank to buy them. The central bank then pays the government with money it creates, and the government uses that money to finance its deficit. This process is called **debt monetization**.

Most of the time and in most countries, deficits are financed primarily through borrowing rather than through money creation. But, at the start of hyperinflations, two changes usually take place.

The first is a budget crisis. The source is typically a major social or economic upheaval:

- It may come from a civil war or a revolution, which destroys the state's ability to collect taxes, as in Nicaragua in the 1980s.
- It may come, as in the case of the hyperinflations in Table 23–1, from the aftermath of a war, which leaves the government with both smaller tax revenues and the large expenditures needed for reconstruction. This is what happened in Germany in 1922 and 1923. Burdened with payments for the war (called "war reparations") it had to pay to Allied forces, Germany had a budget deficit equal to more than two-thirds of its expenditures.
- It may come from a large adverse economic shock—for example, a large decline in the price of a raw material that is both the country's major export and its main source of revenues. As we shall see in the In Depth box on Bolivian hyperinflation, this is what happened in Bolivia in the 1980s. The decline in the price of tin, Bolivia's principal export, was one of the main causes of the Bolivian hyperinflation.

The second change is the government's increasing unwillingness or inability to borrow from the public or from abroad to finance its deficit. The reason is the size of the deficit itself. Worried that the government may not be able to repay the debt in the future, potential lenders start asking the government for higher and higher interest rates. Sometimes, foreign lenders decide to stop lending to the government altogether. As a result, the government increasingly turns to the other source of finance—money creation. Eventually, most of the deficit is financed by money creation.

How large is the rate of money growth needed to finance a given deficit? To answer, let's assume the deficit is financed entirely by money creation:

$$\Delta M = \$ \text{ deficit}$$

This equation tells us that the government (through the central bank) must create enough new money to cover the nominal deficit. M is the nominal money stock, measured, say, at the end of each month. (In the case of hyperinflation, variables change quickly enough that it is useful to divide time into months, rather than quarters or years.) ΔM is the change in the nominal money stock from the end of last month to the end of this month—nominal money creation during this month. "$ deficit" is the budget deficit, measured in nominal terms.

If we divide both sides of the equation by the price level during the month, P, and denote the real deficit by "deficit" without a dollar sign, we get

$$\frac{\Delta M}{P} = \text{deficit} \qquad (23.1)$$

The revenues from money creation, $\Delta M/P$, are called **seignorage**. The word is revealing: The right to issue money was a precious source of revenues for the "seigneurs" of the past: They could buy the goods they wanted by issuing their own money and using it to pay for the goods. Equation (23.1) says the government must create enough money so that seignorage is enough to finance the real deficit.

By multiplying top and bottom of $\Delta M/P$ by M, we can rewrite seignorage as

$$\underbrace{\text{Seignorage}}_{\dfrac{\Delta M}{P}} = \underbrace{\text{Money growth}}_{\dfrac{\Delta M}{M}} \times \underbrace{\text{Real money balances}}_{\dfrac{M}{P}} \qquad (23.2)$$

We are taking a shortcut here. What should be on the left-hand side of the equation is H, the monetary base—the money created by the central bank—not M, the money stock. I ignore the distinction here, as it does not play an important role in the argument that follows.

PATHOLOGIES II: HIGH INFLATION

Seignorage is the product of money growth ($\Delta M/M$) times real money balances (M/P). The larger the real money balances held in the economy, the larger the amount of seignorage corresponding to a given rate of money growth.

Remember that income is a flow. Y here is real income per month.

To think about relevant magnitudes, it is convenient to divide both sides of equation (23.2) by real income, Y (measured at a monthly rate)

$$\frac{\Delta M/P}{Y} = \frac{\Delta M}{M}\left(\frac{M/P}{Y}\right) \tag{23.3}$$

This equation says that the ratio of seignorage to real income [$(\Delta M/P)/Y$] is equal to the rate of money growth ($\Delta M/M$) times the ratio of real money balances to real income [$(M/P)/Y$]. Suppose the government is running a budget deficit equal to 10% of real income. If it finances the deficit through money creation, then seignorage must be equal to 10% of real income as well. Suppose people hold real balances equal to two months of income, so that $(M/P)/Y = 2$. Then, equation (23.3) tells us, the monthly growth rate of money must be equal to 10%/2 = 5%.

To summarize: The revenues from money creation are called seignorage. Seignorage is equal to the product of money growth and real money balances. For given real money balances, higher seignorage requires higher money growth.

Does this imply that the government can finance a deficit equal to 20% of real income through a money growth rate of 10%, a deficit of 40% of real income through money growth of 20%, and so on? No. As money growth increases, so does inflation. And, as inflation increases, the opportunity cost of keeping money increases, leading people to reduce their real money balances. In terms of equation (23.2), an increase in $\Delta M/M$ leads to a decrease in M/P, so that an increase in money growth does not generate a proportional increase in seignorage. What is crucial here is how much people adjust their real money balances in response to inflation, and it is the issue to which we turn next.

23-2 | Inflation and Real Money Balances

What determines the amount of real money balances that people are willing to hold?

Recall the LM relation we have used so far

$$\frac{M}{P} = \$Y\,L(i)$$
$$(-)$$

Higher real income leads people to hold larger real money balances. A higher nominal interest rate increases the opportunity cost of holding money rather than bonds and leads people to reduce their real money balances.

This characterization holds in both stable economic times and times of hyperinflations. But in times of hyperinflation, we can simplify it further. Here's how. First, rewrite the LM relation using the relation between the nominal and the real interest rate,

See the discussion of nominal and real interest rates in section 14-1.

$$i = r + \pi^e$$

$$\frac{M}{P} = Y\,L(r + \pi^e)$$

Real money balances depend on real income, Y, on the real interest rate, r, and on expected inflation, π^e. All three variables move during a hyperinflation, but expected inflation moves much more than the other two variables: During a typical hyperinflation, actual inflation—and presumably expected inflation—may move from close to 0% to 50% a month or more. Thus, it is not a bad approximation to assume that both income and the real interest rate are constant, and focus just on the movements in expected inflation. So we write

$$\frac{M}{P} = \bar{Y} L(\bar{r} + \pi^e) \qquad (23.4)$$

where the bars over Y and r mean that we now take both income and the real interest rate as constant. In times of hyperinflation, equation (23.4) tells us, we can think of real money balances as depending primarily on expected inflation. As expected inflation increases and it becomes more and more costly to hold money, people will reduce their real money balances.

Indeed, during a hyperinflation people find many ways of reducing their real money balances. When the monthly rate of inflation is 100%, for example, keeping currency for a month implies losing half of its real value (because things cost twice as much a month later). **Barter**, the exchange of goods for other goods rather than for money, increases. Payments

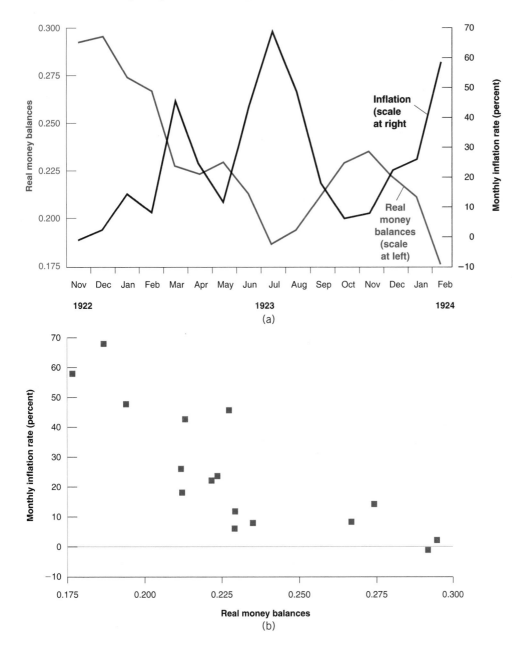

FIGURE 23–1

Inflation and Real Money Balances in Hungary, November 1922 to February 1924

At the end of the Hungarian hyperinflation, real money balances stood at roughly half their pre-hyperinflation level.

for wages become much more frequent—often twice weekly. Once people are paid, they rush to stores to buy goods. Although the government often makes it illegal to use other currencies than the one it is printing, people shift to foreign currencies as stores of value. And even if it is illegal, an increasing proportion of transactions takes place in foreign currency. During the Latin American hyperinflations of the 1980s, people shifted to U.S. dollars. The shift to dollars has become so widespread in the world that it has a name: **dollarization** (the use of dollars in another country's domestic transactions).

By how much do real money balances actually decrease as inflation increases? Figure 23–1 examines the evidence from the Hungarian hyperinflation of the 1920s and provides some insights.

Figure 23-1(a) plots real money balances and the monthly inflation rate from November 1922 to February 1924. Note how movements in inflation are reflected in opposite movements in real money balances. The short-lived decline in Hungarian inflation from July to October 1923 is reflected in an equally short-lived increase in real money balances. At the end of the hyperinflation in February 1924, real money balances stand at a little more than half their level at the beginning.

Figure 23–1(b) presents the same numbers, but in the form of a scatter diagram. It plots monthly real money balances on the horizontal axis against inflation on the vertical axis. (We do not observe expected inflation, which is clearly the variable we would like to plot, so I use actual inflation instead.) Note how the points nicely describe a downward-sloping demand for money: As actual inflation—and presumably expected inflation, as well—increases, the demand for money strongly decreases.

To summarize: Increases in inflation lead people to decrease their demand for money, leading in turn to a decrease in real money balances.

23-3 | Deficits, Seignorage, and Inflation

We have looked at the relation between seignorage, money growth, and real money balances (equation [23.2]), and the relation between real money balances and inflation (equation [23.4]). Combining them gives

$$\text{seignorage} = \left(\frac{\Delta M}{M}\right)\left(\frac{M}{P}\right)$$

$$= \left(\frac{\Delta M}{M}\right)[\bar{Y} L(\bar{r} + \pi^e)] \tag{23.5}$$

The first line repeats equation (23.2): Seignorage equals the rate of money growth times real money balances. And the second line incorporates what we learned in equation (23.4): Real money balances depend negatively on expected inflation.

Using this relation, we can now show how the need to finance a large budget deficit can lead not only to *high inflation*, but also, as is the case during hyperinflations, *high and increasing inflation*.

The Case of Constant Money Growth

Suppose the government chooses a *constant* rate of money growth and maintains that rate forever. (Clearly, this is not what happens during hyperinflations, where the rate of money growth typically increases over the course of the hyperinflation; we shall get more realistic later.) How much seignorage will this constant rate of money growth generate?

If money growth is constant forever, then inflation and expected inflation must eventually be constant as well. Assume output growth equals zero. Then, actual and expected inflation must equal money growth

$$\pi^e = \pi = \frac{\Delta M}{M}$$

Replacing π^e by $\Delta M/M$ in equation (23.5) gives

$$\text{Seignorage} = \frac{\Delta M}{M}\left[\overline{Y}L\left(\overline{r} + \frac{\Delta M}{M}\right)\right] \qquad (23.6)$$

Note that money growth has two opposite effects on seignorage.

- On one hand, given real money balances, money growth increases seignorage. This is reflected by the first term on the right of equation (23.6): An increase in $\Delta M/M$ increases seignorage.
- On the other hand, an increase in money growth increases inflation and thus decreases real money balances. This is reflected by the presence of $\Delta M/M$ in the second term on the right of equation (23.6).

$\Delta M/M\uparrow \Rightarrow$ Seignorage $\uparrow$

$\Delta M/M\uparrow \Rightarrow \pi\uparrow \Rightarrow \pi^e\uparrow \Rightarrow$
$L(\overline{r} + \pi^e)\downarrow \Rightarrow M/P\downarrow \Rightarrow$
Seignorage ?

Thus, the net effect of money growth on seignorage is ambiguous. The empirical evidence is that the relation between seignorage and money growth is hump-shaped, as drawn in Figure 23–2: At low rates of money growth, such as those we observe in Europe or the United States today, an increase in money growth leads to a small reduction in real money balances. Thus, it leads to an increase in seignorage. When money growth (and therefore inflation) becomes very high, however, the reduction in real money balances induced by higher money growth becomes larger and larger. Eventually, there is a rate of money growth—point A in Figure 23–2—beyond which further increases in money growth *decrease* seignorage.

The shape of the relation in Figure 23–2 may look familiar to those of you who have studied the economics of taxation. Income tax revenues equal the *tax rate on income* times income—the *tax base*. At low tax rates, the tax rate has little influence on how much people work, and tax revenues increase with the tax rate. But as tax rates increase further, some people start working less or stop declaring part of their income, and the tax base decreases. As the income tax reaches very high levels, increases in the tax rate lead to a decline in tax revenues. Obviously, tax rates of 100% lead to no tax revenue at all: Why work if the government takes all your income? This relation between tax revenues and the tax rate is often called the **Laffer curve**, after the economist Arthur Laffer, who argued in the early 1980s that a cut in U.S. tax rates would lead to more tax revenues. He was clearly wrong about where the United States was on the curve: The effect of the decrease in tax rates was to lower tax revenues, not increase them. But the general point still stands: When tax rates are high enough, a further increase in the tax rate can indeed lead to a decrease in tax revenues.

See chapter 20 for a discussion of the effects of the tax cuts of 1981 to 1983 on the U.S. budget and the U.S economy.

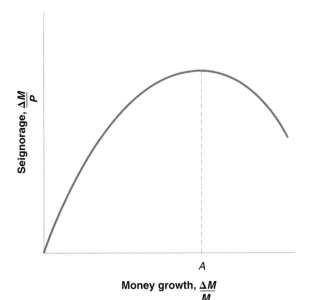

FIGURE 23–2

Seignorage and Money Growth

Seignorage is first an increasing function, then a decreasing function of money growth.

There is more than a simple analogy here. Inflation can be thought of as a tax on money balances. The tax rate is the rate of inflation, π, which reduces the real value of money holdings. The tax base is real money balances, M/P. The product of these two variables, $\pi(M/P)$, is called the **inflation tax**. There is a subtle difference with other forms of taxation: What the government receives from money creation at any point in time is not the inflation tax, but rather seignorage: $(\Delta M/M)(M/P)$. However, the two are closely related. When money growth is constant, inflation must eventually be equal to money growth, so that

$$\text{Inflation tax} = \pi \left(\frac{M}{P} \right)$$
$$= \left(\frac{\Delta M}{M} \right) \left(\frac{M}{P} \right)$$
$$= \text{Seignorage}$$

What rate of money growth leads to the *most seignorage*, and how much seignorage does it generate? These are the questions that Philip Cagan asked in a classic paper on hyperinflations written in 1956. In one of the earliest uses of econometrics, Cagan estimated the relation between the demand for money and expected inflation (equation [23.4]) during each of the hyperinflations in Table 23–1. Then, using equation (23.6), he computed the rate of money growth that maximized seignorage, and the associated amount of seignorage. The answers he obtained are given in the first two columns of Table 23–3. The third column repeats the actual money growth numbers from Table 23–1.

This table shows something very interesting: In all seven hyperinflations, actual average money growth (column 3) far exceeded the rate of money growth that maximizes seignorage (column 1). Compare the actual rate of money growth in Hungary after World War II, 12,200%, to the rate of money growth that would have maximized seignorage, 32%. This would seem to be a serious problem for the story we have developed so far. If the reason for money creation was to finance the budget deficit, why was the actual rate of money growth so much higher than the number that maximizes seignorage? The answer lies in the dynamics of the economy's adjustment to high money growth. We now turn to it.

Dynamics and Increasing Inflation

Return to the argument we just developed: *If maintained forever*, a higher rate of money growth will *eventually* lead to a proportional increase in both actual and expected inflation, and lead to a decrease in real money balances. If money growth is higher than the amount that maximizes seignorage, the increase in money growth will lead to a decrease in seignorage.

TABLE 23–3 Money Growth and Seignorage

	Monthly Rate of Money Growth Maximizing Seignorage (%)	Implied Seignorage (% of output)	Actual Monthly Rate of Money Growth (%)
Austria	12	13	31
Germany	20	14	314
Greece	28	11	220
Hungary I	12	19	33
Hungary II	32	6	12,200
Poland	54	4.6	72
Russia	39	0.5	49

Source: Philip Cagan, "The Monetary Dynamics of Hyperinflation," in Studies in the Quantity Theory of Money, Milton Friedman ed. (Chicago: University of Chicago Press, 1956).

The crucial words in the argument are "if maintained forever" and "eventually." Consider a government that needs to finance a suddenly much larger deficit, and decides to do so by creating money. As the rate of money growth increases, it may take a while for inflation and expected inflation to adjust. Even as expected inflation increases, it will take a while longer for people to fully adjust their real money balances: Creating barter arrangements takes time, the use of foreign currencies in transactions develops slowly, and so on.

Let's state this conclusion more formally. Recall our equation for seignorage

$$\text{Seignorage} = \left(\frac{\Delta M}{M}\right)\left(\frac{M}{P}\right)$$

In the short run, an increase in the rate of money growth ($\Delta M/M$) may lead to little change in real money balances (M/P). Put another way, if it is willing to increase money growth sufficiently, a government will be able, *in the short run*, to generate nearly any amount of seignorage that it wants, far in excess of the numbers in the second column of Table 23–3. But over time, as prices adjust and real money balances decrease, this government will find that the same rate of money growth yields less and less seignorage. So, if the government keeps trying to finance a deficit larger than that shown in the second column of Table 23–3 (for example, if Austria tries to finance a deficit that is more than 13% of GDP), it will find that it cannot do so with a constant rate of money growth. The only way it will succeed is by continually *increasing* the rate of money growth. This is why actual money growth exceeds the numbers in the first column, and why hyperinflations are nearly always characterized by increasing money growth and inflation.

There is also another effect at work, which we have ignored until now, but goes in the same direction. We have taken the deficit as given. But as inflation becomes very high, the budget deficit typically becomes larger. Part of the reason has to do with lags in tax collection. This effect is known as the **Tanzi–Olivera effect**, for Vito Tanzi and Julio Olivera, two economists who have emphasized its importance. As taxes are collected on past nominal income, their real value goes down with inflation. For example, if income taxes are paid this year on income received last year, and if the price level is 10 times higher than last year's, the actual tax rate is only one-tenth that of the official tax rate. Thus, high inflation typically decreases real government revenues, making the deficit problem worse. The problem is often compounded by other effects on the expenditure side: Governments often try to slow inflation by prohibiting firms under state control from increasing their prices, although their costs are increasing with inflation. The direct effect on inflation is small at best, but the firms then run a deficit that must in turn be financed by the government, further increasing the budget deficit. As the budget deficit increases, so does the need for more seignorage, and so does the need for even higher money growth.

Hyperinflations and Economic Activity

We have focused so far on movements in money growth and inflation—which clearly dominate the economic scene during a hyperinflation. But hyperinflations affect the economy in many other ways.

Initially, higher money growth leads to an *increase* in output. The reason is that it takes some time for increases in money growth to be reflected in inflation, and during that time, the effects of higher money growth are expansionary: As we saw in chapter 14, the initial effects of an increase in nominal money growth are actually to *decrease* nominal and real interest rates, leading to an increase in demand and an increase in output.

But as inflation becomes very high, the adverse effects of hyperinflation dominate:

- The transaction system becomes less and less efficient. One famous example of inefficient exchange is the story of people using wheelbarrows to carry the currency needed for transactions at the end of the German hyperinflation.
- Price signals become less and less useful. Because prices change so often, it is difficult for consumers and producers to assess the relative prices of goods and to make informed

Here is a joke told in Israel during the high inflation of the 1980s: "Why is it cheaper to take the taxi rather than the bus? Because in the bus, you have to pay the fare at the beginning of the ride. In the taxi, you pay only at the end." ▶

We have discussed here ▶ the costs of very high inflation. The discussion today in OECD countries is about the costs of, say, 5% inflation versus 0%. The issues are quite different in that case, and we return to it in chapter 26.

decisions. The evidence shows that the higher the rate of inflation, the higher the variation in the relative prices of different goods. Thus, the price system, which is crucial to the functioning of a market economy, also becomes less and less efficient.

- Swings in the inflation rate also become larger. It becomes harder to predict what inflation will be in the near future, whether it will be, say, 500% or 1,000% over the next year. Borrowing at a given nominal interest rate becomes more and more of a gamble. If you borrow at, say, 1,000% for a year, you may end up paying a real interest rate of 500% or 0%: A large difference! The result is that borrowing and lending typically come to a near stop in the last months of hyperinflation, leading to a large decline in investment.

So, as inflation increases and its costs become larger, there is typically an increasing consensus that it should be stopped. This takes us to the last section of this chapter, how hyperinflations actually end.

23-4 | How Do Hyperinflations End?

Hyperinflations do not die a natural death. Rather, they have to be stopped through a **stabilization program**.

The Elements of a Stabilization Program

What needs to be done to end a hyperinflation follows from our analysis of the causes of hyperinflation.

- There must be a fiscal reform and a credible reduction of the budget deficit. This reform must take place both on the expenditure side and on the revenue side.
  On the expenditure side, reform typically implies reducing the subsidies that have often mushroomed during the hyperinflation. Obtaining a temporary suspension of interest payments on foreign debt also helps decrease expenditures. An important component of stabilization in Germany in 1923 was the reduction in reparation payments—precisely those payments that had triggered the hyperinflation in the first place.
  On the revenue side, what is required is not so much an increase in overall taxation than a change in the composition of taxation. This is important: During a hyperinflation, people are in effect paying a tax, the inflation tax. Stabilization implies replacing the inflation tax with other taxes. The challenge is to put in place and collect these other taxes. This cannot be done overnight, but it is essential that people become convinced that it will be done and that the budget deficit will be reduced.

This is what Argentina did ◀ in 1991, adopting a currency board and fixing the exchange rate at one dollar for one Argentinian peso. See the discussion of currency boards in chapter 22. ▶

- The central bank must make a credible commitment that it will no longer automatically monetize the government debt. This credibility may be achieved in several ways. The central bank can be prohibited, by decree, from buying any government debt, so that no monetization of the debt is possible. Or the central bank can peg the exchange rate to the currency of a country with low inflation. An even more drastic step is to officially adopt dollarization, to make a foreign currency the country's official currency. This step is drastic because it implies giving up seignorage altogether, and is often perceived as a decrease in the country's independence.

An Israeli finance minister ▶ was fired in the 1980s for proposing such a measure as part of a stabilization program. His proposal was perceived as an attack on the sovereignty of Israel.

- Are other measures needed as well? Some economists believe that **incomes policies**— that is, wage and price guidelines or controls—should be used, in addition to fiscal and monetary measures, to help the economy reach a new lower rate of inflation. Incomes policies, they argue, help coordinate expectations around a new lower rate of inflation. If firms know wages will not increase, they will not increase prices. If workers know prices will not increase, they will not ask for wage increases, and inflation can be eliminated more easily.
  Others believe credible deficit reduction and central bank independence are all that is required. They argue that the appropriate policy changes, if credible, can lead to drastic changes in expectations and thus to the elimination of expected and actual inflation nearly

overnight. They point to the potential dangers of wage and price controls. Governments may end up relying on the controls, and may not take the painful but needed fiscal policy measures, leading ultimately to failure. Also, if the structure of relative prices is distorted to start with, price controls run the risk of maintaining these distortions.

Stabilization programs that do not include incomes policies are called **orthodox**; those that do are called **heterodox** (because they rely on both monetary–fiscal changes and incomes policies). The hyperinflations of Table 23–1 were all ended through orthodox programs. Many of the more recent Latin American stabilizations have relied on heterodox programs.

Can Stabilization Programs Fail?

Can stabilization programs fail? Yes. They can fail, and they often do. Argentina went through five stabilization plans from 1984 to 1989 before succeeding in 1990. Brazil only succeeded in 1995, in its sixth attempt in 12 years.

Sometimes failure results from a botched or half-hearted effort at stabilization. A government puts wage controls in place, but does not take the measures needed to reduce the deficit and money growth. Wage controls cannot work if money growth continues, and the stabilization program eventually fails.

Sometimes failure results from political opposition. If social conflict was at the root of the hyperinflation, it still may be present and just as hard to resolve at the time of stabilization. Those who lose from the fiscal reform needed to decrease the deficit will oppose the stabilization program and may force the government to retreat. Often workers who see an increase in the price of public services or an increase in taxation, but who do not fully perceive the decrease in the inflation tax, strike or even riot, leading to failure of the stabilization plan.

Failure can also result from the anticipation of failure. Suppose the exchange rate is fixed to the dollar as part of the stabilization program. Also suppose participants in financial markets anticipate that the government will soon be forced to devalue. To compensate for the risk of devaluation, they require very high interest rates to hold domestic rather than U.S. bonds. These very high interest rates cause a large recession. The recession in turn forces the government to devalue, validating the markets' initial fears. If instead markets had believed that the government would maintain the exchange rate, the risk of devaluation would have been lower, interest rates would have been lower, and the government would have been able to proceed with stabilization. To many economists, the successes and failures of stabilization plans appear to have such an element of self-fulfilling prophecy. Even well-conceived plans work only if they are expected to work. In other words, luck and good public relations both play a role.

The Costs of Stabilization

We saw in chapter 9 how the U.S. disinflation of the early 1980s was associated with a large recession and a large increase in unemployment. We saw in chapter 22 that the European disinflations of the 1980s may have come with an even larger unemployment cost. We might therefore expect the much larger disinflations associated with the end of a hyperinflation to be associated with very large recessions or even depressions. This is typically not the case.

To understand why, recall our discussion of disinflation in section 9-3. We argued that there were three reasons why inflation might not decrease as fast as money growth, leading to a recession. The first was the fact that wages are typically set in nominal terms for some period of time (up to three years in the United States) and, as a result, many of them are already determined when the decision to disinflate is made. The second was that wage contracts are typically staggered, making it difficult to implement a slowdown in all wages at the same time. The third was credibility.

Hyperinflation eliminates the first two problems. During hyperinflation, wages and prices are changed so often that both nominal rigidities and the staggering of wage decisions become nearly irrelevant.

This argument was particularly relevant in the stabilizations in Eastern Europe in the early 1990s, where, because of central planning, the initial structure of relative prices was very different from that in a market economy. Imposing wage or price controls would have prevented relative prices from adjusting to their appropriate market value.

This is a variation on the theme of self-fulfilling exchange rate crises developed in chapter 21.

Remember that the rate of real money growth equals the rate of nominal money growth minus the rate of inflation. If inflation decreases by less than nominal money growth, this implies negative real money growth. This decrease in the real money stock then leads to high interest rates, which can trigger a recession.

The Bolivian Hyperinflation of the 1980s

In the 1970s, Bolivia achieved strong output growth, in large part because of high world prices for its exports: tin, silver, coca, oil, and natural gas. But by the end of the decade, the economic situation started deteriorating. The price of tin declined. Foreign lending, which had financed a large part of Bolivian spending in the 1970s, was sharply curtailed as foreign lenders started worrying about repayment. Partly as a result, and partly because of long-running social conflicts, political chaos ensued. From 1979 to 1982, the country had 12 presidents, nine military and three civilian.

When the first freely elected president in 18 years came to power in 1982, he faced a nearly impossible task. U.S. commercial banks and other foreign lenders were running scared. They surely did not want to make new loans to Bolivia, and they wanted the previous loans to be repaid. Net private (medium- and long-term) foreign lending to the Bolivian government had decreased from 3.5% of GDP in 1980 to −0.3% in 1982, and decreased to −1.0% in 1983. Because the government felt it had no other choice, it turned to money creation to finance the budget deficit.

Inflation and Budget Deficits. The next three years were characterized by the interaction of steadily higher inflation and budget deficits.

Table 1 gives the budget numbers for the period 1981 to 1986. Because of the lags in tax collection, the effect of rising inflation was to dramatically reduce real tax revenues. And the government's attempt to maintain low prices for public services was the source of large deficits for state-run firms. As these deficits were financed by subsidies from the state, the result was a further increase in the budget deficit. In 1984, the budget deficit reached a staggering 31.6% of GDP.

The result of higher budget deficits and the need for higher seignorage was to increase money growth and inflation. Inflation, which had run at an average 2.5% a month in 1981, increased to 7% in 1982 and to 11% in 1983. As shown in Figure 1, which gives Bolivia's monthly inflation rate from January 1984 to April 1986 (the vertical line indicates the beginning of stabilization), inflation kept increasing in 1984 and 1985, reaching 182% in February 1985.

Stabilization. There were many attempts at stabilization along the way. Stabilization programs were launched in November 1982, November 1983, April 1984, August 1984, and February 1985. The April 1984 package was an orthodox program involving a large devaluation, an announcement of tax reform, and an increase in public-sector prices. But the opposition of trade unions was too strong, and the program was abandoned.

After the election of a new president, yet another attempt at stabilization was made in September 1985. This one proved successful. It was an orthodox stabilization plan, organized around the elimination of the budget deficit. Its main features were

- *Fiscal policy*: Public-sector prices were increased; food and energy prices were increased; public-sector wages were frozen; and a tax reform, aimed at reestablishing and broadening the tax base, was announced.
- *Monetary policy*: The official exchange rate of the peso was adjusted to what the black market rate had been prestabilization. The exchange rate was set at 1.1 million pesos to the dollar, up from 67,000 pesos to the dollar the month before (a 1,600% devaluation). The exchange rate was then left to float, within limits.
- *Reestablish international creditworthiness*: Negotiations were started with international organizations and commercial banks to restructure the debt. An agreement with foreign creditors and the IMF was reached nine months later, in June 1986.

As in the previous attempt at stabilization, the unions called a general strike. In response, the government declared a state of siege, and the strike was quickly disbanded. After hyperinflation and so many failed attempts to control it, public opinion was clearly in favor of stabilization.

TABLE 1	Revenues, expenditures, and the deficit, as a percentage of Bolivian GDP					
	1981	**1982**	**1983**	**1984**	**1985**	**1986**
Revenues	9.4	4.6	2.6	2.6	1.3	10.3
Expenditures	15.1	26.9	20.1	33.2	6.1	7.7
Budget balance (−: deficit)	−5.7	−22.3	−17.5	−31.6	−4.8	2.6

Revenues and expenditures of the central government.
Source: Jeffrey Sachs, "The Bolivian Hyperinflation and Stabilization," *National Bureau of Economic Research*, working paper No. 2073, November 1986, Table 3.

The effects on inflation were dramatic. For a few weeks the inflation rate was actually negative! Inflation did not remain negative for very long, but the average monthly rate of inflation was below 2% during 1986 to 1989. As the table shows, the budget deficit was drastically reduced in 1986, and the average deficit was below 5% of GNP for the rest of the decade.

Did stabilization have a negative effect on output? It probably did. Real interest rates remained very high for more than a year after stabilization. The full effect of these high real interest rates on output is hard to establish, however. At the same time stabilization was implemented, Bolivia was hit with further large declines in the price of tin and natural gas.

In addition, a major campaign against narcotics had the effect of disrupting coca production. How much of the Bolivian recession of 1986 was due to stabilization, and how much was due to these other factors, is difficult to assess.

References

The material in this box draws largely from Jeffrey Sachs, "The Bolivian Hyperinflation and Stabilization," NBER working paper, 1986. Sachs was one of the architects of the stabilization program.

See also Juan Antonio Morales, "The Transition from Stabilization to Sustained Growth in Bolivia," in Michael Bruno et al., eds., *Lessons of Economic Stabilization and its Aftermath*, (Cambridge, MA: MIT Press, 1991).

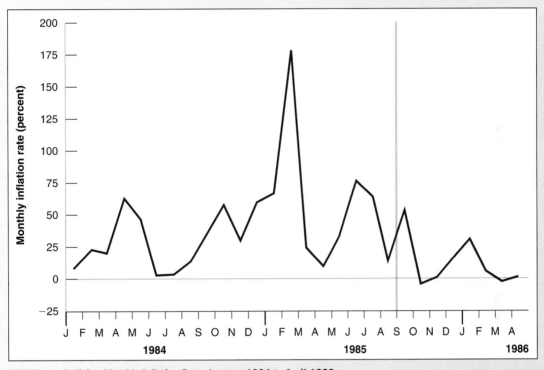

FIGURE 1   **Bolivian Monthly Inflation Rate, January 1984 to April 1986**

But the issue of credibility remains. The fact that even coherent programs may not succeed implies that no program is fully credible from the start. If, for example, the government decides to fix the exchange rate, a high interest rate initially may be needed to maintain the parity. Those programs that turn out to be successful are those in which the government maintains the program, and where increased credibility leads to lower interest rates over time. But, even in that case, the initial high interest rate often leads to a recession. Overall, the evidence is that most, but not all, hyperinflations involve some cost in output. Much of the current research focuses on how stabilization packages should be designed to reduce this cost: orthodox versus heterodox, restrictions on money growth or fixing of the exchange rate, and so on.

23-5 | Conclusions

We argued in chapter 22 that there is no unique high unemployment pathology. We characterized the Great Depression as a sharp decrease in activity followed by a long and strong recovery, and high European unemployment as a long and more insidious illness, with prospects for only a slow recovery. By contrast, this chapter shows that there is a clear hyperinflation pathology. High inflation has the feel of an intense but short-lived illness. Its causes are largely common across episodes: Hyperinflations come from the governments' inability to control their budget in the face of major shocks, economic or political. In addition, their symptoms are largely common across episodes: accelerating inflation and progressively larger real costs until stabilization is attempted and eventually achieved.

SUMMARY

- Hyperinflations are periods of high inflation. The most extreme took place after World War I and World War II in Europe. But Latin America has had episodes of high inflation as recently as the early 1990s.

- High inflation comes from high money growth. High money growth comes from the combination of large budget deficits and the inability to finance them through borrowing, either from the public or from abroad.

- The revenues from money creation are called seignorage. Seignorage is equal to the product of money growth and real money balances. The smaller real money balances, the higher the required rate of money growth, and therefore the higher the rate of inflation required to generate a given amount of seignorage.

- Hyperinflations are typically characterized by increasing inflation. There are two reasons for this. One is that higher money growth leads to higher inflation, inducing

people to reduce real money balances, requiring even higher money growth (and thus leading to even higher inflation) to finance the same real deficit. The other is that higher inflation often increases the deficit, which requires higher money growth, and even higher inflation.

- Hyperinflations are ended through stabilization programs. To be successful, stabilization programs must include fiscal measures aimed at reducing the deficit and monetary measures aimed at reducing or eliminating money creation as a source of financing for the deficit. Some stabilization plans also include wage and price guidelines or controls.

- A stabilization program that imposes wage and price controls without changes in fiscal and monetary policy will fail. But even coherent and well-conceived programs do not always succeed. Anticipation of failure may lead to failure of even a coherent plan.

KEY TERMS

- hyperinflation, 447
- debt monetization, 449
- seignorage, 449
- barter, 451
- dollarization, 452
- Laffer curve, 453

- inflation tax, 454
- Tanzi–Olivera effect, 455
- stabilization program, 456
- incomes policies, 456
- orthodox stabilization program, 457
- heterodox stabilization program, 457

QUESTIONS & PROBLEMS

An asterisk denotes a harder problem.

1. **TRUE/FALSE/UNCERTAIN**

a. In the short run, governments can finance a deficit of any size through money growth.

b. The inflation tax is always equal to seignorage.

c. Hyperinflations may distort prices, but have no effect on real output.

d. The solution to ending hyperinflations is simple: Institute a wage and price freeze, and inflation will stop.

e. As inflation is generally good for those who borrow money, hyperinflations are the best times in which to take out large loans.

f. Budget deficits usually shrink during hyperinflations.

2. SEIGNORAGE

Assume that money demand takes the following form:

$$\frac{M}{P} = Y[1 - (r + \pi^e)]$$

where $Y = 1,000$ and $r = 0.1$.

a. Assume that in the short run, π^e is constant and equal to 25%. Compute the amount of seignorage if the rate of money growth, $\Delta M/M$, equals

i. 25%.

ii. 50%.

iii. 75%.

b. In the medium run, $\pi^e = \pi = \Delta M/M$. Compute the amount of seignorage associated with the three rates of money growth in question (a). Explain why the answers differ from those in (a).

***c.** In the medium run, what is the rate of money growth that maximizes seignorage?

3. THE TANZI-OLIVERA EFFECT

How would each of the following change the Tanzi-Olivera effect?

a. Requiring monthly instead of yearly tax payments by households.

b. Assessing greater penalties for underwitholding of taxes from monthly paychecks.

c. Decreasing the income tax, and increasing the sales tax.

4. STABILIZATION

You are an economic advisor to a country suffering a hyperinflation. Discuss the following statements made by politicians debating the proper course for stabilization.

a. "This crisis will not end until workers begin to pay their fair share of taxes."

b. "The central bank has demonstrated that it cannot responsibly wield its power to create money, so we have no choice but to adopt a currency board."

c. "Price controls are necessary to end this madness."

d. "Stabilization will require a large recession and substantial increase in unemployment."

FURTHER READINGS

For more on the German hyperinflation, read Steven Webb, *Hyperinflation and Stabilization in the Weimar Republic* (New York: Oxford University Press, 1989).

Two good reviews of what economists know and don't know about hyperinflation are Rudiger Dornbusch, Federico Sturzenegger, and Holger Wolf, "Extreme Inflation: Dynamics and Stabilization," *Brookings Papers on Economic Activity*, 1990:2, 1–84, and Pierre Richard Agenor and Peter Montiel, *Development Macroeconomics* (Princeton, NJ: Princeton University Press, 1995), Chapters 8 to 11. Chapter 8 makes for easy reading; the other chapters are more difficult.

The experience of Israel, which underwent high inflation and stabilization in the 1980s, is described in Michael Bruno, *Crisis, Stabilization and Economic Reform* (New York: Oxford University Press, 1993), especially Chapters 2 to 5. Michael Bruno was the head of Israel's central bank for most of that period.

Much recent research has focused in particular on how to end hyperinflations. One of the classic articles is "The Ends of Four Big Inflations," by Thomas Sargent, in Robert Hall, ed., *Inflation: Causes and Effects* (Chicago: NBER and the University of Chicago, 1982), 41–97. In that article, Sargent argues that a credible program can lead to stabilization at little or no cost in terms of activity.

Rudiger Dornbusch and Stanley Fischer, "Stopping Hyperinflations, Past and Present," *Weltwirtschaftlichers Archiv*, 1986:1, 1–47, gives a very readable description of the end of hyperinflations in Germany, Austria, Poland, and in Italy in 1947, Israel in 1985, and Argentina in 1985.

CHAPTER 24

Pathologies III: Transition in Eastern Europe, and the Asian Crisis

We focus in this chapter on two of the major macroeconomic events of the 1990s.

The first, which started in the early 1990s and is ongoing, is the transition from central planning to a market economy in Eastern Europe. With the start of the transition came a large decline in output. Some countries have recovered and are now growing. But in others, including Russia, output is still declining, and it is not clear when the recovery will start.

The second is known as "the Asian crisis." One of the main success stories of the last quarter of the twentieth century was the high sustained growth of many Asian countries. But, in 1997, a crisis triggered a sharp recession in many of these countries. At this point, the worst appears to be over, but it is not clear if and when these countries will return to their pre-crisis growth rates.

The purpose of this chapter is twofold. First, to explain what happened, what mechanisms were at work in each case, and what the future may hold. Second, to show you how understanding these two complex events requires us to use many of the tools we have developed in earlier chapters. As you read this chapter, you will see how, to make sense of what happened, you need to combine what you learned about the short run, the medium run, and the long run in the core. In the case of Russia: the effects of budget deficits on inflation, and the role of the state in promoting growth. In the case of Asia: the mechanics of exchange rate crises, and the sources of high Asian growth.

24-1 | Transition in Eastern Europe

For most of the post–World War II period, the economies of Eastern Europe were centrally planned. The government sent production plans to firms telling them what to produce and how to produce it. Prices were determined not by the market, but by the central planner, and played little or no role in production or consumption decisions.

Starting in the 1970s, some countries—in particular, Hungary—introduced reforms aimed at giving firms incentives to produce more efficiently, sometimes allowing for a limited role for prices. But the first fundamental reform was introduced in Poland in January 1990. After winning the elections in 1989, *Solidarity*—the trade union that the communist regime had banned earlier—decided to abandon central planning and shift to a market economy. In January 1990, in what has been called an economic **big bang**, it removed controls on nearly all prices and implemented a macroeconomic stabilization plan. Since then, all the countries of Eastern Europe have moved in the same direction. Central planning is gone. What has taken its place is less clear, however, and varies from country to country.

Twelve of them, Armenia, Azerbaijan, Belarus, Georgia, Kazakhstan, Krgyzstan, Moldova, Russia, Tajikistan, Turkmenistan, Ukraine, and Uzbekistan have formed a loose alliance called the *Commonwealth of Independent States*—CIS for short. Three Baltic states (Estonia, Latvia, and Lithuania) have gone their own way.

Looking at the evolution of all the countries in transition would be too large a task: There are simply too many. Fifteen countries have emerged from the breakup of the former Soviet Union alone, each with its own transition dynamics. And transition is not limited to Eastern Europe. China and Vietnam are also moving away from central planning. Of all the countries that were centrally planned in the 1980s, only Cuba and North Korea have so far resisted the tide. To keep things manageable, I shall focus here on five countries: three Central European countries—the Czech Republic, Hungary, and Poland—and two from the former Soviet Union—Russia and Ukraine. Table 24–1 gives their basic characteristics, and where they stood in transition at the end of 1998.

Note that GDP is measured in PPP terms. See chapter 10 for a definition and a discussion.

The two columns on the left give population and GDP per capita for each country. The five countries are middle-income countries. GDP per capita in the Czech Republic, the highest in the list, is roughly the same as GDP per capita in Portugal.

The two columns on the right report on progress in two important dimensions of transition.

- The first is **price liberalization**, the degree to which prices are decontrolled and allowed to clear markets. Firms need price signals to know what to produce. The table shows that this step has been largely achieved in all countries—this is indeed a dramatic departure from central planning.

- The second is **privatization**, the transfer of state-owned firms to private owners—owners with the incentives to maximize profit and to respond to price signals. The table indicates

TABLE 24–1 Characteristics and Progress in Transition, in Five Eastern European Countries

	Population (millions)	GDP Per Capita ($ PPP)	Price Liberalization	Privatization
Czech Republic	10.3	9,770	3	4
Hungary	10.2	6,410	3+	4
Poland	38.6	5,400	3+	3+
Russia	147.5	4,480	3−	3+
Ukraine	51.8	2,400	3	2+

Note: GDP per capita numbers are for 1995. The other numbers refer to 1998. The numbers for price liberalization and privatization are indices, constructed as follows:
Price liberalization refers to restrictions on price setting by firms. 1: Most prices still controlled; 2: price controls still important; 3: comprehensive price liberalization; 4: comprehensive price liberalization and antitrust legislation in place.
Privatization refers to the privatization of large firms. 1: Little done; 2: some program in place, and some sales; 3: more than 25% of large firms privatized; 4: more than 50% of large firms privatized.
Source: *Transition Report*, European Bank for Reconstruction and Development, November 1998.

progress has been made in all countries, with the Czech Republic in the lead, and Ukraine trailing behind. (Different countries have taken different approaches to privatization. See the Global Macro box "Privatization in the Czech Republic and Russia.")

If, as is widely believed, central planning was highly inefficient, we might have expected price liberalization and privatization, and more generally the move to a market economy, to lead to rapid and large increases in output. Also, given their largely similar progress on both price liberalization and privatization, we might have expected most countries to have roughly similar evolutions. Figure 24–1 shows that we would have been wrong on both counts. The figure shows the evolution of real GDP in each of the five countries since 1989 (In each country, GDP is normalized to equal 1 in 1989.) The figure yields two clear conclusions.

- The start of transition was associated with a large decline in measured output in all countries. Note the use of "measured output" here: As we shall soon discuss, some of the decline reflects measurement problems. But much of the decline is real.
- Whereas output turned around after a few years in the three Central European countries, this has not been the case in either Russia or Ukraine. At the end of 1998, measured GDP stood at 98% of its pretransition level in the Czech Republic, at 94% in Hungary, and at 117% in Poland. In contrast, it stood at only 55% of its pretransition level in Russia, and

GLOBAL MACRO

Privatization in the Czech Republic and Russia

When transition started, most firms formally belonged to the state. One of the tasks faced by governments was to establish private ownership. In thinking about privatization, governments had various objectives. They wanted

1. To establish a fair distribution of ownership rights. After all, these firms belonged implicitly to all citizens before transition; it was fair that they belong to all of them explicitly after the transition.
2. To establish an efficient structure of ownership. Study of firms in Western economies suggests it is important that there be at least a few large owners. When a firm is owned by many small shareholders, managers are freer to do what they want, which may not always be in the owners' best interests.
3. To proceed quickly, so as not to leave the state firms in ownership limbo, which would prevent restructuring.
4. To obtain revenues from the sale of state firms, so as to make it easier to finance new spending and avoid budget deficits.

The problem with these objectives is that they are partly incompatible. For example, a fair distribution naturally leads to many small owners; an efficient structure requires a few large owners. Getting substantial revenues from privatization is inconsistent with proceeding quickly: Selling firms at a good price is complicated and requires time. The result of these conflicting objectives is that different countries took different approaches toward privatization.

The Czech Republic adopted a privatization method known as **voucher privatization**. People were given vouchers allowing them to bid for shares of state firms. They had the choice of either bidding directly or selling their vouchers to privately created investment funds, which then used the vouchers to bid for the shares. About three-quarters of the vouchers were sold to about 260 funds. Each investment fund typically has a large stake in a few firms. The hope was that as large shareholders, these funds would force managers to restructure the firms. The evidence is that this is happening, but much more slowly than was hoped.

In Russia, people were also given vouchers that they could either sell in a market for vouchers or use to bid for shares of firms. During the 20 months in which vouchers were traded, their price varied from $4 to $20. One important difference from the Czech Republic was that the government gave the firms' insiders, that is, the firms' managers and workers, a large proportion of the shares in the newly privatized firms. The reason was political: The Russian government was much weaker politically than the Czech government, and could not have passed privatization without the consent of the firms' insiders. The hope of the government was that the managers and the workers would eventually sell their shares to outsiders, and this would lead to restructuring. The fear was that the managers and workers would in fact control the firms, and be reluctant to restructure. At this time, it appears that firms are still largely controlled by insiders, and that little restructuring has taken place.

Reference

For more on privatization in Russia, see Maxim Boycko, Andrei Shleifer, and Robert Vishny, *Privatizing Russia* (Cambridge, MA: MIT Press, 1995).

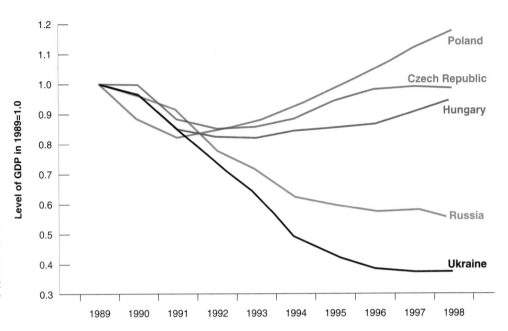

FIGURE 24-1

The Evolution of GDP in Five Eastern European Countries

Transition was associated with a large initial decrease in real GDP. Although the three Central European countries have turned around, this has not yet been the case in Russia or Ukraine.

at 37% in Ukraine. These last two numbers are amazingly low: At the trough of the Great Depression in the United States in 1933, real GDP stood at 66% of its predepression (1929) level!

This figure sets the stage for the three issues on which we focus in the rest of the section:

- By how much has output really declined?
- Why did output decline?
- Why have some countries recovered and not others?

By How Much Has Output Declined?

There are two main reasons to suspect that some of the decline in output reflects measurement error rather than a true decline:

- Some of the goods produced under central planning were practically useless. But their prices, which were set by the central planner and did not reflect the forces of demand and supply, were positive. With price liberalization, demand for these goods dropped and the production of these goods stopped. A decline in the production of useless goods clearly should not be counted as a decline in GDP; but, because these goods had (an incorrect) positive price to start, the decline in their production was registered as a decline in output.
- A large informal economy has emerged, an economy whose activity is not recorded in official statistics. Much of the growth has taken place in very small firms. Because the surveys needed to monitor the activity of small firms are only slowly being put in place, these firms' activity is underreported. And these firms are typically not eager to report their activity to official authorities because some of what they do may not be legal, and because reporting implies paying taxes, from profit taxes to social security contributions — something they would rather avoid.

One way of measuring activity may be to measure electricity consumption: Even informal activities use electricity. In Russia and Ukraine, electricity consumption has decreased less than officially measured GDP, suggesting an increase in the size of informal activity.

How important are these two sources of measurement errors? The consensus is that they account for some of the decline in measured output. In Poland, for example, estimates are that the decrease in output in 1990, the first year of transition, was closer to 7% than to 11.6%, the official estimate. And there is evidence that measurement error has played an important role, especially in the countries of the former Soviet Union. A recent study estimates that when growth in the informal economy is taken into account, the decline in Russian GDP since 1989 has been "only" 22%, compared to 45% using official numbers.

Thus, even allowing for measurement error, it appears that most countries suffered a large decline in output at the beginning of transition, and that output in Russia today is lower than it was pretransition.

Why Did Output Decline?

In the core, we saw that in the short run a decline in output can come either from adverse shifts in aggregate demand or from shifts in aggregate supply. Although there is not complete agreement, most economists believe that most of the initial decline in output was caused mostly by adverse aggregate supply shocks. More specifically, they argue that the main cause of the initial output decline was the enormous *structural change*, which was triggered by transition. They argue that one of the immediate effects of transition was to sharply decrease the demand for the goods produced by state firms. Demand shifted to new products and to new firms. But new firms, which for the most part did not exist pretransition, faced many constraints and could expand production only slowly. The net result was therefore an initial decrease in total output.

To explore this argument in more detail, we must give up an assumption we have maintained until now. When thinking about the goods markets, we assumed the economy produced only one type of good, or equivalently that there was only one sector in the economy; the reason was to avoid having to think about many goods, and about supply and demand for each good. To explore the argument, we now need to relax this assumption. We need to think of an economy with at least two sectors, one composed of state firms, and the other composed of new private firms.

Figure 24–2 provides a starting point by looking at the labor market in an economy with two sectors, sector 1 and sector 2. The real wage is measured on the vertical axis. Employment in sector 1 is measured from the origin (point O) on the horizontal axis, going from left to right. The demand for labor in sector 1 is given by the downward-sloping relation *SS* (I use the letter *S* because, later on, I shall interpret sector 1 as the state sector). For example, at wage W/P, employment in sector 1 is given by N_1. The lower the real wage, the higher the level of employment in sector 1.[1]

See chapter 7.

What follows extends the model of the labor market in chapter 6 to two sectors. Instead of one labor demand (equivalently, one price-setting relation), there are now two—one for the state sector, and one for the private sector.

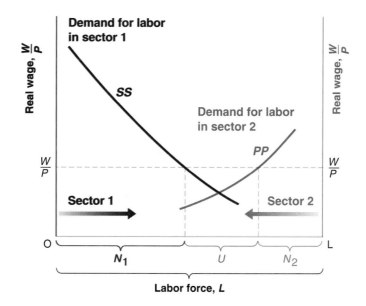

FIGURE 24–2

Employment and Unemployment in an Economy with Two Sectors

Employment in each sector is a decreasing function of the real wage.

[1] **DIGGING DEEPER.** In drawing the demand for labor in each sector as downward sloping, we implicitly assume decreasing returns to labor, so that higher employment requires a lower real wage. In chapter 6, we assumed instead constant returns to labor, so the corresponding relation was horizontal. This assumption was fine there, but we need to relax it here: As will be clear, we want to capture the notion that it may be impossible to employ all workers, even at a very low wage.

Now draw point L on the horizontal axis so that the distance OL measures the labor force. Then measure employment in sector 2 by the distance from point L, going from right to left. The demand for labor in sector 2 is given by PP (I use the letter P because, later on, I shall interpret sector 2 as the private sector). It is also downward sloping—as we go from right to left. The lower the real wage, the higher the level of employment in sector 2. For example, at wage W/P, employment in sector 2 is given by N_2.

Now assume the real wage is the same in both sectors and is W/P in Figure 24–2. Then, employment in sector 1 is equal to N_1, employment in sector 2 is equal to N_2. Because the labor force is given by L, unemployment is given by $U = L - N_1 - N_2$.

Let's now apply this framework to the transition. Before transition started, most of the employment was in the state sector, the sector composed of the large firms producing under the central plan. The private sector was small, and unemployment was officially equal to

Despite the official num-▶ zero. This initial position is captured in Figure 24–3. Think now of sector 1 as the state sec-
bers, there was some un- tor. Think of sector 2 as the private sector. SS gives the demand for labor in the state sector;
employment, but it was PP gives the demand for labor in the private sector. The real wage is W/P. At that wage, em-
quite small. ployment in the state sector is equal to N_S, employment in the private sector is equal to N_P, unemployment is equal to zero.

The initial effect of transition was to sharply reduce the demand for labor in the state sector and to increase it in the private sector. The net effect was a decrease in employment and output, and an increase in unemployment. Let's examine each of these effects.

- Many state firms experienced sharp decreases in demand. With price liberalization, many of the goods they produced were no longer in demand. With the decline in defense spending, there was a sharp drop in the demand for defense-related goods, an effect particularly important in the former Soviet Union. Trade arrangements among centrally planned economies collapsed in 1991, leading many state firms to lose their Eastern European export markets. There were other effects as well, which can be thought of as the effects of *disorganization*: Many state firms, which had relied on the central planner to provide them with intermediate inputs and to find buyers for their products, did not know how to operate in a market economy, where to find their inputs, or how to sell their products. In effect, this disorganization made them less productive. The result of all these changes was a large adverse shift in the demand for labor by state firms; this is represented as a shift to the left, from SS to SS' in Figure 24–4.
- Why the demand for goods produced by state firms decreased is no great mystery. But why didn't demand shift to goods produced by the new private sector, leading to an increase in private employment sufficient to offset the decrease in state employment? The answer is that the private sector could not grow fast enough.

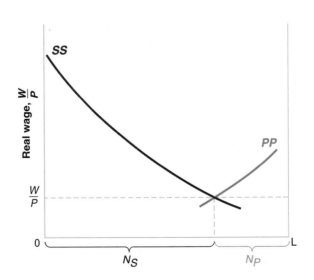

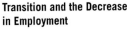

Transition and the Decrease in Employment

Transition led initially to a large decrease in the demand for labor in the state sector, and to a smaller increase in the demand for labor in the private sector. As a result, unemployment increased.

Some services, such as small-scale retail trade, can be provided with little or no capital and little expertise. These grew very quickly. But production of new goods typically requires capital and expertise, and both were absent at the beginning of transition. Because the banking system also lacked the expertise to make loans, and because would-be entrepreneurs had no past credit record to be assessed, they could not obtain credit to buy new capital. Because entrepreneurial skills were not useful under central planning, most would-be entrepreneurs lacked the knowledge and the skills needed to create and run new firms. As a result, the increase in employment in the private sector was insufficient to offset the decrease in employment in the state sector.

In terms of Figure 24–4, there was an increase in the demand for labor from the private sector, a shift to the left from *PP* to *PP'*. But, at a given real wage W/P, the net effect of the shifts in *SS* and *PP* was to decrease total employment and, by implication, total output. Thus, the initial effect of the transition was to increase unemployment from zero to *U'*.

Why didn't wages decrease enough to maintain the high level of employment? The first answer is that in fact, real wages did decrease in most countries at the beginning of transition. The second answer is that even if wages had decreased much more, there probably would still have been unemployment. This is the case in Figure 24–4: As I have drawn it, the economy still would have some unemployment even at zero wages.

Why Have Some Countries Recovered and Not Others?

We have focused so far on the initial phase of transition. After the initial output decline, the hope was that the transition economies would start recovering: The new private sector would expand. As state firms were privatized, they would restructure and start expanding as well. This is what has happened in many of the Central European countries. But further east, including Russia and Ukraine, output has continued to decline, and recovery is not yet in sight. Let's explore why.

The Czech Republic, Hungary, and Poland. What has happened in Central European countries, such as the Czech Republic, Hungary and Poland, is captured in Figure 24–5.

- The demand for labor in the new private sector has steadily increased, leading to a steady shift of *PP* to the left.
- Most state firms have been privatized. Some have started to restructure. Restructuring has complex effects on employment: Initially, it may lead to plant closings and a further decrease in employment. But it also allows firms first to survive and then to grow: Eventually, *SS* shifts to the right. There is some evidence that such a shift has started in some Central European countries.

Within a few weeks of the start of economic reform in Poland in January 1990, thousands of farmers and other small-scale vendors were selling their goods directly to consumers on the sidewalks of the capital, Warsaw.

Warning: These issues are controversial. It is also fair to point out that economists predicted neither the size of the initial output decline, nor the differences in the size of the decline across countries.

FIGURE 24-5

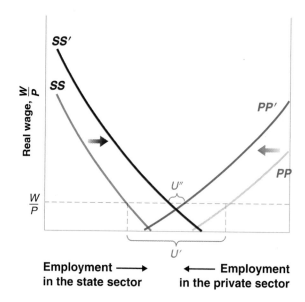

Transition in Central Europe: The Recovery

Private sector employment has increased. State sector employment has increased, although by less. Unemployment has decreased.

Although output growth was positive in Poland in 1992 and 1993 (2.6% in 1992, 3.8% in 1993), labor productivity growth was larger than output growth, implying negative employment growth, and an increase in unemployment.

Together, the shifts in *SS* and *PP* have led to an increase in output and a decrease in unemployment, from *U'* to *U'''*. In Poland, output growth turned positive in 1992, and has averaged 5.6% a year since 1992. The unemployment rate, which had been roughly equal to zero before transition, peaked at 16% in 1994, and has decreased since. In 1998, it stood at just under 10%. The growth performance of the Czech Republic and Hungary has been less impressive; output in both countries started growing from 1994, but, at the end of 1998, (measured) output was still slightly below its pretransition level.

Why aren't Central European countries growing faster? There are two main constraints at work:

● One is still the lack of domestic expertise in most aspects of business. In principle, this constraint could be offset by **foreign direct investment (FDI)**, the purchase of existing firms or the development of new plants by foreign firms. Foreign firms can bring in the experience and the capital that are lacking domestically. Because Central Europe is geographically close to Western markets, because it has a highly educated labor force and low wages compared to OECD countries, one would have expected foreign firms, especially Western European firms, to invest and create new plants at a very fast pace in Central Europe. This has been relatively more the case in Hungary, where foreign direct investment was 5% of GDP in 1997. In Poland and the Czech Republic, however, even though foreign investment has increased since the beginning of transition, it remains quite small, around 2% of GDP.

To get some perspective on this, in 1996, foreign direct investment in all of Central and Eastern Europe (400 million people) was roughly equal to foreign direct investment in Mexico (100 million people).

● Another constraint is that before they can expand production and employment, most state firms need to undergo drastic restructuring. And restructuring so far has been slow for three reasons.

Privatization is necessary but not sufficient for restructuring: If a firm is owned by many small shareholders, they may not be organized enough to replace an incompetent manager, or to force the manager to restructure. For more on this issue, see the Global Macro box "Privatization in the Czech Republic and Russia."

First, restructuring involves large amounts of capital: Many plants are technologically obsolete and need to be replaced altogether.

Second, restructuring typically involves an initial further decrease in employment: Some plants must be shut down, and some workers must be laid off. The prospect of layoffs has often led to strong opposition by workers, who, given the often high unemployment rate, care very much about job security. In Poland, for example, these concerns led to a very slow pace of privatization until the mid-1990s.

Third, restructuring requires that someone in the firm have both strong incentives and the authority to do it. But in many countries, privatization has proceeded slowly, and in many firms—privatized or still in state hands—no one is yet in a position to make and implement such decisions.

For all these reasons, it will take many years—probably a few decades—before even the more successful transition countries achieve a standard of living comparable to those of the average OECD country.

Russia and Ukraine. As we saw in Figure 24–1, things have been much worse in Russia and Ukraine. I shall concentrate on Russia in what follows, but similar explanations apply to Ukraine and other former Soviet Union countries.

The private sector has not grown (at least the formal private sector; we mentioned earlier that informal activity appears to have increased substantially). The state firms have not been restructured; both their output and their employment have steadily declined. Except for 1997 when GDP growth was positive (and small), GDP growth has been consistently negative in Russia since the beginning of transition. Why have things been so bad? There are many factors at work, but most economists agree that they can be traced to the same source, namely the weakness of the Russian state in the transition.

The state has been unable to define and to enforce *property rights*. An entrepreneur thinking about creating a new firm, or an investor thinking of investing in a project, wants to make sure that she will be able to get and keep the profits from the investment. If the laws are unclear, or if the application of the law is poor, she may well decide not to invest: How can she be sure that her suppliers will honor their contracts and deliver the required inputs at the agreed upon price? How can she be sure that the buyers of the goods she produces will pay on time, or even pay at all? If the officials in charge of applying the law are corrupt, or if Mafia-like organizations dominate economic activity, investment will also come to a stop: Why invest, if bribes to corrupt officials or side payments to the Mafia eliminate profits in the end? All these problems have been present in Russia. As a result, investment as a proportion of GDP has fallen dramatically. And in 1996, foreign direct investment was less than 1% of GDP.

> What follows is an example of the importance of property rights for growth, an issue discussed in section 12-4.

The state has also been unable or unwilling to eliminate transfers to state firms, even after they were privatized. Under central planning, state firms traditionally relied on subsidies when they were making losses. This is what Janos Kornai, a Hungarian economist and a long-time advocate of economic reform in centrally planned economies, called the **soft budget constraint**. Part of the transition requires convincing these firms that the budget constraint is now *hard*, that they will no longer get subsidies from the state to cover their losses. This has been achieved—often with difficulty—in most Central European countries. It has not been achieved in Russia. This is shown in Table 24–2.

The first line in Table 24–2 shows official subsidies to firms as a proportion of GDP since 1992. Just looking at subsidies, there would appear to have been much progress: Official subsidies, which were running at more than 10% of GDP in 1992, have substantially decreased. But the second line, which gives the evolution of **tax arrears** (unpaid taxes by firms), gives a more accurate picture of what has happened. More and more firms have stopped paying the taxes they owe the state. Tax arrears were equal to more than 10% at the end of 1996 (the last year for which we have the official number), and the evidence suggests that the problem has grown worse since. This increase in tax arrears, and more generally the

TABLE 24–2	Subsidies to Firms, Tax Arrears, Budget Deficits, and Inflation in Russia, 1992–1998						
	1992	**1993**	**1994**	**1995**	**1996**	**1997**	**1998**
Subsidies (% of GDP)	10.4	3.0	1.8	1.3	—	—	—
Tax arrears (% of GDP)	—	1.7	2.5	3.5	10.0	—	—
Budget deficit (% of GDP)	−21.6	−7.4	−10.4	−5.7	−8.2	−7.5	−9.0
Inflation (% per year)	2,506	840	204	128	22	11	190

Source: Transition Report, EBRD, November 1997 and April 1998; Economics of Transition, November 1998.

inability of the government to impose a hard budget constraint on firms, has had two main macroeconomic implications:

- It has decreased the incentives of firms to restructure. Rather than trying to make profits, managers in many firms have focused instead on obtaining transfers, implicit or explicit, from the state. Most firms are still producing mediocre goods with obsolete capital, and their output is still declining.
- The lack of revenues has led to a large budget deficit. This is shown in the third line of Table 24–2. The budget deficit, which reached 21.6% of GDP in 1992, was reduced to 5.7% of GDP in 1995, but increased again thereafter. In 1998, it stood at 9% of GDP.

Recall that a budget deficit can be financed either by bonds or by money creation. Only to the extent that it is financed by money creation will it lead to high money growth and high inflation.

We saw in chapter 23 how large budget deficits can lead to high inflation. Russia provides the most recent example of this proposition. Note first (from the last line in the table) that inflation, which had run at over 2,500% a year in 1992, decreased to a very low 11% in 1997. How was such a dramatic reduction achieved, given that the deficits remained so large? The answer is that starting in 1994, the Russian government decided to finance its deficit by issuing bonds rather than by printing money. Given the obvious risk that it would be unable to repay the bonds, the Russian government was able to sell these bonds only by paying an extremely high rate of interest, further increasing the deficit.

See section 21-2 on exchange rate crises. Investors will hold domestic bonds only if they expect to earn the same return on domestic and foreign bonds. If they expect the domestic government will not pay the interest it has promised on the bonds, they will want to sell the bonds and get out of the domestic currency, triggering an exchange rate crisis.

In August 1998, it became clear to the foreign creditors that sooner or later the Russian government would not be able to repay. This triggered an exchange rate crisis. To maintain the exchange rate, the Russian government would have had to increase interest rates to levels it simply could not afford. It decided instead to let the ruble float and to suspend payment on the bonds. Within a few days, the ruble went from 6 to 9 rubles per dollar, a 50% depreciation. This was followed by a long political crisis, and the eventual appointment of a new prime minister. This appointment, however, has not solved the problem. As of early 1999, most economists believe that the budget deficit will remain high for some time, and the Russian government will finance part of it through money creation. Most of the forecasts are for a period of higher inflation, until the high inflation triggers a successful stabilization plan.

When will Russia turn itself around? It is clear that the solution to the current crisis implies raising government revenues and balancing the budget. But our discussion makes clear that raising revenues is not simply a matter of raising tax rates. If firms already do not pay the taxes they owe, raising tax rates will do nothing. The government must find ways to make firms pay taxes. More generally, it must find ways to make state firms live within their budget constraint, to improve property rights, to limit corruption of state officials, and to enforce the laws. This is a tall order for any government to take on, and this is why most observers do not expect fast growth in Russia any time soon.[2]

24-2 | The Asian Crisis

For economists studying growth, much of the focus for the last quarter of the twentieth century was on the **Asian miracle**—the very high and sustained growth achieved in many Asian countries. In 1997 however, the Asian miracle gave way, in a number of these countries, to the **Asian crisis**, a sharp shift from high growth to a deep recession.

See "The Secrets of Growth" in section 12-4.

Table 24–3 tells the basic story for the four countries most affected by the crisis, Indonesia, Malaysia, Korea, and Thailand. The growth rate, which had averaged around 7% a year in all four countries from 1970 to 1996, turned small and negative in Thailand in

---

[2]**DIGGING DEEPER.** Why have governments acted so differently in Central Europe, and in Russia or Ukraine? This is a difficult question. Here are some tentative answers. (1) While reformers were democratically elected in Central Europe, reform was largely imposed from the top in Russia, and pushed by a small group of reformers. (2) Russia, in contrast to Central Europe, never had a market economy, and was under communism for more than 70 years. (3) The managers of the firms were more powerful in Russia than in Central Europe from the start. (4) Policy mistakes were made in Russia along the way.

TABLE 24–3	Output Growth in East Asian Countries, 1970–1998		
	1970–1996	**1997**	**1998**
Indonesia	6.8	4.7	−15.5
Malaysia	7.4	7.8	−4.7
Korea	8.4	5.5	−6.5
Thailand	7.5	−0.4	−7.0

Growth rate: annual rate of growth of GDP (in percent).
Source: *OECD Economic Outlook*, December 1998.

1997, and large and negative in all four countries in 1998. Most forecasts are for a return to positive growth in 1999 or 2000. But nobody is predicting whether and when these countries will be able to return to the high growth rates of the past.

What triggered the Asian crisis? The immediate cause is an exchange rate crisis. The first country to be attacked was Thailand in July 1997. The Thai government did what most governments do in this case: It first increased the interest rate, and promised to defend the parity at any cost. It then concluded that the cost was too high and gave up, allowing for a large depreciation of the baht (the Thai currency). Within a few months, the same scenario was repeated in Korea, in Indonesia, and in Malaysia. Figure 24–6 shows the behavior of the exchange rate vis-à-vis the dollar in the four countries from January 1997 to December 1998. (The exchange rates are plotted from the point of view of the United States—that is, Asian currency in terms of dollars. A depreciation of an Asian currency corresponds to a decline of the exchange rate on the graph.) In July 1998, the Thai baht, the Korean won, and the Malaysian ringgit were down to 60% of their January 1997 levels, and the Indonesian rupiah was down to 15%. Since then, exchange rates have recovered slightly.

These events raise two sets of questions:

- Why was there an exchange rate crisis? Why then? Why in countries that until then had been taken as role models by other low- and middle-income countries?
- Why has the crisis had such a dramatic effect on output? One might have guessed that such large depreciations might lead to a boom in exports and a boom in output. So why was there such a sharp recession?

> Recall the discussion of exchange rate crises in section 21-2.

> That a real depreciation leads (if the Marshall–Lerner condition holds) to an improvement in the trade balance and an increase in output was one of the main conclusions of chapter 19.

FIGURE 24–6

The Evolution of Exchange Rates: Indonesia, Malaysia, Thailand, and Korea, January 1997 to December 1998

In 1997 and early 1998, all four currencies suffered large depreciations. Since then, exchange rates have recovered slightly.

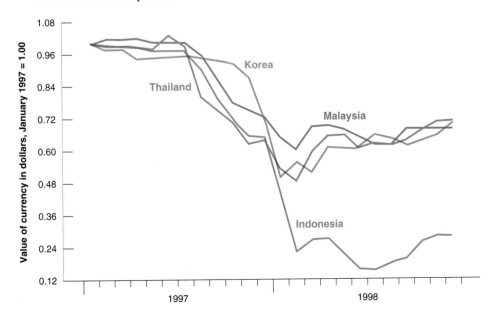

Why the Crisis?

The Asian crisis was not predicted. With the benefit of hindsight, was it predictable? Even after the fact, and despite an enormous amount of research, there is little agreement on the answer. Some economists argue that the crisis was predictable, that these Asian economies were suffering from serious problems that sooner or later would have led to a crisis. In other words, they point to *fundamentals* as the ultimate source of the crisis. Others argue that the crisis was instead largely a case of *self-fulfilling expectations*: If the foreign investors had not panicked, there would have been no crisis, and no reason to panic in the first place. Let's look at these two positions.

Recall our discussion of self fulfilling exchange rate crises in section 21-2.

The Case for Fundamentals. For many years before the crisis, the four countries had run both large trade and current account deficits. The numbers for 1996 are shown in Table 24–4. In 1996, three of the four countries had a large trade deficit. And all four had a current account deficit, ranging from 3.3% of GDP in Indonesia to 8.5% of GDP in Thailand.

From chapter 18: The current account deficit equals the trade deficit plus net income payments to the rest of the world. That the current account deficit exceeded the trade deficit in all four countries in 1996 means that each country was, on net, paying interest to the rest of the world: Each country was a net debtor, having borrowed in the past to finance current account deficits.

Large trade or current account deficits are often danger signals, indicating the need for macroeconomic adjustment, possibly including a depreciation. Until the crisis, the Asian trade deficits were not seen however as a problem but as a sign of strength. To understand why, we must return to the identity relating the trade balance, investment, saving, and the budget surplus we saw in chapter 19

$$NX = S + (T - G) - I$$

The trade balance (NX) equals total saving—private (S) plus public ($T - G$)—minus investment (I). Thus, a trade deficit (a negative value of NX) can have three underlying causes:

- Low private saving (a low value of S)
- Government dissaving—or equivalently, a budget deficit—(a negative value of $T - G$)
- High investment (a high value of I)

Whether one should worry about a large trade deficit depends on where it comes from. If consumers or the government go on a spending binge (high consumption given income, and thus low S, or a negative value of $T - G$), there are good reasons to worry: How will they repay in the future? But if the trade deficit reflects a high level of investment, then there may be no reason to worry: High investment means high output in the future and thus the ability to repay in the future.

Here is an analogy: You may be willing to lend to a firm if the funds are used to buy a machine. You may be more reluctant to do so if the funds are used to finance a new office for the company's boss.

Table 24–4 shows that this last case was clearly the relevant one for all four countries. In 1996, the ratio of investment to GDP ranged from 30.8% for Indonesia to 41.7% for Thailand. (By way of comparison, the ratio of investment to GDP in the United States in 1996 was 15%.) Also, in all four countries the government was running a budget surplus. This means the proximate source of the trade deficits was high investment, not low saving.

Those who argue that the crisis was due to a problem with fundamentals do not question these facts. But they argue that these high investment rates were in fact not the good news

TABLE 24–4	Trade, Current Account, Investment Rates, and Budget Balances: Indonesia, Korea, Malaysia, and Thailand, 1996 (percent of GDP)			
	Indonesia	**Korea**	**Malaysia**	**Thailand**
Trade balance	−1.1	−4.4	0.5	−6.6
Current account balance	−3.3	−4.8	−3.7	−8.5
Investment rate	30.8	38.4	41.5	41.7
Budget balance	1.2	0.4	0.7	0.9

Source: Giancarlo Corsetti, Paolo Pesenti and Nouriel Roubini, "What Caused the Asian Currency and Financial Crisis?" mimeo, September 1998, New York University.

most observers thought they were at the time. To understand their argument, we must return to the analysis of the long run we developed in the core.

See section 12-1 on growth and technological progress.

In chapter 12, we saw that what determines the rate of growth of a country in the long run is its rate of technological progress. But we also saw that a country can grow faster for some time if it is willing to invest a larger and larger proportion of its output. The intuition is simplest in the case where technological progress is zero. A country where there is no technological progress cannot sustain positive growth forever. But it can sustain it for a while, by increasing the capital used by each worker. As increasing capital per worker requires investing an ever increasing share of output, growth must eventually come to an end.

Some economists believe that this is what hides behind the high Asian growth rate in the last 25 years. They argue that the "Asian miracle" reflects in large part very high rates of investment, and that the high growth rate was doomed. They also argue that while investments were becoming increasingly questionable, foreign investors were still willing to invest because they felt that the governments would bail them out if the investments turned sour. Under this argument, what happened in 1997 is that foreign investors opened their eyes, realized the problems facing these Asian countries, realized that governments might not bail them out, and decided to get out. Fundamentals caused the crisis.

The Case for Self-Fulfilling Expectations. Many economists are skeptical that the argument we just presented can fully explain what happened. They point out that standard decompositions of growth between the role of capital accumulation and technological progress point to continuing high technological progress in many Asian countries. More generally, they point out that all countries, including highly successful ones, have many flaws and problems, and that it is too easy to find culprits after any crisis.

They suggest that the crisis was instead a case of self-fulfilling expectations. They point to two features of foreign lending in Asia that increased the likelihood of such a self-fulfilling crisis. First, foreign lending was in large part short-term lending. Second, foreign lending was largely lending to banks, rather than directly to firms or to the government.

Here is how perceptions can change: Before the crisis, the tight relations between banks and firms in Asia were often cited as one of the factors behind high growth. This tight relation and the exchange of information that came with it, the argument went, allowed firms to get the funds they needed. Since the crisis, the very same relations have been condemned as "crony capitalism"—too-friendly relations between lenders and borrowers, that have led to bad loans and misbehavior.

Before we present the logic of the argument, Table 24−5 gives the basic facts. In 1996, 78% of the Korean debt vis-à-vis the rest of the world was debt owed by Korean banks to foreign investors. And 50% of debt vis-à-vis the rest of the world was short-term debt, debt that borrowers might have to repay on short notice. The corresponding numbers were high for the other three countries as well.

The implication of these two characteristics of foreign debt—bank debt, and short term dept—is that when the foreign creditors panicked, the result was not one but two runs, one on banks, and the other on the currency.

Recall the description of bank runs in chapter 4. Banks borrow short term (their liabilities are often *demand deposits*), and use the funds to make loans to firms. Even when all the loans are sound and will eventually be repaid, if all depositors want their funds at once, the bank will be unable to comply: Firms cannot repay their loans right away. Thus, if some

Look at the Focus box "Bank Runs" in chapter 4.

TABLE 24−5	Foreign Debt and Its Composition: Indonesia, Korea, Malaysia, Thailand, 1996			
	Indonesia	Korea	Malaysia	Thailand
Foreign debt (as % of GDP)	56	28	40	50
Banks' debt (as % of total debt)	40	78	73	85
Short-term debt (as % of total debt)	25	50	27	41
Short-term debt (as % of reserves)	176	203	41	99

Source: Giancarlo Corsetti, Paolo Pesenti and Nouriel Roubini, "What Caused the Asian Currency and Financial Crisis?" mimeo, September 1998, New York University.

depositors want their funds back, it is rational for other depositors to worry and try to get their funds back as well, leading to a bank run.

Now go back to the Asian crisis. Suppose that even if all short-term foreign creditors had decided to get their funds out of Asian banks and back into dollars, banks had been able to call back their loans to firms, and the central bank had had enough foreign reserves to sell dollars against domestic currency to any foreign lender who wanted out. Then there would have been no justification for a run. The foreign creditors who wanted out would have been able to get their funds back from banks and to sell the domestic currency for dollars. Other creditors would have stayed in.

But, for the reasons we discussed earlier, banks could not pay back all their short-term foreign creditors at once. And the central bank did not have enough reserves to sell dollars against foreign currency to all foreign short-term creditors. Very few governments have such large reserves. As the last line of Table 24–5 shows for both Indonesia and Korea, short-term debt was about twice as large as reserves.

The stage was then set for runs both on the domestic banks and on the currency. And this is exactly what happened. Foreign creditors tried to get their funds out of banks, leading to a bank run, and a banking crisis. And as they tried to get out of domestic currency, they triggered an exchange rate crisis as well. After a while, the government had no choice but to give up defending the parity, and let the currency depreciate, often, as we saw earlier, by a large amount. This made things worse for banks. As they had borrowed in dollars, a depreciation implied a further increase in liabilities in terms of domestic currency, worsening the bank crisis, leading more foreign creditors to want their funds back, leading to further depreciation, and so on. By creating a bank crisis as well as an exchange crisis, the decision of foreign creditors to get out was much more destructive than it would have been absent a banking crisis. The result was an economic crisis, which, after the fact, largely justified the fears of foreign creditors in the first place.

Which interpretation of the crisis is right? As is often the case, the right answer is probably both. There were increasing problems in several countries, so foreign creditors were right to start worrying. But there is little question that once some of them decided to take their funds out, the result was both a bank run and an exchange rate crisis, leading to a much worse outcome than was justified by fundamentals alone.

Why Did the Exchange Rate Crisis Lead to a Recession?

Why did the exchange rate crisis cause such a sharp decrease in output in all four countries in 1998? After all, based on what we saw in chapter 19, we would have expected the large depreciation that the countries experienced to lead to an increase in the demand for domestic goods, and an increase in output. Why did the opposite happen?

One reason is that before governments gave up on the parity, they tried to defend it by increasing interest rates, often to very high levels. Although these high interest rates turned out not to be sufficient to maintain the parity, they were more than sufficient to have a large negative effect on investment, leading to a sharp contraction in output.

Now that the exchange rate crisis is over, most governments have decreased interest rates to much lower levels. One would therefore expect the adverse effect of high interest rates to gradually disappear, and the positive effect of the large depreciation to gradually dominate, leading to a turnaround in output. This is indeed what happened during the previous major exchange rate crisis of the 1990s, the Mexican crisis of 1994: A sharp recession in 1995 was followed by sustained growth thereafter. (See the Global Macro box "The Mexican Crisis of 1994.")

We can hope that the same mechanisms will be at work in Asia. There is, however, at least one reason to worry that the recession may last longer than it did in Mexico. As we saw earlier, Asia has experienced not only an exchange rate crisis, but also a financial crisis. Many banks are bankrupt, and unable to make new loans. This implies that many firms are unable to borrow. One surprising fact is that the volume of exports from these Asian coun-

In contrast to a standard bank run, the liabilities of Asian banks to foreigners were not demand deposits, but short-term loans. As these short-term loans became due, foreign investors did not renew them, asking instead for payment of both principal and interest. Banks were unable to comply, leading other investors to question whether they would themselves be paid, thus leading them not to renew their loans, and so on.

See the Focus box "Money versus Bank Credit" in chapter 22, for a discussion of the same mechanism during the Great Depression in the United States.

tries has not increased in 1998 as much as one would have predicted based on the large depreciations. One hypothesis is that some exporters have not been able to expand production. Doing so would have required adding capital and borrowing—something they could not do. Thus, in the spring of 1999, most forecasts are that it may take some time for the countries to repair the damage done by the crisis, and that their recession may last longer than Mexico's.

What Are the Lessons from the Asian Crisis?

Every crisis leads to a reexamination of the way the economy works, and to proposals for change. The Asian crisis is no exception. It has led to two intense debates:

- The pros and cons of **capital controls**. If the foreign debt of Asian countries had been primarily long-term rather than short-term debt, the potential for a bank run and an exchange

The Mexican Crisis of 1994

In the second half of the 1980s, Mexico embarked on both macroeconomic stabilization and economic reform. One of the elements of the program was the reduction of inflation. After a successful reduction of the inflation rate from 159% in 1987 to about 20% in 1991, the Mexican government decided to maintain a roughly constant exchange rate of the peso vis-à-vis the dollar. This decision proved to be one of the causes of the peso crisis of December 1994.

Although the nominal exchange rate vis-à-vis the dollar was approximately constant from 1990 on, inflation in Mexico remained substantially higher than in the United States. The result was a substantial real appreciation of the peso: This is shown in Table 1, which gives the nominal and the real exchange rates between Mexico and the United States for 1990 to 1994. By 1994, Mexican goods were 22% more expensive relative to U.S. goods than they had been five years earlier. The effect of this real appreciation was, unsurprisingly, a large trade deficit. As Table 1 shows, the Mexican trade deficit reached 7.2% of GDP by 1994.

During 1994, it became increasingly clear to many economists and to foreign investors that overvaluation of the peso was becoming a serious issue, and that a devaluation probably could not be avoided. In December, fear of a devaluation led to large capital outflows. Mexico tried to maintain the parity by increasing interest rates. But it was too late. The peso had to be devalued by 50% in December 1994. One year later, in December 1995, the peso stood at 7.75 pesos to the dollar, compared to 3.45 pesos in November 1994. The reason the depreciation was so large is that, as in the case of the Asian crisis, many foreign investors decided to get out of the country altogether. Those who stayed required high interest rates. Short-term nominal interest rates in 1995 averaged 60%; with inflation running at 30%, these implied high real interest rates.

In 1994 and 1995, the Mexican economy was thus subject to two strong shocks, each with opposite effects on output. First, the peso devaluation, leading to an increase in competitiveness and an increase in demand for domestic goods. Second, the large increase in real interest rates, leading to a decrease in demand. The net effect was a decline in GDP of 6.3% in 1995. Since 1996, however, real interest rates have been lower, and the real depreciation has led to a boom in exports and a boom in output. Output growth was 5.1% in 1996 and 6.9% in 1997. The crisis is now mostly a bad memory. The question is whether the same scenario will play out in Asia.

TABLE 1	Nominal and real exchange rates between Mexico and the United States, 1990–1994				
	1990	**1991**	**1992**	**1993**	**1994**
Nominal exchange rate (E)	2.81	3.01	3.09	3.11	3.37
U.S. price level (P^*)	100.0	100.2	100.8	102.3	103.6
Mexican price level (P)	100.0	120.5	136.7	148.8	158.9
Real exchange rate (EP^*/P)	100.0	89.0	80.0	78.0	78.0
Mexican trade balance/GDP (%)	−1.8	−3.8	−6.4	−5.4	−7.2

Nominal exchange rate: dollar in terms of pesos. The U.S. and Mexican price levels are producer price indexes, equal to 100 in 1990. The real exchange rate is normalized to 100 in 1990. Minus signs in the last line denote a trade deficit.

rate crisis would have been more limited, and there may have been no crisis. This has prompted calls for restrictions on short-term foreign debt, making it costly for foreign creditors to lend short term, and for domestic borrowers to borrow short term from foreigners. Many economists agree that the case for restrictions on short-term foreign lending has some merits; most believe, however, that such restrictions may be hard to implement in practice.

- The role of the International Monetary Fund—the IMF. During the crisis, the IMF played two major roles. First, it helped the countries design a macroeconomic package, with both short-run measures as well as structural reforms. Second, and conditional upon adoption of the package, it lent funds to the countries to allow them to defend the exchange rate or to limit the depreciation of their currency. Both roles have been heavily criticized. Some have argued that the specific policy package it asked countries to adopt was wrong. Some

GLOBAL MACRO

What Should Be The Role of the IMF?

During the Asian crisis, the IMF played two major roles:

- It asked the countries under attack to take measures aimed at fighting the crisis and improving the economy. Based on its experience in previous crises, it asked for an increase in interest rates and a fiscal contraction. It also asked for several structural reforms, ranging from deregulation, to fighting corruption, to bank reform, to trade reform.

- Conditional upon adoption of these measures, it lent funds to help the countries limit the depreciation of their currency. The total amounts were very large, around 100 billion dollars for the four countries at which we have looked.

The logic behind both roles was, on the one hand, to reassure investors that the right policies were being implemented, and on the other to provide funds to allow the countries to go through the crisis without too much damage. This strategy has come under heavy criticism.

Some of the criticisms have been aimed at the specifics of the package. Wouldn't it have been wiser not to increase interest rates so much and let the exchange rate depreciate sooner? Why ask countries that already had a fiscal surplus to embark on further fiscal contraction? This may have been the right measure in other crises, but was not obviously the right one in this case.

Some of the criticisms have been about the role of the IMF in general:

- Some have questioned the length of the list of reforms. If the purpose of the reforms was to reassure foreign investors, was such a long list really needed? Wasn't the IMF trying to use the crisis to impose a larger agenda on Asian countries? And if so, should this really be its role?

- Some have argued that if the purpose was to avoid runs, the IMF actually should have made more funds available to Asian countries. Although the funds were large, they were not available instantaneously to the

countries, and they were typically not large enough to pay short-term foreign creditors if they all decided to leave. The IMF, the argument goes, should have made enough funds available to avoid the possibility of runs.

- Some have argued instead that the IMF should not have been involved in lending to these countries, and, more generally, should not be involved in lending large sums to countries in trouble. The sums that the IMF would need to lend are too large to be feasible. Instead, the IMF, the argument goes, should be involved in coordinating the foreign creditors. If a potential run is the problem, convincing creditors to shift from short-term debt to longer-term debt is the solution. If a country is unable to pay foreign creditors, then the IMF could play the role that bankruptcy courts play domestically: helping creditors to reach an agreement among themselves and with the debtor country.

Critics of the IMF clearly raise the right questions. But the answers are far from clear cut. What is the minimal list of reforms that will convince foreign investors to stay? We do not know. When an exchange rate crisis starts, is there enough time to coordinate creditors? Isn't it essential to have an institution such as the IMF in a position to make funds available quickly to a country in trouble? If the IMF did not use its own funds, what incentives would it have to make sure that reforms are implemented? The discussion will surely continue.

References

For two prominent critiques of the role of the IMF, read Martin Feldstein, "Reforming the IMF," *Foreign Affairs*, March/April 1998, and Steven Radelet and Jeffrey Sachs, "The East Asian Crisis: Diagnosis, Remedies, and Prospects," *Brookings Papers on Economic Activity*, 1998:1, 1–90. For a defense of the IMF, read Stanley Fischer, "Lessons From a Crisis," *The Economist*, October 3, 1998.

have argued that the list of structural reforms it asked for was far too long. Some have argued that the IMF should have lent more, others that it should have lent less. These criticisms are discussed in the Global Macro box, "What Should Be the Role of the IMF?"

SUMMARY

Transition in Eastern Europe

- Most countries that operated under central planning have moved toward becoming market economies. The first to break away from central planning was Poland in 1990, followed by the other countries of Eastern Europe.

- Transition was associated in all countries with a large decrease in output. The state sector suffered a large decline in output. Growth in the new private sector was hampered by many factors, in particular a lack of capital, a poorly functioning banking system, and a lack of expertise and experience.

- Several countries, especially those in Central Europe, have turned around, and are now growing. The private sector is growing fast. State firms have been largely privatized, and are slowly being restructured.

- Other countries, including Russia, are still doing poorly. Even when they have been privatized, ex-state firms rely on transfers from the state. They have not restructured, and their output and employment are still declining. Poorly protected property rights are slowing down private sector growth.

- The lack of tax revenues has led to a large budget deficit in Russia. This deficit has triggered high levels

of money creation, and many economists forecast high inflation in the near future.

The Asian Crisis

- In 1997, several Asian countries went from high growth rates to a deep recession. The immediate cause was an exchange rate crisis. Economists disagree about the causes of the crisis:

- Some believe that the crisis had fundamental causes. They argue that high Asian growth was increasingly sustained through very high investment rates, and was coming to an end. The realization by foreign investors that this was the case triggered the crisis.

- Others believe that the crisis was largely a case of self fulfilling expectations. They point out that a large proportion of foreign debt was bank debt and short-term debt. Both characteristics allowed for the possibility of bank and exchange rate runs. Both happened in 1997.

- High interest rates and the banking crisis have both led to a sharp output decline. The depreciation should now lead to an increase in demand and in output. It is not clear whether and when these countries will return to the high growth rates of the past.

KEY TERMS

- big bang, 464
- price liberalization, 464
- privatization, 464
- voucher privatization, 465
- foreign direct investment (FDI), 470

- soft budget constraint, 471
- tax arrears, 471
- Asian miracle, 472
- Asian crisis, 472
- capital controls, 477

QUESTIONS & PROBLEMS

An asterisk denotes a harder problem.

1. TRUE/FALSE/UNCERTAIN

a. The fact that output has decreased so much in countries that have gone from central planning to a market economy shows that central planning was not so bad after all.

b. Although times in transition economies are bad, economic conditions are much better than they were in the United States during the Great Depression.

c. The slow pace of privatization in some transition economies is irresponsible; large state firms should be sold to foreign investors immediately.

d. The decline in direct subsidies to state firms in Russia indicates significant progress in transition to a market economy.

e. There can be no growth in Russia until corruption is eliminated.

2. TRUE/FALSE/UNCERTAIN

a. Trade deficits for Asian economies in the 1990s were good news as they reflected high rates of investment.

b. Mexico in 1995 is a good example of a self-fulfilling exchange rate crisis.

c. The very high investment rates in Asia before the crisis suggest that Asian countries may well have been on the wrong side of the golden rule level of capital.

3. CATCHING UP

Poland's GDP per capita in 1995 was around $5,000 (in PPP terms), compared to an average of $20,000 for the five richest OECD countries. If growth of GDP per capita in Poland exceeds OECD growth by 2% a year, how long will it take for Poland to have a GDP per capita:

a. One-half of the OECD countries.
(*Hint*: look at "the rule of 70" in chapter 10.)

b. Equal to that of the OECD countries.

c. Do you think it will really take that long? Why, or why not?

4. FACING AN EXCHANGE RATE CRISIS

Suppose an economy is described by the *IS*, the *LM*, and the arbitrage equations derived in chapter 20:

$$IS: \quad Y = C(Y - T) + I(Y, i) + G + NX\left(Y, Y^*, \frac{E^e}{1 + i - i^*}\right)$$

$$LM: \quad \frac{M}{P} = Y L(i)$$

$$\text{Arbitrage:} \quad E = E^e/(1 + i - i^*)$$

a. Explain why E^e and i^* enter the *IS* relation.

b. Characterize the equilibrium graphically, using the same two graphs as in Figure 20–2(a) and 20–2(b).

c. Suppose that financial investors start anticipating a depreciation in the future, so E^e increases. Show the effect on the *IS* curve in Figure 20–2(a) and on the relation between the interest rate and the exchange rate in Figure 20–2(b). Explain in words.

d. Show the effects on equilibrium output and on the equilibrium exchange rate. Does output go up or down? Explain in words.

e. Suppose the central bank decides to maintain the parity. From Figure 20–2(b) what must happen to the interest rate? How must the *LM* curve shift? What happens to ouput? Explain in words.

*f. It is argued that during the Asian crisis, one effect of the depreciation was in fact to decrease demand. Many of the debts vis-à-vis the rest of the world were expressed in dollars, so that a depreciation had the effect of increasing their value in domestic currency, decreasing the wealth of consumers, and decreasing demand. How would you modify the *IS* equation to reflect this additional effect?

*g. With this additional effect added to the *IS* equation, redo (d). Explain in words.

FURTHER READINGS

On Transition

For a description of the start of transition in Poland, read *Poland's Jump to the Market Economy* (Cambridge, MA: MIT Press, 1993), by Jeffrey Sachs, a Harvard economist who played a big part in the design of Polish economic reform.

A very useful document, both in terms of analysis and basic numbers, is the *Annual Transition Report* of the European Bank for Reconstruction and Development, a bank created for the purpose of helping the transition in Eastern Europe.

On the Asian Crisis

For a presentation of the view that the Asian crisis was due mainly to fundamentals, read "The Myth of Asia's Miracle" (Foreign Affairs, November/December 1994), by Paul Krugman, from MIT. (Note that this was written before the crisis.) Read also "What happened to Asia?", January 1998 (Krugman's web page: http://web.mit.edu/krugman/www/). Krugman's argument is based in large part on the work of Alwyn Young, which we saw in the In Depth box "Hong Kong and Singapore: A Tale of Two Cities" in chapter 12.

Nouriel Roubini, from New York University, has created a web page on the Asian crisis (www.stern.nyu.edu/~nroubini/asia/AsiaHomepage.html). All the articles mentioned in section 24-2 (and many more) can be found at this page.

Back to Policy

Nearly every chapter of this book has looked at the role of policy. The next three chapters put it all together.

CHAPTER 25

Chapter 25 asks two questions: Given the uncertainty about the effects of macroeconomic policies, wouldn't it be better not to use policy at all? And, even if policy potentially can be useful, can we trust policy makers to carry out the right policy? Bottom line: Uncertainty limits the role of policy; policy makers do not always do the right thing. But, with the right institutions, policy can help and should be used.

CHAPTER 26

Chapter 26 looks at monetary policy. It reviews what we have learned, chapter by chapter, and then focuses on two issues. The first is the optimal rate of inflation: High inflation is bad, but how low a rate of inflation should the central bank aim for? The second is the design of policy: Given a target rate of inflation, how should the central bank be willing to deviate from the target to stabilize output? The chapter ends with a description of the way monetary policy is conducted in the United States today.

CHAPTER 27

Chapter 27 looks at fiscal policy. Again, it reviews what we have learned, and then looks more closely at the mechanics of debt, taxes, and spending implied by the government budget constraint. Having done so, it considers several issues, from how wars should be financed, to the dangers of high debt levels. It ends with a description of the current budget situation in the United States, and a discussion of the problems on the horizon.

CHAPTER 25 | Should Policy Makers Be Restrained?

A recurrent theme of this book has been that macroeconomic policy has an important role to play. The right mix of fiscal and monetary policy can, I have argued, help a country out of a recession, improve its trade position without increasing activity and igniting inflation, slow down an overheating economy, stimulate investment and capital accumulation, and so on.

This theme, however, is clearly at odds with growing demands that policy makers be tightly restrained. In the European Union, countries that have adopted the Euro are required to keep their budget deficit under 3% of GDP. In the United States, the first item in the "Contract with America," the program drawn by Republicans for the mid-term U.S. elections in 1994, was the introduction of a balanced-budget amendment to the Constitution (Fig. 25-1). With the elimination of the U.S. budget deficit in the second half of the 1990s, the push for a balanced budget amendment has weakened. However, if deficits were to return, the issue would surely again command center stage. Monetary policy is also under fire. For example, the charter of the central bank of New Zealand, written in 1989, defines monetary policy's role as the maintenance of price stability, to the exclusion of any other macroeconomic goal.

Arguments for restraints on policy fall in two general categories:

1. Policy makers may have good intentions, but they end up doing more harm than good.
2. Policy makers do what is best for them, which is not necessarily what is best for the country.

This chapter develops and examines these arguments in the context of macroeconomic policy in general. Chapters 26 and 27 then examine monetary policy and fiscal policy in more detail.

House Republican

Contract with America

A Program for Accountability

We've listened to your concerns and we hear you loud and clear. If you give us the majority, on the first day of Congress, a Republican House will:

Force Congress to live under the same laws as every other American
Cut one out of three Congressional committee staffers
Cut the Congressional budget

Then, in the first 100 days there will be votes on the following 10 bills:

1. Balanced budget amendment and the line item veto: It's time to force the government to live within its means and restore accountability to the budget in Washington.

2. Stop violent criminals: Let's get tough with an effective, able, and timely death penalty for violent offenders. Let's also reduce crime by building more prisons, making sentences longer and putting more police on the streets.

3. Welfare reform: The government should encourage people to work, not have children out of wedlock.

4. Protect our kids: We must strengthen families by giving parents greater control over education, enforcing child support payments, and getting tough on child pornography.

5. Tax cuts for families: Let's make it easier to achieve the American Dream: save money, buy a home, and send their kids to college.

6. Strong national defense: We need to ensure a strong national defense by restoring the essentials of our national security funding.

7. Raise the senior citizens' earning limit: We can put an end to government age discrimination that discourages seniors from working if they want.

8. Roll back government regulations: Let's slash regulations that strangle small business and let's make it easier for people to invest in order to create jobs and increase wages.

9. Common-sense legal reform: We can finally stop excessive legal claims, frivolous lawsuits, and overzealous lawyers.

10. Congressional term limits: Let's replace career politicians with citizen legislators. After all, politics shouldn't be a lifetime job.

(Please see reverse side to know if the candidate from your district has signed the Contract as of October 5, 1994.)

If We Break This Contract, Throw Us Out, We Mean It.

FIGURE 25-1

The Contract with America

25-1 | Uncertainty and Policy

A blunt way of stating the first argument in favor of policy restraints is that those who know little should do little. The argument has two parts: first, that macroeconomists, and by implication the policy makers who rely on their advice, know little; and second, that they should therefore do little.

How Much Do Macroeconomists Actually Know?

Macroeconomists are like doctors treating cancer. They know a lot, but there is also a lot they don't know.

Take an economy with high unemployment, where the central bank is considering the use of monetary policy to increase economic activity. Think of the sequence of links between an increase in money and an increase in output—all the questions the central bank faces when deciding whether and by how much to increase the money supply:

- Is the current high rate of unemployment a sign that unemployment is above the natural rate, or a sign that the natural rate has increased (chapters 6, 7, and 22)? If the economy is too close to the natural rate, isn't there a risk that monetary expansion will lead to a decrease in unemployment below the natural rate and an increase in inflation (chapters 8 and 9)?
- By how much will the change in the money supply decrease the short-term interest rate (chapter 4)? What will be the effect of the decrease in the short-term interest rate on the long-term interest rate (chapter 15)? By how much will stock prices increase (chapter 15)? By how much will the currency depreciate (chapters 20 and 21)?

- How long will it take for lower long-term interest rates and higher stock prices to affect investment and consumption spending (chapter 16)? How long will it take for the J-curve effects to work themselves out and for the trade balance to improve (chapter 19)? What is the danger that the effects come too late, when the economy has already recovered?

When assessing these questions, central banks—or macroeconomic policy makers in general—do not operate in a vacuum. They rely in particular on macroeconometric models. The equations in these models give estimates of how these individual links have looked in the past. But different models give different answers. This is because they have different structures, different lists of equations, and different lists of variables.

Figure 25–2 shows an example of this diversity. This example comes from a study commissioned in the early 1990s by the Brookings Institution—a research institute in Washington, D.C.—asking the builders of the 12 main macroeconometric models each to answer a similar set of questions. (The models are described in the Focus box "Twelve Macroeconometric Models.") The goal was to see how different the answers would be across models. One question was

> *Consider a case where the U.S. economy is growing at its normal growth rate, and where unemployment is at its natural rate; call this the* baseline *case. Suppose now that over the period of a year, the Fed increases money faster than in the baseline, so that after a year, nominal money is 4% higher than it would have been in the baseline case. From then on, nominal money grows at the same rate as in the baseline case, so that the level of nominal money remains 4% higher than it would have been without the change in monetary policy. Suppose further that interest rates in the rest of the world remain unchanged. What will happen to U.S. output?*

A description of the models and of the study is given in Ralph Bryant et al., *Empirical Macroeconomics for Interdependent Economies* (Washington, DC: Brookings Institution, 1988). The study shows the effects not only of monetary policy, but also of fiscal policy. (The simulation described in the text is simulation E in the supplemental volume.)

Figure 25–2 shows the deviation of output from the baseline predicted by each of the 12 models. All 12 models predict that output will increase for some time after the increase in money. After one year, the average deviation of output from the baseline is positive. But the range of answers is large, from nearly 0% to close to 3%; even leaving out the most extreme prediction, the range is still more than 1%. Two years out, the average deviation is 1.2%;

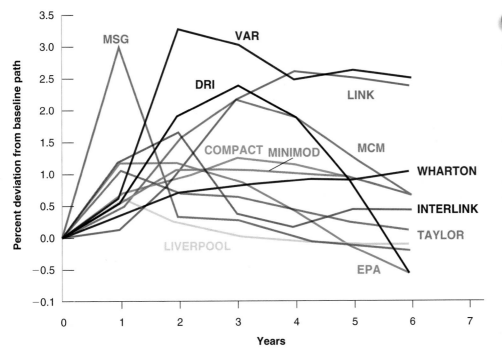

FIGURE 25-2

The Response of Output to a Monetary Expansion: 12 Predictions from 12 Models

Although all 12 models predict that output will increase for some time in response to a monetary expansion, the range of answers regarding the size and the length of the output response is large.

again leaving out the most extreme prediction, the range is still 2%. And six years out, the average deviation is 0.6%, and the answers range from -0.5% to 2.5%. In short, if we measure uncertainty by the range of answers from this set of models, there is substantial uncertainty about the effects of policy.

Should Uncertainty Lead Policy Makers to Do Less?

Should uncertainty about the effects of policy lead policy makers to do less? In general, the answer is: Yes. Consider the following example, which builds on the simulation we just looked at.

Suppose the U.S. economy is in recession. The unemployment rate is 7% and the Fed is considering using monetary policy to expand output. To concentrate on uncertainty about the effects of policy, let's assume the Fed knows everything else for certain. Based on its forecasts, it *knows* that absent changes in monetary policy, unemployment will still be 7% next year. It knows that the natural rate of unemployment is 5%, and therefore the unemployment rate is 2% above the natural rate. And it knows, from Okun's law, that 1% more output growth for a year leads to a reduction in the unemployment rate of 0.4%.

Under these assumptions, the Fed knows that if it could achieve 5% more output growth over the coming year, the unemployment rate a year from now would be lower by 0.4 times $5\% = 2\%$, thus down to its natural rate of 5%. By how much should the Fed increase the money supply?

Taking the average of the responses from the different models in Figure 25–2, an increase in the money supply of 4% leads to a 0.85% increase in output in the first year. Equivalently, a 1% increase in the money supply leads to a $0.85/4 = 0.21\%$ increase in output.

Suppose the Fed takes this average relation as holding with *certainty*. What it should then do is straightforward. To return the unemployment rate to the natural rate in one year requires 5% more output growth. And 5% output growth requires the Fed to increase money

In the real world, of course, the Fed does not know any of these things with certainty. It can only make forecasts. It does not know the exact value of the natural rate, or the exact coefficient in Okun's law. Introducing these sources of uncertainty would reinforce our basic conclusion.

by 5%/0.21 = 23.8%. The Fed should therefore increase the money supply by 23.8%. If the economy's response is equal to the average response from the 12 models, this increase in money will return the economy to the natural rate of unemployment within a year.

Suppose the Fed actually increases money by 23.8%. But let's now take into account uncertainty, as measured by the range of responses of the different models in Figure 25–2. Recall that the range of responses of output to a 4% increase in money after one year varies from 0 to 3%; equivalently, a 1% increase in money leads to a range of increases in output from 0 to 0.75%. These ranges imply that an increase in money of 23.8% leads, across models, to an output response anywhere between 0% and (23.8% × 0.75) = 17.9%. These output numbers imply in turn a decrease in unemployment anywhere between 0% and 7%, or values of the unemployment rate a year hence anywhere between 7% and 0%!

The conclusion is clear: Given the range of uncertainty about the effects of monetary policy on output, increasing money by 23.8% would be irresponsible. If the effects of money on output are as strong as suggested by one of the 12 models, unemployment by the end of the year could be 5% below the natural rate, leading to enormous inflationary pressures. Given this uncertainty, the Fed should increase money by much less than 23.8%. For example, increasing money by 10% leads to a range for unemployment a year hence of 7% to 4%, clearly a safer range of outcomes.[1]

Uncertainty and Restraints on Policy Makers

Let's summarize what we have learned so far. There is substantial uncertainty about the effects of macroeconomic policies. This uncertainty should lead policy makers to be more cautious, to use less active policies. Policies should be aimed broadly at avoiding prolonged recessions, slowing down booms, and avoiding inflationary pressure. The higher unemployment or inflation, the more active the policies should be. But they should stop well short of **fine tuning**, of trying to achieve constant unemployment or constant output growth.

These conclusions would have been controversial 20 years ago. Back then, there was a heated debate between two groups of economists. One group, headed by Milton Friedman from Chicago, argued that because of long and variable lags, activist policy was likely to do more harm than good. The other group, headed by Franco Modigliani from MIT, had just built the first generation of large macroeconometric models and believed that economists' knowledge of the economy was becoming good enough to allow for increasingly fine tuning of the economy. Today, most economists recognize there is substantial uncertainty about the effects of policy. They also accept the implication that this uncertainty should lead to less active policies.

> Friedman and Modigliani are the same two economists who independently developed the modern theory of consumption (chapter 16).

Note that what we have developed so far is an argument for *self-restraint by* policy makers, not for *restraints on* policy makers. If policy makers understand the implications of uncertainty—and there is no reason to think they don't—they will, on their own, follow less active policies. There is no reason to impose further restraints, such as the requirement that money growth be constant or that the budget be balanced. Let's now turn to arguments for restraints on policy makers.

25-2 | Expectations and Policy

One reason the effects of macroeconomic policy are uncertain is the interaction of policy and expectations. How a policy works, and sometimes whether it works at all, depends not only on how it affects current variables but also on how it affects expectations about the fu-

---

[1]**DIGGING DEEPER.** This example relies on the notion of *multiplicative uncertainty*—that because the effects of policy are uncertain, more active policies lead to more uncertainty. See William Brainard, "Uncertainty and the Effectiveness of Policy," *American Economic Review*, May 1967, 411–425.

ture (the main theme of chapter 17). However, the importance of expectations for policy goes beyond uncertainty about the effects of policy. This brings us to a discussion of games:

Until the 1970s, macroeconomic policy was seen in the same way as the control of a complicated machine. Methods of **optimal control**, developed initially to control and guide rockets, were increasingly being used to design macroeconomic policy. Economists no longer think this way. It has become clear that the economy is fundamentally different from a machine, even a very complicated one. Unlike a machine, the economy is composed of people and firms who try to anticipate what policy makers will do, who react not only to current policy but also to expectations of future policy. Hence, macroeconomic policy must be thought of as a **game** between policy makers and the economy. So, when thinking about policy, what we need is not **optimal control theory** but rather **game theory**.

Let's clarify semantics. When economists say "game," they do not mean "entertainment," they mean **strategic interactions** between **players**. In the context of macroeconomic policy, the players are the policy makers and "the economy"—more concretely, the people and the firms in the economy. The strategic interactions are clear: What people and firms do depends on what they expect policy makers to do. In turn, what policy makers do depends on what is happening in the economy.

Game theory is becoming an important tool in all branches of economics. The 1994 Nobel prize in economics was awarded to three game theorists, John Nash from Princeton, John Harsanyi from Berkeley, and Reinhard Selten from Germany.

Game theory has given economists many insights, often explaining how some apparently strange behavior makes sense when one understands the nature of the game being played. One of these insights is particularly important for our discussion of restraints here: Sometimes you can do better in a game by giving up some of your options. To see why, let's start with an example from outside economics, governments' policies toward hijackers.

Hijackings and Negotiations

Most governments have a stated policy that they will not negotiate with plane hijackers. The reason for this stated policy is clear: to deter hijacking by making it unattractive to hijack planes.

Suppose, despite the stated policy, a hijacking takes place. Now that the hijacking has taken place anyway, why not negotiate? Whatever compensation the hijackers demand is likely to be less costly than the alternative—the likelihood that lives will be lost if the plane has to be taken by force. So the best policy would appear to be: Announce that you will not negotiate, but, if a hijacking happens, negotiate nevertheless.

Upon reflection, it is clear this would in fact be a very bad policy. Hijackers' decisions do not depend on the stated policy, but on what they expect will actually happen if they hijack a plane. If they know that negotiations will actually take place, they will rightly consider the stated policy as irrelevant. And hijackings will take place.

So what is the best policy? Despite the fact that once hijackings have taken place, negotiations typically lead to a better outcome, the best policy is for governments to commit *not* to negotiate. By giving up the option to negotiate, they are likely to prevent hijackings in the first place.

A refresher: Given labor market conditions, and given their expectations of what prices will be, firms and workers set nominal wages. Given the nominal wages they have to pay, firms then set prices. Thus, prices depend on expected prices and labor market conditions. Equivalently, price inflation depends on expected price inflation and labor market conditions. This is what is captured in equation (25.1).

Let's now turn to a macroeconomic example, based on the relation between inflation and unemployment. As you will see, exactly the same logic is involved.

Inflation and Unemployment Revisited

Recall the relation between inflation and unemployment we derived in chapter 8 (equation [8.7], with the time indexes omitted)

$$\pi = \pi^e - \alpha(u - u_n) \tag{25.1}$$

Inflation (π) depends on expected inflation (π^e) as embodied in wages set in labor contracts, and on the difference between the actual unemployment rate and the natural unemployment rate ($u - u_n$). The coefficient α captures the effect of unemployment on inflation, given expected inflation: When unemployment is above the natural rate, inflation is lower than expected; when it is below the natural rate, inflation is higher than expected.

Suppose the Fed announces it will follow a monetary policy consistent with zero inflation. On the assumption that wage setters believe the announcement, expected inflation (π^e) as embodied in wage contracts is equal to zero, and the Fed faces the following relation:

$$\pi = -\alpha(u - u_n) \qquad (25.2)$$

For simplicity, I assume the Fed can choose the rate of inflation exactly. In doing so, I ignore uncertainty about the effects of policy (the topic of section 25-1, but not a central issue here).

If the Fed follows through on its announced policy of zero inflation, expected and actual inflation will both be equal to zero, and unemployment will be equal to the natural rate.

Zero inflation and unemployment equal to the natural rate is not a bad outcome. But it would seem the Fed can actually do even better. Recall from chapter 8 that in the United States, α is roughly equal to 1. So equation (25.2) implies that by accepting just 1% inflation, the Fed can achieve an unemployment rate of 1% below the natural rate. Suppose the Fed—and everybody else in the economy—finds the trade-off attractive, and decides to decrease unemployment by 1% in exchange for an inflation rate of 1%. This incentive to deviate from the announced policy once the other player has moved—in this case, once wage setters have set the wage—is known in game theory as the **time inconsistency** of optimal policy. In our example, the Fed can improve the outcome this period by deviating from its announced policy of zero inflation: By accepting some inflation, it can achieve a substantial reduction in unemployment.

The natural rate of unemployment, despite its name, has no claim to being natural or best in any sense (see chapters 6 and 8). It may be perfectly reasonable for the Fed and everyone else in the economy to prefer an unemployment rate lower than the natural rate.

Unfortunately, this is not the end of the story. Seeing that the Fed has increased money by more than it announced it would, wage setters are likely to wise up and begin to expect positive inflation of 1%. If the Fed still wants to achieve an unemployment rate 1% below the natural rate, it now has to accept 2% inflation. However, if it does, wage setters are likely to increase their expectations of inflation further, and so on.

The eventual outcome is likely to be high inflation. Because wage setters understand the Fed's motives, expected inflation catches up with actual inflation, and the Fed must eventually be unsuccessful in its attempt to achieve unemployment below the natural rate. In short, attempts by the Fed to make things better lead in the end to things being worse. The economy ends up with the *same unemployment rate* as would have prevailed if the Fed had followed its announced policy, but with *much higher inflation*.

How relevant is this example? Very relevant. Reread chapter 8. One can read the history of the Phillips curve and the increase in inflation in the 1970s as coming precisely from the Fed's attempts to maintain unemployment below the natural rate, leading to higher and higher expected and actual inflation. In that light, the shift of the original Phillips curve can be seen as the adjustment of wage setters' expectations to the central bank's behavior.

So what is the best policy in this case? It is for the Fed to make a credible commitment that it will not to try to decrease unemployment below the natural rate. By giving up the option of deviating from its announced policy, the Fed can achieve unemployment equal to the natural rate and zero inflation. The analogy with the hijacking example is clear: By credibly committing not to do something that would appear desirable at the time, policy makers can achieve a better outcome: no hijackings in our earlier example, no inflation here.

Establishing Credibility

How can a central bank credibly commit not to deviate from its announced policy?

One way to establish its credibility is for the central bank to give up—or to be stripped by law of—its policy-making power. For example, the mandate of the bank can be defined by law in terms of a simple rule, such as setting money growth at 0% forever.

Such a law surely takes care of the problem of time inconsistency. But such a tight restraint comes close to throwing the baby out with the bathwater. We want to prevent the central bank from pursuing too high a rate of money growth in an attempt to lower unemployment below the natural rate. But—subject to the restrictions discussed in section 25-1—we still want the central bank to be able to expand the money supply when unemployment is far above the natural rate and contract the money supply when unemployment is far below the natural rate. Such actions become impossible under a constant-money-growth rule. There are indeed better ways to deal with time inconsistency. In the case of monetary policy, our discussion suggests one way this can be done:

1. Make the central bank independent. Appointing central bankers for longer terms and making it harder to fire them will make them more likely to resist political pressure to decrease unemployment below the natural rate.

2. Then choose a "conservative" central banker, somebody who dislikes inflation and is unwilling to accept more inflation in exchange for less unemployment when unemployment is at the natural rate. When the economy is at the natural rate, such a central banker simply will not be tempted to embark on a monetary expansion. Thus, the problem of time inconsistency will disappear altogether.

Appointing as the head of the central bank someone who does not have the same preferences as the people as a whole might seem like a solution that only game theorists would concoct. But this is actually the way many countries have been responding to the problem of time consistency in monetary policy. In many countries in the last two decades, central banks have been given more independence. And governments typically have appointed central bankers who are more "conservative" than the governments themselves—central bankers who appear to care more about inflation and less about unemployment than the government. (See the Focus box "Was Alan Blinder Wrong in Speaking the Truth?")

Figure 25–3 suggests that this approach has been quite successful. The vertical axis gives the average annual inflation rate in 18 OECD countries for the period 1960 to 1992. The horizontal axis gives the value of an index of "central bank independence," constructed by looking at several legal provisions in the bank's charter—for example, whether and how the government can remove the head of the bank. There is a striking inverse relation between the two variables, as summarized by the regression line: More central bank independence is systematically associated with lower inflation.

One can reasonably argue this does not prove that central bank independence leads to lower inflation. It may be that countries that dislike inflation tend both to give more independence to their central bankers and have lower inflation. (This is another example of the difference between correlation and causality, discussed in Appendix 3 at the end of the book.)

Time Consistency and Restraints on Policy Makers

Let's summarize what we have learned in this section: We have examined arguments for putting restraints on policy makers, based on the issue of time inconsistency. We have looked at the case of monetary policy. But similar issues arise in the context of fiscal policy as well, for example, in the case of debt repudiation, an issue we shall discuss in chapter 27.

FOCUS

Was Alan Blinder Wrong in Speaking the Truth?

In the summer of 1994, President Clinton appointed Alan Blinder, an economist from Princeton, vice-chairman (in effect, second in command) of the Federal Reserve Board. A few weeks later Blinder, speaking at an economic conference, indicated his belief that the Fed has both the responsibility and the ability, when unemployment is high, to use monetary policy to help the economy recover. This statement was badly received. Bond prices decreased, and most newspapers ran editorials critical of Blinder.

Why was the reaction of markets and newspapers so negative? It was surely not that Blinder was wrong. There is no doubt that monetary policy can and should help the economy out of a recession. Indeed, the Federal Reserve Bank Act of 1978 requires the Fed to pursue full employment as well as low inflation.

The reaction was negative because, in terms of the argument we developed in the text, Blinder revealed by his words that he was not a conservative central banker, that he cared about unemployment as well as about inflation. With the unemployment rate equal to 6.1%, close to what was thought to be the natural rate at the time, markets interpreted Blinder's statements as suggesting that he might want to decrease unemployment below the natural rate. Interest rates increased because of higher expected inflation, and so bond prices decreased.

The moral of the story is clear. Whatever views central bankers may hold, they should try to look and sound conservative. . . . This is why many heads of central banks are reluctant to admit, at least in public, the existence of any trade-off between unemployment and inflation, even in the short run.

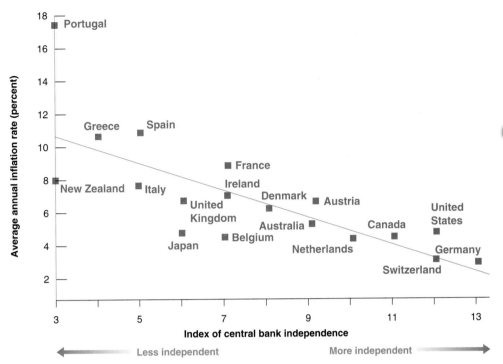

FIGURE 25-3

Inflation and Central Bank Independence

Across OECD countries, the higher the degree of central bank independence, the lower the rate of inflation.
Source: Vittorio Grilli, Donato Masciandaro, and Guido Tabellini, "Political and Monetary Institutions and Public Financial Policies in the Industrial Countries," *Economic Policy*, October 1991, 341–392.

When issues of time inconsistency are relevant, tight restraints on policy makers—such as a fixed-money-growth rule in the case of monetary policy—can provide a coarse solution. But the solution may have large costs if it prevents the use of macroeconomic policy altogether. Better ways typically involve designing better institutions (such as an independent central bank) that can reduce the problem of time inconsistency without eliminating monetary policy as a macroeconomic policy tool.

25-3 | Politics and Policy

We have assumed so far that policy makers were *benevolent*—they tried to do what was best for the economy. However, much public discussion challenges that assumption: Politicians or policy makers, the argument goes, do what is best for themselves, and this is not always what is best for the country.

You have heard the arguments: Politicians avoid the hard decisions, they pander to the electorate, partisan politics leads to gridlock, and nothing ever gets done. Discussing the flaws of democracy goes far beyond the scope of this book. What we can do here is to review briefly how these arguments apply to macroeconomic policy, then look at the empirical evidence, and see what light it sheds on the issue of policy restraints.

Games between Policy Makers and Voters

Many macroeconomic measures involve trading off short-run losses against long-run gains—or, symmetrically, short-run gains against long-run losses.

Take, for example, tax cuts. By definition, tax cuts lead to lower taxes today. They are also likely to lead to an increase in activity, and so an increase in pretax income, for some time. But unless they are matched by equal decreases in government spending, they lead to a larger budget deficit and to the need for an increase in taxes in the future. If voters are shortsighted, the temptation for politicians to cut taxes may prove irresistible. Politics may lead to systematic deficits, at least until the level of government debt has become so high that politicians are scared into action.

The tax cuts implemented by the Reagan administration both decreased tax rates and increased activity in the early 1980s in the United States (chapter 20). But they also led to a long sequence of deficits, which took nearly two decades to eliminate. We shall look at the relation between current and future taxes more formally when we examine the implications of the government budget constraint in chapter 27.

Now move on from taxes to macroeconomic policy in general. Again suppose that voters are shortsighted. If the politicians' main goal is to please voters and get reelected, what better policy than to expand aggregate demand before an election, leading to higher growth and lower unemployment? True, growth in excess of the normal growth rate cannot be sustained, and eventually the economy must return to the normal level of output: Higher growth must be followed by lower growth later. But with the right timing and shortsighted voters, higher growth can win the elections. Thus, we might expect a clear **political business cycle**, with higher growth on average before elections than after elections.

From Okun's law, output growth in excess of normal growth leads to a decline in unemployment rate below the natural rate. In the medium run, we know that the unemployment rate must increase back to the natural rate. This in turn requires output growth below normal growth for some time. See chapter 9 (in particular, Table 9–1).

The arguments we have just laid out are familiar; in one form or another, you surely have heard them before. And their logic is convincing. So it may come as a surprise that they do not fit the facts very well.

For example, our discussion of taxes might lead you to expect that budget deficits and high government debt have always been and will always be with us. Figure 25–4, which gives the evolution of the ratio of government debt to GDP in the United States since 1900, shows this is not the case. Note how the first three buildups in debt all happened in very special circumstances: World War I, the start of the Great Depression, and World War II. These were times of unusual declines in output or unusually high military spending. Note also how from the end of the World War II to the end of the 1970s, the ratio of debt to GDP steadily *decreased*. By 1979, the ratio of debt to GDP was 33%, down from 130% in 1946.

The relation between the deficit, debt, and GDP is explored in detail in chapter 27.

True, the steady increase in debt from the early 1980s to the mid-1990s fits the argument of shortsighted politicians quite well. During that time, the ratio of debt to GDP steadily increased, from a low of 31.6% in 1981 to a high of 68.2% in 1995. But since then, the deficit has steadily decreased, and the ratio of debt to GDP is now falling. Explaining the behavior of debt over a period of 15 years through the behavior of shortsighted politicians raises the issue of why things were different before 1981, and also after 1995. The broader historical record suggests that by itself, shortsightedness does not explain much of the past evolution of deficits and debt.

Chapter 27 will examine alternative—and empirically more successful— explanations for the evolution of government debt, both over time and across countries.

Return to the political-business-cycle argument that policy makers try to get high output growth before the elections so they will be reelected. If the political business cycle were important, we would expect to see faster growth before elections than after. Table 25–1 gives GDP growth rates for each of the four years of each U.S. administration since President Truman in 1948. It is indeed the case that growth has been highest on average in the last year

FIGURE 25–4

The Evolution of the U.S. Ratio of Government Debt to GDP, 1900–1998

The three major buildups of debt since 1900 have been associated with World War I, the start of the Great Depression, and World War II. *Source: Historical Statistics of the United States,* Department of Commerce; and *Economic Report of the President* (1999).

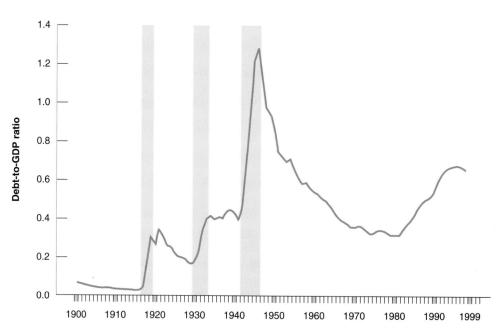

TABLE 25-1	Growth During Democratic and Republican Administrations (percent per year)			
	Year			
	First	**Second**	**Third**	**Fourth**
Democratic				
Truman	0.0	8.5	10.3	3.9
Kennedy/Johnson	2.6	5.3	4.1	5.3
Johnson	5.8	5.8	2.9	4.1
Carter	4.7	5.3	2.5	−0.2
Clinton I	2.3	3.5	2.3	3.4
Clinton II	3.9	3.5		
Average: Democratic	3.2	5.3	4.4	3.3
Republican				
Eisenhower	4.0	−1.3	5.6	2.1
Nixon	2.4	−0.3	2.8	5.0
Nixon/Ford	5.2	−0.5	−1.3	4.9
Reagan I	1.9	−2.5	3.6	6.4
Reagan II	3.6	3.0	2.7	3.0
Bush	2.5	1.2	−0.7	2.6
Average: Republican	3.3	−0.1	2.1	4.0
Average	3.3	2.6	3.2	3.7

Source: Alberto Alesina, "Macroeconomics and Politics," *NBER Macroeconomics Annual*, 1988, 13–61, Table 4. Updated.

of an administration. But the average difference across years is small: 3.7% in the last year of an administration versus 3.3% in the first year. (There are other interesting features in the table, such as the difference between Republican and Democratic administrations; we return to these shortly.) There is little evidence of manipulation of the macroeconomy to win elections.

Games between Policy Makers

Another line of argument focuses not on games between politicians and voters, but rather on games between political parties. For example, take the issue of budget deficit reduction in the United States. Despite the fact that by the mid-1980s large budget deficits were perceived as one of the main macroeconomic problems facing the United States, it took another 15 years before the deficit was eliminated. Some of the delays were part of the normal democratic process: Deficit reductions involve making painful decisions, and forging a consensus takes time. But other factors seemed to be at work too. Although agreeing on the need for deficit reduction, the two political parties differed on how it should be done. Because they believe in a smaller role for government, Republicans focused on decreases in spending. In contrast, Democrats were more open to increases in taxes. Each side held out, hoping the other side would give in.

Game theorists refer to these situations as **wars of attrition**. The hope that the other side will give in leads to long and often costly delays. Such wars of attrition are endemic in fiscal policy. Deficit reduction often takes place long after it would be best. This is particularly visible during episodes of hyperinflation. As we saw in chapter 23, hyperinflations come from monetary finance of large budget deficits. Although the need to reduce those deficits is usually recognized early on, support for stabilization programs—which include the elimination of those deficits—typically comes only when inflation has reached such high levels that economic activity is severely affected.

Wars of attrition are not limited to fiscal policy: You may remember the 1998 NBA strike in the United States, where more than half of the season was cancelled because owners and players could not reach an agreement.

Another example of a game between political parties is the movements in economic activity brought about by the alternation of parties in power. Republicans typically worry more than Democrats about inflation and less than Democrats about unemployment. So we would expect Democratic administrations to show stronger growth—and thus less unemployment and more inflation—than Republican administrations. This prediction appears to fit the facts quite well. Look at Table 25–1 again. The most striking contrast in growth rates is in the second year of each administration. During the second year of each Democratic administration since Truman, growth has been very high. During the second year of each Republican administration, growth has been very low. In four out of six Republican administrations, growth in the second year has been negative.

An intriguing question: Why is the effect so much stronger in the administration's *second* year? The theory of unemployment and inflation we developed in chapter 9 suggests a plausible answer. There are lags in the effects of policy, so it takes about a year for a new administration to affect the economy. And sustaining higher growth than normal for too long would lead to increasing inflation, so even a Democratic administration would not want to sustain higher growth throughout its term. Thus, growth rates tend to be much closer to each other during the second halves of Democratic and Republican administrations than during first halves.

Back to the Balanced-Budget Amendment

Let's end this chapter with one of the issues we started with, the case for and against a balanced-budget amendment. What have we learned?

First, despite common beliefs, the picture of politicians pandering to shortsighted voters does not fit the broad evidence on the evolution of deficits and debt. The large peacetime U.S. budget deficits of the 1980s and 1990s are the exception rather than the rule. Fiscal policy is not typically characterized by chronic deficits.

This is not to say that all is well, or that the political process always delivers the best macroeconomic policy decisions. Hard decisions are often delayed. Wars of attrition between parties, and indirectly between their different constituencies, seem endemic in fiscal policy. Deficit reductions often come late, only after debt has increased to high levels.

Do these problems justify the addition of a balanced-budget amendment to the U.S. Constitution? To most economists, the answer is no. Their arguments go as follows:

The Case Against a Balanced-Budget Amendment. A balanced-budget amendment would eliminate the problem of deficits. But it would also eliminate the use of fiscal policy as a macroeconomic policy instrument. This is too high a price to pay.

The evidence suggests the problem is not that politicians systematically want deficits. Rather, it appears to be that politicians find it difficult to agree on and implement a deficit-reduction plan when it is needed. Deficit control and reduction can be achieved with looser constraints than a constitutional amendment.

Consider the case for automatic spending cuts when the deficit gets too large (a looser constraint on policy than a balanced-budget amendment). Suppose the budget deficit is too large, and it is desirable to cut spending across the board by 5%. Members of Congress may find it difficult to explain to their constituency why their favorite spending program was cut by 5%. Now suppose the deficit triggers automatic across-the-board spending cuts of 5% without any congressional action. Knowing that other programs will be cut, members of Congress may accept cuts in their favorite programs more easily. They may also be better able to deflect the blame for the cuts: Members of Congress who succeed in limiting the cuts to their favorite program to, say, 4% can then return to their constituents and claim success in having avoided even larger cuts.

The Case for a Balanced-Budget Amendment To some economists, however, the answer is yes, a balanced-budget amendment is necessary. These economists are typically more skeptical of the usefulness of macroeconomic policy in general, and of fiscal policy in particular. They worry that running deficits during recessions may have adverse effects on financial markets, hindering rather than helping the recovery (a potentially perverse effect of policy we discussed in chapter 17). Because of the lags involved in the legislative process, they are also skeptical of Congress's ability to change fiscal policy in time to stabilize the economy. So they are willing to give up fiscal policy as a macroeconomic instrument.

These economists are also skeptical of any rules that Congress may impose upon itself, but can undo by a vote later on. This leads them to conclude that nothing short of a constitutional amendment can do the job of ending deficits forever.

In the light of this debate, the decrease in the budget deficit in the 1990s is particularly interesting. Is it due, as the opponents of a strict balanced budget amendment argue, to the use of cleverly designed but flexible rules to decrease the deficit? Or is it due, as proponents of a strict balanced budget amendment argue, to luck, namely to unusually strong growth of output, resulting in high government revenues, in the United States in the 1990s? I explore the issue in the in Depth box "Did Rules Help Reduce the U.S. Budget Deficit?" My reading of the evidence is that growth explains much of the reduction in the deficit, but that rules have helped. At least for a country such as the United States, a balanced budget amendment is not needed; more flexible rules can do the job.

See two related boxes: "Monetary Contraction and Fiscal Expansion: The United States in the Early 1980s" in chapter 20, and "The Clinton–Greenspan Policy Mix" in chapter 5.

IN DEPTH

Did Rules Help Reduce the U.S. Budget Deficit?

Figure 1 on page 496 shows the evolution of the budget deficit as a ratio to GDP in the United States since 1980. (Because this is the way the budget numbers are constructed and presented, the years in the figure and in the rest of the box are fiscal rather than calendar years. The fiscal year runs from October 1 of the preceding calendar year to September 30 of the current calendar year. For example, fiscal year 1998 runs from October 1997 to September 1998.) Deficits increased sharply in the early 1980s, reaching 6.1% of GDP in 1983. They then went down and up again, reaching 4.7% in 1992. Since 1992, however, they have decreased steadily, and in 1998, the U.S. budget was in surplus, for the first time in 30 years.

We saw in chapter 20 how the deficits started: with the large tax cuts under the Reagan administration. The question we focus on here is how the deficits were reduced, and eventually, eliminated.

The Gramm–Rudman–Hollings Bill

The first serious attempt to reduce the deficit took place in 1985. Frustrated by Congress's inability to achieve deficit reduction, two Republican senators, Senators Gramm and Rudman, and one Democratic senator, Senator Hollings, jointly introduced a bill aimed at forcing deficit reduction through restraints on the budget process.

The bill easily passed the Senate and the House. Its principle was simple. The bill set ceilings for the deficit in each fiscal year, with the goal of eliminating the deficit by 1991. If the budget proposed by Congress implied a

deficit above the ceiling, a procedure known as *sequestration* automatically went into effect, with spending on all programs cut by the same percentage so as to achieve the target deficit.

Several spending programs were excluded from the cuts, mainly interest payments on the debt, Social Security benefits, and some low-income transfer programs. There were also *escape clauses* to prevent deficit reduction from standing in the way of macroeconomic stabilization. For example, if projected growth was below 3%, the deficit ceiling was relaxed in proportion to the difference between projected growth and 3%.

How did Gramm–Rudman–Hollings (GRH) work in practice? It had a short and checkered history:

The first obstacle was a constitutional challenge on the grounds that GRH took too much power away from the legislative bodies. The bill was declared unconstitutional by the Supreme Court in 1986. But the ruling was based largely on technicalities, and a second GRH bill, which avoided the problems mentioned by the Court, was passed in 1987. The occasion was used, however, to increase the ceilings, and move the target date for zero deficit to 1993!

The later history of GRH was full of loopholes, optimistic forecasts, and other gimmicks:

● Because the GRH ceiling applied only to the coming year's budget, Congress systematically shifted spend-

(continued)

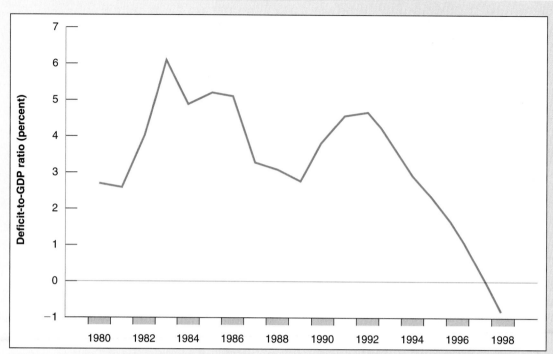

FIGURE 1   U.S. Deficit, 1980–1998 (percent of GDP)

ing to the previous year's budget. This creative accounting made the deficit in the previous fiscal year look worse. But it allowed the current year's budget to satisfy the GRH ceilings more easily.

- Public assets were sold, and proceeds from sales counted as revenues, reducing the measured deficit but doing little to reduce the true deficit. (We discuss the role of asset sales further in chapter 27.)
- Optimistic projections for economic activity were used. The result was optimistic projections for revenues and thus optimistically low projections for deficits.

In view of all these gimmicks, how effective was GRH in reducing deficits? Table 1 gives the initial ceilings (GRH I), the revised ceilings (GRH II), and the actual deficits—both in current dollars and in ratio to GDP—for each fiscal year

from 1986 to 1990, the year in which GRH was replaced by another set of rules (more on this shortly).

In each of the fiscal years 1987 to 1989, the budget adopted by Congress satisfied the GRH ceiling. In each of those years, however, the realized deficit was larger than the GRH ceiling, by anywhere between $6 billion in 1987 to $16 billion in 1989. Nevertheless, the period was characterized by a steady decrease in the ratio of the deficit to GDP, from 5.1% in 1986 to 2.8% in 1989.

In 1990, however, the actual deficit was $121 billion above the GRH ceiling. There were two main reasons. First, economic activity was lower than forecast when the budget had been passed; GDP growth was only 1.2% in 1990. And the government was faced with a savings-and-loan crisis: Many S&L institutions had become insolvent, and the government had to make good on its promise to insure depositors against losses.

TABLE 1   Gramm–Rudman–Hollings ceilings and actual deficits

Fiscal Year	Deficit Ceiling Under: GRH I	GRH II	Actual Deficit	Actual Deficit Ratio to GDP %
	(billions of current dollars)			
1986	172		221	5.1
1987	144		150	3.3
1988	108	144	155	3.1
1989	72	136	152	2.8
1990	36	100	221	3.9

Both phenomena—unusually low growth and the S&L crisis—justified a higher deficit. Nevertheless, because the actual deficit was so much higher than the ceiling, GRH had lost its credibility. A new system of rules, known as the *Budget Enforcement Act of 1990*, was introduced.

The Budget Enforcement Act of 1990

This new set of rules differed from GRH in several ways:

- First, it imposed constraints only on spending. Spending was divided into two categories, discretionary spending (roughly, spending on goods and services, including defense) and mandatory spending (roughly, transfer payments to individuals). Constraints, called *caps*, were set on discretionary spending for the following five years. These caps were set in such a way that they required a small but steady decrease in real terms in discretionary spending. Explicit provisions were made for emergencies. For example, spending on Operation Desert Storm in 1991 was not subject to the caps.

- Second, any new transfer program could be adopted only if it could be shown not to increase deficits in the future (either by raising new revenues, or by decreasing spending on some other existing program). This rule is known as the pay-as-you-go or *PAYGO* rule.

By focusing on spending rather than on the deficit itself, this set of rules had one important implication. If there was a recession, hence a decrease in revenues, the deficit could increase without triggering a decrease in spending. This happened in 1991 and 1992 when, because of the recession, the deficit increased—despite the fact that spending satisfied the constraints imposed by the caps. The shift in focus had in turn two desirable effects: allowing for a larger fiscal deficit during a recession—a good thing from the point of view of macrostabilization—but also putting less pressure to break the rules during a recession—a good thing from a political point of view.

On the surface, it would appear the Budget Enforcement Act of 1990 (extended by new legislation in 1993 and 1997) was a great success: By 1998, the deficit was gone. Looking more closely, however, the answer is more ambiguous. Table 2 gives the evolution of total spending, of total revenues, and of the deficit, for each fiscal year from 1990 to 1998, together with the decomposition of spending between discretionary (itself decomposed into defense and nondefense) and mandatory spending (given as the difference between columns (4) and (3)).

Looking first at total spending, revenues, and the deficit in columns (4) to (6), it is clear that the reduction in the deficit from 1990 to 1998 was due in nearly equal parts to a decrease in spending and to an increase in tax revenues. The increase in tax revenues can be attributed mostly to growth. Because the income tax is progressive—the tax rate increases with the level of income—steady growth increases tax revenues as a proportion of GDP; this is what happened in the 1990s. Turning to the decrease in spending, a comparison of columns (4) (total spending) and (3) (discretionary spending) shows that the decrease in spending, from 22% in 1990 to 19.7% in 1998, is more than fully accounted for by the decrease in discretionary spending, from 8.8% in 1990 to 6.6% in 1998. This would appear to be good news for rules, as discretionary spending is the part of spending that was subject to caps. But a look at column (1) suggests that another factor deserves most of the credit: the end of the cold war, and the resulting decrease in defense spending, from 5.3% to 3.2%.

Does this mean the Budget Enforcement Act had no effect? Probably not. In its absence, judging from past trends, both the non-defense part of spending and mandatory spending would probably have risen substantially as a proportion of GDP. They did not.

What lessons should we draw from the U.S. experience? That restraints can help, but that good design of these restraints is essential. It is important both to limit loopholes and to allow for realistic escape clauses (cases where the rules are suspended). But some loopholes may

(continued)

| TABLE 2 | Federal spending, revenues, and deficit, 1990–1998 (percent of GDP) |

Year	Discretionary Expenditures			Expenditures	Revenues	Deficit
	Defense (1)	Nondefense (2)	Total (3)	Total (4)	Total (5)	(6)
1990	5.3	3.5	8.8	22.0	18.2	3.8
1991	5.5	3.6	9.1	22.6	18.0	4.6
1992	4.9	3.8	8.7	22.5	17.8	4.7
1993	4.5	3.8	8.3	21.8	17.8	4.0
1994	4.1	3.8	7.9	21.4	18.4	3.0
1995	3.8	3.8	7.6	21.1	18.8	2.3
1996	3.5	3.6	7.1	20.7	19.3	1.6
1997	3.4	3.5	6.9	20.1	19.8	0.3
1998	3.2	3.4	6.6	19.7	20.5	−0.8

actually make restraints more flexible and thus more acceptable. One can read the outcomes from 1986 to 1989 in that light: Despite the use of creative accounting and optimistic forecasts, the ratio of the deficit to GDP was steadily reduced. Realistic escape clauses or exceptions are also important. In view of low growth and the S&L crisis, the deficit of 1990 was largely justified. But because it was so much larger than the GRH ceiling, GRH's credibility was destroyed, and another system had to be put in place. This system was more flexible and, combined with growth, eventually achieved its goal.

SUMMARY

- There is substantial uncertainty about the effects of macroeconomic policies. This uncertainty should lead policy makers to be more cautious, to use less active policies. Policies must be broadly aimed at avoiding prolonged recessions, slowing down booms, and avoiding inflationary pressure. The higher the level of unemployment or inflation, the more active the policies should be. But they should stop short of fine tuning, of trying to maintain constant unemployment or constant output growth.

- Using macroeconomic policy to control the economy is fundamentally different from controlling a machine. Unlike a machine, the economy is composed of people and firms who try to anticipate what policy makers will do, who react not only to current policy but also to expectations of future policy. In this sense, macroeconomic policy can be thought of as a game between policy makers and the economy.

- When playing a game, it is sometimes better for a player to give up some of his options. For example, when a hijacking occurs, it is best to negotiate with hijackers. But a government that credibly commits to not negotiating with hijackers—that gives up the option of negotiation—is actually more likely to deter hijackings in the first place.

- The same argument applies to various aspects of macroeconomic policy. By credibly committing not to use monetary policy to decrease unemployment below its natural rate, a central bank can alleviate fears that money growth will be high, and in the process decrease both expected and actual inflation. When issues of time inconsistency are relevant, tight restraints on policy makers—such as a fixed-money-growth rule in the case of monetary policy—can indeed provide a coarse solution. But the solution may have large costs if it prevents the use of macroeconomic policy altogether. Better methods typically involve designing better institutions (such as an independent central bank) that can reduce the problem of time inconsistency without eliminating monetary policy as a macroeconomic policy tool.

- Another argument for putting restraints on policy makers is that they may play games either with the public or among themselves, and these games may lead to undesirable outcomes. Politicians may try to fool a shortsighted electorate by choosing policies with short-run benefits but large long-term costs—for example, large budget deficits. Political parties may delay painful decisions, hoping that the other party will make the adjustment and take the blame. These problems exist, although they are less prevalent than is usually perceived. In such cases, tight restraints on policy, such as a constitutional amendment to balance the budget, provide a coarse solution. Better ways typically involve better institutions and better ways of designing the process through which policy and decisions are made.

KEY TERMS

- fine tuning, 487
- optimal control, 488
- game, 488
- optimal control theory, 488
- game theory, 488

- strategic interactions, 488
- players, 488
- time inconsistency, 489
- political business cycle, 492
- wars of attrition, 493

An asterisk denotes a harder problem.

1. TRUE/FALSE/UNCERTAIN

a. There is so much uncertainty about the effects of monetary policy that we would be better off not using it.

b. Elect a Democrat as president if you want low unemployment.

c. There is clear evidence of political business cycles in the United States: low unemployment around elections, higher unemployment the rest of the time.

d. Rules are ineffective in reducing budget deficits.

e. It would be good to put a device on planes that would prevent all communications with the outside in the event the plane was hijacked.

2. TIME CONSISTENCY

Has the problem of "time consistency" ever arisen in your personal life? Who were the players in that "game"?

3. DESIGNING POLICY TO WIN ELECTIONS

You are an advisor to a newly elected president. She will face new elections four years from now. Inflation last year was 3% and the unemployment rate was equal to the natural rate. The Phillips curve is given by:

$$\pi_t = \pi_{t-1} - \alpha(u_t - u_n)$$

a. Assume you can use fiscal and monetary policy to achieve any unemployment rate you want for each of the next four years. Write a short memo to the president indicating what unemployment and inflation rates she should try to achieve.

b. How would you change the content of your memo if the Phillips curve is given by

$$\pi_t = \pi_t^e - \alpha(u_t - u_n)$$

and the evidence is that people form rational expectations?

4. DEALING WITH TERRORISTS

What measures (constitutional amendments, legal procedures, technological devices) would you put in place to deal with terrorists who hijack a plane?

5. DEMOCRATS AND REPUBLICANS

There are two parties: the Democrats, who care a lot more about unemployment than inflation, and the Republicans, who care a lot more about inflation than unemployment.

The Phillips curve is given by:

$$\pi_t = \pi_t^e - \alpha(u_t - u_n)$$

where π_t^e denotes expectations held in year $t - 1$ for inflation in year t.

There are elections at the end of this year. Democrats and Republicans have an equal chance of winning and being in power next year.

a. Describe how people will form expectations of inflation for next year.

b. Given these expectations, describe what happens to inflation and unemployment next year if the Democrats win.

c. Given these expectations, describe what happens to inflation and unemployment next year if the Republicans win.

d. Do these results fit the evidence in Table 25–1? Why or why not?

e. Suppose now that everybody expects Democrats to win the elections. Suppose the Democrats indeed win. What happens to inflation and unemployment next year? Explain.

*6. CUTTING THE BUDGET: THE PRISONER'S DILEMMA

Suppose there is a budget deficit. It can be reduced by cutting defense spending or by cutting welfare programs or by cutting both.

The Democrats have to decide whether to support cuts in welfare programs. The Republicans have to decide whether to support cuts in defense spending. Each party has to decide what to do, without knowing the decision of the other party.

The possible outcomes can be represented in the table on the next page.

To understand how to read this table, look at the bottom left corner. If Democrats vote for welfare cuts, and

		Welfare cuts	
		Yes	**No**
Defense	**Yes**	(R = 1, D = 1)	(R = −2, D = 3)
cuts	**No**	(R = 3, D = −2)	(R = −1, D = −1)

Republicans vote against cuts in defense spending, the outcome is that the Republicans are very happy, the Democrats unhappy. The Republicans get 3 (a high positive number) and the Democrats get −2. Make sure you understand each of the four outcomes.

a. If the Republicans decide to cut defense spending, what is the best response of the Democrats? Given this response, how much will the Republicans get?

b. If the Republicans decide not to cut defense spending, what is the best response of the Democrats? Given this response, how much will the Republicans get?

c. What will the Republicans do? What will the Democrats do? Will the budget deficit be reduced? Why or why not? (This is an example of a game known as the prisoner's dilemma in game theory.) Is there a way to improve the outcome?

FURTHER READINGS

A leading proponent of the view that governments misbehave and should be tightly restrained is James Buchanan, from George Mason University. Buchanan received the Nobel prize in 1986 for his work on public choice. Read his book with Richard Wagner, *Democracy in Deficit: The Political Legacy of Lord Keynes* (New York: Academic Press, 1977).

The argument that time consistency is a central issue for policy was first developed by Finn Kydland, from Carnegie Mellon, and Edward Prescott, from Minnesota, in "Rules Rather than Discretion: The Inconsistency of Optimal Plans," *Journal of Political Economy*, 85(3), June 1977, 473–492.

For a survey of the politics of fiscal policy, read Alberto Alesina and Roberto Perotti, "The Political Economy of Budget Deficits," *IMF Staff Papers*, 1995. Look also at James Poterba, "Do Budget Rules Work?" in Alan Auerbach, ed., *Fiscal Policy. Lessons from Economic Research*, (Cambridge: MIT Press, 1997).

For more on the politics of monetary policy, read Alberto Alesina and Lawrence Summers, "Central Bank Independence and Macroeconomic Performance: Some Comparative Evidence," *Journal of Money, Credit and Banking*, May 1993, 289–297.

We invite you to visit the Blanchard page on the Prentice Hall Web site at:

http://www.prenhall.com/blanchard

for this chapter's World Wide Web exercises

CHAPTER

Monetary Policy:
A Summing Up

Nearly every chapter has had something to say about monetary policy. This chapter puts it all together and ties up the remaining loose ends.

Let's first briefly review what we have learned (the Focus box "Monetary Policy: What We Have Learned and Where" gives a more detailed summary):

- In the short run, monetary policy affects output as well as its composition: An increase in money leads to a decrease in interest rates and a depreciation of the currency. These lead to an increase in the demand for goods and an increase in output.
- In the medium run and the long run, monetary policy is neutral: Changes in the level of money eventually lead to proportional increases in prices, leaving output and unemployment unaffected. Changes in the rate of money growth lead to corresponding changes in the inflation rate.

We therefore can think of monetary policy as involving two basic decisions. The first is deciding what the average rate of money growth, and by implication the average inflation rate, should be. The second is deciding how much to deviate from this average rate of money growth to reduce fluctuations in output. In this context, this chapter explores two issues:

1. The optimal inflation rate. There is no question that high inflation is costly. But how low should inflation be? Should central banks aim for an average inflation rate of, say, 4%, or aim for price stability, or even aim for deflation (negative inflation)?
2. The design of monetary policy. Once the central bank has decided what rate of inflation it wants to achieve, how should it design monetary policy? Given that it directly controls money growth, should it announce a target rate for money growth? Or should it announce a target rate of inflation and try to hit it as best as it can? In the short run, how much should it be willing to deviate from whatever target it has announced if, say, the economy goes into recession?

Having explored these issues, the chapter ends by looking at what the U.S. central bank—the Fed—actually does, how it designs and carries out monetary policy, and how well it has done in the recent past.

Monetary Policy: What We Have Learned and Where

- In chapter 4 we looked at the determination of money demand and money supply, and the effects of monetary policy on the interest rate.

  We saw how an increase in the money supply (achieved through an open market operation) leads to a decrease in the interest rate.

- In chapter 5 we looked at the short-run effects of monetary policy on output.

  We saw how an increase in money leads, through a decrease in the interest rate, to an increase in spending, and to an increase in output.

- In chapter 7 we looked at the effects of changes in money on output and prices, not only in the short run but also in the medium run.

  We saw that in the medium run, money is neutral: Changes in money are fully reflected in changes in prices.

- In chapter 9 we looked at the relation between money growth, inflation, and unemployment.

  We saw that in the medium run, money growth is reflected one for one in inflation, leaving the unemployment rate unaffected. We looked at alternative disinflation strategies. Based on the U.S. disinflation in the early 1980s and other disinflations around the world, we concluded that disinflations typically come at a cost of higher unemployment for some time.

- In chapter 14 we introduced a distinction between the nominal interest rate and the real interest rate.

  We saw how higher money growth leads to a lower nominal interest rate in the short run, but to a higher nominal interest rate—and an unchanged real interest rate—in the medium run.

- In chapter 17 we returned to the short-run effects of monetary policy on output, taking into account the effects of monetary policy on expectations.

  We saw that monetary policy affects the short-term nominal interest rate, but that spending depends primarily on both current and expected future short-term real interest rates. We saw how, as a result, the effects of monetary policy on output depend on how expectations respond to policy.

- In chapter 20 we looked at the effects of monetary policy in an economy with open goods and financial markets.

  We saw how, in an open economy, monetary policy affects spending and output not only through interest rates, but also through the exchange rate. An increase in money leads both to a decrease in the interest rate and a depreciation, and both increase spending and output.

- In chapter 21 we discussed the pros and cons of different monetary policy regimes, of flexible versus fixed exchange rates. We discussed the pros and cons of adopting a common currency such as the Euro.

  In the appendix, we looked further at the effects of monetary policy on interest rates and exchange rates, taking into account the role of expectations in financial and foreign-exchange markets.

- In chapter 22 we looked at monetary policy in the Great Depression. We saw how a contraction in nominal money, bank failures, and deflation were all important sources of the large decline in output from 1929 to 1933. Then, looking at unemployment in Europe, we examined the argument that disinflation may not only increase the unemployment rate above the natural rate, but also increase the natural rate for some time.

- In chapter 23 we studied hyperinflations and looked at the conditions under which such episodes arise, and eventually end.

  We focused on the relation between budget deficits, money growth, and inflation. We saw how large budget deficits can lead to high money growth rates, and to hyperinflation.

- In chapter 25 we looked at the problems facing macroeconomic policy in general, and monetary policy in particular.

  We saw that uncertainty about the effects of policy should lead to more cautious policies. We saw that even well-intentioned policy makers may sometimes not do what is best, and that there is a case for restraints on policy makers. We also looked at the case for making the central bank independent, and appointing a conservative central banker.

- In this chapter we discuss the issues of the optimal inflation rate, the choice and the use of targets for monetary policy. We conclude the chapter by looking at how the Fed actually conducts monetary policy in the United States today.

Table 26–1 shows that inflation has steadily gone down in rich countries since the early 1980s. In 1998, average inflation in the OECD was 3.3%, down from 10.5% in 1981. Twenty four countries (out of 29) had an inflation rate below 5%; there were only two in 1981.

Does this imply most central banks have now achieved their goal? Or should they aim for an even lower rate, perhaps 0%? The answer depends on the costs and benefits of inflation.

The Costs of Inflation

We saw in chapter 23 how very high inflation, say 30% a month or more, can thoroughly disrupt economic activity. The debate in OECD countries today, however, is not about the costs of inflation rates of 30% a month or more. Rather, it centers on the advantages of, say, 0% versus 4% inflation a year. Within that range, economists identify four main costs of inflation: shoe-leather costs, tax distortions, money illusion, and inflation variability.

Shoe-Leather Costs. In the medium run, a higher inflation rate leads to a higher nominal interest rate, thus to a higher opportunity cost of holding money. As a result, people decrease their money balances by making trips to the bank more often—thus the expression **shoe-leather costs**. These trips would be avoided if inflation were lower, and people could be doing other things instead, working more or enjoying more leisure.

> In the medium run, the real interest rate is not affected by inflation. Thus, an increase in inflation is reflected one for one in an increase in the nominal interest rate (chapter 14).

During hyperinflations, shoe-leather costs can become quite large. But their importance in times of moderate inflation is limited. If an inflation rate of 4% leads people to go to the bank one more time every month, or to do one more transaction between their money market fund and their checking account every month, this hardly qualifies as a major cost of inflation.

Tax Distortions. The second cost of inflation comes from the interaction between the tax system and inflation. Consider, for example, the taxation of capital gains. Taxes on capital gains are typically based on the change in the dollar price of the asset between the time it was purchased and the time it is sold. This implies that the higher the rate of inflation, the higher the tax. An example will make this clear.

Suppose inflation has been running at π a year for the last 10 years. Suppose you bought your house for $50,000 ten years ago, and you are selling it today for $50,000 times $(1 + \pi)^{10}$—so its real value is unchanged. If the capital-gains tax is 30%, the *effective tax rate* on the sale of your house—defined as the ratio of the tax you pay to the price for which you sell your house—is

$$(30\%) \frac{50,000(1 + \pi)^{10} - 50,000}{50,000(1 + \pi)^{10}}$$

> The numerator of the fraction equals the sale price minus the purchase price. The denominator is the sale price.

Because you are selling your house for the same real price for which you bought it, your real capital gain is zero and you should not be paying any tax. Indeed, if $\pi = 0$—if there has been no inflation—then the effective tax rate is 0%. But if $\pi = 4\%$, then the effective tax rate is 9.7%: Despite the fact that your real capital gain is zero, you end up paying a high tax.

TABLE 26–1 Inflation Rates in the OECD, 1981–1998					
Year	**1981**	**1985**	**1990**	**1995**	**1998**
OECD average[1]	10.5%	6.5%	5.9%	5.1%	3.3%
Number of countries with inflation below 5%[2]	2	11	16	20	24

[1]Average of GDP deflator inflation rates, using relative GDPs as weights.
[2]Out of 29 countries.

The problems extend beyond capital-gains taxes. Although the real rate of return on an asset is the real interest rate, not the nominal interest rate, income for the purpose of income taxation includes nominal interest payments, not real interest payments. Or, to take yet another example, until the early 1980s in the United States, the income levels corresponding to different income-tax rates were not increased automatically with inflation. As a result, people were pushed into higher tax brackets as their nominal income—but not necessarily their real income—increased over time, an effect known as *bracket creep*.

Some economists argue ▶ the costs of bracket creep were in fact much larger. As tax revenues steadily increased, there was little pressure on the government to control spending. The result, they argue, was an increase in the size of government in the 1960s and 1970s far beyond what would have been desirable.

You may argue this cost is not a cost of inflation per se, but rather the result of a badly designed tax system. In the example of the house we just discussed, the government could eliminate the problem if it *indexed* the purchase price to the price level—that is, it adjusted the purchase price for inflation since the time of purchase—and computed the tax on the difference between the sale price and the adjusted purchase price. Under that computation, there would be no capital gains and therefore no capital-gains tax to pay. But because tax codes rarely allow for such systematic adjustment, the inflation rate matters and leads to distortions.

Money Illusion. The third cost comes from *money illusion*, the notion that people appear to make systematic mistakes in assessing nominal versus real changes. Many computations that would be simple under price stability become more complicated when there is inflation. In comparing their income this year to their income in the past, people have to keep track of the history of inflation. In choosing between different assets or deciding how much to consume or save, they have to keep track of the difference between the real interest rate and the nominal interest rate. Casual evidence suggests that many people find these computations difficult and often fail to make the relevant distinctions. Economists and psychologists have gathered more formal evidence, and it suggests that inflation often leads people and firms to make incorrect decisions (see the Focus box "Money Illusion.") If this is the case, then a simple solution is to have no inflation.

Inflation Variability. The last cost comes from the fact that higher inflation is typically associated with *more variable inflation*. And more variable inflation means financial assets such as bonds, which promise fixed nominal payments in the future, become riskier.

Take a bond that pays $1,000 in 10 years. With constant inflation over the next 10 years, the real value of the bond in 10 years is known with certainty. But with variable inflation, the real value of $1,000 in 10 years becomes uncertain. Saving for retirement becomes more difficult. For those who have invested in bonds, lower inflation than expected means a better retirement; but higher inflation may mean poverty. This is one of the reasons retirees, for whom part of income is fixed in dollar terms, typically worry more about inflation than other groups in the population.

You may argue, as in the case of taxes, that these costs are not due to inflation per se, but rather to the financial markets' inability to provide assets that protect their holders against inflation. Rather than issuing only nominal bonds (bonds that promise a fixed nominal amount in the future), governments or firms could also issue *indexed bonds*—bonds that promise a nominal amount adjusted for inflation, so people do not have to worry about the real value of the bond when they retire. Indeed, as we saw in chapter 15, several governments have now introduced such bonds. Indexed bonds now play an important role in the United Kingdom, where, over the last 20 years, people increasingly have used them to save for retirement. Indexed bonds were introduced in the United States only in 1997. Although they account for only a small proportion of U.S. government bonds at this point, their role will surely increase in the future.

The Benefits of Inflation

Inflation is actually not all bad. One can identify three benefits of inflation: (1) seignorage, (2) the option of negative real interest rates for macroeconomic policy, and (3) (somewhat paradoxically) the use of the interaction between money illusion and inflation in facilitating real wage adjustments.

There is a lot of anecdotal evidence that many people fail to adjust properly for inflation in financial computations. Recently, economists and psychologists have started looking at money illusion more closely. In a recent study, two psychologists, Eldar Shafir from Princeton and Amos Tversky from Stanford, and one economist, Peter Diamond from MIT, designed a survey aimed at finding the presence and the determinants of money illusion. Among the many questions they asked of people in various groups (people at Newark International Airport, people at two New Jersey shopping malls, and a group of Princeton undergraduates) is the following:

Suppose Adam, Ben, and Carl each received an inheritance of $200,000 and each used it immediately to purchase a house. Suppose each sold his house one year after buying it. Economic conditions were, however, different in each case:

- During the time Adam owned his house, there was a 25% deflation—the prices of all goods and services decreased by approximately 25%. A year after Adam bought the house, he sold it for $154,000 (23% less than he had paid).
- During the time Ben owned his house, there was no inflation or deflation—the prices of all goods and services did not change significantly during the year. A year after Ben bought the house, he sold it for $198,000 (1% less than he had paid).

- During the time Carl owned his house, there was a 25% inflation—the prices of all goods and services increased by approximately 25%. A year after Carl bought the house, he sold it for $246,000 (23% more than he had paid).

Please rank Adam, Ben, and Carl in terms of the success of their house transactions. Assign "1" to the person who made the best deal, and "3" to the person who made the worst deal.

It is clear that, in nominal terms, Carl clearly made the best deal, followed by Ben, followed by Adam. But what is relevant is how they did in real terms—adjusting for inflation. And in real terms, the ranking is reversed: Adam, with a 2% real gain, made the best deal, followed by Ben (with a 1% loss), followed by Carl (with a 2% loss).

The survey's answers were the following:

Rank	Adam	Ben	Carl
1st	37%	17%	48%
2nd	10%	73%	16%
3rd	53%	10%	36%

Carl was ranked first by 48% of the respondents, and Adam was ranked third by 53% of the respondents. These answers are very suggestive of money illusion. In other words, people have a hard time adjusting for inflation.

Seignorage. Money creation—the ultimate source of inflation—is one of the ways in which the government can finance its spending. Put another way, money creation is an alternative to borrowing from the public or raising taxes.

Typically, the government does not "create" money to pay for its spending. Rather, it issues and sells bonds, and spends the proceeds. But if the bonds are bought by the central bank, which then creates money to pay for them, the result is the same: Other things being equal, the revenues from money creation—that is, *seignorage*—allow the government to borrow less from the public or to lower taxes.

How large is seignorage in practice? When looking at hyperinflation in chapter 23, we saw that seignorage is often an important source of government finance in countries with very high inflation rates. But its importance in OECD economies today, and for the range of inflation rates we are considering, is much more limited. Take the case of the United States: The ratio of the monetary base—the money issued by the Fed (see chapter 4)—to GDP is about 6%. An increase in money growth of 4% per year (which eventually leads to a 4% increase in inflation) would lead therefore to an increase in seignorage of 4% × 6%, or 0.24% of GDP. This is a small amount of revenues to get in exchange for 4% more inflation.

Therefore, while the seignorage argument is sometimes relevant (for example, in economies that do not yet have a good fiscal system in place), it seems hardly relevant in the discussion of whether OECD countries today should have, say, 0% versus 4% inflation.

Let H denote the monetary base. Then

$$\frac{\text{Seignorage}}{Y} = \frac{\Delta H}{PY}$$

$$= \frac{\Delta H}{H} \frac{H}{PY}$$

$\Delta H/H$: Rate of growth of the monetary base

H/PY: Ratio of the monetary base to (nominal) GDP

The Option of Negative Real Interest Rates. A positive inflation rate allows the monetary authority to achieve *negative real interest rates*, an option that may be very useful for macroeconomic policy when an economy is in recession. Let's look at this more closely.

The nominal interest rate on a bond cannot be negative. If it were, bondholders would be better off holding money rather than bonds. Thus, the lowest possible nominal interest rate is zero.

$$r = i - \pi^e$$
$$i \geq 0 \Rightarrow r \geq -\pi^e$$
$$\pi^e < 0 \text{ (deflation)} \Rightarrow r > 0$$

The real interest rate equals the nominal rate minus expected inflation (see chapter 14). If inflation and expected inflation are positive, then the real interest rate can be negative. But if they are equal to zero, the lowest value the real interest rate can take is zero. And if there is actual and expected deflation, the real interest rate must remain positive. So the lower the rate of inflation, the higher the floor on the real interest rate, the more limited the role of monetary policy in increasing demand and ending a recession.

As we discussed in chapter 22, this was indeed one of the adverse implications of deflation during the Great Depression: Expected deflation implied high real interest rates, despite low nominal interest rates. And today, because inflation is very low in many countries, the issue is resurfacing. Indeed, this is one of the issues facing Japan today. Faced with a sharp decrease in economic activity, the central bank has decreased short-term nominal interest rates nearly to zero. But with the decrease in activity, inflation has turned into deflation, leading to positive real interest rates. The Japanese economy would benefit from lower real interest rates. But this is not an option: the Japanese central bank cannot decrease nominal interest rates below zero.

Other countries may face the same problem in the future. In early 1999, most OECD countries have inflation rates close to zero, and low nominal interest rates—less than 5%. If there was a sharp decrease in demand, the most the central banks could decrease the nominal interest rate—and by implication the real interest rate—would be by 5% or less. This might not be enough to avoid a recession. (In the recession of 1990–1991, the Fed decreased the nominal interest rate by 7%. Still, this was not enough to avoid the recession.)

Money Illusion Revisited. Paradoxically, the presence of money illusion provides at least one argument for having a positive inflation rate.

To see why, consider two situations. In the first, inflation is 4% and somebody's wage increases by 1% in dollar terms. In the second, inflation is 0% and the wage is decreased by 3% in dollar terms. Both lead to the same decrease in the real wage, namely 3%. There is some evidence, however, that many people will accept the real wage cut more easily in the first than in the second case.

Why is this example relevant to our discussion? Because, as we saw in chapter 13, the constant process of change that characterizes modern economies means some workers must sometimes take a real pay cut. Thus, the argument goes, the presence of inflation allows for these downward real-wage adjustments more easily than no inflation. This argument is plausible. Economists have not established its importance; but, because so many economies now have very low inflation, we soon may be in a position to test it.

A fight between metaphors: Because inflation makes these real wage adjustments easier to achieve, some economists say inflation "greases the wheels" of the economy. Others, emphasizing the adverse effects of inflation on relative prices, say that inflation instead "puts sand" in the economy.

The Optimal Inflation Rate: The Current Debate

At this stage, the debate in OECD countries is between those who think some inflation (say, 4%) is fine and those who want to achieve price stability—that is, 0% inflation.

Those who are happy with an inflation rate around 4% emphasize that the costs of 4% versus 0% inflation are small and that the benefits of some inflation are worth keeping. They argue some of the costs of inflation could be avoided by indexing the tax system and issuing more indexed bonds. They also say that going from current rates of inflation to 0% would require some increase in unemployment for some time, and that this transition cost may well exceed the eventual benefits.

Those who want to aim for 0% argue that if inflation is bad, it should be eliminated, and that there is no reason to stop at 4% inflation just because we happen to be there. They make the point that 0% is a very different target rate from all others: It corresponds to price stability. This is desirable in itself. Knowing the price level will be the same in 10 or 20 years as it is today simplifies several complicated decisions, and eliminates the scope for money illusion. Also, given the time consistency problem facing central banks (discussed in chapter 25) credibility and simplicity of the target inflation rate are important. Price stability may achieve these goals better than a target inflation rate of 4%.

The debate is not settled. For the time being, most central banks appear to be aiming for low but positive inflation—that is, inflation rates between 2% and 4%.

Once a central bank has decided what rate of inflation it wants to achieve, it still faces two issues:

- What target should it announce? Should it announce a target rate for money growth (which it controls) or should it announce a target for inflation (which is what it cares about, but does not control directly)?
- Once it has chosen a target, how closely should it try to meet it? For example, in the short run, how much weight should it put on meeting the target versus getting the economy out of a recession?

Money Growth and Inflation Revisited

Consider the following two propositions: (1) In the medium run and the long run, inflation is determined by the growth rate of the money stock. (2) The central bank controls the growth rate of the money stock.

Together, the two propositions suggest a simple rule for monetary policy: Compute the growth rate of the money stock consistent with the desired rate of inflation, and announce this growth rate as the target. By meeting its money growth target, the central bank will then achieve its desired rate of inflation.

As appealing as this rule sounds, it runs into a serious problem: It does not work! Even over long periods of time, it turns out that there is no tight relation between the rate of growth of the money stock and the rate of inflation. Sure, the two generally move together: If money growth is high, inflation will also be high; and if money growth is low, inflation will be low. Recall how much inflation and money growth move together during episodes of hyperinflation (chapter 23). But the relation is not tight enough that, by choosing a rate of money growth, the central bank can achieve precisely its desired rate of inflation.

This proposition is shown in Figure 26–1, which plots 10-year averages of the inflation rate (using the CPI as the price index) against 10-year averages of the growth rate of the money stock ($M1$) from 1970 to 1998 (for example, the value of the inflation rate for 1998 is the average inflation rate for 1989–1998). The reason for using 10-year averages should be clear: In the short run, changes in money growth affect mostly output, not inflation. It is only in the medium run that a relation between money growth and inflation should emerge. Taking 10-year averages of both money and inflation is a way of looking for the presence of

From chapter 4: $M1$ is the sum of currency and checkable deposits. The Fed does not directly control $M1$. What it controls is H, the monetary base; but it can choose H to achieve any value of $M1$ it wants. So it is reasonable to think of the Fed as controlling $M1$.

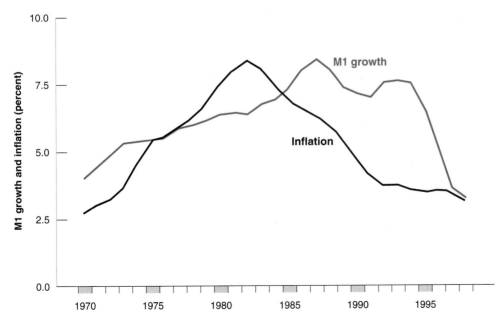

FIGURE 26–1

$M1$ Growth and Inflation: 10-Year Averages, 1970–1998

There is no tight relation between $M1$ growth and inflation, even in the medium run.

such a medium-run relation. Figure 26–1 shows that for the United States since 1970, the relation between $M1$ growth and inflation has not been very tight. True, both went up at the beginning of the period, and both have come down since. But note, for example, how inflation started declining in the early 1980s, whereas money growth remained high for another decade, and has only come down in the 1990s.

From Money to Monetary Aggregates

Why is there no tight relation between money growth and inflation? The answer is because of *shifts in the demand for money.* An example will help here. Suppose, as the result of the introduction of credit cards, people decide to hold only half the amount of money they used to hold before; in other words, the real demand for money decreases by half. In the medium run, the real money stock must also decrease by half. For a given nominal money stock, the price level must double. So, even if the nominal money stock is constant, there will be a period of inflation as the price level doubles. During this period, there will be no tight relation between money growth (which is zero) and inflation (which is positive).

The reason the demand for money shifts over time goes beyond the introduction of credit cards. To understand why, we must challenge an assumption we have maintained until now, namely, that there was a sharp distinction between money and other assets. In fact, there are many financial assets that are close to money. They cannot be used for transactions—at least not without substantial restrictions—but they can be exchanged for money at little cost. In other words, they are very **liquid**; this makes them potentially attractive substitutes for money. Shifts between money and these assets are the main factor behind shifts in the demand for money.

Take, for example, *money market fund shares.* Money market funds are financial intermediaries that hold as assets short-maturity securities (typically, Treasury bills) and have deposits (or shares, as they are called) as liabilities. The funds pay depositors an interest rate close to the T-bill rate minus the administrative costs of running the fund. Deposits can be exchanged for money on notice and at little cost. Most money market funds allow depositors to write checks but only above a certain amount, typically $500. Because of this restriction, money market funds are not included in $M1$. When these funds were introduced in the mid-1970s, people were able for the first time to hold a very liquid asset while receiving an interest rate close to that on T-bills. Money market funds quickly became very attractive, increasing from nothing in 1973 to $321 billion in 1989. Many people reduced the balances on their bank accounts and moved to money market funds. In other words, there was a large negative shift in the demand for money.

The presence of shifts between money and other liquid assets have led central banks to construct measures that include not only money, but also other liquid assets. These aggregates are called **monetary aggregates**, and typically come under the names of $M2$, $M3$, and so on. In the United States, $M2$—which is also sometimes called **broad money**—includes $M1$ (currency and checkable deposits), plus money market mutual fund shares, money market deposit accounts (the same as money market shares, but issued by banks rather than money market funds), and time deposits (deposits with an explicit maturity of a few months to a few years, and with a penalty for early withdrawal).

The construction of $M2$ and other monetary aggregates would appear to offer a solution to our earlier inflation targeting problem. If most of the shifts in the demand for money are between $M1$ and other assets within $M2$, the demand for $M2$ should be more stable than the demand for $M1$, and so there should be a tighter relation between $M2$ growth and inflation than between $M1$ growth and inflation. Thus, the central bank should target $M2$ growth. Although this is the approach taken by many central banks, it is not without problems:

- The relation between $M2$ growth and inflation is tighter than between $M1$ growth and inflation; but it is still not very tight. This is shown in Figure 26–2, which plots 10-year averages of the inflation rate and of the rate of growth of $M2$. The evolution of $M2$ growth is

From chapter 5, equation (5.3) (the *LM* equation): The real money supply (the left side) must be equal to the real demand for money (the right side)

$$\frac{M}{P} = YL(i)$$

If, as a result of the introduction of credit cards, the real demand for money halves, then

$$\frac{M}{P} = \frac{1}{2}YL(i)$$

For a given level of output and a given interest rate, M/P must also halve. Given M, this implies that P must double.

For comparison, checkable deposits were equal to $560 billion in 1989.

In 1998, $M2$ was equal to about $4.4 billion, compared to $1.1 billion for $M1$.

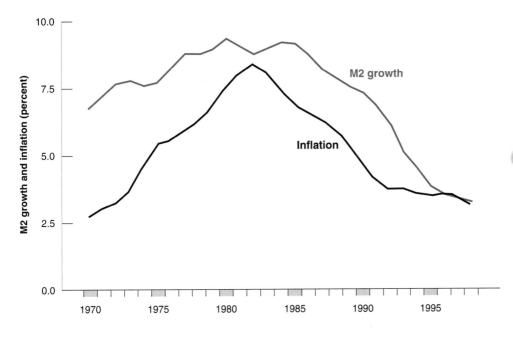

FIGURE 26–2

M2 Growth and Inflation: 10-Year Averages, 1970–1998

Although the relation between *M2* growth and inflation is tighter than the relation between *M1* growth and inflation, it is still not very tight.

closer to that of inflation than was the case for *M1* growth. But the fit is still not tight. Note, for example, how *M2* growth was nearly 5% above inflation in the 1970s, and how this difference has disappeared over time. Put another way, a given rate of *M2* growth is associated with 5% more inflation than it was in the 1970s.

- More importantly, although the Fed controls *M1*, it does not control *M2*. For example, if people decide to shift from holding T-bills directly to holding them indirectly, through money market funds, this will increase *M2*. There is, however, little the Fed can do about it. Thus, *M2* is a strange target: It is neither under the direct control of the Fed, nor what the Fed ultimately cares about.

These two problems have led an increasing number of central banks to shift from the targeting of some monetary aggregate to **inflation targeting**. The logic is simple: Inflation may not be under the control of the central bank, but at least it is what the central bank and the public ultimately care about.

First to adopt inflation targeting was New Zealand in 1990, which set a target range for inflation of 0% to 2%, later extended to 0% to 3%. Next was Canada in 1991, setting a target range for inflation of 0% to 2%. Since then, some form of inflation targeting has been adopted by, among others, the United Kingdom, Sweden, Israel, and Spain.

Taylor's Rule

Once the central bank has chosen and announced a target, say, an inflation target, how closely should it try to meet that target?

Suppose the target for inflation is 2%, but the current inflation rate is 5%. Should the central bank try to decrease inflation to 2% as fast as it can, or should it decrease it slowly? The fact that, in the short run, money growth affects both output and inflation suggests that the answer should be: Not too fast. Decreasing inflation quickly is likely to require a sharp recession, something the central bank should try to avoid. How slowly or how fast should the central bank go toward the target? In answer to this question, John Taylor from Stanford University, has suggested a rule that the central bank may want to follow. **Taylor's rule** is as follows:

Let π be the rate of inflation, and π^* be the target rate of inflation. Let i be the nominal interest rate, and i^* be the target nominal interest rate—the nominal interest rate associated with the target rate of inflation π^* in the medium run. Let u be the unemployment rate, and u_n be the natural unemployment rate.

Think of the central bank as choosing the nominal interest rate, i (recall from chapter 5 that by controlling the money stock, the central bank can achieve any short-term nominal

As we saw in chapter 14: In the medium run, the real interest rate is given, so the nominal interest rate moves one for one with the inflation rate: If $r = 3\%$ and the target inflation rate $\pi^* = 2\%$, then the target nominal interest rate $i^* = 3\% + 2\% = 5\%$. If the target inflation rate π^* is 0%, then $i^* = 3\% + 0\% = 3\%$.

interest rate it wants). Then, Taylor argued, the central bank should follow the following rule

$$i = i^* + a(\pi - \pi^*) - b(u - u_n)$$

where a and b are positive coefficients. Let's look at what the rule says:

This ignores the difference between expected inflation and actual inflation. A more precise statement is that the nominal interest rate must increase more than one for one with expected inflation:

$i\uparrow > \pi^e\uparrow \Rightarrow r(\equiv i - \pi^e)\uparrow$

- If inflation is equal to target inflation ($\pi = \pi^*$), and the unemployment rate is equal to the natural rate ($u = u_n$), then the central bank should set the nominal interest rate i equal to its target value i^*. This way, the economy can stay on the same path, with inflation equal to the target, and unemployment equal to the natural rate.

- If inflation is higher than the target ($\pi > \pi^*$), the central bank should increase the nominal interest rate above i^*. This higher interest rate will increase unemployment, and this increase in unemployment will lead to a decrease in inflation.

   The coefficient a should therefore reflect how much the central bank cares about unemployment versus inflation. The higher a, the more the central bank will increase the interest rate in response to inflation; the more the economy will slow down; the faster inflation will return to the target.

   In any case, Taylor pointed out, a should be larger than one. Why? Because what matters for spending is the real interest rate, not the nominal interest rate. When inflation increases, the central bank, if it wants to decrease spending and output, must increase the *real* interest rate. In other words, it must increase the nominal interest rate more than one for one with inflation.

What values of a and b would a central bank choose if it cared only about inflation?

- If unemployment is higher than the natural rate ($u > u_n$), the central bank should decrease the nominal interest rate. The lower nominal interest rate will increase activity, leading to a decrease in unemployment. Like the coefficient a, the coefficient b should reflect how much the central bank cares about unemployment relative to inflation. The higher b, the more the central bank will be willing to deviate from target inflation to keep unemployment close to the natural rate.

   In stating this rule, Taylor did not argue that it should be followed blindly: Many other events, such as an exchange rate crisis, or the need to change the composition of spending and thus the mix between monetary and fiscal policy, justify changing the nominal interest rate for reasons other than those included in the rule. But, he argued, the rule provides a useful way of thinking about monetary policy: Choose a target rate of inflation, and then try to achieve it taking into account not only current inflation but also current unemployment. Interestingly, researchers looking at the behavior of both the Fed in the United States, and the Bundesbank in Germany, have found that despite the fact that these two central banks surely did not think of themselves as following Taylor's rule, this rule describes their behavior over the last 15 to 20 years quite well.

26-3 | The Fed in Action

The Fed's web site (http://www.federalreserve.gov/) gives a lot of information about how the Fed is organized, and what it does.

Having discussed the design of monetary policy in general, let's end this chapter by looking at how the Fed actually carries out monetary policy in the United States.

The Mandate of the Fed

The mandate of the Federal Reserve System was most recently defined in the **Humphrey–Hawkins Act**, passed by Congress in 1978. The act requires the Fed to

> *maintain long-run growth of the monetary and credit aggregates commensurate with the economy's long-run potential to increase production, so as to promote effectively the goals of maximum employment, stable prices, and moderate long-term interest rates.*

There is one important point behind the heavy official language: The Fed has a mandate not only to achieve low inflation but also to stabilize economic activity.

The Organization of the Fed

The Federal Reserve System is composed of three parts:

- A set of 12 **Federal Reserve Districts**, each with a Federal Reserve District Bank. The main functions of these regional banks are to manage check clearing and supervise banking and financial activities in the district.
- The **Board of Governors**, located in Washington, D.C. The board has seven members, including the chairman of the Fed. Each governor is appointed by the U.S. president for a nonrenewable term of 14 years and must be confirmed by the U.S. Senate. The chairman is appointed by the U.S. president for a renewable term of four years. The Board of Governors is in charge of the design of monetary policy.
- The **Federal Open Market Committee (FOMC)**, also located in Washington. The committee has 12 members. Five are Federal Reserve District Bank presidents, and the other seven are the governors. The principle behind this composition is that Federal Reserve Bank presidents are more likely to be attuned to the economic situation in their districts, the governors more attuned to national trends and evolutions. The main function of the committee is to give instructions to the **Open Market Desk**, the desk in charge of open market operations—the purchase and sale of bonds by the Fed—in New York City.

This description might suggest that the Fed is a complex organization with many centers of power. The reality is simpler: The chairman is typically very powerful. And the most important decisions are made by the Federal Open Market Committee.

We discussed in chapter 25, the importance of central bank independence. The Fed is one of the most independent central banks in the world. The main control lever available to the U.S. president and Congress is the nomination and confirmation of the chairman every four years. But during his four-year tenure, the chairman is largely free to choose monetary policy as he thinks best. The Fed's budget is not subject to congressional oversight, so Congress cannot put pressure on the Fed by threatening to cut its funding. The chairman of the Fed must testify twice a year to Congress to explain the stance of monetary policy. Members of Congress often complain and grumble about the Fed's decisions, but there is not much they can actually do about it.

See Figure 25–3.

The Instruments of Monetary Policy

We saw in chapter 4 that we can think of the interest rate as being determined by the demand and supply for central bank money. Recall the equilibrium condition (equation [4.11]) is given by

$$H = [c + \theta(1 - c)] \$Y L(i) \qquad (26.1)$$

On the left side is H, the supply of central bank money—equivalently, the monetary base. On the right side is the demand for central bank money—the sum of the demand for currency by people, and the demand for reserves by banks. Think of it this way:

See chapter 4.

- Start with $\$Y L(i)$, the overall demand for money (currency and checkable deposits). This demand depends on income and the opportunity cost of holding money, the interest rate on bonds.
- The parameter c is the proportion of money people want to hold in the form of currency. Thus, $c \$Y L(i)$ is the demand for currency by people.
- What people do not hold in currency, they hold in the form of checkable deposits. Checkable deposits are therefore a fraction $(1 - c)$ of the overall demand for money, thus, $(1 - c) \$Y L(i)$. The parameter θ denotes the ratio of reserves held by banks to checkable deposits. The demand for reserves by banks is then $\theta(1 - c) \$Y L(i)$.
- Adding the demand for currency, $c \$YL(i)$, and the demand for reserves by banks, $\theta(1 - c) \$Y L(i)$, gives the total demand for central bank money—the right side of the equation.

The equilibrium interest rate is such that the supply and the demand for central bank money are equal. The Fed has three instruments at its disposal to affect this interest rate. The first, *reserve requirements*, affects the demand for reserves, and thus the demand for central bank money. The other two, *lending to banks* and *open market operations*, affect the supply of central bank money.

Reserve Requirements. The Fed determines **reserve requirements**, the minimum amount of reserves that banks must hold in proportion to checkable deposits. Even without such requirements, banks would want to hold some reserves to be able to satisfy their depositors' demand for cash. But the Fed typically sets reserve requirements above the level that banks would choose. The current requirement is that banks hold reserves equaling 10% of their checkable deposits.

By changing reserve requirements, the Fed changes the amount of reserves banks must hold for a given amount of demand deposits, and thus the demand for central bank money. An increase in reserve requirements leads to an increase in the demand for central bank money, leading to an increase in the equilibrium interest rate. Symmetrically, a decrease in the reserve requirement leads to a decrease in the interest rate.

Increases in reserve requirements can force banks to take drastic actions to increase their reserves, such as recalling some of the loans they have made. For this reason, the Fed has become increasingly reluctant to use reserve requirements as an instrument of macroeconomic policy, preferring to rely on its other instruments instead.

Lending to Banks. The Fed can also lend to banks (an instrument we ignored in chapter 4). How much it lends and under what conditions is called the Fed's **discount policy**. The rate at which it lends to banks is called the **discount rate**. When the Fed lends to banks, it is said to lend through the **discount window**.

From the point of view of the Fed, lending to banks is very similar to buying bonds in an open market operation. In both cases, the Fed creates money and thus increases H, the monetary base. In lending to banks, it receives in exchange a claim on the bank. In open market operations, it acquires a government bond, a claim on the government.

Until the introduction of open market operations in the 1930s, the discount policy was the Fed's main instrument. But its role has steadily declined in favor of open market operations. The Fed typically discourages banks from borrowing from the discount window except for short-run or seasonal reasons. Changes in the discount rate still play a role, but mostly as a signal of the Fed's intentions. Financial markets often interpret a decrease in the discount rate as a signal that the Fed is going to follow a more expansionary policy. Through its effect on expectations of future interest rates, a decrease in the discount rate often leads to a decrease in medium- and long-term interest rates.

Open Market Operations. The Fed's third and main tool is *open market operations*, in which the Fed buys and sells bonds in the bonds market. Open market operations are carried out by the Open Market Desk in New York and are typically conducted in the market for short-term Treasury bills.

When the Fed buys bonds, it pays for them by creating money, increasing H; when it sells bonds, it decreases H. Over the years, the Fed has found open market operations to be the most convenient and flexible way of changing the supply of central bank money, and thus of changing the interest rate. Open market operations are today the main instrument of U.S. monetary policy.

The Practice of Policy

How does the Fed decide what policy to follow? A good place to start is with the meetings of the FOMC, which take place about every six weeks. For these meetings, the Fed staff prepares forecasts and simulations of the effects of alternative monetary policies. The forecasts

---

An increase in θ increases the demand for reserves by banks, increasing the demand for central bank money. Given an unchanged supply, the interest rate must increase to decrease the demand for central bank money and maintain equilibrium.

From chapter 15: Medium- and long-term interest rates are weighted averages of expected short-term interest rates. A decrease in the discount rate, which leads participants in financial markets to expect lower short-term interest rates in the future, leads to a decline in long-term interest rates.

For more on open market operations, review chapter 4.

show what is likely to happen to the economy under an unchanged monetary policy and what the major sources of uncertainty appear to be. They also show the evolution of the economy under alternative monetary policies (for example, under various assumptions about the growth of the monetary base).

The FOMC then decides on the course of monetary policy. Once a year, it announces target ranges for the growth of a number of monetary aggregates over the following year. Currently, the Fed announces target ranges for two monetary aggregates, $M2$ and $M3$. The target range for $M2$ has remained the same since 1994, 1% to 5%. Then, at each meeting during the year, it issues a general directive to the open market desk about what to do during the following six weeks. The conduct of open market operations between FOMC meetings is left to the manager of the Open Market Desk. The manager focuses on the interest rate in the market for central bank money, the *federal funds market*. In that market, banks that have excess reserves (reserves in excess of what they are required to hold) lend overnight to banks that have insufficient reserves. The rate in that market is called the *federal funds rate*. As new information comes in, indicating, for example, that the economy is stronger or weaker than expected, the manager (in consultation with the FOMC members) intervenes to change the federal funds rate as he or she sees best, until the next FOMC meeting.

Could the Conduct of U.S. Monetary Policy Be Improved?

Given our discussion of the shortcomings of targeting monetary aggregates in section 26-2, one must ask, How close does the Fed come to maintaining the monetary aggregates within their target ranges? The answer is given in Figure 26–3, which plots for each year since 1975 the actual value of $M2$ growth for the year, as well as the target range set for $M2$ growth at the beginning of the year.

Clearly, the Fed does not always hit its target range: Actual $M2$ growth has ended out of the range for 9 out of the last 24 years! Note in particular how in the late 1990s, $M2$ growth has increased from the bottom of the target range to far above the target range. Given that inflation has remained very low, overshooting the target has not worried financial market participants, who attribute the high growth rate in $M2$ to shifts in the demand for $M2$. But these sharp swings in $M2$ growth surely reinforce the case we discussed earlier for shifting to inflation targeting. What is the point of announcing a range for $M2$ if you miss the range so often?

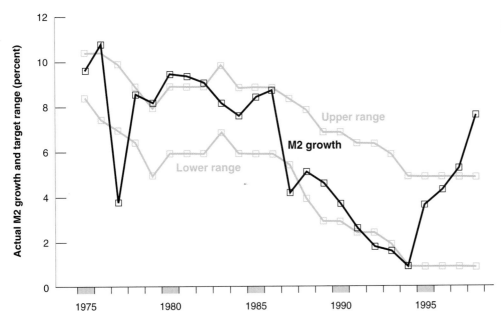

FIGURE 26–3

$M2$ Growth, 1975–1998: Actual Growth Rate and Target Growth Range

Actual $M2$ growth has ended out of the target range for 9 out of the last 24 years.

More generally, we may ask: Could the conduct of monetary policy in the United States be improved? At the time of this writing, nearly all economists would agree that the record of monetary policy over the last 20 years in the United States has been outstanding. Since the early 1980s, the Fed has used monetary policy successfully, first to achieve and then to maintain low inflation, and to stabilize output. Much of the credit goes to Alan Greenspan, the current chairman of the Fed. Without an explicit inflation target, Greenspan has convinced financial markets that the Fed is committed to low inflation. At the same time, he has shown a willingness to use interest rates to stabilize activity whenever it is needed. A sharp decrease in interest rates in the early 1990s probably reduced the depth of the 1990–1991 recession. In late 1998, as uncertainty associated with the Asian crisis seemed to decrease U.S. consumer and business confidence, a decrease in the federal funds rate was widely interpreted as a commitment on the part of the Fed to help sustain activity if this turned out to be needed. This decrease appeared to play a central role in reestablishing confidence. By the end of 1998, Greenspan was widely hailed as one of the heroes of the year, single-handedly responsible for avoiding a world-wide recession.

Some of the compliments may be exaggerated, but there is no doubt that the record of monetary policy under Alan Greenspan has been very good. Should one leave well enough alone? Some economists do not think so. They argue it is unwise to have policy depend so much on one individual, that one cannot be sure that the next chairman of the Fed will be able to achieve the same mix of credibility and flexibility. Improvements in the design of policy, such as the shift to inflation targeting, can and should be made. They may not be needed now, but they cannot hurt and may be useful in the future.

SUMMARY

On the Optimal Rate of Inflation

- Inflation is down to very low levels in most OECD countries. One question facing central banks is whether they should try to achieve zero inflation—that is, price stability.

- The main arguments for zero inflation are the following:
  - Inflation, together with an imperfectly indexed tax system, leads to tax distortions.
  - Because of money illusion, inflation leads people and firms to make incorrect decisions.
  - Higher inflation typically comes with higher inflation variability, creating more uncertainty and making it more difficult for people and firms to make the right decisions about the future.
  - As a target, price stability has a simplicity and a credibility that a positive inflation target does not have.

- There are also arguments for maintaining low but positive inflation.
  - Revenues from money growth (seignorage) allow for lower taxes elsewhere. However, this argument is quantitatively unimportant when comparing inflation rates of 0% versus, say, 4%.

  - Positive actual and expected inflation allow the central bank to achieve negative real interest rates, an option that can be useful when fighting a recession.
  - Positive inflation allows firms to achieve real wage cuts when needed without requiring nominal wage cuts.
  - A further decrease from the current positive rate of inflation to zero would imply an increase in unemployment for some time, and this transition cost may exceed whatever benefits come from zero inflation.

On the Design of Monetary Policy

- Once a central bank has decided what rate of inflation it wants to achieve, it faces two issues. First, should it choose a target for money growth or for inflation? Second, how closely should it try to meet the target?

- Because of shifts in the demand for money, the relation between $M1$ growth and inflation is not tight. Thus, targeting $M1$ growth would lead to large movements in inflation.

- Growth rates of monetary aggregates that include money and other liquid assets, such as $M2$, move more closely with inflation. But the relation is still not very tight. And more importantly, these larger aggregates are not under the control of the central bank.

- These problems have led several central banks to shift to inflation targeting. The issue is then how close the central bank should try to stay to the target.

- Taylor's rule gives a useful way of thinking about how the central bank should operate. The central bank should move its interest rate in response to two main factors: the deviation of the inflation rate from its target, and the deviation of the unemployment rate from the natural rate. A central bank that follows this rule will stabilize activity and achieve its target inflation rate in the medium run.

On the Fed

- The Federal Reserve System is composed of three parts: 12 Federal Reserve Districts; a Board of Governors, with seven members including the chairman; and the Federal Open Market Committee, composed of the seven members of the Board of Governors and five Federal Reserve District Bank presidents. Open market operations are the main instrument of monetary policy. The other two, reserve requirements and discount policy, are used infrequently.

- Once a year, the Federal Open Market Committee announces target ranges for the monetary aggregates. These target ranges are used to signal the general course of monetary policy. The Fed does not feel bound by these ranges and often ends up outside the range, if it feels that circumstances warrant it.

- Decisions about the course of monetary policy are made every six weeks by the Federal Open Market Committee. Daily decisions about open market operations are left to the manager of the Open Market Desk in New York City, in consultation with members of the Federal Open Market Committee.

- The record of monetary policy in the United States in the recent past is very good: Since the early 1980s, the Fed has used monetary policy successfully, first to achieve low inflation, and to stabilize output.

KEY TERMS

- shoe-leather costs, 503
- liquid, 508
- monetary aggregates, 508
- broad money (*M2*), 508
- inflation targeting, 509
- Taylor's rule, 509
- Humphrey–Hawkins Act, 510
- Federal Reserve Districts, 511

- Board of Governors, 511
- Federal Open Market Committee (FOMC), 511
- Open Market Desk, 511
- reserve requirements, 512
- discount policy, 512
- discount rate, 512
- discount window, 512

QUESTIONS & PROBLEMS

[Web] indicates that the question requires access to the Internet.

1. TRUE/FALSE/UNCERTAIN

a. The most important argument for a positive rate of inflation in OECD countries is seignorage.

b. The Fed should target *M2* growth.

c. Fighting inflation should be the Fed's only purpose.

d. Announcing target ranges for money growth would limit the flexibility and therefore the usefulness of monetary policy.

e. We would do just as well if we replaced the chairman of the Fed by Taylor's rule.

f. The higher the inflation rate, the higher the effective tax rate on income.

2. MONEY DEMAND SHIFTS

How would each of the following affect the demand for $M1$ and $M2$?

a. Banks reduce penalties on early withdrawal from time deposits.

b. The government forbids the use of money market funds for check-writing purposes.

c. The U.S. government legislates a tax on all ATM transactions.

d. Congress decides to impose a tax on all transactions in short-term government securities.

3. NOMINAL INTEREST RATES, INFLATION, AND TAXES

Suppose you have a mortgage of $50,000. Consider two cases:

i. Expected inflation is 0%; the nominal interest rate on your mortgage is 4%.

ii. Expected inflation is 10%; the nominal interest rate on your mortgage is 14%.

a. What is the real interest rate you are paying on your mortgage in each case?

b. Suppose you can deduct nominal mortgage interest payments from your income before paying the income tax (as is the case in the United States). Assume the tax rate is 25%. Thus, for each dollar you pay in mortgage interest, you pay 25 cents less in taxes, in effect getting a subsidy from the government for your mortgage costs. Compute, in each case, the real interest rate you are paying on your mortgage, taking into account this subsidy.

c. "In the United States, inflation is good for homeowners." Discuss this statement.

4. $M2$ AND $M1$

Suppose that $M1$ growth is very high, but $M2$ growth is equal to zero. Should you worry about inflation? Explain.

5. MONETARY POLICY IN ACTION

Using equation (26.1), show three ways in which monetary policy can decrease the interest rate, given the level of output. In each case, explain how it works.

6. NEGATIVE REAL INTEREST RATES

"The worry that with deflation, real interest rates cannot be negative, is misplaced. Fiscal policy can decrease the cost of borrowing as much as it wants, by offering subsidies to borrowers." Discuss this statement.

7. MINUTES OF THE FEDERAL OPEN MARKET COMMITTEE [Web]

Access the web site of the Board of Governors of the Federal Reserve and read the most recent minutes of the Federal Open Market Committee (at http://www.bog.frb.fed.us/fomc/).

a. What has happened to the growth rate of $M2$ since the last meeting?

b. Does the FOMC seem to be more worried about a slowdown in growth or a pickup in the pace of inflation?

c. What is happening to the benchmark federal funds rate?

d. Was the Committee's action unanimously approved by all its members? If not, why did some members disagree?

FURTHER READINGS

For evidence of nominal wage rigidity and the scope for inflation to facilitate real wage adjustments, see the results of a survey of managers by Alan Blinder and Don Choi, in "A Shred of Evidence on Theories of Wage Rigidity," *Quarterly Journal of Economics*, 1990, 1003–1016.

For a discussion of the pros and cons of low inflation, look at George Akerlof, William Dickens, and George Perry. "The Macroeconomics of Low Inflation", *Brookings Papers on Economic Activity*, 1996–1.

For more detail on how the Fed operates, read Glenn Hubbard, *Money, the Financial System, and the Economy* (Reading, MA: Addison-Wesley, 1997).

"Modern Central Banking," written by Stanley Fischer for the 300th anniversary of the Bank of England, published in *The Future of Central Banking*, Forrest Capie, Stanley Fischer, Charles Goodhart and Norbert Schnadt, eds., (Cambridge: Cambridge University Press, 1995), provides a very nice discussion of the current issues in central banking. Read also "What Central Bankers Could Learn from Academics—and Vice Versa," by Alan Blinder, *Journal of Economic Perspectives*, Spring 1997, 3–19.

On inflation targeting, read "Inflation Targeting: A New Framework for Monetary Policy?" by Ben Bernanke and Frederic Mishkin, *Journal of Economic Perspectives*, Spring 1997, 97–116.

For more on the Taylor rule, read John Taylor, "Discretion versus Policy Rules in Practice," *Carnegie Rochester Conference Series on Public Policy 39* (Amsterdam: North-Holland, 1993), 195–214.

CHAPTER 27 | Fiscal Policy. A Summing Up

In this chapter, we do for fiscal policy what we did for monetary policy in chapter 26—review what we have learned and tie up remaining loose ends.

Let's first briefly review what we have learned (the Focus box "Fiscal Policy: What We Have Learned and Where" gives a more detailed summary).

- In the short run, a budget deficit (triggered, say, by a decrease in taxes) increases demand and output. What happens to investment is ambiguous.

- In the medium run, output returns to its natural level. The interest rate and the composition of spending are different, however. The interest rate is higher; investment is lower.

- In the long run, lower investment implies a lower capital stock, and therefore a lower level of output.

In deriving these conclusions, however, we did not pay close attention to the government budget constraint, that is, to the relation between debt, deficits, government spending, and taxes. This chapter's first task is to do just that, to look at the government's budget constraint and its implications. Having done so, we examine several fiscal policy issues where this constraint plays an important role, from the proposition that deficits do not really matter to the dangers of accumulating very high levels of public debt. Finally, we return to the U.S. budget and the problems on the horizon.

- In chapter 3 we looked at the role of government spending and taxes in determining demand and output in the short run.

  We saw how, in the short run, increases in government spending and decreases in taxes both increase output.
- In chapter 5 we looked at the short-run effects of fiscal policy on output and the interest rate.

  We saw how a fiscal contraction leads to decreases in both output and the interest rate. We also saw how fiscal and monetary policy can be used to affect both the level and the composition of output.
- In chapter 7 we looked at the effects of fiscal policy in the short and medium run.

  We saw that in the medium run (taking the capital stock as given), changes in fiscal policy have no effect on output and are simply reflected in a different composition of spending.
- In chapter 11 we looked at how saving, and thus budget deficits, affect the level of capital accumulation and the level of output in the long run.

  We saw how, once capital accumulation is taken into account, larger deficits decrease capital accumulation, leading to a lower level of output in the long run.
- In chapter 17 we looked at the short-run effects of fiscal policy, taking into account not only its direct effects through taxes and government spending, but also its effects on expectations.

  We saw how the effects of a deficit reduction on output depend on expectations of future fiscal and monetary policy. We also saw how a deficit reduction may, in some circumstances, be expansionary, even in the short run.

- In chapter 19 we looked at the effects of fiscal policy when the economy is open to trade.

  We saw how fiscal policy affects both output and the trade balance, and examined the relation between budget deficits and trade deficits. We saw how fiscal policy and exchange-rate adjustments can be used to affect both the level and the composition of output.
- In chapter 20 we looked at the role of fiscal policy in an economy with open goods and financial markets.

  We saw how in the presence of international capital mobility, the effects of fiscal policy depend on the exchange-rate regime. Fiscal policy has a much stronger effect on output under fixed exchange rates than under flexible exchange rates.
- In chapter 23 we looked at the relation between fiscal policy, money growth, and inflation.

  We saw how budget deficits must be financed either by borrowing or by money creation. When money creation becomes the main source of finance, the result of large deficits is high money growth and hyperinflation.
- In chapter 25 we looked at the problems facing fiscal policy makers, from uncertainty about the effects of policy to issues of time consistency and credibility.

  We discussed the pros and cons of restraints on the conduct of fiscal policy, such as a constitutional amendment to balance the budget.
- In this chapter we look further at the implications of the budget constraint facing the government and discuss current issues of fiscal policy in the United States.

27-1 | The Government Budget Constraint

Suppose that starting from a balanced budget, the government cuts taxes, creating a deficit. What will happen to debt over time? Will the government need to increase taxes later? If so, by how much?

To answer these questions, we must start with the definition of the budget deficit. We can write the budget deficit in year t as

$$\text{deficit} = rB_{t-1} + G_t - T_t \tag{27.1}$$

All variables are in real terms. B_{t-1} is government debt at the end of year $t - 1$, or equivalently, at the beginning of year t; r is the real interest rate, which I shall take to be constant here. Thus, rB_{t-1} equals the real interest payments on the existing government debt. G_t is government spending on goods and services during year t. T_t is taxes minus transfers during year t. In words: The budget deficit equals spending, including interest payments on the debt, minus taxes net of transfers.

Note two characteristics of equation (27.1):

Do not confuse the words "deficit" and "debt." (Many journalists and politicians do.) Debt is a *stock*, what the government owes as a result of past deficits. The deficit is a flow, how much the government borrows in a given year.

- We measure interest payments as real interest payments—the product of the *real* interest rate times existing debt—rather than as actual interest payments—the product of the nominal interest rate times existing debt. As we discuss in the Focus box "Inflation Accounting and the Measurement of Deficits," this is the correct way of measuring interest payments. However, official measures of the deficit include actual (nominal) interest payments and are therefore incorrect. The correct measure of the deficit is sometimes called the **inflation-adjusted deficit**.
- For consistency with our definition of G as spending on goods and services earlier, G does not include transfer payments. Transfers are instead subtracted from T, so that T stands for taxes minus transfers. Official measures of government spending add transfers to spending on goods and services, and define revenues as taxes, not taxes net of transfers. These are only accounting conventions. Whether transfers are added to spending or subtracted from taxes makes a difference to the measurement of G and T, but clearly does not affect the measure of the deficit.

Let G denote spending on goods and services, Tr denotes transfers, and Tax denotes total taxes. Then,

Deficit = G + Tr − Tax

This can be rewritten in two (equivalent) ways:

Deficit = G − (Tax − Tr)

The deficit is equal to spending on goods and services, minus net taxes—total taxes minus transfers. This is the way we write it in the text:

Deficit = (G + Tr) − Tax

The deficit is equal to total spending—spending on goods and services plus transfers—minus total taxes. This is the way the government reports spending and revenues.

The **government budget constraint** then simply states that the *change in government debt during year t* is equal to the *deficit during year t*

$$B_t - B_{t-1} = \text{deficit}_t$$

If the government runs a deficit, government debt increases. If the government runs a surplus, government debt decreases.

Using the definition of the deficit, we can rewrite the government budget constraint as

$$B_t - B_{t-1} = rB_{t-1} + G_t - T_t \tag{27.2}$$

The government budget constraint links the change in debt to the initial level of debt (which affects interest payments) and to current government spending and taxes.

It is often convenient to decompose the deficit into the sum of two terms:

- Interest payments on the debt, rB_{t-1}.
- The difference between spending and taxes, $G_t - T_t$. This second term is called the **primary deficit** (equivalently, $T_t - G_t$ is called the **primary surplus**).

Using this decomposition, we can rewrite equation (27.2) as

$$\underbrace{B_t - B_{t-1}}_{\text{Change in the debt}} = \underbrace{rB_{t-1}}_{\text{Interest payments}} + \underbrace{G_t - T_t}_{\text{Primary deficit}}$$

Or, moving B_{t-1} to the right and reorganizing

$$B_t = (1 + r)B_{t-1} + \underbrace{G_t - T_t}_{\text{Primary deficit}} \tag{27.3}$$

Debt at the end of year t equals $(1 + r)$ times debt at the end of year $t - 1$, plus the primary deficit during year t, $(G_t - T_t)$. This relation will prove very useful in what follows.

Current versus Future Taxes

Let's look at the implications of a one-year decrease in taxes for the path of debt and future taxes. Start from a situation where, until year 1, the government has balanced its budget, so that debt is equal to zero. During year 1, the government decreases taxes by 1 for one year. Thus, debt at the end of year 1, B_1, is equal to 1. What happens thereafter? Let's consider different cases.

FOCUS

Official measures of the budget deficit are constructed as nominal interest payments, iB, plus spending on goods and services, G, minus taxes net of transfers, T (I have dropped the time indices, which are not needed here)

$$\text{official measure of the deficit} = iB + G - T$$

This is an accurate measure of the *change in nominal debt*. If it is positive, the government is spending more than it receives, and must therefore issue new debt. If it is negative, the government buys debt back.

But it is not an accurate measure of the *change in real debt*, the change in how much the government owes, expressed in terms of goods rather than dollars. To see why not, suppose the official measure of the deficit is equal to zero, so the government neither issues nor buys back debt, and the amount of nominal debt remains the same. Suppose inflation is positive and equal to 10%. Then, at the end of the year, the real value of the debt has decreased by 10%. If we define—as we should—the deficit as the change in the real value of the debt of the government, the government is in fact running a budget surplus equal to 10% times the initial level of debt.

More generally, if B is debt and π is inflation, the official measure of the deficit overstates the correct measure by an amount equal to πB. Put another way, the correct measure of the deficit is obtained by subtracting πB from the official measure

$$\begin{aligned}\text{correct measure of the deficit} &= iB + G - T - \pi B \\ &= (i - \pi)B + G - T \\ &= rB + G - T\end{aligned}$$

where $r = i - \pi$ is the real interest rate. The correct measure of the deficit is thus equal to real interest payments plus government spending minus taxes net of transfers, the measure we have used in the text. (Note that r is equal here to the nominal interest rate minus *actual* inflation, and should be more accurately called the "realized real interest rate," to distinguish it from the real interest rate, which is equal to the nominal interest rate minus *expected* inflation.)

The difference between the official and the correct measures of the deficit equals πB. So, the higher the rate of inflation, π, or the higher the level of debt, B, the more inaccurate the official measure is. In countries in which both inflation and debt are high, the official measure may record a very large budget deficit, when in fact real government debt is actually decreasing. This is why you should always do the inflation adjustment before deriving conclusions about the position of fiscal policy.

Figure 1 plots the official and the inflation-adjusted measures of the budget deficit for the United States from 1968 to 1998. The official measure shows a deficit in every year except two, 1969 and 1998. The inflation-adjusted measure shows, instead, alternating deficits and surpluses until the late 1970s. However, both measures show how much worse the deficit became after 1980, and how things have improved in the 1990s. Today, with inflation running at about 2% a year, and the U.S. ratio of debt to GDP equal to roughly 40%, the difference between the two measures is roughly equal to 2% times 40%, or 0.8% of GDP. Put another way, an official budget deficit of 0.0% of GDP corresponds in fact to a budget surplus of 0.8%.

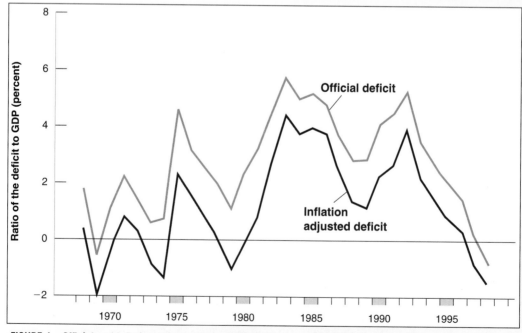

FIGURE 1   Official and Inflation-Adjusted Budget Deficits for the United States, 1968–1998

Full Repayment in Year 2. Suppose the government decides to repay the debt fully during year 2. From equation (27.3), the budget constraint for year 2 is given by

$$B_2 = (1 + r)B_1 + (G_2 - T_2)$$

If the debt is fully repaid during year 2, then debt at the end of year 2 is equal to zero: $B_2 = 0$. Replacing B_1 by 1 and B_2 by 0 in the preceding equation gives

$$T_2 - G_2 = (1 + r)$$

To repay the debt fully during year 2, the government must run a primary surplus equal to $(1 + r)$. It can do so in one of two ways: a decrease in spending or an increase in taxes. I shall assume here and in what follows that the adjustment comes through taxes, so that the path of spending is unaffected. It follows that the decrease in taxes by 1 below normal during year 1 must be offset by an increase in taxes by $(1 + r)$ above normal during year 2. The path of taxes and debt corresponding to this case is given in Figure 27–1(a) (assuming a value for r of 10%). The black bars represent taxes during each year—as deviations from their initial level, and the red lines represent the level of debt at the end of each year.

Full repayment in year 2:

$T_1 \downarrow$ by 1

$\Rightarrow T_2 \uparrow$ by $(1 + r)$

Full Repayment in Year t. Now suppose the government decides to wait until year t to increase taxes and repay the debt. So from year 2 to year $t - 1$, the primary deficit is equal to zero. Let's work out what this implies for the level of debt at the beginning of year t (equivalently, the end of year $t - 1$).

During year 2, the primary deficit is zero. So, from equation (27.3), debt at the end of year 2 is

$$B_2 = (1 + r)B_1 + 0 = (1 + r)$$

where the second equality follows from the fact that $B_1 = 1$.

With the primary deficit still equal to zero during year 3, debt at the end of year 3 is

$$B_3 = (1 + r)B_2 + 0 = (1 + r)(1 + r) = (1 + r)^2$$

Solving for debt at the end of year 4 and so on, it is clear that as long as the government keeps a primary deficit equal to zero, debt grows at a rate equal to the interest rate, and thus debt at the end of year $t - 1$ is given by

$$B_{t-1} = (1 + r)^{t-2} \tag{27.4}$$

Despite the fact that taxes are cut only in year 1, debt keeps increasing over time, at a rate equal to the interest rate. The reason is simple: Although the primary deficit is equal to zero, debt is now positive, and so are interest payments on the debt. Each year, the government must issue more debt to pay the interest on existing debt.

In year t, the year in which the government decides to repay the debt, the budget constraint is

$$B_t = (1 + r)B_{t-1} + (G_t - T_t)$$

If debt is fully repaid during year t, then B_t (debt at the end of year t) is zero. Replacing B_t by zero, and B_{t-1} by its expression from equation (27.4), gives

$$0 = (1 + r)(1 + r)^{t-2} + (G_t - T_t)$$

Reorganizing and bringing $G_t - T_t$ to the right implies

$$T_t - G_t = (1 + r)^{t-1}$$

Add exponents:
$(1 + r)(1 + r)^{t-2} =$
$(1 + r)^{t-1}$ (see Appendix 2).

To pay back the debt, the government must run a primary surplus equal to $(1 + r)^{t-1}$ during year t. If the adjustment is done through taxes, the initial decrease in taxes of 1 during year 1 leads to an increase in taxes of $(1 + r)^{t-1}$ during year t. The path of taxes and debt corresponding to this case is given in Figure 27–1(b).

Full repayment in year t:

$T_1 \downarrow$ by 1
$\Rightarrow T_t \uparrow$ by $(1 + r)^{t-1}$

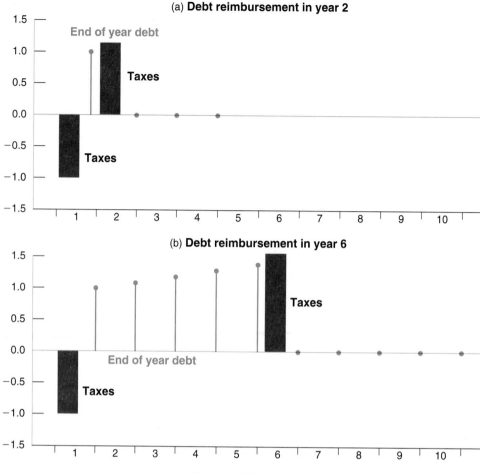

(a) **Debt reimbursement in year 2**

(b) **Debt reimbursement in year 6**

FIGURE 27-1

Tax Cuts, Debt Repayment, and Debt Stabilization

(a) If debt is fully repaid during year 2, the decrease in taxes of 1 in year 1 requires an increase in taxes equal to $(1 + r)$ in year 2. (b) If debt is fully repaid during year t, the decrease in taxes of 1 in year 1 requires an increase in taxes equal to $(1 + r)^{t-1}$ during year t. (c) If debt is stabilized from year 2 on, then taxes must be permanently higher by r from year 2 on.

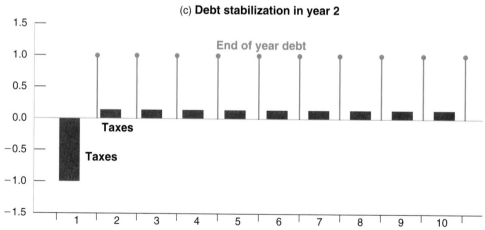

(c) **Debt stabilization in year 2**

This example yields our first basic conclusion. If spending is unchanged, a decrease in taxes must eventually be offset by an increase in taxes in the future. The longer the government waits to increase taxes or the higher the real interest rate, the higher the eventual increase in taxes.

Debt and Primary Surpluses

We have assumed so far that the government fully repays the debt. Let's now look at what happens to taxes if the government only stabilizes the debt. (Stabilizing the debt means changing taxes or spending so that debt remains constant.)

Suppose that the government decides to stabilize the debt from year 2 on. Stabilizing the debt from year 2 on means that debt at the end of year 2 and thereafter remains at the same level as at the end of year 1.

From equation (27.3), the budget constraint for year 2 is

$$B_2 = (1 + r)B_1 + (G_2 - T_2)$$

Under our assumption that debt is stabilized in year 2, $B_2 = B_1 = 1$. Replacing in the preceding equation

$$1 = (1 + r) + (G_2 - T_2)$$

Bringing $G_2 - T_2$ to the left side and reorganizing

$$T_2 - G_2 = (1 + r) - 1 = r$$

To avoid a further increase in debt during year 1, the government must run a primary surplus equal to real interest payments on the existing debt. It must do so in following years as well: Each year, the primary surplus must be sufficient to cover interest payments, and thus to leave the debt level unchanged. The path of taxes and debt is shown in Figure 27–1(c): Debt remains at 1 from year 1 on. Taxes are permanently higher from year 1 on, by an amount equal to r; equivalently, from year 1 on, the government runs a primary surplus equal to r.

The logic of this argument extends directly to the case where the government waits until year t to stabilize. Whenever the government stabilizes, it must from then on run a primary surplus sufficient to pay interest on the debt.

This example yields our second basic conclusion. The legacy of past deficits is higher government debt. To stabilize the debt, the government must eliminate the deficit. To do so, it must run a primary surplus equal to the interest payments on the existing debt.

◀ Stabilizing the debt from year 2 on:

$T_1 \downarrow$ by 1
 $\Rightarrow T_2, T_3, \ldots \uparrow$ by r

The Evolution of the Debt-to-GDP Ratio

We have focused so far on the evolution of the level of debt. But in an economy in which output grows over time, it makes more sense to focus instead on the ratio of debt to output. To see how this change in focus modifies our conclusions, we need to go from equation (27.3) to an equation that gives the evolution of the **debt-to-GDP ratio**—the **debt ratio** for short.

To do this, first divide both sides of equation (27.3) by real output, Y_t, to get

$$\frac{B_t}{Y_t} = (1 + r)\frac{B_{t-1}}{Y_t} + \frac{G_t - T_t}{Y_t}$$

Next rewrite B_{t-1}/Y_t, as $(B_t/Y_{t-1})(Y_{t-1}/Y_t)$ (in other words, multiply top and bottom by Y_{t-1})

$$\frac{B_t}{Y_t} = (1 + r)\left(\frac{Y_{t-1}}{Y_t}\right)\frac{B_{t-1}}{Y_{t-1}} + \frac{G_t - T_t}{Y_t}$$

We are nearly where we want to be: All the terms in the equation are now in terms of ratios to GDP, Y. We can simplify further. Assume that output growth is constant and denote the growth rate of output by g, so Y_{t-1}/Y_t can be written as $1/(1 + g)$. Use the approximation $(1 + r)/(1 + g) = 1 + r - g$. We can then rewrite the equation as

$$\frac{B_t}{Y_t} = (1 + r - g)\frac{B_{t-1}}{Y_{t-1}} + \frac{G_t - T_t}{Y_t}$$

Finally, move B_{t-1}/Y_{t-1} to the left to get

$$\frac{B_t}{Y_t} - \frac{B_{t-1}}{Y_{t-1}} = (r - g)\frac{B_{t-1}}{Y_{t-1}} + \frac{G_t - T_t}{Y_t} \qquad (27.5)$$

Start from
 $Y_t = (1 + g)Y_{t-1}$.
Divide both sides by
 Y_t
to get
 $1 = (1 + g)Y_{t-1}/Y_t$.
Reorganize to get
 $Y_{t-1}/Y_t = 1/(1 + g)$

◀ This approximation is derived as proposition 6 in Appendix 2 at the end of the book.

The change in the debt ratio is equal to the sum of two terms. The first is the difference between the real interest rate and the growth rate times the initial debt ratio. The second is the ratio of the primary deficit to GDP.

Compare equation (27.5), which gives the evolution of the ratio of debt to GDP, to equation (27.2), which gives the evolution of debt itself. The difference is the presence of $r - g$ in equation (27.5) compared to r in equation (27.2). The reason for the difference is simple: Suppose the primary deficit is zero. Debt will then increase at a rate equal to the real interest rate, r. But if GDP is growing as well, the ratio of debt to GDP will grow more slowly; it will grow at a rate equal to the real interest rate minus the growth rate of output, $r - g$.

The Evolution of the Debt Ratio in the OECD.
Equation (27.5) implies that the increase in the ratio of debt to GDP will be larger

- the higher the real interest rate;
- the lower the growth rate of output;
- the higher the initial debt ratio;
- the higher the ratio of the primary deficit to GDP.

All four factors have played a role in the evolution of the debt-to-GDP ratio over the last four decades in the OECD countries:

- The 1960s was a decade of strong growth, so strong that the average growth rate exceeded the average real interest rate in most countries. As a result, $(r - g)$ was negative, and most countries were able to decrease their debt ratios without having to run large primary surpluses.
- The 1970s was a period of lower growth, but of very low (often negative) real interest rates. (Nominal interest rates were high in the 1970s. But inflation was even higher, leading to negative real interest rates.) Thus, $(r - g)$ was again negative on average, and the result was a further decrease in the debt ratio in most OECD countries.
- The situation changed drastically in the early 1980s. Real interest rates increased and growth rates decreased. To avoid an increase in their debt ratios, OECD countries would have had to run large primary surpluses. They did not and the debt ratios increased rapidly.
- In the 1990s, real interest rates remained high and growth rates remained low. It became increasingly clear that most countries had no alternative to stabilize their debt ratios than to run larger primary surpluses. Most OECD countries have now done so. At the end of the 1990s, most countries are now running a primary surplus sufficient to imply a steady decline in their debt ratios.

Table 27–1 gives the evolution of the ratio of debt to GDP for the United States and the European Union, as well as for Italy, Belgium, and Greece, from 1981 to 1998, together with a forecast for 2000.

TABLE 27–1 Debt and Primary Surpluses for the United States, the European Union, and Selected Countries, 1981–2000 (percent of GDP)

| Country | Debt/GDP | | | Primary Surplus/GDP |
	1981	1998	2000 (forecast)	1998
United States	21.6	42.0	36.0	3.5
European Union	24.0	56.7	55.6	2.3
Italy	56.4	107.0	102.8	5.0
Belgium	82.2	114.7	109.0	5.8
Greece	27.1	108.7	104.7	6.8

Except for Greece, "Debt" is net debt, that is, financial liabilities of the government minus financial assets held by the government.

Source: OECD Economic Outlook, December 1998, Tables 32, 34, 35.

If two variables (here debt and GDP) grow at rates r and g, respectively, then their ratio (here the ratio of debt to GDP) will grow at rate $(r - g)$. See proposition 8 in Appendix 2.

1960s:
high g, low r ⟹ B/Y ↓

1970s:
lower g, very low r
⟹ B/Y ↓

1980s:
low g, high r ⟹ B/Y ↑

1990s:
low g, high r, primary surplus > 0 ⟹ B/Y →

Note how much the debt ratio has increased in both the United States and the European Union since the early 1980s, but also how things have now turned around, and the debt ratio is now declining. As shown in the last column, the reason for the turnaround is that both the United States and the European Union countries are now running primary surpluses.

Note also how steep the increase in the debt ratio has been in Italy, Belgium, and Greece. All three countries now have debt ratios in excess of 100% of GDP. But, even in these countries, things have turned around, and large primary surpluses are also leading to a steady decline in the debt ratio.

To summarize: We have looked at the government budget constraint. We have seen that the change in the ratio of debt to GDP can be expressed as the sum of the primary deficit to GDP plus the ratio of debt to GDP times the real interest rate minus the growth rate. In the 1980s, high interest rates, low growth, and primary deficits all contributed to an increase in debt in most OECD countries. In the 1990s, countries have reacted by running large primary surpluses, and the debt-to-GDP ratio is now falling in most OECD countries.

For more on the reduction of deficits in Europe, see the discussion of the Maastricht treaty—which puts a ceiling on deficits in Euroland countries—in chapter 21. For more on the reduction of deficits in the United States, see chapter 25.

27-2 | Four Issues in Fiscal Policy

Having looked at the mechanics of the government budget constraint, we can now take up four issues in which this constraint plays an important role.

Ricardian Equivalence

How does taking into account the government budget constraint affect the way we should think of the effects of deficits on output?

One extreme view is that once this constraint is taken into account, neither deficits nor debt has an effect on economic activity! This argument is known as the **Ricardian equivalence** proposition. David Ricardo, a nineteenth-century English economist, was the first to articulate its logic. His argument was further developed and given prominence in the 1970s by Robert Barro, then at Chicago, now at Harvard University. For this reason, the argument is also known as the **Ricardo–Barro proposition**.

The best way to understand the proposition's logic is to use the example of tax changes from section 27-1. Suppose that the government decreases taxes by 1 this year. And at the same time, it announces that to repay the debt, it will increase taxes by $(1 + r)$ next year.

What will be the effect of the initial tax cut on consumption? A plausible answer is that it will have no effect at all. Why? Because consumers realize that the tax cut is not much of a gift: Lower taxes this year are exactly offset, in present value, by higher taxes next year. Put another way, their human wealth—the present value of after-tax labor income—is unaffected. Current taxes go down by 1, but the present value of next year's taxes goes up by $(1 + r)/(1 + r) = 1$, and the net effect of the two changes is exactly equal to zero.

We can look at the same result another way, by looking at saving rather than consumption. To say that consumers do not change consumption in response to the tax cut is the same as saying that *private saving increases one for one with the deficit*. Thus, the Ricardian equivalence proposition says that if a government finances a given path of spending through deficits, private saving will increase one for one with the decrease in public saving, leaving total saving unchanged. The total amount left for investment will not be affected. Over time, the mechanics of the government budget constraint imply that government debt will increase. But this increase will not come at the expense of capital accumulation.

Under the Ricardian equivalence proposition, the long sequence of deficits and the increase in government debt that characterized the OECD for most of the last 20 years are no cause for worry. As governments were dissaving, the argument goes, people were saving more in anticipation of the higher taxes to come. The decrease in public saving was offset by an equal increase in private saving. Total saving was therefore unchanged, and so was investment. OECD economies have the same capital stock today that they would have had if there had been no increase in debt. High debt is thus no cause for concern.

Although Ricardo stated the logic of the argument, he believed there were many reasons why it would not hold in practice. In contrast, Barro argues that the argument is not only logically correct, but is also a good description of reality.

See chapter 16 for a definition of human wealth and a discussion of its role in consumption.

How seriously should you take the Ricardian equivalence proposition? Most economists would answer, "Seriously, but not seriously enough to think that deficits and debt are irrelevant." A major theme of this book has been that expectations matter, that consumption decisions depend not only on current income but also on future income. If it were widely believed that a tax cut this year is going to be followed by an offsetting increase in taxes *next year*, the effect on consumption probably would be small. Many consumers would save most or all of the tax cut in anticipation of higher taxes next year. (Replace "year" by "month" or "week" and the argument becomes even more convincing.)

Tax cuts rarely come, however, with the announcement of tax increases a year later. Consumers have to guess when and how taxes will eventually be increased.

The increase in taxes in year t is $(1 + r)^{t-1}$. The discount factor for a dollar in year t is $1/(1 + r)^{t-1}$. Thus, the value of the increase in taxes in year t as of today is $(1 + r)^{t-1}/(1 + r)^{t-1} = 1$.

This fact does not by itself invalidate the Ricardian equivalence argument: No matter when taxes will be increased, the government budget constraint still implies that the present value of future tax increases must always be equal to the decrease in taxes today. Take the second example we looked at in section 27-1 (see Figure 27–1b) in which the government waits t years to increase taxes, and thus increases them by $(1 + r)^{t-1}$. The present value in year 0 of this expected tax increase is $(1 + r)^{t-1}/(1 + r)^{t-1} = 1$—exactly equal to the original tax cut. The change in human wealth from the tax cut is still zero.

But insofar as future tax increases appear more distant and their timing more uncertain, consumers are more likely to ignore them. This may be the case because they expect to retire before taxes go up, or, more likely, because they just do not think that far into the future. In either case, Ricardian equivalence is likely to fail.

So, it is safe to conclude that budget deficits have an important effect on activity. In the short run, larger deficits are likely to lead to higher demand and higher output. In the long run, higher government debt lowers capital accumulation and thus lowers output.

Deficits, Output Stabilization, and the Cyclically Adjusted Deficit

Note the analogy with monetary policy: The fact that higher money growth leads in the long run to more inflation does not imply higher money growth should never be used for output stabilization.

The fact that deficits have long-run adverse effects on capital accumulation and output does not imply deficits should not be used for output stabilization. Rather, it implies that deficits during recessions should be offset by surpluses during booms, so as not to lead to a steady increase in debt.

Ignore output growth in this section, and thus ignore the distinction between stabilizing the debt and stabilizing the debt-to-GDP ratio. (If you want, check that the arguments here extend in a straightforward way to the case where output is growing.)

To help assess whether fiscal policy is on track, economists have constructed deficit measures that tell them what the deficit would be, under existing tax and spending rules, if output were at its natural level. Such measures come under many names, from **full-employment deficit**, to **mid-cycle deficit**, to **standardized employment deficit**, to **structural deficit** (the term used by the OECD). I shall use **cyclically adjusted deficit**, the term I find the most intuitive. Such a measure gives a simple benchmark by which to judge the direction of fiscal policy: If the actual deficit is large but the cyclically adjusted deficit is equal to zero, then current fiscal policy is consistent with no systematic increase in debt over time. Debt will increase as long as output is below its natural level; but as output returns to its natural level, deficits will disappear and the debt will stabilize.

This does not imply that the goal should be to maintain a cyclically adjusted deficit equal to zero at all times. In a recession, the government may want to run a deficit large enough that even the cyclically adjusted deficit is positive. In that case, the fact that the cyclically adjusted deficit is positive provides a clear warning: The return of output to its natural level will not be enough to stabilize the debt, and the government will have to take specific measures to decrease the deficit at some point in the future.

The theory underlying the cyclically adjusted deficit is simple. The practice has proven tricky. To see why, we need to look at how measures of the cyclically adjusted deficit are constructed. Construction requires two steps. First, establish how much lower the deficit would be if output were, say, 1% higher. Second, assess how far away output is from its natural level.

The first step is straightforward. A reliable rule of thumb is that a 1% decrease in output leads automatically to an increase in the deficit of 0.5% of GDP. This increase occurs because most taxes are proportional to output, whereas most government spending does not depend on the level of output. That means a decrease in output, which leads to a decrease in revenues and not much change in spending, naturally leads to a larger deficit. If output is, say, 5% below its natural level, the deficit as a ratio to GDP will be about 2.5% larger than it would be if output were at its natural level. (This effect of activity on the deficit has been called an **automatic stabilizer**: A recession naturally generates a deficit, and therefore a fiscal expansion that partly counteracts the recession.)

The second step is more difficult. Recall from chapter 6 that the natural level of output is the output level that would be produced if the economy were operating at the natural rate of unemployment. Too low an estimate of the natural rate of unemployment will lead to too high an estimate of the natural level of output, therefore to too optimistic a measure of the cyclically adjusted deficit. This explains in part what happened in Europe in the 1980s. Based on the assumption of an unchanged natural unemployment rate, the cyclically adjusted deficits did not look bad in the 1980s. If European unemployment had returned to its level of the 1970s, the increase in output would have been sufficient to reestablish budget balance in most countries. But, it turned out, much of the increase in unemployment reflected an increase in the natural unemployment rate, and unemployment remained very high throughout the 1980s. As a result, most of the decade was characterized by high deficits and a large increase in debt-to-GDP ratios.

◄ Look at our earlier discussion of the evolution of the debt ratio in the OECD.

◄ See the discussion of high European unemployment in chapter 22.

Wars and Deficits

Wars typically bring about large budget deficits. As we saw in chapter 25, the two largest increases in U.S. government debt in the twentieth century were during World War I and World War II. (We further examine the case of World War II in the Focus box "Deficits, Consumption, and Investment in the United States During World War II.")

◄ Look at the two peaks associated with World War I and World War II in Figure 25–4.

Is it right for governments to rely so much on deficits to finance wars? After all, war economies are usually operating at low unemployment, so the output stabilization reasons for running deficits we examined earlier are irrelevant. The answer, nevertheless, is yes. In fact, there are two good reasons to run deficits during wars. The first is distributional: Deficit fi-

---

FOCUS

Deficits, Consumption, and Investment in the United States During World War II

In 1939, the share of U.S. government spending on goods and services in GDP was 15%. By 1944, it had increased to 45%! The increase was due to increased spending on national defense, which went from 1% of GDP in 1939 to 36% in 1944.

Faced with such a massive increase in spending, the U.S. government reacted with large tax increases. For the first time in U.S. history, the individual income tax became a major source of revenues; individual income tax revenues, which were equal to 1% of GDP in 1939, had increased to 8.5% in 1944. But the tax increase was still far less than the increase in expenditures. The increase in federal revenues, from 7.2% of GDP in 1939 to 22.7% in 1944, was only a little more than half the increase in expenditures.

The result was a sequence of large budget deficits. By 1944, the federal deficit reached 22% of GDP. The ratio of debt to GDP, already high at 53% in 1939 because of the deficits the government had run during the Great Depression, stood at 110%.

Was the increase in government spending achieved at the expense of consumption or private investment? (As we

saw in chapter 18, it could in principle have come from higher imports and a current account deficit. But the United States had nobody to borrow from during the war. Indeed, it was lending to some of its allies: Transfers from the U.S. government to foreign countries were equal to 6% of U.S. GDP in 1944.)

The 30% increase in the share of GDP going to government purchases was met in large part by a 23% decrease in the share of consumption in GDP—from 74% to 51%. Part of the decrease in consumption may have been in anticipation of higher taxes after the war; part was also the result of the unavailability of many consumer durables; and patriotism probably played a role in leading people to save more and buy the war bonds issued by the government to finance the war. But the increase in government purchases was also met by a 6% decrease in the share of (private) investment in GDP—from 10% to 4%. Part of the burden of the war was passed on in the form of lower capital accumulation to those living after the war.

nance is a way to pass some of the burden of the war to those alive after the war, and it seems only fair for future generations to share in the sacrifices the war requires. The second is more narrowly economic: Deficit spending helps reduce tax distortions. Let's look at each reason.

Passing on the Burden of the War. Wars lead to large increases in government spending. Consider the implications of financing this increased spending either through increased taxes or through higher deficits. To distinguish this case from our earlier discussion of output stabilization, let's also assume that output is fixed at its natural level.

Suppose the government relies on deficit finance. With government spending up sharply, there will be a very large increase in the demand for goods. Given our assumption that output does not increase, interest rates will have to increase enough so as to maintain equilibrium. Investment, which depends on the interest rate, will decrease sharply.

Suppose instead that the government finances the spending increase through an increase in income taxes. Consumption will decline sharply. Exactly how much depends on consumers' expectations. The longer they expect the war to last, the longer they expect higher taxes to last, and the more they will decrease consumption. In any case, the increase in government spending will be partly offset by a decrease in consumption. Interest rates will increase by less than they would have under deficit finance. Investment will decrease by less.

Assume that the economy is closed, so that $Y = C + I + G$. Suppose that G goes up, and Y remains the same. Then, $C + I$ must go down. If taxes are not increased, most of the decrease comes from a decrease in I. If taxes are increased, most of the decrease comes from a decrease in C.

In short, for a given output, the increase in government spending requires either a decrease in consumption or a decrease in investment. Whether the government relies on tax increases or deficits determines whether consumption or investment does most of the adjustment.

How does all this affect who bears the burden of the war? The more the government relies on deficits, the smaller the decrease in consumption during the war and the larger the decrease in investment. Lower investment means a lower capital stock after the war, and so lower output after the war. By reducing capital accumulation, deficits become a way of passing some of the burden of the war onto future generations.

Reducing Tax Distortions. There is another argument for running deficits, not only during wars but, more generally, in times when government spending is exceptionally high. Think, for example, of reconstruction after an earthquake, or of the costs involved in the reunification of Germany in the early 1990s.

See the Global Macro box "German Unification and the German Monetary–Fiscal Tug-of-War" in chapter 5.

The argument is as follows: If the government were to increase taxes in line with the increase in spending, tax rates would have to be very high. Very high tax rates can lead to very high distortions. Faced with very high income tax rates, people work less or engage in illegal, untaxed activities. Rather than moving the tax rate up and down to maintain a balanced budget, it is better (from the point of view of reducing distortions) to maintain a relatively constant tax rate, to *smooth taxes*. **Tax smoothing** implies running large deficits when government spending is exceptionally high and small surpluses the rest of the time.

The Dangers of Very High Debt

We now have seen two costs of high government debt—lower capital accumulation, and higher tax rates and higher distortions. The recent experience of a number of countries points to yet another cost: High debt can lead to vicious circles and makes the conduct of fiscal policy extremely difficult.

To see why this is so, return to equation (27.5), which gives the evolution of the debt ratio over time:

$$\frac{B_t}{Y_t} - \frac{B_{t-1}}{Y_{t-1}} = (r - g)\frac{B_{t-1}}{Y_{t-1}} + \frac{(G_t - T_t)}{Y_t}$$

Take a country with a high debt ratio, say, 100%. Suppose the real interest rate is 3%, the growth rate 2%. The first term on the right is $(3\% - 2\%) \times 100\% = 1\%$ of GDP. Suppose further that the government is running a primary surplus of 1%, thus just enough to keep the debt ratio constant [the right side of the equation equals $1\% + (-1\%) = 0\%$].

Now suppose financial investors start requiring a higher interest rate to hold government bonds. This may be because they are not sure the government will be able to keep the deficit under control and repay the bonds in the future. The specific reason does not matter here. For concreteness, suppose the domestic interest rate increases from 3% to, say, 6%.

Now assess the fiscal situation: $r - g$ is now $6\% - 2\% = 4\%$. With the increase in $r - g$ from 1% to 4%, the government must increase its primary surplus from 1% to 4% of GDP just to keep the debt-to-GDP ratio constant. Now come the potential vicious circles.

Suppose the government takes steps to avoid an increase in the debt ratio. The spending cuts or tax increases are likely to prove politically costly, generating even more political uncertainty and the need for an even higher interest rate. Also, the sharp fiscal contraction is likely to lead to a recession, decreasing the growth rate. Both the increase in the interest rate and the decrease in growth further increase $r - g$, making it even harder to stabilize the debt ratio.

Alternatively, suppose the government proves unable or unwilling to increase the primary budget surplus by 3% of GDP. Debt then starts increasing, leading financial markets to become even more worried and require an even higher interest rate. The higher interest rate leads to even larger deficits, an even faster increase in the debt ratio, and so on.

In short, the higher the ratio of debt to GDP, the larger the potential for explosive debt dynamics. Even initially unfounded fears that the government may not fully repay the debt can easily become self-fulfilling: By increasing the interest rate the government must pay on its debt, these fears can lead the government to lose control of its budget, and lead to an increase in debt to a level such that the government is unable to repay the debt, validating initial fears.

If this reminds you of our discussion of exchange rate crises, and the possibility of self-fulfilling crises, you are right. Very much the same mechanisms are at work: Expectations that a problem may arise lead to the emergence of the problem, validating initial expectations. Indeed, in some crises, both mechanisms are at work. In the Brazilian crisis of 1998, fears of a devaluation of the *real* (the Brazilian currency) forced Brazil to increase interest rates to very high levels. These interest rates led to much larger budget deficits, raising questions about whether the Brazilian government could repay its debt, further increasing interest rates. Eventually, Brazil had no choice but to devalue. It did so in early 1999.

◄ Exchange rate crises were studied in chapter 21.

If a government decides that the debt ratio is too high, how and how fast should it reduce it? The answer is through many years, even many decades, of surpluses. The historical reference here is that of England in the nineteenth century. By the end of its war against Napoleon in the early 1800s, England had run up a debt ratio in excess of 200% of GDP. It spent most of the nineteenth century reducing the ratio, so that by 1900 the ratio stood at only 30% of GDP.

The prospect of many decades of fiscal austerity is unpleasant. Thus, when debt ratios are very high, an alternative solution keeps coming up—**debt repudiation**. The argument is a simple one. Repudiating the debt—canceling it in part or in full—is good for the economy. It allows for a decrease in taxes and thus a decrease in distortions. It decreases the risk of vicious circles. The problem with repudiation however is the problem of time inconsistency that we studied in chapter 25. If the government reneges on its promises to repay the debt, it may find it very difficult to borrow again for a long time in the future; financial markets will remember what happened and be reluctant to lend again. What seems best today may be unappealing in the long run. Debt repudiation is very much a last resort, to be used when everything else has failed.

To summarize: We have looked at four issues that directly involve the government budget constraint:

1. Ricardian equivalence—the proposition that a larger deficit is offset by an equal increase in private saving, so deficits have no effect on demand and output. We have concluded that Ricardian equivalence does not usually hold, and that deficits decrease capital accumulation and output in the long run.

2. The use of cyclically adjusted deficits—measures that tell us what the deficit would be, under existing tax and spending rules, if output were at its natural level. If the cyclically

adjusted deficit is positive, this signals that sooner or later, changes will have to be made to tax and spending rules.

3. The use of deficit finance in times of wars. We have seen how running deficits during wars shifts some of the burden of the war from people living during the war to those living after the war. Deficits also help smooth taxes and reduce tax distortions.

4. The dangers of very high debt ratios. We have seen how high debt ratios increase the risk of fiscal crises, with high interest rates leading to large deficits, and large deficits leading in turn to higher interest rates.

27-3 | The U.S. Budget Deficit

Let's conclude this chapter by looking at the U.S. budget. Table 27–2 gives the basic budget numbers for 1998.

Some of the numbers may not be the same as those you have seen in the press. The reason is that there are many different definitions of "expenditures," "revenues," and "deficit." Some numbers refer to the budget of the federal government only, and some consolidate the accounts of federal, state, and local governments. As a whole, state and local governments typically run surpluses: In 1998, the combined surplus of state and local governments was $145 billion, or about 1.7% of GDP. The surplus for the government as a whole—federal, state, and local—was therefore equal to the surplus of the federal government, 0.8% of GDP, plus the surplus of state and local governments, 1.7%, so 0.8% + 1.7% = 2.5% of GDP.

I shall focus here only on the federal budget. Even here, there are two sets of numbers:

- The government uses its own accounting system and, because this is the system used to present and discuss the budget in Congress, these are the numbers you are most likely to encounter when reading newspapers.

Many states operate under rules that prevent them from running deficits.

TABLE 27–2	U.S. Federal Budget: Revenues and Expenditures, 1998 (percent of GDP)		
Revenues	21.7		
Personal taxes		10.1	
Corporate profit taxes		2.4	
Indirect taxes		1.1	
Social insurance contributions		8.1	
Expenditures, excluding interest payments	18.2		
Consumption expenditures		5.4	
Defense			3.5
Nondefense			1.9
Transfers		9.6	
Grants to state/local governments		2.7	
Other spending		0.5	
Primary surplus (1)	3.5		
Net interest payments (2)	2.7		
Real interest payments (3)		1.9	
Inflation component		0.8	
Official surplus: (1) minus (2)	0.8		
Inflation adjusted surplus: (1) minus (3)	1.6		
Memo item: Debt-to-GDP ratio	42.0		

April 1999, *Source: Survey of Current Business*, Tables 3–2 and 3–7.

- An alternative accounting system is provided in the national income and product accounts (NIPA); it provides a more economically meaningful set of budget numbers. The numbers in Table 27–2 are NIPA numbers.

Here are the main differences between the government and the NIPA numbers:

- The government budget numbers are presented by *fiscal year*. The fiscal year runs from October 1 of the preceding calendar year to September 31 of the current calendar year. The NIPA numbers are for calendar years.
- The government budget numbers are presented in two categories: "on-budget" and "off-budget." The most important off-budget item is Social Security. In fiscal year 1998 the on-budget deficit was \$30 billion. This deficit was more than offset by an off-budget surplus of \$99 billion, leading to a combined surplus of \$99 − \$30 = \$69 billion; the main source of the off-budget surplus was an excess of Social Security taxes over Social Security benefits.
- By separating the Social Security system from the rest of the budget, the on-budget/off-budget distinction serves a useful political purpose. It is, however, a meaningless distinction from an economic viewpoint. The NIPA measure makes no such distinction; the NIPA deficit corresponds most closely to the sum of the on-budget and off-budget deficits.
- The two accounting systems differ in how they treat the sale of government assets. Government accounts treat asset sales as revenues. The NIPA accounts correctly recognize that asset sales bring revenues today, but reduce revenues in the future; thus, asset sales are not included in revenues in the NIPA accounts.
- The two accounting systems differ in the way they treat government investment. Government accounts count all expenditures, including investment purchases such as aircraft carriers. The NIPA accounts, which measure current rather than capital expenditures, exclude investment but include depreciation on existing government-owned capital.

For more details on the differences, read *The Economic and Budget Outlook: Fiscal Years 2000–2009* (Washington DC: Congressional Budget Office, January 1999), Appendix D (or access it at the web site http://www.cbo.gov/).

We saw in chapter 25 that such sales were used to make the deficit numbers consistent with the Gramm–Rudman–Hollings restrictions in the late 1980s.

So when you hear a deficit number, ask, Federal, or federal, state, and local? Government or NIPA accounts? If government accounts, on-budget, off-budget, or the sum of the two?

Finally, you are likely to encounter two numbers for (federal) government debt. The first is *gross debt*, the sum of the federal government's financial liabilities. When Congress votes to increase the debt ceiling, this is the number to which the ceiling applies. At the end of 1998, gross debt was equal to \$5.5 trillion, or 65% of GDP. The second, and more relevant, number is *net debt*, or, equivalently, *debt held by the public*. At the end of 1998, net debt was only \$3.6 trillion, or 42% of GDP. Where did the difference come from? \$1.9 trillion of government debt was held not by the public but by government agencies; for example, about \$0.8 trillion was held by the Social Security Trust Fund.

Let's now look at the numbers in Table 27–2. In 1998, federal revenues were 21.7% of GDP. Expenditures excluding interest payments were 18.2% of GDP, so the federal government was running a primary surplus of 3.5% of GDP.

Interest payments on the debt held by the public were 2.7%. The official surplus was therefore equal to 3.5% − 2.7% = 0.8%. We know, however, this measure is incorrect (see section 27-1 and the Focus box therein). The correct measure, the sum of the primary surplus minus *real* interest payments, was 3.5% − 1.9% = 1.6%. The government was running a surplus of 1.6%. Will this surplus last? Is the Federal budget truly in good shape, or are there reasons to worry? For the next 10 years, the federal budget outlook appears very good. But, looking over the longer run, say, the next 60 years, there are problems on the horizon. Waiting for the problems to appear would be dangerous; it is important to start doing something now. Let us look at these problems more closely.

The Budget Outlook Until 2009

Every year, the **Congressional Budget Office** of the U.S. Congress (**CBO**) constructs and publishes budget projections for the following 10 years. These projections are based on forecasts for the major macroeconomic variables together with the assumption that spending and tax rules already in place will continue to apply in the future. CBO projections of budget

TABLE 27–3	Projected Surpluses and Debt Levels, Federal Government: Fiscal Years 1998–2009 (percent of GDP)		
	1998 (actual)	**2003** (projected)	**2009** (projected)
Surplus	0.8	2.0	2.8
Debt	42.0	29.0	9.0

Source: The Economic and Budget Outlook: Fiscal Years 2000–2009, Congressional Budget Office, Table 2–3.

surpluses and debt levels for the federal government for fiscal years 1998 to 2009 are given in Table 27–3.

The numbers in Table 27–3 suggest the federal budget is in very good shape. Under current spending and tax rules, the total (official) surplus is projected to increase from 0.8% of GDP in 1998 to 2.8% of GDP in 2009. As a result, debt held by the public is projected to fall from 42% of GDP in 1998 to 9% of GDP in 2009. If such a decrease actually takes place, this will reduce the debt ratio to its lowest level since World War I.

Despite these impressive numbers, some economists argue that the government should go further and generate even larger surpluses. They rely on two separate arguments. The first is that the U.S. saving rate is still very low and should be increased. One way to increase it is to increase public saving—equivalently, run larger budget surpluses. The second argument is that the numbers in Table 27–3 reflect the calm before the storm. Looking further into the future, changes in demographics imply large increases in spending in several government programs, increases to which the government should start responding now. Let's consider both arguments in turn.

Surpluses and the Low U.S. Saving Rate

The U.S. saving rate is one of the lowest among OECD countries: In 1998, the U.S. saving rate was 17.2% of GDP, about 3 percentage points below the OECD average. Should this low saving rate be a matter of concern? We discussed the issue in general in chapter 11. The saving rate does affect the level of capital and the level of output in the long run. A higher saving rate would lead over time to a higher standard of living in the future.

If we believe that the United States, as a nation, is not saving enough for the future, there is a strong argument for taking measures to increase private saving, or offsetting low private saving by higher public saving. This is the first argument for running even larger budget surpluses than are currently projected.

However, this advice raises an intriguing issue. If the government ran even larger surpluses than those projected in Table 27–3, the government's net debt position would decrease even faster than it does in Table 27–3, and could well become negative. Is this feasible? Could the government have a negative net debt position? The answer is yes. As the government ran surpluses, it could first buy back all of its debt, and when this was done, start buying private bonds or stocks. Or—and this would be more likely to be the case—it could do both at the same time, that is, leave some amount of government debt in the economy, and use the surpluses to buy private bonds or equities. In any case, the government would turn from being a net debtor to being a net creditor. This would be historically unusual, but is perfectly feasible.

Surpluses and The Aging of America

About half of U.S. federal spending is on **entitlement programs**. These are programs that require the payment of benefits to all who meet the eligibility requirements established by law. The three largest programs are Social Security (which provides benefits to retirees),

These numbers are projections (constructed assuming existing tax and spending rules) rather than forecasts (which would try to predict how the rules might be changed): If the projections show very large deficits in the future, it is likely that Congress will react and reduce deficits below these projections. If the projections show very large surpluses, the temptation may be irresistible for Congress either to decrease taxes or to increase spending beyond current rules and thus reduce surpluses below projections.

For the effects of the saving rate on output in the long run, review chapter 11.

There are several OECD countries where the government is a net creditor: The ratio of net debt to GDP is equal to −6% in Finland, −24% in Korea, and −43% in Norway.

Medicare (which provides health care to retirees), and Medicaid (which provides health care to the poor).

Table 27–4 shows current and projected spending on each of these three programs, as a percent of GDP, from 1998 to 2060. The projections are again from the Congressional Budget Office, and are constructed using economic forecasts and current rules (including future changes in rules if these changes have already been incorporated into the law) for each program.

The numbers are dramatic. Under existing rules, Social Security benefits are projected to increase from 4% of GDP in 1998 to 7% in 2060. Medicare benefits are projected to increase from 2% to 7%, Medicaid benefits from 1% to 3%. If nothing is done, the ratio of entitlement spending to GDP is projected to increase by more than 10% of GDP over the next 60 years.

These projected increases have two sources:

- The first and main one is the *aging of America*, the rapid increase in the proportion of people over 65 that will take place as the Baby Boom generation starts reaching retirement age, from year 2010 on. The *old age dependency ratio*—the ratio of the population 65 years old or more to the population between 20 and 64 years old—is projected to increase from about 20% in 1998 to more than 40% in 2060. This evolution explains the projected growth of Social Security benefits, and a good part of the increase in Medicare.
- The second, which accounts for the rest of the growth of Medicare and most of the growth in Medicaid, is the steadily increasing cost of health care.

Can these increases in entitlement spending be offset by decreases in other expenditures? The answer is no. From Table 27–2, you can see that even if *all* expenditures other than transfers were eliminated, there still would not be enough to cover the projected increase in entitlement spending: In 1998, total expenditures excluding interest payments and transfers, were equal to 18.2% − 9.6% = 8.6% of GDP, less than the 10% of the projected increase in entitlement spending.

It is therefore clear that major changes in entitlement programs will have to take place. Social Security benefits may have to be reduced (relative to projections), the provision of medical care will have to be limited (again, relative to projections). There is also little doubt that taxes, such as the payroll taxes used to finance Social Security, will have to be increased.

It is also clear that waiting to act until spending starts increasing would be waiting too long. The cut in benefits or the increase in tax rates needed to finance entitlement programs would be too large. Just to finance projected Social Security benefits, the payroll tax rate would have to increase from approximately 12% today to about 20% in 2060. Financing Medicare and Medicaid increases would require further and even larger increases in the tax rate. Thus, there is a general agreement that the government should not wait, but should start taking measures now.

What should these measures do? They have to combine tax increases and benefit reductions to increase surpluses now and accumulate assets in anticipation of future spending in

TABLE 27–4	Projected Spending on Social Security, Medicare, and Medicaid, 1998–2060 (percent of GDP)			
	1998	2010	2040	2060
Social Security	4.0	5.0	7.0	7.0
Medicare	2.0	3.0	6.0	7.0
Medicaid	1.0	2.0	3.0	3.0
Total	7.0	10.0	16.0	17.0

Source: The Economic and Budget Outlook: Fiscal Years 1998–2060, Congressional Budget Office, January 1999, Table 2–5.

See the Focus box "Social Security, Social Security Reform, and Capital Accumulation in the United States" in chapter 11.

the future. This is the approach that has been taken in dealing with Social Security. Since 1983, Social Security contributions have exceeded Social Security benefits, leading to surpluses and the accumulation of assets in a **Social Security trust fund**. Assets in this trust fund are now equal to about 10% of GDP.

How does such accumulation help in dealing with future increases in spending? Decumulation of these assets later on can delay the date at which taxes have to be increased or benefits decreased. Indeed, if accumulation in the fund is large enough, it may avoid the need for tax increases or benefit cuts altogether. An example will help here. Suppose that the real interest rate is equal to 3%. Then, if the trust fund accumulated assets in an amount equal to 100% of GDP, real interest payments would be equal to 3% of GDP, an amount sufficient to cover the whole projected increase in Social Security benefits as a percentage of GDP from 1998 to 2060.

This section has concentrated on the United States. But similar problems, namely, the aging of the population and the increase in medical costs, are affecting all OECD countries.

Under current assumptions, however, the trust fund does not come close to reaching such a level. It is projected to reach about 20% of GDP in 2020, then to decline and be equal to zero by 2030. Thus, there is a need to do more, not only for Social Security but, as we have seen, for Medicare and Medicaid programs as well. What to do and how to do it are likely to remain the main items on the budget agenda for the foreseeable future.

SUMMARY

- The government budget constraint gives the evolution of government debt as a function of spending and taxes. One way of expressing the constraint is that the change in debt (the deficit) is equal to the primary deficit plus interest payments on the debt. The primary deficit is the difference between government spending on goods and services, G, and taxes net of transfers, T.

- If government spending is unchanged, a decrease in taxes must be offset by an increase in taxes in the future. The longer the government waits to increase taxes or the higher the real interest rate, the higher the eventual increase in taxes.

- The legacy of past deficits is higher debt. To stabilize the debt, the government must eliminate the deficit. To do so, it must run a primary surplus equal to the interest payments on the existing debt.

- Under the Ricardian equivalence proposition, a larger deficit leads to an equal increase in private saving. Thus, deficits have no effect on demand and output. The accumulation of debt does not affect capital accumulation. In reality, Ricardian equivalence fails, and larger deficits lead to higher demand and higher output in the short run. The accumulation of debt leads to lower capital accumulation, and thus to lower output in the long run.

- To stabilize the economy, the government should run deficits during recessions, and surpluses during booms. The cyclically adjusted deficit tells what the

deficit would be, under existing tax and spending rules, if output were at its natural level.

- Deficits are justified in times of high spending, such as wars. Relative to an increase in taxes, they lead to higher consumption and lower investment during wars. They therefore shift some of the burden of the war from people living during the war to those living after the war. They also help smooth taxes and reduce tax distortions.

- Several European countries have very high debt-to-GDP ratios. In addition to reducing capital and requiring higher taxes and thus tax distortions, high debt ratios increase the risk of fiscal crises.

- In 1998, the U.S. budget showed a small surplus. Forecasts for the following 10 years showed increasing surpluses. Some economists believe, however, that the government should run even larger surpluses. They rely on two arguments:
  —The U.S. saving rate is low. Larger public saving (larger surpluses) would increase national saving, increase capital accumulation, and increase output in the long run.
  —America is aging. The proportion of retirees will increase steadily over the next 70 years in the United States. This implies that spending on several entitlement programs will increase a lot in the future, and that we should start increasing taxes today.

QUESTIONS & PROBLEMS

1. TRUE/FALSE/UNCERTAIN

a. Tax smoothing and deficit finance help spread the burden of war across generations.

b. The government can never have a negative debt position.

c. The current budget surpluses for the United States will not last.

d. If Ricardian equivalence holds, an increase in income taxes will affect neither consumption nor saving.

e. The ratio of debt to GDP cannot exceed 100%. If it did, more than GDP would be needed to pay interest on the debt.

2. BUDGET NUMBERS

Consider an economy where the official budget deficit is 4% of GDP; the debt-to-GDP ratio is 100%; the nominal interest rate is 10%; and the inflation rate is 7%.

a. What is the primary deficit/surplus?

b. What is the inflation-adjusted deficit/surplus?

c. Suppose the unemployment rate is 2% above the natural rate. What is the cyclically adjusted, inflation-adjusted deficit/surplus?

d. Suppose the unemployment rate is equal to the natural rate. Suppose that the normal growth rate is 2%. Is the debt-to-GDP ratio going up or down?

e. If things continue as in (d), what will be the debt-to-GDP ratio in 10 years?

3. FISCAL CRISES

Suppose that in the economy described in the previous problem, financial investors worry that the level of debt is too high, and that a devaluation may come. They start expecting a devaluation of 20% with probability of 0.5 within a year.

a. If the foreign interest rate remains equal to 10%, what happens to the domestic interest rate?

b. Suppose that inflation remains the same. What happens to the domestic real interest rate? What is likely to happen to the growth rate?

c. What happens to the official budget deficit? To the inflation adjusted deficit?

d. Suppose the growth rate decreases from 2% to −2%. What happens to the change in the debt ratio?

e. Were the investors right to worry?

4. WARS AND DEFICITS

"A deficit during a war can be a good thing. First, the deficit is temporary, so after it is over, the government can go right back to its old level of spending and taxes. Second, given that the evidence supports Ricardian equivalence proposition, the deficit will stimulate the economy during wartime, helping to keep the unemployment rate low." Identify four distinct mistakes in this reasoning.

5. SOLVING THE PROBLEMS OF SOCIAL SECURITY

"It may have made sense in the 1930s to force people to save to make sure they would have enough to live on in their old age. But now, people are much more aware of the need to save for retirement. It does not make sense for the government to continue to act as 'big brother.'

So the solution to the Social Security problem is in fact quite simple. Allow young people, say, everybody under the age of 25 today, to save what they want and how they want; in other words, let them out of the Social Security system. Then, what happens to them is their problem. And there is no longer a problem of financing Social Security."

Discuss.

The modern statement of the Ricardian equivalence proposition is Robert Barro, "Are Government Bonds Net Wealth?" *Journal of Political Economy*, December 1974, 1095–1117.

The *Guide to the Federal Budget*, by Stanley Collender, published every year by the Urban Institute Press, in Washington D.C., is one of the most useful descriptions of the budget process and the budget numbers.

Each year, the Congressional Budget Office, an office of the U.S. Congress, publishes *The Economic and Budget Outlook* for the current and future fiscal years (the January 1999 edition gives the outlook for fiscal years 1999 to 2009). The document provides a clear and unbiased presentation of the current budget, of current budget issues, and of budget trends. (It is also available at http://www.cbo.gov/)

A good introduction to the issues of Social Security reform is given in *Social Security Reform*, edited by Steven Sass and Robert Triest, published by the Federal Reserve Bank of Boston, June 1997.

For a discussion of what may happen to the budget surplus in the future, read Alberto Alesina, "The Political Economy of the Budget Surplus in the U.S.", *Journal of Economic Perspectives*, forthcoming 2000.

We invite you to visit the Blanchard page on the Prentice Hall Web site at:

http://www.prenhall.com/blanchard

for this chapter's World Wide Web exercises

CHAPTER 28

Epilogue: The Story of Macroeconomics

I have spent 27 chapters presenting the framework that most economists use to think about macroeconomic issues and the major conclusions they draw, as well as the issues on which they disagree. How this framework has been built over time is a fascinating story. It is the story I want to tell in this chapter.

28-1 | Keynes and the Great Depression

John Maynard Keynes

The history of modern macroeconomics starts in 1936, with the publication of Keynes's *General Theory of Employment, Interest, and Money*. As he was writing the *General Theory*, Keynes confided to a friend: "I believe myself to be writing a book on economic theory which will largely revolutionise—not, I suppose at once but in the course of the next ten years, the way the world thinks about economic problems."

Keynes was right. The book's timing was one of the reasons for its immediate success. The Great Depression was not only an economic catastrophe, but also an intellectual failure for the economists working on **business cycle theory**—as macroeconomics was then called. Few economists had a coherent explanation for the Depression, for either its depth or its length. The economic measures taken by the Roosevelt administration in the New Deal had been based on instinct rather than on economic theory. The *General Theory* offered an interpretation of events, an intellectual framework, and a clear argument for government intervention.

The *General Theory* emphasized **effective demand**—what we now call *aggregate demand*. In the short run, Keynes argued, effective demand determines output. Even if output eventually returns to its natural level, the process is slow at best. Indeed, one of Keynes's most famous quotes is, "In the long run, we are all dead."

In the process of deriving effective demand, Keynes introduced many of the building blocks of modern macroeconomics:

- The multiplier, which explains how shocks to demand can be amplified and lead to larger shifts in output.
- **Liquidity preference** (the term Keynes gave to the demand for money), which explains how monetary policy can affect interest rates and effective demand.
- The importance of expectations in affecting consumption and investment; and the idea that *animal spirits* (shifts in expectations) are a major factor behind shifts in demand and output.

Finally, the *General Theory* was more than a treatise for economists. It offered clear policy implications, and they were in tune with the times. Waiting for the economy to return by itself to its natural level was irresponsible. In the midst of a depression, trying to balance the budget was not only stupid, it was dangerous. Active use of fiscal policy was essential to return the country to high employment.

28-2 | The Neoclassical Synthesis

Within a few years, the *General Theory* had transformed macroeconomics. Not everybody was converted, and few agreed with it all. But most discussions became organized around it.

By the early 1950s, a large consensus had emerged, based on an integration of many of Keynes's ideas and the ideas of earlier economists. This consensus was called the **neoclassical synthesis**. To quote from Paul Samuelson in the 1955 edition of his textbook, *Economics*, the first modern economics textbook:

> In recent years, 90 per cent of American economists have stopped being "Keynesian economists" or "Anti-Keynesian economists." Instead, they have worked toward a synthesis of whatever is valuable in older economics and in modern theories of income determination. The result might be called neo-classical economics and is accepted, in its broad outlines, by all but about five per cent of extreme left-wing and right-wing writers.

The neoclassical synthesis was to remain the dominant view for another 20 years. Progress was astonishing, and the period from the early 1940s to the early 1970s can be called the golden age of macroeconomics.

Progress on All Fronts

The first order of business after publication of the *General Theory* was to formalize mathematically what Keynes meant. Although Keynes knew mathematics, he had avoided using math in the *General Theory*. One result was endless controversies about what Keynes meant and whether there were logical flaws in some of his arguments.

The IS-LM Model. Several formalizations of Keynes's ideas were offered. The most influential one was the *IS-LM* model, developed by John Hicks and Alvin Hansen in the 1930s and early 1940s. The initial version of the *IS-LM* model—which was actually very close to the version presented in chapter 5 of this book—was criticized for emasculating many of Keynes's insights: Expectations played no role, and the adjustment of prices and wages was altogether absent. Yet the *IS-LM* model provided a basis from which to start building, and as such it was immensely successful. Discussions became organized around the slopes of the *IS* and *LM* curves, what variables were missing from the two relations, what equations for prices and wages should be added to the model, and so on.

Franco Modigliani

Theories of Consumption, Investment, and Money Demand. Keynes had emphasized the importance of consumption and investment behavior, and of the choice between money and other financial assets. Major progress was soon made along all three fronts.

In the 1950s, Franco Modigliani (then at Carnegie Mellon and now at MIT) and Milton Friedman (then at the University of Chicago and now at the Hoover Institution at Stanford) independently developed the theory of consumption we saw in chapter 16. Both insisted on the importance of expectations in determining current consumption decisions.

James Tobin, from Yale, developed the theory of investment, based on the relation between the present value of profits and investment. The theory was further developed and tested by Dale Jorgenson, from Harvard. We saw this theory in chapter 16.

James Tobin

Tobin also developed the theory of the demand for money, and more generally the theory of the choice between different assets based on liquidity, return, and risk. His work has become the basis not only for an improved treatment of financial markets in macroeconomics, but also for the theory of finance in general.

Growth Theory. In parallel with the work on fluctuations, there was a renewed focus on growth. In contrast to the stagnation in the pre–World War II era, most countries were growing fast in the 1950s and 1960s. Even if they experienced fluctuations, their standard of living was increasing rapidly. The growth model developed by MIT's Robert Solow in 1956, which we saw in chapters 11 and 12, provided a framework to think about the determinants of growth. It was followed by an explosion of work on the roles of saving and technological progress in growth.

Robert Solow

Macroeconometric Models. All these contributions were integrated in larger and larger macroeconometric models. The first U.S. macroeconometric model, developed by Lawrence Klein from the University of Pennsylvania in the early 1950s, was an extended *IS* relation, with 16 equations. With the development of the National Income and Product Accounts (making available better data) and the development of econometrics and computers, the models quickly grew in size. The most important effort was the construction of the MPS model (MPS stands for MIT–Penn–SSRC, for the two universities and the research institution—the Social Science Research Council—involved in its construction), developed during the 1960s by a group of people led by Franco Modigliani. Its structure was an expanded version of the *IS-LM* model, plus a Phillips curve mechanism. But its components—consumption, investment, and money demand—all reflected the tremendous theoretical and empirical progress made since Keynes.

Keynesians versus Monetarists

With such rapid progress, many macroeconomists came to believe that the future was bright. The nature of fluctuations was increasingly well understood; the development of models

Lawrence Klein

allowed for a better use of policy. The time when the economy could be fine tuned, and recessions all but eliminated, seemed not far in the future.

This optimism was met with skepticism by a small but influential minority, the **monetarists**. Their intellectual leader was Milton Friedman. Although Friedman saw much progress being made—and was himself the father of one of the major contributions, the theory of consumption—he did not share in the general enthusiasm. He believed that the understanding of the economy remained very limited. He questioned the motives of governments as well as the notion that they actually knew enough to improve macroeconomic outcomes.

In the 1960s, debates between "Keynesians" and "monetarists" dominated the economic headlines. The debates centered around three issues: the effectiveness of monetary versus fiscal policy, the Phillips curve, and the role of policy.

Milton Friedman

Monetary versus Fiscal Policy. Keynes had emphasized *fiscal* rather than *monetary* policy as the key to fighting recessions. And this had remained the prevailing wisdom. The *IS* curve, many argued, was quite steep: Changes in the interest rate had little effect on demand and output. Thus, monetary policy did not work very well. Fiscal policy, which affects demand directly, could affect output faster and more reliably.

Friedman strongly challenged this conclusion. In a 1963 book titled *A Monetary History of the United States, 1867–1960*, Friedman and Anna Schwartz painstakingly reviewed the evidence on monetary policy and the relation between money and output in the United States over a century. Their conclusion was not only that monetary policy was very powerful, but that movements in money did explain most of the fluctuations in output. They interpreted the Great Depression as the result of a tragic mistake in monetary policy, a decrease in the money supply due to bank failures—a decrease that the Fed could have avoided by increasing the monetary base, but had not. (We discussed this interpretation in chapter 22.)

Friedman and Schwartz's challenge was followed by a vigorous debate and by intense research on the respective effects of fiscal and monetary policy. In the end, a consensus was in effect reached. Both fiscal and monetary policies clearly had effects. And if one cared about the composition of output and took into account the openness of the economy, the best policy was typically a mix of the two.

The Phillips Curve. The second debate focused on the Phillips curve. The Phillips curve was not part of the initial Keynesian model. But because it provided such a convenient (and apparently reliable) way of explaining the movement of wages and prices over time, it had become part of the neoclassical synthesis. In the 1960s, based on the empirical evidence up to then, many Keynesian economists believed that there was a reliable trade-off between unemployment and inflation, even in the long run.

Edmund Phelps

Milton Friedman and Edmund Phelps (from Columbia University) strongly disagreed. They argued that the existence of such a long-run trade-off flew in the face of basic economic theory. They argued that the apparent trade-off would quickly vanish if policy makers actually tried to exploit it—that is, if they tried to achieve low unemployment by accepting higher inflation. As we saw in chapter 8 when we studied the evolution of the Phillips curve, Friedman and Phelps were most definitely right. By the mid-1970s, the consensus was indeed that there was no long-run trade-off between inflation and unemployment.

The Role of Policy. The third debate centered on the role of policy. Much less certain that economists knew enough to stabilize output and that policy makers could be trusted to do the right thing, Friedman argued for the use of simple rules, such as steady money growth (a rule we discussed in chapter 26). Here is what he said in 1958:

> *A steady rate of growth in the money supply will not mean perfect stability even though it would prevent the kind of wide fluctuations that we have experienced from time to time in the past. It is tempting to try to go farther*

and to use monetary changes to offset other factors making for expansion and contraction. . . . The available evidence casts grave doubts on the possibility of producing any fine adjustments in economic activity by fine adjustments in monetary policy—at least in the present state of knowledge. There are thus serious limitations to the possibility of a discretionary monetary policy and much danger that such a policy may make matters worse rather than better.

Political pressures to "do something" in the face of either relatively mild price rises or relatively mild price and employment declines are clearly very strong indeed in the existing state of public attitudes. The main moral to be drawn from the two preceding points is that yielding to these pressures may frequently do more harm than good.

Source: Milton Friedman, "The Supply of Money and Changes in Prices and Output," Testimony to Congress, 1958.

As we saw in chapter 25, this debate on the role of macroeconomic policy has not been settled. The nature of the arguments has changed somewhat, but they are still with us today.

28-3 | The Rational Expectations Critique

Despite the battles between Keynesians and monetarists, macroeconomics around 1970 looked like a successful and mature field. It appeared successful at explaining events, at guiding policy choices. Most debates were framed within a common intellectual framework. But, within a few years the field was in crisis. The crisis had two sources.

Robert Lucas

One was events. By the mid-1970s, most countries were experiencing *stagflation*, a word created at the time to denote the simultaneous existence of high unemployment and high inflation. Macroeconomists had not predicted stagflation. After the fact and after a few years of research, a convincing explanation was provided, based on the effects of adverse supply shocks on both prices and output. (We discussed the effects of such shocks in chapter 7.) But it was too late to undo the damage to the discipline's image.

The other was ideas. In the early 1970s, a small group of economists—Robert Lucas from Chicago; Thomas Sargent, then at Minnesota and now at Chicago; and Robert Barro, then at Chicago and now at Harvard—led a strong attack against mainstream macroeconomics. They did not mince words. In a 1978 paper, Lucas and Sargent stated

Thomas Sargent

That the predictions [of Keynesian economics] were wildly incorrect, and that the doctrine on which they were based was fundamentally flawed, are now simple matters of fact, involving no subtleties in economic theory. The task which faces contemporary students of the business cycle is that of sorting through the wreckage, determining what features of that remarkable intellectual event called the Keynesian Revolution can be salvaged and put to good use, and which others must be discarded.

Source: "After Keynesian Economics," in *After the Phillips Curve*: Persistence of High Inflation and High Unemployment (Boston: Federal Reserve Bank of Boston, 1978).

The Three Implications of Rational Expectations

Lucas and Sargent's main argument was that Keynesian economics had ignored the full implications of the effect of expectations on behavior. The way to proceed, they argued, was to assume that people formed expectations as rationally as they could, based on the information they had. Thinking of people as having *rational expectations* had three major implications, all highly damaging to Keynesian macroeconomics.

Robert Barro

The Lucas Critique. The first implication was that existing macroeconomic models could not be used to help design policy. Although these models recognized that expectations affect behavior, they did not incorporate expectations explicitly. All variables were assumed to depend on current and past values of other variables, including policy variables. Thus, what the models captured was the set of relations between economic variables as they had held in the past, under past policies. Were these policies to change, Lucas argued, the way people formed expectations would change as well, making estimated relations—and, by implication, simulations generated using existing macroeconometric models—poor guides to what would happen under these new policies. This critique of macroeconometric models became known as the **Lucas critique**. To take again the history of the Phillips curve as an example, the data up to the early 1970s had suggested a trade-off between unemployment and inflation. As policy makers tried to exploit that trade-off, it disappeared.

Rational Expectations and the Phillips Curve. The second implication was as follows: When rational expectations were introduced in Keynesian models, these models actually delivered the very un-Keynesian conclusion that deviations of output from its natural level were short-lived, much more so than Keynesian economists claimed. This argument was based on a reexamination of the aggregate supply relation.

In Keynesian models, the slow return of output to its natural level came from the slow adjustment of prices and wages through the Phillips curve mechanism. An increase in money, for example, led first to higher output and to lower unemployment. Lower unemployment then led to higher nominal wages and to higher prices. The adjustment continued until wages and prices had increased in the same proportion as nominal money, until unemployment and output were back at their natural levels.

This adjustment, Lucas pointed out, was highly dependent on wage setters' backward-looking expectations of inflation. In the MPS model, for example, wages responded only to current and past inflation, and to current unemployment. But once the assumption was made that wage setters had rational expectations, the adjustment was likely to be much faster. Changes in money, to the extent that they were anticipated, might have no effect on output: For example, anticipating an increase in money of 5% over the coming year, wage setters would increase the nominal wages set in contracts for the coming year by 5%. Firms would in turn increase prices by 5%. The result would be no change in the real money stock, and no change in demand or output.

Within the logic of the Keynesian models, Lucas therefore argued, only *unanticipated changes in money* should affect output. Predictable movements in money should have no effect on activity. More generally, if wage setters had rational expectations, shifts in demand were likely to have effects on output for only as long as wages were set in nominal terms, a year or so. Even on its own terms, the Keynesian model did not deliver a convincing theory of the long-lasting effects of demand on output.

Optimal Control versus Game Theory. The third implication of rational expectations was as follows: If people and firms had rational expectations, it was wrong to think of policy as the control of a complicated but passive system. Rather, the right way was to think of policy as a game between policy makers and the economy. The right tool was not *optimal control*, but *game theory*. And game theory led to a different vision of policy. A striking example was the issue of *time inconsistency*, discussed by Finn Kydland and Edward Prescott (then at Carnegie Mellon, now at the University of Minnesota), an issue that we discussed in chapter 25: Good intentions on the part of policy makers could actually lead to disaster.

To summarize: When rational expectations were introduced, (1) Keynesian models could not be used to determine policy, (2) Keynesian models could not explain long-lasting deviations of output from its natural level, and (3) the theory of policy needed to be redesigned, using the tools of game theory.

The Integration of Rational Expectations

As you might guess from the tone of Lucas and Sargent's quote, the intellectual atmosphere in macroeconomics was tense in the early 1970s. But within a few years, a process of integration (of ideas, not people, because tempers remained high) had started, and it was to dominate the 1970s and the 1980s.

Fairly quickly, the idea that rational expectations was the right working assumption gained wide acceptance. This did not happen because all macroeconomists believe that people, firms, and participants in financial markets always form expectations rationally. But rational expectations appears to be a natural benchmark, at least until economists have made more progress in understanding whether and how actual expectations systematically differ from rational expectations.

Work then started on the challenges raised by Lucas and Sargent.

Robert Hall

The Implications of Rational Expectations. First, there was a systematic exploration of the role and the implications of rational expectations in goods, financial, and labor markets. Much of what was discovered has been presented in this book already. Here are two examples:

- Robert Hall, then from MIT and now at Stanford, showed that if consumers are very foresighted (in the sense defined in chapter 16), then changes in consumption should be unpredictable: The best forecast of consumption next year would be consumption this year! Put another way, changes in consumption should be very hard to predict. This result came as a surprise to most macroeconomists at the time, but it is in fact based on a simple intuition: If consumers are very foresighted, they will change their consumption only when they learn something new about the future. But by definition, such news cannot be predicted. This consumption behavior, known as the **random walk of consumption**, has served as a benchmark in consumption research ever since.
- Rudiger Dornbusch from MIT showed that the large swings in exchange rates under flexible exchange rates, which had previously been thought of as the result of speculation by irrational investors, were fully consistent with rationality. We saw his analysis in chapter 21: Changes in monetary policy can lead to long-lasting changes in interest rates; changes in current and expected interest-rate differentials between two countries can lead to large changes in the exchange rate. Dornbusch's model, known as the *overshooting* model of exchange rates, has become the benchmark in discussions of exchange-rate movements.

Rudiger Dornbusch

Stanley Fischer

Wage and Price Setting. Second, there was a systematic exploration of the determination of wages and prices, going far beyond the Phillips curve relation. Two important contributions were made by MIT's Stanley Fischer and John Taylor, then at Columbia University and now at Stanford. Both showed that the adjustment of prices and wages in response to changes in unemployment can be slow *even under rational expectations*.

They pointed to an important characteristic of both wage and price setting, the **staggering** of wage and price decisions. In contrast to the simple story we told earlier, where all wages and prices increased simultaneously in anticipation of an increase in money, actual wage and price decisions are staggered over time. So there is not one sudden synchronized adjustment of all wages and prices to an increase in money. Rather, the adjustment is likely to be slow, with wages and prices adjusting to the new level of money through a process of leapfrogging over time. Fischer and Taylor thus showed that the second issue raised by the rational-expectations critique could be resolved, that a slow return of output to its natural level is consistent with rational expectations in the labor market.

The Theory of Policy. Third, thinking about policy in terms of game theory led to an explosion of research on the nature of the games being played, not only between policy makers and the economy but also between policy makers—between political parties, or between the central bank and the government, or between governments of different countries. One of the

John Taylor

major achievements of this research has been the development of a way of thinking more rigorously about such fuzzy notions as "credibility," "reputation," and "commitment." At the same time, there has been a distinct shift in focus from "what governments should do" to "what governments actually do," and thus a focus on the political constraints that economists should take into account when advising policy makers.

To summarize: By the end of the 1980s, the challenges raised by the rational-expectations critique had led to a complete overhaul of macroeconomics. The basic structure had been extended to take into account the implications of rational expectations, or more generally, of forward-looking behavior by people and firms. Indeed, what I have presented in this book is what I see as the synthesis that has emerged, and that now constitutes the common framework of macroeconomics. In the last section of this chapter, I shall summarize what I see as the basic set of propositions on which most macroeconomists agree. But before I do so, I want to turn briefly to current research. Much of it is still too speculative to have made it into the book, but no doubt some of it will do so soon.

28-4 | Current Developments

Today, three groups dominate the research headlines: the new classicals, the new Keynesians, and the new growth theorists. (Note the generous use of the word "new." Unlike producers of laundry detergents, economists stop short of using "new and improved." But the subliminal message is the same.)

New Classical Economics and Real Business Cycle Theory

The rational-expectations critique was more than just a critique of Keynesian economics. It also offered its own interpretation of fluctuations. Instead of relying on imperfections in labor markets, on the slow adjustment of wages and prices, and so on, to explain fluctuations, Lucas argued, macroeconomists should see how far they could go in explaining fluctuations as the effects of shocks in competitive markets with fully flexible prices and wages.

This is the research agenda that has been pursued by the **new classicals**. The intellectual leader is Edward Prescott, and the models he and his followers have developed are known as **real business cycle (RBC)** models. These models assume that output is always at its natural level. Thus, all fluctuations in output are movements of the natural level of output, as opposed to movements away from the natural level of output.

Edward Prescott

Where do these movements come from? The answer proposed by Prescott is technological progress. As new discoveries are made, productivity increases, leading to an increase in output. The increase in productivity leads to an increase in the wage, which makes it more attractive to work, leading workers to work more. Productivity increases therefore lead to increases in both output and employment, as we indeed observe in the real world.

The RBC approach has been criticized on many fronts. As we discussed in chapter 12, technological progress is the result of very many innovations, each of which takes a long time to diffuse. It is hard to see how this process could generate anything like the large short-run fluctuations in output that we observe in practice. It is also hard to think of recessions as times of technological *regress*, times in which productivity and output both go down. Finally, as we have seen, there is very strong evidence that changes in money, which have no effect on output in RBC models, in fact have strong effects on output in the real world.

At this point, most economists do not believe that the RBC approach provides a convincing explanation of major fluctuations in output. The approach has nevertheless proved useful. It has drilled in the correct point that not all fluctuations in output are deviations of output from its natural level. At a more technical level, it has provided several new techniques for solving complex models, which are widely used in research today. It is likely to evolve rather than disappear. Already, some recent RBC models have started introducing nominal rigidities, allowing for the effects of money on output.

New Keynesian Economics

The term **new Keynesians** denotes a loosely connected group of researchers who share a common belief that the synthesis that has emerged in response to the rational-expectations critique is basically correct. But they also share the belief that much remains to be learned about the nature of imperfections in different markets, and about the implications of those imperfections for macroeconomic evolutions.

One line of research has focused on the determination of wages in the labor market. We discussed in chapter 6 the notion of *efficiency wages*—the idea that wages, if perceived by workers as too low, may lead to shirking, problems of morale within the firm, difficulties in recruiting or keeping good workers, and so on. One influential researcher in this area has been George Akerlof from Berkeley, who has explored the role of "norms," the rules that develop in any organization—in this case, the firm—to assess what is fair or unfair. This research has led him and others to explore issues previously left to research in sociology and psychology, and to examine their macroeconomic implications.

George Akerlof

Another line of new Keynesian research has explored the role of imperfections in credit markets. Except for a discussion of the role of banks in the Great Depression and in the current Japanese recession, I have typically assumed in this book that the effects of monetary policy worked through interest rates, and that firms and people could borrow freely at the quoted interest rate. In practice, most people and many firms can borrow only from banks. And banks often turn down potential borrowers, despite their willingness to pay the posted interest rate. Why this happens, and how it affects our view of how monetary policy works, has been the subject of much research, in particular by Ben Bernanke of Princeton.

Yet another direction of research is **nominal rigidities**. As we saw earlier in this chapter, Fischer and Taylor have shown that with staggering of wage or price decisions, output can deviate from its natural level for a long time. This conclusion raises several issues. If staggering is indeed responsible, at least in part, for fluctuations, why don't wage setters/price setters synchronize decisions? Why aren't prices and wages adjusted more often? Why aren't all prices and wages changed, say, on the first day of each week? In tackling these issues, Akerlof and N. Gregory Mankiw, from Harvard University, have derived a surprising and important result, often referred to as the **menu cost** explanation of output fluctuations.

Each wage or price setter is largely indifferent about when and how often he changes his own wage or price (for a retailer, changing the prices on the shelf every day or every week does not make much difference to profits). Even small costs of changing prices—such as those involved in printing a new menu, for example—may lead to infrequent and staggered price adjustment. This staggering leads to slow adjustment of the price level, and to large aggregate output fluctuations in response to movements in aggregate demand. In short, decisions that do not matter much at the individual level (how often to change prices or wages) lead to large aggregate effects (slow adjustment of the price level, and large effects of shifts in aggregate demand on output).

New Growth Theory

After being one of the most active topics of research in the 1960s, growth theory experienced an intellectual slump. Since the mid-1980s, however, growth theory has made a strong comeback. The set of new contributions goes under the name of **new growth theory**.

Two economists, Robert Lucas (the same Lucas who spearheaded the rational-expectations critique) and Paul Romer (from Berkeley), have played an important role in defining the issues. When growth theory faded in the late 1960s, two issues were left largely unresolved. The first was the determinants of technological progress. The second was the role of increasing returns to scale—whether, say, doubling capital and labor may actually lead to more than a doubling of output. These are the two major issues on which new growth theory has concentrated. The discussions of technological progress in chapter 12, and of the interaction between technological progress and unemployment in chapter 13, reflect some of the advances economists have made on this front. The work of Alwyn Young (from the

Paul Romer

University of Chicago) on growth in fast-growing Asian countries, which we discussed in chapter 12, is a good example of this new research.

To summarize, current research is proceeding mainly on three fronts. First (the New Classical approach): Identifying how much of the fluctuations can be thought of as movements in the natural level of output and in the natural unemployment rate. Second (the New Keynesian approach): Identifying the precise nature of market imperfections and nominal rigidities that give rise to deviations of output from its natural level. Third (the New Growth theory): Identifying the factors responsible for technological progress and growth in the long run.

28-5 | Common Beliefs

As we come to the end of this book, let me state the basic set of propositions on which most macroeconomists agree:

- In the short run, shifts in aggregate demand affect output. Higher consumer confidence, a larger budget deficit, and faster growth of money are all likely to increase output and employment, and to decrease unemployment.
- In the medium run, output returns to its natural level. This natural level depends on the natural rate of unemployment (which, together with the size of the labor force, determines the level of employment), on the capital stock, and on the state of technology.
- In the long run, two main factors determine the evolution of the level of output. The first is capital accumulation, the second the rate of technological progress.
- Monetary policy affects output in the short run, but not in the medium or the long run. A higher rate of money growth eventually translates one for one into a higher rate of inflation.
- Fiscal policy has both short-run, medium-run and long-run effects on activity. Higher deficits are likely to increase output in the short run. However, they are likely to decrease capital accumulation and output in the long run.

These propositions leave room for disagreement:

- One is the length of the short run, the period of time over which aggregate demand affects output. At one extreme, real business cycle theorists start from the assumption that output is always at its natural level: The short run is very short. At the other, theories of hysteresis in unemployment (which we explored in chapter 22) imply that the effects of demand may be extremely long-lasting, that the short run may really be very long.
- Another is the role for policy. Although conceptually distinct, it is largely related to the first. Those who believe that output returns quickly to its natural level are typically willing to impose tight rules on both monetary and fiscal policy, from constant money growth to the requirement of a balanced budget. Those who believe that the adjustment is slow typically believe in the need for more flexible stabilization policies.

But, behind these disagreements, there is a largely common framework in which most research is conducted and organized. The framework gives us a way of interpreting events and discussing policy. This is what I have done in this book.

SUMMARY

- The history of modern macroeconomics starts in 1936, with the publication of Keynes's *General Theory of Employment, Interest and Money*. Keynes's contribution was formalized in the *IS-LM* model by John Hicks and Alvin Hansen in the 1930s and early 1940s.

- The period from the early 1940s to the early 1970s can be called the golden age of macroeconomics. Among the major developments were the development of the theories of consumption, investment, money demand, and portfolio choice; the development of

- growth theory; and the development of large macroeconometric models.

- The main debate during the 1960s was between Keynesians and monetarists. Keynesians believed that developments in macroeconomic theory allowed for better control of the economy. Monetarists, led by Milton Friedman, were more skeptical of the ability of governments to help stabilize the economy.

- In the 1970s, macroeconomics experienced a crisis. There were two reasons. The first was the appearance of stagflation, which came as a surprise to most economists. The second was a theoretical attack led by Robert Lucas. Lucas and his followers showed that when rational expectations were introduced, (1) Keynesian models could not be used to determine policy, (2) Keynesian models could not explain long-lasting deviations of output from its natural level, and (3) the theory of policy needed to be redesigned, using the tools of game theory.

- Much of the 1970s and 1980s was spent integrating rational expectations into macroeconomics. As is reflected in this book, macroeconomists are now much more aware of the role of expectations in determining the effects of shocks and policy, and of the complexity of policy, than they were two decades ago.

- Current research in macroeconomic theory is proceeding along three lines. New classical economists are exploring the extent to which fluctuations can be explained as movements in the natural level of output, as opposed to movements away from the natural level of output. New Keynesian economists are exploring the role of market imperfections in fluctuations. New growth theorists are exploring the role of R&D and of increasing returns to scale in growth.

- Despite the differences, there exists a set of propositions on which most macroeconomists agree. The main two are: In the short run, shifts in aggregate demand affect output. In the medium run, output returns to its natural level.

KEY TERMS

- business cycle theory, 538
- effective demand, 538
- liquidity preference, 538
- neoclassical synthesis, 538
- monetarists, 540
- Lucas critique, 542
- random walk of consumption, 543

- staggering, 543
- new classicals, 544
- real business cycle (RBC) models, 544
- new Keynesians, 545
- nominal rigidities, 545
- menu costs, 545
- new growth theory, 545

FURTHER READINGS

The two classics are J. M. Keynes, *The General Theory of Employment, Money and Interest* (London: Macmillan Press, 1936), and Milton Friedman and Anna Schwartz, *A Monetary History of the United States, 1867–1960* (Princeton, NJ: Princeton University Press, 1963). Be warned: The first makes for hard reading, and the second is a heavy volume.

For an account of macroeconomics in textbooks since the 1940s, read Paul Samuelson's "Credo of a Lucky Textbook Author," *Journal of Economic Perspectives*, Spring 1997, 153–160.

In the introduction to *Studies in Business Cycle Theory* (Cambridge, MA: MIT Press, 1981), Robert Lucas develops his approach to macroeconomics, and gives a guide to his contributions.

The paper that launched real business cycle theory is Edward Prescott, "Theory Ahead of Business Cycle Measurement," *Federal Reserve Bank of Minneapolis Review*, Fall 1986, 9–22. It is not particularly easy reading.

For more on new Keynesian economics, read David Romer, "The New Keynesian Synthesis," *Journal of Economic Perspectives*, Winter 1993, 5–22.

For more on new growth theory, read Paul Romer, "The Origins of Endogenous Growth," *Journal of Economic Perspectives*, Winter 1994, 3–22. A more complete treatment is given in Charles Jones, *An Introduction to Economic Growth* (New York: W.W. Norton, 1997).

In a lighter mode, for a well-written set of essays on many economists and their ideas, read David Warsh, *Economic*

Principles: Masters and Mavericks of Modern Economics, (New York: Free Press, 1993).

For more on how macroeconomists, from Robert Solow to Robert Lucas, view macroeconomics, read Brian Snowdown and Howard Vane, "Conversations with Leading Economists, Interpreting Modern Macroeconomics" (Northampton, MA: Edward Elgar, 1999).

If you want to learn more about macroeconomic issues and theory:

Most economics journals are heavy on mathematics and are hard to read. But a few make an effort to be more friendly. The *Journal of Economic Perspectives* in particular has nontechnical articles on current economic research and issues. The *Brookings Papers on Economic Activity*, published twice a year, analyze current macroeconomic problems. So does *Economic Policy*, published in Europe, which focuses more on European issues.

Most regional Federal Reserve banks also publish reviews with easy-to-read articles; these reviews are available free of charge. Among these are the *Economic Review* published by the Cleveland Fed, the *Economic Review* published by the Kansas City Fed, the *New England Economic Review* published by the Boston Fed, and the *Review* published by the Minneapolis Fed.

More advanced treatments of current macroeconomic theory—roughly at the level of a first graduate course in macroeconomics—are given by David Romer, *Advanced Macroeconomics* (New York: McGraw-Hill, 1995) and by Olivier Blanchard and Stanley Fischer, *Lectures on Macroeconomics* (Cambridge, MA: MIT Press, 1989).

Appendix 1: An Introduction to National Income and Product Accounts

This appendix introduces the basic structure and the terms used in the national income and product accounts. The basic measure of aggregate activity is gross domestic product, or GDP. The **national income and product accounts (NIPA**, or simply **national accounts)** are organized around two disaggregations of GDP. The first looks at *income*: Who receives what? The other looks at *product*: What is produced, and who buys it?

The Income Side

Table A–1 looks at the income side of GDP—who receives what.

The top part of the table (lines 1 through 9) goes from GDP to national income, the sum of the incomes received by the different factors of production:

- The starting point, in line 1, is **gross domestic product**, or **GDP**. It is defined as *the market value of the goods and services produced by labor and property located in the United States*.

- The next three lines take us from GDP to **GNP**, the **gross national product** (line 4). GNP is an alternative measure of aggregate output. It is defined as *the market value of the goods and services produced by labor and property supplied by U.S. residents*.

Until recently, most countries used GNP rather than GDP as the main measure of aggregate activity. The emphasis in the U.S. national accounts shifted from GNP to GDP in 1991. The difference between the two comes from the distinction between "located in the United States" (used to define GDP) and "supplied by U.S. residents" (used to define GNP). For example, profit from a U.S.–owned plant in Japan is not included in U.S. GDP, but is included in U.S. GNP.

TABLE A–1 GDP: THE INCOME SIDE, 1998 ($ BILLIONS)

FROM GROSS DOMESTIC PRODUCT TO NATIONAL INCOME:

1. **Gross domestic product** (GDP)	8,511	
2. Plus: receipts of factor income from the rest of the world		+269
3. Minus: payments of factor income to the rest of the world		−290
4. Equals: **Gross national product**	8,490	
5. Minus: consumption of fixed capital		−908
6. Equals: **Net national product**	7,582	
7. Minus: indirect taxes		−655
8. Minus: other		+67
9. Equals: **National income**	6,994	

THE DECOMPOSITION OF NATIONAL INCOME:

10. Compensation of employees	4,981	
11. Wages and salaries		4,154
12. Supplements to wages and salaries		827
13. Corporate profits	825	
14. Net interest	449	
15. Proprietors' income	577	
16. Rental income of persons	162	

Source: Survey of Current Business, April 1999, tables 1–9 and 1–14.

Thus, to go from GDP to GNP, we must first add **receipts of factor income from the rest of the world**, which is income from U.S. capital or U.S. residents abroad (line 2), and then subtract **payments of factor income to the rest of the world**, which is income received by foreign capital and foreign residents in the United States (line 3). In 1998, payments to the rest of the world exceeded receipts from the rest of the world by $21 billion, so GNP was smaller than GDP by $21 billion.

- The next step takes us from GNP to **net national product**, or **NNP** (line 6). The difference between GNP and NNP is the depreciation of capital, which is called **consumption of fixed capital** in the national accounts.

- Finally, lines 7 to 9 take us from NNP to **national income** (line 9), defined as the *income that originates in the production of goods and services supplied by residents of the United States*.

  The main step in going from NNP to national income is to subtract **indirect taxes** (line 7) (sales taxes) that decrease the amount left for factor income—the payments going to the various factors of production. There are also a few other corrections, which sum to $67 billion in line 8. Most of them you can safely ignore. One, however, deserves a short discussion.

  National income is actually constructed in two independent ways. One is from the top down, starting from GDP constructed from the product side and going through the steps we have just gone through in Table A–1. The other is from the bottom up, by adding the different components of factor income (compensation of employees, corporate profits, and so on). The two measures typically differ, and the difference is called the *statistical discrepancy*. In 1998, national income computed from the top down was less than national income computed from the bottom up by $76 billion. The statistical discrepancy is a reminder of the statistical problems involved in constructing the national income accounts.

The bottom part of the table (lines 10–16) disaggregates national income into different types of income.

- **Compensation of employees** (line 10), or labor income, is by far the largest component, accounting for 71% of national income. It is the sum of wages and salaries (line 11) and of supplements to wages and salaries (line 12). These range from employer contributions for social insurance (by far the largest item) to such exotic items as employer contributions to marriage fees to justices of the peace.

- **Corporate profits** (line 13) are revenues minus costs (including interest payments) and minus depreciation.

- **Net interest** (line 14) is the interest paid by firms minus the interest received by firms, plus interest received from the rest of the world minus interest paid to the rest of the world.

  In 1998, most of net interest represented net interest paid by firms: The United States received about as much in interest from the rest of the world as it paid to the rest to the world. Thus, the sum of corporate profits plus net interest paid by firms was approximately $825 billion + $449 billion = $1,274 billion, or about 18% of national income.

- **Proprietors' income** (line 15) is the income received by persons who are self-employed. It is defined as *the income of sole proprietorships, partnerships, and tax-exempt cooperatives*.

- **Rental income of persons** (line 16) is equal to the income from the rental of real property, minus depreciation on this real property. Houses produce housing services; rental income measures the income received for these services.

  If the national accounts counted only actual rents, rental income would depend on the proportion of apartments and houses that were rented versus owner occupied. For example, if everybody became the owner of the apartment or the house in which they lived, rental income would go to zero, and thus measured GDP would drop. To avoid this problem, national accounts treat houses and apartments as if they were all rented out. Thus, rental income is constructed as actual rents plus *imputed* rents on those houses and apartments that are owner occupied.

Before we move to the product side, Table A–2 shows how we can go from national income to personal disposable income—the income available to consumers after they have received transfers and paid taxes.

- Not all national income (line 1) is distributed to persons. Some of the corporate profits are retained by firms. So the first step is to subtract all corporate profits (line 2, also line 13 in Table A–1), and add back that part of profits that is distributed to persons, *personal dividend income* (line 3).

- Similarly, not all interest payments paid by firms go to persons. Some go to banks, some go abroad. So the next step is to subtract all net interest payments by firms and by the rest of the world (line 4, also line 14 in Table A–1), and add back all interest payments received by persons (line 5).

TABLE A–2 FROM NATIONAL INCOME TO PERSONAL DISPOSABLE INCOME, 1998 ($ BILLIONS)

1.	**National income**	**6,994**	
2.	Minus: corporate profits		−825
3.	Plus: personal dividend income		+263
4.	Minus: net interest		−449
5.	Plus: personal interest income		+765
6.	Plus: government and business transfers		+1145
7.	Minus: contributions for social insurance		−767
8.	Equals: **Personal income**	7,126	
9.	Minus: personal tax and nontax payments		−1098
10.	Equals: **Personal disposable income**	6,028	

Source: Survey of Current Business, April 1999, tables 1–9 and 2–1.

- Finally, people receive income not only from production, but also from transfers (line 6). Transfers accounted for $1,145 billion in 1998, of which all but $28 billion came from the government. From these transfers must be subtracted contributions for social insurance paid by workers, $767 billion (line 7).

- The net result of these adjustments is **personal income**, the income actually received by persons (line 8). **Personal disposable income** (line 10) is then equal to personal income minus personal tax

and nontax payments (line 9). In 1998, personal disposable income was equal to $6,027 billion, or about 71% of GDP.

The Product Side

Table A–3 looks at the product side of the national accounts, at who buys what.

Let us start with the three components of domestic demand: consumption, investment, and government spending.

TABLE A–3 GDP: THE PRODUCT SIDE, 1997 ($ BILLIONS)

1.	**Gross domestic product**	**8,511**		
2.	Personal consumption expenditures	**5,807**		
3.	Durable goods		725	
4.	Nondurable goods		1,662	
5.	Services		3,420	
6.	Gross private domestic fixed investment	**1,308**		
7.	Nonresidential		938	
8.	Structures			247
9.	Producers' durable equipment			691
10.	Residential		370	
11.	Government purchases	**1,487**		
12.	Federal		521	
13.	National Defense			341
14.	Nondefense			180
15.	State and local		966	
16.	Net exports	**−151**		
17.	Exports		959	
18.	Imports		−1,110	
19.	Changes in business inventories	**60**		

Source : Survey of Current Business, April 1999, table 1–1.

- Consumption, called **personal consumption expenditures** (line 2), is by far the largest component of demand, accounting for 68% of GDP. It is defined as *the sum of goods and services purchased by persons resident in the United States.*

  In the same way that they include imputed rental income on the income side, national accounts include imputed housing services as part of consumption. Owners of a house are assumed to consume housing services, for a price equal to the imputed rental income of that house.

  Consumption is disaggregated into three components: purchases of **durable goods** (line 3), **nondurable goods** (line 4), and **services** (line 5). Durable goods are commodities that can be stored and have an average life of at least three years; automobile purchases are the largest item here. Nondurable goods are commodities that can be stored but have a life of less than three years. Services are commodities that cannot be stored, so must be consumed at the place and time of purchase.

- Investment is called **gross private domestic fixed investment** (line 6). It is the sum of two very different components:

  Nonresidential investment (line 7) is the purchase of new capital goods by firms. These may be either **structures** (line 8)—mostly new plants—or **producer durable equipment** (line 9)—such as machines, computers, or office equipment.

  Residential investment (line 10) is the purchase of new houses or apartments by persons.

- **Government purchases** (line 11) are equal to purchases of goods by the government plus compensation of government employees. (Government employees are thought of as selling their services to the government.)

  Government purchases are the sum of purchases by the federal government (line 12) (which themselves can be disaggregated between spending on national defense [line 13] and nondefense spending [line 14]) and purchases by state and local governments (line 15).

  Note that government purchases do not include transfers from the government, or interest payments on government debt. These do not correspond to purchases of either goods or services, and so are not included here. This means that the number for government purchases you see in Table A–3 is substantially smaller than the number you typically hear for government spending—which includes transfers and interest payments.

- The sum of consumption, investment, and government purchases gives the demand for goods by U.S. firms, U.S. persons, and the U.S. government. If the United States were a closed economy, this would be the same as the demand for U.S. goods. But because the U.S. economy is open, the two numbers are different. To get to the demand for U.S. goods, we must make two adjustments. First, we must add the foreign purchases of U.S. goods, **exports** (line 17). Second, we must subtract U.S. purchases of foreign goods, **imports** (line 18). In 1998, exports were less than imports by $151 billion. Thus, **net exports** (or equivalently the **trade balance**), was equal to minus $151 billion (line 16).

- Adding consumption, investment, government purchases, and net exports gives the total purchases of U.S. goods. Production may, however, be less than those purchases if firms satisfy the difference by decreasing inventories. Or production may be greater than purchases, in which case firms accumulate inventories. The last line of Table A–3 gives **changes in business inventories** (line 19), also sometimes called (rather misleadingly) "inventory investment." It is defined as the *change in the physical volume of inventories held by business.* The change in business inventories can be positive or negative. In 1998, it was positive: U.S. production was higher than total purchases of U.S. goods by $60 billion.

A Warning

National accounts give an internally consistent description of aggregate activity. But underlying these accounts are many choices of what to include and what not to include, where to put some types of income or spending, and so on. Here are three examples:

- Work within the home is not counted in GDP. If, for example, two women decide to babysit each other's children rather than to take care of their own children and pay each other for the babysitting services, measured GDP will go up, whereas true GDP clearly does not change. The solution would be to count work within the home in GDP, the same way that we impute rents for owner-occupied housing. But, so far, this has not been done.

- The purchase of a house is treated as an investment, and housing services are then treated as part of consumption. Contrast this with the treatment of automobiles. Despite the fact that they provide services for a long time—although not as long a time as houses do—purchases of automobiles are not treated as investment. They are treated as consumption and appear in the national accounts only in the year in which they are bought.

- Firms' purchases of machines are treated as investment. The purchase of education is treated as consumption of education services. But education is clearly in part an investment: People acquire it in part to increase their future income.

The list could go on. However, the purpose of these examples is not to make you conclude that national accounts are wrong. Most of the accounting decisions we just saw were made for good reasons, often because of data availability or for simplicity of treatment. Rather, the point is that to use national accounts best, you should understand their logic, but also understand the choices that have been made and thus understand their limitations.

KEY TERMS

- national income and product accounts (NIPA), or national accounts, A1
- gross domestic product (GDP), A1
- gross national product (GNP), A1
- receipts of factor income from the rest of the world, A2
- payments of factor income to the rest of the world, A2
- net national product (NNP), A2
- consumption of fixed capital, A2
- national income, A2
- indirect taxes, A2
- compensation of employees, A2
- corporate profits, A2
- net interest, A2
- proprietors' income, A2
- rental income of persons, A2
- personal income, A3
- personal disposable income, A3
- personal consumption expenditures, A4
- durable goods, A4
- nondurable goods, A4
- services, A4
- gross private domestic fixed investment, A4
- nonresidential investment, A4
- structures, A4
- producer durable equipment, A4
- residential investment, A4
- government purchases, A4
- exports, A4
- imports, A4
- net exports, or trade balance, A4
- changes in business inventories, A4

FURTHER READING

For more details, read the introduction to *National Income and Product Accounts of the United States*, Volume 2, *1959–1988*, U.S. Department of Commerce, (Washington, DC: Bureau of Economic Analysis). For an update, read "A Guide to the NIPAs," *Survey of Current Business*, Bureau of Economic Analysis, March 1998.

Appendix 2: A Math Refresher

This appendix presents the mathematical tools and the mathematical results that are used in the book.

Geometric Series

Definition. A geometric series is a sum of numbers of the form:

$$1 + x + x^2 + \cdots + x^n$$

where x is a number that may be greater or smaller than one, and x^n denotes x to the power n, that is, x times itself n times.

Examples of such series are

- The sum of spending in each round of the multiplier (chapter 3). If c is the marginal propensity to consume, then the sum of increases in spending after n rounds is given by

$$1 + c + c^2 + \cdots + c^{n-1}$$

- The present discounted value of a sequence of payments of 1 each year for n years (chapter 14), when the interest rate is equal to i:

$$1 + \frac{1}{1+i} + \frac{1}{(1+i)^2} + \cdots + \frac{1}{(1+i)^{n-1}}$$

We usually have two questions we want to answer when encountering such a series. The first one is what the sum is. The second is whether the sum explodes as we let n increase, or reaches a finite limit. The following propositions tell you what you need to know to answer these questions.

Proposition 1 tells you how to compute the sum:

Proposition 1:

$$1 + x + x^2 + \cdots + x^n = \frac{1 - x^{n+1}}{1 - x} \quad \text{(A.1)}$$

The proof is as follows. Multiply the sum by $(1 - x)$, and use the fact that $x^a x^b = x^{a+b}$ (that is: one has to add exponents when multiplying):

$$(1 + x + x^2 + \cdots + x^n)(1 - x)$$
$$= 1 + x + x^2 + \cdots + x^n$$
$$\quad - x - x^2 - \cdots - x^n - x^{n+1}$$
$$= 1 \qquad\qquad\qquad\qquad - x^{n+1}$$

All the terms on the right except for the first and the last cancel. Dividing both sides by $(1 - x)$ gives equation (A.1).

This formula can be used for any x and any n. If, for example, x is 0.9 and n is 10, then the sum is equal to 6.86. If x is 1.2 and n is 10, then the sum is equal to 32.15.

Proposition 2 tells you what happens as n gets large:

Proposition 2: If x is less than one, the sum goes to $1/(1 - x)$ as n gets large. If x is equal to or greater than one, the sum explodes as n gets large.

The proof is as follows. If x is less than one, then x^n goes to zero as n gets large. Thus, from equation (A.1), the sum goes to $1/(1 - x)$. If x is greater than one, then x^n becomes larger and larger as n increases, $1 - x^n$ becomes a larger and larger negative number, and the ratio $(1 - x^n)/(1 - x)$ becomes a larger and larger positive number. Thus, the sum explodes as n gets large.

Application from chapter 14: Consider the present value of a payment of $1 forever, starting next year, when the interest rate is equal to i. The present value is given by

$$\frac{1}{(1 + i)} + \frac{1}{(1 + i)^2} + \cdots \quad \text{(A.2)}$$

Factoring out $1/(1 + i)$, rewrite this present value as:

$$\frac{1}{(1 + i)}\left[1 + \frac{1}{(1 + i)} + \cdots\right]$$

The term in brackets is a geometric series, with $x = 1/(1 + i)$. As the interest rate i is positive, x is less than one. Applying proposition 2, when n gets large, the term in brackets is thus equal to

$$\frac{1}{1 - \dfrac{1}{(1 + i)}} = \frac{(1 + i)}{(1 + i - 1)} = \frac{(1 + i)}{i}$$

Replacing the term in brackets in the previous equation by $(1 + i)/i$ gives:

$$\frac{1}{(1 + i)}\left[\frac{(1 + i)}{i}\right] = \frac{1}{i}$$

The present value of a sequence of payments of one dollar a year forever, starting next year, is thus equal to one over the interest rate. If i is equal to 5%, the present value is equal to $20.

Useful Approximations

Throughout the book, I use several approximations that make computations easier. These approximations are most reliable when the variables x, y, z below are small, say, between 0% and 10%. The numerical examples in propositions 3 through 10 that follow are based on the values $x = 0.05$ and $y = 0.03$.

Proposition 3:

$$(1 + x)(1 + y) \approx (1 + x + y) \qquad (A.3)$$

The proof is as follows: Expanding $(1 + x)(1 + y)$ gives $(1 + x)(1 + y) = 1 + x + y + xy$. If x and y are small, then the product xy is very small and can be ignored as an approximation (for example, if $x = 0.05$ and $y = 0.03$, then $xy = 0.0015$). So $(1 + x)(1 + y)$ is approximately equal to $(1 + x + y)$.

For the values x and y above, for example, the approximation gives 1.08 compared to an exact value of 1.0815.

Application from chapter 18: Arbitrage between domestic and foreign bonds leads to the following relation:

$$(1 + i_t) = (1 + i_t^*)\left(1 + \frac{(E_{t+1}^e - E_t)}{E_t}\right)$$

Using proposition 3 on the right-hand side of the equation gives

$$(1 + i_t^*)\left(1 + \frac{(E_{t+1}^e - E_t)}{E_t}\right)$$

$$\approx \left(1 + i_t^* + \frac{(E_{t+1}^e - E_t)}{E_t}\right)$$

Replacing in the arbitrage equation gives

$$(1 + i_t) \approx \left(1 + i_t^* + \frac{(E_{t+1}^e - E_t)}{E_t}\right)$$

Subtracting 1 from both sides gives

$$i_t \approx i_t^* + \frac{(E_{t+1}^e - E_t)}{E_t}$$

The domestic interest rate is approximately equal to the foreign interest rate plus the expected rate of depreciation of the domestic currency.

Proposition 4:

$$(1 + x)^2 \approx 1 + 2x \qquad (A.4)$$

The proof follows directly from proposition 3, with $y = x$. For the value of $x = 0.05$, the approximation gives 1.10, compared to an exact value of 1.1025.

Application from chapter 15: From arbitrage, the relation between the two-year interest rate and the current and expected one-year rates is given by:

$$(1 + i_{2t})^2 = (1 + i_{1t})(1 + i_{1t+1}^e)$$

Using proposition 4 for the left-hand side of the equation gives

$$(1 + i_{2t})^2 \approx 1 + 2\, i_{2t}$$

Using Proposition 3 for the right-hand side of the equation gives

$$(1 + i_{1t})(1 + i_{1t+1}^e) \approx 1 + i_{1t} + i_{1t+1}^e$$

Replacing in the original relation gives

$$1 + 2\, i_{2t} = 1 + i_{1t} + i_{1t+1}^e$$

Or, reorganizing:

$$i_{2t} = \frac{(i_{1t} + i_{1t+1}^e)}{2}$$

The two-year rate is approximately equal to the average of the current and expected one-year rates.

Proposition 5:

$$(1 + x)^n \approx 1 + nx \qquad (A.5)$$

The proof follows by repeated application of propositions 3 and 4. For example, $(1 + x)^3 = (1 + x)^2(1 + x) \approx (1 + 2x)(1 + x)$ by proposition 4, $\approx (1 + 2x + x) = 1 + 3x$ by proposition 3.

The approximation becomes worse as n increases, however. For example, for $x = 0.05$ and $n = 5$, the approximation gives 1.25, compared to an exact value of 1.2763. For $n = 10$, the approximation gives 1.50, compared to an exact value of 1.63.

Application: In chapter 21, we saw that arbitrage between n-year U.S. bonds and n-year German bonds implies:

$$(1 + r_{nt})^n = \left(\frac{1}{\epsilon_t}\right)(1 + r_{nt}^*)^n (\epsilon_{t+n}^e)$$

From proposition 5, it follows that

$$(1 + r_{nt})^n \approx (1 + nr_{nt})$$

and

$$(1 + r_{nt}^*)^n \approx (1 + nr_{nt}^*)$$

Note also that we can rewrite the two terms in ϵ on the right in the arbitrage equation as

$$\frac{\epsilon_{t+n}^e}{\epsilon_t} = 1 + \frac{(\epsilon_{t+n}^e - \epsilon_t)}{\epsilon_t}$$

Replacing these three expressions in the arbitrage relation gives

$$(1 + nr_{nt}) \approx (1 + nr_{nt}^*)\left(1 + \frac{(\epsilon_{t+n}^e - \epsilon_t)}{\epsilon_t}\right)$$

From proposition 3, it follows that

$$(1 + nr_{nt}) \approx \left(1 + nr_{nt}^* + \frac{(\epsilon_{t+n}^e - \epsilon_t)}{\epsilon_t}\right)$$

Or, simplifying:

$$n(r_{nt} - r_{nt}^*) \approx \frac{(\epsilon_{t+n}^e - \epsilon_t)}{\epsilon_t}$$

The expected rate of real dollar depreciation over the next n years is approximately equal to n times the difference between the nth year U.S. and German real interest rates.

Proposition 6:

$$\frac{(1 + x)}{(1 + y)} \approx (1 + x - y) \qquad \text{(A.6)}$$

The proof is as follows. Consider the product of $(1 + x - y)(1 + y)$. Expanding this product gives $(1 + x - y)(1 + y) = 1 + x + xy - y^2$. If both x and y are small, then xy and y^2 are very small, so $(1 + x - y)(1 + y) \approx (1 + x)$. Dividing both sides of this approximation by $(1 + y)$ gives the proposition above.

For the values of $x = 0.05$ and $y = 0.03$, the approximation gives 1.02, while the correct value is 1.019.

Application from chapter 14: The real interest rate is defined by:

$$(1 + r_t) \equiv \frac{(1 + i_t)}{(1 + \pi_t^e)}$$

Using Proposition 6 gives

$$(1 + r_t) \approx (1 + i_t - \pi_t^e)$$

Simplifying:

$$r_t \approx i_t - \pi_t^e$$

This gives us the approximation we use at many points in the book: The real interest rate is approximately equal to the nominal interest rate minus expected inflation.

These approximations are also very convenient when dealing with *growth rates*. Define the rate of growth of x by $g_x \equiv \Delta x/x$, and similarly for z, g_z and for y, g_y. The numerical examples below are based on the values $g_x = 0.05$ and $g_y = 0.03$.

Proposition 7: If $z = xy$, then,

$$g_z \approx g_x + g_y \qquad \text{(A.7)}$$

The proof is as follows. Let Δz be the increase in z when x increases by Δx and y increases by Δy. Then, by definition,

$$z + \Delta z = (x + \Delta x)(y + \Delta y)$$

Divide both sides by z, so that

$$\frac{(z + \Delta z)}{z} = \frac{(x + \Delta x)}{x} \frac{(y + \Delta y)}{y}$$

where I have used on the right hand side the fact that dividing by z is the same as dividing by xy. Simplifying gives

$$\left(1 + \frac{\Delta z}{z}\right) = \left(1 + \frac{\Delta x}{x}\right)\left(1 + \frac{\Delta y}{y}\right)$$

Or, equivalently,

$$(1 + g_z) = (1 + g_x)(1 + g_y)$$

From proposition 3, $(1 + g_z) \approx (1 + g_x + g_y)$, or, equivalently, $g_z \approx g_x + g_y$.

For the values of g_x and g_y above, the approximation gives $g_z = 8\%$, while the correct value is 8.15%.

Application from chapter 13: Let the production function be of the form $Y = NA$, where Y is production, N is employment, and A is productivity. Denoting the growth rates of Y, N, and A by g_Y, g_N, and g_A respectively, Proposition 7 implies $g_Y \approx g_N + g_A$: The rate of output growth is approximately equal to the rate of employment growth plus the rate of productivity growth.

Proposition 8: If $z = x/y$, then

$$g_z \approx g_x - g_y \qquad \text{(A.8)}$$

The proof is as follows. Let Δz be the increase in z, when x increases by Δx and y increases by Δy. Then, by definition:

$$z + \Delta z = \frac{x + \Delta x}{y + \Delta y}$$

Dividing both sides by z and using the fact that $z = x/y$ gives

$$1 + \Delta z/z = \frac{1 + (\Delta x/x)}{1 + (\Delta y/y)}$$

Or, substituting:

$$1 + g_z = \frac{1 + g_x}{1 + g_y}$$

From proposition 6, $(1 + g_z) \approx (1 + g_x - g_y)$, or, equivalently, $g_z \approx g_x - g_y$.

For the values of $g_x = 0.05$ and $g_y = 0.03$, the approximation gives $g_z = 2\%$, while the correct value is 1.9%.

Application from chapter 9: Let aggregate demand be given by $Y = \gamma M/P$, where Y is output, M is nominal money, P is the price level, and γ is a constant parameter. It follows from propositions 7 and 8 that

$$g_y \approx g_\gamma + g_M - \pi$$

where π is the rate of growth of prices, equivalently the rate of inflation. As γ is constant, g_γ is equal to zero. Thus,

$$g_y \approx g_M - \pi$$

The rate of output growth is approximately equal to the rate of growth of nominal money minus the rate of inflation.

Functions

I use functions informally in the book, as a way of denoting how a variable depends on one or more other variables.

In some cases, I look at how a variable Y moves with a variable X. I write this relation as

$$Y = f(X)$$
$$+$$

A plus sign below X indicates a positive relation: An increase in X leads to an increase in Y. A minus sign indicates a negative relation: An increase in X leads instead to a decrease in Y.

In some cases, I allow the variable Y to depend on more than one variable. For example, I allow Y to depend on X and Z:

$$Y = f(X, Z)$$
$$(+, -)$$

The signs indicate that an increase in X leads to an increase in Y, and that an increase in Z leads to a decrease in Y.

An example of such a function is the investment function in chapter 5:

$$I = I(Y, i)$$
$$(+, -)$$

This equation says that investment, I, increases with production, Y, and decreases with the interest rate, i.

In some cases, it is reasonable to assume that the relation between two or more variables is a **linear relation**. A given increase in X always leads to the same increase in Y. In that case, the function is given by:

$$Y = a + bX$$

The parameter a is called the **intercept**: It gives the value of Y when X is equal to zero. The parameter b is called the **slope**: It tells us by how much Y increases when X increases by 1.

The simplest linear relation is the relation $Y = X$, which is represented by the 45-degree line and has a slope of one. Another example of a linear relation is the consumption function introduced in chapter 3:

$$C = c_0 + c_1 Y_D$$

where C is consumption and Y_D is disposable income. The parameter c_0 tells us what consumption would be if disposable income were equal to zero. The parameter c_1 tells us by how much consumption increases when income increases by 1 unit; c_1 is called the propensity to consume.

KEY TERMS

- linear relation, A9
- intercept, A9
- slope, A9

Appendix 3: An Introduction to Econometrics

How do we know that consumption depends on disposable income? How do we know the value of the propensity to consume? To answer these questions, and, more generally, to estimate behavioral relations and find out the values of the relevant parameters, economists use *econometrics*—the set of statistical techniques designed for use in economics. Econometrics can get fairly mathematical, but the basic principles behind econometric techniques are simple. This appendix shows you these basic principles.

To do so, I shall use as an example the consumption function introduced in chapter 3, and I shall concentrate on estimating c_1, the propensity to consume out of disposable income.

Changes in Consumption and Changes in Disposable Income

The propensity to consume tells us by how much consumption changes for a given change in disposable income. A natural first step is simply to plot changes in consumption versus changes in disposable income and see how the relation between the two looks like. This is done in Figure A–1.

The vertical axis in Figure A–1 measures the annual change in consumption minus the average annual change in consumption since 1960. More precisely, let C_t denote consumption in year t. Let ΔC_t denote $C_t - C_{t-1}$, the change in consumption from year $t-1$

to year t. Let $\overline{\Delta C}$ denote the average annual change in consumption since 1960. The variable measured on the vertical axis is constructed as $\Delta C_t - \overline{\Delta C}$. A positive value of the variable represents an increase in consumption larger than average, a negative value an increase in consumption smaller than average.

Similarly, the horizontal axis measures the annual change in disposable income, minus the average annual change in disposable income since 1960, $\Delta Y_{Dt} - \overline{\Delta Y_D}$.

A particular square in the figure gives the deviations of the change in consumption and disposable income from their respective means for a particular year between 1960 and 1998. In 1998, for example, the change in consumption was higher than average by $144 billion, the change in disposable income was higher than average by $66 billion dollars. (For our purposes, it is not important to know which year each square refers to, just what the set of points in the diagram looks like. So, except for 1998, the years are not indicated in Figure A–1.)

Figure A–1 suggests two main conclusions:

- First, there is a clear positive relation between changes in consumption and changes in disposable income. Most of the points lie in the upper-right and lower-left quadrants of the figure: When disposable income increases by more than average, consumption also typically increases by more than average; when disposable income increases by less than average, so typically does consumption.
- Second, the relation between the two variables is good but not perfect. In particular, some points lie

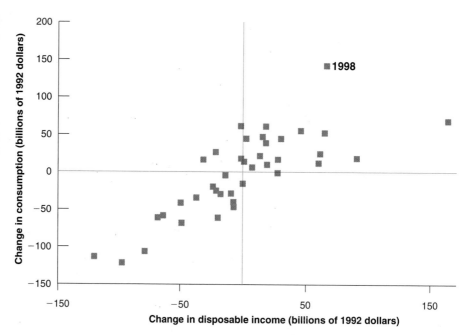

FIGURE A–1

Changes in Consumption versus Changes in Disposable Income, 1960–1998

There is a clear positive relation between changes in consumption and changes in disposable income.

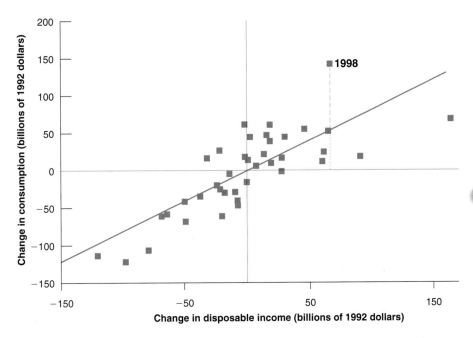

Changes in Consumption and Changes in Disposable Income. The Regression Line

The regression line is the line that fits the scatter of points best.

in the upper-left quadrant: These correspond to years when smaller-than-average changes in disposable income were associated with higher-than-average changes in consumption.

Econometrics allows us to state these two conclusions more precisely and to get an estimate of the propensity to consume. Using an econometrics software package, we can find the line that fits the cloud of points in Figure A–1 best. This line-fitting process is called **ordinary least squares (OLS)**. (The term "least squares" comes from the fact that the line has the property that it minimizes the sum of the squared distances of the points to the line—thus it gives the "least" "squares." The word "ordinary" comes from the fact that this is the simplest method used in econometrics.) The estimated equation corresponding to the line is called a **regression**, and the line itself is called the **regression line**.

In our case, the estimated equation is given by

$$(\Delta C_t - \overline{\Delta C}) = 0.83(\Delta Y_{Dt} - \overline{\Delta Y_D}) + \text{residual}$$
$$\overline{R}^2 = 0.61 \quad (A3.1)$$

The regression line corresponding to this estimated equation is drawn in Figure A–2. Equation (A3.1) reports two important numbers (econometrics packages give more information than reported above; a typical printout, together with further explanations, is given in the Focus box "A Guide to Understanding Econometric Results"):

- The first is the estimated propensity to consume. The equation tells us that an increase in disposable income of $1 billion above normal is typically

associated with an increase in consumption of $0.83 billion above normal. In other words, the estimated propensity to consume is 0.83. It is positive but smaller than 1.

- The second important number is $\overline{R}^2$, which is a measure of how well the regression line fits:

  Having estimated the effect of disposable income on consumption, we can decompose the change in consumption for each year into that part that is due to the change in disposable income—the first term on the right in equation (A3.1)—and the rest, which is called the **residual**. For example, the residual for 1998 is indicated in Figure A–2 by the vertical distance from the point representing 1998 to the regression line.

  If all the points in Figure A–2 were exactly on the estimated line, all residuals would be equal to zero; all changes in consumption would be explained by changes in disposable income. As you can see, however, this is not the case. $\overline{R}^2$ is a statistic that tells us how well the line fits. $\overline{R}^2$ is always between 0 and 1. A value of 1 would imply that the relation between the two variables is perfect, that all points are exactly on the regression line. A value of 0 would imply that the computer can see no relation between the two variables. The value of $\overline{R}^2$ of 0.61 in equation (A3.1) is high, but not very high. It confirms the message from Figure A–2: Movements in disposable income clearly affect consumption, but there is still quite a bit of movement in consumption that cannot be explained by movements in disposable income.

Correlation versus Causality

What we have established so far is that consumption and disposable income typically move together. More formally, we have seen that there is a positive **correlation**—the technical term for "co-relation"—between annual changes in consumption and annual changes in disposable income. And we have interpreted this relation as showing **causality**—that an increase in disposable income causes an increase in consumption.

We need to think again about this interpretation. A positive relation between consumption and disposable income may reflect the effect of disposable income on consumption. But it may also reflect the effect of consumption on disposable income. Indeed, the model we developed in chapter 3 tells us that if, for any reason, consumers decide to spend more, then output, and thus income and, in turn, disposable income, will increase. If part of the relation between consumption and disposable income comes from the effect of consumption on disposable income, interpreting equation (A3.1) as telling us about the effect of disposable income on consumption is not right.

An example will help here: Suppose consumption does not depend on disposable income, so that the true value of c_1 is equal to zero. (This is not very realistic, but it will make the point most clearly.) So draw the consumption function as a horizontal line (a line with a slope of zero) in Figure A–3. Next, suppose disposable income is equal to Y_D, so that the initial combination of consumption and disposable income is given by point A.

Now suppose that because of improved confidence, consumers increase their consumption, so that the consumption line shifts up. If demand affects output, then income and in turn disposable income increase, so that the new combination of consumption and disposable income will be given by, say, point B. If, instead, consumers become more pessimistic, the consumption line shifts down, and so does output, leading to a combination of consumption and disposable income given by point D.

If we look at that economy, we observe points A, B, and D. If, as we did earlier, we then draw the best-fitting line through these points, we estimate an upward-sloping line, such as CC', and so estimate a positive value for the propensity to consume, c_1. Remember, however, that the true value of c_1 is zero. Why do we get the wrong answer—a positive value for c_1 when the true value is zero? Because we interpret the positive relation between disposable income and consumption as showing the effect of disposable income on consumption, where in fact the relation reflects the effect of consumption on disposable income: Higher consumption leads to higher demand, higher output, and so higher disposable income.

There is an important lesson here, *the difference between correlation and causality*. The fact that two variables move together does not imply that movements in the first variable cause movements in the second variable. Perhaps the causality runs the other way: Movements in the second variable cause movements in the first variable. Or perhaps, as is likely to be the

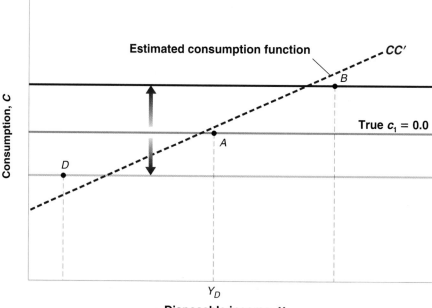

FIGURE A–3

A Misleading Regression

The relation between disposable income and consumption comes from the effect of consumption on income rather than from the effect of income on consumption.

A Guide to Understanding Econometric Results

In your readings, you may run across results of estimation using econometrics. Here is a guide, which uses the slightly simplified, but otherwise untouched computer output for the equation (A3.1):

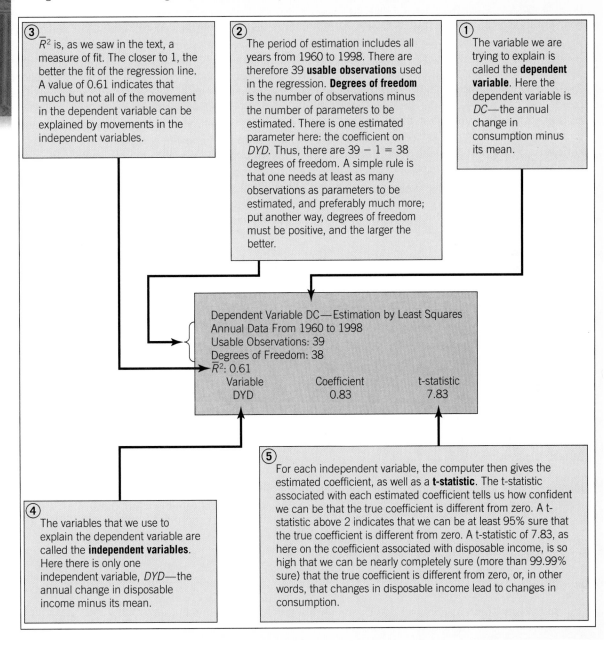

③ $\bar{R}^2$ is, as we saw in the text, a measure of fit. The closer to 1, the better the fit of the regression line. A value of 0.61 indicates that much but not all of the movement in the dependent variable can be explained by movements in the independent variables.

② The period of estimation includes all years from 1960 to 1998. There are therefore 39 **usable observations** used in the regression. **Degrees of freedom** is the number of observations minus the number of parameters to be estimated. There is one estimated parameter here: the coefficient on *DYD*. Thus, there are $39 - 1 = 38$ degrees of freedom. A simple rule is that one needs at least as many observations as parameters to be estimated, and preferably much more; put another way, degrees of freedom must be positive, and the larger the better.

① The variable we are trying to explain is called the **dependent variable**. Here the dependent variable is *DC*—the annual change in consumption minus its mean.

Dependent Variable DC—Estimation by Least Squares
Annual Data From 1960 to 1998
Usable Observations: 39
Degrees of Freedom: 38
$\bar{R}^2$: 0.61

Variable	Coefficient	t-statistic
DYD	0.83	7.83

④ The variables that we use to explain the dependent variable are called the **independent variables**. Here there is only one independent variable, *DYD*—the annual change in disposable income minus its mean.

⑤ For each independent variable, the computer then gives the estimated coefficient, as well as a **t-statistic**. The t-statistic associated with each estimated coefficient tells us how confident we can be that the true coefficient is different from zero. A t-statistic above 2 indicates that we can be at least 95% sure that the true coefficient is different from zero. A t-statistic of 7.83, as here on the coefficient associated with disposable income, is so high that we can be nearly completely sure (more than 99.99% sure) that the true coefficient is different from zero, or, in other words, that changes in disposable income lead to changes in consumption.

case here, the causality runs both ways: Disposable income affects consumption, *and* consumption affects disposable income.

Is there a way out of the correlation-versus-causality problem? If we are interested—and we are—in the ef-

fect of disposable income on consumption, can we still learn that from the data? The answer is, yes, but only by using more information.

Suppose that we *knew* that a specific change in disposable income was not caused by a change in consumption. Then, by looking at the reaction of consumption to *this* change in disposable income, we could learn how consumption responds to disposable income; we could estimate the propensity to consume.

This answer would seem to simply assume away the problem: How can we know that a change in disposable income is not due to a change in consumption? In fact, sometimes, we can. Suppose, for example, that the government embarks on a major increase in defense spending, leading to an increase in demand and, in turn, an increase in output. In that case, if we see both disposable income and consumption increase, we can safely assume that the movement in consumption reflects the effect of disposable income on consumption, and thus estimate the propensity to consume.

This example suggests a general strategy:

- Find exogenous variables—that is, variables that affect disposable income but are not in turn affected by it.

- Look at the change in consumption in response not to all changes in disposable income—as we did in our earlier regression—but to those changes in disposable income that can be explained by changes in these exogenous variables.

By doing so, we can be confident that what we are estimating is the effect of disposable income on consumption, and not the other way around.

The problem of finding such exogenous variables is known as the **identification problem** in econometrics. These exogenous variables, when they can be found, are called **instruments**. Methods of estimation that rely on the use of such instruments are called **instrumental variable methods**.

When equation (A3.1) is estimated using an instrumental variable method—using changes in government defense spending as the instrument—rather than ordinary least squares as we did earlier, the estimated equation becomes

$$(\Delta C_t - \overline{\Delta C}) = 0.52(\Delta Y_{Dt} - \overline{\Delta Y_D}) + \text{residual}$$
$$\overline{R}^2 = 0.52$$

Note that the coefficient on disposable income, 0.52, is smaller than 0.83 in equation (A3.1). This decrease in the estimated propensity to consume is exactly what we would expect: Our earlier estimate in equation (A3.1) reflected not only the effect of disposable income on consumption, but also the effect of consumption back on disposable income. The use of instruments eliminates this second effect, which is why we find a smaller estimated effect of disposable income on consumption.

This short introduction to econometrics is no substitute for a course in econometrics. But it gives you a sense of how economists use data to estimate relations and parameters, and to identify causal relations between economic variables.

KEY TERMS

- ordinary least squares (OLS), A11
- regression, A11
- regression line, A11
- residual, $\overline{R}^2$, A11
- correlation, A12
- causality, A12
- dependent variable, A13
- independent variable, A13
- usable observations, A13
- degrees of freedom, A13
- t-statistic, A13
- identification problem, A14
- instruments, A14
- instrumental variable methods, A14

GLOSSARY

above the line, below the line In the balance of payments, the items in the *current account* are above the line drawn to divide them from the items in the *capital account,* which appear below the line.

accelerationist Phillips curve See *modified Phillips curve.*

adaptive expectations A backward-looking method of forming expectations by adjusting for past mistakes.

adjusted nominal money growth Nominal money growth minus normal output growth.

aggregate demand relation The demand for output at a given price level. It is derived from equilibrium in goods and financial markets.

aggregate output Total amount of output produced in the economy.

aggregate private spending The sum of all nongovernment spending. Also called *private spending.*

aggregate production function The relation between the quantity of aggregate output produced and the quantities of inputs used in production.

aggregate supply relation The price level at which firms are willing to supply a given level of output. It is derived from equilibrium in the labor market.

animal spirits A term introduced by Keynes to refer to movements in investment that could not be explained by movements in current variables.

anticipated money Movements in nominal money that could have been predicted based on the information available at some time in the past.

appreciation (nominal) An increase in the price of the domestic currency in terms of a foreign currency. Corresponds to a decrease in the exchange rate.

appropriability (of research results) The extent to which firms benefit from the results of their research and development efforts.

arbitrage The proposition that the expected rates of return on two financial assets must be equal. Also called *risky arbitrage* to distinguish it from *riskless arbitrage,* the proposition that the actual rates of return on two financial assets must be the same.

Asian crisis The financial and economic crisis in Asia which started in 1997.

Asian miracle The fast growth in many Asian countries over the last 20 to 30 years.

automatic stabilizer The fact that a decrease in output leads, under given tax and spending rules, to an increase in the budget deficit. This increase in the budget deficit in turn increases demand and thus stabilizes output.

autonomous spending That component of the demand for goods that does not depend on the level of output.

balance of payments A set of accounts that summarize a country's transactions with the rest of the world.

balanced budget A budget in which taxes are equal to government spending.

balanced growth The situation in which output, capital, and effective labor all grow at the same rate.

band (for exchange rates) The limits within which the exchange rate is allowed to move under a fixed exchange rate system.

bank reserves Holdings of central bank money by banks. The difference between what banks receive from depositors and what they lend to firms or hold as bonds.

bank run Simultaneous attempts by depositors to withdraw their funds from a bank.

bargaining power The relative strength of each side in a negotiation or a dispute.

barter The exchange of goods for other goods rather than for money.

base year When constructing real GDP by evaluating quantities in different years using a given set of prices, the year to which this given set of prices corresponds.

behavioral equation An equation that captures some aspect of behavior.

big bang The simultaneous implementation of many reforms at once.

bilateral exchange rate The real exchange rate between two countries.

Board of Governors The group of seven members that governs the Federal Reserve System and is in charge of the design of monetary policy.

bond A financial asset that promises a stream of known payments over some period of time.

bond rating The assessment of a bond based on its default risk.

broad money See *M2.*

budget deficit The excess of government expenditures over government revenues.

business cycle theory The study of macroeconomic fluctuations.

business cycles See *output fluctuations.*

capital account In the balance of payments, a summary of a country's asset transactions with the rest of the world.

capital accumulation Increase in the capital stock.

capital controls Restrictions on the foreign assets domestic residents can hold and on the domestic assets foreigners can hold.

cash flow The net flow of cash a firm is receiving.

causality A relation between cause and effect.

central bank money Money issued by the central bank. Also known as the *monetary base* and *high-powered money.*

central parity The reference value of the exchange rate around which the exchange rate is allowed to move under a fixed exchange rate system. The center of the *band.*

changes in business inventories In the national income and product accounts, the change in the physical volume of inventories held by businesses.

checkable deposits Deposits at banks and other financial institutions against which checks can be written.

churning The concept that new goods make old goods obsolete, that new production techniques make older techniques and worker skills obsolete, and so on.

collective bargaining Bargaining about wages between firms and unions.

compensation of employees In the national income and product accounts, the sum of wages and salaries and of supplements to wages and salaries.

confidence band When estimating the dynamic effect of one variable on another, the range of values where we can be confident the true dynamic effect lies.

Congressional Budget Office (CBO) An office of Congress in charge of constructing and publishing budget projections.

constant returns to scale The proposition that a proportional increase (or decrease) of all inputs leads to the same proportional increase (or decrease) in output.

consumer confidence index An index computed monthly that estimates consumer confidence regarding current and future economic conditions.

Consumer Price Index (CPI) The cost of a given list of goods and services consumed by a typical urban dweller.

consumption (C) Goods and services purchased by consumers.

consumption function A function that relates consumption to its determinants.

consumption of fixed capital Depreciation of capital.

contractionary open market operation An open market operation in which the central bank sells bonds to decrease the money supply.

controlled experiment A set of test conditions in which one variable is altered while the others are kept constant.

convergence The tendency for countries with lower output per capita to grow faster, leading to convergence of output per capita across countries.

coordination (of macroeconomic policies between two countries) The joint design of macroeconomic policies to improve the economic situation in the two countries.

corporate bond A bond issued by a corporation.

corporate profits In the national income and product accounts, firms' revenues minus costs (including interest payments) and minus depreciation.

correlation A measure of the way two variables move together. A positive correlation indicates that the two variables tend to move in the same direction. A negative correlation indicates that the two variables tend to move in opposite directions. A correlation of zero indicates that there is no apparent relation between the two variables.

cost of living index The average price of a consumption bundle.

coupon bond A bond that promises multiple payments before maturity and one payment at maturity.

coupon payments The payments before maturity on a coupon bond.

coupon rate The ratio of the coupon payment to the face value of a coupon bond.

crawling peg An exchange rate mechanism in which the exchange rate is allowed to move over time according to a pre-specified formula.

creative destruction The proposition that growth simultaneously creates and destroys jobs.

credibility The degree to which people and markets believe that a policy announcement will actually be implemented and followed through.

credit channel The channel through which monetary policy works by affecting the amount of loans made by banks to firms.

currency Coins and bills.

currency board An exchange rate system in which: (i) the central bank stands ready to buy or sell foreign currency at the official exchange rate; (ii) it cannot engage in open market operations, that is buy or sell government bonds.

current account In the balance of payments, the summary of a country's payments to and from the rest of the world.

Current Population Survey (CPS) A large monthly survey of U.S. households used in particular to compute the unemployment rate.

current yield The ratio of the coupon payment to the price of a coupon bond.

cyclically adjusted deficit A measure of what the government deficit would be under existing tax and spending rules, if output were at its natural level. Also called a *full-employment deficit, midcycle deficit, standardized employment deficit,* or *structural deficit.*

debt finance Financing based on loans or the issuance of bonds.

debt monetization The printing of money to finance a deficit.

debt ratio See *debt-to-GDP ratio.*

debt repudiation A unilateral decision by a debtor not to repay its debt.

debt-to-GDP ratio The ratio of debt to gross domestic product. Also called simply the *debt ratio.*

decreasing returns to capital The property that increases in capital lead to smaller and smaller increases in output as the level of capital increases.

decreasing returns to labor The property that increases in labor lead to smaller and smaller increases in output as the level of labor increases.

default risk The risk that the issuer of a bond will not pay back the full amount promised by the bond.

deflation Negative inflation.

degrees of freedom The number of usable observations in a *regression* minus the number of parameters to be estimated.

demand deposit A bank account that allows depositors to write checks or get cash on demand, up to an amount equal to the account balance.

demand for domestic goods The demand for domestic goods by people, firms, and governments, both domestic and foreign. Equal to the domestic demand for goods plus net exports.

dependent variable A variable whose value is determined by one or more other variables.

depreciation (nominal) A decrease in the price of the domestic currency in terms of a foreign currency. Corresponds to an increase in the exchange rate.

depreciation rate A measure of how much usefulness a piece of capital loses from one period to the next.

depression A deep and long-lasting recession.

devaluation An increase in the exchange rate in a fixed exchange-rate system.

discount bond A bond that promises a single payment at maturity.

discount factor The value today of a dollar (or other national currency unit) at some time in the future.

discount policy The conditions under which the Fed lends to banks.

discount rate (1) The interest rate used to discount a sequence of future payments. Equal to the nominal interest rate when discounting future nominal payments, to the real interest rate when discounting future real payments. (2) The interest rate at which the Fed lends to banks.

discount window Metaphorically, the window where the Fed lends to banks. More generally, the means by which the Federal Reserve Bank lends to banks.

discouraged worker A person who has given up looking for employment.

disinflation A decrease in inflation.

disposable income The income that remains once consumers have received transfers from the government and paid their taxes.

dividends The portion of a corporation's profits that the firm pays out each period to shareholders.

dollar GDP See *nominal GDP*

dollarization The use of dollars in domestic transactions in a country other than the United States.

domestic demand for goods The sum of consumption, investment, and government spending.

dual labor market A labor market that combines a *primary labor market* and a *secondary labor market.*

durable goods Commodities that can be stored and have an average life of at least three years.

duration of unemployment The period of time during which a worker is unemployed.

dynamics Movements of one or more economic variables over time.

econometrics Statistical methods applied to economics.

effective demand Synonym for *aggregate demand.*

effective labor The number of workers in an economy times the state of technology.

effective real exchange rate See *multilateral exchange rate.*

efficiency wage The wage at which a worker is performing a job most efficiently or productively.

endogenous variable A variable that depends on other variables in a model and is thus explained within the model.

entitlement programs Programs that require the payment of benefits to all who meet the eligibility requirements established by law.

equilibrium The equality between demand and supply.

equilibrium condition The condition that supply be equal to demand.

equilibrium equation An equation that represents an equilibrium condition.

equilibrium in the goods market The condition that the supply of goods be equal to the demand for goods.

equity finance Financing based on the issuance of shares.

equity premium Risk premium required by investors to hold stocks rather than short-term bonds.

Euro The new European currency, which will replace national currencies in 11 countries in 2002.

European central bank (ECB) The central bank, located in Frankfurt, in charge of determining monetary policy in the Euro zone.

European Monetary System (EMS) A fixed exchange rate system in place in most of the countries of the European Union, from 1978 to 1999.

European Union A political and economic organization of 15 European nations. Formerly called the European Community.

Eurosclerosis A term coined to reflect the belief that Europe suffers from excessive rigidities, especially in the labor market.

exchange rate mechanism (ERM) The rules that determined the bands within which the member countries of the European Monetary System had to maintain their bilateral exchange rate.

exogenous variable A variable that is not explained within a model but rather is taken as given.

expansion A period of positive GDP growth.

expansionary open market operation An open market operation in which the central bank buys bonds to increase the money supply.

expectations hypothesis The hypothesis that financial investors are risk neutral, which implies expected returns on all financial assets have to be equal.

expectations-augmented Phillips curve See *modified Phillips curve.*

expected present discounted value The value today of an expected sequence of future payments. Also called *present discounted value* or *present value.*

experiment A test carried out under controlled conditions to assess the validity of a model or hypothesis.

exports (X) The purchases of domestic goods and services by foreigners.

face value (on a bond) The single payment at maturity promised by a discount bond.

fad A period of time during which, for reasons of fashion or overoptimism, financial investors are willing to pay more than the fundamental value of a stock.

Fed accommodation A change in the money supply by the Fed to maintain a constant interest rate in the face of changes in money demand or in spending.

federal deposit insurance Insurance provided by the U.S. government that protects each bank depositor up to $100,000 per account.

federal funds market The market where banks which have excess reserves at the end of the day lend them to banks which have insufficient reserves.

federal funds rate The interest rate determined by equilibrium in the Federal funds market. The interest rate affected most directly by changes in monetary policy.

Federal Open Market Committee (FOMC) A committee composed of the seven governors of the Fed, plus five District Bank presidents. The FOMC directs the activities of the *Open Market Desk.*

Federal Reserve Bank (Fed) The U.S. central bank.

Federal Reserve Districts The twelve regional districts that constitute the Federal Reserve System.

fertility of research The degree to which spending on research and development translates into new ideas and new products.

financial intermediary A financial institution that receives funds from people and/or firms, and uses these funds to make loans or buy financial assets.

financial investment The purchase of financial assets.

financial markets The markets in which financial assets are bought and sold.

financial wealth The value of all of one's financial assets minus all financial liabilities. Sometimes called *wealth* for short.

fine tuning A macroeconomic policy aimed at precisely hitting a given target, such as constant unemployment or constant output growth.

fiscal consolidation See *fiscal contraction.*

fiscal contraction A policy aimed at reducing the budget deficit through a decrease in government spending or an increase in taxation. Also called *fiscal consolidation.*

fiscal expansion An increase in government spending or a decrease in taxation, which lead to an increase in the budget deficit.

fiscal policy A government's choice of taxes and spending.

fiscal year An accounting period of 12 months. In the United States, the period from October 1 of the previous calendar year to September 30 of the current calendar year.

Fisher effect or **Fisher hypothesis** The proposition that in the long run an increase in nominal money growth is reflected in an identical increase in both the nominal interest rate and the inflation rate, leaving the real interest rate unchanged.

Fisher hypothesis See *Fisher effect.*

fixed exchange rate An exchange rate between the currencies of two or more countries that is fixed at some level and adjusted only infrequently.

fixed investment See *investment (I).*

float The exchange rate is said to float when it is determined in the foreign exchange market, without central bank intervention.

floating exchange rate An exchange rate determined in the foreign-exchange market without central bank intervention.

flow A variable that can be expressed as a quantity per unit of time (such as income).

forecast error The difference between the actual value of a variable and a forecast of that variable.

foreign direct investment The purchase of existing firms or the development of new firms by foreign investors.

foreign exchange Foreign currency; all currencies other than the domestic currency of a given country.

foreign-exchange reserves Foreign assets held by the central bank.

four tigers The four Asian economies of Singapore, Taiwan, Hong Kong, and South Korea.

full-employment deficit See *cyclically adjusted deficit.*

fully funded social security system Retirement system in which the contributions of current workers are invested in financial assets, with the proceeds (principal and interest) given back to the workers when they retire.

fundamental value (of a stock) The present value of expected dividends.

G-7 The seven major economic powers in the world: the United States, Japan, France, Germany, the United Kingdom, Italy, and Canada.

game *Strategic interactions* between *players.*

game theory The prediction of outcomes from *games.*

GDP deflator The ratio of nominal GDP to

real GDP; a measure of the overall price level. Gives the average price of the final goods produced in the economy.

GDP in current dollars See *nominal GDP*

GDP in terms of goods See *real GDP*

GDP in constant dollars See *real GDP*

GDP adjusted for inflation See *real GDP*

GDP in chained (1992) dollars See *real GDP*

GDP growth The growth rate of real GDP in year t; equal to $(Y_t - Y_{t-1})/Y_{t-1}$.

general equilibrium A situation in which there is equilibrium in all markets (goods, financial, and labor).

geometric series A mathematical sequence in which the ratio of one term to the preceding term remains the same. A sequence of the form $1 + c + c^2 + \cdots + c^n$.

gold standard A system in which a country fixed the price of its currency in terms of gold and stood ready to exchange gold for currency at the stated parity.

golden-rule level of capital The level of capital at which long-run consumption is maximized.

government bond A bond issued by a government or a government agency.

government budget constraint The budget constraint faced by the government. The constraint implies that an excess of spending over revenues must be financed by borrowing, and thus leads to an increase in debt.

government purchases In the national income and product accounts, the sum of the purchases of goods by the government plus compensation of government employees.

government spending (G) The goods and services purchased by federal, state, and local governments.

government transfers Payments made by the government to individuals that are not in exchange for goods or services. Example: Social Security payments.

Great Depression The severe worldwide depression of the 1930s.

gross domestic product (GDP) A measure of aggregate output in the national income accounts. (The market value of the goods and services produced by labor and property located in the United States.)

gross national product (GNP) A measure of aggregate output in the national income accounts. (The market value of the goods and services produced by labor and property supplied by U.S. residents.)

gross private domestic fixed investment In the national income and product accounts, the sum of nonresidential investment and residential investment.

growth The steady increase in aggregate output over time.

hedonic pricing An approach to calculating real GDP that treats goods as providing a collection of characteristics, each with an implicit price.

heterodox stabilization program A stabilization program that includes incomes policies.

high-powered money See *central bank money.*

hires Workers newly employed by firms.

housing wealth The value of the housing stock.

human capital The set of skills possessed by the workers in an economy.

human wealth The labor-income component of wealth.

Humphrey-Hawkins Act A 1978 act of the U.S. Congress defining the goals of monetary policy.

hyperinflation Very high inflation.

hysteresis In general, the proposition that the equilibrium value of a variable depends on its history. With respect to unemployment: the proposition that a long period of sustained actual unemployment leads to an increase in the equilibrium rate of unemployment.

identification problem In econometrics, the problem of finding whether correlation between variables X and Y indicates a causal relation from X to Y, or from Y to X, or both. This problem is solved by finding exogenous variables, called *instruments,* that affect X and do not affect Y directly, or affect Y and do not affect X directly.

identity An equation that holds by definition, denoted by the sign $\equiv$.

imports (Q) The purchases of foreign goods and services by domestic consumers, firms, and the government.

income The flow of revenue from work, rental income, interest, and dividends.

incomes policies Government policies that set up wage and/or price guidelines or controls.

independent variable A variable that is taken as given in a relation or in a model.

index number A number, such as the GDP deflator, that has no natural level and is thus set to equal some value (typically 1 or 100) in a given period.

indexed bond A bond that promises payments adjusted for inflation.

indirect taxes Taxes on goods and services. In the United States, primarily sales taxes.

industrial policy A policy aimed at helping specific sectors of an economy.

inflation A sustained rise in the general level of prices.

inflation rate The rate at which the price level increases over time.

inflation targeting The conduct of monetary policy so as to achieve a given inflation rate over time.

inflation tax The product of the rate of inflation and real money balances.

inflation-adjusted deficit The correct economic measure of the budget deficit: The sum of the *primary deficit* and real interest payments.

instrumental variable methods In econometrics, methods of estimation that use *instruments* to estimate causal relations between different variables.

instruments In econometrics, the exogenous variables that allow the identification problem to be solved.

intercept In a linear relation between two variables, the value of the first variable when the second variable is equal to zero.

interest parity condition See *uncovered interest parity relation.*

intermediate good A good used in the production of a final good.

International Monetary Fund (IMF) The principal international economic organization. Publishes the *World Economic Outlook* annually and the *International Financial Statistics (IFS)* monthly.

inventory investment (I_s) The difference between production and sales.

investment (I) Purchases of new houses and apartments by people, and purchases of new capital goods (machines and plants) by firms.

investment income In the current account, income received by domestic residents from their holdings of foreign assets.

IS curve A downward-sloping curve relating output to the interest rate. The curve corresponding to the *IS relation,* the equilibrium condition for the goods market.

IS relation An equilibrium condition stating that the demand for goods must be equal to the supply of goods, or equivalently that investment must be equal to saving. The equilibrium condition for the goods market.

J-curve A curve depicting the initial deterioration in the trade balance caused by a real depreciation, followed by an improvement in the trade balance.

junk bond A bond with a high risk of default.

labor force The sum of those employed and those unemployed.

labor hoarding The practice of retaining workers during a period of low product demand rather than laying them off.

labor in efficiency units See *effective labor.*

labor market rigidities Restrictions on

firms' ability to adjust their level of employment.

labor productivity   The ratio of output to the number of workers.

Laffer curve   A curve showing the relation between tax revenues and the tax rate.

lagged value   The value of a variable in the preceding time period.

layoffs   Workers who lose their jobs either temporarily or permanently.

leapfrogging   Advancing on and then overtaking the leader. Used to describe the process by which economic leadership passes from country to country.

life cycle theory of consumption   The theory of consumption, developed initially by Franco Modigliani, that emphasizes that the planning horizon of consumers is their lifetime.

linear relation   A relation between two variables such that a one-unit increase in one variable always leads to an increase of n units in the other variable.

liquid asset   An asset that can be sold easily and at little cost.

liquidity preference   The term introduced by Keynes to denote the demand for money.

liquidity trap   The case where nominal interest rates are close to zero, and monetary policy cannot therefore decrease them further.

LM curve   An upward-sloping curve relating the interest rate to output. The curve corresponding to the *LM relation*, the equilibrium condition for financial markets.

LM relation   An equilibrium condition stating that the demand for money must be equal to the supply of money. The equilibrium condition for financial markets.

logarithmic scale   A scale in which the same proportional increase represents the same distance on the scale, so that a variable that grows at a constant rate is represented by a straight line.

long run   A period of time extending over decades.

long-term bond   A bond with maturity of 10 years or more.

Lucas critique   The proposition, put forth by Robert Lucas, that existing relations between economic variables may change when policy changes. An example is the apparent trade-off between inflation and unemployment, which may disappear if policy makers try to exploit it.

M1   The sum of currency, traveler's checks, and checkable deposits—assets that can be used directly in transactions. Also called *narrow money*.

M2   *M1* plus money market mutual fund shares, money market and savings deposits, and time deposits. Also called *broad money*.

M3   A *monetary aggregate* constructed by the Fed and broader than *M2*.

macroeconomics   The study of aggregate economic variables, such as production for the economy as a whole, or the average price of goods.

Maastricht treaty   A treaty signed in 1991 that defined the steps involved in the transition to a common currency for the European Union.

marginal propensity to consume (*mpc*, or *c₁*)
The effect on consumption of an additional dollar of disposable income.

marginal propensity to import   The effect on imports from an additional dollar in income.

marginal propensity to save   The effect on saving of an additional dollar of disposable income. (Equal to one minus the marginal propensity to consume.)

Marshall–Lerner condition   The condition under which a real depreciation leads to an increase in net exports.

maturity   The length of time over which a financial asset (typically a bond) promises to make payments to the holder.

medium run   A period of time between the *short run* and the *long run*.

medium-term bond   A bond with maturity of one to 10 years.

menu cost   The cost of changing a price.

merchandise trade   Exports and imports of goods.

microeconomics   The study of production and prices in specific markets.

midcycle deficit   See *cyclically adjusted deficit*.

model   A conceptual structure used to think about and interpret an economic phenomenon.

models of endogenous growth   Models in which accumulation of physical and human capital can sustain growth even in the absence of technological progress.

modified Phillips curve   The curve that plots the change in the inflation rate against the unemployment rate. Also called an *expectations-augmented Phillips curve* or an *accelerationist Phillips curve*.

monetarism, monetarists   A group of economists in the 1960s, led by Milton Friedman, who argued that monetary policy had powerful effects on activity.

monetary aggregate   The market value of a sum of liquid assets. *M1* is a monetary aggregate that includes only the most liquid assets.

monetary base   See *central bank money*.

monetary contraction   A change in monetary policy, which leads to an increase in the interest rate. Also called "monetary tightening".

monetary expansion   A change in monetary policy, which leads to a decrease in the interest rate.

monetary–fiscal policy mix   The combination of monetary and fiscal policies in effect at a given time.

monetary tightening   See *monetary contraction*.

money   Those financial assets that can be used directly to buy goods.

money illusion   The notion that people appear to make systematic mistakes in assessing nominal versus real changes.

money market funds   Financial institutions that receive funds from people and use them to buy short-term bonds.

money multiplier   The increase in the money supply resulting from a one-dollar increase in central bank money.

multilateral exchange rate (multilateral real exchange rate)   The real exchange rate between a country and its trading partners, computed as a weighted average of bilateral real exchange rates. Also called the *trade-weighted real exchange rate* or *effective real exchange rate*.

multiplier   The ratio of the change in an *endogenous variable* to the change in an *exogenous variable* (for example, the ratio of the change in output to a change in autonomous spending).

Mundell-Fleming model   A model of simultaneous equilibrium in both goods and financial markets for an open economy.

narrow banking   Restrictions on banks that would require them to hold only short-term government bonds.

narrow money   See *M1*.

national accounts   See *national income and product accounts*

national income   In the United States, the income that originates in the production of goods and services supplied by residents of the United States.

national income and product accounts   The system of accounts used to describe the evolution of the sum, the composition, and the distribution of aggregate output.

National Industrial Recovery Act (NIRA)   A New Deal program that asked industries to sign codes of behavior, to establish minimum wages, and not to impose further wage cuts.

National Recovery Administration (NRA)   The administration in charge of the set of programs designed to help the U.S. economy recover from the Great Depression.

natural experiment   A real-world event that can be used to test an economic theory.

natural level of employment The level of employment that prevails when unemployment is equal to its natural rate.

natural level of output The level of production that prevails when employment is equal to its natural level.

natural rate of unemployment The unemployment rate at which price and wage decisions are consistent.

neoclassical synthesis A consensus in macroeconomics, developed in the early 1950s, based on an integration of Keynes's ideas and the ideas of earlier economists.

net capital flows Capital flows from the rest of the world to the domestic economy minus capital flows to the rest of the world from the domestic economy.

net exports The difference between exports and imports. Also called the *trade balance.*

net interest In the national income and product accounts, the interest paid by firms minus the interest received by firms, plus interest received from the rest of the world minus interest paid to the rest of the world.

net national product (NNP) Gross national product minus capital depreciation.

net transfers received In the current account, the net value of foreign aid received minus foreign aid given.

neutrality of money The proposition that an increase in nominal money has no effect on output or the interest rate but is reflected entirely in a proportional increase in the price level.

new classicals A group of economists who interpret fluctuations as the effects of shocks in competitive markets with fully flexible prices and wages.

New Deal The set of programs put in place by the Roosevelt administration to get the U.S. economy out of the Great Depression.

new growth theory Recent developments in growth theory that explore the determinants of technological progress and the role of increasing returns to scale in growth.

new Keynesians A group of economists who believe in the importance of nominal rigidities in fluctuations, and are exploring the role of market imperfections in explaining fluctuations.

nominal exchange rate The price of foreign currency in terms of domestic currency. The number of units of domestic currency you can get for one unit of foreign currency.

nominal GDP The sum of the quantities of final goods produced in an economy times their current price. Also known as *dollar GDP* and *GDP in current dollars.*

nominal interest rate Interest rate in terms of the national currency (in terms of dollars in the United States). Tells us how many

dollars one has to repay in the future in exchange for one dollar today.

nominal rigidities The slow adjustment of nominal wages and prices to changes in economic activity.

non-accelerating inflation rate of unemployment (NAIRU) The unemployment rate at which inflation neither decreases nor increases. See *natural rate of unemployment.*

nondurable goods Commodities that can be stored but have an average life of less than three years.

nonemployment rate The ratio of population minus employment, to population.

nonhuman wealth The financial and housing component of wealth.

noninstitutional civilian population The number of people potentially available for civilian employment.

nonresidential investment The purchase of new capital goods by firms: *structures* and *producer durable equipment.*

normal growth rate The rate of output growth needed to maintain a constant unemployment rate.

North American Free Trade Agreement (NAFTA) An agreement signed by the United States, Canada, and Mexico in which the three countries agreed to establish all of North America as a free-trade zone.

not in the labor force Number of people who are neither employed nor looking for employment.

n-year interest rate See *yield to maturity.*

Okun's law The relation between GDP growth and the change in the unemployment rate.

Open Market Desk The Federal Reserve agency in charge of open market operations. Located in New York City.

open market operation The purchase or sale of government bonds by the central bank for the purpose of increasing or decreasing the money supply.

openness in factor markets The opportunity for firms to choose where to locate production and for workers to choose where to work and whether or not to migrate.

openness in financial markets The opportunity for financial investors to choose between domestic and foreign financial assets.

openness in goods markets The opportunity for consumers and firms to choose between domestic and foreign goods.

optimal control The control of a system (a machine, a rocket, an economy) by means of mathematical methods.

optimal control theory The set of mathematical methods used for *optimal control.*

ordinary least squares A statistical method

to find the best fitting relation between two or more variables.

Organization for Economic Cooperation and Development (OECD) An international organization that collects and studies economic data for many countries. Most of the world's rich countries belong to the OECD.

orthodox stabilization program A stabilization program that does not include incomes policies.

output fluctuations Movements in output around its trend.

output per capita A country's gross domestic product divided by its population.

overnight interest rate The interest rate charged for lending and borrowing overnight.

overshooting The large movement in the exchange rate triggered by a monetary expansion or contraction.

panel data set A data set that gives the values of one or more variables for many individuals or many firms over some period of time.

paradox of saving The result that an attempt by people to save more may lead both to a decline in output and to unchanged saving.

parameter A coefficient in a behavioral equation.

participation rate The ratio of the labor force to the noninstitutional civilian population.

patent The legal right granted to a person or firm to exclude anyone else from the production or use of a new product or technique for a certain period of time.

pay-as-you-go social security system Retirement system in which the contributions of current workers are used to pay benefits to retirees.

payments of factor income to the rest of the world In the United States, income received by foreign capital and foreign residents in the United States.

peg The exchange rate to which a country commits under a fixed exchange rate system.

permanent income theory of consumption The theory of consumption, developed by Milton Friedman, that emphasizes that people make consumption decisions based not on current income, but on their notion of permanent income.

personal consumption expenditures In the national income and product accounts, the sum of goods and services purchased by persons resident in the United States.

personal disposable income *Personal income* minus personal tax and nontax payments. The income available to consumers after they have received transfers and paid taxes.

personal income The income actually received by persons.

Phillips curve The curve that plots the relation between (1) movements in inflation and (2) unemployment. The original Phillips curve captured the relation between the inflation rate and the unemployment rate. The modified *Phillips curve* captures the relation between (1) the change in the inflation rate and (2) the unemployment rate.

players The participants in a *game*. Depending on the context, players may be people, firms, governments, and so on.

point-year of excess employment A difference between the actual unemployment rate and the natural unemployment rate of one percentage point for one year.

policy mix See *monetary–fiscal policy mix.*

political business cycle Fluctuations in economic activity caused by the manipulation of the economy for electoral gain.

postindustrial economies Economies in which the manufacturing sector's share of gross domestic product is small.

present value See *expected present discounted value.*

price level The general level of prices in an economy.

price liberalization The process of eliminating subsidies, decontrolling prices and allowing them to clear markets.

price-setting relation The relation between the price chosen by firms, the nominal wage, and the markup.

primary deficit Government spending, excluding interest payments on the debt, minus government revenues. (The negative of the *primary surplus.*)

primary labor market A labor market where jobs are good, wages are high, and turnover is low. Contrast to the *secondary labor market.*

primary surplus Government revenues minus government spending, excluding interest payments on the debt.

private saving (S) Saving by consumers. The value of consumers' disposable income minus their consumption.

private spending See *aggregate private spending.*

privatization The transfer of state-owned firms to private ownership.

producer durable equipment Durable goods such as machines, computers, and office equipment purchased by firms for production purposes.

producer price index (PPI) A price index of domestically produced goods in manufacturing, mining, agricultural, fishing, forestry, and electric utility industries.

production function The relation between

the quantity of output and the quantities of inputs used in production.

profitability The expected present discounted value of profits.

propagation mechanism The dynamic effects of a *shock* on output and its components.

proprietors' income In the national income and product accounts, the income of sole proprietorships, partnerships, and tax-exempt cooperatives.

propensity to consume (c_1) The effect of an additional dollar of disposable income on consumption.

propensity to save The effect of an additional dollar of disposable income on saving (equal to one minus the propensity to consume)

public saving Saving by the government; equal to government revenues minus government spending. Also called the *budget surplus.* (A *budget deficit* represents public dissaving.)

purchasing power Income in terms of goods.

purchasing power parity (PPP) A method of adjustment used to allow for international comparisons of GDP.

quits Workers who leave their jobs in search of better alternatives.

quotas Restrictions on the quantities of goods that can be imported.

$\overline{R}^2$ A measure of fit, between zero and one, from a *regression.* An $\overline{R}^2$ of zero implies that there is no apparent relation between the variables under consideration. An $\overline{R}^2$ of 1 implies a perfect fit: all the *residuals* are equal to zero.

random walk The path of a variable whose changes over time are unpredictable.

random walk of consumption The proposition that, if consumers are foresighted, changes in their consumption should be unpredictable.

rate of growth of multifactor productivity See *Solow residual.*

rational expectations The formation of expectations based on rational forecasts, rather than on simple extrapolations of the past.

rational speculative bubble An increase in stock prices based on the rational expectation of further increases in prices in the future.

real appreciation An increase in the relative price of domestic goods in terms of foreign goods. A decrease in the real exchange rate.

real business cycle (RBC) models Eco-

nomic models that assume that output is always at its natural level. Thus all output fluctuations are movements of the natural level of output, as opposed to movements away from the natural level of output.

real depreciation A decrease in the relative price of domestic goods in terms of foreign goods. An increase in the real exchange rate.

real exchange rate The relative price of foreign goods in terms of domestic goods.

real GDP A measure of aggregate output. The sum of quantities produced in an economy times their price in a base year. Also known as *GDP in terms of goods, GDP in constant dollars, GDP adjusted for inflation.* The current measure of real GDP in the United States is called *GDP in (chained) 1992 dollars.*

real GDP in chained (1992) dollars See *real GDP.*

real interest rate Interest rate in terms of goods. Tells us how many goods one has to repay in the future in exchange for one good today.

realignment Adjustment of parities in a fixed exchange-rate system.

receipts of factor income from the rest of the world In the United States, income received by U.S. capital or U.S. residents abroad.

recession A period of negative GDP growth. Usually refers to at least two consecutive quarters of negative GDP growth.

regression The output of *ordinary least squares.* Gives the equation corresponding to the estimated relation between variables, together with information about the degree of fit and the importance of the different variables.

regression line The best-fitting line corresponding to the equation obtained by using *ordinary least squares.*

rental cost of capital See *user cost.*

rental income of persons In the national income and product accounts, the income from the rental of real property, minus depreciation on this property.

research and development (R & D) Spending aimed at discovering and developing new ideas and products.

reservation wage The wage that would make a worker indifferent to working or becoming unemployed.

reserve ratio The ratio of bank reserves to checkable deposits.

reserve requirements The minimum amount of reserves that banks must hold in proportion to checkable deposits.

residential investment The purchase of new homes and apartments by people.

residual The difference between the actual

value of a variable and the value implied by the *regression line*. Small residuals indicate a good fit.

revaluation A decrease in the exchange rate in a fixed exchange-rate system.

Ricardian equivalence The proposition that neither government deficits nor government debt have an effect on economic activity. Also called the *Ricardo–Barro proposition*.

Ricardo-Barro proposition See *Ricardian equivalence*.

risk averse A person is risk averse if he/she prefers to receive a given amount for sure to an uncertain amount with the same expected value.

risk neutral A person is risk neutral if he/she is indifferent between receiving a given amount for sure or an uncertain amount with the same expected value.

risk premium The difference between the interest rate paid on a bond and the interest rate paid on a given bond with the highest rating.

riskless arbitrage See *arbitrage*.

risky arbitrage See *arbitrage*.

sacrifice ratio The number of point-years of excess unemployment needed to achieve a decrease in inflation of 1 percent.

saving The sum of private and public saving, denoted by S.

saving rate The proportion of income that is saved.

savings The accumulated value of past saving. Also called *wealth*.

scatter diagram A graphic presentation that plots the value of one variable against the value of another variable.

secondary labor market A labor market where jobs are poor, wages are low, and turnover is high. Contrast to the *primary labor market*.

seignorage The revenues from the creation of money.

separations Workers who are leaving or losing their jobs.

services Commodities that cannot be stored and thus must be consumed at the place and time of purchase.

severance payments Payments made by firms to laid-off workers.

share A financial asset issued by a firm that promises to pay a sequence of payments, called dividends, in the future. Also called *stock*.

shocks Movements in the factors that affect aggregate demand and/or aggregate supply.

shoe leather costs The costs of going to the bank to take money out of a checking account.

short run A period of time extending over a few years at most.

short-term bond A bond with maturity of one year or less.

simulation The use of a model to look at the effects of a change in an exogenous variable on the variables in the model.

skill-biased technological progress The proposition that new machines and new methods of production require skilled workers to a greater degree than in the past.

social security trust fund The funds accumulated by the U.S. social security as a result of surpluses in the past.

slope In a linear relation between two variables, the amount by which the first variable increases when the second increases by one unit.

soft budget constraint The granting of subsidies to firms that make losses, thus decreasing the incentives for these firms to take the measures needed to generate profits.

Solow residual The excess of actual output growth over what can be accounted for by the growth in capital and labor.

stabilization program A government program aimed at stabilizing the economy (typically stopping high inflation).

stagflation The combination of stagnation and inflation.

staggering of wage decisions The fact that different wages are adjusted at different times, making it impossible to achieve a synchronized decrease in nominal wage inflation.

standardized employment deficit See *cyclically adjusted deficit*.

state of technology The degree of technological development in a country or industry.

statistical discrepancy A difference between two numbers that should be equal, based on differences in sources or methods of construction.

steady state In an economy without technological progress, the state of the economy where output and capital per worker are no longer changing. In an economy with technological progress, the state of the economy where output and capital per effective worker are no longer changing.

stock A variable that can be expressed as a quantity at a point in time (such as wealth). Also a synonym for *share*.

stocks An alternative term for *inventories*.

strategic interactions An environment in which the actions of one player depend on and affect the actions of another player.

structural change In the context of transition: The sharp shifts in the structure of demand, leading to sharp shifts in the structure of production as transition takes place.

structural deficit See *cyclically adjusted deficit*.

structural rate of unemployment See *natural rate of unemployment*.

structures In the national income and product accounts, plants, factories, office buildings, and hotels.

supply siders A group of economists in the 1980s who believed that tax cuts would increase activity by enough to increase tax revenues.

Tanzi-Olivera effect The adverse effect of inflation on tax revenues and in turn on the budget deficit.

tariffs Taxes on imported goods.

Taylor's rule A rule, suggested by John Taylor, telling a central bank how to adjust the nominal interest rate in response to deviations of inflation from its target, and of the unemployment rate from the natural rate.

tax smoothing The principle of keeping tax rates roughly constant, so that the government runs large deficits when government spending is exceptionally high and small surpluses the rest of the time.

technological progress An improvement in the state of technology.

technological unemployment Unemployment brought about by technological progress.

technology gap The differences between states of technology across countries.

term structure of interest rates See *yield curve*.

time inconsistency In game theory, the incentive for one player to deviate from his previously announced course of action once the other player has moved.

Tobin's q The ratio of the value of the capital stock, computed by adding the stock market value of firms and the debt of firms, to the replacement cost of capital.

total wealth The sum of human wealth and nonhuman wealth.

tradable goods Goods that compete with foreign goods in either domestic or foreign markets.

trade balance The difference between exports and imports. Also called *net exports*.

trade deficit A negative trade balance; that is, imports exceed exports.

trade surplus A positive trade balance; that is, exports exceed imports.

trade-weighted real exchange rate See *multilateral exchange rate*.

transfers See *government transfers*.

Treasury bill (T-bill) A U.S. government bond with a maturity of up to one year.

Treasury bond A U.S. government bond with a maturity of 10 years or more.

Treasury note A U.S. government bond with a maturity of one to 10 years.

***t*-statistic** A statistic associated with an estimated coefficient in a regression that indicates the level of confidence that the true coefficient differs from zero.

twin deficits The budget and trade deficits that have characterized the United States since the early 1980s.

unanticipated money Movements in nominal money that could not have been predicted based on the information available at some time in the past.

uncovered interest parity relation An arbitrage relation stating that domestic and foreign bonds must have the same expected rate of return, expressed in terms of the domestic currency.

underground economy That part of a nation's economic activity that is not measured in official statistics, either because the activity is illegal or because people and firms are seeking to avoid taxes.

unemployment rate The ratio of the number of unemployed to the labor force.

union density The proportion of the work force that is unionized.

usable observation An observation for which the values of all the variables under consideration are available for *regression* purposes.

user cost of capital The cost of using capital over a year, or a given period of time. The sum of the real interest rate and the depreciation rate. Also called the *rental cost of capital*.

value added The value a firm adds in the production process, equal to the value of its production minus the value of the intermediate inputs it uses in production.

velocity The ratio of nominal income to money; the number of transactions for a given quantity of money, or the rate at which money changes hands.

voucher privatization A method of privatization in which the government grants vouchers to private citizens allowing them to bid for shares in state-owned firms.

wage indexation A rule that automatically increases wages in response to an increase in prices.

wage-price spiral The mechanism by which increases in wages lead to increases in prices, which lead in turn to further increases in wages, and so on.

wage setting relation The relation between the wage chosen by wage setters, and the unemployment rate.

war of attrition Occurs when both parties to an argument hold their grounds, hoping that the other party will give in.

wealth See *financial wealth*.

yield curve The relation between yield and maturity for bonds of different maturities. Also called the *term structure of interest rates*.

yield to maturity The constant interest rate that makes the price of an *n*-year bond today equal to the present value of future payments. Also called the *n-year interest rate*.

INDEX

Footnotes are indicated by the italicized letter n following the page number.

Symbols Used in This Book

Symbol	Term	Introduced in Chapter
$(\ )^d$	superscript ^{d} means demanded	
$(\ )^e$	superscript ^{e} means expected	
A	Aggregate private spending	17
	Also: Labor productivity/States of technology	6, 12
α	Effect on the inflation rate of the unemployment rate, given expected inflation	8
B	Bonds	27
β	Effect of an increase in output growth on the unemployment rate	9
C	Consumption	3
CU	Currency	4
c	Proportion of money held as currency	4
c_0	Consumption when disposable income equals zero	3
c_1	Propensity to consume	3
D	Checkable deposits	4
	Also: Real dividend on a stock	15
$\$D$	Nominal dividend on a stock	15
δ	Depreciation rate	11
E	Nominal exchange rate (price of foreign currency in terms of domestic currency)	18
$\overline{E}$	Fixed nominal exchange rate	20
E^e	Expected future exchange rate	18
ε	Real exchange rate	18
G	Government spending	3
g_A	Growth rate of technological progress	12
g_K	Growth rate of capital	12
g_m	Growth rate of nominal money	9
g_N	Growth rate of population	12
g, g_y	Growth rate of output	9
$\overline{g}_y$	Normal rate of growth of output	9
H	High powered money/monetary base/central bank money	4
	Also: Human capital	11
I	Fixed investment	3
$\overline{I}$	Investment, taken as exogenous	3
I_S	Inventory investment	3
i	Nominal interest rate	4
i_1	One-year nominal interest rate	15
i_2	Two-year nominal interest rate	15
i^*	Foreign nominal interest rate	18
K	Capital stock	10